1965

Y0-DTI-594

Our Favorite Salads

FAVORITES FROM HOME ECONOMICS TEACHERS

T.B.
321

TABLE OF CONTENTS

ACKNOWLEDGMENTS

We wish to thank the many home economics teachers who submitted their favorite recipes for inclusion in this book. We regret that lack of space made it impossible to include all of them.

We wish also to express our appreciation for the use of photographs supplied us by the following: Cover — Tuna Research Foundation (recipe on page 336); Inside Front Cover — United Fresh Fruit and Vegetable Association (recipe on page 125); and Inside Back Cover — Brussels Sprouts Marketing Program (recipe on page 300).

Title and order blank page photographs were supplied by the following: McCormick and Company, Inc.; National Dairy Council; Chiffon Margarine; Keith Thomas Company; National Macaroni Institute; Processed Apples Institute; Western Iceberg Lettuce; Knox Gelatin; McIlhenny Company (Tabasco); National Kraut Packers Association; California Avocado Advisory Board; South African Rock Lobster Service Corporation; and Seven Seas Salad Dressings.

© Favorite Recipes Press, 1968
Post Office Box 3177
Montgomery, Alabama 36109
Library of Congress Catalog Card No. 68-30672

INTRODUCTION

Americans are salad lovers. Most homemakers wouldn't think of serving a main meal without a salad. In fact, many wise homemakers often make salad the meal itself.

The home economics teachers who contributed recipes for Our Favorite Salads are most aware of the benefits of salads. These teachers know salads are packed with vitamins and minerals and are perfect for the weight-conscious. Hearty salads are naturals for those trying to put weight on and light salads are the answer to how to get a good food without eating the calories.

In this collection of Our Favorite Salads, you'll find delicious salads galore. The pages are filled with recipes for fruit, vegetable, seafood and meat salads, green ones and congealed ones. There's even a section on party and foreign salads for those extra-special occasions.

Mary Ann Richards

Anne Weiss — Executive Editor

Maureene Buck — Associate Editor   Edna Maggelet — Assistant Editor
Dee Bryant — Associate Editor   Joyce Miller — Assistant Editor
Lynne Guran — Associate Editor   Janell Webster — Assistant Editor

BOARD OF ADVISORY EDITORS

Mrs. Ruth McRae Carlson
Washington, D. C.

Ruth Stovall
State Supervisor
Home Economics Education
Alabama

Anne G. Eifler
Supervisor, School Lunch
and Nutrition, Pennsylvania

Barbara Gaylor
Home Economics & Family
Life Education Service,
Michigan

Kathryn Gill
Chief, Home Economics
Education, Wisconsin

Betty Lou Hoffman
State Advisor
Future Homemakers of
America, Montana

Catherine B. Myers
State Supervisor
Home Economics Education
New Mexico

Blanche Portwood
State Supervisor
Home Economics Education
Oklahoma

Clio S. Reinwald
Coordinator, Home
Economics & School Food
Service, Pennsylvania

Frances Rudd
Director, Home Economics
Arkansas

Dorothy Schnell
Chief, Bureau
of Homemaking Education
California

Imogene Van Overschelde
Supervisor, Home
Economics Education,
South Dakota

Helen H. Wilson
State Supervisor
Home Economics
Idaho

SALADS ARE IN GOOD TASTE

Salads at one time were considered strictly summer fare, and this wasn't many years ago. Now, though, homemakers have learned to vary the contents of salads so they have an honored place at the table every day.

Neither was it too long ago that salads consisted solely of greens garnished with tomatoes, sometimes cucumbers, scallions and perhaps a little green pepper and celery.

Today there are as many salads as there are ideas . . . attractive side dishes of fruit or vegetables; big, elegant main dishes . . . great for family, tops for company.

Which salad goes with which meal? That depends on the rest of the meal. A small, crisp green or fruit salad is an excellent accompaniment to a hearty meal. If the salad is to be the meal itself, choose one that contains generous amounts of meat, seafood, poultry, eggs or cheese.

A rule of thumb for choosing salads: Light salads go with heavy, hearty meals; heavy salads with light meals or by themselves. Tart salads are particularly good with seafood. Fruit salads are delicious as appetizers, desserts or as side dishes.

Special occasions call for special salads. Try potato salad or a tangy bean salad for the Fourth of July. Spicy apple salad is perfect for Labor Day; Christmas calls for cranberry salad. Try rich-looking tomato aspic on Valentine's (molded in a heart shape, of course) and maybe a congealed cherry salad on Washington's birthday.

Salad Making Hints

Dash your salads generously with color, being sure the color combinations are pleasing. Ingredients also should complement each other in texture, form and flavor.

Mix vegetables and fruit for an unusual taste treat. Or try soft and firm-textured foods together.

To enhance flavor of salads, sprinkle lemon juice on fruits, seafoods, meats, poultry or vegetables. The lemon juice also keeps salad foods from developing unattractive brown spots.

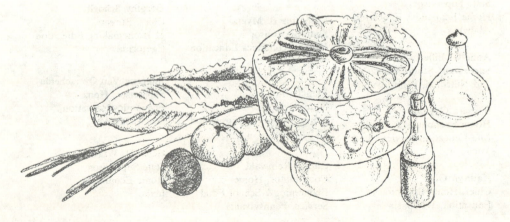

THE BEST SALADS

1. Choose the appropriate salad.
   a. Light salad with hearty meal.
   b. Tart salad with fish.
   c. Hearty or hot salad for main course.
   d. Fruit salad as appetizer, dessert, or meat accompaniment.

To Wash Greens . . .

All greens must be washed thoroughly before using. Discard any bruised or wilted leaves.

To wash iceberg lettuce, cut out the core. Hold the lettuce under cold running water so the water runs into the opening.

The running water should cause leaves to separate. Shake off excess water and dry thoroughly.

Leaf lettuce, endive, spinach, etc., should be washed one leaf at a time. Swish each leaf in water. Allow water to drain off. Roll up in a clean tea towel to absorb excess moisture. Wrap and store in refrigerator until ready to use.

Salad Etiquette

Q: Where would I place individual salads?
A: First course salads should be in the center of each place, for formal serving on a large plate. Main course salads should be placed at left of dinner plate. If the table is crowded, place directly above forks. In this case the bread and butter plate should be omitted.

Q: Is it proper to have salad on the table at the beginning of the meal?
A. Yes. Place your salad just before seating your guest.

Q: How should I serve a platter of salad or a bowl of mixed greens?
A: It may be passed provided it is easy to handle and servings can be easily removed. It is permissible for the hostess to serve individual salad plates and pass them around.

Q: Should dressing always be passed?
A: Pass your dressing if none has already been added to the salad.

Q: Is a salad fork always necessary?
A: A dinner salad may be eaten with the same fork as the main course.

Q: Where does the salad fork appear in the table setting?
A: This depends on when the salad is to be served during the meal. For the first course, the fork is at the extreme left. If with the main course or following it, the fork is inside the dinner fork just at left of the dinner plate.

CLASSIC SALAD

The simplest salad, a tossed green one, is also the most classic. Dressing tossed greens keynotes simplicity; oil, vinegar and seasonings are accepted dressing ingredients.

Rub the salad bowl with a clove of garlic or toss a chapon in with the salad. (A chapon is a small piece of stale or toasted bread rubbed with a cut clove of garlic. This is always removed before serving salad.)

Use a variety of greens in artful combinations, two or more to a salad. After washing in cold water, dry greens gently and thoroughly so not even a drop of water clings to them. Tear, do not cut, into bite-size pieces and heap in the salad bowl.

Carry to the table along with premixed dressing or — if you prefer to mix dressing at the table — with the salt, pepper, oil, vinegar and mustard you will use. The usual proportion of oil to vinegar is three parts oil to one part vinegar.

In either case, dress the salad only at the very last minute, and use just enough dressing to coat each leaf—no more. Toss gently but repeatedly. You want to coat each leaf evenly and completely without "bruising" the salad. Serve immediately on chilled plates.

What else goes into the salad bowl? Absolutely nothing if you belong to the "greens only" cult. If you prefer to have a combination of flavors, occasionally try bits of celery, avocado, carrot, green pepper, even onion rings in your salads. Take care not to repeat the rest of the menu, though. If, for instance, a salad is to be served with a tomato-dominated dish, you'll not want tomatoes in the salad.

In any case, keep a sharp eye on the tomatoes. They make salads soggy unless you cut them in advance, drain off excess juice, and add them to the greens at the last minute.

Ways To Improvise

Add any of these to greens:

1. Artichokes, cut small
2. Avocado, in thin slices
3. Carrot, grated raw
4. Cauliflowerets, raw
5. Cheese, crumbled
6. Cucumber slices or sticks
7. Ham, in slivers
8. Mushrooms, (uncooked) in thin slices
9. Radish slices
10. Red onion rings
11. Shrimp, whole or broken
12. Tiny cheese balls

THE SALAD BOWL

As much, possibly more, has been written or said about the bowl as the salad itself . . . whether it absolutely must be of wood or whether another kind can be used, whether to rub it with garlic before tossing the salad in it, even whether this great bowl should ever touch water.

The most practical course seems to be: Use whatever bowl suits your wishes.

Classic wood fits most occasions, whether you're serving salad at a backyard barbecue or a sit-down supper party.

To protect your fine wood bowl, wash it with a damp cloth or swish it quickly in cool water. Dry at once. Every three or four months, rub the inside of the bowl with olive or salad oil. Wipe it clean. This will keep the bowl's venerable patina.

For the ultimate in formality, use your silver bowl—protected by a glass liner, of course.

Ceramic bowls are a favorite for a cheerful family dinner or for everyday. To prevent chipping, though, handle the bowl carefully.

Stainless steel bowls are sleek and modern. These bowls, which never need polishing, may be used for all types of salads.

Clear glass bowls are ideal for showing off a fresh fruit salad, but they become unpleasantly smudged with oil in tossed salad. Ovenproof bowls are essential for hot salads. An added touch—slip the bowl into a decorative holder before putting it on the table.

Wilted Greens

For salad with a twist, try wilted greens. Bacon drippings give the sweet-sour dressing a very special flavor. Serve wilted greens in your ovenproof bowl or a stainless steel one.

6 slices bacon	4 tsp. sugar
Bacon drippings	½ tsp. salt
½ c. sliced green onion	8 c. leaf lettuce, torn
¼ c. vinegar	6 radishes, thinly sliced
¼ c. water	1 hard-cooked, egg chopped

Cook bacon and drain. Place lettuce in warm serving bowl. Pour warm drippings from skillet over lettuce. Heat vinegar, water, sugar, salt, pepper and green onions in skillet. Pour over greens. Toss until thoroughly mixed. Garnish with radish slices and chopped egg. Serve at once.

MAIN DISH SALADS

The perfect-almost-any-time-salad is the main dish one. It is the answer to what to serve at bridge luncheons, suppers, baby or bridal showers, for your own lunch or when you're having a few friends in. It's ideal for a spur-of-the-minute meal, too, since preparation and service are so easy.

A main dish salad is a meal in itself—nutritious and filling. These salads usually are built around meat, eggs, fish or cheese combined with salad greens and a tangy or spicy dressing.

A light main course salad, though, may be just a generous serving of fruit topped with sherbet or cottage cheese.

Usually a main dish salad menu includes soup, the salad, bread, dessert and beverage.

Because canned meats are used so often in main dish salads, remember these tips. For easy slicing, chill the meat well, remove both ends from the can, push the contents out in one piece, then slice as desired. Canned meats may be sliced several hours ahead of serving if the slices are tightly wrapped and refrigerated.

Cube, sliver or slice luncheon meats, corned beef or small sausages and add to tossed green salads, potato, macaroni or cabbage salads.

In preparing bread to accompany the salad, use packaged mix—it's a real time-saver. Hard rolls and French bread are both excellent with salads. Vary these with garlic butter, a sprinkling of poppy, sesame or celery seeds, or a topping of grated cheese.

Special Occasions

Colorful fruit arrangements, gelatin molds or unusual frozen salads are ideal for special occasion salads. Gelatin and frozen salads are especially well suited for entertaining when so much of the food must be prepared in advance.

Serve these salads on a special tray or platter—your most elegant silver, china or crystal, for example. Garnish the salad neatly and attractively.

Pile dressing or mayonnaise high in the center of a large gelatin ring for an impressive salad.

Fancy party sandwiches or tiny rolls usually accompany dessert salads.

TO ACCOMPANY MEALS...

The most often served salads are those that accompany a main course. Frequently today, the accompaniment salad is a first course appetizer. It may also garnish a main dish serving platter or be served right along with the rest of the meal.

These salads are served in small to medium-sized portions. They are carefully chosen to complement the rest of the menu in color, texture and flavor. They may be varied easily by the dressing or topping. This way, the salads adapt to luncheon, supper or dinner menus.

There are several ways to serve these accompaniment salads. Individual salads arranged on greens on a large platter may be passed. A small salad for each person makes an attractive place setting.

Arrange on small plates or in wooden bowls and put to the left of the dinner plate. Crisp, tossed green salads, fruit or vegetable arrangements garnished with greens are attractive in a large salad bowl.

Cheese sticks, bread sticks or appetizer crackers are good when salads are served at the begininng of the meal. If the salad is served with the main course, have assorted breads or dinner rolls.

Special Suggestions

To dress up accompanying salads, try these suggestions:

1. Use canned pineapple chunks with a fruit salad. Lift them from the can and while still wet with syrup, dip in chopped nuts.

2. Roll balls of cream cheese in slivered or chopped nuts, plain or toasted coconut for a fruit salad topping.

3. Dip apple or banana slices in pineapple juice or syrup to prevent them from turning dark.

4. Garnish meat platters with whole spiced peaches, crab apples or apricots. These are especially tasty with canned meats.

QUICKIE VEGETABLE SALADS

1. On lettuce leaf, heap green beans marinated in French dressing. Top with pimento.
2. Diced celery and grated raw carrots mixed with nuts or raisins.
3. Garden peas combined with sliced celery, cheese cubes and French dressing.
4. Sliced tomatoes covered with cucumber slices and onion rings.
5. Tomato juice molded with shredded cabbage and celery.
6. Asparagus spears marinated in French dressing, garnished with tomatoes.
7. Thinly sliced radishes and turnips and raw cauliflowerets.
8. Mound of cottage cheese with diced green pepper, cucumber and onions.
9. Sliced beets and onion rings marinated in French dressing.
10. Mixed canned vegetables marinated in Italian dressing. Serve on lettuce bed.
11. On leaf of lettuce, place asparagus sprinkled with grated cheese.
12. Cherry tomatoes, cucumber slices and sliced spring onions.
13. Marinated green beans and hard-cooked egg slices.
14. Red beans, onion rings and shredded cabbage.
15. Stuff tomato with cottage cheese; sprinkle with minced chives, parsley or toasted almonds.

Easy Main Dishes

Hearty main dish salads should be colorful and crisp—filled with protein to keep your energy going.

Tomato Aspic with Slaw

Soften 1 envelope of unflavored gelatin in ¼ cup cold tomato juice. Heat 1¾ cups tomato juice to a boil. Add 1 teaspoon grated onion, 1 tsp. salt, and softened gelatin. Stir till gelatin dissolves. Pour into ring mold and chill till firm. Unmold ring on serving plate. Fill center with cabbage slaw to which has been added diced corned beef or luncheon meat. Other fillings that can be used are cottage cheese, potato salad, egg, chicken or tuna salad.

Red Bean Salad

While beans are still hot, combine 2½ c. cooked beans with 1½ c. coarsely cut celery; 1 c. sliced, on the bias, sweet Spanish onions; ½ c. sliced sweet pickles; ½ c. small cubes sharp cheddar cheese, if desired. Add 1 tbsp. sweet pickle liquid and ½ c. or more oil and vinegar dressing. Allow to stand in refrigerator several hours or overnight. Garnish with rings of onion or green pepper, hard-cooked egg slices.

Ham Salad

Combine 1 c. of cooked cubed ham; 4 hard-cooked eggs, chopped; ½ c. diced celery; ½ c. diced cucumber pickles; with mayonnaise to taste. Serve in lettuce cups. Garnish with paprika.

SPARKLING FRUIT SALAD

1. Add chilled orange pieces to green salad.
2. Avocado slices, grapefruit sections and a sprinkling of pomegranate seeds.
3. Top pineapple slices with sliced and scored bananas and peanuts.
4. Top peach halves with cottage cheese and chopped chives or onions.
5. Put pear halves together with cream cheese. Top with a cherry or watercress.
6. Top apricot halves with softened cream cheese and chopped dates or nuts.
7. Crushed pineapple molded in gelatin.
8. Avocado cubes and melon balls.
9. Diced fresh pineapple, strawberries and a sprinkling of finely chopped mint.
10. Combine orange or grapefruit sections, avocado slices and red apples.

Fruit Platter for Lunch

Place canned peach halves cut side up on salad greens in center of large plate. Fill with fruit cocktail. Spread pineapple slices with cottage cheese and top with another pineapple slice, sandwich style. Fill centers with cottage cheese. Cut bananas in half. Slice from tip inwards. Arrange slices in fan shape. (Bananas may be dipped in pineapple syrup for added flavor.) Arrange pineapple and banana fans around peaches. Garnish with salad greens.

Hints for Serving Fruit

Brighten the edges of pineapple rings by dipping them in paprika.

Decorate fruit salad with candied fruit.

Substitute orange for vinegar in mint sauce and serve with fruit salad.

Soften cream cheese with canned fruit syrup and use as a fruit salad topping.

Thin mayonnaise with canned fruit syrup for a dressing.

To prevent discoloration of fruit, slice with stainless steel knife at the last moment. Or sprinkle with lemon juice or powdered ascorbic or citric acid preparations (may be bought in drug store), and store in refrigerator until serving time.

SEASONING SALADS

Add seasonings or cheese to salads to give them a tasty lift. The chart below will guide you in using seasonings which complement the salad.

Store herbs and spices tightly covered away from heat. They keep best in a cool, but not cold, place. A soon as they lose their delicate aroma, replace them. They have lost flavor, too.

Refrigerate cheeses for best keeping. Serve them, however, at room temperature for the most distinctive flavor. Exceptions are cream, cottage and Neufchatel cheese which should be chilled when served.

HERBS	USE WITH
BASIL	Tomato and green salads; fresh tomato slices
CARAWAY	Coleslaw; beet and potato salads
CHIVES	Potato, cucumber, mixed vegetable and green salads
DILLI SEED	Coleslaw; potato and cucumber salads
MARJORAM	French dressing; mixed green and chicken salads
MINT	Fruit, cabbage and celery salads; slaw
MUSTARD	Potato salad; French and oil/vinegar dressings
OREGANO	Potato, mixed green and seafood salads; tomato aspic
PARSLEY	Greens, vegetables, shellfish salads
ROSEMARY	French dressing or mayonnaise for chicken or potato salads
SAVORY	Mixed green, green vegetables, potato and tomato salads; aspic
TARRAGON	Chicken, seafood, vegetable and mixed green salads; oil/vinegar dressings
THYME	Aspic; tomato and beet salads; mayonnaise and herb dressings

CHEESE	USE WITH
AMERICAN CHEDDAR	Tossed salads, dressings, appetizers
BLEU	Tossed salads, dressings, appetizer spreads
BRICK	Salads, appetizers
CAMEMBERT	Fruit salads, appetizer spreads
COTTAGE	Fruit, vegetable salads
CREAM	Fruit, vegetable salads, dressings, appetizer spreads
GORGONZOLA	Salads, dressings
GOUDA	Appetizers
MUENSTER	Raw vegetable appetizers
NEUFCHATEL	Salads, in dips
PROVOLONE	Appetizers
RICOTTA	Salads, appetizers
ROQUEFORT	Dressings, appetizers
SWISS	Fruit, vegetable salads

SPICES	USE WITH
ALLSPICE	Fruit salads; fruit salad dressings
GINGER	Pear salads
MACE	Whipped cream dressings for fruit salads
PAPRIKA	French dressings, garnish for green salads
CAYENNE PEPPER	Salad dressings; meat, fish and vegetable salads

APPETIZERS SET THE STAGE

Hors d'oeuvres are intended to excite the taste buds, but never, never to satisfy the appetite. You must approach your hors d'oeuvre or appetizer as though you were "setting the stage" for things to come.

Appetizers provide a very simple way to balance and vary a menu, to say nothing of giving the hostess a chance to be artistic and decorative. Follow the rule of opposites when planning your hors d'oeuvres. Bland or substantial main courses require crisp and tart appetizers. Vegetable or salad hors d'oeuvres complement a meal rich in protein or carbohydrates.

Appetizers may be hot or cold — take your choice. You only have to be sure that those to be served cold are indeed crisp and cold, not lukewarm and wilted. Hot appetizers should be piping hot.

CANAPÉS or Hors d'oeuvres?

In American food talk the terms hors d'oeuvre, appetizer and canape are often used interchangeably. It is true that both hors d'oeuvres and canapes are appetizers; however, there is a difference.

Canapes — Morsels of food with a base of bread, pastry or crackers. Finger food.

Hors d'oeuvre — Can be served hot or cold but is always eaten at the table, with a knife and fork.

Appetizer — Any finger food that does not have a base, and is eaten before the meal.

Spiced cold fish and shellfish are the most effective of all spurs to appetite and thirst.

MAKING YOUR OWN DRESSINGS

Bottled dressings are very convenient for today's busy homemaker. But it really takes so little time to create your own dressing, you might give it a try.

A light French dressing—oil, vinegar or lemon juice and seasonings—is the undisputed queen of dressings, appropriate on any salad. Mayonnaise, whipped or sour cream, and cooked dressing are all excellent and can be used in any way your taste dictates.

Never be afraid to experiment when making dressings. Vary the seasonings according to the ingredients, and who knows—you may create something very new and special.

Basic Ingredients

To make good dressings, you need certain staples. Oil and vinegar go in almost all dressings. The seasonings you choose depend on the flavor you want to achieve.

Oil

Some people insist on fruity Italian oil; others prefer the more delicate French type. Olive oil is used widely, but a good vegetable oil has more food value.

Vegetable oils are made from corn, cotton seed, peanuts and soy beans. Regardless of the type oil you choose, top quality is essential.

Vinegar

"Use a little at a time" is your guide for vinegar. Strength in vinegars differs so much you just have to try a little, then a little more, until you get exactly the flavor you want. Old-fashioned cider vinegar has a mild, sweet taste. For distinctiveness in dressings, use tarragon, wine, pear, garlic or other specially seasoned vinegar.

Seasonings

Regular table salt is fine for dressings; it won't cake. Freshly-ground black pepper is the best choice. Use dried or fresh herbs sparingly. A little goes a long way.

Garlic, too, has a habit of making itself well known if you use too much. Go lightly on it, whether you use fresh garlic, powdered dry garlic or garlic salt.

Other Salad Standbys

A variety of seasonings should be kept on hand in small amounts to add interest to every type of salad. Essential are celery salt, onion salt, minced onion and onion juice.

Adding distinctive flavor to both salads and dressings are horseradish; pickle relish; caraway, sesame, celery and mustard seeds. Don't overlook fresh and dried herbs like sage, mint, basil, chives, oregano, marjoram, dill, thyme. Use a sharp steak sauce or red pepper sauce for zest.

Crunchy nuts and raisins give a pleasing texture and taste contrast to meat, fish and fruit salads and aspics.

CHEESE	Amount	Calories
Blue or Roquefort type	1 oz.	105
Cheddar or American:		
Ungrated	1-in. cube	70
Grated	1 cup	445
Cottage cheese:		
Uncreamed	1 cup	195
Creamed	1 cup	240
Cream cheese	1 oz.	105
Parmesan, dry, grated	1 tbsp.	20
Swiss, natural	1 oz.	105

MEAT, POULTRY, FISH, SHELLFISH, RELATED PRODUCTS

	Amount	Calories
Bacon, broiled or fried crisp, drained	1 slice	50
Chicken, cooked:		
Meat and skin, broiled	3 oz. without bone	190
Canned, boneless	3 oz.	170
Ham, baked, lean and fat	3 oz.	245
Boiled ham, sliced	1 oz.	65
Crab meat, canned	3 oz.	85
Salmon pink, canned	3 oz.	120
Shrimp, canned, meat only	3 oz.	100
Tuna, canned in oil, drained	3 oz.	170

NUTS, RELATED PRODUCTS

	Amount	Calories
Almonds, shelled	¼ cup	210
Brazil nuts, broken pieces	¼ cup	190
Cashew nuts, roasted	¼ cup	190
Coconut, flaked, packaged	¼ cup	150
Peanut halves, roasted, salted	¼ cup	210
Peanut butter	1 tbsp.	95
Pecans:		
Halves	5 halves	70
Chopped	¼ cup	185
English Walnut:		
Halves	6 halves	65
Chopped	¼ cup	165

VEGETABLES AND VEGETABLE PRODUCTS

	Amount	Calories
Beans:		
Kidney, dried, canned	½ cup	115
Lima, cooked	½ cup	90
Snap, green, cooked	¾ cup	25
Beets, cooked, diced	1 cup	70

Cabbage:	AMOUNT	CALORIES
Raw:		
Finely shredded	½ cup	12
Cole slaw with mayonnaise	½ cup	85
Cooked	¾ cup	25
Carrots:		
Raw:		
Whole, 5½ x 1 in. (25 thin strips)	1 carrot	20
Grated	½ cup	20
Cooked, diced	½ cup	20
Cauliflower, raw, flower buds	⅓ cup	10
Celery, raw:		
Stalk, small inner	3 stalks	10
Pieces, diced	1 cup	17
Cucumbers, 7½ x 2 in.:		
Raw, pared	1 cucumber	30
Raw, pared, center slice, ⅛-in. thick	6 slices	1
Endive, curly (including escarole)	2 oz.	10
Lettuce, headed, raw:		
Head, loose leaf, 4-in. diameter	1 head	30
Head, compact, 1 lb.	1 head	60
Leaves	2 large or 4 small	5
Mushrooms, canned, solids and liquid	½ cup	20
Onions:		
Mature:		
Raw, 2½-in. diameter	1 onion	40
Young, green, small, without tops	6 onions	20
Parsley, raw, chopped	1 tbsp.	1
Peas, green:		
Cooked	½ cup	55
Canned, drained	½ cup	70
Peppers, green, raw:	1 med.	15
Chopped	1 tbsp.	2
Canned, pimentos, medium	1 med.	10
Potatoes, medium, boiled		
Peeled after boiling	1 potato	105
Peeled before boiling	1 potato	80
Potato chips, 2-in. diameter	10 chips	115
Radishes, raw, small, without tops	4 radishes	5
Sauerkraut, canned, including liquids	1 cup	45
Tomatoes:		
Raw, medium, about 3 per lb.	1 tomato	35
Tomato juice, canned	½ cup	25
Tomato catsup	1 tbsp.	20

FRUIT AND FRUIT PRODUCTS

Apples, raw, medium, about 3 per lb.	1 apple	70
Apple juice, fresh or canned	½ cup	60
Applesauce, canned:		
Sweetened	½ cup	115
Unsweetened	½ cup	50

	AMOUNT	CALORIES
Apricots:		
Raw, about 12 per lb.	3 apricots	55
Canned, heavy syrup (pack)	4 halves	105
Dried, uncooked halves	10 small	100
Avocados, raw:		
California varieties	½ avocado	185
Florida varieties, peeled, pitted	½ avocado	185
Bananas, raw, medium	1 banana	85
Blackberries, fresh	¾ cup	40
Blueberries, fresh	⅔ cup	60
Cantaloupes, medium	½ melon	60
Cherries:		
Fresh raw: sour, sweet, hybrid	1 cup	65
Canned, sour, red, pitted	½ cup	105
Cranberries, fresh	1 cup	50
Dates, fresh and dried, pitted, cut	2 cups	40
Figs:		
Fresh, 1½ in. diameter	3 figs	90
Dried, large, 2 x 1 inch	1 fig	60
Fruit cocktail, canned in syrup	½ cup	95
Grapefruit:		
White, medium	½ grapefruit	55
Pink or red, medium	½ grapefruit	60
Raw, sections, white	½ cup	4
Grapes:		
American slip skin	1 cup	65
European adherent skin	1 cup	95
Green seedless	1 bunch	80
Lemons, medium	1 lemon	20
Lemon juice:		
Fresh	¼ cup	15
Fresh	1 tbsp.	4
Canned, unsweetened	¼ cup	15
Limes, medium	1 lime	15
Lime Juice:		
Fresh	¼ cup	15
Fresh	1 tbsp.	4
Oranges, fresh:		
Navel, California	1 orange	60
Other varieties	1 orange	75
Orange juice:		
Fresh:		
California Valencia, summer	1 cup	120
Florida varieties:		
Early and midseason	1 cup	100
Late season	1 cup	110
Canned, unsweetened	1 cup	120
Frozen concentrate:		
Undiluted, Unsweetened, 6 oz. can	1 can	85
Water added	1 cup	110
Orange and grapefruit juice:		
Frozen concentrate, water added	1 cup	110

Peaches:	Amount	Calories
Fresh:		
Whole, medium, 2-in. diameter	1 peach	35
Sliced	1 cup	65
Canned, heavy syrup pack	1 cup	200
Frozen:		
Carton, 4 oz.	1 carton	99
Can, 16 oz.	1 can	355
Pears:		
Fresh, 3 x 2½-in. diameter	1 pear	100
Canned, heavy syrup pack	1 cup	195
Pineapple:		
Fresh, diced	¾ cup	55
Canned, syrup pack:	10 med. with	
Chunks	2 tbsp. juice	75
Crushed	½ cup	95
Sliced	2 small or	
	1 large slice	
	and 2 tbsp.	
	juice	90
Pineapple juice, canned	¾ cup	105
Plums:		
Fresh, 2-in. diameter	1 plum	25
Canned, syrup pack	3 with 2	
	tbsp. juice	100
Prunes, dried, medium:		
Uncooked	4 prunes	70
Cooked, unsweetened	4 with 2	
	tbsp. juice	95
Prune juice, canned	½ cup	100
Raisins, dried	1 tbsp. scant	30
Raspberries, red:		
Fresh	¾ cup	50
Frozen, 5 oz. carton	1 carton	138
Strawberries:		
Red, capped	¾ cup	40
Frozen, halves	5 oz.	155
Frozen, whole	5 oz	131
Tangerines, medium	1 tangerine	40
Watermelon, 4 x 8-in. wedge	1 wedge	115

FATS AND OILS

Oils, salad or cooking	1 tbsp.	125
Salad dressings:		
Bleu Cheese	1 tbsp.	80
French	1 tbsp.	60
Italian	1 tbsp.	85
Home-cooked, boiled	1 tbsp.	30
Mayonnaise	1 tbsp.	105
Thousand Island	1 tbsp.	75

Source: Yearbook of Agriculture, U.S. Department of Agriculture

SALAD MAKING TERMS

ANTIPASTO — Italian appetizer assortment.

ASPIC — A clear, savory jelly used in molds or to garnish cold dishes.

BIENFATIQUE — French term. A salad of greens tossed until limp, or with a hot dressing.

BLANCH — To parboil in water for a minute; or to pour water over food and then drain it almost immediately.

CANAPE — A small appetizer of bread or toast topped with a savory mixture.

CHAPON — A small cube of stale French bread rubbed with garlic and tossed with the salad greens to add a hint of flavor.

CHILL — To keep in a refrigerator until cold but not frozen.

CHOP — To cut into small pieces.

CUBE — To cut into small dice.

CUT — To chop or slice.

DICE — Cut into small squares.

FLAKE — To break into small pieces with a fork.

GARNISH — To decorate a dish by adding small amounts of food or herbs for color or flavor.

GRATE — To reduce to particles by rubbing on or grinding in a grater.

HORS D'OEUVRES — French appetizer course. An assortment of small portions of meat, fish, egg, vegetables.

JULIENNE — Food cut in long thin strips.

MINCE — To chop finely or put through a mincer or press.

MOLD — To shape in a mold. A gelatin-stiffened mixture set in a mold.

PARE — To remove the skin of fruit or vegetable with a knife or parer.

PIT — To remove kernel of fruit.

TOSS — To mix with light strokes, lifting with a fork and spoon. To flip in the air.

ABBREVIATIONS

Cup	.................................c.	Large	................................lge.
Tablespoon	.......................tbsp.	Package	.........................pkg.
Teaspoon	...........................tsp.	Small	...............................sm.
Pound	...................................lb.	Dozen	...........................doz.
Ounce	.................................oz.	Pint	.................................pt.

MEASUREMENTS

3 tsp. = 1 tbsp.

2 tbsp. = ⅛ c.

4 tbsp. = ¼ c.

8 tbsp. = ½ c.

16 tbsp. = 1 c.

5 tbsp. + 1 tsp. = ⅓ c.

⅝ c. = ½ c. + 2 tbsp.

⅞ c. = ¾ c. + 2 tbsp.

4 oz. = ½ c.

8 oz. = 1 c.

2 c. granulated sugar = 1 lb.

3½ c. powdered sugar = 1 lb.

2¼ c. brown sugar = 1 lb.

4 c. sifted all-purpose flour = 1 lb.

1 lb. butter = 2 c. or 4 sticks

1 qt. = 4 c.

A Few Grains = less than ⅛ tsp.

Pinch is as much as can be taken between tip of finger and thumb

CAN CONTENTS

Average Contents	Can Size
1 c.	8 oz.
1¾ c.	No. 300
2 c.	No. 303
2½ c.	No. 2
3½ c.	No. 2½

Accompaniments,
Appetizers & Beverages

RECIPE FOR CHEESE TRAY FOR FALL ON PAGE 22

BLENDER CRANBERRY RELISH

2 c. frozen cranberries
1 orange
1 c. sugar

Rinse and drain cranberries quickly. Wash orange; slice into 6 or 8 sections. Remove seeds and excess membrane. Place cranberries and orange sections with rinds in blender; turn on high speed until well blended. Empty into a quart container; stir in sugar. Store in refrigerator to be used as needed; keeps well. Limes may be substituted for the orange. Yield: 3 1/2 cups.

Mrs. Bonita Liles Williams
Kingston H.S.
Kingston, Arkansas

CANDIED MINT LEAVES

Mint leaves
1 egg white
6 drops of peppermint oil
½ c. sugar

Remove stems from mint; coat both sides with egg white. Combine peppermint oil and sugar; dip leaves in sugar, coating well. Place on waxed paper or in slow oven to dry. A good garnish for fruit salads or cocktails.

Mrs. Patricia Charpentier, New London H.S.
New London, New Hampshire

CHEESE TRAY FOR FALL

Edam cheese
Gouda cheese
Brick cheese
Swiss cheese slices
Provolone cheese
Camembert cheese
Caraway seed cheese
Blue cheese wedge
Muenster cheese
American cheese
Lettuce
Assorted crackers
Fall fruit

Peel Edam cheese; cut several wedges and arrange in center of large tray. Cut Gouda in wedges and slices, leaving red wax on; overlap at one side of tray. Slice several pieces from piece of brick cheese and arrange at end of tray. Overlap slices of Swiss cheese at front of tray and pile sticks of Provolone cheese next to it. Remove foil from Camembert and arrange at front of tray. Slice and overlap caraway cheese at side of tray; arrange wedge of blue cheese and Muenster. Pile cubes of American cheese at back of tray next to Edam and garnish tray with crisp lettuce or galax leaves. Serve with a basket of assorted crackers and fall fruit such as grapes, apples and pears. Serve hot chocolate or spiced chocolate, as an accompaniment.

Photograph for this recipe on page 21.

CRANBERRY RELISH

2 c. finely chopped cranberries
1 c. miniature marshmallows
1 flat can crushed pineapple, drained
½ pt. heavy cream, whipped

Combine chopped cranberries and marshmallows; cover and refrigerate overnight. Add pineapple. Just before serving fold in whipped cream. Serve with chicken or turkey. Yield: 8 servings.

Mrs. Della O. Lindsay
Riverside H.S.
Boardman, Oregon

A CUP OF FRIENDSHIP

1 c. maraschino cherries, cut in halves
1 c. pineapple, cut in small pieces
1 c. peaches, cut in small pieces
3 c. sugar

Drain all fruit and mix with sugar. Store in an apothecary jar or other covered container with loose-fitting lid 2 weeks or until the fruit is fermented. Do not refrigerate. To keep supply replenished, add 1 cup fruit and 1 cup sugar every 2 weeks, rotating kinds of fruit; fruit cocktail may be substituted for peaches. Chopped bananas and pecans may be mixed with portion of the fruit to be served; do not add them to entire mixture.

Mrs. Patsy Robertson, Ridgeroad, Jr. H.S.
North Little Rock, Arkansas

DEVILED EGGS

6 hard-cooked eggs
2 tbsp. mayonnaise
½ tsp. salt
¼ tsp. pepper
1 tbsp. sweet pickle, chopped
1 tsp. finely chopped onion

Slice eggs in half lengthwise; remove yolks. Mash yolk with fork. Add remaining ingredients; blend well and place in egg whites. Garnish with sliced stuffed olives, paprika or parsley. Chill before serving. Yield: 6 servings.

Mrs. Anna Marie Acosta, Carencro H.S.
Carencro, Louisiana

DEVILED EGGS

6 hard-cooked eggs
½ tsp. salt
¼ tsp. pepper
½ tsp. dry mustard
3 tbsp. mayonnaise

(Continued on next page)

Cut eggs in halves; slip yolks out. Mash yolks with fork; add salt, pepper, mustard and mayonnaise. Blend well; heap yolk mixture lightly in whites. Serve with salads or cold meats.

Mrs. Catherine R. Trotter, Independence H.S.
Independence, Louisiana

PICKLED EGGS

3 doz. hard-cooked eggs
2 pt. white vinegar
10 whole allspice
1 tbsp. salt
1 tsp. powdered ginger or 1 root
2 cloves of garlic
2 bay leaves
1 pod red pepper

Remove shells from eggs; arrange in large glass jar. Simmer vinegar and spices about 15 minutes. Pour over eggs; cover. May be eaten after 24 hours but flavor improves with standing. Will keep indefinitely in refrigerator. If desired, add small onions, carrot sticks, ripe olives, 1-inch squares sharp cheddar cheese or cauliflower. Excellent as garnish, accompaniment or appetizer with crackers.

Mrs. Blanche Young, Dial Jr. H.S.
Pine Bluff, Arkansas

PICKLED EGGS

6 hard-cooked eggs
2 c. vinegar, sweet pickle juice or
    beet pickle juice

Remove shells; place eggs in quart jar. Pour vinegar over eggs; store in refrigerator 48 hours before using. Cut in wedges. Serve on vegetable plate or as garnish. Red color of beet juice gives eggs a very different and unique touch.

Mrs. Wayne Weishaar, Lemmon H.S.
Lemmon, South Dakota

STUFFED EGGS

6 hard-cooked eggs
12 cubes ham, olives or pimento (opt.)
3 tbsp. softened butter or margarine
Dash of Worcestershire sauce
Salt and pepper to taste
2 tbsp. mayonnaise or salad dressing

Slice eggs in half; cut small slice from rounded side. Remove yolks. Arrange egg whites on rack; place a cube of ham in each cavity. Beat yolks with electric mixer; add remaining ingredients.

Blend until very smooth; place in whites. Anchovy paste, lemon juice or dry mustard may be added to yolk mixture. Yield: 12 halves.

Mrs. Kathryn Williams, Ruidoso H.S.
Ruidoso, New Mexico

STUFFED EGGS CURRY

1 doz. eggs, hard-cooked
1 c. mayonnaise
1 tsp. chicken-seasoned stock base
¼ tsp. instant onion powder
¼ tsp. white pepper
1 tsp. curry powder (or more)
½ tsp. salt
1 c. finely minced cooked or canned
    chicken (opt.)
Little tidbits for toppings, capers,
    anchovies, olive slices, pimento and
    sliced onion

Carefully cut hard-cooked eggs in half crosswise; slice a small cap off the ends. Remove yolk and mash or force through a sieve. Add mayonnaise, stock base, onion powder, pepper, curry powder, salt and chicken. Mix thoroughly. Refill egg white, piling yolk mixture high. Cap with smaller portion of white and top each with rolled anchovies, ripe or stuffed olives, capers, pimento and onion. If desired, the caps may be tinted with food color and may be secured with colored toothpicks. Yield: 24.

Photograph for this recipe on page 383.

GARLIC MARINATED MUSHROOMS

2 c. canned button mushrooms
⅓ c. vinegar
2 tbsp. water
¾ c. olive oil
1 envelope Italian Good Seasons salad
    mix
1 lge. clove of garlic, quartered

Drain mushrooms; add to dressing made of remaining ingredients. Marinate in closed jar overnight. Yield: 8-10 servings.

Mrs. Doris Schlumpf, Durand Unified H.S.
Durand, Wisconsin

MARY'S CHUNK PICKLES

10 to 12 whole cucumbers
4 c. vinegar
8 c. sugar
2 tbsp. mixed pickling spices
5 tsp. salt

23

(Continued on next page)

Place cucumbers in pan; cover with freshly boiling water for 4 mornings. Cut in chunks on 5th day; make syrup of remaining ingredients. Bring to boil; pour over cucumbers. Let stand 2 days. Bring all to boil on 3rd day; seal in hot, sterilized jars.

Mrs. Joy L. Manson
Parishville-Hopkinton Central H.S.
Parishville, New York

MINTED GRAPES

1 bunch seedless green grapes
½ c. honey
2 tbsp. lime juice
2 tbsp. finely snipped mint

Wash and stem enough grapes to fill 4 parfait or sherbet glasses; peel if desired. Stir together honey, lime juice and mint; refrigerate grapes in marinade until ready to serve. Spoon into glasses; garnish with sprig of mint. Yield: 4 servings.

Mrs. Ruth H. Winslow, H. Wilson Thorpe Jr. H.S.
Hampton, Virginia

MUSHROOM PICKLES

⅔ c. tarragon vinegar
½ c. salad oil
1 med. garlic clove, minced
1 tbsp. sugar
1 ½ tsp. salt
Dash of freshly ground pepper
2 tbsp. water
Dash of bottled hot pepper sauce
1 med. onion, sliced, separated in rings
2 6-oz. cans broiled mushrooms, drained

Combine first 8 ingredients; add onion and mushrooms. Cover; refrigerate 8 hours, stirring several times. Drain before serving.

Mrs. Dorothy Felts, East Rowan Sr. H.S.
Salisbury, North Carolina

RELISHED CARROTS

½ c. apple vinegar
½ c. salad oil
¾ c. sugar
1 can whole baby canned carrots
1 tbsp. chopped pimento
½ c. green pickle relish

Heat vinegar, salad oil and sugar; add carrots. Let set overnight in refrigerator; drain. Add pimento and pickle relish. Yield: 6 servings.

Mrs. Billye Freeland, Eastwood H.S.
El Paso, Texas

STRAWBERRIES

1 15-oz. can sweetened condensed milk
1 3 ½-oz. can Angel Flake coconut
1 6-oz. box strawberry Jell-O
½ c. finely chopped pecans
1 5-oz. pkg. red sugar crystals
1 3-oz. pkg. slivered almonds
3 to 4 drops of green cake coloring

Combine milk, coconut, Jell-O and nuts; let stand overnight in refrigerator. Roll; shape into strawberries. Roll in red sugar crystals. Dilute green coloring with small amount of water; add almond and tint. Insert almonds in strawberries as stems. Yield: 50-60 servings.

Francis Reeves, Wilmer-Hutchins H.S.
Hutchins, Texas

SWEDISH CUCUMBERS

1 7-in. cucumber, unpeeled
½ c. white vinegar
2 tbsp. water
Generous dash of white pepper
2 tbsp. sugar
¼ tsp. salt
1 tbsp. chopped parsley

Slice cucumber very thin. Place in glass dish. Combine vinegar, water, pepper, sugar and salt; pour over cucumber. Sprinkle with parsley; allow to stand 2 to 3 hours in refrigerator before serving. Yield: 10 servings.

Opal M. House, Orland H.S.
Orland, California

SWEET AND SOUR MUSHROOMS

1 lb. fresh mushrooms
3 c. water
½ tsp. salt
1 tsp. pickling spice
¾ c. white vinegar
¼ tsp. white pepper
3 tbsp. catsup
½ c. sugar
4 tbsp. cornstarch

Wash mushrooms; simmer water, 1 teaspoon salt and pickling spice for 12-15 minutes. Drain; reserve liquid. Mix vinegar, remaining salt,

24

(Continued on next page)

white pepper, catsup, sugar, cornstarch and 1 cup mushroom liquid until well dissolved; cook over medium heat, s t i r r i n g constantly, until thickened. Add mushrooms; s i m m e r about 5 to 8 minutes until mushrooms are thoroughly hot. Cool; store in refrigerator overnight. Serve hot or cold. Excellent for buffet supper. Yield: 8-10 servings.

Mrs. Gloriann Martinson Katabi
Watsonville H.S.
Watsonville, California

UNCOOKED TOMATO RELISH

    1 peck underripe tomatoes
    2 c. chopped celery
    6 lge. white onions, chopped
    2 green peppers, chopped
    2 c. sugar
    ⅓ c. salt
    2 oz. mustard seed
    1 qt. vinegar

Peel tomatoes with knife; chop. Drain in colander overnight. Add celery, onions, and peppers. Mix sugar, salt, mustard seed and vinegar; pour over vegetables. Chill o v e r n i g h t or longer. This salad-relish may be sealed in sterilized jars and kept for w e e k s uncooked and w i t h o u t refrigeration. Yield: 25 servings.

Mrs. Le Nora Hudson, Okla. Sch. for Deaf
Sulphur, Oklahoma

BISCUIT PIZZAS

    1 can biscuits
    1 can tomato paste
    ¼ tsp. oregano
    Salt to taste
    Pepper to taste

Grease round cake pan for each pizza or use large cookie sheet for several pizzas. Pull each bisquit out to about the size of a saucer or as large as possible without holes. Combine remaining ingredients with tomato paste mixture and desired garnishes. Bake at 350 degrees about 12 to 15 minutes. Cheese, sausages, mushrooms or olives may be used for garnishes. Yield: 10 servings.

Mrs. Connie McClure, Nimitz Jr. H.S.
San Antonio, Texas

CHEESE COCKTAIL BISCUITS

    1 c. grated sharp cheddar cheese
    ½ c. butter or margarine
    ½ tsp. Worcestershire sauce
    1 ½ c. flour

    ½ tsp. salt
    Dash of cayenne pepper
    Large red peanuts

Blend cheese and butter together; mix until light. Add remaining ingredients; knead to form smooth dough. Pinch off pieces of dough and roll into 3/4 inch balls. Place peanut in center of each ball. Arrange on ungreased baking sheet. Bake at 375 degrees 12 to 15 minutes. May be made ahead and refrigerated. Yield: 3 dozen biscuits.

Mrs. J. D. Wolf, Leigh H.S.
San Jose, California

CHEESE DELIGHT

    1 4-oz. can peeled green chilies, diced
    1 4-oz. can pimentos, diced
    2 hard-cooked eggs, mashed with fork
    ½ lb. cheddar cheese, grated
    1 8-oz. can tomato sauce
    French rolls or English muffins

Combine all ingredients for filling in order given. Spread on rolls. Place on cookie sheet. Heat in 350-degree oven until cheese melts, about 12 minutes. Mixture may be spread on bite-sized pieces of white bread.

Mrs. Betty Lou Davis, Washington Jr. H.S.
Dinuba, California

CHEESE DOLLARS

    ½ c. butter or margarine
    3 oz. very sharp cheddar cheese, grated
    1 c. flour
    ⅛ tsp. red pepper
    ¼ tsp. salt

Cream butter and cheese together; add remaining ingredients. Shape into 1 1/2-inch roll. Wrap in aluminum foil; chill well. Slice into 1/8 inch slices. Bake at 400 degrees for 6 minutes. Yield: 3 dozen canapes.

Jo Anne Kralich, Pompano Beach Jr. H.S.
Pompano Beach, Florida

CHEESE PUFFS

    1 loaf thick white bread, sliced
    8 oz. cream cheese
    ½ lb. cheddar cheese
    ½ lb. butter or margarine
    4 egg whites, stiffly beaten

Trim crusts from bread; cut into 1-inch cubes. Melt cheeses and butter in top of double boiler over hot water. Cool; fold in egg whites. Dip

(Continued on next page)

bread cubes into mix; coat well. Place on cookie sheet. Refrigerate overnight or freeze. Brown at 400 degrees until puffy and light brown. Serve immediately. Yield: 11 dozen puffs.

Mrs. Shirley Absher, Cement H.S.
Cement Oklahoma

CUCUMBER SANDWICHES
Cucumbers, peeled and thinly sliced
Vinegar
Salt to taste
Pepper to taste
Sliced onion
1 cake cream cheese
Mayonnaise
Fresh bread slices

Soak cucumbers overnight in vinegar, salt, pepper, and sliced onion. Soften cream cheese at room temperature; mash and add 1 tablespoon mayonnaise. Spread bread with additional mayonnaise, then cream cheese. Place 4 cucumber slices and 1 thin onion slice on each slice of bread. Trim crust from bread and cut sandwiches into quarters. Chill in refrigerator until serving time.

Mrs. Blanche Young, Dial H.S.
Pine Bluff, Arkansas

HOT CURRY-CHEESE CANAPES
¾ lb. cream cheese
2 egg yolks
⅓ c. onion, finely chopped
¼ tsp. curry powder
Dash of salt and pepper
Cream
1 loaf bread, thinly sliced

Combine all ingredients for spread. Cut rounds of bread, about 4 per slice. Spread with cheese-curry mixture. Place on cookie sheet. Cover with plastic wrap. Refrigerate. Brown in broiler, about 4 inches below heating element, until lightly browned, about 8 to 12 minutes. Serve hot. Yield: 5 dozen canapes.

Margaret Jordan, Sr. H.S.
White Plains, New York

HOT CHEESE TARTS
1 c. mayonnaise
3 tbsp. Parmesan cheese
1 loaf party-sized rye bread
1 to 2 red onions

Combine mayonnaise with 3 tablespoons cheese. Spread thin layer of mixture on bread. Slice onions thinly; place 1 slice on each slice of bread. Spread top with additional cheese mixture; sprinkle with additional Parmesan cheese. Bake at 450 degrees a short time. Yield: 12-24 servings.

Mrs. Wayne L. Furman, Sr. H.S.
Wellsboro, Pennsylvania

OLIVE-CHEESE SHORTIES
6 tbsp. butter
1 ⅓ c. shredded sharp cheddar cheese
1 ½ tsp. parsley flakes
⅛ tsp. onion powder
Dash of cayenne pepper
⅔ c. flour
24 olives, stuffed or black

Cream butter and cheese until smooth; blend in seasonings. Gradually add flour. Mix until smooth. Drop by teaspoons into ungreased cookie sheet. Place olive firmly on center of each ball. Bake at 400 degrees for 15 to 20 minutes. Yield: 24 shorties.

Gaynelle C. James, Gardner SW H.S.
Gardner, Illinois

OLIVE WHIRLIGIGS
1 c. shredded sharp process American cheese
3 tbsp. butter or margarine, softened
Dash of cayenne or Tabasco sauce
½ c. sifted all-purpose flour
½ c. chopped, stuffed green olives

Blend cheese, butter and cayenne; stir in flour. Roll dough between waxed paper to 10 x 6-inch rectangle, about 1/8 inch thick. Sprinkle pastry with chopped olives. Roll up, beginning with long side, as for jelly roll, lifting waxed paper slightly with each turn. Seal edge. Wrap roll in waxed paper. Chill at least 1 hour. Cut into 1/4-inch slices. Place about 2 inches apart on ungreased cookie sheet. Bake in 400-degree oven for 10 minutes or until edges are slightly browned. Serve hot. Yield: 40 canapes.

Mrs. Robert C. Powell, Atkinson H.S.
Atkinson, Illinois

SPRINGER CHEESE DELIGHTS

3 oz. cream cheese
¼ lb. grated sharp cheddar cheese
¼ lb. butter
2 egg whites, beaten
Bread cubes

Melt cheeses and butter in double boiler; fold in egg whites. Cut bread into 1-inch cubes; dip into cheese mixture. Place on cookie sheet and refrigerate overnight. Bake at 350 degrees 10 to 12 minutes. Yield: 4 dozen canapes.

Mrs. Ellen M. Schenck, Wilson H.S.
West Lawn, Pennsylvania

PARMESAN CRISPS

8 slices white bread
¾ c. grated Parmesan cheese
¾ tsp. chili powder
¾ c. butter, melted

Trim crusts from bread. Cut each slice into 6 sticks. Place on baking sheet; toast in preheated 375-degree oven 3 minutes. Combine cheese and chili powder. Coat sticks with melted butter; roll in cheese mixture. Place sticks on baking sheet. Bake 3 to 4 minutes longer or until golden brown. Serve warm. Yield: 48 sticks.

Mrs. Gordon Louis Moore, Sidney Lanier H.S.
San Antonio, Texas

ROLL-UPS

6 to 7 slices fresh white bread
4 oz. cheese
1 egg, beaten slightly
2 tbsp. milk
Deep fat for frying

Cut crusts from bread; roll bread thin with rolling pin. Roll bread tightly around finger of cheese. Place on pan, cut side down; cover with damp paper towel. Cut each roll-up in two crosswise; dip into egg-milk mixture. Fry in 1 1/2-inches 370-degree fat. Serve hot. Yield: 12-14 roll-ups.

Mrs. Evelyn Blake, Andrew Lewis H.S.
Salem, Virginia

TOASTED CARAWAY-CHEESE CANAPES

1 egg
1 8-oz. pkg. cream cheese
2 sm. onions, chopped finely
1 tsp. salt

¼ tsp. pepper
½ tsp. chives
8 tsp. caraway seeds
24 slices party rye bread

Beat egg and mix with softened cream cheese, onions, salt, pepper and chives until well blended. Spread mixture on bread slices. Sprinkle with caraway seeds. Freeze on flat surface. Pack in containers with freezer paper between layers. Return to freezer. Broil 4 inches from broiler until lightly browned. Serve hot. Yield: 24 canapes.

Mrs. Colleen T. Key, Lebanon H.S.
Lebanon, Tennessee

BACON BUNS

2 pkg. dry yeast
¼ c. warm water
¾ c. plus 1 tsp. sugar
2 c. milk
¾ c. plus 2 tbsp. butter
7 c. sifted flour
3 beaten eggs
1 tsp. salt
½ tsp. nutmeg
½ med. onion, chopped
1 lb. bacon slices, diced
1 lb. Canadian bacon, diced
Pepper to taste

Dissolve yeast in warm water. Add 1 teaspoon sugar; let work. Scald milk; add 3/4 cup butter and remaining sugar. Cool. Place cooled mixture in large bowl of mixer. Add 3 or 4 cups flour; add yeast mixture, eggs, salt and nutmeg. Add remaining flour; knead if necessary. Place in greased bowl; cover. Let rise until doubled. Saute onion in remaining butter; add remaining ingredients for filling. Pat dough into eight dozen 3-inch circles. Add 1/2 teaspoon bacon mixture to each circle. Fold over; seal and shape into crescent. Let rise. Brush with remaining egg. Bake at 400 degrees for 15 minutes. Garlic powder may be substituted for onion. Yield: 8 dozen rolls.

Doris Everson, Whittier Jr. H.S.
Sioux Falls, South Dakota

BAMBINO'S BABY PIZZAS

1 3-oz. can tomato paste
½ tsp. garlic salt
Oregano
⅛ lb. mozzarella cheese
⅛ lb. pepperoni sausage
Melba toast rounds

Preheat oven to 400 degrees. Combine tomato paste, garlic salt and 1/8 teaspoon oregano. Cut cheese and pepperoni into tiny cubes. Spoon small amounts of sauce onto melba toast rounds. Top with cheese and sausage cubes. Sprinkle with

(Continued on next page)

27

dash of oregano. Place on baking sheet. Bake 3 to 5 minutes or until cheese melts. Serve hot. Yield: 3 dozen pizzas.

Mrs. Linda Hair, Pearce Jr. H.S.
Austin, Texas

BROILED MEAT PUFFS

12 refrigerated biscuits
2 egg whites
½ tsp. salt
1 c. chopped cooked chicken or turkey
½ c. mayonnaise
1 tbsp. finely diced celery
1 tbsp. chopped pimento
Dash of pepper

Pull each biscuit apart to make 3 thin biscuits. Bake on ungreased cookie sheet at 400 degrees for 8 to 10 minutes or until golden brown. Beat egg whites and salt until stiff peaks form. Fold in remaining ingredients. Spread each biscuit with 1 tablespoon meat mixture. Bake at 475 degrees or broil for 3 to 5 minutes until golden brown. Watch carefully. Serve hot. May be prepared ahead, refrigerated 1 to 3 hours, then browned just before serving. Yield: 36 puffs.

Nancy M. Kinn, Arlington-Green Isle H.S.
Arlington, Minnesota

CHIPPED BEEF ROLL-UPS

2 sm. jars chipped beef
10 green olives, chopped
1 tbsp. mayonnaise
1 3-oz. pkg. cream cheese

Spread slices of beef out carefully. Mix olives and mayonnaise with softened cream cheese. Spread cheese mixture on slices of beef; layer beef and cheese mixture alternately in 3 to 5 layers. Roll jelly roll fashion; wrap and refrigerate. Slice in thin rounds. Mixture keeps well refrigerated or frozen. Yield: 24 rounds.

Mrs. G. G. Craig, Jr., Alvaton H.S.
Alvaton, Kentucky

CHEESE PASTRY SHELLS

1 c. sifted flour
½ tsp. salt
¼ c. shortening
1 c. grated sharp cheese
4 tsp. water
White sauce

Preheat oven to 425 degrees. Sift flour and salt together. Cut in shortening and grated cheese until mixture is mealy. Stir in water. Press firmly into smooth ball with hands. Roll out about 1/8-inch thick. Cut into tiny rounds and press into small muffin cups or tart shell molds. Bake 8 to 10 minutes. Fill shells with sauce and broil 2 minutes.

WHITE SAUCE:

2 tbsp. butter
2 tbsp. flour
½ tsp. salt
⅛ tsp. pepper
1 c. milk
1 can crab meat or cooked shrimp

Melt butter over low heat in heavy saucepan. Blend in flour and seasonings. Cook over low heat, stirring until mixture is smooth and bubbly. Remove from heat. Stir in milk. Bring to a boil, stirring constantly. Boil 1 minute. Add crab meat. Yield: 2 1/2 to 3 dozen shells.

Gail Epperson, Slidell Sr. H.S.
Slidell, Louisiana

CIRCLE SANDWICHES

5 to 7 slices bread, crusts removed
1 pkg. cream cheese
2 tbsp. lemon juice
1 to 2 tbsp. milk
1 can Vienna sausage

Line bread on piece of waxed paper or Saran wrap; overlap edges. Roll with rolling pin until bread loses its spring and pieces are rolled together. Mix cream cheese, lemon juice and milk together until consistency to spread. Spread on bread; place Vienna sausages in center. Bring sides of bread together and finger press until sides hold together. Roll in Saran or waxed paper; refrigerate 24 hours. Slice in small slices and serve. Olives may be substituted for sausage. Yield: 15 to 20 sandwiches.

Mrs. Mary Belle Tuten, Bernice H.S.
Bernice, Louisiana

HAM MOUNDS

6 slices white bread
Prepared mustard
Bread and butter pickles
1 can deviled ham

Spread bread lightly with mustard; cut each slice into four squares. Arrange squares on baking sheet; top each with pickle slice and mound of deviled ham. Broil in oven until bread is toasted and meat is heated through. Yield: 24 servings.

Mrs. W. H. Livingstone, Middleton Reg. H.S.
Middleton, Nova Scotia, Canada

DEVILED BISCUITS

1 pkg. refrigerated biscuits
¼ c. butter or margarine
1 4-oz. can deviled ham
¼ c. grated Parmesan cheese

Snip biscuits into quarters. Arrange in two 8-inch pie plates. Heat butter and deviled ham; stir until blended. Pour ham mixture over biscuits, being sure they are coated. Sprinkle with cheese. Bake in 400-degree oven about 15 minutes or until golden. Serve hot as appetizers or hot bread.

Mary E. Massie, Colonial Heights H.S.
Colonial Heights, Virginia

HOT LOBSTER CANAPES

1 can lobster
¼ tsp. paprika
1 tsp. prepared mustard
½ tsp. Worcestershire sauce
3 drops Tabasco sauce
3 tbsp. sherry
½ c. mayonnaise
Small toast rounds or crackers

Drain lobster; mince meat very fine. Add seasonings, sherry, and mayonnaise. Pile mixture onto toast rounds. Place under broiler until bubbly. Filling may be prepared ahead, spread on toast and broiled just before serving.

Mrs. Karlene J. Nahaney, Boothbay Reg. H.S.
Boothbay Harbor, Maine

MANHATTAN PIZZAS

8 oz. grated cheddar cheese
4 strips bacon, chopped
¼ c. onion, chopped
½ c. catsup
24 slices snack caraway rye bread

Combine cheese, bacon, onion and catsup. Spread cheese mixture on rye bread. Place under broiler until cheese melts and begins to bubble. Yield: 12 servings.

Joan Klingbeil, Cumberland H.S.
Cumberland, Wisconsin

MEXICAN APPETIZERS

3 c. plus 2 tbsp. flour
3 tsp. chili powder
1 ½ tsp. salt
1 c. shortening
6 ½ tbsp. cold water
¼ c. finely chopped onion
Chopped green pepper
1 clove of garlic, crushed
½ lb. ground beef
1 tbsp. butter
⅓ c. catsup

Sift 3 cups flour, 2 teaspoons chili powder and salt together into mixing bowl. Cut in shortening until size of peas; sprinkle with water. Mix and shape into ball. Refrigerate. Brown onion, green pepper, garlic and ground beef in butter; blend in catsup, remaining flour and remaining chili powder. Cook, stirring constantly until mixture thickens. Remove from heat. Divide pastry in half. Roll out about 1/16 inch thick. Cut 60 2-inch circles. Place on ungreased baking sheet. Spoon 1 teaspoon filling on each circle. Roll out remaining dough and cut 60 circles. Place on filled circles; seal edges with fork. Bake in 400-degree oven for 15 to 18 minutes or until lightly browned. Serve warm or cold. Yield: 6 circles.

Mrs. J. G. Bowman, Eagleton Jr. H.S.
Maryville, Tennessee

MOCK PIZZA

1 med. onion
1 can Spam
8 oz. cheese
1 can chili, without beans
Sesame crackers

Chop onion and Spam fine. Combine cheese and chili; add chopped ingredients. Spread mixture on crackers; place under broiler until cheese melts. Bun halves may be substituted for crackers. Yield: 50 canapes.

Mrs. Dallas Sturlaugson, Maddock H.S.
Maddock, North Dakota

PIZZA APPETIZERS

1 lb. hot sausage
2 6-oz. cans tomato paste
½ c. tomato sauce
½ c. finely chopped onion
¼ c. chopped stuffed olives
¼ c. chopped green pepper
½ tsp. salt
½ tsp. pepper
½ tsp. sweet basil
½ tsp. oregano
½ tsp. rosemary
½ lb. grated sharp cheddar cheese
Crackers

Shape sausage by teaspoonfuls. Cook over medium heat until pink is gone. Pour off grease. Add remaining ingredients except cheese and crackers. Cook over low heat for 20 minutes. Spread on crackers. Top with grated cheese. Bake in 350-degree oven until cheese is melted.

(Continued on next page)

Serve hot. Pizza mix may be stored in refrigerator 2 to 3 days before serving. French bread may be substituted for crackers, slicing lengthwise, before spreading with mixture. Yield: 40 servings.

Kathryn Hill, Comanche H.S.
Comanche, Texas

RIGATONI APPETIZERS

    1 pkg. Lawry's spaghetti sauce mix
    1 8-oz. can tomato sauce
    1 ½ c. water
    1 ¼ lb. lge. rigatoni
    ½ lb. ground beef
    ¼ c. finely chopped onion
    1 tsp. Lawry's seasoned salt
    ¼ tsp. Lawry's seasoned pepper
    ¼ c. grated mozzarella cheese
    ¼ c. ricotta cheese

Blend spaghetti sauce mix, tomato sauce and water in saucepan. Bring to a boil; reduce heat and simmer 25 minutes. Cover and set aside. Cook rigatoni according to package directions, but cooking only 8 to 9 minutes. Rinse immediately with cold water. Place ground beef and onion in skillet. Sprinkle with salt and pepper. Brown until ground beef is crumbly. Remove from heat and add cheeses immediately. Combine thoroughly. Stuff each rigatoni with meat mixture. Place in a small shallow baking dish. Pour prepared spaghetti sauce over stuffed rigatoni. Bake in 350-degree oven 10 to 15 minutes. Serve with cocktail picks.

Mrs. Esther Darst Minton
South Mountain H.S.
Phoenix, Arizona

SMALL PIZZA CANAPE

    2 sm. English muffins or cooked
      refrigerated biscuits
    4 tsp. chili sauce
    Sharp cheddar or mozzarella cheese
      strips
    ½ tsp. oregano
    4 pieces sausage, pepperoni or anchovy
      fillet
    Olive oil

Tear muffins in two, fairly evenly. Toast on flat sides only, at least 5 inches below broiler heat. Spread each muffin half with 1 teaspoon chili sauce, cheese and dash of oregano. Top each with piece of sausage. Drizzle small amount oil over top. Return to broiler and toast until the cheese is thoroughly melted. Yield: 5 servings.

Mrs. Sherri Day, West H.S.
Anchorage, Alaska

SHRIMP PATE

    1 c. shrimp
    ½ sm. onion, minced
    ¼ . melted butter
    1 tbsp. lemon juice
    ¼ c. salad dressing
    ¼ tsp. salt
    ¼ tsp. pepper

Mash shrimp; add remaining ingredients. Serve on garlic melba rounds.

Agnes J. Demick, Wolcott Jr. H.S.
Warren, Michigan

SMOKY SALMON

    1 7 ¾-oz. can salmon, drained and
      flaked
    ¼ c. mayonnaise or salad dressing
    1 tbsp. lemon juice
    1 tsp. horseradish
    1 tsp. grated onion
    ¼ tsp. liquid smoke
    Pastry for 1 crust
    Paprika

Combine salmon, mayonnaise and seasonings; mix thoroughly. Divide pastry in half. Roll very thin in circles about 9 inches in diameter. Spread each circle with 1/2 cup salmon mixture. Cut into 16 wedge-shaped pieces. Roll in jelly-roll fashion, beginning at round edge. Place rolls on 15 x 10 x 1-inch baking pan. Prick top to allow steam to escape; sprinkle with paprika. Bake in 450-degree oven for 10 to 15 minutes or until lightly browned. Yield: 32 rolls.

Mrs. Nadine D. Hendricks, Johnston H.S.
Austin, Texas

TINY BURGERS

    ½ lb. ground beef
    1 tsp. prepared horseradish
    ½ tsp. garlic salt
    ½ tsp. onion salt
    ¼ tsp. monosodium glutamate
    Salt and pepper to taste
    40 Triscuits or other crackers
    Grated Parmesan cheese

Combine ground beef, horseradish, garlic salt, onion salt, monosodium glutamate, salt and pepper. Spread one scant teaspoon meat mixture on each cracker. Sprinkle with cheese. Broil for 3 minutes about 3 to 4 inches from heat. Yield: 40 burgers.

Mrs. Judith Anderson, Stillwater Sr. H.S.
Stillwater, Minnesota

TEEN TOASTS

1 sm. pkg. cream cheese
1 tbsp. grated onion
3 tbsp. milk
1 loaf fresh bread, crusts removed
½ lb. bacon

Mix cream cheese, onion and milk until smooth. Spread mixture on bread slices; roll each slice as for jelly roll. Wrap each roll in 1/2 slice bacon. Refrigerate. Broil, turning until bacon is done. Serve immediately. Yield: 10 servings.

Mrs. Corinne Morse, Middle School
Amesbury, Massachusetts

TUNA-SOUR CREAM FILLING

1 7-oz. can albacore tuna
¼ c. chopped celery
2 tbsp. chopped onion
4 tsp. lemon juice
½ tsp. horseradish
6 tbsp. sour cream
Salt and pepper to taste

Mix all ingredients for open-faced sandwiches or appetizers. Garnish as preferred. Yield: 6-8 servings.

Mrs. Diane Caviezel, Enumclaw Jr. H.S.
Enumclaw, Washington

NACHOS

Cooked pinto beans
Toasted corn tortillas, quartered
Jalapeno peppers
American cheese

Mash cooked beans and fry in small shortening. Toast or fry tortillas. Spread beans on tortillas. Place on pan; add thin strips of peppers. Top with thin cheese slices. Bake in 425 to 450-degree oven for about 3 minutes. Serve hot.

Mrs. Eddith M. Davis, Bowie H.S.
El Paso, Texas

PEANUT BUTTER STICKS

1 lb. loaf fine grained bread
2 c. smooth peanut butter
¾ c. salad oil

Trim crusts from bread with sharp knife. Cut off one 3/4 inch crosswise strip from each slice. Cut remainder of slice into 4 strips lengthwise. Lay strips flat, close together in large, shallow pan. Toast strips and crusts for 1 hour to 1 hour and 30 minutes at 250 degrees. Make fine uniform crumbs of crusts in chopper or blender. Blend peanut butter with salad oil until consistency of medium cream sauce. Dip toasted strips into peanut butter, scraping off excess. Roll strips in crumbs. Set aside to dry. Pack in airtight can. Sticks will remain fresh 2 to 3 weeks. Yield: 30 sticks.

Mrs. Essie Bill Curtis, Macon County H.S.
Montezuma, Georgia

SOUFFLED CRACKERS

Soda crackers
Melted butter
Sesame seeds

Place soda crackers in ice water; let soak 10 to 15 minutes. Lift crackers carefully from water with pancake turner. Place small amount of butter and small amount of sesame seeds on each cracker. Place crackers on greased cookie sheet. Bake in 400-degree oven until light and crisp, about 30 to 40 minutes.

Mrs. Yvonne Lindrum, Montebello Jr. H.S.
Montebello, California

APPETIZER CHEESE MOUSSE

2 tsp. unflavored gelatin
¼ c. cold water
2 c. dairy sour cream
2 tsp. Italian dressing mix
¼ c. crumbled blue cheese
1 c. small curd cream-style cottage
    cheese

Soften gelatin in cold water; place over boiling water and stir until dissolved. Stir into sour cream; add dressing mix, blue cheese and cottage cheese. Beat with electric or rotary beater until well blended. Pour into 3 1/2-cup ring mold or small loaf pan. Chill until firm. Unmold; garnish with parsley and carrot curls. Serve with crisp crackers. Yield: 12 servings.

Mrs. Robert C. Powell, Atkinson H.S.
Atkinson, Illinios

CHEESE APPETIZER

2 lge. pkg. cream cheese
1 sm. cube bleu cheese
1 c. ground pecans
1 ground garlic button
Chili powder

31

(Continued on next page)

Cheese Hors D'Oeuvres

Mix first 4 ingredients thoroughly; shape into 2 rolls. Roll each in chili powder. Cover with waxed paper and chill for 24 hours. Slice and serve on crackers. Yield: 16 servings.

Mrs. Ruby W. Harkey, San Saba H.S.
San Saba, Texas

CHEESE BALL

2 8-oz. pkg. cream cheese
½ lb. sharp cheddar cheese, grated
1 finely chopped pimento
1 tbsp. finely chopped green pepper
1 tsp. onion juice
2 tsp. Worcestershire sauce
Dash of cayenne pepper
½ tsp. soy sauce
Chopped nuts

Mix all ingredients except nuts. Roll into ball or log. Place in waxed paper and chill for 12 hours. Roll in nuts or chopped parsley before serving. Serve with assorted crackers.

Louise Hall, Amador Co. H.S.
Sutter Creek, California

CHEESE BALL

3 3-oz. pkg. cream cheese
2 jars sharp cheese spread
1 jar Roka blue cheese
2 tbsp. wine vinegar
1 clove of garlic
Chopped pecans

Allow cheeses to soften at room temperature. Mix cheeses in large bowl until well blended, adding vinegar and garlic. Refrigerate until firm. Remove garlic clove. Shape into ball; roll in pecans. Serve with assorted crackers.

Mrs. Don Jackson, Bad Axe H.S.
Bad Axe, Michigan

CHEESE BALL

2 c. shredded cheddar cheese
1 3-oz. pkg. cream cheese
3 tbsp. mayonnaise
½ tsp. Worcestershire sauce
1 tsp. sherry extract
Dash of onion salt
Dash of garlic salt
Dash of celery salt
¼ c. chopped ripe olives
3 tbsp. minced dried beef
3 tbsp. minced fresh parsley

Combine cheeses, mayonnaise, Worcestershire sauce, sherry extract and onion, garlic and celery salts; blend until smooth. Add olives; cover and chill until firm. Shape cheese mixture into ball. Combine dried beef and parsley; roll ball in mixture. Cover and chill. Finely chopped pecans or chopped ripe olives may be substituted for dried beef. Yield: 20 servings.

Ramona Lawton, Mercer Jr. H.S.
Garden City, Georgia

CHEESE BALL

½ lb. American cheese, cubed
½ lb. sharp cheddar cheese, cubed
2 4-oz. pkg. blue cheese, cubed
½ c. mayonnaise
2 tsp. Worcestershire sauce
1 tbsp. chopped onion
1 tbsp. chopped sweet pickle
½ c. chopped pecans
½ c. chopped parsley

Let cubed cheese stand at room temperature for 2 hours. Cream well with electric mixer; blend in next 4 ingredients. Place in small bowl and cover with waxed paper; refrigerate for at least 6 hours. Remove from bowl; roll into ball size of grapefruit. Combine remaining ingredients; roll ball in mixture until covered completely. Cheese ball will keep in refrigerator for 2 weeks.

Mrs. Mildred Parr, Phoenix H.S.
Phoenix, Oregon

CHEESE BALLS

4 egg whites, beaten stiffly
1 ½ c. grated cheese
½ tsp. red pepper
½ tsp. salt
Cracker crumbs

Mix first 4 ingredients well; roll in cracker crumbs. Let stand in refrigerator until cold. Fry in hot fat until light brown. Yield: 4 dozen balls.

Jean Cook, Clarksdale H.S.
Clarksdale, Mississippi

CHEESE DREAMS

1 c. sifted plain flour
1 tsp. cayenne pepper
½ tsp. salt
1 8-oz. pkg. sharp cheese, softened
1 stick oleo
1 ½ c. cornflakes, crushed slightly

32

(Continued on next page)

Sift flour, pepper and salt together; add cheese and oleo. Mix well; add cornflakes. Roll into small balls. Place on cookie sheet. Mash each ball with fork; bake for 12 to 15 minutes at 350 degrees. Sprinkle with paprika. Yield: 8-10 servings.

Mrs. C.D. Huston, Greenwood Jr. H.S.
Greenwood, Mississippi

CHEESE LOG

½ lb. mild or sharp cheese, grated
1 8-oz. pkg. cream cheese, softened
Dash of onion juice
Dash of garlic salt
Dash of Worcestershire sauce
1 c. toasted nuts, crushed

Mix grated cheese with cream cheese; add seasonings to taste and half the nuts. Form into log or ball; roll in remaining nuts. Chill until firm enough to slice. Serve with crackers. Yield: 10-12 servings.

Mrs. Dorothy J. Evans, Ouachita Parish H.S.
Monroe, Louisiana

CHEESE LOG

1 lb. sharp cheese, grated
2 8-oz. pkg. cream cheese
1 tbsp. mayonnaise
1 ½ tsp. red pepper
1 tsp. garlic powder
1 tsp. onion powder
1 tbsp. Worcestershire sauce
Salt to taste (opt.)
1 c. coarsely chopped pecans

Cream cheeses with electric mixer; add mayonnaise and beat for 10 minutes. Add remaining ingredients except pecans; beat for 5 minutes longer. Shape into 7 x 1 1/2-inch roll; roll in chopped nuts. Roll in waxed paper and chill for 2 hours. Slice and serve with crackers. Yield: 25 servings.

Delores S. Barber, Scotland H.S.
Laurinburg, North Carolina

CHEESE PUFFS

1 3-oz. pkg. cream cheese
¼ lb. sharp cheddar cheese
1 stick butter
2 egg whites, beaten stiffly
1 sm. loaf white bread, cut into 1-inch cubes

Melt cheeses and butter in double boiler; add to egg whites. Dip bread cubes into mixture, coating

well. Place on cookie sheet. Refrigerate overnight or place in cold place. Bake at 400 degrees for 10 to 15 minutes or until golden brown. Yield: 10-12 servings.

Mrs. Ethyl Dahler, Central H.S.
LaCrosse, Wisconsin

CHEESE SNACKS

1 ½ c. sifted flour
½ tsp. red pepper
½ tsp. paprika
½ tsp. salt
½ lb. grated sharp cheese
½ lb. margarine
1 tbsp. Worcestershire sauce
Pecan halves
1 egg white, slightly beaten

Sift dry ingredients together into bowl; blend in cheese and margarine until smooth. Add Worcestershire sauce. Form into 3/4-inch balls; place on ungreased cookie sheet. Mash with bottom of glass covered with damp cloth. Press pecan half on each; brush pecan with egg white. Bake at 325 degrees for 20 to 25 minutes. Yield: 50 snacks.

Mrs. Patsy Evans, Bridge City H.S.
Bridge City, Texas

CHEESE SPREAD

1 tsp. garlic salt
3 tbsp. Worcestershire sauce
1 6-oz. can tomato paste
1 lb. mild cheddar cheese, grated
1 lb. sharp cheddar cheese, grated
1 ½ c. (about) beer

Stir garlic salt, Worcestershire sauce and tomato paste into cheeses; add beer to form smooth paste. Serve with crackers, potato chips or rye bread rounds. Yield: 40-50 servings.

Mrs. Mary Esther Rowe, Swartz Creek H.S.
Swartz Creek, Michigan

CHEESE STRAWS

¼ lb. extra sharp cheddar cheese
½ lb. oleo, softened
½ tsp. salt
Dash of red pepper
2 c. flour

Combine all ingredients; mix thoroughly. Press through star tip on cookie press onto cookie sheet. Bake for 10 minutes at 400 degrees. Cool. Store in airtight container. Yield: 90 straws.

Mrs. Sue Rogers, Krum Sch.
Krum, Texas

CHEESE STRAWS

½ lb. cheddar cheese, grated
1 ½ sticks butter
2 c. flour
¼ tsp. salt
¼ to ½ tsp. cayenne pepper

Mix cheese and butter; add remaining ingredients, mixing well. Force through cookie press onto ungreased baking sheet. Bake at 350 degrees for 12 to 15 minutes. Yield: 25 straws.

Mrs. Dorothy J. Evans, Ouachita Parish H.S.
Monroe, Louisiana

CHEESE STRAWS

1 stick margarine
1 glass Old English cheese
1 ½ c. sifted flour
1 tsp. paprika
1 tsp. salt
½ tsp. red pepper

Cream together margarine and cheese; add flour, paprika, salt and red pepper. Mix well. Place in cookie press. Line cookie sheet with aluminum foil. Snake cheese mixture onto foil, using star tip. Bake at 300 degrees for 25 minutes. Do not brown. Cool on cooling rack. Cut or break into serving pieces. Store in airtight can. Yield: 8-10 servings.

Frances W. McKinzie, Lufkin H.S.
Lufkin, Texas

CHEESE STRAWS

1 c. butter or oleo
1 lb. sharp cheese, grated
3 c. unsifted flour
3 tsp. baking powder
2 tsp. salt
1 tsp. red pepper

Cream oleo and cheese. Sift together flour, baking powder, salt and red pepper; blend with cheese mixture. Shape with pastry tube. Bake for 30 to 40 minutes at 325 degrees. Yield: 3 dozen.

Louise Curry, Richfield H.S.
Waco, Texas

COCONUT-CHEESE BALLS

1 8-oz. pkg. cream cheese, softened
3 tbsp. whole cranberry sauce, drained
½ tsp. grated orange rind
⅛ tsp. salt
Flaked coconut

Combine all ingredients except coconut. Chill slightly. Shape into bite-sized balls; roll in coconut. Serve with assorted crackers. Yield: 30-40 servings.

Mrs. Nina Grooce, Forbush H.S.
East Bend, North Carolina

CHEESE AND WALNUT BALLS

1 c. cheddar cheese, grated
2 tbsp. flour
½ tsp. salt
½ tsp. chili powder
Pinch of oregano
Tabasco sauce
1 egg white, beaten stiff but not dry
Walnuts, chopped fine

Mix together cheese, flour, salt, chili powder, oregano, and Tabasco sauce; fold in egg white. Form into small balls; roll in walnuts. Chill. Fry in deep hot fat until brown. Serve on hors d'oeuvre picks. Yield: 2-3 dozen.

Emma Lou Leftwich, Mt. Pleasant H.S.
Mt. Pleasant, Texas

CRISPY CHEESY WAFERS

1 ½ sticks margarine
12 oz. very sharp cheese, grated
2 c. flour
2 c. Rice Krispies
½ tsp. salt

Cream margarine; add cheese. Mix flour, Rice Krispies and salt; add to margarine mixture. Shape into walnut-sized balls. Place on cookie sheet; flatten with bottom of small glass. Bake in 350-degree oven for 10 to 12 minutes or until firm.

Katharine Rigby, Starr-Washington Sch.
Union Furnace, Ohio

DEVILED CHEESE BITES

1 3-oz. pkg. cream cheese, softened
2 oz. blue cheese, crumbled
1 2 ¼-oz. can deviled ham
¼ c. chopped pecans
Onion juice
½ c. snipped parsley
Thin pretzel sticks

Blend cream cheese, blue cheese, deviled ham, pecans and few drops onion juice; chill. Shape into small balls; roll in parsley. Chill until serving time. Stick pretzel stick into each ball. Yield: 2 dozen.

Frances Harrison, Ruston H.S.
Ruston, Louisiana

EDAM NUGGETS

1 c. Edam cheese, grated
2 tbsp. finely chopped celery
⅛ tsp. dry mustard
2 tbsp. cream or ale
Finely chopped parsley

Combine all ingredients except parsley; blend well. Shape into small balls; roll in parsley. Yield: 16 balls.

Margaret M. Stouffer, South Western H.S.
Hanover, Pennsylvania

GOOD CHEESE BALL

½ lb. sharp cheddar cheese, grated
1 lge. pkg. cream cheese
4 oz. Roquefort or blue cheese
1 glass Old English cheese
1 c. chopped nuts
½ c. sherry
¼ c. chopped parsley

Have cheeses at room temperature. Combine cheeses, 1/2 cup chopped nuts, sherry and 2 tablespoons parsley in bowl; mix with wooden spoon until well blended. Add more sherry if needed. Form into large ball or cake. Combine remaining nuts and parsley; roll ball in mixture. Cover with Saran wrap and chill. Mixture may be packed into Saran wrap-lined cake pan sprinkled with nuts and parsley. Yield: 25 servings.

Emily Truitt Duley, Frederick Sasscer H.S.
Upper Marlboro, Maryland

HOT CHEESE PUFFS

1 c. shredded cheddar cheese
3 tbsp. soft butter
½ c. flour
1 tsp. paprika
½ tsp. Worcestershire sauce
Dash of cayenne pepper
Salt to taste
24 med. stuffed olives

Preheat oven to 400 degrees. Cream cheese and butter; blend in flour, paprika, Worcestershire sauce, cayenne and salt. Mold about 1 teaspoonful dough around each olive, covering completely. Place on ungreased cookie sheet. Bake at 400 degrees for 12 minutes or until golden brown. Walnuts, pecans or cocktail franks may be substituted for olives. Yield: 24 servings.

Mrs. David Hetrick, Cardinal Stritch H.S.
Oregon, Ohio

HOLIDAY CHEESE BALL

¼ c. milk
1 3-oz. pkg. blue cheese
¼ c. cubed cheddar cheese
1 sm. onion wedge
1 tsp. Worcestershire sauce
2 3-oz. pkg. cream cheese, cubed
½ c. chopped pecans

Puree milk and blue cheese in blender; add cheddar cheese and onion. Blend until smooth; add Worcestershire sauce and cream cheese, blending thoroughly. Shape into 3-inch ball and chill. Roll in chopped nuts before serving. Yield: 6 servings.

Mrs. Wade H. Harris, Seagrove H.S.
Seagrove, North Carolina

KAY'S CHEESE BALL

½ lb. American process cheese
4 oz. sharp cheddar cheese
2 4-oz. pkg. blue cheese
¼ c. mayonnaise
2 tsp. Worcestershire sauce
1 tbsp. finely chopped onion
1 tbsp. finely chopped sweet pickle
½ c. finely chopped nuts
½ c. chopped parsley

Let cheeses stand at room temperature until soft. Cream cheeses with mayonnaise, Worcestershire sauce, onion and sweet pickle. Place in small bowl and cover with waxed paper; refrigerate for about 6 hours. Remove from bowl; roll into grapefruit-sized ball. Roll ball in nut and parsley mixture. Keeps in refrigerator for 2 weeks or in freezer for 6 months.

Anna Margaret Kalhar, Fisher Jr. H.S.
Cheney, Washington

MEXICAN CHEESE ROLLS

2 8-oz. pkg. cream cheese
8 slices pimento cheese
1 tsp. garlic powder
½ c. ground pecans
Chili powder

Mix first 3 ingredients in blender or electric mixer until smooth. Add pecans. Shape into 2 small rolls, 1 1/2-inches in diameter. Roll in chili powder until red. Refrigerate. Slice into small rounds; serve on crackers or chips. Yield: 8 servings.

Mrs. Pauline Moxley, McAllen H.S.
McAllen, Texas

NUTTY CHEESE SPREAD

1 8-oz. pkg. cream cheese
1 5-oz. jar process sharp cheese spread
2 5-oz. jars process Roquefort cheese spread
1 sm. onion, minced
1 clove of garlic, minced
½ c. chopped pecans or walnuts

Have cheeses at room temperature. Beat together until light, fluffy and well blended; beat in onion and garlic. Chill. Shape into ball; roll in nuts until well coated. Keep in refrigerator or freezer until ready to serve. Yield: 25 servings.

Mrs. Janet Prentice, Chico Sr. H.S.
Chico, California

OLIVE-CHEESE NUGGETS

¼ lb. sharp natural cheddar cheese, shredded
¼ c. soft butter or margarine
¾ c. sifted flour
⅛ tsp. salt
½ tsp. paprika
24 to 30 med. stuffed green olives

Blend cheese with butter. Sift flour, salt and paprika into cheese-butter mixture; mix to form dough. Shape around olives, using about 1 teaspoonful dough for each. Place on ungreased baking sheet. Bake at 400 degrees for 12 to 15 minutes or until light golden brown. Serve hot or cold. Yield: 2-2 1/2 dozen.

N. Sharon Fraser, South Lake Sr. H.S.
St. Clair Shores, Michigan

OLIVE-FILLED CHEESE BALLS

½ lb. softened, sharp cheddar cheese
2 tbsp. soft butter or margarine
½ c. flour
Dash of cayenne
25 stuffed green olives or large pitted ripe olives

Grate cheese fine; add butter and mix well. Add flour and cayenne; mix well. Wrap about 1 tablespoonful mixture around each olive, completely covering. Bake for 15 minutes in 350-degree oven. Serve hot. May be mixed in blender if desired. Yield: 25 balls.

Catherine G. Ward, G. P. Babb Jr. H.S.
Forest Park, Georgia

SPICY CHEESE ROLL

1 lb. cheddar cheese
1 8-oz. pkg. cream cheese
1 tsp. onion salt
1 tsp. garlic salt
1 tbsp. Worcestershire sauce
1 tsp. Tabasco sauce
Paprika

Grind or blend cheeses; mix well. Add remaining ingredients except paprika. Shape into log, about 1 1/2-inches in diameter; roll in paprika. Chill until firm or overnight. Slice and serve on crackers. Yield: 2 dozen.

Mrs. Carla Sue Park, Dayton H.S.
Dayton, Texas

TASTY CHEESE BALL

4 3-oz. pkg. cream cheese
½ lb. Old English cheese, grated
½ lb. blue moon or cheddar cheese, grated
2 tsp. steak sauce
1 tsp. prepared mustard
1 sm. onion, grated

Soften cheeses. Add steak sauce, mustard and onion. Form into ball; cover with waxed paper and refrigerate. Yield: 15-18 servings.

Mrs. Joan Moore, Alden Comm. Sch.
Alden, Iowa

FRUIT KABOBS

3 apricot halves
3 maraschino cherries
3 pineapple chunks
3 fresh strawberries
Avocado half
Lemon juice

Drain fruit; spear on 3 toothpicks. Sprinkle avocado with lemon juice; serve on bed of lettuce with fruit dressing.

Mrs. Beverlee Williams, Campbell H.S.
Campbell, California

APPETIZER MEATBALLS

1 lb. ground beef
1 tsp. salt
½ c. cornflakes
¼ tsp. pepper
¼ c. catsup
1 tbsp. Worcestershire sauce
¼ c. finely chopped onion
½ c. evaporated milk

Mix all ingredients thoroughly; shape into 3 dozen tiny meatballs, using 1 teaspoon mixture for each. Place in foil-lined 13 x 9 x 3/4-inch pan. Bake in 400-degree oven for 12 to 15 minutes. Insert toothpick in each meatball. Serve with hot barbecue sauce for dipping.

Marjorie Harrington, Foxborough H.S.
Foxborough, Massachusetts

BACON-LIVER ROLLS

6 fresh chicken livers
6 thin strips bacon

Wrap chicken livers with bacon strips; fasten with toothpick. Broil until bacon is crisp. Yield: 6 rolls.

Mrs. Dorothy M. Ham, Brantley Co. H.S.
Nahunta, Georgia

BROILED CHICKEN LIVERS

Water chestnuts, ⅓ for each chicken liver
Chicken livers, as needed
Bacon, ⅓ slice for each liver
Soy sauce
Brown sugar

Fold chestnut in chicken liver; wrap with bacon. Secure with toothpicks; marinate at least 4 hours in soy sauce. Dip each liver in brown sugar; broil about 15 minutes. Serve immediately.

Mrs. C. D. Huston, Greenwood Jr. H.S.
Greenwood, Mississippi

HOT DOGS IN SWEET-N-SOUR SAUCE

1 doz. hot dogs
6 oz. currant jelly
6 oz. prepared mustard

Cook hot dogs; slice diagonally. Mix jelly and mustard; melt in electric skillet until well blended. Add hot dogs; simmer. Keep warm; serve on toothpicks. Yield: 10-12 servings.

Mrs. Ella Passarelli, Chichester Sr. H.S.
Boothwyn, Pennsylvania

CRAB MEAT-BACON ROLLS

½ c. tomato juice
1 well-beaten egg
1 c. dry bread crumbs
Dash of salt
Dash of pepper
½ tsp. chopped parsley
½ tsp. chopped celery leaves
1 6½-oz. can crab meat, flaked
12 slices bacon, halved

Combine tomato juice and egg; add crumbs, seasonings, parsley, celery leaves and crab meat. Mix thoroughly; roll into finger lengths. Wrap each roll with 1/2 slice bacon; fasten with toothpick. Broil, turning frequently; brown evenly. Yield: 2 dozen.

Linda Gail Pack, Pisgah H.S.
Canton, North Carolina

MARINATED SHRIMP

2 med.-sized cans deviled shrimp
1 5-oz. bottle Worcestershire sauce

Drain shrimp; rinse gently under cold water. Place in bowl; add Worcestershire sauce. Let stand in refrigerator 6 to 10 hours; drain and serve on toothpicks. Yield: 6 servings.

Mrs. Clarice Schorzman, Ritzville H.S.
Ritzville, Washington

PICKLED SHRIMP KABOBS

2 to 2½ lb. fresh or frozen shrimp in shells
½ c. celery leaves
¼ c. mixed pickling spices
1 tbsp. salt
2 c. sliced onion
7 bay leaves
1½ c. salad oil
¾ c. white vinegar
3 tbsp. capers and juice
2½ tsp. celery seed
1½ tsp. salt
Few drops of bottled hot pepper sauce
Green pepper pieces
Pineapple chunks

Cover shrimp with boiling water; add celery leaves, pickling spices and salt. Cover, simmer for 5 minutes. Drain; peel and devein shrimp under cold water. Alternate shrimp, onion and bay leaves in large shallow dish. Combine salad oil, vinegar, capers and juice, celery seed, salt and pepper sauce; mix well and pour over shrimp. Cover; chill at least 24 hours, spooning marinade over shrimp occasionally. Spear a shrimp, a piece of green pepper and a pineapple chunk for each appetizer kabob. Shrimp will keep about a week in refrigerator. Yield: 4 1/2 cups.

Mrs. Nickerson, Warner Sch.
Warner, Alberta, Canada

NEAPOLITAN APPETIZER TRAY

Chicory
1 3-oz. tin smoked oysters
1 4½-oz. can ripe black olives
1 4½-oz. jar artichoke hearts
1 6-oz. jar pepper piccalilli
1 6-oz. jar eggplant in vinegar
1 4-oz. jar pimentos
1 3-oz. jar marinated mushrooms
1 2-oz. tin flat fillets of anchovies in
olive oil

Make spokes of chicory on large serving plate; place oysters in center. Arrange olive, artichokes, piccalilli, eggplant, pimentos and mushrooms in clockwise manner between chicory strips. Roll anchovies; place on platter to balance arrangement. The success of this dish depends upon colorful arrangement. Yield: 4-6 servings.

Mrs. Louise Stellato, Bishop Reilly H.S.
Fresh Meadows, New York

AVOCADO-STUFFED CELERY

1 avocado
1 ½ tsp. lemon juice
1 3-oz. pkg. cream cheese
¼ tsp. grated lemon peel
½ tsp. Worcestershire sauce
¼ tsp. salt
Dash of pepper
Celery stalks

Pare avocado; mash well. Sprinkle with lemon juice; blend in cheese, lemon peel, Worcestershire sauce, salt and pepper. Stuff celery stalks; cut into 2-inch to 3-inch pieces. Garnish with pimento, if desired. Yield: 1 cup stuffing.

Mrs. Shelley Langley, Coppell H.S.
Coppell, Texas

BLUSHING CELERY CIRCLES

1 6-oz. can tomato paste
2 3-oz. pkg. cream cheese
Dash of oregano
1 tsp. prepared mustard (opt.)
1 stalk celery

Blend tomato paste with softened cream cheese and oregano. Add mustard if mixture seems dry. Separate celery stalk; wash each piece and pat dry. Stuff cavities with cheese mixture. Press pieces together to form original shape of stalk. Wrap in waxed paper; chill 3 to 4 hours. Slice in 1/4-inch slices, horizontally across entire stalk; arrange on tray. Garnish with celery leaves or parsley. Yield: 6-8 servings.

Mrs. Inez F. Klein, Malverne Sr. H.S.
Malverne, New York

STUFFED PICKLES

1 3-oz. pkg. cream cheese
2 tbsp. salad dressing
1 tbsp. Worcestershire sauce
½ c. chopped walnuts
3 lge. dill pickles

Blend cheese, salad dressing, Worcestershire sauce and nuts until smooth. Core pickles with corer; stuff centers with cheese mixture. Chill 1 hour or until cheese is firm; slice crosswise. Yield: 6-8 servings.

Mrs. William Hamlet, East Lake Jr. H.S.
Chattanooga, Tennessee

ZIPPY POTPOURRI

1 c. broccoli buds
1 c. cauliflowerets
1 c. thin carrot sticks
1 c. thin celery sticks
1 c. mayonnaise
1 tsp. red horseradish
½ tsp. mustard
Dash of Worcestershire sauce

Prepare vegetables; place each in separate section of serving platter. Combine remaining ingredients; let stand 1 hour to blend. Place dip in center of vegetables.

Mrs. Rita Rummelsburg, South Side Jr. H.S.
Rockville Centre, New York

CATAWBA COCKTAIL

1 bottle cherries
1 bottle grape juice, chilled
1 bottle ginger ale, chilled

Place a cherry in small serving glasses. Half fill with grape juice; finish filling with ginger ale. Yield: 15 servings.

Mrs. Jean Head, Etowah H.S.
Attalla, Alabama

CRANBERRY CRUSH

1 qt. cranberries
3 c. boiling water
1 tsp. baking soda
2 c. sugar
½ c. orange juice
1 tbsp. lemon juice

Cook cranberries in boiling water until berries burst. Stir in baking soda. Remove greenish acid froth which rises with skimmer. Add sugar. Cook 10 minutes. Put through coarse sieve to remove skins. Add orange juice and lemon juice. Freeze. Yield: 6-8 servings.

Mrs. Winifred Iverson, Riggs Sr. H.S.
Pierre, South Dakota

FLOATING ORANGES

2 mandarin oranges
½ c. maraschino cherries
1 8-oz. can sweetened orange juice, chilled

Peel oranges; remove seeds. Slice; chill in covered container. Place 2 cherries in each cube section of ice cube tray; fill tray with water and freeze. Place frozen cubes in serving glasses; fill with orange juice and add several orange slices. Yield: 4 servings.

Mrs. Marguerite S. Morris, West Bolivar H.S.
Rosedale, Mississippi

FRUIT ALE

2 c. orange juice
2 c. grape juice
2 c. apple juice
½ c. lemon juice
¾ c. sugar
1 8-oz. bottle Seven-Up

Combine fruit juices; chill. Add Seven-Up just before serving. Yield: 8 servings.

Sister Angeline Tetreault, Academie Assumption
Edmonton, Alberta, Canada

FRUIT SLUSH

2 to 3 bananas, mashed
2 oranges, juice and pulp
2 lemons, juice and pulp
1 8-oz. can crushed pineapple
1 c. sugar
½ tsp. orange rind and lemon rind
1 pt. ginger ale

Combine all ingredients; stir until sugar is completely dissolved. Pour into refrigerator tray; freeze to slush stage. Serve as appetizer, non-sweet dessert, or breakfast beverage. Yield: 8-10 servings.

Mrs. Thordis K. Danielson, New Rockford H.S.
New Rockford, North Dakota

LIME ICE

2 ¼ c. sugar
1 qt. water
Juice of 6 limes
Juice of 1 lemon

Grated lemon rind
Apricot and pear pieces
Ginger ale

Dissolve sugar in water; boil 10 minutes. Strain lime and lemon juice; add to syrup. Add rind; mix thoroughly. Freeze; place in cocktail or sherbet glasses. Arrange apricot and pear over ice; pour ginger ale over top. Yield: 8 servings.

Eulyn Dynes, Phillips Independent H.S.
Borger, Texas

MULLED FRUIT JUICE

6 c. fruit juice of choice
½ c. orange juice
½ lemon, sliced
2 tbsp. honey
10 whole cloves
6 whole allspice
2 cinnamon sticks

Combine ingredients in large saucepan. Cover; simmer about 10 minutes. Remove from heat; let stand 30 minutes. Reheat when ready to serve; strain before serving. Yield: 1 1/2 quarts.

Mrs. Frances Eldridge, Central Sr. H.S.
Clifton, Illinois

SLUSH

1 12-oz. can frozen orange juice
1 c. sugar
1 No. 2 can crushed pineapple
2 crushed bananas
1 sm. bottle maraschino cherries
2 c. ginger ale

Combine all ingredients; freeze to slush stage. Serve in cups or sherbet dishes. Yield: 8-10 servings.

Mrs. Joan F. Moore, Alden Comm. H.S.
Alden, Iowa

SPICED CRANBERRY COCKTAIL

1 c. water
1 c. sugar
1 cinnamon stick
1 tsp. ginger
1 tsp. allspice
1 tsp. whole cloves
2 c. cranberry juice
½ c. lemon juice
2 c. apple juice
Red food coloring

39

(Continued on next page)

Steep water, sugar and spices for 30 minutes; cool. Add juices and enough coloring to make mixture a bright red; strain. Place in freezer; freeze about 1 1/2 hours. Serve as frosty cocktail juice. Yield: 10-12 servings.

Carla Sue Park, Dayton H.S.
Dayton, Texas

TASTY EYE OPENER

3 c. V-8 juice
½ tsp. Worcestershire sauce
Dash of Tabasco sauce
½ c. water

Combine all ingredients; simmer about 5 to 10 minutes. Garnish with sour cream. Yield: 4-6 servings.

Mrs. Virginia H. Brown, Soddy-Daisy Jr. H.S.
Daisy, Tennessee

ALMOND TEA

2 c. sugar
3 pt. water
½ lemon rind, grated
Juice of 3 lemons
2 c. strong tea
1 tsp. almond flavoring
1 tsp. vanilla

Combine sugar, 2 pints water and lemon rind; boil for 5 minutes. Cool; add remaining ingredients. Stir well. May be served hot or iced. Yield: 18 servings.

Naoma Brown, East H.S.
Aurora, Illinois

RUSSIAN TEA

3 sticks cinnamon
1 tsp. whole cloves
½ tsp. whole allspice
1 c. water
3 tbsp. tea, scalded in 1 qt. boiling water
1 ½ c. orange juice
½ c. fresh lemon juice
1 ½ c. sugar
Red food coloring

Ball together cinnamon, cloves, allspice and cold water; let stand 10 minutes. Combine ingredients; stir to dissolve sugar. Add food coloring to give desired tint. Yield: 10-12 servings.

Mrs. Dixie Dunn Ruby, Charles Town H.S.
Charles Town, West Virginia

INSTANT RUSSIAN TEA

1 ½ c. sugar
3 tsp. cinnamon
½ tsp. cloves
2 c. Tang
½ c. instant tea
2 tbsp. instant lemonade

Mix sugar and spices; add remaining ingredients and mix well. Store in air-tight container. Place 1 scant tablespoon mix to 1 cup freshly boiled water; stir well. Serve with thinly sliced lemon or small piece of peppermint stick candy if desired. May be iced. Yield: 66 servings.

Mrs. Wendell Utley, Magnolia Sr. H.S.
Magnolia, Kansas

TOMATO JUICE COCKTAIL

1 14-oz. can tomato juice
½ tsp. grated onion
1 tsp. chopped celery
2 tbsp. lemon juice
¼ tsp. Worcestershire sauce
½ tsp . sugar
½ tsp. salt
½ tsp. horseradish (opt.)

Combine all ingredients; chill 1 hour. Strain; serve in glasses. Yield: 4 servings.

Mrs. Wanda Newlin, Atwood-Hammond H.S.
Atwood, Illinois

TOMATO-PINEAPPLE JUICE

1 can pineapple juice
1 can tomato juice

Fill glass about half with pineapple juice; tip glass and add equal amount of tomato juice slowly. The juices should stay separate to give a two-toned effect.

Mrs. Betty Debus, Peetz H.S.
Peetz, Colorado

VEGETABLE COCKTAIL

2 c. tomato juice
1 c. carrot juice
1 tsp. grated onion
1 tsp. grated celery
1 tsp. grated bell pepper

Combine all ingredients; chill before serving. May be added to 1 package lemon Jell-O and molded into salad. Yield: 6 servings.

Mrs. Fernette Honaker, Menaul Presb. H.S.
Albuquerque, New Mexico

Dips and Sauces

RECIPE FOR HOLLANDAISE SAUCE ON PAGE 55

Avocado Dips

AVOCADO COCKTAIL DIP

1 lge. avocado, halved
2 tsp. lemon juice
1 tsp. grated onion
4 tbsp. mayonnaise
Few drops of Tabasco
Salt to taste

Remove flesh from avocado; reserve 1 shell. Mash avocado; add lemon juice, onion, mayonnaise, Tabasco and salt. Blend thoroughly; pile into avocado shell. Surround with potato chips. Yield: 4 servings.

Lucy H. Dunn, Jerome Sr. H.S.
Jerome, Idaho

AVOCADO DIP

2 ripe avocados, halved
1 c. sour cream
¼ tsp. salt
2 tbsp. prepared horseradish (opt.)

Remove seeds and peel from avocados. Mash pulp with wooden spoon; beat until smooth. Stir in remaining ingredients. Yield: 2 cups.

Mrs. Joel Ferrell, Brinkley H.S.
Brinkley, Arkansas

AVOCADO DIP

1 ripe avocado
2 tbsp. chopped onion
¼ tsp. garlic salt
¼ c. sour cream

Peel and mash avocado; mix in onion, garlic salt and sour cream. Use immediately. Yield: 2 servings.

Shari Bolander, Del Norte H.S.
Del Norte, Colorado

AVOCADO DIP

1 c. mashed avocado
1 8-oz. pkg. cream cheese
3 tbsp. lemon juice
1 tsp. finely chopped onion
1 tsp. salt
Dash of Worcestershire sauce
Potato chips

Gradually add avocado to cream cheese, blending until smooth. Add lemon juice, onion, salt and Worcestershire sauce; mix well. Serve with potato chips or raw vegetables. Yield: 1 1/2 cups.

Eileen H. MacDonald, Jenifer Jr. H.S.
Lewiston, Idaho

AVOCADO DIP

1 ripe avocado
1 tbsp. garlic salt
Few drops of lemon juice
1 sm. carton sour cream

Mash avocado; add garlic salt and lemon juice. Mix well. Add avocado mixture to sour cream; blend well.

Mrs. Kathy Hufstedler, Pampa H.S.
Pampa, Texas

AVOCADO DIP

2 avocados, mashed
2 oz. cream cheese
¼ c. chopped onion
1 tsp. lemon juice
½ c. mayonnaise

Combine avocados and cream cheese, blending until smooth. Add remaining ingredients. Stir until blended. Yield: 10 servings.

Lloydine Denton, Stualen Sparkman H.S.
Sparkman, Arkansas

GUACAMOLE

2 ripe avocados
1 tsp. salt
1 tbsp. lemon juice
1 lge. green chili
1 tsp. onion or onion salt
1 chopped tomato

Blend all ingredients thoroughly except tomato in blender or by hand. Add tomato. Yield: 4 servings.

Louise Smith, Dextor Municipal Sch.
Dexter, New Mexico

GUACAMOLE DIP

1 avocado, peeled and seed removed
¼ c. mayonnaise
1 tsp. lemon juice
¼ c. chopped onion
1 tsp. salt
1 tsp. Worcestershire sauce

Place all ingredients in blender; turn on low speed. Blend until smooth. Serve with corn chips as dip, or on lettuce loaf with tomato wedges. Yield: 2 servings.

Lou Helen Gill, James Logan H.S.
Union City, California

GUACAMOLE

2 med.-sized avocados
1 tbsp. lemon juice
1 tbsp. grated onion
1 tsp. salt
¼ tsp. chili powder
⅓ c. mayonnaise or salad dressing
4 slices bacon (opt.)
Paprika (opt.)
Parsley (opt.)

Combine avocados, lemon juice, onion, salt and chili powder. Spread with mayonnaise sealing edges to bowl; chill. Stir in mayonnaise at serving time. Fry bacon crisp; crumble. Add to dip. Garnish with paprika and parsley. Serve with corn chips. Yield: 5 servings.

Mrs. Kay Fulton, Farmington H.S.
Farmington, Arkansas

GUACAMOLE DIP

1 can taco sauce
2 tsp. lemon juice
1 green onion
2 ripe avocados, peeled and seed removed
¼ tsp. garlic salt
½ tsp. salt
2 tbsp. green chilies

Place all ingredients in blender in order given. Blend on high speed until smooth. Yield: 6 servings.

Mrs. Novella Mae Melton, Roswell H.S.
Roswell, New Mexico

MUSHROOM-AVOCADO DIP

1 avocado, peeled and seed removed
1 pt. sour cream
1 pkg. cream of mushroom soup mix
1 tsp. lemon juice

Mash avocado; add remaining ingredients. Blend until smooth.

Jean Daniels, Excelsior H.S.
Norwalk, California

QUICK DIP

1 avocado, peeled and seed removed
1 lge. can bean dip

Mash avocado; add bean dip. Blend until smooth.

Rubie Williams, Anton Sch.
Anton, Texas

CHILI CHIP DIP

1 1-lb. can vegetarian beans
2 tbsp. hot dog relish
1 tbsp. minced parsley
1 tbsp. chili powder
½ c. sour cream

Beat beans with electric mixer until smooth. Add relish, parsley and chili powder, mixing well. Stir in sour cream. Chill several hours or overnight. Sprinkle with paprika. Serve with raw vegetables or potato chips. Yield: 2 1/2 cups.

Treva L. Kelly, Riverside-Brookfield H.S.
Riverside, Illinois

FIESTA BEAN DIP

2 c. hot, cooked red or pinto beans
1 c. grated sharp cheddar cheese
2 tbsp. minced onion
1 lge. clove of garlic, mashed
1 jalapeno, finely chopped
1 tsp. jalapeno liquid

Press beans through sieve or mash until smooth. Place in sauce pan. Stir in enough bean liquid to thin mixture to dipping consistency. Add remaining ingredients, mixing well. Cook over very low heat until cheese is melted. Serve hot with tortillas. Makes good sandwich spread when cold.

Mrs. Thelma McClain, Bremond H.S.
Bremond, Texas

BLENDER DIP

1 8-oz. pkg. cream cheese
½ c. Parmesan cheese
¼ tsp. garlic salt
¼ c. pecans

Blend cream cheese in blender until smooth; add Parmesan cheese and garlic salt. Mix until well blended. Add pecans; blend only until mixed. Pour into mold; chill until firm. Yield: 12 servings.

Mrs. Emily Bierschwale, Junction H.S.
Junction, Texas

BLUE CHEESE DIP

4 oz. blue cheese
1 8-oz. pkg. cream cheese, softened
¼ c. evaporated milk
3 tbsp. pimento
⅓ c. chopped green pepper
¼ tsp. garlic salt

Add blue cheese to cream cheese; beat until creamy. Stir in remaining ingredients. Chill

(Continued on next page)

dip until 30 minutes before serving. Sprinkle with paprika, if desired. Yield: 2 cups.

Mrs. G. G. Craig, Jr., Alvaton H.S.
Alvaton, Kentucky

CHEDDAR DUNK

½ lb. aged cheese
2 tbsp. cream
½ tsp. dry mustard
  or 1 tbsp. prepared
1 tbsp. Worcestershire sauce

Beat all ingredients together until fluffy, adding more cream, if necessary. Serve with assorted crackers and raw vegetables.

Gaynelle C. James, Gardner S.W. H.S.
Gardner, Illinois

CHEESE AND CELERY DIP

2 tbsp. margarine
2 tbsp. flour
1 10-oz. can condensed cream of
  celery soup
½ c. grated cheese
Pinch of paprika

Melt margarine in saucepan; add flour. Blend until smooth; cook for 1 minute. Add soup and cheese; stir well until boiling. Pour into hot dish; keep hot while serving. Garnish with paprika. Serve with potato chips, crackers, short sticks of celery or cubes or pineapple. Yield: 10 servings.

Mrs. Patricia Race, Lockeport Reg. H.S.
Lockeport, Nova Scotia

CHEESE DIP

1 envelope Good Seasons cheese-garlic
  salad dressing mix
1 ½ tsp. onion juice
2 c. creamed cottage cheese
½ to ⅔ c. light cream

Add salad dressing mix and onion juice to cottage cheese; mix well. Thin with cream to desired consistency. Serve with assorted crackers. Yield: 2 1/2 cups.

Mrs. Ruby Roach, Adair Co. H.S.
Columbia, Kentucky

CHEESE DIP

2 8-oz. pkg. cream cheese
1 tbsp. mayonnaise
1 tsp. garlic salt
1 8-oz. bottle Picante hot sauce

Blend cream cheese, mayonnaise and garlic salt; add hot sauce. Blend together until well blended in blender or small bowl of mixer. Less hot sauce may be used for milder dip. Serve with Fritos or corn chips. Yield: 8-12 servings.

Frances W. McKinzie, Lufkin H.S.
Lufkin, Texas

CHILI DIP

1 c. cottage cheese
1 pkg. Chili Con Queso Dip Mix
½ tsp. chili powder

Combine all ingredients in mixing bowl. Mix at high speed until cheese is smooth. Let stand overnight. Serve with potato chips or Doritos. Yield: 3 servings.

Mrs. Arva McCarty Knight, Bellevue H.S.
Bellevue, Texas

CHILI CON QUESO DIP

⅔ c. chopped onion
3 tbsp. oil
1 sm. can Rotel tomatoes with chilies,
  broken into sm. pieces
4 tsp. paprika
3 tsp. chili powder
½ clove of garlic
3 tbsp. flour
¼ c. cold water
1 lb. brick cheese
⅓ lb. sharp process cheese
Salt and red pepper to taste

Saute onion in oil but do not brown. Add tomatoes, paprika, chili powder and garlic. Make paste of flour and water; stir into tomato mixture. Simmer 10 minutes over low flame. Add cheeses, salt and pepper. Heat until cheese is melted. Serve warm. May be refrigerated and reheated later. Yield: 3 pints.

Mrs. Ruth Gill, Tuloso-Midway H.S.
Corpus Christi, Texas
Juno Brooke Mulder, French High
Beaumont, Texas

COCKTAIL DIP FOR FRESH VEGETABLES

1 c. mayonnaise
4 tsp. soy sauce
1 tsp. powdered ginger
2 tbsp. chopped chives
2 tbsp. milk
1 tsp. vinegar

Combine all ingredients; place in refrigerator. Marinate for at least 12 hours before using. Serve with raw cauliflower, celery or radishes.

Mrs. Frank Marcus, West H.S.
Davenport, Iowa

COTTAGE-BORSCH CRACKER DIP

1 c. sm. curd cottage cheese
1 tbsp. crumbled bleu cheese
½ c. shredded beets
1 tbsp. lemon juice
½ tsp. salt

Beat cottage and bleu cheese in mixer until smooth. Add remaining ingredients, mixing well. Chill. Serve with potato chips, Fritos or crackers. Yield: 1 1/4 cups.

Mrs. Brooksie Rentz, Brookland-Cayce H.S.
Cayce, South Carolina

CUCUMBER DIP

1 lge. cucumber, unpeeled
1 pkg. cream cheese
1 tsp. salt
¼ tsp. white pepper

Grate cucumber; blend with cheese, salt and pepper. Refrigerate for at least 1 hour to mellow flavor. Serve with fancy crackers or potato chips. May be tinted green for special occasions. Yield: 4 servings.

Mrs. Bill P. Edwards, Camden H.S.
Camden, Arkansas

CUCUMBER DIP

½ pt. sour cream or yogurt
Cream cheese, softened
1 tsp. vinegar
2 tsp. celery salt
2 tbsp. chopped chives
1 med. cucumber, about 1 ½ cups,
    peeled and finely chopped

Mix sour cream with cream cheese. Add vinegar, celery salt and chives. Fold in cucumber. Chill. Yield: 2 3/4 cups.

Martha R. Phillips, Kennett H.S.
Conway, New Hampshire

DEVIL'S DIP

1 pkg. frozen, chopped broccoli
¼ c. sliced mushrooms
¼ c. chopped celery
¼ c. chopped onion
3 tbsp. margarine
1 can mushroom soup
1 6-oz. pkg. garlic cheese, cut into
    sm. pieces
Tabasco

Cook broccoli according to directions on package; drain. Saute mushrooms, chopped celery and onion in margarine until soft but not brown. Add soup, broccoli and cheese. Cook slowly, stirring constantly, until cheese is melted and well blended. Add a dash of Tabasco. Pour into chafing dish. Serve with Fritos. Yield: 10 servings.

Mable Moorhouse, Belen H.S.
Belen, New Mexico

DUNKING BOWL DIP

½ lb. cream cheese
2 tbsp. grated onion
1 clove of garlic
1 tbsp. chopped parsley
½ cucumber, med. size, grated
1 tsp. dill
½ tsp. salt

Stir cheese with wooden spoon to soften. Add remaining ingredients, mixing well. Add cream, if necessary, for dipping consistency. Pour dip into dunking bowl. Place bowl in center of large tray; surround with ice. Fill red cabbage leaf cups with carrot and celery curls, cherry tomatoes with stems, radish roses, thinly sliced cauliflower, green onions and ripe olives. Garnish with parsley and turnip daisies.

Mrs. Yvonne Lindrum, Montebello Jr. H.S.
Montebello, California

SPRING GARDEN DIP

1 c. sour cream
½ c. mayonnaise
1 tsp. salt
1 tsp. sugar
½ c. minced green onion
Radish roses
¼ c. minced radishes
¼ c. minced cucumbers, well drained
¼ c. minced green peppers
1 clove of garlic, thoroughly crushed
Carrot, celery, zucchini or white turnip
    sticks

Combine all ingredients; blend. Pour into small bowl. Place in center of large serving plate; surround with crisp carrots, celery, zucchini, turnips and radish roses. Yield: 2 1/2 cups.

Mrs. Dorothy Fernandes, St. Joseph H.S.
Hilo, Hawaii

CURRY DIP

1 c. mayonnaise
1 tsp. grated onion
1 tsp. prepared horseradish
1 tsp. tarragon vinegar
¼ tsp. curry powder

(Continued on next page)

Combine all ingredients; blend well. Chill; serve surrounded with crisp cauliflower flowerets, broccoli, or other crisp vegetables. Yield: 1 cup.

Mrs. David Richmond, Fed. Hocking Local H.S. Stewart, Ohio

CURRY DIP

    1 pt. mayonnaise
    2 tsp. curry powder
    3 dashes of Tabasco sauce

Combine ingredients; place in refrigerator for 8 hours or overnight. Serve with raw vegetable sticks.

Mrs. Anne Livingston, Foster Sr. H.S. Seattle, Washington

CURRY DIP
WITH FRESH VEGETABLES

    1 c. mayonnaise
    1 tsp. grated onion
    1 tsp. garlic salt
    1 tsp. tarragon vinegar
    1 tsp. horseradish
    1 tsp. curry

Combine all ingredients in order listed. Serve with green pepper strips, celery sticks, cauliflower pieces, carrots strips and radishes.

Mrs. Elizabeth Bruton, Mercy H.S. University City, Missouri

SOUR CREAM DIP

    2 c. thick sour cream
    2 tbsp. chopped parsley
    2 tbsp. chopped chives
    1 tsp. dried herbs
    ⅛ tsp. curry powder
    ½ tsp. salt
    ¼ tsp. paprika

Combine all ingredients; place in hollowed-out red cabbage, grapefruit, eggplant or pineapple.

Margaret M. Stouffer, South Western H.S. Hanover, Pennsylvania

DILL DIP

    1 c. sour cream
    1 c. mayonnaise
    1 tsp. dillweed
    1 tsp. Beau Monde
    1 tbsp. dried parsley
    1 tbsp. dried onion flakes

Blend all ingredients until smooth. Chill at least 2 hours before serving. Yield: 10-12 servings.

Mrs. Thelma Leigh, Quincy Jr. Sr. H.S. Quincy, California

DILLY DIP

    8 oz. cream cheese, room temperature
    1 pt. cottage cheese
    ½ c. chopped dill pickle
    ¼ c. dill pickle juice
    ¼ tsp. garlic salt

Blend cream cheese and cottage cheese with mixer until smooth. Add pickle, juice and garlic salt; mix until blended. Chill. Serve with potato chips or crackers. Yield: 15 servings.

Mrs. Irma Haley, Castleford H.S. Castleford, Idaho

DILL PICKLE DIP

    1 8-oz. pkg. cream cheese, room
      temperature
    3 tbsp. dill pickle juice
    3 tbsp. finely grated dill pickles

Combine all ingredients in small mixing bowl; mix at low speed until all ingredients are combined. Serve with crackers and chips. Yield: 10 servings.

Mrs. Charlotte Faris, Abingdon H.S. Abingdon, Virginia

EASY SOUR CREAM DIP

    1 pkg. sour cream mix for baked
      potatoes
    ¼ c. milk
    ½ pt. sour cream

Mix sour cream mix and milk until free from lumps. Blend into sour cream. Chill for at least 30 minutes. Serve. Yield: 8 servings.

Rose Mary Seale, Sparkman H.S. Sparkman, Arkansas

GREEN CHILI DIP

    1 sm. can chopped green chili
    1 c. sour cream
    Garlic salt

Stir green chili into sour cream. Add garlic salt to taste. Cream may be added if too thick. Serve with potato chips. Amount of green chili may be altered to taste. Yield: 1 cup.

Jane Parnell, Fort Sumner H.S. Fort Sumner, New Mexico

HERB-CHEESE DIP

1 c. cottage cheese
½ tsp. grated onion
3 tbsp. milk
Dash of pepper
½ tsp. dried sage
½ tsp. celery salt
1 tbsp. lemon juice

Combine all ingredients in blender; blend for 1 second.

Alberta Ball Bickerdike, East Pike Sch.
Milton, Illinois

HOSTESS DIP

1 8-oz. pkg. cream cheese
3 tbsp. milk
2 tsp. lemon juice
1 tsp. Worcestershire sauce
1 tbsp. mayonnaise
1 tsp. horseradish mustard
¾ tsp. garlic salt
½ tsp. paprika
Corn chips

Combine cream cheese and milk, blending until smooth. Add lemon juice, Worcestershire sauce, mayonnaise, mustard, garlic salt and paprika; mix well. Serve with corn chips. Yield: 20 servings.

Mrs. Keith Acker
West Branch-Rose City Area Schs.
West Branch, Michigan
Mrs. Dorothy B. Byrd
South Gwinnett H.S.
Snellville, Georgia

HOT CHEESE DIP

2 c. light cream
2 tsp. dry mustard
1 tbsp. Worcestershire sauce
4 whole cloves of garlic
1 tsp. salt
1 ½ lb. shredded med.-sharp cheddar cheese
3 tbsp. flour

Combine all ingredients except cheese and flour in earthware, glass or enamel saucepan. Heat slowly, stirring with wooden spoon. Mix cheese and flour; add gradually to milk mixture, stirring until melted. Serve warm with ham, crackers or chips. Yield: 10 servings.

B. J. Womack, Andrew Jackson H.S.
Jacksonville, Florida

HOT CHEESE DIP

½ lb. Velveeta cheese
¼ c. Ro-tel tomatoes with chili peppers

Melt cheese in top of double boiler; add tomatoes with chili peppers. Mix well; pour into serving dish. Serve with Fritos. Yield: 8 servings.

Mrs. Variel Garner, Moody H.S.
Moody, Texas

HOT CHEESE DUNK

1 can condensed cheddar cheese soup
2 tbsp. catsup
⅛ tsp. powdered oregano
⅛ tsp. garlic or onion powder
Toast squares, crackers or chips

Stir soup until smooth; blend in catsup, oregano and garlic. Heat, stirring often. Invite guests to spear toast squares with fork and dunk. Yield: 1 1/2 cups.

Mrs. Ronald Haney, Wallace Co. H.S.
Sharon Springs, Kansas

HOT PEPPER DIP

1 lge. onion, finely chopped
1 4-oz. can Ortega whole California chilies
1 7-oz. can Ortega Salsa
1 can whole packed tomatoes, well drained
1 lb. Velveeta cheese, cubed

Saute onion, peppers, salsa and tomatoes until very dry. Blend in cheese until smooth. May be refrigerated as long as two weeks.

Claudine Bettercourt, Lemoore Union H.S.
Lemoore, California

GARLIC-CHEESE DIP

1 3-oz. pkg. cream cheese
2 c. cottage cheese
1 tsp. lemon juice
2 or 3 dashes of Tabasco sauce
2 cloves of garlic, minced
¼ c. (or more) milk

Combine all ingredients; blend with electric mixer or blender until smooth. Add milk until of proper consistency for dip.

Betsy Blake, Bridgeport H.S.
Bridgeport, Washington

GARLIC-CHEESE DIP

1 8-oz. pkg. cream cheese
1 5-oz. pkg. sharp cheddar cheese
  spread
Milk
Garlic salt to taste
Celery
Carrots
Onions
Radishes

Combine cream cheese and cheddar cheese spread at room temperature. Gradually add milk while creaming until mixture has smooth dip consistency; add garlic salt to taste. Chill for 1 hour. Serve with chilled celery and carrot sticks, onion stalks, and radishes.

Carol Pohl, Kelseyville H.S.
Kelseyville, California

GARLIC DIP FOR VEGETABLES

¾ c. mayonnaise
7 drops of garlic juice
2 tbsp. lemon juice

Combine all ingredients; blend well. Serve with carrot strips, cauliflower flowerets and radishes. Yield: 6-8 servings.

Helen White, Wilmot Sch.
Wilmot, Arkansas

JALAPENO-CHEESE DIP

1 lb. Velveeta cheese, room
  temperature
1 med. onion, grated
2 to 4 jalapeno peppers, chopped
1 c. mayonnaise

Break cheese into pieces in electric mixer bowl; add onion and jalapeno peppers. Beat until smooth and creamy; add mayonnaise. Beat until creamy. Let stand at room temperature to develop flavor. Serve at room temperature with corn chips, tostadas, celery, carrot sticks or crackers. Dip may be made ahead of time and frozen. Yield: 8-10 servings.

Mrs. Nellie Hoggatt, Perryton Jr. H.S.
Perryton, Texas

BACON BIT DIP

10 slices bacon
1 ½ tsp. instant minced onion
1 ½ tsp. water
1 ½ c. sour cream

Fry bacon until crisp. Drain on paper towels. Crumble. Mix onion and water together and let stand for 5 minutes. Blend bacon and onion with sour cream; cover and chill.

Mrs. Daniel B. Snead, Glenn Vocational H.S.
Birmingham, Alabama

SWEDISH CANAPE DIP

1 8-oz. pkg. cream cheese
1 tbsp. horseradish
Pinch of salt
6 slices bacon, fried until crisp

Mash cream cheese; add horseradish, salt and bacon. Serve as dip. Yield: 15 servings.

Ada Colquhoun, Pershing Co. H.S.
Lovelock, Nevada

TURKISH DELIGHT

6 strips bacon
1 med. onion, chopped
2 lb. Velveeta cheese
1 No. 202 can tomatoes, drained
Garlic powder to taste
1 can El Paso green chili, finely chopped

Cook bacon until crisp. Remove from fat. Cook onion in remaining fat. Add cheese, garlic powder and tomatoes. Add chili last. Thin with tomato juice, if necessary. Cook 2 hours. Pour into chafing dish. Serve with Fritos.

Elizabeth Kanis, Nashoba Reg. H.S.
Bolton, Massachusetts

DEVIL DIP

1 3-oz. can deviled ham
1 c. salad dressing
1 tbsp. catsup
1 tbsp. Worcestershire sauce
Dash of onion salt

Mix all ingredients together; chill. Serve with favorite chip. Yield: 6 servings.

Barbara J. Suttner, Chenoa H.S.
Chenoa, Illinois

DEVILED HAM DIP

1 can deviled ham
2 tbsp. mayonnaise
3 tbsp. cream
½ tsp. onion
¼ tsp. salt

48

(Continued on next page)

Whip deviled ham to smooth consistency with mixer. Add mayonnaise, cream, onion and salt. Beat well; chill. Yield: 8 servings.

Doris Herlick, Big Fork H.S.
Big Fork, Montana

Mash liverwurst with fork; add remaining ingredients. Mix well. Chill; serve on potato chips or cracker rounds. Yield: 2 cups.

Mrs. Margie Gilchrist, Stephen F. Austin Jr. HS
Borger, Texas

DEVILED HAM-CHEESE DIP

1 4½-oz. can deviled ham
¼ c. grated Swiss cheese
2 tbsp. relish
½ tsp. Tabasco
1 tbsp. mayonnaise

Combine deviled ham and cheese; stir in relish, Tabasco and mayonnaise. Serve with potato chips or crackers. Yield: 2/3 cup.

Mrs. Janell Samford, C. O. Wilson Jr. H.S.
Nederland, Texas

HAM-CHEESE FONDUE

½ lb. cheddar cheese
1 4¼-oz. can deviled ham
2 tsp. prepared mustard
1 tsp. Worcestershire sauce

Melt cheese; stir in deviled ham, mustard and Worcestershire sauce. Serve hot.

Marie K. Jaspers, Pomeroy H.S.
Pomeroy, Washington

TANGY DEVILED HAM DIP

1 3-oz. pkg. cream cheese
1 2¼-oz. can deviled ham
1 c. tomato catsup

Soften cream cheese; add deviled ham. Combine thoroughly. Add catsup; mix thoroughly. Chill; serve. Yield: 2 cups.

Mrs. Kathaleen M. Rice, Jim Ned H.S.
Tuscola, Texas

LIVERWURST DIP

½ lb. liverwurst
½ c. mayonnaise
2 tsp. prepared mustard
3 tbsp. crushed potato chips
2 tbsp. pickle relish
¼ tsp. paprika
¼ tsp. salt
⅛ tsp. pepper

MEXICAN CHEESE DIP

2 tbsp. butter
2 tbsp. flour
1 No. 303 can chili peppers with tomatoes
2 lb. Velveeta cheese, grated

Melt butter in 2-quart saucepan on low temperature; stir in flour. Add chili pepper and tomatoes; bring to a boil over medium sheet. Add cheese; reduce heat to low, stirring until mixture is blended. Serve hot or cold with chips, Fritos, cauliflowerettes or celery sticks. Yield: 30 servings.

Ruth A. Nesmith, Rio Hondo H.S.
Rio Hondo, Texas

BEER AND CHEESE DIP

1 lb. process American cheese
2 oz. dry onion soup mix
¾ to 1 c. beer

Melt cheese in top of double boiler; blend in onion soup mix well. Pour beer in gradually, stirring until well blended. Serve warm with crackers, pretzels or potato chips. Yield: 12 servings.

Esther F. Intermill, Chassell H.S.
Chassell, Michigan

SNAPPY CHEESE

2 or 3 cloves of garlic, chopped
1 sm. onion, chopped fine
Paprika to color cheese
2 lb. Old English cheese
⅓ bottle Tabasco sauce
1 can beer, leave open 24 hours

Mix garlic, onion and paprika with cheese; add Tabasco sauce and beer. Beat with electric mixer about 10 minutes or until creamy.

Wilma Durbin Wood, Amanda Jr. High
Middletown, Ohio

CHARLIE'S DIP

½ c. cream cheese
½ c. cream-style cottage cheese

(Continued on next page)

2 tbsp. cream
2 tbsp. minced onion
2 tbsp. caraway seed
4 tbsp. capers
Salt and pepper to taste

Blend cottage cheese in blender until smooth; add remaining ingredients. Blend well. Serve. Yield: 1 cup.

Mrs. Margaret Huelskamp, Bedford Comm. HS
Bedford, Iowa

EASY COTTAGE CHEESE DIP

1 12-oz. carton cream-style sm. curd
   cottage cheese
1 ½ tsp. instant minced onion
½ tsp. seasoned salt
1 tbsp. finely chopped pimento or parsley
   (opt.)

Combine first 3 ingredients; mix well with electric mixer or blender. Chill 5 to 6 hours. Add pimento or parsley. Serve with potato chips, corn chips, celery or carrot strips for dunking or serve on baked potatoes. Yield: 15 to 20 servings.

Ghlee Kershner, Montpelier H.S.
Montpelier, Indiana

EVERYBODY'S FAVORITE DIP

1 8-oz. pkg. cream cheese, softened
⅓ c. chili sauce
⅓ c. catsup
½ med. onion, diced fine
1 tbsp. dried parsley
Milk (opt.)

Blend all ingredients with fork or in blender. Add small amount of milk if too thick. Serve with chips, crackers or raw vegetables.

Mrs. Marcy Ginther, Harding H.S.
St. Paul, Minnesota

NIPPY CHEESE DIP

1 8-oz. pkg. cream cheese
¾ tsp. Lawry's seasoned salt
1 tbsp. grated onion and juice
1 tsp. Worcestershire sauce
2 tbsp. catsup
3 tbsp. mayonnaise

Soften cheese; add remaining ingredients in order given. Blend thoroughly. Serve with potato or corn chips. Yield: 8 servings.

Anna Lee Wells, Flat Gap H.S.
Flat Gap, Kentucky

ONION DIP

1 carton cottage cheese
1 pkg. dry onion soup mix
1 c. mayonnaise

Pour cottage cheese into small mixing bowl. Beat at whipping speed until creamy in texture. Add onion soup mix and blend well. Add mayonnaise and continue beating until desired consistency for dip or sandwich filling. Yield: 8-10 servings.

Mary Ella Porter, Como-Pickton H.S.
Como, Texas

ONION SOUP DIP

8 oz. sour cream
1 envelope onion soup
Cream

Blend sour cream for a few seconds; add onion soup. Add cream for desired consistency. Yield: 6-8 servings.

Mrs. Mary Adams, Carr Creek H.S.
Carr Creek, Kentucky

SNAPPY DIP

1 8-oz. pkg. cream cheese
¼ c. dried minced onion
¼ c. catsup
1 tsp. Worcestershire sauce
¼ c. mayonnaise

Soften cream cheese. Add remaining ingredients and refrigerate. Yield: 1 cup.

Mrs. Dianne Rader, Rich Central H.S.
Olympia Fields, Illinois

SLIM DIP

1 tbsp. instant minced onion
1 tsp. seasoned salt
2 pt. cartons sm. curd cottage cheese
1 or 2 tbsp. finely chopped parsley or
   pimento

Combine onion, seasoned salt and cottage cheese; beat until well blended. Refrigerate for 5 to 6 hours to blend flavors. Stir in parsley or pimento. Yield: 3 cups.

Mrs. Dorothy Smith, Virginia H.S.
Virginia, Illinois

QUICK AND LOW DIP

1 pt. low calorie sour cream
   substitute
1 envelope onion soup mix

(Continued on next page)

Stir ingredients together with fork. Let stand 30 minutes in refrigerator. Serve with chips. Yield: 8-10 servings.

Mrs. Violet N. Tabler, Moon Sr. H.S.
Coraopolis, Pennsylvania

PINEAPPLE-CHEESE DIP

2 8-oz. pkg. softened cream cheese
1 c. crushed pineapple
2 tbsp. chopped onion
2 tbsp. chopped green pepper
1 c. chopped pecans
2 tsp. seasoned salt

Thoroughly combine all ingredients. Serve with corn chips.

Mrs. Sunny Stephens, Poteet H.S.
Poteet, Texas

PIMENTO DIP

1 lb. sharp cheese
1 can pimento
1 c. salad dressing

Grate cheese on coarse side of grater; add pimentos and salad dressing. Add additional dressing, if necessary; dip should be consistency of whipped cream. Serve with wheat crackers. Yield: 25 servings.

Mrs. Kathryn D. Brown, Quakertown Jr. H.S.
Quakertown, Pennsylvania

RAREBIT DIP

¼ c. margarine
½ c. chopped celery
½ c. chopped green pepper
2 tbsp. chopped onion
¼ c. flour
½ tsp. salt
1 c. milk
1 ½ c. cubed American cheese
1 10-oz. can Ro-tel tomatoes

Melt margarine over low flame. Add celery, green pepper and onion; saute until tender. Stir in flour and salt. Add milk. Cover. Cook over low flame, stirring occasionally until thickened. Add cheese, stirring until melted. Gradually stir in Ro-tel tomatoes. Serve over deep fried noodles or with chips. Good hot or cold. Yield: 1 quart.

Mrs. Alma Crawley, Furr Jr.-Sr. H.S.
Houston, Texas

RIPE OLIVE DIP

1 8-oz. pkg. cream cheese
½ c. sour cream
1 sm. can chopped ripe olives
3 tbsp. finely chopped celery
3 tbsp. finely chopped pecans
Few dashes of onion powder or finely minced onion

Soften cheese; add sour cream. Beat well. Blend in remaining ingredients. May be used also as party sandwich spread. Yield: 10 servings.

Mrs. Marian G. Craddock, Colorado H.S.
Colorado City, Texas

ROQUEFORT CHEESE WHIP

1 c. cottage cheese
½ c. mayonnaise
¼ c. grated Roquefort cheese

Place ingredients in bowl; whip with electric beater. Serve with potato chips or use a dressing for lettuce.

Marjory Fuller, Seitz Jr. H.S.
Riverview, Michigan

RO-TEL DIP

2 8-oz. pkg. cream cheese
1 can Ro-tel tomatoes and green chilies

Soften cream cheese at room temperature. Cream until very soft. Add tomatoes with chilies. Beat until blended. Refrigerate until ready to serve. Yield: 2 cups.

Mrs. Pat Bandy, Huckabay H.S.
Stephenville, Texas

CLAM DUNK

1 8-oz. pkg. cream cheese, softened
2 tsp. lemon juice
1 8-oz. can minced clams, drained
2 tsp. chili sauce (opt.)
2 tsp. Worcestershire sauce
1 tsp. salt
⅛ tsp. pepper
Dash of hot pepper sauce
Paprika

Blend cheese and lemon juice. Add clams and remaining ingredients except paprika; mix well. Sprinkle with paprika; chill. Serve with garlic rounds. Yield: 1 1/2 cups.

Shirley J. Bonomo, Spring Valley H.S.
Spring Valley, Wisconsin
Mrs. Beverly A. Reed, Stamford Central Sch.
Stamford, New York

Seafood Dips

DIPSY CLAM CREAM

1 pkg. garlic salad dressing mix
1 pt. heavy sour cream
1 8-oz. can minced clams, drained

Mix all ingredients well; marinate in refrigerator for at least 1 hour. Serve with assorted crackers, celery or carrot sticks or cauliflowerets. Yield: 6-8 servings.

Mrs. B. Sachs, Westlake H.S.
Thornwood, New York

CRAB DIP

1 8-oz. pkg. cream cheese
¼ c. cream
2 tsp. Worcestershire sauce
3 tbsp. lemon juice
¼ tsp. onion juice
Dash of salt
Pepper to taste
⅛ tsp. Tabasco sauce
1 clove of garlic, minced
1 tbsp. pimento, chopped
1 ½ 7 ½-oz. cans crab meat

Beat cheese; add cream. Beat until smooth. Add Worcestershire sauce, lemon juice, onion juice, salt, pepper, Tabasco, garlic and pimento. Remove boney bits from crab; chop into fine pieces. Stir into cheese mixture. Chill until ready to serve. Serve with assorted crackers, potato chips, carrot sticks or celery.

Louise Hall, Amador County H.S.
Sutter Creek, California

CRAB MEAT DIP

¾ lb. cream cheese with chives
1 can crab meat, undrained
1 med. tomato, diced
3 tbsp. mayonnaise

Soften cream cheese with liquid from crab meat; mix in remaining ingredients. Chill; serve with assorted crackers. Will keep for 2 to 3 days in refrigerator. Yield: 6-10 servings.

Mrs. Emily X. McGuigan, Portsmouth H.S.
Portsmouth, Rhode Island

HOT CRAB MEAT DIP

1 8-oz. pkg. cream cheese, softened
1 can crab meat, bones removed
1 tbsp. crab juice
1 tsp. lemon juice
½ tsp. curry powder

Mix cream cheese and crab; add juices and curry powder. Press into baking dish. Bake for 25 minutes in 350-degree oven or until it bubbles. Serve with crackers or chips.

Mary Lloyd Faulkner, Manville H.S.
Manville, New Jersey

SARDINE DIP

1 can sardines, mashed
½ sm. onion, grated
¼ c. mayonnaise
4 crackers, crumbled
Worcestershire sauce
1 tbsp. horseradish

Combine all ingredients; mix well. Pile into center of plate; surround with crackers. Yield: 6 servings.

Foye Davis, Horatio H.S.
Horatio, Arkansas

CHRISTMAS DIP

1 10-oz. can frozen condensed cream of shrimp soup
1 8-oz. pkg. cream cheese
2 tbsp. chopped parsley
1 tbsp. finely chopped green pepper
1 tsp. chopped pimento
1 tsp. chili powder

Thaw soup by placing unopened can in pan of hot water for about 30 minutes. Combine with cheese; beat just until smooth with beater. Add remaining ingredients; chill. Yield: 2 cups.

Carolyn Lewis, Bonneville H.S.
Ogden, Utah

GARLIC-SHRIMP DIP

2 cans frozen shrimp soup
1 jar garlic cheese spread
1 can sm. shrimp, rinsed
1 sm. can mushroom pieces

Melt soup and cheese over low heat; stir occasionally. Add shrimp and mushroom pieces to cheese mixture; mix well. Serve warm or place in fondue dish. Serve with potato chips or crackers. Yield: 2 cups.

Donna J. Pomerenke, Walnut Grove Pub. Sch.
Walnut Grove, Minnesota

SHRIMP DIP

6 oz. cream cheese, softened
1 tsp. grated onion
1 tsp. lemon juice
Mayonnaise or sour cream
1 c. chopped shrimp

Blend cheese, onion, lemon juice and enough mayonnaise for desired consistency; add shrimp. Serve on chips or crackers.

Frances Rudd, Advisory Ed., Home Ec. Ed.
State Dept. of Ed.
Little Rock, Arkansas

SHRIMP DIP

1 5-oz. can shrimp, drained and mashed
1 4-oz. pkg. cream cheese, softened
⅓ c. sour cream
¼ c. minced dill pickle
¼ c. minced pimento
½ tsp. salt
1 tsp. paprika
½ tsp. vinegar
3 drops Tabasco sauce

Combine all ingredients; blend until smooth. Chill well before serving. Serve with crackers or potato chips. Yield: 2 cups.

Helen Krueger, Prince Rupert Sr. Secondary
British Columbia, Canada

SHRIMP SOUP DIP

1 can frozen condensed cream of shrimp
  soup, thawed
1 3-oz. pkg. cream cheese, softened
1 tsp. lemon juice
¼ tsp. garlic powder

Combine all ingredients in blender container; blend until smooth. Serve with crackers, chips or raw vegetables. Yield: 1 1/2 cups.

Mrs. Marcia Miller, Petoskey H.S.
Petoskey, Michigan

YOGURT-SHRIMP DIP

¾ c. creamed cottage cheese
¾ c. plain yogurt
¼ tsp. salt
2 tbsp. black olives, chopped
1 4-oz. can broken shrimp, drained

Blend cottage cheese until smooth in electric blender. Add yogurt and salt; mix well. Stir in olives and shrimp. Serve as dip for carrot sticks, cauliflower pieces and celery sticks, or as dressing for lettuce salads.

Pamela Redd, Magrath H.S.
Magrath, Alberta, Canada

TUNA DIP

1 can grated tuna
½ c. mayonnaise
1 tbsp. grated onion
1 sm. pkg. cream cheese
1 tbsp. Worcestershire sauce
⅛ tsp. Tabasco sauce

Mix all ingredients well. Use as dip with potato chips, spread on crackers or for open-faced sandwiches.

Mrs. Rachel Nicholson, Union H.S.
Union, Mississippi

ZIPPY TUNA DIP

8 oz. pkg. cream cheese
½ c. sour cream
1 tbsp. finely chopped green onion
2 tbsp. cream-style horseradish
½ tsp. salt
1 6½-oz. can tuna, drained
1 tsp. Worcestershire sauce
Dash of pepper

Mix cream cheese until soft; stir in sour cream. Add remaining ingredients and stir until mixed. Serve with crackers and chips.

Ramona Lawton, Mercer Jr. H.S.
Garden City, Georgia

SMOKED EGG DIP

6 hard-cooked eggs, finely chopped
1 tbsp. soft butter
1 ¼ tsp. Liquid Smoke
1 ½ tsp. lemon juice
1 tsp. mustard
1 ½ tsp. Worcestershire sauce
1 drop of Tabasco sauce
¾ tsp. salt
½ tsp. dried minced onions

Combine ingredients. Blend until smooth in mixer. Refrigerate 4 hours. Whip to soften 30 minutes before serving.

Mrs. Marilyn B. Hoffman, Oxford H.S.
Oxford, Mississippi

SPIFFY DIP

3 tbsp. milk
1 8-oz. pkg. cream cheese, softened
1 tsp. Worcestershire sauce
1 tbsp. mayonnaise
2 tsp. lemon juice
1 tsp. horseradish mustard
½ tsp. paprika
¾ tsp. garlic salt

Gradually add milk to cream cheese; add remaining ingredients. Stir until well blended. Serve with potato chips, corn chips, dip crackers or raw vegetable sticks. Yield: 1 cup.

Mrs. Betty K. Thomas, J. I. Carter Jr. H.S.
Arlington, Texas

STRAWBERRY DIPS

1 qt. fresh strawberries
1 c. dairy sour cream
Powdered sugar

Carefully wash strawberries; do not hull. To serve, dip strawberries in sour cream and powdered sugar. Yield: 6 servings.

Margaret Molitor, Goodrich H.S.
Goodrich, Michigan

VEGETABLE DIP

1 tsp. B.V. paste
1 8-oz. jar cream cheese
1 jar Roka blue cheese
1 pt. mayonnaise
1 med. onion, grated

Have all ingredients at room temperature. Melt B.V. paste over hot water; add remaining ingredients. Mix until smooth. Serve with crisp, cold raw vegetables. Yield: 3 cups.

Ona Keas, Midwest City H.S.
Midwest City, Oklahoma

VEGETABLE DIP

1 c. mayonnaise
1 c. catsup
1/3 c. lemon juice
1 tbsp. dry mustard
2 tbsp. horseradish, drained
1 tbsp. sugar
1/2 tsp. Worcestershire sauce
1/4 tsp. pepper
1/2 tsp. salt

Combine all ingredients; mix well. Chill in refrigerator to allow mixture to thicken. May be kept in tightly closed container in refrigerator for several days. Yield: 2 cups.

Mabel V. Garst, Eaton H.S.
Eaton, Ohio

YOGURT DIP

1 clove of garlic
6 walnut halves
1 tbsp. olive oil
1 c. yogurt
Salt and pepper to taste
Dash of lemon juice
1 cucumber, peeled and diced

Mash garlic and walnut meats with olive oil. Stir in yogurt, salt and pepper. Flavor with lemon juice and stir in cucumber. Chill. Serve with crisp crackers. Yield: 6 servings.

Ruby A. Lesch, Wayzata Jr. H.S.
Wayzata, Minnesota

ZIPPY DIP

1 pt. sour cream
1 tsp. dried parsley flakes
1/2 tsp. garlic salt
1/4 tsp. seasoned salt
1/8 tsp. seasoned pepper
1/4 tsp. oregano
1/4 tsp. cayenne pepper
1/4 tsp. chili powder

Combine all ingredients. Serve with warmed tortilla chips.

Susan Holbrook, Blackford H.S.
San Jose, California

DEVIL SAUCE

1/4 c. molasses
1/4 c. prepared mustard
1/4 c. brown sugar
3/4 c. vinegar
1/2 c. canned pineapple juice
1/4 c. Worcestershire sauce
1/2 tsp. Tabasco

Combine molasses, mustard and brown sugar; mix well. Add vinegar, pineapple juice, Worcestershire sauce and Tabasco; mix well. Serve with oven-braised short ribs, as a barbecue sauce or on leftover roast. Yield: 1 3/4 cups.

Mrs. Reva Wilson, Drummond H.S.
Drummond, Montana

BARBECUE SAUCE

1 chopped onion
2 tbsp. salad oil
2 tbsp. vinegar
1 c. catsup
1/2 c. water
1/2 tsp. prepared mustard
3 tbsp. Worcestershire sauce
1/2 c. lemon juice

Cook onion in oil until yellow; add remaining ingredients. Simmer 30 minutes. Serve over diced, cooked pork. Yield: 1 pint.

Norine E. Sipe, Goffstown H.S.
Goffstown, New Hampshire

BLACKBERRY SAUCE
FOR COLD HAM

2 tsp. dry mustard
1 tsp. paprika
1 tsp. ginger
1/2 tsp. salt
2 tbsp. water
2 tbsp. lemon juice
Juice and rind of 2 oranges
1/2 c. blackberry jelly

Mix dry ingredients; add water, juices and orange rind. Let stand for 30 to 45 minutes. Add blackberry jelly and heat slowly. Use as a sauce for cold, sliced baked ham. Yield: 4 servings.

Augusta H. Dennis, Billingsley H.S.
Billingsley, Alabama

CHOCOLATE GOUP SAUCE

1 c. sugar
2 tbsp. (rounded) cocoa
1 tbsp. (rounded) flour
Pinch of salt
1 ½ c. milk

Mix dry ingredients; add to milk. Cook, stirring constantly, until mixture boils and coats spoon. Cool. Serve over white, yellow or chocolate cake topped with whipped cream. Yield: 6 servings.

Mrs. Jean Evans, Wallace Pub. Sch.
Wallace, Nebraska

CREOLE SAUCE

3 tbsp. chopped onion
3 tbsp. chopped green pepper
2 tbsp. butter or margarine
1 c. seasoned tomato sauce
1 3 or 4-oz. can sliced mushrooms
½ tsp. salt
¼ tsp. pepper

Cook onion and green pepper in butter until tender but not brown. Add tomato sauce, drained mushrooms, salt and pepper. Simmer over low heat for 10 minutes. Serve over boiled shrimp, steak, salmon loaf or meat loaf. Yield: 4-6 servings.

Thelma McClain, Bremond H.S.
Bremond, Texas

CUMBAK SAUCE

1 c. mayonnaise
½ c. Wesson oil
½ c. catsup
¼ c. chili sauce
1 tsp. Worcestershire sauce
1 tsp. paprika
1 tsp. mustard
1 sm. onion, grated
1 garlic button, grated
Juice of 1 lemon
1 tbsp. water

Measure all ingredients into pint jar. Shake well. Serve as dressing for lettuce salad or as sauce for seafood. Yield: 1 pint.

Mrs. Patsy C. Johnston, Calhoun H.S.
Calhoun, Louisiana

DUNKING SAUCE

1 c. mayonnaise
½ c. catsup
1 ½ tbsp. tarragon vinegar

2 to 3 dashes Tabasco
3 tbsp. horseradish
2 tbsp. lemon juice
¼ tsp. onion juice
½ tsp. dry mustard
1 tsp. Worcestershire sauce
1 tsp. salt
1 tbsp. finely minced chives
1 tbsp. finely minced parsley

Combine all ingredients; store in covered jar in refrigerator until ready to use. Yield: 2 cups.

Mrs. Blanche W. Truesdale, Ruffin H.S.
Ruffin, North Carolina

FRESH APPLESAUCE

2 chopped apples
2 tbsp. pineapple juice
2 tbsp. red hots

Blend together apples, pineapple juice and red hots. Apples may be pared or unpared as desired. Yield: 6-8 servings.

Mrs. Novella Mae Melton, Roswell H.S.
Roswell, New Mexico

HOLLANDAISE SAUCE

3 egg yolks
2 to 3 tbsp. lemon juice
¼ tsp. salt
½ c. soft safflower oil margarine

Blend together egg yolks, lemon juice and salt in small saucepan; add margarine. Stir constantly over very low heat until margarine melts and sauce thickens. Serve hot or at room temperature. Any leftover sauce can be stored in the refrigerator. To serve, stir in a little hot water. Yield: Approximately 3/4 cup sauce.

Photograph for this recipe on page 41.

HORSERADISH SAUCE

½ c. whipping cream
3 tbsp. mayonnaise
1 tbsp. vinegar
2 tbsp. horseradish, drained
1 tsp. prepared mustard
½ tsp. salt

Whip cream; fold in mayonnaise. Stir in vinegar slowly; add remaining ingredients. Chill. Serve with ham or freeze and serve on lettuce as a salad. Yield: 6 servings.

Mrs. Virginia Claypool, Marshall H.S.
Marshall, Illinois

267 LEMON TOPPING

1 c. milk
1 pkg. instant lemon pudding
½ pt. whipping cream

Add milk to pudding; beat with rotary beater until thick. Whip the cream and fold into pudding. Spread on congealed salad. Yield: 12 servings.

Mrs. Eleanor Puckett, North Mecklenburg H.S. Huntersville, North Carolina

MUSHROOM-CHEESE SAUCE

¼ c. cream of mushroom soup
¼ c. shredded cheddar cheese

Combine soup and cheese in saucepan; cover and place over low heat until hot. Stir to blend; pour over cooked asparagus or other vegetables. Yield: 4 servings.

Mrs. Carol Canada, Colcord H.S. Colcord, Oklahoma

ONION BUTTER

¼ c. butter
1 tsp. Worcestershire sauce
¼ tsp. dry mustard
¼ tsp. cracked pepper
2 tbsp. minced onion
2 tbsp. snipped parsley

Combine butter, Worcestershire sauce, dry mustard and pepper; cream until fluffy. Stir in onion and parsley. Serve on hot hamburgers or steaks. Yield: 1/3 cup.

Mrs. Karen Rackow, Southern Door High Brussels, Wisconsin

PINEAPPLE SAUCE

1 c. sugar
¼ c. flour
⅛ tsp. nutmeg (opt.)
1 No. 2 can pineapple chunks
1 tbsp. butter
¼ to ½ tsp. cinnamon (opt.)

Mix sugar, spices and flour. Drain juice from pineapple and add to sugar and flour; cook until thick. Pour over pineapple; add butter. Yield: 6 servings.

Mrs. Jo Lucas, Bellevue Comm. Sch. Bellevue, Iowa

SEAFOOD SAUCE

1 c. catsup
1 tbsp. lemon juice
1 tsp. horseradish

Combine all ingredients. Chill. Serve with shrimp or other seafood. Yield: 6 servings.

Mrs. Helen Calfee, Gibbs H.S. Corryton, Tennessee

SHRIMP COCKTAIL SAUCE

½ c. tomato catsup
¼ c. lemon juice
1 tbsp. Worcestershire sauce
2 tbsp. horseradish
¼ tsp. Tabasco sauce
¼ tsp. salt
1 tbsp. minced onion
1 tbsp. minced celery

Combine ingredients as listed; chill thoroughly. Serve as a dip for boiled shrimp or on individual cocktail servings. Yield: 4 servings.

Mrs. Mary E. McGee, Stockdale High Stockdale, Texas

SPICY SAUCE FOR BAKED HAM

1 tsp. dry mustard
¼ tsp. powdered cloves
¼ tsp. powdered cinnamon
2 tbsp. cider or malt vinegar
1 c. crabapple jelly

Mix mustard, cloves, cinnamon and vinegar in top of double boiler. Add jelly; heat over boiling water, stirring occasionally, until jelly melts. Spoon over slices of hot baked ham. Yield: 8 servings.

Mrs. C. Norton, Sutherland Jr. Secondary North Vancouver, British Columbia

TARTAR SAUCE

½ c. mayonnaise
1 tbsp. minced onion
1 tbsp. chopped pickle
1 tbsp. chopped olives
1 tbsp. capers
1 tbsp. chopped parsley

Blend all ingredients. Serve as accompaniment to hot or cold fish and cold meats. Yield: 3/4 cup.

Mrs. Hazel L. Seaton, Twiggs County H.S. Danville, Georgia

Salad
Dressings

RECIPE FOR FLUFFY DATE SALAD DRESSING ON PAGE 72

AGNES' SALAD DRESSING

    1 can tomato sauce
    ½ c. vinegar
    ¾ c. sugar
    ½ c. salad oil
    1 tsp. grated onion
    ½ tsp. prepared mustard

Place all ingredients in quart jar. Shake until thick and well blended. Store in refrigerator. Yield: 1 pint.

Mrs. Weldon Russell, Howard H.S.
Howard, Kansas

APRICOT NECTAR SALAD DRESSING

    ½ c. sugar
    ⅛ tsp. salt
    2 tbsp. flour
    1 egg, slightly beaten
    1 c. apricot nectar
    1 c. heavy cream, whipped or equivalent
     of low carlorie topping

Combine sugar, salt and flour in top of double boiler. Stir in egg. Add apricot nectar gradually. Cook over boiling water, stirring constantly, until thickened. Cool and fold in cream. Delicious on fresh fruit salad. Yield: 1 pint.

Helen Firkus, Neenah Sr. H.S.
Neenah, Wisconsin

AVOCADO SALAD DRESSING

    1 med. avocado
    3 tbsp. vinegar
    1 pkg. onion salad dressing mix
    1 c. sour cream

Peel and slice avocado; place in blender. Add vinegar and salad dressing mix; cover and blend 30 seconds. Add sour cream; blend 30 seconds longer. Yield: 1 1/2 cups.

Mrs. Oleta M. Smith, O'Donnell H.S.
O'Donnell, Texas

AVOCADO-CHEESE DRESSING

    1 c. sm. curd cottage cheese
    1 med. avocado, peeled and cut into
     pieces
    ½ tsp. grated lemon rind
    1 tbsp. lemon juice
    ½ c. mayonnaise
    ½ tsp. salt
    ½ tsp. Worcestershire sauce

Mix all ingredients in electric blender until smooth. Press cottage cheese and avocado through sieve if no blender available. Mix with remaining ingredients. Yield: 2 cups.

Nancy Graham, Big Piney H.S.
Big Piney, Wyoming

AVOCADO SALAD DRESSING

    1 egg
    ½ tsp. dry mustard
    ½ c. salad oil
    ¼ tsp. Tabasco sauce
    Juice of 2 lemons
    1 tbsp. Worcestershire sauce
    2 avocados
    2 fresh green onions, chopped
    ½ tsp. salt
    ½ tsp. pepper
    Garlic salt to taste
    ½ c. mayonnaise

Blend egg and mustard together; add oil. Mix thoroughly; add Tabasco sauce, lemon juice and Worcestershire sauce. Mash avocado; add onions, salt, pepper and garlic salt. Mix well and add mayonnaise. Chill for 2 hours. Serve over lettuce. Yield: 6-8 servings.

Mrs. Margaret M. Elliott, Edcouch-Elsa H.S.
Edcouch, Texas

AVOCADO SALAD DRESSING

    1 med. avocado, well ripened
    1 tbsp. lemon juice
    ½ tsp. salt
    ½ tsp. chili powder
    ¼ tsp. black pepper
    Dash of cayenne (opt.)
    ¼ c. mayonnaise

Peel avocado; remove seed. Mash with lemon juice to smooth consistency or blend in blender. Add seasonings and mayonnaise; mix well. Serve over sliced tomatoes, lettuce or seafood salads. Yield: 1 1/4 cups.

Mrs. Ruth Yelvington, Mildred H.S.
Corsicana, Texas

BEVI'S CHEM LAB SPECIAL

    ½ c. honey
    1 ½ c. catsup
    1 c. wine vinegar
    ½ to ¾ c. oil
    2 tsp. lemon juice
    1 med. onion, grated
    1 clove of quartered garlic
    2 tsp. salt
    1 ½ tsp. mustard

(Continued on next page)

½ tsp. paprika
1 tsp. celery seed
1 tsp. Worcestershire sauce

Combine all ingredients. Shake until honey is dissolved. Mixture will thicken upon refrigeration. Garlic can be left in, depending on strength desired. Yield: 3 cups.

Chris Spindt, San Rafael H.S.
San Rafael, California

BLEU CHEESE DRESSING

1 pt. salad dressing
1 bud of garlic, chopped
½ c. salad oil
1 sm. can evaporated milk
8 to 10 oz. bleu cheese

Combine first 4 ingredients in blender; add half the cheese. Blend well. Crumble remaining cheese into mixture. Refrigerate; chill for 3 days before using. Yield: 12 servings.

Mrs. Charles W. Hord, Cen. H.S.
Murfreesboro, Tennessee

BLEU CHEESE DRESSING

1 4-oz. pkg. cream cheese
½ pt. sour cream
½ pt. mayonnaise
1 4-oz. pkg. bleu cheese
½ tsp. parsley flakes
¼ tsp. garlic salt
¼ tsp. onion salt
1 tsp. lemon juice
½ tsp. Worcestershire sauce

Combine cream cheese, sour cream, mayonnaise, bleu cheese and seasonings; blend thoroughly. Cover; refrigerate. Yield: 3 cups.

Mrs. Donna L. Hoffbuhr, Lebanon Jr. H.S.
Lebanon, Oregon

BLEU CHEESE DRESSING

1 box cultured sour cream
¼ lb. blue cheese
1 tbsp. salad dressing
¼ tsp. garlic salt

Blend all ingredients together; let stand for 2 hours before serving. Keeps several weeks in refrigerator. Serve on green salads. Yield: 32 servings.

Mrs. Aleen Hartman, Manderson-Hyottville H.S.
Manderson, Wyoming

BLUE CHEESE DRESSING

4 5-oz. pkg. blue cheese
1 c. mayonnaise
2 c. sour cream
2 tsp. lemon juice
1 tsp. salt
1 tsp. pepper
Dash of garlic salt
½ tsp. monosodium glutamate
½ tsp. Worcestershire sauce
1 tbsp. minced onion
Dash of paprika
2 to 4 tbsp. milk

Mix all ingredients in blender or bowl. Refrigerate to blend flavors. Yield: 3 1/2 cups.

Mrs. Dorothy Zimmerman, Canby Pub. H.S.
Canby, Minnesota

BLUE CHEESE DRESSING

3 4-oz. pkg. blue cheese
⅔ c. evaporated milk
¼ tsp. powdered garlic or 1 clove of garlic, ground
½ tsp. powdered onion or 1 sm. onion, chopped
1 tsp. Worcestershire sauce
½ c. mayonnaise

Heat cheese and milk together. Remove from heat; blend in remaining ingredients. Refrigerate. Yield: 1 pint.

Margaret Kalhar, Fisher Jr. H.S.
Cheney, Washington

CREAMY BLEU CHEESE DRESSING

1 c. mayonnaise
1 c. sour cream
7 oz. bleu cheese
2 tbsp. lemon juice
Garlic salt to taste
Seasoned salt to taste
¼ tsp. coarse black pepper
½ c. coffee cream

Blend mayonnaise and sour cream. Crumble cheese; add to sour cream mixture. Add remaining ingredients except cream; blend well. Add enough cream for desired consistency. Yield: 3 cups.

Margaret Schlotz, Waldport H.S.
Waldport, Oregon

BLUE CHEESE SHAKE-UP

1 oz. blue cheese, crumbled
½ tsp. salt
½ tsp. dry mustard

(Continued on next page)

½ tsp. paprika
Dash of cayenne
½ c. salad oil
3 tbsp. salad vinegar

Combine ingredients in jar; cover. Shake well. Toss with green salads. Yield: 3/4 cup.

Mrs. Gerry Fanning, East Jr. H.S.
Tullahoma, Tennessee

BLUE CHEESE-FRENCH DRESSING

1 can tomato soup
½ c. vinegar
⅓ c. oil
⅓ c. sugar
1 tbsp. Worcestershire sauce
1 tsp. dry minced onion
1 tsp. salt
1 tsp. paprika
1 tsp. dry mustard
¼ tsp. Tabasco sauce
¼ lb. blue cheese, crumbled

Place all ingredients in 1-quart jar; shake well. keep in cool place in covered container. Yield: 20-30 servings.

Phyllis P. Nash, Conestaga Sr. H.S.
Berwyn, Pennsylvania

DANISH DRESSING

1 8-oz. pkg. cottage cheese
2 tbsp. blue cheese
2 tbsp. milk

Combine ingredients in blender or small bowl. Beat until smooth. Cover; chill overnight. Serve. Yield: 1 1/4 cups.

Mrs. Barbara Segura, S.F. Austin Jr. H.S.
Galveston, Texas

SOUTHERN SALAD DRESSING

½ c. cornstarch
1 ½ c. boiling water
½ clove, chopped
1 garlic button
1 pt. mayonnaise
½ c. chopped olives
½ c. chopped pickles
1 tbsp. vinegar
¾ wedge bleu cheese
Salt to taste

Add cornstarch to boiling water; cool. Add clove, garlic, mayonnaise, olives, pickles, vinegar, bleu cheese and salt. Blend well. Yield: 4 cups.

Beda Sue Hogue, Fourche Valley, H.S.
Briggsville, Arkansas

TANGY BLUE CHEESE DRESSING

¼ c. blue cheese, room temperature
⅛ tsp. salt
¼ tsp. black pepper
⅓ c. cream
½ c. mayonnaise
⅓ c. vinegar
½ tsp. Worcestershire sauce

Combine cheese, salt, pepper; cream with fork. Gradually beat in cream, mayonnaise, vinegar and Worcestershire sauce; blend well. Cover; chill in refrigerator for several hours. Serve on green salad or with tomatoes.

Mrs. Billy Marks, Bodenham H.S.
Pulaski, Tennessee

TASTY BLEU CHEESE DRESSING

½ lb. bleu cheese
⅓ c. tarragon vinegar
5 c. mayonnaise
Garlic to taste
¼ med. onion chopped or dry minced onion
4 drops Tabasco sauce
Celery seed to taste

Blend all ingredients together by hand; do not use electric blender. Refrigerate. Yield: 2 quarts.

Mrs. Paulinda King Hall, Walker H.S.
Atlanta, Georgia

BUTTERMILK SALAD DRESSING

¼ c. plus 2 tbsp. sugar
¼ c. vinegar
¾ tbsp. garlic powder
1 ½ tsp. parsley flakes
¾ tsp. salt
¼ c. plus 2 tbsp. ground onions
1 pt. Miracle Whip salad dressing
½ c. salad oil
½ c. buttermilk

Combine all ingredients; store in refrigerator.

Mrs. Alvenia Nimmo, Burns Flat H.S.
Burns Flat, Oklahoma

CAESAR DRESSING

1 3-oz. pkg. blue cheese
1 pkg. Caesar dip mix
¼ c. mayonnaise

Soften blue cheese to room temperature; add remaining ingredients. Blend thoroughly. Yield: 1 cup.

Mrs. William D. Bowen, Parsons, Jr. H.S.
Parsons, Kansas

CAESAR SALAD DRESSING

1 egg
¾ c. salad oil
¼ c. lemon juice
1 tsp. salt
¼ tsp. black pepper
1 tbsp. Worcestershire sauce
¼ c. grated Parmesan Cheese

Place whole egg in boiling water for 1 minute. Break into bowl; beat until fluffy. Continue beating at high speed, adding oil gradually. Reduce speed; add remaining ingredients. Yield: 12 servings.

Mrs. Anne Stalter, Riverside Park Jr. H.S.
Springfield, Vermont

CELERY SEED DRESSING

½ c. sugar
1 tbsp. flour
½ tsp. mustard
1 tsp. paprika
1 tsp. salt
½ c. vinegar
1 tbsp. grated onion
1 c. salad oil
1 tsp. celery seed

Mix sugar, flour and seasoning; add vinegar. Cook until slightly thickened; add onion. Cook; beat in oil gradually. Mix in celery seed. Yield: 1 pint.

Mrs. Mary B. McGlone, St. Rose Academy H.S.
Vincennes, Indiana

CELERY SEED DRESSING

10 tbsp. sugar
½ tsp. grated onion
1 tsp. salt
1 tsp. dry mustard
⅓ c. white vinegar
1 c. vegetable oil
1 tbsp. celery seed

Mix sugar, onion, salt and mustard in small electric mixer bowl. Add vinegar and oil alternately by spoonfuls, beating all the while with electric mixer. Add celery seeds; stir in by hand. Store in refrigerator.

Gladys E. Bloomfield
Cambie Jr. Secondary H.S.
Richmond, British Columbia, Canada

CELERY SEED DRESSING

½ c. sugar
1 tsp. dry mustard
1 tsp. salt

2 tsp. grated onion
⅓ c. salad vinegar
1 tbsp. celery seed

Combine all ingredients; beat until thick and creamy, about 10 minutes. Pour into bottle; chill. Excellent for citrus fruit salads.

Mrs. Wayne Weishaar, Lemmon H.S.
Lemmon, South Dakota

CELERY SEED DRESSING

1 lightly beaten egg
1 tbsp. onion juice or powder
1 c. sugar
1 tsp. salt
1 tbsp. dry mustard
⅓ c. vinegar
1 tbsp. celery seed
1 pt. Wesson oil

Mix first 7 ingredients; add oil slowly while mixing. Yield: 1 1/2 pints.

Velva Johnson, Adams H.S.
Adams, Minnesota

CELERY SEED DRESSING WITH CATSUP

1 ¼ c. sugar
1 ½ tsp. salt
1 ½ tsp. paprika
1 ½ tsp. grated onion
½ c. catsup
½ c. vinegar
1 ½ c. salad oil

Combine sugar, salt, paprika, onion and catsup in mixing bowl. Beat at slow speed; add vinegar and oil slowly, alternating a small amount of each at a time. Be careful not to break emulsion. Beat until thick; add celery seed. Yield: 3 cups.

Sister M. Vincent Werner, Andale H.S.
Andale, Kansas

CELERY SEED DRESSING WITH LEMON

½ c. sugar
1 tsp. celery seed
1 tsp. salt
1 tsp. dry mustard
1 tsp. paprika
⅓ c. lemon juice
¾ c. salad oil

Combine all ingredients except salad oil. Gradually add salad oil, beating with an electric or rotary beater until thick. Yield: 1 1/2 cups.

Elaine M. Krick, Jefferson H.S.
Alexandria, Minnesota

Salad Dressings

CHEF'S DRESSING

½ c. buttermilk
2 tbsp. cream-style cottage cheese
¼ tsp. salt
¼ tsp. French's mustard
1 drop Tabasco sauce
½ sm. white onion, sliced
1 tbsp. minced parsley
½ tbsp. minced chives

Place all ingredients in blender; cream until smooth. Yield: 6 servings.

Mrs. Mary J. Higgins, Marietta H.S.
Marietta, Georgia

CHEF'S SALAD DRESSING

1 c. salad dressing
½ c. catsup
2 tbsp. lemon juice
1 tsp. Worcestershire sauce
Salt, pepper and garlic salt to taste
4 tbsp. soft butter

Combine all ingredients except butter; stir to smooth consistency. Add butter. Mix until butter is size of small peas. Serve over chef's salad.

Mrs. James J. Sullivan
East Grand Forks Sr. H.S.
East Grand Forks, Minnesota

COOKED DRESSING

1 ½ tsp. salt
1 ½ tsp. dry mustard
¼ c. plus 2 tbsp. sugar
Dash of cayenne pepper
3 tbsp. flour
6 eggs
2 ¼ c. milk
1 c. vinegar
Butter (opt.)

Mix dry ingredients in top of double boiler. Beat eggs and milk together in small bowl; add to dry ingredients gradually, stirring out lumps. Stir in vinegar slowly. Cook over simmering water, stirring constantly, until thick. Stir in butter; cool. Store, covered, until ready to use. Yield: 1 1/2 quarts.

Mrs. Bette D. Jenness
Linesville-Conneaut-Summit Joint Sch.
Linesville, Pennsylvania

COOKED SALAD DRESSING

3 eggs, beaten
1 to 1 ¼ c. sugar
1 tsp. cornstarch
½ c. diluted vinegar
3 to 4 tbsp. cream or canned milk
5 tbsp. mayonnaise

Combine eggs, sugar, cornstarch and vinegar in top of double boiler; cook until thick. Add milk and mayonnaise. Serve with potato salad.

Mrs. Ruth W. Thearle, North Hagerstown H.S.
Hagerstown, Maryland

COOKED SALAD DRESSING

½ c. vinegar
½ c. sugar
1 tbsp. dry mustard
1 dessert spoon cornstarch or 3 tbsp. flour
1 tsp. salt
Dash of cayenne pepper
2 eggs, beaten
1 c. milk or 1 sm. can evaporated milk
1 tbsp. butter

Heat vinegar. Mix dry ingredients; add eggs and milk. Add milk mixture to hot vinegar slowly, stirring constantly. Cook in double boiler until done, about 20 to 25 minutes, stirring constantly until thick. Remove from heat; add butter. Beat with egg beater until smooth. Additional milk may be added, if a thinner dressing is desired.

Mrs. Thomas Lye, Bloomfield Jr. H.S.
Halifax, Nova Scotia, Canada

COTTAGE CHEESE DRESSING

½ c. French dressing
½ c. mayonnaise
¼ c. cottage cheese

Fold French dressing into mayonnaise; lightly fold in cottage cheese. Chill; serve with fruit, vegetable or mixed green salads. Yield: 1/4 cups.

Mrs. Carol Wisnewski, Stratford H.S.
Stratford, Wisconsin

CRANBERRY SALAD DRESSING

1 tbsp. sugar
1 tsp. (scant) dry mustard
1 tsp. salt
Dash of paprika
4 egg yolks, beaten very lightly
4 tbsp. lemon juice
12 marshmallows
1 c. whipping cream

62

(Continued on next page)

Beat dry ingredients into egg yolks; add lemon juice. Cook in double boiler, stirring constantly, until thick. Remove from heat; beat in marshmallows until smooth. Cook for 2 minutes longer. Whip cream; fold in just before serving.

Mrs. Eloise Guerrant, Robert Lee H.S.
Robert Lee, Texas

CREAM CHEESE DRESSING
    1 3-oz. pkg. cream cheese
    3 hard-cooked eggs, chopped
    1/3 to 1/2 c. parsley, chopped
    3 tbsp. vinegar
    9 tbsp. salad oil
    1 c. catsup

Stir cream cheese until of soft creamy consistency; add remainder ingredients. Blend well. Serve with hearts of lettuce. Yield: 1 pint.

Mrs. Lyman Shaw, Bloomington H.S.
Bloomington, Illinois

CREAM DRESSING
    1/2 pt. whipping cream, whipped
    1/4 c. sugar
    1/4 c. vinegar
    Salt to taste

Combine all ingredients thoroughly. Serve over salad made of lettuce, spinach and Bermuda onions. Yield: 6 servings.

Wanda M. Stacke, Sr. H.S.
Marshfield, Wisconsin

CREAM-GARLIC DRESSING
    1/4 c. wine vinegar
    1/4 c. tarragon vinegar
    1 1/2 c. corn or cottonseed oil
    1 tsp. salt
    3 tbsp. sugar
    2 cloves of garlic
    1/4 c. milk
    3 oz. cream cheese

Blend all ingredients in electric blender. Serve over tossed salad. Add 1/4 to 1/2 cup bleu cheese for variation. Yield: 2 1/2 cups.

Grace Lamusga, Hosterman Jr. H.S.
Robbinsdale, Minnesota

CREAMY RIVER DRESSING
    3 eggs
    1 qt. salad oil
    1 qt. buttermilk

    5 to 6 tbsp. dry mustard
    2 to 4 tbsp. garlic salt
    1 tbsp. salt

Place eggs in blender; blend. Add remaining ingredients; blend. Store in refrigerator. Yield: 2 quarts.

Ann Good, Inola H.S.
Inola, Oklahoma

CURRY SALAD DRESSING
    1/2 tsp. beef-flavored gravy base
    1/4 c. hot water
    1 c. mayonnaise
    1 clove of garlic
    1 tbsp. curry powder
    1/4 tsp. Worcestershire sauce
    6 to 8 drops bottled hot pepper sauce

Stir together gravy base and hot water; blend in mayonnaise. Insert toothpick in garlic; stir in garlic, curry powder, Worcestershire and pepper sauce. Chill for several hours or overnight. Remove garlic clove before serving. Serve over mixed greens.

Alberta Ball Bickerdike, East Pike Sch.
Milton, Illinois

DUTCH CUPBOARD DRESSING FOR DANDELION GREENS
    4 slices bacon, diced
    1/2 c. sugar
    1/2 tsp. salt
    1 tbsp. cornstarch
    1 egg
    1/4 c. vinegar
    1 c. water
    1 sm. onion, chopped

Fry bacon until browned. Mix sugar with salt and cornstarch. Add beaten egg, vinegar and water. Add to fat and bacon. Cook until thick, stirring constantly. Add onion to dressing before placing it on greens. Yield: 1 pint.

Mrs. Joann Ketterer, United Local H.S.
Hanoverton, Ohio

AMERICAN-STYLE FRENCH DRESSING

½ c. olive and or vegetable oil
2 tbsp. vinegar
2 tbsp. lemon juice
½ tsp. salt
¼ tsp. dry mustard
¼ tsp. paprika

Beat all ingredients together with rotary beater or shake well in tightly covered jar. Store in covered jar in refrigerator. Shake well before using. Yield: 1/2 cup.

Mrs. Marilyn Ehlers, Tuttle H.S.
Tuttle, Oklahoma
Marguerite K. German, Copper Basin H.S.
Copperhill, Tennessee

CHILI FRENCH DRESSING

½ c. vegetable oil
¼ c. catsup
¼ c. chili sauce
¼ c. vinegar
½ c. sugar
1 ½ tbsp. Worcestershire sauce
½ sm. onion, finely chopped or grated
Pinch of salt

Combine all ingredients; beat for about 5 to 7 minutes or until thick. Store in refrigerator. Yield: 10 servings.

Patricia M. O'Brien, Duchesne Academy
Omaha, Nebraska

CREAMY FRENCH DRESSING

1 tsp. salt
½ tsp. dry mustard
3 to 4 tbsp. sugar
3 tbsp. catsup
¼ c. evaporated milk
½ c. corn oil
3 tbsp. vinegar

Measure all ingredients except vinegar into mixing bowl; beat with mixer until smooth and well blended. Add vinegar all at once, beating until thoroughly mixed. Store in refrigerator. Yield: 1 1/4 cups.

Mrs. Velma Clark, Brimfield H.S.
Brimfield, Illinois

FAVORITE SALAD DRESSING

1 c. catsup
1 c. sugar
½ c. vinegar
½ c. salad oil
¼ tsp. garlic powder
1 tbsp. Worcestershire sauce

Combine all ingredients in quart jar; cover and shake thoroughly. Store in refrigerator.

Mrs. Rubye R. Hill, Thomson Comm. H.S.
Thomson, Illinois

FRENCH DRESSING

1 clove of garlic
1 sm. onion
½ tsp. salt
1 tbsp. Worcestershire sauce
⅓ c. sugar
⅓ c. catsup
¼ c. vinegar
1 c. corn oil

Grate clove of garlic 3 times over grater; repeat process with onion. Add remaining ingredients to garlic and onion; beat well. Store in refrigerator. Yield: 1 pint.

Mrs. Clara M. Trout, Oakland Comm. Sch.
Oakland, Iowa

FRENCH DRESSING

½ c. catsup
¼ c. vinegar
⅔ c. sugar
1 onion, grated
½ tsp. paprika
1 c. oil
1 tsp. Worcestershire sauce
½ tsp. salt
⅛ tsp. pepper

Combine all ingredients in quart jar; shake to mix well. Store in refrigerator. Yield: 1 quart.

Betty Rogers, West Holt H.S.
Atkinson, Nebraska

FRENCH DRESSING

½ c. vinegar
1 tbsp. sugar
1 tsp. mustard
3 tsp. salad lift
⅛ tsp. salt
1 c. vegetable oil
⅓ c. catsup

Combine vinegar, sugar, mustard, salad lift and salt; mix well until all spice lumps are broken. Add oil and catsup. Pour mixture into bottle or jar. Store in refrigerator. Shake well before using.

Mrs. Dorothy Beeler, Beaver City H.S.
Beaver City, Nebraska

FRENCH DRESSING

1 c. catsup
1 c. sugar
1 c. salad oil
½ c. vinegar
Salt and pepper to taste

Place all ingredients in blender or jar; mix well. Store in refrigerator.

Ann Marie Marshall, Columbus H.S.
Columbus, Wisconsin

FRENCH DRESSING

2 c. salad oil
⅔ c. catsup
1 sm. onion, cut into chunks
2 tsp. salt
1 c. sugar
2 tsp. celery seed
⅔ c. vinegar

Place all ingredients in blender; Mix on high speed for about 30 seconds or until well blended. Chill. Yield: 1 quart.

Mrs. Mina F. Robinson, Perry H.S.
Perry, Kansas

FRENCH SALAD DRESSING

1 c. salad oil
½ c. catsup
2 tbsp. chopped onion
½ c. sugar
1 tsp. salt
Juice of 1 lemon
1 tbsp. vinegar

Combine all ingredients in bowl; beat with rotary beater until well mixed. Shake well before using. Store in refrigerator. Yield: 2 cups.

Mrs. Marjorie Steagall, Scio H.S.
Scio, Oregon

FRENCH SALAD DRESSING

1½ c. sugar
½ c. vinegar
1 tbsp. (heaping) mustard
½ tsp. salt
¾ tsp. celery seed
1 bottle tomato catsup
1 med. onion, grated
2 c. corn oil

Combine all ingredients except oil; beat well. Add oil; beat until thick. Refrigerate.

Mary Rae Burgett, Hanston H.S.
Hanston, Kansas

MARY'S FRENCH DRESSING

1 c. catsup
1 c. salad oil
⅓ c. vinegar
3 tbsp. sugar
3 tsp. salt
2 tsp. paprika
3 tbsp. minced onion

Combine all ingredients. Place in blender until thick or mix with electric mixer. One clove of garlic may be substituted for onion. Use 2 to 3 tablespoons chili or Tabasco sauce and enough catsup to fill 1 cup, if desired.

Mrs. Katherine McIlquham, Chippewa Falls H.S.
Chippewa Falls, Wisconsin

MY FAVORITE
CREAMY FRENCH DRESSING

1 c. powdered sugar
½ c. catsup
½ c. salad oil
¼ c. vinegar
1 tsp. Worcestershire sauce
1 tsp. grated onion
½ tsp. salt
½ tsp. dry mustard
1 clove of garlic, minced or 1 tsp.
  garlic salt

Place all ingredients in small mixer bowl; beat thoroughly. Beat in blender, if desired. Store in refrigerator.

Fern A. Soderholm, Willmar Jr. H.S.
Willmar, Minnesota

QUICK MIX FRENCH DRESSING

1 c. mayonnaise
1 tsp. sugar
Salt to taste
2 tsp. salad vinegar
½ c. catsup
¼ tsp. Tabasco sauce
1 tsp. Worcestershire sauce

Blend mayonnaise, sugar, and salt; add remaining ingredients one at a time until uniform in color. Chill. Yield: 1 1/2 cups.

Mrs. Virginia Grider, Liberty H.S.
Liberty, Kentucky

RED FRENCH DRESSING

⅓ c. sugar
1 tsp. dry onion
½ tsp. dry garlic
⅓ c. cider vinegar
⅓ c. catsup
1 c. salad oil

65

(Continued on next page)

French Dressings

Combine all ingredients in order listed in pint jar; shake well. Place in blender; beat well at high speed. Shake well before using. Store in refrigerator. Yield: 1 pint.

Mrs. Della O. Lindsay, Riverside H.S.
Boardman, Oregon

RUBY RED DRESSING

½ c. salad oil
½ c. tarragon vinegar
½ c. catsup
½ c. chili sauce
½ c. sugar
½ med. onion, minced
1 clove of garlic, crushed
Dash of Tabasco sauce
Dash of Worcestershire sauce

Combine all ingredients; shake well in jar or place in blender until mixed. Chill.

Mrs. Marcy Ginther, Harding H.S.
St. Paul, Minnesota

TASTY FRENCH DRESSING

1 c. oil
¼ c. vinegar
¾ c. catsup
½ c. sugar
½ tsp. salt
½ tsp. paprika
½ tsp. dry mustard
½ sm. onion, minced

Combine all ingredients in bottle or jar; shake to mix thoroughly. Refrigerate. Yield: 1 pint.

Gertrude Hogan, Cotton H.S.
Cotton, Minnesota

CREAMY FRENCH DRESSING

4 tbsp. sugar
2 tsp. salt
2 tsp. dry mustard
¼ tsp. pepper
1 ½ tsp. paprika
¼ tsp. oregano
6 tbsp. vinegar
4 tbsp. mayonnaise
1 ½ c. oil
1 tsp. Worcestershire sauce

Place sugar, salt, mustard, pepper, paprika and oregano in bowl; add vinegar and mayonnaise and mix. Add oil, mixing well; add Worcestershire sauce and beat until well blended. Store in jar in refrigerator until ready to use. Yield: 6 servings.

Sister Mary Ignatius, Madonna H.S.
Chicago, Illinois

CREAMY FRENCH DRESSING

1 tbsp. paprika
1 tsp. salt
1 tsp. sugar
Dash of cayenne
⅓ c. vinegar
1 egg
1 c. salad oil

Combine dry ingredients; add vinegar and egg, beating well. Add oil in slow stream, beating constantly with electric or rotary beater until thick. Store in refrigerator until ready to use. Yield: 1 2/3 cups.

Mrs. Paulinda King Hall, Walker H.S.
Atlanta, Georgia

FAVORITE FRENCH DRESSING

½ c. vinegar
1 c. salad oil
1 tsp. salt
2 tsp. paprika

Measure all ingredients into pint fruit jar; cover tightly and refrigerate. Shake well before using. Yield: 1 1/2 cups.

Mrs. Ruth L. Smith, Hillman Comm. Sch.
Hillman, Michigan

FRENCH DRESSING

1 med. onion, grated
⅓ c. tarragon or wine vinegar
1 c. oil
⅓ tsp. (scant) salt
⅓ tsp. dry mustard
⅓ c. sugar

Combine all ingredients in jar; cover and shake well. Refrigerate for several days before using. Catsup or mayonnaise may be added, if desired. Yield: 1 pint.

Marian S. Russell, Northwestern H.S.
Hyattsville, Maryland

SAVORY FRENCH DRESSING

½ c. sugar
1 ½ tsp. paprika
1 ½ tsp. salt
1 tsp. mustard
½ c. vinegar
1 c. vegetable oil

Combine all ingredients in jar; cover and shake well. Refrigerate until ready to use.

Mrs. Erma Arrington, Clintwood H.S.
Clintwood, Virginia

FRENCH DRESSING

1 tsp. salt
½ to 2 tsp. sugar
¼ to 1 tsp. paprika
1 tsp. celery salt
Dash of pepper
½ c. fresh lemon juice
¼ c. vinegar
1 ½ c. salad oil

Measure all ingredients into quart jar; cover and shake until well blended and creamy. Refrigerate. Shake well before using. One teaspoon chili sauce, 1 tablespoon chopped chutney or green pepper, 1 beet chopped or 1 hard-boiled egg, grated may be added to 1 cup dressing. Yield: 2 1/4 cups.

Mrs. Shirley Newcombe, Bangor John Glenn Sch.
Bay City, Michigan

FRENCH DRESSING

½ c. salad oil
2 tbsp. lemon juice
2 tbsp. vinegar
½ tsp. salt
1 clove of garlic
½ tsp. dry mustard
½ tsp. paprika
1 tsp. sugar
Dash of cayenne

Combine all ingredients in pint jar; cover and shake well before rising. Store in refrigerator. Yield: 3/4 cup.

Beulah G. Mounger, Morganza H.S.
Morganza, Louisiana

QUICK 'N' EASY FRENCH DRESSING

1 c. oil
⅓ c. vinegar
1 tsp. salt
¼ tsp. pepper
1 tsp. dry mustard
¼ tsp. paprika
1 clove of garlic (opt.)
1 tbsp. sugar

Combine all ingredients in blender; mix thoroughly. Store in refrigerator until ready to use. Yield: 6 servings.

Mrs. Juanita Finlayson, Morningside H.S.
Inglewood, California

SWEET FRENCH DRESSING

¼ c. sugar
1 tsp. salt
1 tsp. dry mustard

1 tsp. celery salt
1 c. salad oil
⅓ c. vinegar or lemon juice

Mix together dry ingredients; add oil in small amounts alternately with vinegar. Store in refrigerator. Shake well before serving. Yield: 1 cup.

Mrs. Jewel Rabb, West Side Sch.
Heber Springs, Arkansas

SWEET FRENCH DRESSING

1 c. vegetable oil
¼ c. vinegar
¼ c. lemon juice
6 tbsp. sifted confectioners' sugar
1 tsp. salt
½ tsp. dry mustard
½ tsp. paprika

Combine all ingredients; mix well with rotary beater or shake well in tightly covered jar. Cover and store in refrigerator. Shake well before serving. Yield: 1 1/2 cups.

Mrs. Patricia Mullins, South Fulton H.S.
South Fulton, Tennessee

SWEET FRENCH DRESSING

½ c. vinegar
1 c. sugar
2 tsp. salt
¼ tsp. paprika
¼ tsp. chili powder or steak sauce
1 tsp. celery seed
1 c. salad oil

Heat vinegar, sugar and salt; bring to boil. Cook until sugar and salt are dissolved, stirring constantly. Cool; add remaining ingredients. Stir or shake well before using. Dressing may be kept in refrigerator for several weeks. Yield: 25 servings.

Pauline J. Harris, Pennsboro H.S.
Pennsboro, West Virginia

TOMATO FRENCH DRESSING

1 c. tomato juice
½ c. corn oil
¼ c. vinegar
2 tbsp. sugar
1 tsp. dry mustard
1 tsp. paprika
1 tsp. salt
1 tsp. Worcestershire sauce
1 clove of garlic

67

(Continued on next page)

Combine all ingredients in bottle or jar; cover tightly and shake well. Chill for several hours. Remove garlic. Shake thoroughly before serving. Yield: 2 cups.

Nanette H. Fisher, El Segundo H.S.
El Segundo, California

TOMATO FRENCH DRESSING

½ c. sugar
2 tsp. paprika
2 tsp. salt
1 10-oz. can tomato juice
½ c. salad oil
½ c. cider vinegar
¼ c. chopped onions
½ tsp. garlic powder

Combine all ingredients; Mix well using mixer or blender. Yield: 1 pint.

Mrs. Luella Wilson, Shaler H.S.
Glenshaw, Pennsylvania

AUDREY'S FRENCH DRESSING

1 10¾-oz. can tomato soup
1½ c. apple cider vinegar
1 c. sugar
2 tsp. salt
1 tsp. minced onion
¼ tsp. garlic powder
2 c. salad oil

Combine all ingredients except oil; blend at medium speed in blender or beat with electric mixer. Add oil in slow, steady stream, continuing to beat. Beat for 3 minutes longer. Store in refrigerator. Yield: 1 1/2 quarts.

Audrey Young, East Troy H.S.
East Troy, Wisconsin

CELERY SEED FRENCH DRESSING

1 10¾-oz. can tomato soup
⅔ c. wine vinegar
½ c. vegetable oil
½ c. sugar
1½ tsp. salt
¼ tsp. paprika
1 tsp. dry mustard
1 tsp. celery seed

Combine tomato soup, vinegar, vegetable oil and sugar; stir until sugar is dissolved and mixture is uniform. Add seasonings. Pour into jar; Refrigerate. Shake well before using. Yield: 3 cups.

Mrs. Ronald Goolsbey, Appleton Sr. H.S. East Appleton, Wisconsin

AUNT GLADY'S FRENCH DRESSING

1 can tomato soup
½ c. corn oil
¾ c. sugar
¾ c. vinegar combined with ¼ c. water
1 tbsp. chopped green pepper
1 tbsp. chopped onion
½ tbsp. Worcestershire sauce

Combine all ingredients in bottle or jar; cover and shake well. Chill.

Mrs. Pat Allen, Bath H.S.
Bath, New Brunswick, Canada

CELERY SEED FRENCH DRESSING

¾ c. sugar
⅛ tsp. garlic salt
1 tbsp. dry mustard
1 tsp. celery seed
1 c. tomato soup
1 c. salad oil
½ c. vinegar
Salt and pepper to taste

Place all ingredients in quart jar; shake well. Store in refrigerator.

Mrs. Roma E. Wood, Cambridge Public Sch.
Cambridge, Nebraska

FRENCH DRESSING

½ c. sugar
½ c. vinegar
½ c. salad oil
1 can tomato soup
1 tsp. dry mustard
1 tbsp. Worcestershire sauce
¼ tsp. onion salt
¼ tsp. garlic salt
¼ tsp. paprika
¼ tsp. salt
¼ tsp. pepper

Combine all ingredients in bottle or jar; shake well. Store in refrigerator. Shake before using.

Donna G. Bennett, North Kamloops Sr. Secondary
North Kamloops, British Columbia, Canada

FRENCH DRESSING

1 tbsp. prepared mustard
½ c. vinegar
1 can tomato soup
1 tsp. salt
½ tsp. paprika
1 tbsp. Worcestershire sauce
1 sm. onion

(Continued on next page)

½ c. salad oil
¾ c. sugar
½ tsp. pepper

Mix mustard and vinegar in quart jar; add remaining ingredients and shake well. Store in refrigerator. Yield: 1 quart.

Mrs. Laura Russell, Freelandville Sch.
Freelandville, Indiana

FRENCH DRESSING

1 can tomato soup
¾ c. vinegar
2 tsp. salt
½ tsp. paprika
1 tbsp. Worcestershire sauce
1 c. vegetable oil
¼ c. sugar
½ tsp. pepper
1 tsp. prepared mustard
1 tsp. onion juice

Measure ingredients into quart jar; shake well. Store in refrigerator until used. Yield: 15 servings.

Mrs. Scott Willock, Alexander H.S.
Albany, Ohio

FRENCH DRESSING

½ c. sugar
1 tsp. salt
1 tsp. dry mustard
1 tsp. paprika
1 to 2 cans condensed tomato soup
½ c. vinegar
1 tbsp. Worcestershire sauce
1 c. salad oil
1 med. onion, diced
1 clove of garlic, diced

Place all ingredients in jar; shake well. Mixture may be put into blender and mixed well, if desired. Store in refrigerator. Yield: 1 quart.

Sandra Cuchna, Webb H.S.
Reedsburg, Wisconsin

RED DRESSING FOR TOSSED SALAD

1 10 ½-oz. can tomato soup
3 c. sugar
3 c. vinegar
3 c. salad oil
3 tsp. salt
3 tsp. paprika
3 tsp. onion salt
3 tsp. dry mustard
¾ tsp. cloves

Mix all ingredients thoroughly. Pour into jars and refrigerate. Yield: 24 servings.

Mrs. Mary D. Moore, Addison Central Sch.
Addison, New York

FRENCH DRESSING

1 can tomato soup
1 c. vinegar
¾ c. salad oil
¾ c. sugar
1 ½ tsp. salt
1 tsp. black pepper
1 tsp. paprika
1 tsp. mustard

Place ingredients in order listed in quart jar; shake well. Store in refrigerator. Shake each time before using. Yield: 1 quart.

Mrs. Marie Edmunds, Bonners Ferry H.S.
Bonners Ferry, Idaho

TOMATO FRENCH DRESSING

1 10 ½-oz. can condensed tomato soup
⅔ c. vinegar
⅔ c. salad oil
2 tbsp. minced onion
2 tbsp. sugar
3 tsp. dry mustard
1 tsp. salt
½ tsp. pepper (opt.)

Combine ingredients in quart jar; shake well. Refrigerate. One medium clove of garlic, minced, may be used, if desired. Yield: 3 cups.

Beatrice Campbell, Leland Consol. Sch.
Leland, Mississippi

TOMATO SOUP FRENCH DRESSING

1 10 ½-oz. can condensed tomato soup
½ c. salad oil
¾ c. sugar
¾ c. vinegar
2 ½ tsp. Worcestershire sauce
½ tsp. salt
½ tsp. paprika
2 tsp. celery seed
½ tsp. dry mustard
1 clove of garlic, minced
1 tbsp. minced onion or 1 tsp. dried
  onion

Mix all ingredients together in quart jar; cover and shake well. Chill. Let stand for at least 12 hours before using. Yield: 3 cups.

Mrs. Janice Lueck, Cadott H.S.
Cadott, Wisconsin

TOMATO FRENCH DRESSING

- ¾ c. sugar
- ¾ c. salad oil
- ¾ c. vinegar
- 1 can tomato soup
- 1 tbsp. grated onion
- 1 tsp. salt
- 1 tsp. dry mustard

Combine all ingredients; beat for 10 minutes. Pour into bottle. Chill for 24 hours before using.

Mrs. Wayne Weishaar, Lemmon H.S.
Lemmon, South Dakota

TOMATO FRENCH DRESSING

- 1 c. sugar
- 1 tsp. salt
- 1 tsp. dry mustard
- ⅔ c. vinegar
- 1 tbsp. Worcestershire sauce
- 1 c. salad oil
- 1 tsp. horseradish
- 1 can condensed tomato soup

Combine all ingredients in bowl; beat with mixer until well mixed. Pour into container and refrigerate. Yield: 1 quart.

Helen Reesor, Colon Comm. Sch.
Colon, Michigan

TOMATO SOUP DRESSING

- 1 can tomato soup
- 1 c. vegetable oil
- 1 c. vinegar
- 1 sm. onion, grated
- 1 tbsp. sugar
- 1 tbsp. Worcestershire sauce
- 1 tsp. dry mustard
- 1 tsp. paprika
- 1 tsp. salt
- 1 clove of garlic, grated

Combine all ingredients in quart jar; cover and shake well. Refrigerate. Yield: 3 1/2 cups.

Barbara Monroe, Adrian H.S.
Adrian, Minnesota

TOMATO SOUP DRESSING

- 1 tbsp. sugar
- 1 tsp. salt
- 1 tsp. dry mustard
- 1 tsp. paprika
- 1 c. salad oil
- 1 c. vinegar
- 1 can condensed tomato soup
- 1 tbsp. Worcestershire sauce
- 1 clove of garlic, minced
- 1 sm. onion, chopped

Combine all ingredients in jar; cover and shake thoroughly. Store in refrigerator. Yield: 4 cups.

Mary Jo Lewis, New Boston H.S.
New Boston, Texas

WESSON FRENCH DRESSING

- 1 tsp. salt
- ½ tsp. sugar
- ¼ tsp. pepper
- ½ tsp. paprika
- ½ tsp. dry mustard
- ¾ c. Wesson oil
- ¼ c. vinegar
- ½ tsp. Worcestershire sauce (opt.)

Measure ingredients into jar in order listed; cover and shake well. Chill. Shake well before using. Yield: 1 cup.

Naomi M. Vaught, Manatee H.S.
Bradenton, Florida

ZESTY FRENCH DRESSING

- ½ c. sugar
- 1 ½ tsp. salt
- 1 ½ tsp. paprika
- 1 tsp. dry mustard
- 1 c. oil
- 1 med. onion, grated fine
- 6 tbsp. vinegar

Mix dry ingredients; stir in oil. Add onion and vinegar; beat well with egg beater or with electric mixer for 2 minutes. Dressing may be mixed in blender until smooth. Yield: 1 1/2 cups.

Mrs. Katy Houghton, Ventura Sch. for Girls
Camarillo, California

ARGYLE SALAD DRESSING

- 2 tbsp. sugar
- 1 tsp. salt
- 1 tsp. mustard
- Pinch of cayenne pepper
- 1 tsp. butter
- 4 egg yolks
- 4 tbsp. vinegar
- 12 marshmallows, chopped
- 1 c. chopped pecans
- 1 c. whipping cream

Mix sugar, salt, mustard, pepper and butter. Add slightly beaten egg yolks and vinegar; cook in double boiler until smooth and thick, 4 to 5 minutes. Remove from heat; cool slightly. Stir in marshmallows and nuts. Just before serving, add stiffly beaten cream. Place generous serving on pear halves or other fruits. Yield: 8-10 servings.

Mrs. Eleanor Weatherford, Tupelo Sr. H.S.
Tupelo, Mississippi

BUTTERCUP FRUIT SALAD DRESSING

1 c. pineapple juice
¼ c. lemon juice
¼ c. flour
¼ c. sugar
½ tsp. salt
3 egg yolks
2 c. miniature marshmallows
½ pt. whipping cream

Blend all ingredients except egg yolks, marshmallows and cream in top of double boiler or saucepan. Cook, stirring constantly, until thickened and smooth. Add a small amount of hot liquid to beaten egg yolks; add egg yolks to mixture. Cook until mixture is thickened. Add marshmallows all at once; stir until marshmallows have melted. Store in covered container in refrigerator. When ready to serve, add cold dressing to cream, whipped until foamy; blend well. Serve with frozen fruit salads. Yield: 20 servings.

Mrs. Helen Goska, West Bend H.S.
West Bend, Wisconsin

CREAMY FRUIT SALAD DRESSING

½ c. pineapple juice
½ c. orange juice
2 tbsp. lemon juice
3 eggs
½ c. sugar
⅛ tsp. salt
1 c. heavy cream or evaporated milk, chilled icy cold and whipped

Mix fruit juices together. Beat eggs until mixed in top of double boiler; add sugar, salt and juices. Cook egg mixture over hot water or over low heat until thickened, stirring constantly. Chill. Fold in whipped cream. Serve immediately on fruit salad. Yield: 2 1/2 cups.

Mrs. Esther Darst Minton, South Mountain H.S.
Phoenix, Arizona

COOKED FRUIT SALAD DRESSING

⅓ c. orange juice
2 tbsp. lemon juice
⅓ c. pineapple juice
2 eggs, slightly beaten
½ c. sugar
¼ tsp. salt
1 c. heavy cream, whipped

Mix fruit juices and beaten eggs; add sugar and salt. Cook over hot water until thickened. Chill and fold in whipped cream. Yield: 2 1/2 cups.

Mrs. Caroline Proctor, Olanta H.S.
Olanta, South Carolina

CREAMY COOKED FRUIT SALAD DRESSING

2 tbsp. melted butter
2 tbsp. bread flour
2 eggs, separated
½ c. plus 2 tbsp. sugar
1 ¾ c. pineapple juice
¼ tsp. salt
1 c. whipping cream (opt.)

Combine butter and flour in heavy saucepan. Mix egg yolks, 1/2 cup sugar and 1/4 cup pineapple juice; blend thoroughly. Add to butter-flour mixture. Beat egg whites; add salt and remaining sugar. Blend gently into butter-flour mixture. Warm remaining pineapple juice; add slowly to mixture. Cook over low heat, stirring constantly, until dressing is thick and smooth. If it curdles, beat with rotary beater. Cool; add cream. Pour over fresh or canned fruit. Yield: 6 servings.

June Patchett, Young America Sch.
Metcalf, Illinois

DRESSING FOR MELON BALL SALADS

1 egg, beaten
1 c. pineapple juice
1 c. sugar
1 tbsp. flour
Dash of salt (opt.)

Combine egg, pineapple juice, sugar, flour and salt in heavy pan or double boiler; bring to a boil over medium heat, stirring constantly. Cool. Dip fruit in dressing before combining for salad, or serve over fruit salad. When used over apples, the apples do not turn dark.

Mrs. Marie Mohr, Wayne H.S.
Wayne, Nebraska

FLUFFY CITRUS SALAD DRESSING

3 tbsp. honey
2 to 3 tsp. lemon, lime or orange juice
½ c. chilled whipping cream

Chill bowl and rotary beater in refrigerator. Just before serving, mix honey and lemon juice together. Beat cream, using chilled bowl and beater, until it piles softly. Blend honey mixture into cream with final few strokes. Serve with any fruit salad. Yield: 1 1/4 cups.

Mrs. Barbara Goedicke
Lindsay Thurber Comp. H.S.
Red Deer, Alberta, Canada

FLUFFY MINT DRESSING

1 c. mayonnaise
½ c. mint-flavored apple jelly
½ c. heavy cream, whipped
Mint leaves (opt.)

(Continued on next page)

Fruit Salad Dressings

Gradually add mayonnaise to jelly; mix until well blended. Fold cream; chill. Serve over unpeeled apple wedges sprinkled with chopped nuts or other fruit salads. Garnish dressing with mint leaves. Yield: 20 servings.

Mrs. Daniel B. Snead, Glenn Vocational
Birmingham, Alabama

FLUFFY DATE SALAD DRESSING

    1 c. dates
    2 eggs
    ¼ c. fresh lemon juice
    ¼ c. sugar
    ⅛ tsp. salt
    1 c. whipping cream
    Fresh or canned fruit for salad
    Crisp salad greens

Cut dates into wedges. Beat eggs in top of double boiler; blend in lemon juice, sugar and salt. Cook, stirring constantly, until thickened. Remove from heat; cool well. Whip cream; fold in egg mixture and dates. Serve over fruit salads on salad greens. Yield: 3 cups dressing.

Photograph for this recipe on page 57.

FRUIT DRESSING

    ½ c. sugar
    1 tsp. flour
    1 egg yolk
    Juice of 1 lemon
    ½ c. unsweetened pineapple juice
    1 c. heavy cream, whipped

Combine sugar, flour and egg yolk; add fruit juices. Cook in top of double boiler until thick. Cool; fold in whipped cream. Yield: 6 servings.

Mrs. Wanda Newlin, Atwood-Hammond H.S.
Atwood, Illinois

FRUIT JUICE DRESSING

    1 c. strained canned fruit juice
    ½ c. orange juice
    ¼ c. lemon juice
    1 tbsp. grated lemon rind
    1 tbsp. grated orange rind
    1 egg, slightly beaten

Mix all ingredients together; cook over low heat, stirring constantly, until mixture boils. Remove from heat; chill thoroughly, serve on fruit salads. Yield: 1 1/2 cups.

Mrs. Gary Petersen, Seward H.S.
Seward, Nebraska

FRUIT SALAD DRESSING

    1 egg
    1 tsp. flour
    Juice from No. 2 can pineapple
    1 tbsp. sugar
    8 marshmallows

Beat egg with flour. Add pineapple juice; add sugar. Heat, stirring constantly, until bubbly. Remove from heat; beat in marshmallows. Store in refrigerator in pint jar. Yield: 8 servings.

Zula Rowland, Washington Co. H.S.
Springfield, Kentucky

FRUIT SALAD DRESSING

    1 c. whipping cream
    1 tbsp. sugar
    ¼ c. frozen orange juice

Beat cream until stiff. Add sugar and frozen orange juice; blend. Serve with fruit salad. Yield: 6-8 servings.

Betty Herbel, Turtle Mountain Comm. Sch.
Belcourt, North Dakota

FRUIT SALAD DRESSING

    2 eggs, beaten
    ⅔ c. sugar
    1 tbsp. flour
    ¼ c. vinegar
    ¾ c. orange or pineapple juice

Combine all ingredients; cook in top of double boiler or over very low heat, stirring constantly, until mixture thickens. Chill in a covered jar. May be served mixed with equal parts of whipped cream, if desired. Yield: 12 servings.

Mrs. Oleta M. Smith, O'Donnell H.S.
O'Donnell, Texas

FRUIT SALAD DRESSING

    ¼ c. sugar
    2 tbsp. flour
    2 eggs
    Dash of salt
    Juice of 1 lemon
    Juice of 1 orange
    Pineapple juice

Mix first 4 ingredients together well; combine lemon and orange juices. Add pineapple juice to make 1 cup liquid. Add to sugar mixture. Cook and stir until thick; add butter. Thin with cream or whipped cream, if desired. Yield: 6-8 servings.

Mrs. Mildred R. Buck, Linden H.S.
Linden, Alabama

GOLDEN FRUIT DRESSING

  2 eggs
  ¼ c. pineapple juice
  ¼ c. sugar
  ¼ c. lemon juice
  ¼ c. orange juice

Beat eggs lightly; beat in pineapple juice. Add sugar; beat in lemon and orange juices. Cook in top of double boiler until thick. Yield: 1 cup.

Mrs. Mary B. McGlone, St. Rose Academy H.S.
Vincennes, Indiana

GOLDEN FRUIT SALAD DRESSING

  3 tbsp. sugar
  ¼ tsp. salt
  1 tbsp. flour
  ¼ c. lemon juice
  ½ c. pineapple juice
  ¼ c. orange juice
  2 egg yolks
  ½ c. whipped cream

Mix sugar, salt and flour. Gradually add fruit juices and place over heat. When hot, reduce heat to simmer; add broken egg yolks. Stir constantly and cook until thick; remove from heat and cool. Fold in whipped cream just before serving. Other fruit juices may be substituted for pineapple. Yield: 2 cups.

Sister M. Del Rey Thieman, St. Mary H.S.
Dell Rapids, South Dakota

HONEY FRENCH DRESSING

  ¼ c. honey
  ¼ c. lemon juice
  ¼ c. salad oil
  ½ c. pear juice
  Dash salt
  ½ tsp. celery seed
  ¼ tsp. dry mustard

Combine all ingredients in jar; shake until well blended. Serve over fruits. Yield: 1 1/4 cups.

Mrs. Charla Mae Filla, Sterling H.S.
Sterling, Colorado

HONEY-LIME DRESSING

  1 6-oz. can frozen limeade
  ¾ c. oil
  ½ c. honey
  ¼ tsp. salt
  2 tsp. celery seeds

Blend limeade, oil, honey and salt. Add celery seeds. Serve over fruits.

Mrs. Vera J. Martin, Eleva-Strum Central
Strum, Wisconsin

HONEY SALAD DRESSING

  ⅓ c. honey
  ⅔ c. sugar
  1 tsp. dry mustard
  ½ tsp. salt
  2 tbsp. vinegar
  1 c. salad oil

Mix honey, sugar, mustard, salt and vinegar. Bring to a full boil; boil 1 minute. Cool slightly; add oil a small amount at a time, beating constantly. Yield: 1 pint.

Dora E. Bean, Deerfield H.S.
Deerfield, Illinois

LEMON AND SHERRY DRESSING

  4 tbsp. lemon juice
  ½ tbsp. salt
  4 tbsp. sugar
  2 tbsp. sherry

Combine lemon juice and salt; stir in sugar slowly. Add sherry. Serve with fruit salad.

Mrs. Novella Melton, Roswell H.S.
Roswell, New Mexico

LINDA'S FRUIT SALAD DRESSING

  2 eggs
  ¼ c. sugar
  ¼ c. pineapple juice
  ¼ c. lemon juice
  1 c. whipped cream

Beat eggs; add sugar, pineapple and lemon juice. Cook in double boiler, stirring constantly, until thickened. Cool. Fold in cream; mix with salad.

Linda J. McCraw, Gaffney Sr. H.S.
Gaffney, South Carolina

LOWELL INN FRUIT DRESSING

  ¾ c. sugar
  1 tsp. salt
  1 tsp. dry mustard
  1 tsp. paprika
  ⅓ c. vinegar
  ¾ c. salad oil
  1 tbsp. grated onion
  1 tsp. celery seed

(Continued on next page)

Combine sugar, salt, mustard, paprika and vinegar. Boil one minute; cool. Add oil, onion and celery seed. Beat well. Serve with fruit salad.

Mrs. Marilyn L. Anderson, Wheaton H.S.
Wheaton, Minnesota

MARASCHINO-CREAM DRESSING

1 3-oz. pkg. cream cheese, softened
2 tbsp. maraschino cherry juice
1 ¼ tsp. vinegar
3 tbsp. minced maraschino cherries

Combine first 3 ingredients; stir in cherries. Serve with fruit salads. Yield: 1/2 cup.

Frances M. Watson, Lake H.S.
Millbury, Ohio

MARSHMALLOW DRESSING

2 egg yolks
1 tsp. sugar
¼ tsp. dry mustard
1 tbsp. vinegar
½ c. miniature marshmallows
½ c. whipping cream, whipped

Beat egg yolks; add sugar, mustard, vinegar and marshmallows. Cook and stir over low heat until marshmallows melt and mixture thickens. Cool thoroughly. Stir until smooth; fold in whipped cream. Yield: 1 cup.

Mrs. Jean F. Goodman, Robert E. Lee Jr. H.S.
Danville, Virginia

NECTAR DRESSING

1 3-oz. pkg. cream cheese
2 tbsp. honey
1 tsp. lemon rind
2 tbsp. lemon juice
¾ tsp. salt
⅛ tsp. cayenne pepper
½ c. salad oil

Combine first 6 ingredients; beat until smooth with rotary beater. Add oil 1 tablespoon at a time, beating well after each addition, until 4 tablespoons have been added. Add remaining oil, 2 tablespoons at a time, beating after each addition, until thoroughly blended. Cover; chill. Beat well again; serve immediately with tart fruit salad. Yield: 1 1/4 cups.

Naomi M. Vaught, Maratee H.S.
Bradenton, Florida

OLD-FASHIONED FRUIT DRESSING

2 eggs
2 tbsp. sugar
2 tbsp. lemon juice
2 tbsp. pineapple juice
1 tbsp. butter
Dash of salt
¾ c. whipping cream, whipped

Beat together eggs, sugar, juices, butter and salt with rotary beater. Cook in saucepan over low heat, stirring constantly, just to boiling. Remove from heat. Cool. Fold in whipped cream. Yield: 8 servings.

Emily Boudreaux, Centerville H.S.
Centerville, Louisiana

OLD-FASHIONED FRUIT DRESSING

2 eggs
2 tbsp. sugar
2 tbsp. vinegar or lemon juice
2 tbsp. pineapple juice
1 tbsp. butter
Dash of salt
¾ c. whipping cream, whipped

Beat first 6 ingredients with rotary beater; cook in saucepan over low heat, stirring constantly, just to boiling. Remove from heat; cool. Fold in whipped cream.

Joanne Weber, East H.S.
Green Bay, Wisconsin

ORANGE SALAD DRESSING

⅓ stick butter
¾ c. sugar
1 tsp. flour
Pinch of salt
2 eggs, well beaten
Grated rind and juice of 2 oranges and
   1 lemon
½ pt. whipping cream

Melt butter in double boiler; add sugar, flour, salt, eggs, juices and rind. Cook until thickened. Cool. Add whipped cream when ready to serve. Serve with frozen or molded fruit salads. Yield: 12 servings.

Mrs. Enos Ann Langston, Angleton H.S.
Angleton, Texas

PINEAPPLE-HONEY DRESSING

½ c. honey
¼ c. lemon juice
¼ tsp. salt
3 tbsp. crushed pineapple

(Continued on next page)

Mix ingredients in order given. Serve with fruit salads. Yield: 3/4 cup.

Jo Anne Tuttle, Spencer Jr. H.S.
Spencer, Iowa

PEARL'S FRUIT SALAD DRESSING

⅔ c. sugar
1 tsp. dry mustard
1 tsp. paprika
1 tsp. celery seed
¼ tsp. salt
⅓ c. honey
5 tbsp. vinegar
1 tbsp. lemon juice
1 tsp. onion
1 c. salad oil

Combine all ingredients in blender; blend at medium speed until well blended. Yield: 2 cups.

Mrs. Pearl Ivers, Tonganoxie H.S.
Tonganoxie, Kansas

PRINCESS DRESSING

30 maraschino cherries
1 c. mayonnaise
1 c. vanilla ice cream

Drain cherries well. Place in blender until pulpy. Add mayonnaise and ice cream; blend and store in refrigerator. Serve with fresh fruit salad. Yield: 2 cups.

Garrah Gibson, Comm. Unit Sch. Dist. 210
Williamsfield, Illinois

ZESTY FRUIT SALAD DRESSING

1 c. sugar
½ c. salad vinegar
4 tbsp. minced celery
2 tbsp. minced green pepper
2 tbsp. minced pimento
¼ c. salad oil
¼ c. grated onion
8 drops Worcestershire sauce
Paprika to taste

Mix sugar and vinegar. Add celery, pepper and pimento; add remaining ingredients. Shake until well blended. Serve with tossed or vegetable salad. Yield: 1 pint.

Helen Firkus, Neenah Sr. H.S.
Neenah, Wisconsin

UNUSUAL SALAD DRESSING

1 c. whipping cream
1 sm. pkg. cream cheese
1 c. miniature marshmallows
1 tbsp. lemon juice

Place all ingredients in bowl and chill together; beat until of smooth spreading consistency. Serve on gelatin fruit salad. Keeps well in the refrigerator for days.

Mrs. Dorothy Anderson, Montrose H.S.
Montrose, South Dakota

FRESH HERB-FLAVORED VINEGAR

½ c. slightly crushed fresh herb leaves, dill, oregano or mint
2 c. white wine vinegar

Place herbs in jar with vinegar; let stand for 4 days. Strain liquid, discarding flavoring ingredients. Bring liquid to boil. Remove from heat; pour into hot sterilized jars. Store in cool dark place for 6 weeks. For variations use 2 cups whole fresh berries; let stand in vinegar for 3 days. Proceed as for herbed vinegar, or slice 1 medium-sized whole orange; let stand in vinegar for 2 days. Proceed as for herbed vinegar. Yield: 2 cups.

Wanda Stacke, Marshfield Sr. H.S.
Marshfield, Wisconsin

GORGONZOLA CHEESE DRESSING

½ tsp. dry mustard
¼ tsp. salt
1 clove of garlic, halved
4 tbsp. wine vinegar
½ c. olive oil
2 oz. crumbled gorgonzola cheese

Mix mustard, salt and garlic thoroughly. Add vinegar; stir. Add oil; stir vigorously. Add cheese; stir. Keep in jar; refrigerate and use as needed.

Mary De Lorne, Oppenheim-Epharatah Cen. H.S.
St. Johnsville, New York

GREEN GODDESS SALAD DRESSING

1 tbsp. lemon juice
½ c. sour cream
1 c. mayonnaise
2 tbsp. tarragon vinegar
2 tbsp. garlic vinegar
1 tbsp. anchovy paste
¼ c. minced onion

(Continued on next page)

Add lemon juice to sour cream; mix with remaining ingredients. S e r v e on green salad, broccoli or asparagus. Yield: 8 servings.

Diana Sanders Moniz, James Monroe H.S.
Sepulveda, California

HATTIE'S SALAD DRESSING

1 ½ c. water
1 c. vinegar
3 eggs
1 c. white sugar
2 tbsp. cornstarch
2 tsp. mustard
1 tsp. salt

Boil water and vinegar. Make paste of remaining ingredients and add to boiling solution, stirring constantly, until m i x t u r e boils. Remove from heat and store in refrigerator. Yield: 3 cups.

Mrs. Mary Ann Goerzen, Sexsmith Public H.S.
Sexsmith, Alberta, Canada

HAWAIIAN HOLLANDAISE SALAD DRESSING

½ c. butter
3 egg yolks
1 ½ tbsp. lemon juice
1 tsp. salt
¼ tsp. pepper
½ c. unsweetened canned pineapple
    juice

Cream butter; add egg yolks, 1 at a time and beat well. Add lemon juice, salt and pepper. Add hot pineapple juice just before serving, a little at a time, beating constantly. Cook in double boiler, stirring constantly, until sauce thickens to consistency of boiled custard. Yield: 1 1/2 cups.

Alice P. Lynum, Jerusalem Ave. Jr. H.S.
North Bellmore, New York

HEALTH DRESSING

⅔ c. salad oil
3 tbsp. sugar
⅓ c. catsup
1 tbsp. lemon juice
½ tsp. onion, grated
⅓ c. vinegar
¾ tsp. salt

Combine all ingredients; shake well. Yield: 1 1/3 cups.

Mrs. Nancy Putney, Sunapee Central H.S.
Sunapee, New Hampshire

HUBBY'S FAVORITE SALAD DRESSING

1 ¼ c. cottage cheese
¼ c. sugar
1 tsp. salt
2 tsp. mustard
1 tsp. paprika
¾ c. oil
¼ c. catsup
⅓ c. vinegar
1 tbsp. Worcestershire sauce
1 tsp. grated onion
Dash of garlic salt

Combine all ingredients in medium-sized bowl; beat with rotary or electric beater until fluffy. Chill and use as needed. Yield: 2 cups.

Mrs. Jane Olcott, Cobleskill Cen. Sch.
Cobleskill, New York

ITALIAN DRESSING

½ c. brown sugar
½ c. vinegar
½ c. catsup
½ c. salad oil
1 clove of garlic, minced
1 sm. onion, minced
Pinch of dry mustard
Salt and pepper to taste

Combine and mix ingredients together.

Mary Ann Jorgensen, North Emery Jr. H.S.
Huntington, Utah

JIFFY SALAD DRESSING

1 c. mayonnaise
1 c. catsup
2 hard-boiled eggs, chopped
6 stuffed olives, sliced

Combine all ingredients and mix well. Salad dressing keeps well in refrigerator. Yield: 6 servings.

Shari Bolander, Del Norte H.S.
Del Norte, Colorado

LETTUCE DRESSING

¾ c. catsup
½ c. mayonnaise
2 tbsp. sugar
1 tsp. mustard
1 tsp. salt
1 tbsp. black pepper
2 buttons of garlic
¼ c. water
2 tbsp. Worcestershire sauce
¼ c. vinegar

(Continued on next page)

Combine catsup, mayonnaise, sugar, mustard, salt and pepper; mix well. Add garlic, water, Worcestershire sauce and vinegar. Yield: 8-10 servings.

Mrs. Josephine P. Clark, Fairview H.S.
Fairview, Tennessee

LOW-CALORIE HERB DRESSING

    1 8-oz. can tomato sauce
    2 tbsp. tarragon vinegar
    1 tsp. onion juice
    1 tsp. Worcestershire sauce
    ½ tsp. salt
    ¼ tsp. dillseed
    ½ tsp. crushed basil

Place all ingredients in jar. Cover and shake well. Chill. Yield: 1 cup.

Mrs. Eleanor Tedford, Wiggins H.S.
Wiggins, Colorado

LOW-CALORIE TOMATO DRESSING

    1 slice soft bread
    1 clove of garlic
    2 c. canned tomatoes
    1 tbsp. vinegar
    1 tsp. liquid Sucaryl
    1 tsp. salt
    1 tsp. paprika

Trim crusts from bread. Cut garlic into pieces; insert in bread and let stand 30 minutes. Remove garlic. Add tomatoes and remaining ingredients to bread. Beat thoroughly. A blender works well for beating together.

Miss Patricia Irvin, Wells H.S.
Wells, Minnesota

FRUIT MAYONNAISE

    2 eggs, beaten until lemon-colored
    ½ c. sugar
    ¼ c. lemon juice
    ¼ c. pineapple juice or orange juice
    1½ c. cream

Combine eggs, sugar, lemon juice and pineapple juice. Cook in double boiler until thick. Chill. Whip cream when ready to serve; fold in dressing. Spoon into mound over salad. Dressing will keep in refrigerator for a week. Yield: 3 cups.

Mrs. Elizabeth B. Martin, Stewart Co. H.S.
Dover, Tennessee

BLENDER BEST YET MAYONNAISE

    2 eggs
    1 tsp. sugar
    ¾ tsp. dry mustard
    ½ tsp. salt
    ½ tsp. paprika
    2 c. salad oil
    1 tbsp. wine vinegar
    2 tbsp. lemon juice

Place eggs in blender; add sugar, mustard, salt and paprika. Cover and mix at high speed for 30 seconds. Push ingredients down with rubber spatula. Cover and start at high speed. Remove cover; start adding oil slowly while appliance is running. Pour in wine vinegar after about 1/4 cup oil has been used. Add more oil slowly. Alternate portions of lemon juice and oil until all ingredients are used. It may be necessary to stop blender and push ingredients down. Yield: 2 1/2 cups.

Barbara Knowlton, Wellman H.S.
Wellman, Texas

COOKED MAYONNAISE

    ¼ c. cornstarch
    1½ c. cold water
    1 egg, unbeaten
    2 tbsp. sugar
    1 tsp. salt
    2 tsp. prepared mustard
    Dash of cayenne
    ¼ c. vinegar or lemon juice
    1 c. salad oil
    ¼ tsp. paprika

Combine cornstarch with water in saucepan. Cook over low heat until mixture is clear, stirring constantly. Set aside. Place egg, sugar, salt, mustard, cayenne, vinegar, salad oil and paprika into deep bowl. Add cornstarch mixture, beating at medium speed until well blended, about 5 minutes. Cool. Keep in refrigerator. Good on slaw, fruit and seafood.

Sarah P. Bowles, Holladay H.S.
Holladay, Tennessee

LEMON FLUFF MAYONNAISE

    1 tbsp. lemon juice
    ½ tsp. grated lemon rind
    ¼ jar Marshmallow Fluff
    1 c. mayonnaise

Stir lemon juice and rind into marshmallow fluff. Add mayonnaise, 1/4 cup at a time, excellent with any fresh fruit salad.

Mrs. Jack C. Montgomery, Fort Gibson H.S.
Fort Gibson, Oklahoma

MAYONNAISE

 1 tsp. mustard
 ½ tsp. salt
 ⅛ tsp. pepper
 ⅛ tsp. paprika
 ¼ tsp. sugar
 1 egg
 2 c. salad oil
 3 tbsp. vinegar

Beat first 6 ingredients. Gradually add 1/2 cup oil, drop by drop, beating constantly. Add vinegar and remaining oil alternately, beating constantly. Refrigerate. Yield: 2 1/2 cups.

Mrs. Shirley Newcombe, Bangor John Glenn H.S.
Bay City, Michigan

NO-COOK MAYONNAISE

 ½ tsp. mustard
 ½ tsp. sugar
 ½ tsp. salt
 Few grains cayenne pepper
 1 egg yolk
 1 tbsp. vinegar
 ¾ c. salad oil
 1 tbsp. lemon juice
 1 tsp. hot water

Place first 5 ingredients in mixing bowl. Blend and add vinegar. Add 3 teaspoons oil, a drop at a time, while beating constantly. Add oil, a teaspoon at a time, until m i x t u r e thickens. Add lemon juice and remaining oil rapidly when very thick. Add water. Chill oil thoroughly for flavors to blend. Yield: 1 cup.

Mrs. Sharon Lawa, Wallis H.S.
Wallis, Texas

SOY MILK MAYONNAISE

 1 c. water
 ½ cup soy milk powder
 1 tsp. salt
 1 tsp. sugar
 ½ tsp. celery salt
 ¼ tsp. garlic salt
 ½ tsp. monosodium glutamate
 1 tsp. paprika
 1 tsp. onion salt
 1 c. (about) oil
 Juice of 2 lemons

Pour water into blender. Add all dry ingredients. Blend at high speed and while blender is operating, pour in oil slowly in a steady stream. When oil begins to stand on top of mixture, stop. Start blender again in order to emulsify the last bit of oil. Pour mixture into container with lemon juice and stir. Yield: 2 cups.

Marilyn Riseberg, Canadian Union College H.S.
College Heights, Alberta, Canada

NIPPY NECTAR DRESSING

 1 3-oz. pkg. cream cheese
 2 tbsp. honey
 1 tsp. grated lemon peel
 2 tbsp. lemon juice
 ½ tsp. salt
 ½ c. salad oil

Soften cream cheese; blend in remaining ingredients, except salad oil. Add oil, 1 tablespoon at a time, beating well after each addition. Chill. Beat again before serving over fruit salad. Yield: 1 cup.

Ginger Clarke, Dake Middle Sch.
Rochester, New York

ORANGE-NUT DRESSING

 ¾ c. orange juice
 6 tbsp. finely chopped pecans or walnuts
 6 tbsp. olive oil
 1 ½ tsp. curry powder
 1 ½ tsp. salt
 1 tbsp. basil wine vinegar
 ¾ tsp.dry mustard

Combine all ingredients; mix well. Serve with tossed green salad. Yield: 1 cup.

Virginia B. McCarthy, Berryville Sch.
Berryville, Arkansas

PINEAPPLE-CHEESE DRESSING

 ⅓ c. sugar
 4 tbsp. cornstarch
 ¼ tsp. salt
 Juice of 1 lemon
 Juice of 1 orange
 1 c. unsweetened pineapple juice
 2 beaten eggs
 2 3-oz. pkg. softened cream cheese

Mix dry ingredients. Add fruit juices and blend. Cook in double boiler 20 minutes, stirring constantly. Slowly stir into eggs and cook 5 minutes, stirring constantly. Beat cream cheese into cooked mixture. Chill. Yield: 2 cups.

Margie Briggs, H.S.
Dansville, Michigan

HONEY-POPPY SEED DRESSING

⅓ c. honey
½ tsp. salt
⅓ c. vinegar
3 tbsp. prepared mustard
1 ¼ c. salad oil
2 ½ tbsp. poppy seeds

Mix all ingredients together in order given. Blend in blender or mixer until oil disappears. Yield: 2 cups.

Mrs. Charla Mae Filla, Sterling H.S.
Sterling, Colorado

POPPY SEED SALAD DRESSING

10 tbsp. sugar
1 tsp. dry mustard
1 tsp. salt
1 c. salad oil
¼ c. vinegar
⅓ c. grated onion
1 tbsp. poppy seeds

Combine all ingredients; mix well. Chill; serve over fresh fruit or avocado and grapefruit salad. Yield: 1 1/2 cups.

Katie Smith, Clute Jr. H.S.
Clute, Texas

POPPY SEED SALAD DRESSING

1 egg
¼ c. sugar
¼ c. lemon juice
1 tsp. dry mustard
½ tsp. paprika
½ tsp. salt
1 tbsp. poppy seed
1 tsp. grated onion
1 ½ c. salad oil
¼ c. honey

Measure first 8 ingredients into blender or mixer. Gradually add salad oil, about 1/4 cup at a time; mix at high speed. Add honey; mix at medium speed. Serve with chilled fruit or mixed fruit and vegetable salads. Yield: 2 cups.

Mrs. Virginia Jamison, Mozelle H.S.
Fisk, Texas

POTATO SALAD DRESSING

1 egg
5 tbsp. vinegar
½ c. sugar
½ tsp. mustard
Salt to taste

Combine ingredients; cook just until thick. Cool; combine with salad ingredients.

Mrs. Jean McOmber, Spring Lake H.S.
Spring Lake, Michigan

QUICK SALAD DRESSING

½ c. salad oil
¼ c. vinegar
½ c. sugar
2 tbsp. prepared mustard
Dash of Worcestershire sauce

Place all ingredients in jar and shake or beat well. May place in blender and mix. Serve on salad greens. Yield: 1 cup.

Mrs. Mary Esther Rowe, Swartz Creek H.S.
Swartz Creek, Michigan

RAVIGOTE

10 sprigs watercress
10 leaves spinach
4 sprigs parsley
1 c. mayonnaise
Salt and nutmeg to taste

Cover watercress, spinach and parsley with boiling water. Let stand 5 minutes. Drain in cold water; drain again. Rub through fine sieve and add to mayonnaise. Season with salt and nutmeg. Serve with seafood salads.

Sister M. Roseleen, O.S.F., Mt. Assisi Academy
Pittsburgh, Pennsylvania

REMOULADE DRESSING

2 hard-cooked egg yolks, sieved
2 buds garlic, crushed
1 ½ tbsp. salad mustard
1 ½ c. mayonnaise
1 tbsp. Worcestershire sauce
2 tbsp. vinegar
Dash of Tabasco sauce
2 tbsp. (heaping) finely chopped parsley
1 tbsp. paprika
Salt and pepper to taste

Combine all ingredients in bowl; mix well. Place in jar; refrigerate 12 hours before serving. Serve on green salad or chilled cooked shrimp or as dip for fresh chilled vegetables. Yield: 1 pint.

Mrs. Earline Baier Alsobrook, Brenham H.S.
Brenham, Texas

CREAMY ROQUEFORT DRESSING

⅓ c. finely chopped green onions and tops
2 c. mayonnaise
2 garlic cloves, grated
½ c. chopped parsley
2 tbsp. anchovy paste
1 c. thick sour cream
½ c. vinegar
2 tbsp. lemon juice
½ lb. Roquefort cheese, crumbled
Salt and pepper to taste

Combine green onions, mayonnaise, garlic and parsley. Blend anchovy paste with sour cream; add to mayonnaise. Thin mixture with vinegar and lemon juice; beat in cheese. Season with salt and pepper; chill. Yield: 12 servings.

Becky Bahnsen, Reed City H.S.
Reed City, Michigan

CREAMY ROQUEFORT WHIRL DRESSING

2 c. mayonnaise
¼ lb. Roquefort cheese
⅔ c. evaporated milk
2 tbsp. sugar
1 tsp. garlic powder
½ tsp. celery salt

Combine all ingredients; mix with beater. Chill until ready to serve. Yield: 3 cups.

Mrs. Barbara Elledge, Grand Prairie Sr. H.S.
Grand Prairie, Texas

THOUSAND ISLAND DRESSING

1 pt. Hellman's mayonnaise
½ bottle chili sauce
2 sm. or 1 lge. pkg. Roquefort or blue cheese, crumbled

Combine mayonnaise and chili sauce; stir in cheese. Yield: 2 pints.

Mrs. Vancel Van Ness, Wheeling H.S.
Wheeling, West Virginia

ROQUEFORT CHEESE DRESSING

1 14½-oz. can evaporated milk
¼ c. vinegar
4 oz. blue or Roquefort cheese
1 qt. mayonnaise

Heat milk, vinegar and cheese until cheese melts; stir in mayonnaise. Blend well; pour into jars. Store in refrigerator until used; will keep indefinitely. Yield: 3 pints.

Mrs. Ethel Parsons, Jackson H.S.
Jackson, California

ROQUEFORT CHEESE DRESSING

½ lb. imported Roquefort cheese
1 c. mayonnaise
½ c. sour cream
Juice of 1 lemon
1 sm. onion, grated

Combine all ingredients. Mix in blender. May be stored in refrigerator indefinitely.

Elizabeth Kanis, Nashoba Reg. H.S.
Bolton, Massachusetts

ROQUEFORT-CREAM DRESSING

½ tsp. garlic salt
½ tsp. celery salt
½ tsp. pepper
½ tsp. paprika
2 tbsp. vinegar
1 pt. sour cream
½ c. mayonnaise
1 tsp. salt
½ lb. Roquefort cheese, crumbled

Blend first 8 ingredients; fold in cheese.

Mrs. Ann Hohman, Juaniata Valley H.S.
Alexandria, Pennsylvania

ROQUEFORT DRESSING

⅓ c. finely chopped onion
2 c. mayonnaise
2 garlic cloves, grated
½ c. chopped parsley
1 c. sour cream
½ c. vinegar
2 tbsp. lemon juice
¼ tsp. salt
½ tsp. pepper
½ lb. blue cheese, crumbled

Combine all ingredients; chill. May be stored in refrigerator. Yield: 1 quart.

Mrs. E. J. Sykes, Pottsville Area H.S.
Pottsville, Pennsylvania

ROQUEFORT DRESSING

1 c. cottage cheese
1 c. buttermilk
1 ½ pt. mayonnaise
4 oz. blue cheese
1 tsp. Worcestershire sauce
½ tsp. garlic salt

Combine all ingredients; beat with mixer or blender. Keep refrigerated. Good on salads, baked potatoes and as dip. Yield: 2 quarts.

Arlene Kendrick, Fort Vancouver H.S.
Vancouver, Washington

ROQUEFORT DRESSING

3 c. mayonnaise
2 ¼ c. sour cream
8 oz. Roquefort cheese, crumbled
Salt

Combine ingredients; mix well. Season to taste with salt, if necessary. Keep under refrigeration until ready to serve. Yield: 1 1/2 quarts.

Mrs. Valerie C. Lewis, Ramona Jr. H.S.
Chino, California

ROQUEFORT DRESSING

1 4-oz. pkg. Roquefort or blue cheese
½ c. mayonnaise
¼ c. catsup

Crumble cheese into pea-sized pieces; combine with mayonnaise and catsup. Serve over hearts of lettuce or tossed salad. Yield: 8-10 servings.

Sabina A. Leiby, Susquenith H.S.
Duncannon, Pennsylvania

ROQUEFORT-SOUR CREAM DRESSING

1 pt. mayonnaise
1 ½ c. sour cream
½ tbsp. lemon juice
1 ½ tbsp. vinegar
½ tbsp. Worcestershire sauce
1 tbsp. onion juice
¼ tsp. white pepper
1 tsp. garlic powder
Few drops of Tabasco sauce
1 pkg. Roquefort cheese (crumbled)

Blend all ingredients with electric mixer. Cover; store in refrigerator. Yield: 4 cups.

Mrs. J. E. Little, Pearland H.S.
Pearland, Texas

QUICK RUSSIAN DRESSING

¼ c. mayonnaise or salad dressing
2 tbsp. to ¼ c. catsup
⅛ tsp. dry mustard
¼ tsp. salt
Dash of garlic salt or onion salt (opt.)

Mix all ingredients; chill. Yield: 1 cup.

Mrs. Margaret Faludi, Oconomowoc Sr. H.S.
Oconomowoc, Wisconsin

QUICK RUSSIAN DRESSING

1 c. salad dressing
½ c. relish
¼ c. catsup

Place salad dressing in small bowl; add relish and catsup. Stir until all ingredients are well blended. Spoon over washed and chilled greens or green salad. Yield: 6 servings.

Mrs. Esther Reynolds, Oneonta Jr. H.S.
Oneonta, New York

RED RUSSIAN DRESSING

1 c. salad oil
¼ c. vinegar
¾ c. sugar
¼ c. catsup
1 can tomato soup
1 tbsp. Worcestershire sauce
1 onion, grated
½ tsp. salt
¼ tsp. pepper

Place all ingredients in a quart jar; shake until well blended. Store in refrigerator. Yield: 20 servings.

Mrs. Helen Goska, West Bend H.S.
West Bend, Wisconsin

RUSSIAN DRESSING

½ tsp. salt
½ tsp. paprika
1 ½ tsp. celery seed
Juice of 1 lemon
1 tbsp. vinegar
1 tbsp. Worcestershire sauce
1 c. salad oil
½ c. catsup
¼ c. grated onion
¼ c. light corn syrup

Combine all ingredients; beat well. Chill. Yield: 2 cups.

Mrs. Sue Rogers, Krum Sch.
Krum, Texas

RUSSIAN DRESSING

1 c. oil
1 c. catsup
½ c. sugar
⅔ c. vinegar
Juice of 2 lemons
2 onions, grated
1 tsp. paprika
2 tsp. salt

Beat together; store in refrigerator. Combine all ingredients; beat well. Store in refrigerator. One-fourth cup oil and 2 tablespoons liquid sweetener may be used instead of 1 cup oil and 1/2 cup sugar for a low-calorie dressing.

Judith Wright, Humboldt H.S.
St. Paul, Minnesota

RUSSIAN DRESSING WITH GARLIC

¼ c. lemon juice
¾ c. salad oil
⅔ c. light cream
2 cloves of garlic
1 tsp. salt
½ tsp. sugar
¼ tsp. pepper
½ tsp. paprika
½ c. condensed tomato soup

Place all ingredients in blender container; whip until blended. Yield: 10-12 servings.

Mrs. Wade H. Harris, Seagrove H.S.
Seagrove, North Carolina

RUSSIAN SALAD DRESSING

1 can tomato soup
½ c. vinegar
½ c. sugar
½ c. salad oil
1 tsp. dry mustard
1 tsp. salt
1 tsp. paprika
1 tbsp. Worcestershire sauce
1 sm. onion, chopped
1 clove of garlic

Combine all ingredients in order given; shake well in jar. Store in refrigerator. Yield: 3 cups.

Vivian Pommer, New Monroe Comm. Sch.
Monroe, Iowa

TANGY RUSSIAN DRESSING

1 envelope Russian salad dressing mix
¼ c. vinegar
2 tbsp. water
½ c. salad oil
1 tsp. horseradish

Prepare salad dressing mix with vinegar, water and oil as directed on package; add horseradish with oil. Chill for at least 1 hour. Serve on appetizers or salads. Yield: 1 cup.

Gail Speron, Dye Jr. H.S.
Flint, Michigan

SALAD DRESSING

1 c. sugar
4 tbsp. flour
1 tsp. salt
2 tsp. dry mustard
11 egg yolks, beaten
1 ½ c. water
1 c. vinegar

Add dry ingredients to egg yolks; add water and vinegar. Mix well. Cook over boiling water until thick. Keep in cool place in covered container. Yield: 3-4 servings.

Loretta Sawin, Chapman H.S.
Chapman, Kansas

SALAD DRESSING

1 c. oil
1 c. granulated sugar
⅔ c. catsup
2 tbsp. grated onion
1 tbsp. salt
½ tbsp. paprika
½ c. vinegar

Combine oil and sugar; stir well. Let stand overnight. Combine oil mixture with catsup, onion, salt, paprika and vinegar; beat with beater. Place in jar; refrigerate. Stir well before placing on salad. Yield: 1 1/2 pints.

Jan Daily, Brookpark Jr. H.S.
Grove City, Ohio

SALAD DRESSING

3 eggs
1 tbsp. paprika
¼ c. horseradish
¼ c. vinegar
¼ c. garlic oil
¼ c. sweet relish
1 tbsp. mustard
1 c. grated Romano cheese
1 qt. all-purpose oil
1 tsp. salt

Beat eggs until fluffy; continue to beat, adding paprika, horseradish, vinegar, garlic oil,

(Continued on next page)

sweet relish, mustard, cheese, all-purpose oil and salt.

LaVerne Stansell, Cary M. Abney H.S.
Waskom, Texas

SALAD DRESSING
    1 c. evaporated milk
    ⅓ c. sugar
    ¼ c. lemon juice

Mix all ingredients and use on fruit salad. Yield: 10 servings.

Mrs. Wilma Tucker, Marion H.S.
Marion, Louisiana

SEVEN-UP SALAD DRESSING
    ¾ c. Kraft mayonnaise
    ½ c. sour cream
    ½ c. Seven-Up
    1 tsp. grated orange rind

Combine mayonnaise and sour cream. Gradually stir in Seven-Up mixing until smooth. Add orange rind and chill thoroughly. Serve over shredded lettuce or fresh fruit salad. Yield: 1 3/4 cups.

Mrs. Esther Williams, Pocatello H.S.
Pocatello, Idaho

SILVER FORK SALAD DRESSING
    ¼ tsp. onion salt
    1 tsp. dry mustard
    1 tsp. lemon juice
    1 tsp. celery seed
    1 tsp. paprika
    1 tbsp. salt
    ¼ c. white sugar
    ½ c. light corn syrup
    ¾ c. oil
    ¼ c. vinegar

Combine first 8 ingredients; mix in blender or electric mixer. Alternately add oil and vinegar, a little at a time, beginning and ending with oil. Beat well; chill. Serve on fruit or vegetable salads. Yield: 1 1/2 cups.

Mary Jo Angelo, Redstone Jr. H.S.
Republic, Pennsylvania

FRUIT ORANGE DRESSING
    1 pt. sour cream
    24 marshmallows, quartered
    6 tbsp. concentrated orange juice

Mix together sour cream and marshmallows. Chill overnight. Beat in orange juice. Serve over fruit salad. Yield: 12-16 servings.

Mrs. Sue Zaloudek, Proviso East H.S.
Maywood, Illinois

CUCUMBER-SOUR CREAM DRESSING
    1 ½ tbsp. cider vinegar
    2 tsp. sugar
    ½ tsp. salt
    1 c. sour cream or yogurt
    1 ½ c. peeled chopped cucumbers

Blend vinegar, sugar and salt in bowl; fold in sour cream and cucumbers. Serve immediately over sliced beets or sliced tomatoes. Yield: 2 1/2 cups.

Linda Treworgy, Greely Jr. J.S.
Cumberland Center, Maine

GOURMET DRESSING
    1 c. sour cream
    1 tbsp. tarragon vinegar
    ½ c. mayonnaise
    ¼ c. chopped green pepper
    ¼ c. chopped onion
    ¼ c. chopped cucumber
    1 garlic clove, diced
    ½ bottle sesame seed
    2 tsp. butter
    1 tsp. Parmesan cheese (opt.)

Mix sour cream, vinegar and mayonnaise; add green pepper, onion, cucumber and garlic. Pour over crisp lettuce. Brown sesame seed in butter; pour over dressing. Sprinkle with Parmesan cheese. Yield: 8 servings.

Mrs. Vanora Fry, Little River H.S.
Little River, Kansas

LAVENDAR DREAM SALAD DRESSING
    ¼ c. grape jelly
    ½ c. sour cream
    ⅛ tsp. salt
    3 tbsp. diced Muenster cheese (opt.)

Beat grape jelly; combine with sour cream and salt. Add cheese. Serve over fruit gelatin or fruit salad. Yield: 6 servings.

Ruth E. Carlson, Donovan H.S.
Donovan, Illinois

SOUR CREAM COOKED DRESSING

1 egg, slightly beaten
¼ c. vinegar
2 tsp. salt
2 tsp. sugar
1 tsp. mustard
⅛ tsp. pepper
1 c. sour cream

Mix egg, vinegar, salt, sugar, mustard and pepper; add to sour cream. Cook and stir until thick in double boiler or small heavy pan over low heat. Remove; serve or chill.

Mrs. Lynda T. Updike, Franklin H.S.
Franklin, Virginia

SOUR CREAM DRESSING

1 c. sour cream
3 tbsp. minced chives or onion
2 tbsp. lemon juice
1 ½ tsp. salt
⅛ tsp. pepper

Mix all ingredients together thoroughly. Serve on baked potatoes, sliced cucumbers or lettuce. Yield: 1 1/4 cups.

Mrs. Catherine R. Trotter, Independence H.S.
Independence, Louisiana

SOUR CREAM ITALIAN DRESSING

1 pkg. Parmesan dressing mix
½ tsp. crushed tarragon
½ tsp. garlic salt
1 tsp. salt
½ tsp. ground peppercorns
¼ c. wine vinegar
2 tbsp. red wine
1 pt. sour cream
1 c. buttermilk
½ c. Parmesan cheese, grated
½ c. cottage cheese (opt.)

Mix dry ingredients with wine and vinegar; allow to stand for about 10 minutes. Add sour cream, buttermilk, Parmesan cheese and cottage cheese; blend thoroughly. Keep in an airtight container in refrigerator for use as needed. Yield: 24 servings.

Mrs. Enid Hedrick, Bolsa Grande H.S.
Garden Grove, California

STRAWBERRY-SOUR CREAM DRESSING

2 c. thick sour cream
1 tsp. salt
½ c. frozen strawberries

Combine sour cream and salt; fold fruit into cream. Serve on fruit or fruit salads. Yield: 2 1/2 cups.

Mrs. Jean Sampson, Channelview H.S.
Channelview, Texas
Nita De Grand, Nacogdoches H.S.
Nacogdoches, Texas
Mrs. Eddie Hilou, Cayuga H.S.
Cayuga, Texas

SPECIAL DRESSING

1 c. mayonnaise
¼ c. catsup
¼ c. buttermilk
1 tbsp. lemon juice
½ tsp. paprika
1 tsp. garlic salt
Salt, pepper and sugar to taste

Combine all ingredients. Place in a covered jar in refrigerator. Will keep for 2 to 3 weeks. Yield: 10-12 servings.

Mrs. Linda M. Manning, Burkeville H.S.
Burkeville, Texas

CABBAGE DRESSING

½ c. sugar
1 egg
1 tsp. salt
1 tbsp. butter
⅛ c. vinegar
1 head cabbage, grated

Mix sugar and egg. Add salt and butter; add water to vinegar to make 1/2 cup. Stir in vinegar. Cook over low heat until mixture boils. Remove and cool. Pour over cabbage just before serving. Will keep in refrigerator for a long time.

Mrs. Nanvy J. Slezak, Seneca Valley H.S.
Harmony, Pennsylvania

CABBAGE SLAW DRESSING

½ tsp. salt
1 tsp. (heaping) prepared mustard
¾ c. sugar
½ c. cold water
¼ c. vinegar
½ lge. head cabbage, grated

Add salt and mustard to sugar; mix well. Add water and stir until sugar is dissolved. Add vinegar and mix well. Pour over cabbage and let stand. Yield: 6-8 servings.

Mary Quinn, Central Jr. H.S.
Superior, Wisconsin

COLESLAW DRESSING

⅓ c. sugar
⅛ tsp. pepper
½ tsp. salt
1 tbsp. grated onion
1 tbsp. vinegar
½ tsp. celery seed
1 tsp. prepared mustard with
  horseradish
1 ½ c. Miracle Whip
Cabbage, shredded

Mix ingredients together, except cabbage; keep in covered jar in refrigerator. Mix with cabbage just before serving. Yield: 2 cups.

Mrs. Dorothy Soderlund, Milaca H.S.
Milaca, Minnesota

COLESLAW DRESSING

⅓ c. mayonnaise
⅛ tsp. salt
Dash of pepper
Pinch of dry mustard
2 tsp. sugar
1 tbsp. vinegar
Dash of red hot sauce or Tabasco sauce

Combine all ingredients. Chill. Serve with any combination of cabbage and other raw vegetables preferred. Yield: 6 servings.

Mrs. Elaine Fineran, Onteora Central H.S.
Boiceville, New York

COLESLAW DRESSING

3 tbsp. sugar
1 tsp. salt
3 tbsp. vinegar
3 tbsp. vegetable oil

Place sugar and salt into small mixing bowl. Add vinegar and vegetable oil. Stir until sugar and salt are dissolved. Pour over coleslaw and toss. Yield: 8 servings.

Mrs. Charlotte Faris, Abingdon H.S.
Abingdon, Virginia

COLESLAW DRESSING

3 tbsp. sugar
½ tsp. salt
Dash of pepper
Dash of paprika
2 tbsp. Miracle Whip
2 tbsp. vinegar
2 tbsp. cream or Milnot

Mix dry ingredients with Miracle Whip. Add vinegar and stir until blended; add cream and mix. Serve on shredded cabbage or coleslaw.

Mrs. R. L. Burton, Beggs H.S.
Beggs, Oklahoma

CREAMY COLESLAW DRESSING

½ c. mayonnaise
1 tbsp. lemon juice
1 tsp. sugar
⅛ tsp. Accent
¼ c. sour cream
2 tsp. celery seed
¼ tsp. salt
Pepper to taste

Place all ingredients in blender. Pour over cabbage when thoroughly mixed. Yield: 1 cup.

Marjorie Bough, Edwardsville Jr. H.S.
Edwardsville, Illinois

CREAM SALAD DRESSING

1 to 2 tbsp. sugar
¼ tsp. salt
⅛ tsp. pepper
¼ tsp. paprika
Dash of cayenne
½ tsp. onion, chopped
½ tsp. green pepper, chopped
3 tbsp. cream, sweet or sour
1 to 2 tbsp. mild vinegar

Mix dry ingredients, onion and green pepper. Add cream. Add vinegar gradually. Beat until thickened. Serve on shredded cabbage or leaf lettuce. Yield: 1/3 cup.

Mrs. Dorothy Lee, Piner Jr. H.S.
Sherman, Texas

SCHLUTER SLAW DRESSING

1 ½ c. salad dressing
1 c. whipping cream, whipped
3 tbsp. vinegar
3 tbsp. sugar
Salt and pepper to taste

Mix all ingredients well. Chill. Yield: 10-12 servings.

Mrs. Sue Rogers, Krum H.S.
Krum, Texas

Salad Dressings

SWEET 'N' SOUR BACON DRESSING

2 slices bacon
1 lge. or 2 sm. eggs
1 tbsp. sugar
¼ tsp. salt
⅛ tsp. pepper
5 tbsp. water
4 tbsp. vinegar

Cut bacon into small pieces; fry in skillet until quite crisp. Mix egg, sugar, salt and pepper in bowl; add water and vinegar. Pour vinegar mixture into skillet with browned bacon; cook until thickened. Cool; pour over broken lettuce leaves in a bowl. Recipe may be doubled and stored in refrigerator. Yield: 1 cup.

Mrs. Ronnie Watson, Johnston Jr. H.S.
Houston, Texas

SWEET-SOUR SALAD DRESSING

2 c. sugar
⅔ c. vinegar
1 c. water
2 tbsp. oil
1 tsp. salt
1 tsp. celery seed
1 sm. onion or clove of garlic (opt.)

Place ingredients all together in shaker or quart jar and mix. Store in refrigerator. Keeps well. Yield: 1 quart.

Mrs. Laura Russell, Freelandville H.S.
Freelandville, Indiana

TANGY SALAD DRESSING

½ c. salad oil
¼ c. vinegar
2 tbsp. sugar
1 tbsp. onion, chopped
½ c. tomato soup

Combine all ingredients; shake well. Cover and refrigerate. Shake before using. Yield: 12 servings.

Mary Joe Whitefield, Lebanon H.S.
Lebanon, Tennessee

TARRAGON CREAM DRESSING

1 tbsp. flour
2 tbsp. sugar
1 tsp. salt
1 tsp. onion salt
⅛ tsp. pepper
½ tsp. tarragon
2 tbsp. salad oil
2 eggs, beaten
⅓ c. lemon juice
1 ⅓ c. evaporated milk

Blend flour with sugar, salt and seasonings in medium saucepan. Stir in salad oil, eggs and lemon juice. Cook and stir over low heat until thickened. Add milk; beat until smooth. Chill before serving. Yield: 2 cups.

Mrs. Iren Kathy Lee, Washington H.S.
El Dorado, Arkansas

TARTAR SAUCE SALAD DRESSING

1 pt. Miracle Whip salad dressing
½ c. chopped stuffed olives
½ c. sweet cucumber pickles
½ c. chopped onions
¼ c. thick cream

Combine all ingredients in large mixing bowl; chill. Serve over tossed green salad, sliced cucumbers or fish. Yield: 35-40 servings.

Mrs. Floyd Craig, Divide H.S.
Nolan, Texas

BETTY'S THOUSAND ISLAND DRESSING

2 tbsp. catsup
¼ c. chopped stuffed olives
1 hard-cooked egg, diced
1 tsp. grated onion
½ tsp. Worcestershire sauce
1 c. mayonnaise

Combine first 5 ingredients; blend into mayonnaise. Chill. Yield: 1 1/2 cups.

Mrs. Betty Rassette, Salina Sr. H.S.
Salina, Kansas

FAY'S THOUSAND ISLAND DRESSING

1 c. salad dressing
½ c. catsup
¼ c. oil
2 tbsp. vinegar
2 tbsp. sweet pickle relish
½ tsp. garlic salt
½ tsp. barbecue seasoning
½ tsp. finely crushed oregano
1 tsp. sugar
1 tbsp. chopped onion
Dash of pepper

Combine all ingredients; blend well. Serve with tossed salad. Yield: 12 servings.

Mrs. Evelyn Fay Grabowski, Plant City Sr. H.S.
Plant City, Florida

MARY'S THOUSAND ISLAND DRESSING

1 c. mayonnaise
¼ c. catsup
1 slice onion
2 sm. sweet pickles
3 sprigs parsley
1 slice green pepper
1 hard-cooked egg, shelled and quartered

Place all ingredients except egg in blender container. Cover; run on low speed until vegetables are coarsely chopped. Add egg; cover container and chop egg. Spoon over tossed greens. Yield: 2 cups.

Mary Davidson, Grant H.S.
Grant, Michigan

QUICK THOUSAND ISLAND DRESSING

¼ c. mayonnaise
1 tbsp. catsup
1½ tbsp. chopped sweet pickle
1 tsp. pickle juice

Blend all ingredients; chill. Serve on tossed salad or cole slaw. Yield: 4 servings.

Judith Irvin, Richlands H.S.
Richlands, North Carolina

THOUSAND ISLAND DRESSING

1 c. mayonnaise
3 tbsp. chili sauce
1 tbsp. chopped green pepper
1 tsp. chopped pimento
1 tsp. chopped chives

Blend all ingredients thoroughly; chill. Serve on lettuce wedges. Yield: 1 1/4 cups.

Mrs. Evelyn Blake, Andrew Lewis H.S.
Salem, Virginia

THOUSAND ISLAND DRESSING

1 c. mayonnaise
2 tbsp. chili sauce
1 tbsp. chopped dill pickle
1 tsp. minced onion
1 hard-cooked egg, chopped

Combine all ingredients; mix well. Keep refrigerated. Yield: 8 servings.

Gladys Fry, Brown Co. H.S.
Mt. Sterling, Illinois

THOUSAND ISLAND DRESSING

2 hard-cooked eggs, coarsely chopped
Dash of salt
⅓ c. drained pickle relish
1 c. mayonnaise
½ c. chili sauce

Combine all ingredients except eggs; blend well. Add eggs; chill in refrigerator.

Mrs. George Sanders, Hoffman Public Sch.
Hoffman, Minnesota

THOUSAND ISLAND DRESSING

3 hard-boiled eggs
1 med. bottle stuffed olives
1 lge. can pimento
1 bottle chili sauce
1 pt. mayonnaise

Run eggs, olives and pimento through food chopper; blend with chili sauce. Fold in mayonnaise. Keeps indefinitely in refrigerator. Yield: 5-6 cups.

Cathernie G. Ward, G.P. Babb Jr. H.S.
Forest Park, Georgia

THOUSAND ISLAND SALAD DRESSING

1 c. mayonnaise
2 tsp. prepared mustard
2 tbsp. catsup
1 tsp. salt
1 tsp. pepper
1 tsp. seasoned salt
1 tsp. garlic salt
1 tsp. onion salt
1 tbsp. finely chopped onion
2 grated boiled eggs

Combine all ingredients; blend well. Chill before serving. Excellent on garden green vegetable salads and fish dishes. Yield: 10 servings.

Mrs. Sharlott M. Valentine, Culkin Jr. H.S.
Vicksburg, Mississippi

THOUSAND ISLAND DRESSING

1 c. salad dressing
½ c. chili sauce
⅓ c. pickle relish
Dash of Salt
2 boiled eggs, coarsely chopped
1 med. onion, chopped
Finely grated celery

(Continued on next page)

Combine all ingredients; blend well. Yield: 3 cups.

Mrs. Shirley Glenn, Centennial Jr. H.S.
Circles Pines, Minnesota

THOUSAND ISLAND SALAD DRESSING

1 c. mayonnaise
⅓ c. chili sauce
⅓ c. chopped cooked or canned beets
¼ c. chopped olives
3 tbsp. chopped green pepper
1 tbsp. chopped onion
2 hard-cooked eggs, chopped

Combine all ingredients; blend well. Serve on lettuce wedges or tossed salad. Yield: 2 cups.

Alberta Hagemann, Thomas Jr. H.S.
Arlington Heights, Illinois

TOSSED SALAD DRESSING

1 c. sugar
½ c. chili sauce
½ c. catsup
½ c. vinegar
1 c. oil
2 or 3 cloves of garlic, minced
1 tsp. salt
½ tsp. pepper

Measure all ingredients into wide mouthed jar; shake well. Chill 5 to 6 hours. Shake well before serving. Yield: 1 1/2 pints.

Mrs. Mary Weaver, Schwenksville Union Sch.
Schwenksville, Pennsylvania

WHITE RIVER

3 eggs
1 qt. Wesson oil
1 qt. buttermilk
5 to 6 tbsp. dry mustard
2 to 4 tbsp. garlic salt
1 tsp. salt

Place eggs in blender; beat until creamy. Add remaining ingredients; blend until creamy. Store in covered container in refrigerator. Yield: 2 quarts.

Ann Good, Inola H.S.
Inola, Oklahoma

OLD-FASHIONED WALDORF DRESSING

1 c. salad dressing
½ c. sugar
¼ c. vinegar

Mix all ingredients until well blended. Set in refrigerator for several days. Will keep, refrigerated, for long period of time. Good served on fruit salad, cabbage slaw or any kind of salad. Yield: 1 pint.

Mrs. Robbie White, Paris Sr. H.S.
Paris, Texas

WALDORF SALAD DRESSING

1 egg
¼ tsp. pepper
¼ tsp. mustard
¼ tsp. turmeric
1 tsp. salt
¼ c. vinegar
Sugar

Beat egg until well mixed. Add remaining ingredients with enough sugar to make one cup of mixture. Cook until dressing begins to thicken. Delicious with any fruit salad or mixed with mayonnaise on cabbage salad. Yield: 1 cup.

Mary J. Strand, Sr. H.S.
Jamestown, New York

YOGURT DRESSING

1 c. yogurt
1 tbsp. lemon juice
1 tbsp. minced onion
2 tsp. sugar
¼ tsp. salt
Dash of cayenne pepper
Dash of cumin powder

Mix all ingredients thoroughly. Serve on Rice Krispies, smoked fish or green salad. Yield: 4 servings.

Mrs. H. Singh, Revelstoke Secondary Sch.
Revelstoke, British Columbia, Canada

ZIPPY DRESSING

1 c. salad dressing
⅓ c. chili sauce
¼ tsp. salt
1 tsp. lemon juice
1 tsp. horseradish
1 sm. onion, chopped fine
1 sm. cucumber, chopped fine

Mix all ingredients; let stand 5 to 6 hours before serving. Yield: 1 1/2 cups.

May Lohmann, Miami H.S.
Miami, Oklahoma

Cereal, Pasta, Egg & Cheese Salads

RECIPE FOR ZIPPY HAM AND MACARONI SALAD ON PAGE 94

BULGUR COLESLAW

1 can bulgur
2 tbsp. vinegar
½ c. mayonnaise
1½ tbsp. grated onion
¾ tsp. celery seed
2¼ tsp. sugar
¾ tsp. salt
⅛ tsp. white pepper
2 c. finely shredded cabbage

Prepare bulgur according to directions on label; chill. Combine next 7 ingredients and mix well. Add cabbage and bulgur; mix well. Serve in lettuce cups; garnish with tomato wedges. Yield: 4-6 servings.

Mrs. Miriam Toth, Castro Valley H.S.
Castro Valley, California

BULGUR SALAD

2½ c. cooked bulgur
3 tbsp. French dressing
3 tbsp. sweet pickle
½ tsp. salt
½ tsp. pepper
1½ c. chopped celery
¼ c. chopped green pepper
2 hard-cooked eggs, diced
1 tsp. chopped onion
⅔ c. mayonnaise

Prepare bulgur. Mix French dressing, pickle, salt and pepper together; combine with cooked bulgur. Add celery, green pepper, eggs, onion and mayonnaise; mix well. Serve on lettuce leaf; garnish with tomato wedges. Yield: 4-5 servings.

Doris R. Becker, Inman H.S.
U.S.D. No. 448
Inman, Kansas

BANANA SUPREME

1 pkg. strawberry Jell-O
½ c. cooked rice
2 bananas
¼ c. lemon juice
1 c. whipping cream
¼ c. sugar
½ tsp. vanilla

Prepare Jell-O according to directions on package. Add rice to Jell-O. Chill until mixture is partially set. Slice bananas finely into lemon juice; stir. Drain any excess juice. Add bananas to Jell-O. Stir. Whip cream. Add sugar and vanilla. Fold cream into Jell-O. Chill until firm. Serve in sherbet dishes. May be poured into pie crust and chilled.

Jean Bauer, Hilda H.S.
Hilda, Alberta, Canada

CURRIED RICE SALAD

3 c. cooked rice
1 c. diced celery
2 tbsp. minced onion
1 tsp. curry powder
½ tsp. dry mustard
¼ tsp. black pepper
Salt to taste
¾ c. salad dressing
1 tbsp. lime or lemon juice
1 8-oz. can crushed pineapple
½ c. chopped salted peanuts or almonds

Toss all ingredients together except nuts. Garnish with nuts. Yield: 6 servings.

Mrs. Ialeen S. Mode, Franklinton H.S.
Franklinton, North Carolina

EGG AND RICE SALAD

4 hard-cooked eggs, grated
1 c. chopped celery
½ c. sweet or dill pickles, chopped
2 c. cold cooked Minute rice
Salt and pepper to taste
1 tbsp. chopped pimento
1 c. shredded cheddar cheese
¾ c. mayonnaise

Combine all ingredients in order listed. Mix well. Yield: 6-8 servings.

Mrs. Viola Johnson, Karnes City H.S.
Karnes City, Texas

FRUIT-MARSHMALLOW-RICE CONFETTI

2 c. cold cooked rice
2 c. miniature marshmallows
2 11-oz. cans mandarin oranges
1 c. drained pineapple tidbits
½ c. maraschino cherries
1 pkg. dessert topping mix

Combine rice, marshmallows, oranges, pineapple and cherries. Refrigerate 1 hour. Prepare dessert topping mix according to package directions. Fold into rice mixture. Refrigerate 1 hour longer. Yield: 8 servings.

Kay F. Bowers, Rollingcrest Jr. H.S.
W. Hyattsville, Maryland

PINEAPPLE-RICE DESSERT

2 c. Minute rice
1 can pineapple chunks, drained well
1 to 2 c. cream
¼ c. sugar
¼ tsp. salt
½ pkg. miniature marshmallows

(Continued on next page)

Cook rice as directed on package. Strain; rinse and cool well. Strain liquid from fruit until fruit is dry. Whip cream slowly; add sugar and salt slowly. Whip until mixture stands in stiff peaks. Combine all ingredients, tossing lightly and folding gently. Garnish with cherry. Yield: 6 servings.

Mrs. Laura Lloyd, Peteterdrac Reg. H.S.
Peteterdrac, New Brunswick, Canada

RICE-FRUIT SALAD

1 ½ c. cooked rice
3 c. unpeeled diced apples
1 c. drained crushed pineapple
2 c. miniature marshmallows
½ c. sugar
¼ tsp. salt
½ tsp. vanilla
1 pkg. dessert topping mix

Mix all ingredients, adding dessert topping last. Add 1/2 cup nuts, if desired. Yield: 10-15 servings.

Mrs. Carol Stuart, Geneseo H.S.
Geneseo, Kansas

RICE-JELL-O SALAD

1 c. rice
1 pkg. lemon Jell-O
1 c. crushed pineapple
1 c. whipped cream
1 c. powdered sugar
½ c. walnuts, crushed
½ c. marshmallows

Boil rice until soft; drain. Let cool. Mix 1 pint hot water with Jell-O; let cool. Add rice, pineapple, cream, sugar, nuts and marshmallows. Mix well and chill. Yield: 10 servings.

Mrs. Evelyn Johnson, Bottineau H.S.
Bottineau, North Dakota

RICE SALAD

1 pkg. lemon Jell-O
2 c. hot water
1 c. rice, cooked
1 sm. can crushed pineapple
10 to 12 marshmallows, cut up
¼ c. sugar
1 c. sweetened whip cream
Dash of salt
Maraschino cherries (opt.)

Dissolve Jell-O in hot water; let stand until syrupy. Beat until foamy. Add rice, pineapple and marshmallows. Fold in whipped cream. Add salt. May be garnished with cherries. Set in refrigerator until firm. Yield: 8-10 servings.

Eileen Brenden, Central H.S.
Glenwood, Minnesota

HOT MACARONI SALAD

1 can button mushrooms
¼ lb. diced bacon
½ c. sugar
2 tbsp. flour
½ tsp. salt
⅛ tsp. pepper
¾ c. cider vinegar
⅔ c. mushroom liquid
7 oz. elbow macaroni
½ c. chopped onion
½ c. chopped celery
½ c. sliced radishes
2 tbsp. chopped parsley

Drain mushrooms, reserve liquid. Fry bacon with mushrooms until crisp. Add sugar, flour, salt and pepper to mushroom mixture; stir to blend. Gradually stir in vinegar and mushroom liquid. Cook until thickened, stirring constantly. Keep hot. Cook macaroni in boiling salted water until tender but firm, about 7 to 8 minutes; drain. Mix lightly with hot dressing, onion and celery. Garnish with radishes and parsley. Serve hot. Yield: 6 servings.

Dorothy Campbell, Deer Park H.S.
Deer Park, Washington

HOT MACARONI SALAD

1 ½ c. cooked elbow macaroni
2 hard-boiled eggs
1 tbsp. chopped onion
1 ½ tbsp. chopped green pepper
1 tbsp. pimento
⅓ c. sour cream
3 tbsp. mayonnaise
½ c. pickle relish
1 tbsp. chopped celery
Salt and pepper to taste

Combine all ingredients. Serve hot. Yield: 6-8 servings.

Sarah Musgrave, Rattan H.S.
Rattan, Oklahoma

MACARONI AND CHEESE SALAD

1 ½ c. cooked elbow macaroni
½ c. cubed American or cheddar cheese
¼ c. sliced green olives

(Continued on next page)

1 diced tomato
½ c. diced celery
¼ c. diced green pepper
3 tbsp. mayonnasie
1 ½ tbsp. cream
1 tsp. salt

Combine all ingredients in bowl. Toss well; chill for several hours. Serve on leaf or head lettuce. Yield: 4 servings.

Mrs. Alice Jean Camigliano, Youngsville H.S.
Youngsville, Pennsylvania

MACARONI-CHEESE TOSS

½ lb. sm. shell macaroni
3 tbsp. clear French dressing
¼ c. sharp cheddar cheese, cubed
3 hard-cooked eggs, cubed
1 c. drained cooked or canned peas
½ c. chopped celery
½ c. sliced green onions
⅓ c. mayonnaise
1 tbsp. prepared mustard
1 ½ tsp. prepared horseradish
½ tsp. Worcestershire sauce
Dash of salt and seasoned salt
Dash of pepper

Cook macaroni in boiling salted water until tender; drain and cool. Pour French dressing over macaroni; set aside. Combine cheese, eggs and vegetables. Blend mayonnaise and seasonings. Add macaroni; toss to mix. Chill. Serve in bowl lined with greens; top with cherry tomatoes. Yield: 8-10 servings.

Mrs. Sharon Schrick, Nortonville H.S.
Nortonville, Kansas

MACARONI SALAD

7 oz. elbow macaroni
½ c. chopped celery
1 tbsp. chopped onion
1 tbsp. chopped green pepper
Chopped pimento
2 tbsp. sweet pickle relish
3 hard-cooked eggs
1 tsp. salt
1 c. cooked peas
¾ c. mayonnaise

Cook macaroni according to directions on package; drain. Rinse in cold water and drain well. Combine celery, onion, green pepper, pimento, relish, eggs, salt and peas in large bowl. Mix in macaroni. Add enough mayonnaise to moisten; blend thoroughly. Serve on crisp lettuce; garnish with wedges of tomato. Yield: 6-8 servings.

Mrs. Carolyn Saxe, Edwards Sr. H.S.
Albion, Illinois

MACARONI SALAD

2 c. cooked macaroni
¼ c. chopped onion
¼ c. sliced celery
¼ c. chopped sweet pickle
1 No. 303 can kidney beans, drained
2 tbsp. pimento
1 tsp. salt
½ tsp. black pepper
½ c. American cheese
3 tbsp. mayonnaise

Cook macaroni as directed on package; drain. Combine with remaining ingredients. Serve on lettuce leaf. Yield: 4-6 servings.

Mrs. Linda M. Manning, Burkeville H.S.
Burkeville, Texas

MACARONI SALAD

7 or 8 oz. elbow, shell or ring macaroni
1 c. cubed cheddar cheese
1 c. sliced pickles
½ c. minced onion
½ c. mayonnaise
1 10 to 12-oz. pkg. frozen peas, cooked
 and drained
Salt to taste

Cook macaroni according to package directions. Drain; rinse with cold water. Add remaining ingredients. Chill. Serve in lettuce cups. Yield: 4-6 servings.

Patricia Anne Manning, Owyhee H.S.
Owyhee, Nevada

MACARONI SALAD

3 c. cooked macaroni
¼ c. chopped green pepper
¼ c. chopped celery
¼ c. chopped pickles
2 hard-cooked eggs, chopped
¼ c. salad dressing

Mix all ingredients with salad dressing to moisten. Serve in bowl or on salad greens. Garnish with tomato wedges, sliced hard-cooked eggs or pickles. Yield: 6 servings.

Sara Thompson, Pineville H.S.
Pineville, Kentucky

MACARONI SALAD

1 c. cooked macaroni
2 tbsp. chopped bell pepper
¼ c. chopped pimentos
2 chopped boiled eggs
2 tbsp. crisp-fried bacon
Salt to taste
2 tbsp. mayonnaise
½ tsp. chopped onion

Toss all ingredients lightly. Chill slightly before serving. Serve with lettuce and crackers.

Delores S. Barber, Scotland H.S.
Laurinburg, North Carolina

MACARONI AND VEGETABLE SALAD

1 ½ c. cooked chilled elbow macaroni
½ c. grated sharp cheddar cheese
½ c. cooked chilled green peas
¼ c. celery
¼ c. green pepper
½ c. shredded cabbage
½ c. grated carrot
Mayonnaise, salt and pepper to taste

Combine all ingredients. Chill 20 to 30 minutes. Serve with cold bologna slices. Yield: 4 servings.

Mrs. W. R. White, Claremont Sr. Secondary Sch.
Victoria, British Columbia, Canada

MAGGIE'S MACARONI SALAD

1 pkg. shell macaroni
1 No. 2 can cut green beans
4 hard-boiled eggs, chopped
1 med. onion, chopped fine
1 tsp. seasoned pepper
¼ tsp. Accent
½ tsp. salt
Mayonnaise to moisten

Prepare macaroni according to package directions; add remaining ingredients in order given. Yield: 10 servings.

Mrs. Martha Harkey, Crystal City H.S.
Crystal City, Texas

MOLDED SALAD

1 pkg. lemon gelatin
½ tsp. salt
1 ½ tbsp. prepared mustard
3 tbsp. vinegar

⅔ c. mayonnaise
1 c. cooked elbow macaroni
⅔ c. chopped cabbage
2 tbsp. green pepper
2 tbsp. pimentos

Prepare gelatin as directed on package. Add salt, mustard and vinegar. Stir together; chill. Add remaining ingredients. Chill. Serve on lettuce. Yield: 4 servings.

Sandra Lord, Old Orchard Beach H.S.
Old Orchard Beach, Maine

OLD-FASHIONED MACARONI SALAD

4 c. cooked elbow macaroni
1 ½ c. sliced celery
½ c. chopped onion
5 or ¼ c. sliced radishes
2 tbsp. minced parsley
1 c. mayonnaise
1 to 2 tbsp. vinegar
2 tsp. prepared mustard
½ tsp. celery seeds
2 tsp. salt
⅛ tsp. pepper

Combine all ingredients; chill. Serve on shredded lettuce; garnish with tomato wedges, sliced olives or carrots. Yield: 6 servings.

Janice C. Wilkes, Bay County H.S.
Panama City, Florida
Mrs. Joan C. Millian, Mem. Jr. H.S.
Valley Stream, New York

TWENTY FOUR-HOUR MACARONI-CREAM SALAD

½ c. sugar
2 tbsp. lemon juice
Pineapple juice
1 egg, beaten
1 apple
1 10-oz. can drained crushed pineapple
½ c. curly shaped macaroni, cooked
½ c. cream, whipped

Boil sugar, lemon juice, pineapple juice and egg in top of double boiler until thick; cool. Add to fruit and macaroni. Let stand 12 to 24 hours in refrigerator. Add whipped cream to serve.

Jean Collins, Washington Jr. High
Brainerd, Minnesota

MARSH-MAC-NUT SALAD

2 c. macaroni
3 bananas, sliced
1 sm. can pineapple tidbits, drained

(Continued on next page)

½ lb. miniature marshmallows
¼ c. chopped maraschino cherries
½ c. walnut pieces
Mayonnaise

Combine macaroni, bananas, pineapple, marshmallows, cherries and walnuts. Add mayonnaise to moisten. Chill well; season to taste with additional lemon juice or salt, if desired. Yield: 12-15 servings.

Mrs. Marian Young, North Bend Public School
North Bend, Nebraska

SALAD SUPREME

1 c. chopped celery
6 tbsp. chopped sweet pickle
6 tbsp. chopped green pepper
6 tbsp. chopped pimento
2 c. cooked macaroni, chilled
1 c. diced sharp cheese
½ c. cooked peas
½ c. salad dressing
Lettuce

Add celery, pickle, green pepper and pimento to macaroni, tossing lightly. Add cheese and peas. Add salad dressing, tossing lightly. Chill thoroughly; serve on lettuce.

Shirley Cline, Rugby H.S.
Rugby, North Dakota

SUMMER MACARONI SALAD

7 to 8 oz. shell or ring macaroni, cooked
1 c. sliced gherkins
1 c. cubed cheddar cheese
½ c. minced onion
½ c. mayonnaise
1 10 to 12-oz. pkg. frozen peas, cooked
   and drained
Salt and pepper to taste

Combine all ingredients; chill. Serve in lettuce cups. Yield: 4-6 servings.

Frances Rodriguez, Espanola H.S.
Espanola, New Mexico

YACHTSMAN'S SALAD

2 c. shell macaroni, cooked
½ c. chopped green pepper
¼ c. chopped onion
¼ c. chopped olives, stuffed or ripe
6 slices crisp bacon, crumbled
4 hard-cooked eggs, chopped
1 tomato, chopped
¼ c. mayonnaise
Salt and pepper to taste

Toss all ingredients together lightly. Chill. Yield: 6-8 servings.

Elizabeth Trennepohl, Angola H.S.
Angola, Indiana

ZIPPY HAM AND MACARONI SALAD

½ lb. boiled ham, sliced about ⅛-inch thick
2 tbsp. salt
3 qt. boiling water
2 c. (8-oz.) elbow macaroni
2 med. tomatoes, coarsely chopped
⅓ c. sliced scallions or green onions
⅓ c. salad oil
3 tbsp. vinegar
1 ½ tsp. dry mustard
2 tsp. sugar
⅛ tsp. pepper

Roll up ham slices tightly, jelly roll fashion; chill. Add 1 tablespoon salt to rapidly boiling water. Gradually add macaroni so that water continues to boil. Cook, uncovered, stirring occasionally, until tender. Drain in colander. Rinse with cold water; drain. Combine macaroni and remaining ingredients plus remaining 1 tablespoon salt; mix well. Chill. Arrange ham rolls on macaroni salad. Garnish as desired. Yield: 4-6 servings.

Photograph for this recipe on page 89.

MAINE SALAD BOWL

1 head lettuce, torn into bite-sized pieces
1 green pepper, chopped
1 sm. onion, chopped
1 med. cucumber, diced
2 tomatoes, diced
6 radishes, sliced thin
¼ c. bleu cheese, crumbled
1 c. crisp Chinese noodles
4 tbsp. French dressing

Combine vegetables and bleu cheese; toss lightly Chill. Add noodles and French dressing just before serving. Toss lightly. Yield: 6-8 servings.

Mrs. Sarah M. Gleason, East Jr. H.S.
East Walpole, Massachusetts

SPINACH-NOODLE TOSS

1 lb. spinach, washed and stems removed
1 lge. onion, sliced and separated into
   rings
1 sm. cauliflower, separated into
   flowerets
1 3-oz. can Chinese noodles

(Continued on next page)

Layer first 3 ingredients in order given in glass salad bowl. Add noodles just before serving; toss at table with favorite oil and vinegar dressing. Yield: 8 servings.

Mrs. Jana Ward, Riverside H.S.
Riverside, New Jersey

BOILED EGG SALAD

    4 hard-boiled eggs, chopped
    1 sm. can pineapple chunks, drained
    ¼ head crisp lettuce, torn into bite-
        sized pieces
    ¼ c. French dressing or 2 tbsp. salad
        dressing

Mix all ingredients together; toss. Add French dressing; mix well. Yield: 4 servings.

Mrs. Dorothy P. Simmons, Crawford H.S.
Arcadia, Louisiana

CARROT-EGG SALAD

    4 raw carrots, ground
    2 hard-cooked eggs, finely chopped
    ¼ tsp. salt
    ¼ c. (about) mayonnaise
    4 lettuce leaves

Combine first three ingredients. Mix with fork. Add mayonnaise. Serve on lettuce. Yield: 4 servings.

Mrs. Grace R. Carroll, Oneonta Jr. H.S.
Oneonta, New York

CHUNKY EGG SALAD

    6 hard-cooked eggs, cut into big pieces
    1 c. sliced celery
    2 tbsp. minced green pepper
    1 tsp. minced onion
    ¼ c. mayonnaise
    ½ tsp. Worcestershire sauce
    Dash of Tabasco
    1 tbsp. vinegar
    1 tsp. salt
    ⅛ tsp. pepper

Combine all ingredients; refrigerate. Serve on greens or thick tomato slices. Garnish with 3 crumbled strips of bacon or 2 chopped stuffed olives. Yield: 6 servings.

Mrs. Melba M. Hackett, Henrico H.S.
Richmond, Virginia
Evelyn B. Willey, Gates Co. H.S.
Gatesville, North Carolina

COLORFUL EGG SALAD

    6 hard-cooked eggs, chopped
    ½ c. celery, diced

    ¼ c. green pepper, diced
    2 to 3 tbsp. pimento, chopped
    ¼ c. salted peanuts
    2 tbsp. chopped ripe olives
    ½ c. mayonnaise
    ¼ tsp. black pepper

Combine all ingredients; serve on lettuce or for sandwich spread. Garnish with olives, nuts, and / or pimento. Yield: 4-6 servings.

Barbara Knowlton, Wellman H.S.
Wellman, Texas

CARNIVAL SALAD

    1 pkg. celery or other vegetable flavored
        gelatin
    2 c. tomato juice
    3 green peppers
    3 eggs, hard cooked

Dissolve gelatin in tomato juice. Remove stem ends and seeds of peppers; place whole egg in each pepper. Fill peppers with tomato gelatin. Chill until set. Slice peppers crosswise to serve. Yield: 10 servings.

Nancy C. Withers, Boyden H.S.
Salisbury, North Carolina

DEVILED EGG MOLD

    1 envelope unflavored gelatin
    ½ c. water
    1 tsp. salt
    2 tbsp. lemon juice
    ¼ tsp. Worcestershire sauce
    ⅛ tsp. cayenne pepper
    ¾ c. mayonnaise
    1 ½ tsp. grated onion
    ½ c. finely diced celery
    ¼ c. finely diced green pepper
    ¼ c. chopped pimento
    4 hard-cooked eggs, chopped

Sprinkle gelatin on water to soften. Place over low heat; stir until gelatin is dissolved. Remove from heat; add salt, lemon juice, Worcestershire sauce and cayenne pepper. Cool. Stir in mayonnaise; fold in remaining ingredients. Turn into 3-cup mold or individual molds; chill until firm. Unmold by dipping mold in warm water to depth of gelatin. Loosen around edge with tip of paring knife. Place serving dish on top of mold; turn upside-down. Shake, holding dish tightly to mold. Garnish with salad greens and green pepper; serve with salad dressing. Yield: 6 servings.

Mrs. Alice Hansberger, Canton Sr. H.S.
Canton, Illinois
Bertha Keller Benthien
Clermont Northeastern H.S.
Batavia, Ohio
Mrs. Florence W. Ponder
Magee Jr. H.S.
Magee, Mississippi

EGG RING

2 tbsp. gelatin
1 ½ c. cold water
2 tbsp. lemon juice
2 tbsp. Worcestershire sauce
2 tbsp. chopped parsley
½ c. catsup
1 pt. mayonnaise
1 doz. hard-cooked eggs, chopped
½ tbsp. minced onion (opt.)

Soak gelatin in cold water for 5 minutes. Set bowl over small amount of hot water until dissolved. Add lemon juice, Worcestershire sauce, parsley and catsup. Let stand until partly set. Add mayonnaise and eggs and onion. Pour into wet ring mold; let stand until set. Unmold on large platter covered with shredded lettuce. Fill center with 1 pound crab meat or chicken.

SAUCE:

½ c. catsup
¼ tsp. salt
2 drops of Tabasco sauce
1 tsp. Worcestershire sauce
2 tbs. lemon juice
1 c. cream

Combine ingredients; pour over mold. Yield: 8-10 servings.

Mrs. Ella Adair, Bryce Valley H.S.
Tropic, Utah

EGG SALAD LOAF

2 envelopes unflavored gelatin
¼ c. cold water
½ c. hot water
2 c. mayonnaise
12 hard-cooked eggs, chopped
2 tsp. grated onion
1 c. celery, chopped
2 tbsp. parsley, chopped
4 tbsp. India relish
2 tbsp. pimento, chopped
2 tbsp. lemon juice
1 ¼ tsp. salt

Soak gelatin in cold water; add to hot water. Stir to dissolve. Beat into mayonnaise. Add remaining ingredients. Pour into loaf or ring mold. Refrigerate for several hours or until set. Yield: 12 servings.

Mrs. Melba Smith, Grandview H.S.
Grandview, Texas

JELLIED EGG SALAD

2 3-oz. pkg. lemon gelatin
1 ¼ c. boiling water
2 c. cold water

3 tbsp. lemon juice
1 c. mayonnaise
4 tbsp. pickle relish, drained
1 tsp. salt
¼ c. chopped onion
2 tbsp. chopped pimento
5 hard-cooked eggs plus 1 hard-cooked
egg white, chopped

Dissolve gelatin in boiling water. Add cold water; chill until s y r u p y. Stir in lemon juice, mayonnaise, pickle relish, salt, onion and pimento. Fold in eggs. Spoon into 2 quart mold. Chill until firm. Garnish with sieved egg yolk. Yield: 8 servings.

Marguerite V. Craig, Evergreen H.S.
Metamora, Ohio

MOLDED EGG SALAD

1 envelope unflavored gelatin
¼ c. cold water
1 c. mayonnaise
4 hard-cooked eggs, chopped
½ c. chopped celery
2 tbsp. green pepper
2 tbsp. pickle relish
1 tbsp. chopped pimento
1 tbsp. lemon juice
1 tsp. salt

Dissolve gelatin in hot water. Add cold water, mayonnaise, eggs, celery, green pepper, relish, pimento, lemon juice and salt. Let set in refrigerator. Cut to serve; top with dressing.

DRESSING:

1 c. whipped cream
1 tbsp. sugar
½ tsp. salt
1 chopped cucumber

Combine first 3 ingredients; fold in cucumber. Chill. Yield: 9 servings.

Mrs. Sarah Ulman, Aurelia Comm. H.S.
Aurelia, Iowa

MUSTARD RING

4 eggs
¾ c. sugar
1 envelope unflavored gelatin
1 ½ tbsp. dry mustard
½ tsp. turmeric
¼ tsp. salt
1 c. water
½ c. white vinegar
1 c. whipping cream

Beat eggs in top of double boiler. Mix sugar and unflavored gelatin thoroughly; stir in mustard, turmeric and salt. Add water and vinegar to eggs.

(Continued on next page)

Stir in sugar mixture; cook over boiling water until slightly thickened, stirring continously. Cool until thick. Whip cream; fold into gelatin mixture. Turn into 1 1/2-quart ring mold. Chill until firm; unmold on salad greens.

Lola Schall, York H.S.
York, Nebraska

DEVILED EGG SALAD

6 hard-boiled eggs
1 tbsp. minced onion
2 tbsp. minced celery
2 tbsp. minced pickle
⅛ tsp. salt
⅛ tsp. pepper
2 tbsp. mayonnaise
1 tbsp. mustard

Cut eggs in half lengthwise. Remove yolks; mash. Add onion, celery, pickle, seasonings, mayonnaise and mustard to moisten. Fill egg whites. Arrange halves on crisp lettuce; sprinkle with paprika, if desired. Yield: 4-6 servings.

Mrs. Altanette Autry, Woodsboro H.S.
Woodsboro, Texas

DEVILED EGG SALAD

6 hard-cooked eggs, sliced lengthwise
1 tsp. finely minced onion
1 tsp. prepared mustard
½ tsp. salt
1 tbsp. catsup
Pinch of black pepper
2 to 3 tbsp. mayonnaise or salad dressing

Remove egg yolks; reserve egg whites. Mash yolks; add remaining ingredients. Whip until fluffy. Pile lightly into whites; garnish as desired. Place 2 to 3 halves on lettuce leaf. Serve with tomato wedges and radish roses.

Mrs. Rubye R. Hill, Thomson Comm. H.S. 301
Thomson, Illinois

EGG SALAD

3 hard-cooked eggs, chopped
¼ c. finely chopped celery
½ tsp. minced onion
3 tbsp. mayonnaise
¼ tsp. salt

Mix all ingredients together; serve on endive or lettuce leaf. Yield: 4 servings.

Mrs. Elvera M. Raff, Longford H.S.
Longford, Kansas

EASTER EGG SALAD

Hard-cooked eggs, 1 for each serving
Few extra yolks, hard-cooked
Mayonnaise
Chopped nuts
Red pimento strips
Raisins
Shredded lettuce

Shell hard-cooked eggs; cut off thin slice lengthwise in order to secure flat base. Mix extra yolks and mayonnaise until of a consistency to use in decorator tube. Apply yolk mixture at proper place for head and wing; add tail. Place small amount over the whole egg. Insert small piece of nut for beak and pimento strip for red comb. Insert raisin for eye; place on bed of shredded lettuce.

Gladys Ketchum, Bryant Sch.
Bryant, Indiana

EGG SALAD

5 med. eggs, hard-boiled
¼ c. chopped onion
½ tsp. salt
¼ tsp. pepper
1 tsp. prepared mustard
¼ c. salad dressing or mayonnaise

Run cold water over eggs to prevent darkening of yolks. Cool; peel shells. Chop eggs finely. Add onion to eggs; add salt, pepper, mustard mayonnaise. Mix well. Refrigerate for 1 hour before serving. Serve on lettuce or as sandwich filling. Yield: 4 servings.

Mrs. Eleanor Ray, Elderton H.S.
Elderton, Pennsylvania

EGG SALAD

6 hard-cooked eggs, chopped
¼ c. chopped green pepper
¼ c. sliced green onions
¼ c. chopped ripe olives
⅓ c. mayonnaise
1 tsp. salt
Dash of pepper

Combine first 4 ingredients; blend mayonnaise with salt and pepper; add to egg mixture. Toss lightly; chill. Use for stuffed tomatoes; or nest in lettuce with ham, cucumber slices and olives. Yield: 6 servings.

Frances Rodriguez, Espanola H.S.
Espanola, New Mexico

EGG SALAD

4 hard-cooked eggs, chopped
¾ c. chopped celery
½ tsp. dry mustard
¼ tsp. salt
¼ tsp. Tabasco
½ c. mayonnaise or salad dressing

Combine eggs and celery in mixing bowl. Add mustard, salt and Tabasco to mayonnaise; blend into egg mixture. Serve on salad greens; garnish with cucumber pickles. Yield: 4 servings.

Mrs. Julia Ausmus, Wynn H.S.
Duff, Tennessee

EGG SALAD

8 hard-cooked eggs
1 tsp. salt
1 tsp. paprika
1 tsp. dry mustard
½ tsp. black pepper
3 tbsp. mayonnaise

Mash eggs or use blender. Add remaining ingredients; mix well. Serve on lettuce leaf or use as sandwich filling. Yield: 6 servings.

Mrs. Pauline Moxley, McAllen H.S.
McAllen, Texas

EGG SALAD OREGANO

½ tsp. oregano
½ tsp. onion salt
¼ tsp. marjoram
¼ tsp. seasoned pepper
¼ c. Italian salad dressing
4 hard-cooked eggs, chopped
1 c. chopped celery
3 tbsp. chopped sweet green pickle
Paprika (opt.)
Olives and radishes (opt.)

Mix all spices and seasonings in salad dressing. Pour into eggs, celery and pickle; mix well. Shape into rounds on lettuce cup with ice cream dipper. Garnish with paprika, olives and radish roses. Yield: 6 servings.

Lula Concepcion, Foothill H.S.
Santa Ana, California

HAPPY HOME EGG SALAD

4 hard-cooked eggs, mashed
¼ to ½ tsp. salt
½ tsp. celery seed
1 tsp. dry minced onion
1 to 2 tbsp. salad dressing

Combine all ingredients. Serve on lettuce. Yield: 3 servings.

Estelle M. Steinberg, West Orange H.S.
West Orange, New Jersey

EGG SALAD SUPREME

½ doz. hard-cooked eggs, diced fine
1 tbsp. chopped pimento
½ c. mild cheddar cheese, diced fine
1 c. celery, diced fine
½ c. mayonnaise
½ c. English walnuts, chopped

Blend all ingredients. Serve on lettuce cup. Yield: 4 servings.

Mrs. Betty Lou James, Western H.S.
Russiaville, Indiana

EGG SALAD IN TOMATO CUPS

4 med.-sized tomatoes
1 3-oz. pkg. cream cheese
Cream
2 tbsp. chopped green onion
¼ c. chopped green pepper
½ med.-sized cucumber, chopped
3 hard-cooked eggs, chopped
¼ c. salad dressing

Peel tomatoes; cut slices from top. Scoop out centers. Sprinkle with salt; invert to chill. Blend cream cheese with enough cream to soften; line tomato cups with cream cheese mixture. Combine remaining ingredients; fill tomato cups. Chill thoroughly. Serve on lettuce with additional salad dressing. Yield: 4 servings.

Mrs. Monna Smith Miller, Lake City H.S.
Lake City, Tennessee

HARD-COOKED EGG SALAD

4 hard-cooked eggs, separated
Italian dressing
2 tsp. minced onion
Cucumber, cubed
Radishes
1 head lettuce
1 lge. tomato, sliced

Mash egg yolks with fork; add dressing until mixture is consistency of very thick cream. Cut egg whites into 1/4 inch cubes; add to yolk mixture. Add onion, small amount of cucumber and radishes. Place thick slice of lettuce on salad plate. Place tomato slice on lettuce. Spoon egg yolks mixture over tomato; serve. Yield: 4 servings.

Mrs. Edna Ruth, Watseka Comm. H.S.
Watseka, Illinois

IMPERIAL SALAD

½ head lettuce
4 chopped hard-boiled eggs
1 c. croutons, browned in butter
   and cooled
½ c. sour cream
¼ c. mayonnaise
2 tbsp. lemon juice
Dash of salt and pepper

Break lettuce into bite-sized pieces. Add eggs and croutons. Combine remaining ingredients; pour over lettuce and toss just before serving. Yield: 4-5 servings.

Susan Valentine, West Liberty-Salem H.S.
West Liberty, Ohio

OLD-TIME EGG SALAD

½ sm. head lettuce
½ bunch leaf lettuce
6 hard-boiled eggs, sliced
1 onion, thinly sliced and separated into
   rings
Cheese
Dash of paprika

Break lettuce into bite-sized pieces in bowl. Top with eggs and onion. Sprinkle with shredded cheese and paprika.

VINEGAR-OIL DRESSING:

¼ c. salad oil
2 tbsp. vinegar
1 ½ tsp. salt
¼ tsp. pepper
1 tsp. Worcestershire sauce
1 tbsp. minced parsley

Combine ingredients. Shake dressing thoroughly; pour over salad. Toss lightly. Yield: 8 servings.

Mrs. Thelma Maxey, Lorenzo H.S.
Lorenzo, Texas

ORIENTAL SALAD

2 hard-cooked eggs, separated
3 tbsp. vinegar
3 tbsp. sugar
3 tbsp. mayonnaise
½ c. ripe olives, cut up
3 pt. coarsely-shredded lettuce
Salt to taste

Mash egg yolks thoroughly; blend with vinegar, sugar and mayonnaise. Add olives and chopped egg whites. Pour over lettuce; mix lightly. Add salt. Yield: 6 servings.

La Verne Stansell, Cary M. Abney H.S.
Waskom, Texas

TOSSED EGG SALAD

1 hard-cooked egg
½ head lettuce
3 tbsp. grated onion
Salt and pepper to taste
Mayonnaise or favorite salad dressing

Mix first four ingredients; toss with mayonnaise. Yield: 6 servings.

Mrs. Louise Chambers
Rochester Indep. Sch. Dist.
Rochester, Texas

TOSSED HARD-COOKED EGG SALAD

⅓ head lettuce
2 to 3 tops of celery stalks
1 tbsp. minced onion
¼ c. chopped celery
2 hard-cooked eggs, diced
¼ c. salad dressing
2 tbsp. prepared mustard
Salt and pepper to taste

Break or tear lettuce into bite-sized pieces; cut celery leaves into small pieces. Combine first 4 ingredients in salad bowl; lightly toss eggs with salad greens. Combine salad dressing, mustard, salt and pepper in small bowl. Combine lightly with egg and lettuce mixture. Yield: 4 servings.

Martha Ann Johnson, Manton H.S.
Manton, Michigan

ASHEVILLE SALAD

2 6-oz. pkg. cream cheese
2 cans cream of tomato soup
1 pkg. plain gelatin
⅓ c. cold water
1 c. celery, onion and green pepper
1 c. mayonnaise
½ c. pecans or other nuts

Combine cheese and soup in small pan; place over low heat until dissolved. Soften gelatin in cold water; add to hot soup mixture. Add remaining ingredients when gelatin mixture cools. Pour into 1 quart mold. Place in refrigerator until congealed. Serve on lettuce with mayonnaise dressing. Yield: 8 servings.

Mrs. Ialeen S. Mode, Franklinton H.S.
Franlinton, North Carolina

BLACK AND WHITE MOLDED SALAD

2 3-oz. pkg. Black Cherry Jell-O
1 lb. lge. curd cottage cheese

(Continued on next page)

Prepare Jell-O by directions on package. When Jell-O begins to set, fold in cottage cheese. Chill until firm. Serve on lettuce leaves. Yield: 6 servings.

Sister M. Constancea, O.S.B., LeBlond H.S.
St. Joseph, Missouri

BLUE CHEESE MOLD

1 tbsp. unflavored gelatin
¼ c. cold water
2 c. cottage cheese
½ c. cream

Dissolve gelatin in cold water. Add remaining ingredients. Chill until firm. Garnish with olives.

Mrs. Jean McOmber, Spring Lake H.S.
Spring Lake, Michigan

BLUE CHEESE SALAD PARFAIT

1 envelope gelatin
¼ c. cold water
1 8-oz. pkg. cream cheese
½ c. salad dressing or mayonnaise
1 tsp. salt
1 c. milk
Lettuce
Canned apricot halves
Canned pineapple slices, halved
Canned pear halves, cut into wedges

Soften gelatin in cold water; dissolve over hot water. Cool. Combine cream cheese and blue cheese, mixing until smooth and well blended. Add salad dressing, salt and gelatin; mix well. Add milk gradually. Pour into fancy 1-quart mold; chill until firm. Unmold on lettuce; garnish with fruits.

Mrs. Elizabeth Bruton, Mercy H.S.
University City, Missouri

CHEESE BALL SALAD

¼ lb. cream cheese
⅓ green sweet pepper or pimento
1 tbsp. mayonnaise
Walnuts
Lettuce

Chop cheese and pepper in food chopper, using fine blade. Blend mixture with mayonnaise. Roll into small balls. Press 1/2 walnut into top of each ball. place 5 balls on each lettuce leaf. Garnish with mayonnaise if desired. May be served as accompaniment to plain green salad. Yield: 4 servings.

Mrs. Anita Spalding, Adelphian Academy
Holly, Michigan

COOL LIME SALAD

1 pkg. lime flavored gelatin
¾ c. boiling water
1 c. buttermilk
1 c. cottage cheese, slightly beaten
1 tbsp. finely chopped onion
1 tbsp. white vinegar
1 tbsp. bottled horseradish
Dash of pepper and paprika
½ c. finely chopped celery
¼ c. thinly sliced sm. radishes
1 tsp. salt

Dissolve gelatin in boiling water. Cool to room temperature. Add buttermilk and cottage cheese, stir until blended. Chill until slightly thickened. Combine remaining ingredients. Fold into slightly thickened gelatin-cheese mixture. Pour into 1-quart mold which has been rinsed with cold water. Chill until firm. Unmold onto crisp green salad. Yield: 6 servings.

Mrs. Louise E. Keller, Rabun County H.S.
Clayton, Georgia

COTTAGE CHEESE-LIME SALAD

1 3-oz. pkg. lime Jell-O
¾ c. boiling water
12 oz. creamed cottage cheese
½ c. cereal cream
½ c. mayonnaise
Few grains of salt and pepper
1 med. carrot, grated
2 tbsp. each, chopped green onion, chopped celery

Dissolve Jell-O in boiling water. Cool. Combine cottage cheese, cream, mayonnaise, salt and pepper. Add carrot, green onion, chopped celery. Combine cheese mixture and cooled Jell-O. Pour into 1-quart mold. Refrigerate immediately. Yield: 8 servings.

Mrs. M. Wilson, Lord Wolseley Sch.
Winnipeo, Manitoba, Canada

COTTAGE CHEESE-VEGETABLE SALAD

1 1-lb. carton sm. curd cottage cheese
1 c. sour cream
1 tbsp. (or more) sugar
¼ tsp. salt
½ c. grated cheddar cheese
¼ c. diced green pepper
½ c. cubed tomatoes

Mix in order given; toss gently. Serve on lettuce leaf. Or use first 4 ingredients; add 3/4 cup fruit. Serve on lettuce leaf. Yield: 6 servings.

Mrs. Irene Wells, Ulysses H.S.
Ulysses, Kansas

LIME JELL-O SALAD

    1 reg. pkg. lime Jell-O
    1 ½ c. hot water
    4-oz. cream cheese, broken into sm.
      pieces
    Pineapple
    1 c. whipping cream

Dissolve Jell-O in hot water. Add cheese, stirring until dissolved. Chill. When Jell-O is consistency of egg white, add pineapple. Whip cream; fold into the Jell-O mixture. Pour into mold. Refrigerate until firm. Yield: 10 servings.

Mrs. Ada Colquhoun, Pershing County H.S.
Lovelock, Nevada

MEAT A GO GO SALAD

    1 pkg. lime gelatin
    1 c. boiling water
    1 tbsp. grated onion
    1 c. diced celery
    1 doz. stuffed olives, chopped
    1 c. cottage cheese
    1 c. salad dressing

Dissolve gelatin in boiling water. Cool. Add remaining ingredients. Pour into small mold. Chill until firm. Perfect accompaniment for meat. Yield: 6 servings.

Norma W. Keeser, Christiansburg H.S.
Christiansburg, Virginia

MOLDED COTTAGE CHEESE AND FRUIT SALAD

    1 tbsp. unflavored gelatin
    ¼ c. cold water
    2 c. cottage cheese
    ⅛ tsp. paprika
    ¾ tsp. salt
    ½ c. light cream
    2 oranges, sectioned
    Lettuce
    1 grapefruit, sectioned
    2 apples, sliced
    French dressing

Soak gelatin in water in small saucepan 5 minutes. Combine next 4 ingredients. Set gelatin over hot water; stir until dissolved. Add gelatin to cheese mixture. Arrange part of orange sections in 9-inch mold, rinsed in cold water. Pour in cheese mixture; chill. Unmold on lettuce. Fill center with remaining fruits. Serve with dressing. Yield: 4-6 servings.

Mrs. Laura Anderson, Sutherlin H.S.
Sutherlin, Oregon

MOLDED CUCUMBER AND COTTAGE CHEESE

    1 3-oz. pkg. lemon Jell-O
    1 c. hot water
    1 c. Miracle Whip salad dressing
    1 pt. cottage cheese
    ½ c. chopped celery
    1 lge. cucumber, peeled and diced
    1 sm. onion, grated
    ½ tsp. salt
    1 tbsp. vinegar
    ½ c. chopped blanched almonds

Dissolve Jell-O in hot water. Cool. Stir in remaining ingredients. Pour immediately into 1 1/2 quart ring mold or individual molds. Chill overnight or until firm. Unmold onto plate. Garnish with crisp greens. Serve with cold cuts, cooked, chilled salmon or shellfish. Yield: 8 servings.

Mrs. Mary Reid, Lord Byng Secondary Sch.
Vancouver, British Columbia, Canada

PIMENTO CHEESE MOLD

    1 pkg. lemon flavored gelatin
    ½ tsp. salt
    1 c. hot water
    1 5-oz. jar pimento cheese spread
    ½ c. salad dressing or mayonnaise
    ¾ c. cold water
    2 to 3 tsp. vinegar
    2 to 3 dashes Tabasco sauce
    ½ c. chopped celery
    ¼ c. finely chopped onion
    2 tbsp. finely chopped green pepper

Dissolve gelatin and salt in hot water. Add cheese spread and salad dressing, beating with electric or rotary beater until smooth. Stir in cold water, vinegar and Tabasco sauce. Chill until partially set. Add remaining ingredients. Pour into individual molds or 3-cup mold. Chill until firm. Unmold. Serve with shrimp or cold cuts. Yield: 4-6 servings.

Ellen F. Dow, Windsor H.S.
Windsor, Vermont

SESAME SALAD

    2 heads leaf lettuce or other salad
      greens
    ⅓ c. sesame seeds
    2 tbsp. butter or margarine
    1 pkg. sliced Swiss cheese, broken into
      sm. pieces

Tear lettuce into small pieces. Brown sesame seeds in butter. Combine lettuce, sesame seeds and cheese. Toss with favorite oil and vinegar dressing. Yield: 4-6 servings.

Marilyn Finger, Round Rock H.S.
Round Rock, Texas

SPRING SALAD

1 3-oz. pkg. lemon Jell-O
½ c. boiling water
1 very sm. onion
1 med. cucumber, peeled
1 carrot
1 12-oz. pkg. cottage cheese
¾ c. mayonnaise

Dissolve Jell-O in boiling water; set aside. Run onion, cucumber and carrot through food chopper. Combine Jell-O, chopped vegetables, cottage cheese and mayonnaise. Pour into desired molds. Yield: 12 servings.

Marilyn Kay Clark, U of Nebraska Sch. of Agri.
Curtis, Nebraska

SUNNY MARSHMALLOW SALAD

1 3-oz. pkg. orange Jell-O
1 c. boiling water
½ c. cold water
1 tbsp. lemon juice
1 8-oz. pkg. cream cheese, softened
1 ½ c. miniature marshmallows

Dissolve orange Jell-O in boiling water. Add cold water and lemon juice. Gradually add Jell-O to cream cheese, mixing until well blended. Chill until almost congealed. Fold in marshmallows. Continue chilling until firm. Yield: 6-8 servings.

Gayla Clouse, Morrison H.S.
Morrison, Tennessee

TOMATO-CHEESE-JELL-O SALAD

1 lge. pkg. lemon Jell-O
1 c. boiling water
1 tbsp. lemon juice
1 c. tomato soup
1 c. salad dressing
1 ½ c. diced celery
1 ½ c. fine curd cottage cheese
2 tbsp. grated onion
¼ tsp. salt
¼ mango pepper, diced

Mix Jell-O, water and lemon juice; cool to syrup stage. Mix soup and salad dressing thoroughly. Combine Jell-O and soup mixture. Add remaining ingredients, mixing well. Pour into mold or glass baking dish. Refrigerate until firm. Yield: 10 servings.

Mrs. Russell Hepler, Salem Center Sch.
Pleasant Lake, Indiana

TOMATO-CREAM CHEESE SALAD

1 can of tomato soup
1 8-oz. pkg. cream cheese
2 envelopes gelatin
½ c. cold water
1 c. salad dressing
1 tsp. onion
1 tsp. green pepper
1 c. chopped celery
1 c. chopped pecans

Heat tomato soup; stir in cream cheese. Dissolve gelatin in cold water; add to soup mixture. Mix in remaining ingredients. Refrigerate until firm.

Mrs. Raye King, Coleman Sch.
Coleman, Texas

TOMATO SOUP SALAD

½ c. cold water
2 envelopes plain gelatin
1 can cream of tomato soup
2 3-oz. pkg. cream cheese
1 ½ c. chopped celery
¾ c. chopped green pepper
1 c. mayonnaise
½ tsp. onion juice
¼ tsp. salt

Pour cold water into small bowl; sprinkle gelatin over top to soften. Heat soup; mix with softened gelatin and cheese. Run hot mixture through sieve; immediately add remaining ingredients. Pour into mold. Refrigerate until set. Yield: 8-10 servings.

Kathryn P. McElroy, La Grange H.S.
La Grange, Texas

TOMATO SOUP SALAD

2 3-oz. pkg. cream cheese
1 can tomato soup
1 pkg. unflavored gelatin
½ c. cold water
½ c. chopped, stuffed olives
½ tsp. salt
3 tbsp. mayonnaise
1 c. chopped celery
1 tbsp. onion juice

Place cream cheese and tomato soup in top of double boiler; stir until cheese melts and mixes with soup. Dissolve gelatin in cold water; add to tomato mixture. Cool. Add remaining ingredients. Pour into molds to congeal. Shrimp or crab meat may be added if desired. Yield: 8 servings.

Mrs. Eleanor Weatherford, Tupelo Sr. H.S.
Tupelo, Mississippi

Frozen Salads

RECIPE FOR APPLE-CHERRY MOUSSE ON PAGE 104

APPLE-CHERRY MOUSSE

2 ½ c. canned apple slices
½ c. sugar
⅛ tsp. salt
½ tsp. mace
½ c. diced maraschino cherries
2 tbsp. maraschino cherry syrup
1 c. heavy cream
Toasted almonds

Chop apples fine; add sugar, salt, mace, cherries and syrup. Let stand for 10 minutes. Whip cream until slightly stiff; fold into apple mixture. Pour into freezing tray of refrigerator; freeze firm. Slice and garnish with whipped cream; sprinkle with toasted almonds. Serve with ladyfingers if desired. Yield: 6-8 servings.

Photograph for this recipe on page 103.

CRANBERRY TIP-TOP SALAD

1 can cranberry sauce
2 tsp. lemon juice
3 oz. cream cheese
½ c. mayonnaise
½ c. powdered sugar
½ pt. whipping cream, whipped
½ c. nuts

Mix cranberry sauce and lemon juice with fork; place in bottom of mold. Soften cream cheese; add mayonnaise and powdered sugar. Fold into whipped cream. Add nuts. Pour on cranberry sauce. Freeze. Serve frozen. Yield: 6-8 servings.

Mrs. Barbara Bradley, Rose Bud H.S.
Rose Bud, Arkansas

CRANBERRY-CREAM CHEESE FROSTIES

1 No. 1 can jellied cranberry sauce
2 tbsp. lemon juice
1 3-oz. pkg. cream cheese
¼ c. mayonnaise
¼ c. confectioners sugar
½ c. chopped walnuts
1 c. heavy cream, whipped

Crush cranberry sauce; add lemon juice. Pour into molds or tray. Combine cream cheese, mayonnaise and sugar; blend. Add nuts. Fold in whipped cream. Spread over cranberry mixture. Freeze until firm. Serve on lettuce. Yield: 6-8 servings.

Virginia Johnson, Dist. 837 H.S.
Madelia, Minnesota

BETTY'S FROZEN CRANBERRY SALAD

1 16-oz. can jellied cranberry sauce
3 tbsp. lemon juice
4 c. heavy cream, whipped
¼ c. mayonnaise
¼ c. confectioners' sugar
1 c. chopped walnuts

Crush cranberry sauce with fork; add lemon juice. Pour into refrigerator tray. Combine remaining ingredients and spread over cranberry mixture. Freeze until firm. Yield: 6-8 servings.

Betty E. Cunes, Williamson Jr.-Sr. H.S.
Tioga, Pennsylvania

FROZEN CRANBERRY SALAD

4 c. cranberries
1 ½ c. water
2 c. sugar
2 to 3 tbsp. lemon juice
2 3-oz. pkg. cream cheese
⅓ c. mayonnaise
½ c. powdered sugar
1 c. English walnuts, chopped
2 c. heavy cream, whipped

Cook cranberries in water until well popped. Put through sieve. Add sugar and cook 5 minutes. Add lemon juice and pour into paper bake cups in muffin tins. Pour 1/2 to 1 inch cranberry mixture into each cup. Set in freezer to chill. Combine remaining ingredients; spread over cranberry mixture. Freeze. May be kept for several weeks. Yield: 24 servings.

Linda Lang, Spring Grove H.S.
Spring Grove, Minnesota

THELMA'S HOLIDAY FREEZE

1 No. 1 can jellied cranberry sauce
1 tbsp. lemon juice
1 3-oz. pkg. cream cheese, softened
¼ c. mayonnaise
¼ c. confectioners' sugar
½ c. walnuts, chopped
1 tsp. grated orange peel
1 c. whipping cream, whipped

Break up cranberry sauce with fork. Stir in lemon juice. Turn into 1-quart freezer tray. Combine cream cheese, mayonnaise and sugar thoroughly; stir in walnuts and orange peel. Fold in whipped cream. Spread evenly over cranberry mixture. Freeze several hours or overnight. Remove from freezer 10 minutes before cutting. Yield: 6 servings.

Opal Carpenter, Mentone H.S.
Mentone, Indiana

FROZEN FRUIT MEDLEY

4 oz. macaroni
2 peeled, sectioned oranges
1 cored, cubed apple
2 sliced bananas
¼ c. chopped walnuts
¼ c. sugar
½ c. sour cream
1 c. whipping cream, whipped

Cook macaroni 5 to 7 minutes; drain and rinse with cold water. Cut each orange section into quarters; combine with apples, bananas and walnuts. Sprinkle with sugar. Mix in sour cream and macaroni; fold in whipped cream. Freeze until firm. Yield: 6-8 servings.

Jacquie Eddleman, Dongola H.S.
Dongola, Illinois

FAVORITE FROZEN FRUIT SALAD

2 3-oz. pkg. cream cheese, softened
1 c. cream, whipped
1 c. drained fruit cocktail
½ c. maraschino cherries, quartered
2 ½ c. miniature marshmallows

Fold cream cheese and cream together; add fruit cocktail, cherries and marshmallows. Blend carefully; place in No. 2 1/2 can. Cover with aluminum foil; freeze overnight. Remove from can; slice. Serve on lettuce leaf. Yield: 8 servings.

M. Judelle Jones, Turlock H.S.
Turlock, California

FROZEN SHERBET SALAD

1 6-oz. or 2 3-oz. pkg. orange gelatin
2 c. hot water
1 pt. orange milk sherbet

Dissolve orange gelatin in hot water; add sherbet. Stir until melted; pour into 2-quart mold. Freeze. Sherbet mixture may be frozen in paper muffin cups. Empty frozen muffins into plastic bag; store in freezer. Serve as dessert with fluff of whipped cream.

STRAWBERRY LAYER:

1 3-oz. pkg. strawberry gelatin
1 10 ½-oz. pkg. frozen strawberries, thawed

Dissolve strawberry gelatin in hot water, day salad is to be served; add juice and berries. Pour over frozen layer; refrigerate for about 30 minutes or until set. Unmold on greens. Yield: 10-12 servings.

Beth Seaver, Doland H.S.
Doland, South Dakota

FROZEN FRUIT SALAD

1 envelope plain gelatin
2 tbsp. lemon juice
¼ c. boiling water
½ c. mayonnaise
1 1-lb. 13-oz. can fruit cocktail, drained
1 c. heavy cream, whipped

Place gelatin, lemon juice and water in blender; cover and blend on high speed for 40 seconds. Add mayonnaise and fruit cocktail; cover and blend for 30 seconds. Pour into tray; freeze until mushy. Place in bowl; beat with rotary beater until smooth. Fold in whipped cream; return to freezer until firm. Cut into bars or squares. Yield: 8 servings.

Mrs. Sharon Schrick, Nortonville H.S.
Nortonville, Kansas

EASY FROZEN SALAD

1 pt. sour cream
1 tbsp. lemon juice
½ c. sugar
1 No. 303 or No. 1 tall can of fruit cocktail, drained

Combine all ingredients; pour into refrigerator tray. Freeze until firm. Yield: 6-8 servings.

Mrs. Lavinia C. Miller, Eau Claire H.S.
Columbia, South Carolina

FROZEN FRUIT SALAD

2 3-oz. pkg. cream cheese
1 c. mayonnaise or salad dressing
1 No. 2 ½ can fruit cocktail, drained
½ c. drained maraschino cherries, quartered
Few drops of red food coloring (opt.)
1 c. heavy cream, whipped

Soften cheese; blend in mayonnaise. Fold in remaining ingredients, adding cream last. Pour into two 1-quart round freezer containers or ice trays; freeze about 6 hours. Slice; place on lettuce. One package orange Jell-O may be added to hasten freezing. Vanilla ice cream may be substituted for cream. Yield: 10-12 servings.

Joy Criner, Avon Park H.S.
Avon Park, Florida

FROZEN FRUIT SALAD

1 No. 2 ½ can fruit cocktail
1 tsp. unflavored gelatin
2 tbsp. lemon juice
1 3-oz. pkg. cream cheese
¼ c. mayonnaise
Dash of salt
⅔ c. whipping cream, chilled
½ c. sugar
½ c. chopped nuts

Drain fruit cocktail. Soften gelatin in lemon juice; dissolve over hot water. Blend cream cheese with mayonnaise and salt; stir in gelatin. Whip cream until stiff, adding sugar gradually; fold in cheese mixture, nuts and fruit cocktail. Pour into waxed paper-lined refrigerator tray; freeze until firm. Turn out onto platter; remove paper. Cut into thick slices; garnish with watercress. Let salad stand at room temperature about 3 to 4 minutes before serving. Yield: 10 servings.

Mrs. Marilyn Bell, Bakersfield H.S.
Bakersfield, California
Mrs. Helen Dunn, Newman H.S.
Newman, Illinois
Louise D. Gurley, Sun Valley H.S.
Monroe, North Carolina

PINK FROZEN SALAD

½ pt. cream, whipped
1 sm. pkg. cream cheese, softened
1 can fruit cocktail, drained
1 c. chopped pecans
1 sm. bottle maraschino cherries, chopped

Combine all ingredients; place in ice tray and freeze. Slice and serve on lettuce leaf. May be wrapped in foil and stored in freezer for several weeks. Small amount of cherry juice may be added for color. Yield: 10-12 servings.

Mrs. Martha Berryhill, Corner H.S.
Warrior, Alabama

ROSY FRUIT COCKTAIL SLICES

2 3-oz. pkg. cream cheese, softened
1 c. mayonnaise
1 c. heavy cream, whipped
1 No. 2 ½ can fruit cocktail, drained
½ c. drained maraschino cherries, quartered
2 ½ c. tiny marshmallows
Few drops red food coloring

Blend cream cheese and mayonnaise; fold in remaining ingredients. Pour into round containers; freeze till firm. Slice; serve on crisp lettuce. Yield: 10-12 servings.

Sister Ramona Ann, St. Mary's Sch.
Holly Springs, Mississippi
Mrs. Katherine Mills Fisher, Anderson H.S.
Austin, Texas

SHORTCUT FROZEN SALAD

1 3 ¾-oz. pkg. instant lemon pudding mix
1 pt. frozen dessert topping, thawed
½ c. mayonnaise or salad dressing
2 tbsp. lemon juice
1 1-lb. can fruit cocktail, drained
1 c. miniature marshmallows
¼ c. chopped pecans

Prepare pudding mix according to package directions; blend in dessert topping, mayonnaise and lemon juice. Fold in remaining ingredients; turn into 9 x 5 x 3-inch loaf pan or 9 x 9 x 2-inch baking pan. Freeze till firm. Yield: 8-10 servings.

Mrs. Etta Champagne, Pettus H.S.
Pettus, Texas

FROZEN PARTY SALAD

1 c. salad dressing
1 8-oz. pkg. cream cheese
2 tbsp. powdered sugar
1 c. chopped apricots
1 c. drained pineapple tidbits
½ c. chopped maraschino cherries
Few drops red food coloring (opt.)
2 c. miniature marshmallows
1 c. heavy cream, whipped
Lettuce

Gradually add salad dressing to cream cheese, mixing until smooth and well blended. Add sugar, fruit and food coloring. Fold in marshmallows and cream. Pour into 9 1/2 x 5 x 3-inch loaf pan. Freeze until firm. Unmold on lettuce covered platter and slice 2 to 3 slices to make it attractive and colorful while serving. Yield: 6-10 servings.

Mrs. Martha Wilson, Ogden Comm. Sch.
Ogden, Illinois
Lillian J. Kissam, Jackson H.S.
Tyler, Texas

PINK FRUIT SALAD

4 lge. bananas
1 pkg. frozen apricots
12 maraschino cherries
2 tbsp. maraschino cherry juice
½ pt. heavy cream, whipped

Mash bananas; drain apricots. Chop cherries; add cherries and juice to bananas and apricots. Fold in whipped cream. Freeze in mold. Yield: 4 servings.

Lois Ellen Lakso, Ketchikan H.S.
Ketchikan, Alaska

FROZEN GRAPEFRUIT SALAD

1 8-oz. pkg. cream cheese
1 c. sour cream
¼ tsp. salt
½ c. sugar
2 c. grapefruit sections
1 avocado, diced
1 c. halved seedless white grapes
½ c. chopped pecans

Soften cream cheese; blend in sour cream. Add salt and sugar; stir until blended. Add grapefruit, avocado, grapes and pecans. Pour into 5 x 9-inch loaf pan; cover. Freeze until firm. Slice; serve on salad greens. Yield: 8 servings.

Sue Kidd, Crockett Jr. H.S.
Odessa, Texas

AVOCADO FRUIT FREEZE

1 lge. avocado
2 tbsp. lemon juice
1 3-oz. pkg. softened cream cheese
2 tbsp. sugar
¼ c. mayonnaise
¼ tsp. salt
1 lb. can pears, drained and diced
¼ c. well-drained, chopped maraschino
    cherries
½ c. whipping cream, whipped

Halve, peel and dice avocado; sprinkle with 1 tablespoon lemon juice. Blend cream cheese, remaining lemon juice, sugar, mayonnaise and salt. Add avocado, pears and cherries; fold in whipped cream. Pour into 3-cup tray or pan; freeze for 6 hours or overnight. Let stand at room temperature about 15 minutes before serving. Garnish with kabobs of maraschino cherries and avocado balls, if desired. Yield: 6-8 servings.

Mrs. Tillie Gandy, Weslaco H.S.
Weslaco, Texas

FROZEN AVOCADO-
CRANBERRY SALAD

1 8-oz. pkg. cream cheese
⅓ c. mayonnaise
½ c. chopped celery
1 9-oz. can crushed pineapple, drained
½ c. cubed avocado, seasoned with ¼ tsp.
    salt and 1 tbsp. lemon juice
12 oz. cubed jellied cranberry sauce
1 c. cream, whipped

Blend cream cheese and mayonnaise; add celery, pineapple, seasoned avocado and cranberry sauce. Fold in whipped cream. Pour into loaf pan; cover with foil. Freeze. Salad may be tinted pink with 1 or 2 drops red food coloring, if desired. Yield: 8-10 servings.

Mrs. Joyce Kaplan, Drew H.S.
Drew, Mississippi

BANANA FROZEN SALAD

2 lge. bananas
2 tbsp. lemon juice
¾ c. sugar
1 2-pt. carton sour cream
2 tbsp. chopped moist cherries
1 No. 2 can crushed pineapple
½ c. chopped pecans

Mash bananas; mix with lemon juice and sugar. Add sour cream, cherries, pineapple and nuts. Pour into mold. Place in deep freeze until frozen. Take out 10 minutes before serving; slice. Yield: 6 servings.

Mrs. Eloise Guerrant, Robert Lee H.S.
Robert Lee, Texas

FROZEN CHERRY SALAD

1 c. pitted sweet cherries
½ c. crushed pineapple
1 banana, sliced
½ c. chopped nuts
½ c. mayonnaise
1 3-oz. pkg. cream cheese
⅛ tsp. salt

Combine fruit and nuts. Blend mayonnaise and cream cheese and salt; fold fruit mixture into cheese mixture. Mix thoroughly; place in refrigerator tray. Freeze. Cut into squares. Serve on crisp salad greens. Yield: 6 servings.

Mrs. Judy H. Carden, Boyden H.S.
Salisbury, North Carolina

FROZEN BLACK CHERRY
SALAD

2 tbsp. pineapple juice
½ c. powdered sugar
½ c. pecans, chopped
¼ tsp. salt
4 marshmallows, cut fine
½ c. mayonnaise
1 can blackberries, well drained
⅔ c. pineapple or other fruit, drained
1 c. cream, whipped

Combine pineapple juice, sugar, pecans, salt, marshmallows; add fruit. Fold mixture into cream; pour into mold. Freeze.

Audrey Swason, Tinley Park H.S.
Tinley Park, Illinois

FROZEN FRUIT SALAD

    1 can crushed drained pineapple
    1 c. pitted Bing cherries, drained
    1 c. miniature marshmallows
    2 tbsp. cherry juice
    1 c. heavy cream, whipped
    ¼ c. maraschino cherries

Combine pineapple, cherries and marshmallows. Add cherry juice to whipped cream; fold in fruit mixture. Arrange maraschino cherries on bottom of greased loaf pan; pour in salad. Freeze until firm. Slice salad and serve on lettuce leaf. Yield: 6-8 servings.

Elena Yatorola, NoRose-Wolcott Cen. Sch. Wolcott, New York

LU'S FROZEN FRUIT SALAD

    2 3-oz. pkg. cream cheese
    2 tbsp. milk
    1 c. crushed pineapple, drained
    ½ c. Royal Anne cherries, pitted and
        sliced
    1 c. juice from pineapple and cherries
    1 pkg. cherry Jell-O
    1 c. whipped cream
    ½ c. mayonnaise
    2 sliced bananas
    2 tbsp. lemon juice
    ½ c. sliced maraschino cherries
    10 lge. marshmallows, cut fine

Soften cream cheese with milk. Combine pineapple and cherries; set aside. Bring juice to a boil; add Jell-O. Set aside to cool. Add cream cheese, whipped cream and mayonnaise to chilled Jell-O. Combine bananas, lemon juice, pineapple mixture, cherries and marshmallows. Fold fruit mixture into Jell-O mixture; pour into 1-pound loaf pan. Freeze. Yield: 12 servings.

Mrs. Shirley Larsen, Bendle H.S. Flint, Michigan

EASTERN FROZEN CRANBERRY SALAD

    1 lb. raw ground cranberries
    2 c. sugar
    1 No. 2 can crushed pineapple, drained
    2 c. miniature marshmallows
    ½ c. broken pecans
    1 pt. whipping cream, whipped

Mix cranberries and sugar; add pineapple, marshmallows and pecans. Fold in whipped cream. Pour into large container or two small molds. Freeze until firm. Remove from freezer a few minutes before serving. Yield: 12 servings.

Mrs. Martha Boyle, Eastern Jr. H.S. Owensboro, Kentucky

FROZEN CRANBERRY FRUIT ROUNDS

    1 1-lb. can jellied cranberry sauce,
        beaten until saucey
    1 No. 2 can drained crushed pineapple
    ½ pt. cultured sour cream
    ¼ c. chopped nuts

Combine above ingredients, reserving cranberry and pineapple cans. Lightly grease the cans; spoon in salad mixture. Cover tightly with foil; freeze for several hours or overnight. Cut out bottom lids of cans, using lids to press out salad. Slice with knife into 1/2 to 3/4 inch slices. Yield: 12-16 servings.

Beth Seaver, Doland H.S. Doland, South Dakota

FROZEN CRANBERRY SALAD

    2 c. raw cranberries, chopped
    1 2-lb. can pineapple chunks
    1 ½ c. sugar
    1 ½ c. miniature marshmallows
    ½ pt. whipping cream

Combine cranberries, pineapple chunks, sugar and marshmallows in large mixing bowl. Chill for 30 minutes. Whip the whipping cream; fold in fruit mixture. Freeze in serving dish. Allow 30 minutes to partially thaw before serving; stir once or twice. Yield: 10-12 servings.

Elise Currieo, Webster H.S. Tulsa, Oklahoma

FROZEN CRANBERRY SALAD

    2 3-oz. pkg. cream cheese
    ¾ c. mayonnaise
    1 c. heavy cream whipped
    1 c. jellied cranberry sauce cubes
    1 9-oz. can crushed pineapple, drained
    ½ c. chopped ripe olives
    ¼ c. chopped celery

Blend cream cheese and mayonnaise together; fold in whipped cream. Fold in cranberry cubes, pineapple, olives and celery. Pour into refrigerator tray and freeze 3 to 4 hours. May be wrapped and stored in deep freeze for 3 to 4 weeks. Top each serving with star of jellied cranberry sauce, if desired. Yield: 5-6 servings.

Lorene L. Arent, Wausa H.S. Wausa, Nebraska

QUICK CRANBERRY SALAD

    1 1-lb. can whole cranberry sauce
    1 sm. can crushed pineapple, drained
    ½ pt. sour cream.

(Continued on next page)

Combine all ingredients; place in 8 x 8-inch cake pan. Freeze. Yield: 9 servings.

Marcia F. Swanson, Henry Co. H.S.
McDonough, Georgia

PINK ARTIC FREEZE

2 3-oz. pkg. cream cheese
2 tbsp. salad dressing
2 tbsp. sugar
1 1-lb. can whole cranberry sauce
1 c. crushed pineapple, drained
½ c. chopped walnuts
1 c. whipping cream, whipped

Soften cheese; blend in salad dressing and sugar. Add fruit and nuts. Fold in whipped cream. Pour into 8 1/2 x 2 1/2-inch loaf pan or individual molds. Freeze firm for 6 hours or overnight. Let stand at room temperature for 15 minutes before serving. Yield: 10-12 servings.

Mrs. Luella Wilson, Shaler H.S.
Glenshaw, Pennsylvania

FROZEN CRANBERRY SALAD

1 c. cranberry sauce, mashed
1 sm. can crushed pineapple
2 bananas, mashed
1 c. pecans
1 sm. carton whipping cream
2 tbsp. sugar
1 tsp. vanilla

Combine cranberry sauce, pineapple, bananas and pecans. Whip cream with sugar and vanilla. Mix all together. Freeze. Yield: 10 servings.

Rubie Williams, Anton Sch.
Anton, Texas

ALASKAN SALAD

½ c. maraschino cherries, chopped
2 c. miniature marshmallows
1 8-oz. pkg. cream cheese, softened
2 tbsp. pineapple juice
¼ c. mayonnaise
1 c. whipping cream
1 No. 2 ½ can crushed pineapple, drained
½ c. chopped dates
1 c. chopped nuts

Mix cherries with marshmallows. Blend cheese, pineapple juice and mayonnaise. Whip cream; fold in all ingredients. Pour into molds or freezer tray and freeze. Yield: 12 servings.

Mrs. Stacie O. Houser, Sun Valley H.S.
Monroe, North Carolina

DATE SOUFFLE SALAD

1 8-oz. pkg. cream cheese
¼ c. maple syrup
1 tbsp. lemon juice
½ c. mashed banana
1 c. crushed pineapple, drained
½ c. dates, chopped
½ c. pecans, chopped
1 c. whipping cream, whipped

Cream cheese; beat in syrup, lemon juice and banana. Stir in pineapple, dates and pecans; fold in whipped cream. Fill 6 to 8 paper muffin cups with mixture. Freeze until firm. Let stand at room temperature for 15 to 20 minutes before serving. Yield: 6-8 servings.

Mary Jane Bertrand, Blackfoot H.S.
Blackfoot, Idaho

FROZEN CHEESE-DATE SALAD

1 3-oz. pkg. cream cheese
¼ c. maple syrup
½ c. cream, whipped
¼ c. dates, chopped
1 ¼ c. bananas
½ c. pineapple
½ c. nuts

Cream cheese until very soft; add syrup gradually. Fold in cream, dates, bananas, pineapple and nuts. Place in freezer. Remove 30 minutes to 1 hour before serving. Yield: 10 servings.

Ora McLeod, Gardiner H.S.
Gardiner, Montana

FROZEN DATE SALAD

1 8-oz. pkg. cream cheese, softened
1 8-oz. can crushed pineapple, drained
1 c. chopped pitted dates
8 maraschino cherries, chopped
1 tbsp. lemon juice
⅛ tsp. salt
½ pt. heavy cream, whipped or pkg.
    topping, whipped
2 tbsp. chopped nuts

Blend cheese and pineapple; add dates, cherries, lemon juice and salt. Fold in whipped cream and nuts. Pour into 1-quart mold or individual molds. Freeze until firm. Unmold onto lettuce leaves. Yield: 8 servings.

Mrs. Aleta B. Nelson, Tidehaven H.S.
Blessing, Texas

Frozen Mixed Fruit Salads

FROZEN DATE SALAD

¼ c. pineapple liquid
1 8-oz. cream cheese, softened
1 8½-oz. crushed pineapple
½ c. chopped pecans
1 8-oz. pkg. dates, sliced
1 c. whipping cream

Add pineapple liquid gradually to softened cream cheese; beat until fluffy. Add pineapple, pecans and dates; mix thoroughly. Whip cream in chilled bowl; fold into date mixture. Spoon into 9-inch square pan or 7 to 8 oiled individual molds. Freeze until firm. Yield: 7-9 servings.

Mrs. Ruth A. Schaffner
Cochrane-Fountain City H.S.
Fountain City, Wisconsin

EASY FROZEN FRUIT SALAD

1 qt. ice cream
½ c. mayonnaise
2 c. red raspberries
1 c. blueberries
1 c. canned crushed pineapple, drained
3 c. mandarin oranges, drained

Soften ice cream in large chilled bowl; blend in mayonnaise. Add fruits; pour into 9 x 5 x 3-inch loaf pan. Freeze for 2 to 3 hours. Unmold onto cold serving platter by dipping into warm water; return to freezer. Slice; serve on lettuce leaf with whipped cream or mayonnaise. Yield: 10-12 servings.

Mary P. Light, King H.S.
Kingsville, Texas

FROZEN FRUIT SALAD

½ c. mayonnaise
1 8-oz. pkg. softened cream cheese
¼ c. sugar
2 tsp. grated orange rind
2 c. sliced bananas
1 c. orange sections
½ c. chopped pitted dates
1 c. whipped cream

Blend together mayonnaise and cream cheese; stir in sugar and orange rind. Fold in bananas, orange sections, dates and whipped cream. Pour into 9-inch square pan and freeze until firm. Cut and serve on lettuce. Garnish with thin orange slice. Yield: 12 servings.

Elizabeth S. Caylor, Asst. State Supvr.
Home Ec. Ed. Ball State U
Muncie, Indiana

FROSTY FRUIT SALAD

6 oz. cream cheese, softened
1 c. sour cream
3½ c. drained chopped canned fruit or fruit cocktail
¼ c. sugar
2 c. miniature marshmallows
1 tsp. grated lemon peel
1 banana, sliced
Greens

Blend cream cheese and sour cream; add fruit, sugar, marshmallows, lemon peel and banana. Freeze in loaf pan or ice cube trays. Serve on greens. Yield: 6 servings.

Sister M. Delrey, St. Mary H.S.
Dell Rapids, South Dakota

PINK FROZEN FRUIT SALAD

2 3-oz. pkg. cream cheese, softened
1 8½-oz. crushed pineapple
1 c. finely chopped dates
¼ c. chopped maraschino cherries
3 tbsp. syrup from cherries
⅛ tsp. salt
½ c. whipped cream
¼ c. chopped nuts

Blend cheese and undrained pineapple; add remaining ingredients. Pour into individual molds. Freeze until firm or overnight. Remove from freezer 20 to 30 minutes before serving. Unmold; garnish with additional cherries. Yield: 6-8 servings.

Mrs. Deborah Longbothum, Mifflinburg H.S.
Mifflinburg, Pennsylvania
Avis Henning, Glasco H.S.
Glasco, Kansas

FROZEN FRUIT SALAD

2 3-oz. pkg. cream cheese
½ tsp. salt
2 tbsp. salad dressing
1 tbsp. lemon juice
½ c. crushed, drained pineapple
½ c. coarsely chopped maraschino cherries
Chopped nuts
2 c. diced bananas
½ c. diced marshmallows
1 c. whipping cream

Mash cheese with fork; blend with salt, salad dressing and lemon juice. Mix well. Fold in pineapple, cherries, nuts, bananas and marshmallows. Whip cream until thickened but not stiff; fold into cheese mixture. Turn into freezing trays. Freeze until firm. Yield: 8 servings.

Mrs. Marie Fuller, Liberty-Eylan Sr. H.S.
Texarkana, Texas

FROSTY NESSELRODE MOUNTAIN

1 8-oz. pkg. cream cheese
½ c. mayonnaise
½ c. pineapple preserves
½ c. golden raisins
½ c. walnuts, chopped
½ c. candied cherries, halved
1 c. whipping cream, whipped

Soften cream cheese; blend with mayonnaise. Add pineapple preserves, raisins, walnuts and cherries. Fold in cream. Pour into 9 x 5 x 3-inch pan. Freeze overnight or for several hours. Serve as dessert or salad. Yield: 8-10 servings.

Bernice Ehrenhard, Hinsdale Central H.S
Hinsdale, Illinois

FROZEN FRUIT SALAD

1 3-oz. pkg. Jell-O, strawberry, lemon, or pineapple-grapefruit gelatin
Dash of salt
1 c. boiling water
1 8 ¾-oz. can pineapple tidbits
¼ c. lemon juice
⅓ c. mayonnaise
1 c. whipping cream
1 med. banana, diced
½ c. halved grapes
¼ c. maraschino cherries, diced
¼ c. chopped nuts

Dissolve Jell-O and salt in boiling water. Drain pineapple. Measure syrup; add water to make 1/2 cup, if necessary. Stir into gelatin with lemon juice. Blend in mayonnaise. Chill until very thick. Whip cream. Fold fruits, nuts and whipped cream into gelatin. Pour into 2 freezing trays or 9 x 5 x 3-inch loaf pan. Freeze until firm at least 3 to 4 hours. To serve, cut in squares or slices. Strawberry, lemon or pineapple-grapefruit gelatin may be substituted for mixed fruit Jell-O. Drained diced orange sections, crushed pineapple or fruit cocktail, a total of almost 2 cups, may be substituted for fruits listed. Yield: 8 servings.

Mrs. Hellen Evans, Adams City H.S.
Commerce City, Colorado
O'dessa H. Cicschke, Carthage H.S.
Carthage, Indiana

FROZEN FRUIT SALAD

1 10 ½-oz. jar maraschino cherries, quartered and drained
2 c. whipped cream or 1 c. pkg. Dream Whip prepared
2 c. mayonnaise
1 tbsp. unflavored gelatin
1 tbsp. cold water
4 tbsp. hot water

Place fruits in large bowl. Fold mayonnaise into cream; fold into fruit mixture. Dissolve gelatin in cold water; add hot water. Stir until dissolved. Fold gelatin mixture into fruit mixture. Pour into 2 regular-sized loaf pans or 1 large pan. Place in freezer until solid. Yield: 20-24 servings.

Winnie C. Perry, Lockport East H.S.
Lockport, Illinois

FROZEN FRUIT SALAD WITH PEARS

1 egg
¼ c. sugar
2 ½ tbsp. flour
½ tsp. salt
2 tbsp. vinegar
¾ c. pineapple juice
1 c. whipped cream
1 can pineapple tidbits
1 can pears, diced
3 bananas, mashed
12 cherries

Beat egg and mix in sugar, flour, salt, vinegar and pineapple juice; cook until thick, stirring constantly. Let set until cooled. Fold in whipped cream; add pineapple, pears, bananas and cherries. Freeze. Yield: 6-8 servings.

Mrs. Dorothy Nichols, West H.S.
West, Texas

FROZEN LEMON CREAM

1 egg, well beaten
¼ c. lemon juice
½ c. sugar
⅛ tsp. shredded lemon peel
½ tsp. vanilla
¼ c.melted margarine
½ c. brown sugar
Pinch of nutmeg
3 c. graham cracker crumbs
¾ c. grated coconut
1 c. heavy cream, whipped

Line bottom and sides of loaf pan with waxed paper, extending edges over rim. Combine first 4 ingredients. Heat and stir over hot, not boiling water until mixture coats spoon, 12 to 15 minutes. Remove from heat; stir in vanilla. Cool thoroughly. Combine margarine, brown sugar, nutmeg, nuts and crumbs; mix until blended. Reserve 3/4 cup crumb mixture for topping. Press remaining crumbs into prepared loaf pan. Fold coconut and whipped cream into cooled lemon mixture. Spoon into pan. Top with reserved crumbs. Press crumbs together lightly. Cover; freeze for 6 hours or overnight. Yield: 8 servings.

Mrs. Ann Hudson, Clinton H.S.
Clinton, Mississippi

FROZEN GRAPE AND FRUIT SALAD

    1 11-oz. pkg. cream cheese
    1 carton whipping cream, whipped
    Food coloring (opt.)
    1 sm. bottle green cherries, chopped fine
    1 sm. bottle red cherries, chopped fine
    1 No. 2 can chunk pineapple
    1 15 ½-oz. can white grapes, halved
    1 c. chopped pecans
    1 tbsp. mayonnaise
    ½ c. sugar

Soften cream cheese; add whipping cream and food coloring, if desired. Add remaining ingredients and blend thoroughly. Place in freezer until frozen. Remove about 1 hour before serving and let thaw in refrigerator.

Johnnye Kennedy, Vonore Sch.
Vonore, Tennessee

FROZEN WALDORF SALAD

    2 eggs, slightly beaten
    ½ c. sugar
    ⅛ tsp. salt (opt.)
    ¼ c. lemon juice
    ½ c. pineapple juice
    ½ c. diced celery
    ½ c. drained crushed pineapple
    2 med. apples, chopped
    ½ c. broken walnuts or pecans
    1 c. cream, whipped

Combine eggs, sugar, salt and juices. Cook over low heat, stirring constantly, until mixture thickens; cool. Add celery, pineapple, apples and walnuts; fold in whipped cream. Spoon into 8-inch square pan; freeze. Cut into squares to serve. Yield: 6-8 servings.

Kate Hodges DeGaris, Pell City H.S.
Pell City, Alabama
Mildred Shaffer, F. J. Reitz H.S.
Evansville, Indiana

FROZEN FRUIT COCKTAIL

    2 3-oz. cream cheese
    ½ c. mayonnaise
    1 c. heavy cream, whipped
    1 No. 2 ½ can fruit cocktail, drained
    1 can sliced peaches, drained
    ½ c. quartered maraschino cherries
    ½ c. tiny marshmallows

Soften cream cheese; blend with mayonnaise. Fold in cream; add remaining ingredients. Remove ends from fruit cans; reseal with heavy aluminum foil. Pour salad mixture into cans; freeze for 4 to 6 hours. Push foil end from bottom to remove; slice salad. Yield: 12 servings.

Mrs. Elizabeth M. Jenkins
East Syracuse-Minoa Cen. H.S.
East Syracuse, New York

EASY FROZEN FRUIT SALAD

    1 pkg. lemon Jell-O or other flavor
    Dash of salt
    1 c. boiling water
    1 sm. can crushed pineapple
    ¼ c. lemon juice
    ⅓ c. mayonnaise
    1 c. whipping cream
    1 med. banana, diced
    ½ c. seeded halved grapes
    1 sm. can fruit cocktail, drained
    ¼ c. chopped nuts

Dissolve Jell-O and salt in boiling water. Drain pineapple, measuring syrup; add water to make 1/2 cup liquid if necessary. Stir liquid into gelatin with lemon juice; blend in mayonnaise. Chill until very thick. Whip cream. Fold fruits, nuts and whipped cream into gelatin mixture; pour into freezing trays or loaf pan. Freeze until firm, at least 3 to 4 hours. Cut in squares or slice to serve. Other fruits may be used. Amount of fruit should total 2 cups. Yield: 8 servings.

Mrs. Rudene Myer, McEachern Jr. H.S.
Powder Springs, Georgia

FROZEN FRUIT-GINGER SALAD

    3 oz. cream cheese
    3 tbsp. mayonnaise
    ¼ c. maraschino cherries, sliced
    ¼ c. chopped dates
    ¼ c. preserved kumquats
    ¼ c. diced pineapple
    1 tbsp. chopped candied ginger (opt.)
    1 c. heavy cream whipped
    ½ c. toasted macadamia nuts
    Lettuce
    Pineapple cream dressing

Beat cheese and mayonnaise together until smooth; combine with fruits and ginger. Fold in whipped cream. Pour into freezing tray or refrigerator; sprinkle with nuts. Freeze 2 hours and 30 minutes to 3 hours or until firm. Cut into squares; serve on lettuce with dressing. Diced oranges may be substituted for dates and bananas for kumquats. Mixture may be frozen in juice cans, sliced and served on tomato or pineapple slices. Watercress may be used for garnish. Yield: 8 servings.

Mrs. Anne Beatty Ransing, Ada Merritt Jr. H.S.
Miami, Florida

ORIENTAL FRUIT FREEZE

    1 3-oz. pkg. cream cheese
    3 tbsp. mayonnaise
    1 tbsp. lemon juice
    ¼ tsp. salt
    ½ c. chopped preserved kumquats
    ½ c. dates, cut up
    ¼ c. quartered maraschino cherries

(Continued on next page)

1 c. crushed pineapple, drained
2 tbsp. finely chopped candied ginger (opt.)
1 c. heavy cream, whipped
¼ c. slivered blanched almonds, toasted

Soften cream cheese; blend in mayonnaise, lemon juice and salt. Stir in fruits and ginger. Fold in whipped cream. Pour into refrigerator tray; sprinkle almonds over top. Freeze until firm. Yield: 6-8 servings.

Mary Sullivan Debevec, Chisholm Sr. H.S.
Chisholm, Minnesota

FROZEN FRUIT SALAD

1 8-oz. pkg. cream cheese
1 c. sugar
2 c. mayonnaise
½ pt. cream, whipped
1 No. 2 ½ can fruit cocktail, drained
1 bottle cherries, drained
1 No. 303 can crushed pineapple, drained

Cream cheese and sugar; add mayonnaise. Blend well; fold in cream. Add fruit. Pour into mold or trays; freeze. Yield: 8 servings.

Marilyn Newton, Cobb Jr. H.S.
Tallahassee, Florida

FROZEN FRUIT SALAD

1 No. 2 can fruit cocktail, drained
1 c. crushed pineapple, undrained
½ c. sugar
1 pkg. gelatin
¼ c. cold water
1 c. whipped cream
⅔ c. mayonnaise
2 bananas, diced
2 tbsp. lemon juice
1 c. miniature marshmallows
1 bottle cherries, drained

Combine fruit cocktail and pineapple; sprinkle with sugar. Place gelatin in water; set in pan of hot water and dissolve. Blend cream and mayonnaise; add to fruit and sugar mixture. Add bananas, lemon juice, marshmallows and cherries. Place in glass dish; freeze. Serve on lettuce. Yield: 10 servings.

Mrs. Nonie Lee Hardage, Carthage Sch.
Carthage, Mississippi

BETTY'S FROZEN FRUIT SALAD

1 lge. pkg. cream cheese
1 c. mayonnaise
1 No. 2 can pineapple, drained
1 jar maraschino cherries, drained
1 No. 2 can fruit cocktail, drained
1 bag miniature marshmallows
Juice of 2 lemons
1 lge. can evaporated milk

Cream cheese; add mayonnaise, fruits, marshmallows and juice of 1 lemon. Place milk in ice tray until crystals form; whip rapidly, gradually adding remaining lemon juice. Fold into fruit mixture; freeze for 12 hours. Yield: 12 servings.

Mrs. Betty M. Dillard, Marion Jr. H.S.
Marion, Virginia

FROZEN FRUIT SALAD

2 8-oz. pkg. cream cheese
½ c. salad dressing
2 tbsp. lemon juice
1 ½ c. fruit cocktail, drained
1 ½ c. pineapple pieces, drained
¾ c. nuts
1 c. marshmallows
½ c. minced cherries
1 c. whipped cream

Soften cream cheese with mixer; add salad dressing and lemon juice. Blend well; add fruit cocktail, pineapple, nuts, marshmallows and cherries. Fold in cream; freeze in 13 x 9 x 3-inch pan. Cut into squares; serve on lettuce.

Mrs. Warren Webb, Columbia Jr. H.S.
Columbia, Kentucky

FROZEN FRUIT SALAD

1 pkg. Jell-O, any flavor
1 c. boiling water
1 3-oz. pkg. cream cheese
2 tbsp. mayonnaise
Dash of salt
1 c. whipping cream
½ c. sugar
1 can fruit cocktail, drained
1 8-oz. can pineapple tidbits, drained
4 tbsp. lemon juice
30 miniature marshmallows

Dissolve Jell-O in boiling water. Blend cream cheese with mayonnaise and salt; stir into Jell-O. Whip cream until stiff, adding sugar gradually; fold in cheese mixture, fruit cocktail, pineapple, lemon juice and marshmallows. Pour into waxed paper-lined refrigerator tray; freeze until firm, about 4 hours. Turn out onto platter; cut into thick slices. Serve on lettuce leaves. Yield: 8 servings.

Mrs. Lee Roy Snapp, Lamar H.S.
Jonesboro, Tennessee

Frozen Mixed Fruit Salads

FROZEN FRUIT SALAD

    1 envelope gelatin
    ¼ c. pineapple juice
    2 eggs, beaten
    ¼ c. lemon juice
    ½ c. sugar
    1 ½ c. whipped cream
    24 marshmallows, cut
    1 lge. can fruit cocktail
    1 lge. can pineapple, cut, drained

Dissolve gelatin in pineapple juice; cook eggs, lemon juice and sugar until thick. Add gelatin; cool. Fold cream, marshmallows and fruit into mixture; freeze. Will keep several weeks in freezer. Yield: 10-12 servings.

Mrs. Louis Ivanish, Malta H.S.
Malta, Montana

FROZEN FRUIT SALAD ELEGANTE

    ¼ pt. whipping cream
    ⅓ c. sugar
    3 bananas, mashed
    1 4-oz. pkg. cream cheese
    ½ pkg. miniature marshmallows
    Juice of ½ lemon
    1 No. 202 can fruit cocktail

Whip cream; fold in sugar. Add remaining ingredients. Mix well; freeze. May be stored for several weeks. Yield: 6-8 servings.

Mrs. Willie Lee Everett, Menard H.S.
Menard, Texas

FROZEN FRUIT AND NUT SALAD

    1 tbsp. unflavored gelatin
    2 tbsp. lemon juice
    1 3-oz. pkg. cream cheese, softened
    ¼ c. mayonnaise
    Dash of salt
    ½ c. sugar
    ½ pt. cream, whipped
    ½ c. chopped walnut meats
    ¼ c. chopped pecans
    ½ c. sm. marshmallows
    1 1-lb. 14-oz. can fruit cocktail, drained
    1 1-lb. 4-oz. can pineapple chunks, drained

Combine gelatin and lemon juice; set in pan of boiling water to dissolve. Combine cream cheese, mayonnaise, salt and sugar in large mixer bowl; beat on low speed. Combine all ingredients; pour into 2 disposable aluminum loaf pans. Freeze until firm; slice and serve on lettuce. Yield: 8-10 servings.

Mrs. Ruth Thorne, Imperial Jr. H.S.
Ontario, California

FROZEN FRUIT SALAD

    1 6-oz. pkg. cream cheese
    1 c. sour cream
    3 ½ c. fruit cocktail, drained
    ¼ c. sugar
    2 c. tiny marshmallows
    1 tsp. grated lemon peel
    1 banana, sliced

Blend cheese with sour cream; add fruit cocktail, sugar, marshmallows, lemon peel and banana. Freeze in loaf pan; slice. Serve on salad greens. Yield: 8 servings.

Mrs. J. W. Williams, Independence H.S.
Independence, Mississippi

COTTAGE FROZEN SALAD

    ½ pt. cream, whipped
    1 pt. cottage cheese, creamed
    ½ c. finely chopped nuts
    ½ c. maraschino cherries
    1 c. crushed pineapple
    1 c. fruit cocktail, undrained

Blend cream and cottage cheese; add 1/4 cup nuts, cherries, pineapple and fruit cocktail. Place in ice cube tray; sprinkle with remaining nuts. Freeze. Yield: 6-8 servings.

Mrs. Rowena Ballew, Richland Sr. H.S.
Fort Worth, Texas

FRUIT SALAD

    1 6-oz. pkg. cream cheese, softened
    1 c. sour cream
    3 ½ c. fruit cocktail, drained
    ¼ c. sugar
    2 c. tiny marshmallows
    1 tsp. grated lemon peel
    1 med. banana, sliced

Blend cream cheese with sour cream; add fruit cocktail, sugar, marshmallows, lemon peel and banana. Freeze in loaf pan. Slice; serve on salad greens. Yield: 8 servings.

Pollyanna Rogers, Howe H.S.
Howe, Oklahoma

FROZEN FRUIT SALAD

    1 No. 2 can crushed pineapple
    1 7 ½-oz. pkg. marshmallows
    1 carton whipping cream
    1 No. 2 can fruit cocktail
    3 bananas, chopped
    ¾ c. nuts
    ¼ c. sugar

(Continued on next page)

Pour pineapple over marshmallows in large bowl; cover and let stand overnight. Whip cream; add all ingredients. Freeze in 10 x 14-inch pan. Omit bananas if freezing for long period. Yield: 12 servings.

Mrs. Cheryl Boyd, Wolfe City H.S.
Wolfe City, Texas

LIME FREEZE

½ c. sugar
1 ⅓ c. water
Juice of 2 limes
1 6-oz. bottle Seven-Up
1 egg white, beaten stiff
Green food coloring
4 mint sprigs
2 maraschino cherries

Add sugar and water to lime juice; stir until sugar is dissolved. Add 7-Up; freeze mixture in refrigerator tray until mushy. Beat egg white until stiff peaks form; fold in frozen mixture. Add green food coloring to mixture. Freeze until mixture is fairly firm, but not solid. Spoon into sherbet glasses; decorate with mint sprigs and maraschino cherries. Yield: 4 servings.

Mrs. J. B. Morris, Gooding H.S.
Gooding, Idaho

FROZEN FRUIT SALAD

3 tbsp. mayonnaise
1 3-oz. pkg. cream cheese
1 tbsp. lemon juice
½ tsp. salt
1 c. orange sections, cut in thirds
1 c. fresh fruit in season
1 c. drained crushed pineapple
1 c. chopped pecans
½ c. maraschino cherries, cut into halves
1 c. whipping cream

Blend mayonnaise and cheese together in bowl; add lemon juice and salt. Combine with orange sections, prepared fresh fruit, pineapple, nuts and maraschino cherries. Whip cream; fold in fruit mixture. Pour into individual molds or freezing trays. Set in freezing compartment until frozen, about 3 hours. Unmold individual salads or cut salad into squares. Serve on lettuce, endive or watercress. Suggested fresh fruits are sliced strawberries or raspberries, halved cherries, diced peaches, pears or bananas. Yield: 10 servings.

Sister Loretta Ann Bertels
St. Elizabeth Academy
St. Louis, Missouri

FROZEN FRUIT SALAD

¾ c. fruit juice
2 eggs, well beaten
¾ c. sugar
¼ tsp. salt
½ pt. cream, stiffly beaten
Bananas,
Pineapple
Maraschino cherries
Mandarin oranges

Heat juice; add eggs, sugar and salt. Cook, stirring constantly, until slightly thickened; remove from stove and cool. Add cream. Add desired amount bananas, pineapple, cherries and oranges. Pour into individual molds and freeze. Yield: 10-12 servings.

Marie Hunt, Fruita Jr.-Sr. H.S.
Fruita, Colorado

FROZEN FRUIT SALAD

1 tbsp. unflavored gelatin
1 c. cold water
⅓ c. mayonnaise
1 c. whipping cream, whipped
1 c. drained canned pineapple chunks
1 c. sliced bananas
1 c. cut-up oranges
½ c. nuts
2 tbsp. lemon juice

Soften gelatin in water. Dissolve over hot water; blend into mayonnaise and whipped cream. Fold in pineapple, bananas, oranges, nuts and lemon juice. Pour into refrigerator tray; freeze until firm. Yield: 8 servings.

Janice A. Kindler, Grand Rapids H.S.
Grand Rapids, Ohio

FROZEN FRUIT AND CHEESE SALAD

2 c. cottage cheese
1 c. sour cream
½ c. mayonnaise
3 tbsp. powdered sugar
Salt to taste
1 c. diced mandarin orange sections
½ c. sliced maraschino cherries
½ c. nutmeats, chopped

Press cottage cheese through sieve. Combine sour cream, mayonnaise, sugar and salt; mix thoroughly with cottage cheese. Add fruits and nuts; toss lightly. Pour into 2 refrigerator trays; freeze until firm. Arrange on salad greens; garnish with orange sections and bits of cherry. This will keep about 2 weeks if wrapped in freezer paper. Remove about 10 to 15 minutes before serving for easy cutting. Yield: 12 servings.

Mrs. Caroline Proctor, Olanta H.S.
Olanta, South Carolina

HONEY-FRUIT SALAD

2 tbsp. sugar
1 tbsp. flour
¼ c. strained honey
2 tbsp. water
⅓ c. fresh lemon juice
1 well beaten egg
1 c. sliced bananas
⅓ c. diced orange sections
¼ c. halved maraschino cherries
1 ¼ c. pineapple tidbits
½ c. sm. marshmallows
⅔ c. evaporated milk

Combine sugar, flour, honey and water; bring to boil. Cook 1 minute. Blend in lemon juice and egg; heat to boiling again and cool. Add bananas, oranges, cherries, pineapple and marshmallows. Beat evaporated milk until stiff in chilled bowl with chilled beaters; fold into fruit mixture. Pour into mold or pan; cover and freeze until firm. May be kept frozen for day or more. Yield: 6 servings.

Mrs. Audrey Buhl, Milaca Pub. Schs.
Milaca, Minnesota

FROZEN CHRISTMAS SALAD

1 3-oz. pkg. cream cheese
1 tbsp. mayonnaise
1 c. canned sweet red cherries
½ c. cut up red maraschino cherries
¼ c. cut up green maraschino cherries
¼ c. cut up orange
1 c. crushed, drained pineapple
1 c. chopped English walnuts
1 c. cream, whipped

Soften cheese; blend with mayonnaise. Add cherries, remaining fruit and nuts. Fold whipped cream into mixture; spoon into loaf pan. Cover tightly. Freeze. Yield: 10-12 servings.

Mrs. Sarabell S. Dunlap, Northeastern Sr. H.S.
Manchester, Pennsylvania

GOLDEN FRUIT FREEZE

1 11-oz. can mandarin orange sections, drained and halved
1 8¾-oz. can crushed pineapple, drained
¼ c. sugar
1 c. sm. curd cream-style cottage cheese
1 2-oz. pkg. dessert topping mix
½ c. milk
1 tsp. vanilla
⅓ c. mayonnaise or salad dressing

Combine fruits and sugar; mix well. Combine cottage cheese, dessert topping mix, milk and vanilla in mixing bowl; beat smooth. Fold in fruit

and mayonnaise. Turn into 8 x 8 x 2-inch pan. Freeze. Let stand at room temperature 15 minutes; cut into squares. Yield: 6-8 servings.

Mrs. Ella Jo Adams, Allen Sr. H.S.
Allen, Texas

FESTIVE FRUIT FREEZE

1 14-oz. can sliced pineapple
1 c. sugar
2 tbsp. flour
½ tsp. salt
2 eggs, beaten
3 tbsp. vinegar
1 c. whipped cream
½ 10-oz. pkg. miniature marshmallows
4 bananas, sliced
1 10-oz. can mandarin oranges, drained
1 14-oz. can fruit cocktail, drained
¼ c. quartered maraschino cherries

Drain pineapple; combine juice with sugar, flour, salt, eggs and vinegar in a saucepan. Cook, stirring, over medium heat until thickened. Cool. Fold in whipped cream. Lightly stir in marshmallows, bananas, mandarin oranges, fruit cocktail and cherries. Cut pineapple slices into chunks; stir in. Spoon into an 18 x 9 x 2 1/2-inch pan. Freeze. Cut into squares and serve on lettuce leaves.

Pamela Redd, Magrath H.S.
Magrath, Alberta, Canada

FROZEN FRUIT SALAD

1 pt. heavy cream
½ c. sugar
¼ c. orange juice
2 c. salad dressing
1 c. diced pineapple
½ c. grapes or white cherries
1 c. diced peaches
½ c. diced oranges
¼ c. diced bananas
¼ c. chopped nutmeats

Whip cream to consistency of custard; fold in remaining ingredients in order listed. Freeze in ice trays. Slice and serve on lettuce. Yield: 10 servings.

Cynthia E. Meier, Brock H.S.
Brock, Nebraska

FROZEN FRUIT LOAF

1 3-oz. pkg. cream cheese
1 9-oz. can crushed pineapple, drained
1 7-oz. bottle Seven-Up

(Continued on next page)

½ c. sugar
1 c. diced peaches
1 c. diced seedless grapes
½ pt. whipping cream
1 ½ c. miniature marshmallows

Soften cream cheese; mix in pineapple. Stir in 7-Up. Sprinkle sugar over peaches and grapes; stir into cheese mixture. Pour into 2-quart refrigerator dish; freeze until partially thickened. Whip cream until stiff; fold cream and marshmallows into fruit mixture. Freeze until solid. Cut into squares and serve on lettuce leaves. Yield: 8 servings.

Elizabeth Treenepohl, Angola H.S.
Angola, Indiana

MERRY CHERRY SALAD

1 c. diced canned peaches and ¼ c. syrup
1 8 ¾-oz. can pineapple tidbits and ¼ c. syrup
½ c. chopped maraschino cherries, drained
1 pkg. strawberry flavored gelatin
1 c. hot water
½ tsp. salt
1 tsp. maraschino cherry syrup
1 tbsp. lemon juice
1 3-oz. pkg. cream cheese, softened
2 tbsp. mayonnaise
1 c. miniature marshmallows
½ c. chilled whipping cream

Butter 9-inch pie pan or individual molds. Chill pan, bowl and rotary beater in refrigerator. Combine peaches, pineapple tidbits and maraschino cherries. Chill in refrigerator. Pour gelatin into bowl. Blend in hot water and salt and stir until gelatin is completely dissolved. Stir in peach, pineapple and cherry syrups and lemon juice. Refrigerate until gelatin is consistency of thick, unbeaten egg white. Beat cream cheese and mayonnaise together until fluffy. Beat until light and fluffy, when gelatin mixture is of desired consistency. Stir several tablespoons into cream cheese. Add gelatin mixture slowly, beating constantly until well blended. Stir in chilled fruit and marshmallows. Heat cream until it is of medium consistency, using chilled bowl and beaters. Fold cream into gelatin mixture. Turn into pie pan and freeze 4 hours. Cut into wedges.

Mrs. Ethel Moses, Hyatt H.S.
Fields, Louisiana

GINGER ALE-FRUIT SALAD

2 tbsp. fruit juices
32 marshmallows
1 ½ c. crushed pineapple, drained
1 lge. bottle cherries, drained
1 c. drained peaches, cut fine
1 c. mayonnaise
2 c. ginger ale
1 c. whipped cream, whipped

Mix fruit juices and marshmallows and melt over low heat until half dissolved. Remove and stir until smooth. Fold in fruit and remaining ingredients except cream. Fold in cream. Freeze without stirring. Yield: 8-12 servings.

Carolyn Whitley, Morgantown Jr. H.S.
Natchez, Mississippi

FROZEN STRAWBERRY-PINEAPPLE SALAD

30 lge. marshmallows, cut into sm. pieces
1 No. 2 ½ can crushed pineapple
2 pkg. frozen strawberries, thawed
3 bananas, cut up
1 c. cream, whipped

Soak marshmallows overnight in crushed pineapple. Add strawberries and bananas; beat thoroughly. Fold in whipped cream; place in pan. Freeze. Yield: 8-10 servings.

Virginia Curran, Swope Jr. H.S.
Reno, Nevada

FROZEN STRAWBERRY SALAD

1 pkg. strawberry gelatin
1 c. boiling water
1 pkg. frozen strawberries, defrosted
1 med. banana, sliced
1 c. seeded Tokay grape halves
4 marshmallows, cut

Dissolve gelatin in hot water; cool but do not allow to jell. Add strawberries, bananas, grape halves and marshmallows. Pour into oiled molds; chill until firm. Unmold; serve on crisp salad greens. Yield: 5-7 servings.

Mrs. Nonie Lee Hardage, Carthage Sch.
Carthage, Mississippi

PEAR SALAD

1 No. 303 can pear halves, drained
1 8-oz. pkg. cream cheese
Pear syrup

Combine pear syrup and cream cheese in blender; blend thoroughly. Slice pears into 4 x 8 pan. Pour cream cheese mixture over pear slices. Freeze. Cut frozen pear mixture into squares to serve; place on salad greens. Yield: 6 servings.

Mrs. Robert Blatchley, Homer Central H.S.
Homer, New York

CREAMY FROZEN FRUIT SALAD

2 3-oz. pkg. cream cheese
1 c. mayonnaise
1 c. heavy cream, whipped
½ c. red maraschino cherries, quartered
½ c. green maraschino cherries, quartered
1 No. 2 can crushed pineapple, drained
2 ½ c. diced marshmallows

Combine cheese and mayonnaise; blend until smooth. Fold in whipped cream, fruit and marshmallows. Pour into 1 quart refrigerator tray. Freeze until firm. Yield: 8-10 servings.

Hilda G. Rohlf, Tallmadge H.S.
Tallmadge, Ohio

FROZEN FRUIT AND CHEESE SALAD

1 c. drained shredded pineapple
1 tbsp. lemon juice
¼ tsp. salt
2 3-oz. pkg. cream cheese
1 c. mayonnaise
1 c. cream, whipped
⅓ c. maraschino cherries, cut into strips or halved

Mix pineapple, lemon juice and salt. Mash cheese with fork; work in mayonnaise gradually. Fold in whipped cream. Combine with pineapple mixture. Add cherries. Pour into refrigerator tray. Freeze without stirring until firm. Do not allow fruit to freeze. Yield: 8 servings.

Mrs. Charlotte Clarke, Central H.S.
Aberdeen, South Dakota
Mrs. Bertha McGee, Nugent Center H.S.
Benoit, Mississippi

FROZEN HAWAIIAN SALAD

2 No. 2 cans crushed pineapple
12 oz. cream cheese
4 ½ c. miniature marshmallows
2 tbsp. mayonnaise
½ c. maraschino cherries, quartered (opt.)
½ c. chopped nutmeats (opt.)
1 pt. whipping cream, stiffly whipped

Heat pineapple; let cool. Soften cream cheese by stirring. Add to cooled pineapple. Stir in marshmallows and mayonnaise. Add cherries and chopped nuts. Fold in whipped cream. Freeze several hours or overnight in square or rectangular pans or in individual molds. Cut into serving portions or turn out onto lettuce leaf. Yield: 40 servings.

Sister Teresa Edward, St. Agnes H.S.
Rochester, New York

FROZEN PINEAPPLE

1 pt. sour cream
1 can crushed pineapple with juice
Juice of 1 lemon
½ c. sugar
Red and green maraschino cherries (opt.)

Mix all ingredients together. Place in freezer overnight or until well frozen. Yield: 8 servings.

Mrs. Phyllis C. Pratt, Canaseraga Central H.S.
Canaseraga, New York

FROZEN PINEAPPLE-CHEESE SALAD

½ pt. whipping cream
¼ c. mayonnaise
1 jar pimento cheese
1 No. 2 can pineapple, crushed
1 c. sm. marshmallows
¼ c. nuts
1 c. maraschino cherries

Whip cream; add mayonnaise and cheese. Blend together. Add pineapple, marshmallows, nuts and cherries. Place in ice tray; place in freezer. Yield: 12 servings.

Maxine King, Unity H.S.
Mendon, Illinois

MARY'S FROZEN FRUIT SALAD

½ c. cream cheese
¼ c. mayonnaise
½ lb. miniature marshmallows
1 c. pineapple, drained
½ c. maraschino cherries, quartered
1 c. heavy cream, whipped

Cream cheese; add mayonnaise, marshmallows, pineapple and cherries. Fold in whipped cream. Pour into mold or glass baking dish; cover with Saran wrap. Freeze. Yield: 10-12 servings.

Mary Hale, Comm. Sch.
Unionville, Tennessee

PERKY SPRING SALAD

2 13-oz. cans crushed pineapple
1 10-oz. pkg. miniature marshmallows
1 pkg. lime Jell-O
1 pt. of cream, whipped
½ pkg. crushed butter mints
1 tbsp. creme de menthe

Combine pineapple, marshmallows and prepared Jell-O; refrigerate overnight. Blend in cream, mints and creme de menthe. Pour into 8 x 12-inch pan. Freeze. Yield: 12-15 servings.

Mrs. Jo Anne Tuttle, Spencer Jr. H.S.
Spencer, Iowa

Fruit Salads

RECIPE FOR CITRUS SALAD ON PAGE 127

CINNAMON APPLES

1 ½ c. sugar
2 c. water
1 sm. pkg. (about 1 c.) red hots
6 lge. cooking apples
1 8-oz. pkg. cream cheese
2 to 3 tbsp. salad dressing
2 to 3 tbsp. chopped nuts

Combine sugar, water and red hots; boil until dissolved. Core and peel apples; place in dissolved sauce and simmer until tender to prick of toothpick. Sauce needs to cover at least 3/4 of the apple as it cooks. Turn apples gently for uniform red color. Remove from sauce when done. Combine remaining ingredients; stuff hollowed core of apple. Garnish with parsley. Yield: 6 servings.

Mrs. Sue S. Reeves, Ames H.S.
Ames, Iowa

CINNAMON-APPLE SALAD

6 firm apples, peeled and cored
1 c. water
1 c. cinnamon drops
2 c. sugar
Chopped nuts
Cream cheese
Mayonnaise

Place apples in open pan on top of stove; pour water, cinnamon drops and sugar over apples. Cook slowly, turning frequently in syrup. Remove apples from syrup when done with strainer; place on crisp lettuce leaf. Fill centers with chopped nuts, cream cheese and mayonnaise. Yield: 6 servings.

Eleanor Waller, Howard Sch.
Nashville, Tennessee

STUFFED APPLE RING SALAD

4 or 5 red apples
Lemon juice or pineapple juice
½ lb. cream cheese
½ c. chopped dates
¼ c. chopped nuts

Wash apples but do not pare; cut in 1/2-inch slices. Remove core, leaving a ring about 1/2 to 1 inch wide. Brush with juice. Mash cream cheese; beat until smooth. Add dates, nuts and small amount of lemon juice; mix well. Place rings on flat surface; fill with cream cheese mixture, spreading smooth with spatula or top each ring with ball of cream cheese. Arrange shredded lettuce; serve with French dressing. Yield: 8 servings.

Mrs. Thelma M. Ash, George Wythe Jr. H.S.
Hampton, Virginia

FRUIT CUP SALAD

3 tart, pared, thinly sliced apples
2 tbsp. lemon juice
2 tbsp. sugar
¼ c. slivered almonds
½ c. sour cream

Coat apples with lemon juice and sugar; place in individual bowls. Saute slivered almonds; drain. Sprinkle over apples; add rounded tablespoon sour cream. Yield: 6 servings.

Mrs. Billie Nowlin
Rising Star H.S.
Rising Star, Texas

APRICOT SALAD

½ c. butter
½ c. sugar
1 egg yolk
1 No. 2 can apricots, drained
½ c. marshmallows, chopped
½ c. chopped nuts

Cream butter and sugar; add egg yolk. Heat slowly, stirring constantly until thick. Pour over apricots and chopped marshmallows; add nuts. Whip cream; fold into apricot mixture. Chill well. Other fruits such as peaches may be used. Yield: 6 servings.

Mrs. Frankie Sue Johnson, Wyandotte H.S.
Wyandotte, Oklahoma

APRICOT SALAD

8 apricot halves, well drained
Salad greens
2 tbsp. chopped celery
2 tbsp. chopped pecans
4 tbsp. salad dressing
4 tbsp. whipped cream
½ tsp. salt

Arrange apricots on salad greens. Combine celery and pecans with salad dressing mixed with whipped cream. Add salt and blend. Garnish apricot halves with salad dressing mixture. Yield: 4 servings.

Mrs. Diane Dilges, Jefferson H.S.
Jefferson, South Dakota

MOLDED APRICOT SALAD

1 lge. can apricots
¼ lb. grated cheddar cheese
1 c. chopped pecans
½ c. sugar
2 tbsp. flour
1 egg

(Continued on next page)

Drain apricots and reserve liquid. Place layer of apricots in oblong casserole; add layer of cheese, layer of pecans. Combine reserved juice with sugar, flour and egg; cook until thick. Pour over fruit-cheese mixture; chill before serving. Yield: 8 servings.

Mrs. Aleta B. Nelson, Tidehaven H.S.
Blessing, Texas

AVOCADO APPETIZER SALAD

2 avocados, halved
Lemon juice
Mayonnaise
Cranberry jelly
Watercress

Drench avocados with lemon juice. Thin mayonnaise with small amount of lemon juice; fill seed cavity. Add 1 spoonful of cranberry jelly. Serve on bed of watercress. Yield: 4 servings.

Dorothy Newman, Hawthorne Cedar Knolls Sch.
Hawthorne, New York

GUACAMOLE

1 to 2 tsp. chili powder
3 tbsp. chili sauce
4 dashes Tabasco sauce
⅓ c. mayonnaise
1 tbsp. lemon juice
1 envelope exotic herbs salad dressing mix
1 sm. grated onion
2 lge. avocados, pureed

Combine all ingredients; mix well. Spoon into quart jar; seal tightly and chill 1 hour. Avocado mixture will darken if not covered tightly. Serve in small mounds on shredded lettuce or romaine. May be used as dip. Yield: 8-12 servings.

Janice Smithson, Wasco Union H.S.
Wasco, California

GUACAMOLE SALAD

1 lge. avocado, peeled, mashed with fork
1 3-oz. pkg. cream cheese
2 tbsp. mayonnaise
1 tbsp. (or more) lemon juice
½ tsp. salt
¼ tsp. pepper
¼ tsp. hot sauce

Mix all ingredients well. Serve on lettuce cups. May be used as hors d' oeuvre spread. Yield: 3 servings.

Mrs. Ora L. Kemple, Caldwell Sr. H.S.
Caldwell, Texas

BANANA GINGERED SALAD

½ c. finely chopped pecans or English walnuts
½ c. finely chopped crystallized ginger
4 bananas
Lettuce
Mayonnaise

Mix nuts and ginger. Roll bananas whole or cut into thirds or fourths in nut-ginger mixture. Arrange on crisp lettuce or shredded Bibb lettuce; drizzle with mayonnaise. Mayonnaise may be thinned with small amount of juice if desired. Yield: 4 servings.

Mrs. Ella Furr Long, Marks H.S.
Marks, Mississippi

BANANA-NUT SALAD

4 ripe bananas
1 head lettuce
½ tsp. mayonnaise
2 tbsp. finely chopped nuts

Cut bananas in half crosswise; remove peelings. Cut each banana half lengthwise. Place 4 or more pieces on lettuce leaf. Place a small amount of mayonnaise on center of banana pieces. Top mayonnaise with nuts, preferably walnuts. Yield: 6 servings.

Mrs. V. S. Trahan, Abbeville H.S.
Abbeville, Louisiana

CRANBERRY SALAD

2 c. fresh cranberries
½ c. coarsely chopped pecans
½ c. sugar
1 c. whipped cream

Chop cranberries fine with food chopper or blender. Mix in pecans and sugar; chill. Fold in whipped cream before serving. Yield: 4 servings.

Sherry Goff, Estancia Municipal Sch.
Estancia, New Mexico

DREAMY SALAD

1 c. flaked coconut
1 c. drained fruit cocktail
1 c. miniature marshmallows
½ c. chopped pecans

Mix all ingredients together; chill for several hours. Yield: 6 servings.

Carol Simpson, Brusly H.S.
Brusly, Louisiana

Mixed Fruit Salads

FRUIT COCKTAIL SALAD

    ½ pt. whipping cream
    1 8-oz. can fruit cocktail
    1 4-oz. pkg. cottage cheese

Whip cream for about 3 minutes. Pour fruit cocktail into bowl; add cottage cheese. Pour in whipped cream. Chill. Serve on lettuce. Yield: 6-8 servings.

Mamie Jean Williams, Glen Allan H.S.
Glen Allan, Mississippi

FRUIT-MALLOW DELIGHT

    1 c. sour cream
    1 c. shredded coconut
    1 c. miniature marshmallows
    1 1-lb. 14-oz. can fruit cocktail, drained

Combine all ingredients. Chill for 2 hours or longer. Spoon into dessert bowls. Yield: 6 servings.

Mrs. Bernice B. Hodges, Bartlett Yancey H.S.
Yanceyville, North Carolina

A GOOD FRUIT SALAD

    1 No. 2½ can fruit cocktail
    1 3-oz. pkg. cream cheese
    1 tbsp. (heaping) mayonnaise
    ¼ c. fruit cocktail juice
    2 c. miniature marshmallows
    ½ c. nuts

Drain fruit cocktail; mix cream cheese with mayonnaise. Add juice. Mix with marshmallows and fruit; add nuts. Chill. Yield: 6 servings.

Mrs. Zelda Austin, Avery H.S.
Avery, Texas

OVERNIGHT SALAD

    2 eggs
    ¼ c. lemon juice
    2 tbsp. butter
    ¼ c. sugar
    1 c. cream, whipped
    1 lge. can fruit cocktail, well drained
    1 sm. pkg. marshmallows

Beat eggs; add lemon juice, butter and sugar. Cook over low heat or in double boiler until thick, stirring constantly. Cool thoroughly. Whip cream and fold into cooked mixture. Add fruit cocktail and marshmallows. Chill overnight. Yield: 6 servings.

Mrs. Eleanore Midahl, Belgrade H.S.
Belgrade, Minnesota

SOUR CREAM DREAM SALAD

    1 c. sour cream
    1 c. miniature marshmallows
    1 No. 2½ can fruit cocktail, well drained

Mix sour cream, marshmallows and fruit cocktail together. Place mixture in 9-inch square pan. Refrigerate for 4 hours or longer. Salad may be prepared day before serving. Yield: 6-8 servings.

June Schellin, Sante Fe H.S.
Sante Fe Springs, California

WHIPPED SURPISE

    1 pkg. whipped topping
    1 5-oz. can fruit cocktail
    ½ c. halved maraschino cherries
    1 tsp. lemon juice
    2 c. miniature marshmallows

Prepare topping; add remaining ingredients. Chill 1 hour and serve. Yield: 6 servings.

Mrs. Gordon MacDonald
Prince of Wales Collegiate Sch.
St. John's, Newfoundland, Canada

AMBROSIA SALAD

    ¾ c. diced oranges
    2 ripe bananas, sliced
    ½ c. seedless grapes
    ¼ c. pitted dates, cut up
    3 tbsp. lemon juice
    ¼ c. flaked coconut
    Mayonnaise
    Whipped cream

Combine first 4 ingredients. Sprinkle with lemon juice; chill. Mix mayonnaise with whipped cream for creamy dressing; fold into fruits. Serve on crisp lettuce, sprinkled with coconut. Yield: 4 servings.

Mrs. Virginia Smith, North H.S.
Evansville, Indiana

AMBROSIA

    3 c. pineapple chunks
    5 med. oranges
    2 fully ripe bananas
    2 c. seedless or seeded grapes, halved
    1 3½-oz. can flaked coconut
    1 c. ginger ale (opt.)
    Whole maraschino cherries

Drain pineapple; reserve juice. Pare and section orange; reserve juice. Slice bananas on bias;

(Continued on next page)

place in orange juice. Place half the fruits in bowl; sprinkle with half the coconut. Top with remaining fruit. Pour reserved pineapple juice over all; chill thoroughly. At serving time, pour ginger ale over all. Sprinkle with remaining coconut; dot with whole maraschino cherries. Yield: 8-12 servings.

Mary Ellen Freer, Canastota Jr.-Sr. H.S.
Canastota, New York

ANISE FRUIT SALAD

1 c. sugar
¼ tsp. aniseed
1 ½ c. water
Dash of salt
1 lb. seedless grapes
4 bananas, sliced
5 apples, diced
1 can mandarin orange sections

Combine sugar, aniseed, water and salt in saucepan; boil 3 to 4 minutes. Cool. Mix fruits together. Pour syrup over fruit. Yield: 12 servings.

Susan Peterson, Amboy Public Sch.
Amboy, Minnesota

APPLE-NUT SALAD

1 c. sugar
4 tbsp. flour
1 c. water
1 well-beaten egg
2 tbsp. vinegar
2 bananas, cubed
4 apples, cubed
½ c. chopped nuts

Mix sugar, flour and water; stir until lump free. Add egg and vinegar; cook until thick or about 2 minutes. Cool. Combine bananas, apples and nuts. Serve with sauce on lettuce leaf. Yield: 6-8 servings.

Mrs. Joye Parish, Marthaville H.S.
Marthaville, Louisiana

APPLE SALAD

6 red apples, chopped
3 tbsp. broken nuts
½ c. chopped dates
2 bananas, diced
1 c. diced pineapple
3 tbsp. mayonnaise

Combine ingredients with mayonnaise; serve on lettuce. Yield: 6 servings.

Mrs. Thelma Bishop Ruddell, Greenville Jr. H.S.
Greenville, West Virginia

APPLE SALAD

1 diced, unpeeled apple
1 tbsp. raisins, washed
1 tbsp. chopped walnuts
2 tbsp. cream
1 tbsp. sugar
2 cherries

Combine apples, raisins, walnuts, cream and sugar. Place in mound on small plate; garnish with cherry. Yield: 2 servings.

Mrs. Mabel I. Rogers, Central Jr. H.S.
Dawson Creek, British Columbia, Canada

APPLE SALAD DELIGHT

3 c. diced apples, unpeeled
1 c. green seedless grapes, halved
½ c. chopped walnuts
⅓ c. chopped almonds
Berry sugar
Mayonnaise
Cream
Nutmeg

Combine apples, grapes and nuts. Sprinkle with small amount of berry sugar. Thin mayonnaise with cream; add to fruit. Top with sprinkling of nutmeg; chill. Serve on lettuce leaves. Yield: 6-8 servings.

F. Pauline Foster, Carstairs H.S.
Carstairs, Alberta, Canada

COTTAGE APPLE SALAD

4 med. apples, quartered, cored and diced
½ c. golden raisins
½ c. chopped walnuts
1 tbsp. sugar
1 tbsp. lemon juice
¼ c. cream-style cottage cheese
¼ c. sour cream

Combine apples, raisins and walnuts. Sprinkle sugar and lemon juice over combination and toss lightly. Blend cottage cheese and sour cream in cup; spoon over apple mixture and toss lightly. Yield: 6 servings.

Mrs. Shirley Glenn, Centennial Jr. H.S.
Circle Pines, Minnesota

STUFFED RED APPLES

2 c. sugar
4 c. water
1 tsp. red food coloring
1 pkg. red hots (opt.)
8 sm. apples, cored
1 6-oz. pkg. cream cheese
½ c. chopped nuts
½ c. chopped raisins
½ c. crushed pineapple
½ c. whole milk

(Continued on next page)

Combine sugar, water, food coloring and red hots; add apples and simmer until tender. Remove apples; pour syrup over top. Let set until apples absorb apple jelly which is formed. Mix cream cheese, nuts, fruit and milk; fill cavities of cooled apples. Yield: 8 servings.

Mrs. Evelyn H. Duke, Caldwell H.S.
Columbia, Louisiana

AVOCADO-PINEAPPLE SALAD

2 avocados
2 tbsp. lemon juice
Lettuce
1 c. well-drained crushed pineapple
1 8-oz. pkg. cream cheese
Dash of salt
Pimento strips
Lemon slices
French dressing

Cut avocados in half crosswise; remove seeds. Slice each half into 3 rings; peel. Sprinkle with lemon juice. Place 2 avocado rings for each serving on lettuce on salad plate. Combine pineapple, cream cheese and salt; blend well. Fill centers of avocado rings with pineapple mixture. Garnish with strips of pimento and lemon slices; serve with French dressing. Cottage cheese may be used instead of cream cheese. Yield: 6 servings.

Mrs. C. M. Dees, Delmar H.S.
Paris, Texas

AVOCADO AND PINEAPPLE SALAD

1 ripe avocado
4 slices fresh or canned pineapple
2 tbsp. olive oil
2 tbsp. lemon or lime juice or vinegar
¼ tsp. salt

Remove peel and pit from avocado; cut avocado and grapefruit into 1/2 inch cubes. Chill. Combine remaining ingredients; shake well and pour over fruit. Serve on lettuce or other salad greens. Yield: 4 servings.

Anne Martin, Lakeview Comm. Schs.
Lakeview, Michigan

AVOCADO SALAD

3 avocados
1 c. pineapple cubes
1 grape, cut in halves
2 oranges, peeled and cut into pieces
French Dressing
Lettuce
Fresh mint

Cut avocados into halves lengthwise; scoop out pulp with French vegetable cutter. Reserve shells. Combine with remaining fruit; marinate in French dressing about 20 minutes. Fill avocado shells; serve on lettuce. Garnish with fresh mint. Add 1/2 cup grapefruit segments if desired. Yield: 6 servings.

Mrs. Annie R. Gonzales, Prescott Jr. H.S.
Baton Rouge, Louisiana

AVOCADO SALAD

4 tbsp. olive oil
4 tsp. fresh lime juice
5 drops Tabasco sauce
⅛ tsp. pepper
Dash of cayenne
¼ tsp. salt
1 tsp. celery salt
2 tsp. sugar
1 to 2 oranges, sectioned, diced
1 grapefruit, sectioned, diced
2 to 4 avocados, halved
Maraschino cherries (opt.)

Combine first 8 ingredients; mix thoroughly. Chill to ripen. Combine orange and grapefruit sections. Shake dressing mixture well; pour over fruit and toss until well coated. Fill avocado cavity with fruit and garnish with cherries if desired. Yield: 4-8 servings.

Niva J. Reddick, Largo Sr. H.S.
Largo, Florida

AVOCADO WITH FRUIT STUFFING

½ pt. sour cream
¼ c. grapefruit juice
1 tsp. vinegar
½ tsp. ginger
½ tsp. tarragon
¼ tsp. salt
¼ tsp. Tabasco sauce
4 tangarines or 1 13-oz. can mandarin
   oranges
6 avocados

(Continued on next page)

Combine sour cream, grapefruit juice, vinegar, ginger, tarragon, salt and Tabasco sauce. Let stand in refrigerator for 1 hour. Cut tangerines in thirds and add just before serving. Cut avocados in half; remove seed but do not peel. Place fruit stuffing in each half. Yield: 12 servings.

Mrs. Jewel Hoogstoel, Endwell Jr. H.S.
Endwell, New York

CALIFORNIA SALAD

2 grapefruit
1 sm. can mandarin oranges
2 lge. avocados
3 tbsp. lemon juice
Lettuce leaves
Green Goddess dressing

Chill grapefruit and orange sections; pare avocados and slice into approximately 12 to 14 slices each. Sprinkle avocado slices with lemon juice; arrange with grapefruit and orange sections on lettuce leaves. Top with Green Goddess dressing, and serve chilled. Yield: 4 servings.

Mrs. Judith G. Blankenship, Merkel H.S.
Merkel, Texas

FRUIT SALAD IN AVOCADO BOATS

3 med.-sized ripe avocados
2 tsp. fresh lime juice
1 c. fresh grapefruit sections
1 c. fresh pineapple wedges
¼ c. olive or salad oil
1 tbsp. vinegar
1 tsp. fresh lemon juice
½ tsp. salt
⅛ tsp. ground black pepper
½ tsp. ground cumin seed

Wash avocados; cut in half and remove seeds. Brush with lime juice to prevent discoloration. Fill cavities with grapefruit and pineapple. Combine remaining ingredients. Beat with rotary beater and serve over salad. Yield: 6 servings.

Photograph for this recipe on inside front cover.

GREEN AND GOLD SALAD

1 c. canned pineapple chunks, drained
1 c. fresh grapefruit sections, drained
1 c. avocado cubes
Lettuce
1 3-oz. pkg. cream cheese
Mayonnaise
Lettuce

Combine fruits; toss lightly. Spoon onto lettuce leaf. Thin softened cream cheese with mayonnaise; serve with fruit. Yield: 6 servings.

Mrs. Ava Bush, Grapeland H.S.
Grapeland, Texas

SUNSHINE SALAD

4 orange sections
4 grapefruit sections
4 slices avocado
3 or 4 romaine leaves
2 strips pimento (opt.)
Salad dressing

Arrange orange, grapefruit and avocado on romaine. Garnish with pimento, if desired. Serve with salad dressing. Yield: 1 serving.

Emily Daniel, Tacisot County Sch.
Tacbotton, Georgia

BANANA-NUT SALAD

2 bananas, sliced
1 8-oz. can pineapple chunks, drained
2 oranges, sectioned
½ c. salted peanuts
1 c. mayonnaise
Maraschino cherries
Lettuce

Combine all ingredients except cherries and lettuce. Chill. Serve on lettuce leaves. Garnish with cherries. Yield: 6 servings.

Mary Malone, Cottage Grove H.S.
Cottage Grove, Tennessee

BANANA AND ORANGE SALAD

1 head lettuce
2 or 3 bananas, sliced
2 oranges, sliced
1 tbsp. sugar
½ c. Miracle Whip salad dressing
3 tbsp. milk

Wash lettuce in cold water; wrap in kitchen towel to dry. Place in refrigerator for 15 minutes for crispness. Break lettuce into bite-sized chunks. Place bananas and oranges in salad bowl. Mix sugar into salad dressing; gradually add milk. Pour over salad.

Carol Ann Krug, Frankenmuth H.S.
Frankenmuth, Michigan

BANANA-PINEAPPLE SALAD

    2 lge. straight bananas
    4 lge. lettuce leaves
    6 slices canned pineapple
    1 tbsp. butter
    2 tsp. flour
    3 tbsp. milk
    1 egg yolk
    2 tbsp. pineapple juice
    2 tbsp. sugar
    ⅛ tsp. salt
    ⅛ tsp. dry mustard
    8 maraschino cherries, halved

Slice bananas lengthwise into equal halves. Place cut side down on lettuce-lined salad plate. Cut each pineapple slice in half. Place 3 halves over each banana like arches, spacing evenly. Melt butter; blend in flour. Add milk; cook over direct heat, stirring constantly, until mixture boils and thickens. Stir in beaten egg yolk; cook 1 minute longer, stirring. Remove from heat; stir in juice, sugar, salt and mustard. Chill. Pour over fruit. Garnish with cherries. Yield: 4 servings.

Mrs. Corinne Schroeder, Healy Memorial H.S.
Trempealeau, Wisconsin

BUCKEMEAL

    2 c. whipping cream
    ½ c. ground oatmeal
    ⅔ c. powdered sugar
    1 tsp. vanilla
    ½ tsp. almond extract
    2 c. grapes
    ½ c. chopped cherries
    2 c. peaches
    2 bananas
    ½ c. pecans
    ½ tsp. ascorbic acid mixture

Whip cream until it stands in peaks. Fold in oatmeal, sugar, vanilla and almond extract. Add grapes, cherries, peaches, bananas and pecans. Add ascorbic acid mixture to keep bananas from turning dark. Fresh fruit is best for this salad. Yield: 8-10 servings.

Mrs. Mary Lee Haby, La Pryor H.S.
La Pryor, Texas

CHERRY-CREAM SALAD

    1 1-lb. can pitted, dark sweet cherries,
        drained
    ½ c. chopped pecans
    2 1-oz. cans mandarin oranges, drained
    1 c. dairy sour cream

Combine all ingredients. Place in mold or pan and chill thoroughly. Garnish with additional cherries, oranges and pecan halves if desired. Yield: 6 servings.

Mrs. Eileen Olson, Siren H.S.
Siren, Wisconsin

BEST YET FRUIT SALAD

    1 No. 3 can pineapple chunks
    1 10-oz. pkg. marshmallows, cut up
    1 lge. and 1 sm. pkg. cream cheese, cubed
    1 No. 3 can Royal Anne cherries, drained
        and pitted
    ½ pt. whipping cream, whipped

Drain pineapple; reserve juice. Heat reserved juice; add marshmallows and cream cheese. Cook until smooth; cool. Add cherries, pineapple and whipped cream; mix well. Pour into individual molds or large dish; refrigerate until chilled or overnight. Serve on crisp lettuce leaf. Yield: 10 servings.

Mrs. Floyd Craig, Divide H.S.
Nolan, Texas

CHERRY SALAD

    1 c. sweet cream or evaporated milk
    1 c. sugar
    3 tbsp. flour
    1 qt. sour cherries, pitted
    4 bananas, sliced
    2 c. miniature marshmallows
    1 c. shredded coconut
    1 c. chopped nuts

Cook first 3 ingredients until thickened over low heat; chill thoroughly. Combine remaining ingredients; fold in chilled dressing. Pour into mold or dish; refrigerate. Yield: 12 servings.

Mrs. Oleta M. Smith, O'Donnell H.S.
O'Donnell, Texas

FESTIVE SALAD

    3 egg yolks, well beaten
    ½ c. cream
    ¼ c. lemon juice
    ⅛ tsp. salt
    1 No. 2½ can Royal Anne cherries, pitted
    1 No. 2 can pineapple, cut into small pieces
    1½ c. almonds, blanched and slivered
    ½ lb. marshmallows, cut into pieces
    1 c. heavy cream, whipped

Combine egg yolks, cream, lemon juice and salt in double boiler; cook over boiling water until thick, stirring constantly. Cool mixture; fold in fruits, nuts, marshmallows and whipped cream. Pour into large shallow pan or bowl; chill for several hours or overnight. Serve on lettuce with cherry garnish. Yield: 12 servings.

Magdalene Beehler, Mount St. Benedict Academy
Crookston, Minnesota

TWENTY FOUR-HOUR SALAD WITH BLACK CHERRIES

3 egg yolks
2 tbsp. sugar
Dash of salt
2 tbsp. vinegar
2 tbsp. pineapple syrup
1 tbsp. butter
1 c. heavy cream, whipped
2 c. black cherries
2 c. miniature marshmallows
2 c. pineapple bits
1 can mandarin oranges

Cook egg yolks, sugar, salt, vinegar, pineapple syrup and butter in double boiler until thick; cool. Fold in whipped cream, cherries, marshmallows, pineapple and oranges. Chill 24 hours. Yield: 12 servings.

Eleanor Sturman, Blue Ridge Sch.
New Milford, Pennsylvania

TWENTY FOUR-HOUR SALAD WITH CHERRIES

2 egg yolks
2 tbsp. sugar
⅓ tsp. salt
¼ c. cream
1 c. drained white cherries, halved
1 c. drained pineapple chunks
1¼ c. miniature marshmallows
1 c. chopped nuts

Combine egg yolks, sugar and salt in double boiler; cook until thick. Cool. Whip cream; add to cooled mixture. Mix with fruits, marshmallows and nuts. Pour into medium mold; chill for 24 hours. Yield: 8 servings.

Dianne Undem O'Neill, Terry H.S.
Terry, Montana

WHITE SALAD

1 No. 2½ can sliced pineapple, cut up
1 No. 2½ can white cherries, pitted and cut up
½ lb. lge. marshmallows, quartered
Juice of 1 lemon
4 egg yolks, beaten
1 c. milk
Pinch of salt
⅛ tsp. dry mustard
1 tsp. cornstarch
1 c. cream, whipped

Combine pineapple, cherries, marshmallows and half the lemon juice. Combine egg yolks, milk, salt, mustard and cornstarch in double boiler;

cook until creamy. Cool; add remaining lemon juice and whipped cream. Combine mixtures in large mold. Chill for 24 hours. Yield: 12 servings.

Mildred H. Dutton, Burlingame H.S.
Burlingame, Kansas

CHRISTMAS DELIGHT SALAD

16 canned peach halves
1 8-oz. pkg. cream cheese
½ c. drained cranberry relish
Salad greens
Frosted grapes

Drain peaches well. Soften cheese with fork; blend in cranberry relish. Connect peach halves with cheese mixture to make 8 whole peaches. Arrange on salad greens on serving plate; garnish with frosted grapes. Yield: 8 servings.

Janell Samford, C. O. Wilson Jr. H.S.
Nederland, Texas

CITRUS SALAD

1 head western iceberg lettuce
2 or 3 lge. oranges
2 ripe pears
1 med. sweet onion, sliced
½ c. mayonnaise or salad dressing
¼ c. honey
1 tbsp. lemon juice
½ tsp. celery seed
¼ tsp. paprika

Core lettuce; wash in cold water and drain well. Place in plastic bag or transparent plastic wrap; refrigerate. Separate 4 outer lettuce leaves and line platter. Shred remaining lettuce and arrange in center. Peel and slice oranges, cartwheel-style. Core and cut pears into thin wedges. Separate onion into rings. Arrange fruit and onion rings over lettuce. Mix together mayonnaise, honey, lemon juice, celery seed and paprika; serve with salad.

Photograph for this recipe on page 119.

CRANBERRY WALDORF

2 c. cranberries
3 c. miniature marshmallows
¾ c. sugar
2 c. diced unpared tart apple
½ c. seedless green grapes
½ c. pecans
¼ tsp. salt
1 c. whipping cream, whipped

(Continued on next page)

Grind cranberries; combine with marshmallows and sugar. Cover and chill overnight. Add apple, grapes, pecans and salt; fold in whipped cream. Chill. Serve in large bowl. Yield: 8-10 servings.

Mrs. Emma Jewel Goodwin, Bertram H.S.
Bertram, Texas

CRANBERRY SALAD

    1 lb. fresh cranberries
    1 c. sugar
    12 marshmallows, quartered
    1 apple, peeled and chopped
    1 c. coarsely chopped walnuts
    1 c. whipping cream

Chop cranberries coarsely in food chopper; add sugar. Drain overnight. Combine marshmallows, apple and nuts with cranberries. Fold in whipped cream. Yield: 8 servings.

Mrs. Edith Conner, Hooks H.S.
Hooks, Texas

CRANBERRY-CREAM SALAD

    1 lb. fresh cranberries
    1 c. sugar
    1 pt. whipping cream
    1 10 ½-oz. pkg. miniature marshmallows
    1 c. crushed pineapple, drained

Grind cranberries; add sugar. Let set in refrigerator for 2 hours. Whip cream; add marshmallows. Set in refrigerator for 2 hours. Mix cranberry and cream mixtures; add pineapple. Place in mold. Refrigerate for several hours. Yield: 8 servings.

Viola Gracey, Travis Jr. H.S.
Snyder, Texas

CRANBERRY DOPE

    1 lb. cranberries
    ¾ c. sugar
    ½ lb. miniature marshmallows
    1 8-oz. can crushed pineapple, drained
    ½ c. chopped pecans
    ½ pt. whipping cream, whipped

Grind cranberries. Sprinkle with sugar; let stand for 10 minutes. Mix marshmallows and pineapple; add nuts. Fold all ingredients together; refrigerate for 4 hours or longer. Yield: 10-12 servings.

Mrs. Doris Swinehart, Necedah Area H.S.
Necedah, Wisconsin

CRANBERRY FLUFF

    2 c. raw cranberries, ground
    3 c. miniature marshmallows
    ¾ c. sugar
    2 c. diced unpared tart apples
    ½ c. seedless green grapes
    ½ c. broken California walnuts
    ¼ tsp. salt
    1 c. heavy cream, whipped

Combine cranberries, marshmallows and sugar. Cover and chill overnight. Add apples, grapes, walnuts and salt. Fold in whipped cream; chill. Turn into serving bowl or spoon into individual lettuce cups. Trim with cluster of green grapes, if desired. Yield: 8-10 servings.

Mrs. Doris Cain, Solomon H.S.
Solomon, Kansas
Janet L. Warner, Las Animas H.S.
Las Animas, Colorado
Elizabeth Stafford, Saratoga H.S.
Saratoga, California

CRANBERRY FLUFF

    2 c. raw cranberries, ground
    2 c. miniature marshmallows
    ¾ c. sugar
    ¾ c. crushed pineapple
    2 c. diced unpeeled tart apples
    ½ c. nuts
    1 c. whipped cream

Combine cranberries, marshmallows and sugar; refrigerate overnight. Add pineapple, apples, nuts and cream. Chill for several hours. Yield: 8-10 servings.

Mrs. Carol Subera, Colby H.S.
Colby, Wisconsin

CRANBERRY-ORANGE RELISH

    ½ lb. cranberries
    1 c. sugar
    ¼ c. orange juice
    1 tsp. grated orange rind
    ¼ c. water
    ¼ c. slivered almonds

Place all ingredients except almonds in saucepan. Cover and cook for 10 to 12 minutes until cranberries burst. Add almonds; cool and refrigerate. Yield: 6 servings.

Mrs. Juanita Willis, Carlsbad Sr. H.S.
Carlsbad, New Mexico

FRESH CRANBERRY SALAD

    2 c. fresh cranberries
    1 c. sugar
    1 c. Tokay grapes
    ¼ c. coarsely chopped walnuts
    ½ c. cream, whipped

(Continued on next page)

Chop cranberries coarsely in food chopper; add sugar. Drain overnight. Cut grapes in half; remove seeds. Add to cranberry mixture; add walnuts. Fold in whipped cream just before serving. Yield: 6 servings.

Mrs. Edith Conner, Hooks H.S.
Hooks, Texas

CRANBERRY SALAD

1 pkg. fresh cranberries
2 c. sugar
1 c. grapes, halved
1 ½ c. marshmallows
½ c. nuts, chopped
½ pt. whipping cream, whipped

Grind cranberries; add sugar. Let stand overnight. Add grapes, marshmallows and chopped nuts; mix. Fold in whipped cream. Chill. Yield: 18 servings.

Janice Kinsch, Melba H.S.
Melba, Idaho

CRANBERRY SALAD

2 No. 300 cans whole cranberry sauce
2 c. miniature marshmallows
2 med. apples, diced
3 bananas, sliced
3 c. mandarin oranges, drained
½ c. pecans, chopped

Combine all ingredients; chill thoroughly. Yield: 14 servings.

Mrs. Robert Blatchley, Homer Central H.S.
Homer, New York

CRANBERRY SALAD

2 c. ground cranberries
1 c. sugar
1 8-oz. can pineapple, drained
1 c. tiny marshmallows
1 c. cream, whipped

Grind cranberries; add remaining ingredients except cream. Fold cream into mixture. Chill and serve. Yield: 6-8 servings.

Sharon Schlafmann, Worthington Sr. H.S.
Worthington, Minnesota

CRANBERRY SALAD

1 lb. fresh cranberries, ground
1 c. sugar
1 pt. whipping cream, whipped

¾ lb. sm. marshmallows
1 No. 2 can drained crushed pineapple
1 c. nuts

Combine cranberries and sugar. Refrigerate 2 hours. Add remaining ingredients; chill. Yield: 12-15 servings.

Mrs. Winnie Carter, Karnack H.S.
Karnack, Texas

HOLIDAY DELIGHT

1 lb. raw cranberries
1 ½ c. sugar
1 lb. Tokay grapes
½ c. walnuts
1 c. miniature marshmallows
2 c. whipping cream, whipped

Wash and stem cranberries; grind. Add sugar to cranberries. Cover and leave overnight in refrigerator. Quarter and seed grapes. Add grapes, nuts, marshmallows and whipped cream just before serving. Yield: 12-15 servings.

Opal M. House, Orland H.S.
Orland, California

INDIA FRUIT SALAD

1 or 2 drops vanilla extract
2 tsp. powdered sugar
½ pt. heavy cream, whipped
1 10-oz. pkg. frozen cranberry relish
1 can pineapple tidbits, drained
2 bananas, sliced
1 orange, sectioned
1 c. bite-sized marshmallows
½ c. chopped nuts

Add vanilla and sugar to cream. Mix remaining ingredients; add to first mixture. Chill until ready to serve. Yield: 12-15 servings.

Mrs. John Leischner, DeLand-Weldon Sr. H.S.
DeLand, Illinois

JUNE'S PARTY SALAD

2 lb. cranberries
4 c. sugar
2 lb. Tokay grapes, seeded
2 c. pecans
3 c. whipping cream, whipped

Grind cranberries; add sugar and mix. Drain cranberries in a colander; add grapes, nuts and whipped cream. Mix thoroughly. Mixture keeps well in refrigerator for several days. Yield: 16-18 servings.

Mrs. Dorothy E. Perryman, Alpine H.S.
Alpine, Texas

LOU'S CRANBERRY SALAD

1 pkg. cranberries
1 c. sugar
1 med. pkg. miniature marshmallows
2 c. chipped apples
1 c. grape halves
½ c. nuts, or coconut
1 pt. whipped cream

Grind cranberries in food grinder. Combine with sugar and marshmallows. Refrigerate for 3 hours or overnight. Add apples, grapes and nuts; mix well. Fold in whipped cream; return to refrigerator until serving time. Yield: 16 servings.

Lynette Taylor, Gentry H.S.
Gentry, Arkansas

PINK FLUFFY
CRANBERRY SALAD

2 c. ground cranberries or 1 lb. can whole cranberry sauce
1 c. sugar
1 pt. whipping cream, whipped
¾ lb. marshmallows, cut into small pieces
1 c. drained crushed pineapple

Combine cranberries and sugar; let stand for 2 hours. Combine cranberry mixture, whipped cream and marshmallows. Fold in pineapple. Pour into loaf pan or mold. Let stand overnight in refrigerator. Salad will keep for several days in refrigerator. Yield: 12 servings.

Mrs. Molly Bedrich, Lancaster H.S.
Lancaster, Texas

QUICK CRANBERRY SALAD

1 pkg. cranberries
¾ c. sugar
2 c. whipped cream
1 lge. can pineapple chunks
½ c. chopped pecans
1 pkg. sm. marshmallows

Cook cranberries until they pop; add sugar. Simmer 5 minutes; cool. Fold in whipped cream, pineapple chunks, nuts and marshmallows. Chill and serve on lettuce cups. Yield: 8 cups.

Mrs. Arthur Ray, Lewis Co. H.S.
Hohenwald, Tennessee

TOP HAT SALAD

Lettuce
1 can whole pineapple slices
1 can molded cranberry sauce
Creamed cottage cheese

Place lettuce leaf, 1 pineapple slice and 1 slice cranberry sauce on each plate; top with cottage cheese.

Lois B. Jenkins, Franklin H.S.
Franklin, Pennsylvania

DELICIOUS FRUIT SALAD

2 c. drained pineapple chunks
2 c. red grapes, halved and seeded
1 c. toasted pecans, chopped
1 c. miniature marshmallows
½ c. mayonnaise
½ c. whipped cream

Combine all ingredients; mix well. Pour into mold or pan; refrigerate until ready to serve. Yield: 8 servings.

Pauline B. Commer, Crowder H.S.
Crowder, Mississippi

DREAMY FRUIT SALAD

1 No. 2 ½ can fruit cocktail
1 11-oz. can mandarin orange segments
1 c. miniature marshmallows
1 c. flaked coconut
1 c. sour cream

Drain fruit cocktail and orange segments. Combine fruit cocktail, orange segments, marshmallows and coconut; fold in sour cream. Chill for several hours to allow flavors to blend. Serve on salad greens. Yield: 8 servings.

Mrs. Nancy Kores, Coronado H.S.
Scottsdale, Arizona
Mrs. Nell Fenoglio, West Covina H.S.
West Covina, California
Dianah Sue Rutliff, Chouteau H.S.
Chouteau, Oklahoma

FAMILY FRUIT SALAD

1 grapefruit, sectioned and cut in chunks
1 orange, sectioned and cut in chunks
2 apples, unpeeled and diced
4 fresh or canned peach halves, diced
4 fresh or canned pear halves, diced
1 c. canned diced pineapple, drained
1 pt. whipped cream or substitute

Combine all fruits; chill several hours. Fold in whipped cream. Serve plain or on lettuce. Yield: 6-8 servings.

Mrs. Virginia J. Darling, Olivet H.S.
Olivet, Michigan

FIVE-CUP SALAD

1 c. orange pulp
1 c. apple, chopped small
1 c. pineapple chunks
1 c. sour cream
1 c. coconut

Peel orange completely, leaving only the pulp. Cut orange into small pieces. Peel apple; cut

(Continued on next page)

into small pieces. Mix fruits, sour cream and coconut thoroughly. Chill. Yield: 10 servings.

Mrs. Katherine Schultz, Fabens H.S.
Fabens, Texas

FIVE-CUP SALAD

1 c. drained pineapple tidbits
1 lge. can mandarin oranges, drained
1 c. miniature marshmallows
1 c. flaked coconut
1 c. sour cream

Mix all ingredients well. Pour into mold or dish; chill for 2 to 3 hours. Serve on bed of lettuce if desired. Yield: 8 servings.

Mrs. Jeanne Callihan, Tecumseh H.S.
Tecumseh, Michigan
Mrs. Donnabelle Pech, Lincoln Community H.S.
Lincoln, Illinois
Mrs. Sandra J. Kotval, Simley Sch.
Inver Grove Heights, Minnesota

FIVE-CUP SALAD

1 c. drained crushed pineapple
1 c. drained mandarin oranges
1 c. black walnut chips
1 c. shredded coconut
1 c. sour cream

Mix first 4 ingredients in dish; add sour cream. Chill and serve. Yield: 6-8 servings.

Mrs. Florence Russell, Napoleon H.S.
Napoleon, Ohio

FIVE-CUP SALAD

1 c. drained mandarin oranges
1 c. drained pineapple chunks
1 c. miniature marshmallows
1 c. grated coconut
1 c. sour cream
½ c. Bing or maraschino cherries

Mix all ingredients; pour into mold or pan. Chill overnight. Serve on lettuce leaf. Yield: 8 servings.

Florence Hughes, Toaz Jr. H.S.
Huntington, New York

FLUFFY FRUIT DELIGHT

½ c. fruit cocktail liquid
16 lge. marshmallows
1 c. heavy cream

1 tsp. vanilla
1 can fruit cocktail, drained
3 bananas, sliced

Heat fruit liquid, stirring in marshmallows until melted. Cool. Whip cream; add vanilla before cream is stiff. Fold in marshmallow mixture, fruit cocktail and bananas. Chill until firm. Garnish with maraschino cherries. Yield: 8 servings.

Mrs. Elizabeth Wilson, Woodstock H.S.
Woodstock, New Brunswick, Canada

FRESH FRUIT SALAD

4 med. bananas, sliced
8 oranges, chopped
1 lb. green or red grapes, seeded and halved
¼ c. walnuts, chopped
1½ c. miniature marshmallows
½ pt. whipping cream
¼ c. sugar
Maraschino cherries

Mix all fruit except cherries together; add nuts and marshmallows. Chill. Whip cream; add sugar. Mix into fruit. Top with cherries. Yield: 8 servings.

Fran Glinsmann, North-Loup Scotia Sch.
Scotia, Nebraska

FRESH FRUIT SALAD

1 No. 2½ can pineapple tidbits
3 oranges, peeled and cut up
3 tbsp. cornstarch
½ c. sugar
3 bananas, sliced

Combine pineapple and oranges. Let set overnight. Drain juice; cook with cornstarch and sugar blended together until thickened. Pour over fruit. When ready to serve, add bananas to salad. Grapes may also be added, if desired. Yield: 6 servings.

Neva Chapin, Janesville Consolidated Sch.
Janesville, Iowa

FRUIT-NUT SALAD

1 can pineapple tidbits
3 bananas, sliced
½ c. salted peanuts
Mayonnaise

Mix fruit and nuts; moisten with mayonnaise. Serve on lettuce leaves. Yield: 4 servings.

Mrs. Darlene Prashar, Astoria H.S.
Astoria, South Dakota

FRUIT SALAD

3 egg yolks
1 tbsp. vinegar
½ tsp. salt
2 tbsp. sugar
2 tbsp. pineapple juice
1 c. whipping cream, whipped
1 No. 2 can pineapple chunks, drained
1 11-oz. can mandarin oranges, drained
6-oz. miniature marshmallows
1 lb. purple grapes

Combine first 5 ingredients; cook until thick. Cool thoroughly. Fold in cream. Add fruit. Refrigerate overnight. Yield: 6-8 servings.

Jo Lucas, Bellevue Comm. Sch.
Bellevue, Iowa

FRUIT SALAD

2 c. sectioned oranges
2 c. halved green grapes
2 c. sliced bananas
2 c. pineapple chunks
2 cups quartered marshmallows
12 maraschino cherries, quartered
1 whole egg
¼ c. lemon juice
2 to 4 tbsp. sugar
1 c. heavy cream

Combine all fruit; set aside. Combine and beat egg, lemon juice and sugar; cook over water until thickened. Cool. Whip cream. Fold in egg mixture. Combine with fruit. Chill. Yield: 12 servings.

Katherine M. Baker, Van Wert H.S.
Van Wert, Ohio

FRUIT SALAD

1 No. 2 can fruit cocktail, drained
1 lge. Delicious apple, diced
1 lge. banana, diced
1 lge. orange, diced
¼ c. maraschino cherries, halved
Whipped cream

Combine fruit cocktail with remaining fruit. Fold cream into fruit or use as topping. Yield: 4-6 servings.

Mrs. Mariann Bielke, Marion I.S.D.
Marion, Texas

FRUIT SALAD

4 or 5 slices pineapple
1 sm. can mandarin oranges
2 red apples, chopped
2 bananas, sliced

6 tbsp. whipping cream
2 to 3 tbsp. sugar
2 tbsp. salad dressing

Cut pineapple into bite-sized pieces; add drained mandarin oranges, apples and bananas. Whip cream; add sugar and salad dressing. Stir to blend; mix with fruit. Serve in lettuce cups. Garnish with a maraschino cherry if desired. Yield: 8-10 servings.

Mrs. Layne M. Storment, Kahlotus H.S.
Kahlotus, Washington

FRUIT SALAD

2 eggs, beaten
4 tbsp. lemon juice
4 tbsp. sugar
2 tbsp. butter
1 c. cream, whipped
1 c. cut marshmallows (opt.)
1 can mandarin oranges
2 c. pineapple, cut into small pieces
2 c. white cherries, cut into halves

Combine eggs, lemon juice and sugar in top of double boiler; cook until thick and smooth, stirring constantly. Remove from heat; add butter. Stir well; let cool. Fold in cream, marshmallows and fruits; pour into mold or pan. Place in refrigerator for 2 hours. Yield: 10-12 servings.

Mrs. Novella Mae Melton, Roswell H.S.
Roswell, New Mexico

FRUIT SALAD BOWL

Crisp salad greens
1 apple, sliced
2 bananas, cut into strips
Lemon juice
1 1-lb. can each pear, apricot halves, drained and chilled
Maraschino cherries, with stems

Line salad bowl with salad greens. Dip apple and banana pieces into lemon juice; arrange in bowl with pears and apricots. Garnish with cherries. Serve with mayonnaise thinned with lemon juice or French dressing. Yield: 4 servings.

Mrs. Ruth P. Nagy, Mineral Co. H.S.
Hawthorne, Nevada

FRUIT SALAD WITH COCONUT

1 can mandarin oranges, drained
1 sm. can chunk pineapple, drained
1 pkg. miniature marshmallows
1 can Angel Flake coconut
2 tbsp. sour cream

(Continued on next page)

132

Mix together first 4 ingredients. Place in mold or pan; chill. Add sour cream just before serving. Yield: 6 servings.

Mrs. Maxine Bohart, Lake Highlands Jr. H.S.
Dallas, Texas

tangerines to fruit cocktail; add coconut, cherries and cherry juice. Mix well. Refrigerate before serving. Yield: 4 servings.

Lynda Dean, Vidor H.S.
Vidor, Texas

FRUIT SALAD MOLD

1 c. pineapple juice
½ c. sugar
2 tsp. flour
2 eggs, beaten
1 tbsp. butter
½ tsp. lemon juice
¾ c. whipped cream
¼ lb. marshmallows, cut finely
1 lb. grapes, cut and seeded
1 can pineapple, diced
¼ lb. pecans or black walnuts, chopped

Combine pineapple juice, sugar, flour, eggs and butter in top of double boiler; cook over hot water until thick, stirring frequently. Add lemon juice; cool. Add whipped cream, marshmallows, fruits and nuts; pour into mold or pan. Refrigerate until ready to serve. Yield: 12 servings.

Mrs. Paul Penton, Harry L. Johnson Sch.
Johnson City, New York

GUMDROP SALAD

½ c. sugar
1 tbsp. flour
1 tbsp. vinegar or juice of 2 lemons
¾ c. crushed pineapple
1 pt. heavy cream, whipped
½ lb. marshmallow, cut up
½ lb. assorted gumdrops, cut-up
1 No 2 ½ can chunk pineapple
1 lb. Tokay grapes, seeded
½ c. nutmeats

Blend sugar and flour; add vinegar and crushed pineapple. Cook in double boiler until thick. Cool. Add remaining ingredients. Mix thoroughly. Place in refrigerator. Chill for 12 to 24 hours. Yield: 6 servings.

Mrs. Joanne Litz, Tulare Western Sch.
Tulare, California

FRUIT SALAD SUPREME

1 lb. marshmallows
4 egg yolks
½ tsp. mustard
1 ½ c. milk
1 lge. can crushed pineapple
4 oranges, peeled, cut up and drained
1 c. chopped black walnuts
1 c. whipped cream

Place marshmallows in large bowl. Combine egg yolks and mustard in saucepan and heat; add milk and cook until thick. Pour over marshmallows; stir well. Add pineapple, oranges, walnuts and whipped cream. Refrigerate overnight or freeze. Yield: 12 servings.

Mrs. Doris Plath, Boone Comm. Sch.
Boone, Iowa

GRANDMA ESSER'S CHRISTMAS SALAD

1 c. crushed pineapple, drained
3 or 4 red apples, cut up
1 10-oz. bag marshmallows, cut up
½ c. chopped walnuts
½ c. sugar
1 tbsp. cornstarch
1 egg yolk
1 c. whipping cream

Drain pineapple; reserve juice. Combine apples, marshmallows and nuts in large bowl with pineapple; mix together lightly. Chill. Cook reserved juice with sugar, cornstarch and egg yolk in double boiler; cool. Add whipped cream. Mix in chilled fruit. Let stand 4 hours or overnight. Garnish with sugared green grapes and mint leaves. Yield: 12-20 servings.

Mrs. Doris Swinehart, Necedah Area H.S.
Necedah, Wisconsin

FRUIT SALAD WITH TANGERINE

3 tangerines
1 can fruit cocktail
½ can coconut
½ bottle cherries
¼ c. cherry juice

Peel tangerines; section. Remove seeds and center membrane; cut each section in half. Add

GRANDMA'S FAVORITE FRUIT SALAD

1 No. 2 ½ can fruit cocktail, drained
2 lge. bananas
1 sm. bunch of grapes, halved and seeded
½ c. chopped walnuts
½ pt. whipping cream

Combine all fruits; add nutmeats. Whip cream; add 6 tablespoons Lemon Sauce. Combine fruit and cream mixtures. Chill. Serve on lettuce leaves. Lemon Sauce is optional.

(Continued on next page)

Mixed Fruit Salads

LEMON SAUCE:

Rind and juice of lge. lemon
6 egg yolks
½ c. (scant) water
½ c. sugar
2 tbsp. butter

Grate lemon rind; set aside. Beat egg yolks lightly. Place yolks, water and lemon juice in top of double boiler; cook until thick, stirring occasionally. Add lemon rind, sugar and butter. Reserve. Yield: 8 servings.

Mrs. Mary D. Moore, Addison Central Sch.
Addison, New York

GRAPE AND PEAR SALAD

Chicory or 8 lge. grape leaves
8 pear halves
6 oz. cream cheese
¼ c. cream
2 lb. white seedless grapes, halved
French dressing or Whipped cream

Cover salad plates with chicory; place pear half, flat side down, on each. Combine cream cheese and cream mixing well; spread generously over pear. Place grapes, to resemble bunch of grapes, flat side down, on pear. Place grape stem in large end of pear. Serve with French dressing. Seeded purple or Tokay grapes may be used. Yield: 8 servings.

Mrs. Lucile Duncan Ryan, Byhalia H.S.
Byhalia, Mississippi

HEAVENLY FRUIT SALAD

1 c. drained mandarin oranges
1 c. drained pineapple chunks
¼ c. maraschino cherries, halved
⅔ c. flaked coconut
1 c. miniature marshmallows
½ c. heavy cream, whipped or 1 c. sour
cream

Combine fruits with coconut and marshmallows; fold cream into mixture. Pour into mold or pan. Chill in refrigerator for several hours or overnight. Yield: 6 servings.

Darlene M. Pohlman, Priest River H.S.
Priest River, Idaho

HOLIDAY FRUIT SALAD

3 oranges, sectioned
2 Delicious apples, unpared and chopped
1 No. 3 can fruit cocktail
1 c. fresh coconut grated

½ c. pecan pieces
1 c. Tokay grapes, seeded
½ c. sugar or sweeten to taste
3 ripe bananas, sliced crosswise

Combine all ingredients in large mixing bowl; cover tightly. Chill for 1 hour. Serve. Excellent accompaniment for roast turkey or baked ham. Yield: 12 servings.

Mrs. Betty K. Thomas, Carter Jr. H.S.
Arlington, Texas

HOT FRUIT SALAD

1 can apricots and juice
1 can drained fruit cocktail
2 or 3 bananas
3 tbsp. brown sugar
Frosted Flakes for topping

Combine fruits and brown sugar. Pour into casserole dish. Bake at 350 degrees for 15 to 20 minutes; remove and cover with flakes. Return to oven; brown cereal. Serve in individual baking dishes. Any additional canned fruit may be added but do not omit apricots. Yield: 8-10 servings.

Mary Ida Hoffman, Meridian Sr. H.S.
Meridian, Mississippi

HUNGARIAN FRUIT SALAD

1 c. crushed pineapple
1 c. sliced bananas
1 c. tangerine sections
Dressing

Combine fruit; add dressing, mixing well. Arrange on lettuce; sprinkle with paprika. Yield: 6 servings.

Lillian J. Kissam, Jackson H.S.
Tyler, Texas

LADY FARE SALAD

1 12-oz. carton cream-style cottage
cheese
6 oz. cream cheese
1 c. green grapes, halved and seeded
½ c. broken pecans
2 tbsp. chopped chives
1 c. heavy cream, whipped

Mash cheeses with fork until smooth; add grapes, pecans and chives. Blend gently; fold in whipped cream. Pour into oiled 1-quart melon mold; chill for 4 to 6 hours. Unmold onto lettuce leaves. Garnish with chopped pistachio nuts and fresh or canned fruits if desired. Yield: 8 servings.

Mrs. Rebecca F. Urraro, Walt Whitman H.S.
Huntington Station, New York

LILY SALAD

1 lb. marshmallows, quartered or
    miniature marshmallows
1 No. 2 ½ can pineapple chunks, drained
1 can mandarin oranges, drained
½ c. pineapple juice
2 egg yolks, well beaten
1 pkg. Dream Whip, whipped

Add marshmallows to pineapple and oranges; mix
well. Bring pineapple juice to boil; pour over
egg yolks. Fold cooked mixture into Dream Whip;
fold in mixed fruit. Pour into mold or dish. Chill
for 24 hours. Yield: 6-8 servings.

Mrs. Shirley Gulbranson, Flandreau Indian H.S.
Flandreau, South Dakota

FRUIT SALAD
FRESH CANTALOUPE

2 c. diced cantaloupe
1 c. pineapple wedges
1 c. sliced fresh strawberries
French dressing
Lettuce

Combine cantaloupe, pineapple and strawberries. Add French dressing to taste; toss
lightly. Serve on chilled lettuce. Yield: 6 servings.

Augusta H. Dennis, Billingsley H.S.
Billingsley, Alabama

FROSTED FRUIT CUP

2 c. ginger ale
1 6-oz. can frozen grape juice concentrate
1 12-oz. can frozen pineapple chunks
⅛ c. maraschino cherry halves
1 c. honeydew cubes
2 c. cantaloupe balls
Mint sprigs

Combine ginger ale and grape juice concentrate;
stir until concentrate dissolves. Pour into 2-
quart refrigerator tray; freeze to a mush, about
1 hour. Thaw pineapple chunks slightly; some
ice crystals should remain. Mix with cherries,
honeydew and canteloupe. Spoon fruit into sherbet
glasses; top with ginger ale mixture. Garnish
with mint sprigs. Yield: 8 servings.

Mrs. Van Johnson, Richardton Pub. Sch.
Richardton, North Dakota

MANALOPE FRUIT CUP

2 cantaloupes, scooped into balls
2 sm. cans mandarin oranges
½ to 1 c. watermelon balls

Scoop out cantaloupes carefully; reserve rinds to
serve as fruit cup, if desired. Mix fruits together;
let set in juices for several hours in refrigerator.
One dozen red or green cherries cut in halves
may be substituted for watermelon. Other fruits
in season may be added. Yield: 4-6 servings.

Mrs. David R. Vanderhei, Grand Rapids Sr. H.S.
Grand Rapids, Minnesota

GRAPE-CANTALOUPE SALAD

1 c. pineapple chunks
½ cantaloupe, cut in ½ x 2-in strips
1 ½ c. seedless green grapes
1 banana, cut in wedges
½ c. minature marshmallows
½ c. fruit dressing

Mix all fruits and marshmallows; toss with
dressing.

Mrs. Mavis Menzies, Arthur Day Jr. H.S.
Winnipeg, Manitoba, Canada

MIM'S SALAD

2 eggs
1 tbsp. dry mustard
Pinch of salt
4 tbsp. brown sugar
4 tbsp. vinegar
½ lb. marshmallows, quartered
1 c. chopped nuts
1 lge. No. 2 can pineapple tidbits, drained
12 maraschino cherries, diced
1 lge. banana, cubed
1 pt. whipping cream, whipped

Cook first 5 ingredients until thick; cool. Combine next 5 ingredients; fold in cream. Add thickened cool mixture. Pour into freezer trays and
freeze. Yield: 12 servings.

Corrine L. Calvin, Poland Jr. H.S.
Poland, Ohio

MOHAVE FRUIT SALAD

2 c. cubed apples
1 c. orange sections
1 ½ c. cubed natural cheddar cheese
½ c. chopped dates
½ c. chopped walnuts
1 tsp. grated orange rind
½ c. mayonnaise or Miracle Whip salad
    dressing

Combine fruit, cheese, dates, nuts and orange
rind. Add mayonnaise; toss lightly. Yield: 4-6
servings.

Jean C. Boychuk, Motley Pub. Schs.
Motley, Minnesota
Mrs. L. O. Freeman, Chickasaw Co. H.S.
Houston, Mississippi

OHIO FRUIT SALAD

1 can peach pie filling
1 c. red California grapes, cut up
1 can mandarin oranges, drained
1 can chunk pineapple, drained

Mix all ingredients together and chill overnight.
Yield: 12 servings.

Hilda G. Rohlf, Tallmadge H.S.
Tallmadge, Ohio

MANDARIN ORANGE SALAD

2 sm. cans mandarin oranges, drained
1 c. coconut, shredded
1 No. 2 can fruit cocktail, drained
1 c. pecans, chopped
1 c. maraschino cherries
2 c. miniature marshmallows
2 c. sour cream

Place all ingredients in refrigerator dish; stir.
Cover. Refrigerate for 24 hours before serving.
Yield: 12 servings.

Mona Faye Fordham, Sikes H.S.
Sikes, Louisiana

ORANGE CUP

1 lge. orange
½ banana, sliced
¼ c. strawberries or other fruit in season
Mint

Slice top off orange; remove orange sections
with grapefruit knife. Combine orange sections
with banana slices and strawberries. Spoon fruit
mixture into orange shell. Top with mint sprigs.
Serve with fruit dressing. Yield: 1 serving.

Mrs. Van Johnson, Richardton Pub. Sch.
Richardton, North Dakota

VOSSLER FRUIT SALAD

1 11-oz. can mandarin orange slices,
    drained
1 can chunk pineapple, drained
1 c. coconut
1 c. marshmallows
1 c. sour cream
2 bananas

Mix orange slices, pineapple chunks, coconut,
marshmallows and sour cream in a large bowl.
Let mixture stand overnight in refrigerator. Add
bananas when ready to serve. Yield: 4 servings.

Mrs. Glen Hickey, Flippin H.S.
Flippin, Arkansas

OVERNIGHT SALAD

1 egg
2 tbsp. lemon juice
2 tbsp. sugar
1 15-oz. can drained pineapple chunks
2 lge. oranges, sectioned or 1 10-oz.
    can mandarin orange sections
1 lge. unpeeled apple, cut into pieces
1 ½ to 2 c. seeded cut grapes, green or
    purple
2 lge. bananas, sliced
½ pt. whipping cream, whipped
Sugar
Vanilla
3 c. miniature marshmallows

Beat egg until light and lemon colored; add lemon
juice and sugar. Cook in heavy saucepan until
thick and smooth, stirring constantly. Cool.
Place pineapple chunks, oranges, apple, grapes
and bananas in large salad bowl; mix gently.
Add egg mixture; mix gently. Flavor cream with
sugar and vanilla. Fold marshmallows and cream
into fruit. Chill 6 to 8 hours or overnight. Yield:
12 servings.

Mrs. Evelyn O'Hara, Waverly Sch.
Stettler, Alberta, Canada

PACIFIC SALAD

1 sm. carton cottage cheese
1 sm. can pineapple tidbits, drained
1 sm. can mandarin oranges, drained
1 c. miniature marshmallows
1 c. coconut
1 sm. carton sour cream

Mix together all ingredients; pour into mold or
dish. Chill. Juice from pineapple may be substituted for sour cream. Yield: 6 servings.

Sarah Henry, Redwater H.S.
Redwater, Texas

A PEACHIE SALAD

4 ripe peaches
½ c. frozen concentrated orange juice
1 c. seedless green grapes
2 bananas, sliced
1 8-oz. can pineapple, drained
2 c. miniature marshmallows
¼ c. sugar

Pare peaches and chop; coat with orange juice.
Add remaining ingredients; toss lightly. Pour
into pan or mold. Chill for several hours. Serve
on lettuce cup. Pineapple juice may be thickened
with 1 tablespoon cornstarch and 1/4 cup sugar
and added just before serving. Yield: 8 servings.

Mrs. Elane F. McCarriar, Hayti H.S.
Hayti, South Dakota

CHILLED FRUIT SALAD

3 bananas, sliced
6 fresh peaches, pared and sliced
½ c. pineapple juice

Combine bananas and peaches; pour in pineapple juice and toss well. Pour into pan or mold. Chill for 30 to 40 minutes. Serve on lettuce leaf if desired. Yield: 4 servings.

Mrs. Sandra V. Ziegler, Sparland H.S.
Sparland, Illinois

RED HOT-PEACH SALAD

1 pkg. red hots
1 can peaches
Cranberry and orange relish

Melt red hots in hot peach juice; cool. Pour over peaches; let soak 24 hours or longer. Fill center with relish or any desired filling. Yield: 4 servings.

Janet Smith, Axtell H.S.
Axtell, Texas

MARSHMALLOW SALAD

1 c. milk
Sugar
4 egg yolks, beaten
1 can white cherries
1 can crushed, drained pineapple
1 c. pears, diced
1 lb. marshmallows
1 ½ tsp. lemon juice
1 c. whipping cream

Cook milk, 3 tablespoons sugar and egg yolks until custard will coat spoon. Cool. Add cherries, pineapple, pears, marshmallows and lemon juice. Whip cream; add sugar to taste. Fold into fruit-custard mixture. Chill for 24 hours.

Edna Doperalski, Wamego H.S.
Wamego, Kansas

MIXED FRUIT SALAD

1 ½ c. sliced bananas
Lemon juice
½ c. cut pineapple
½ c. diced ripe pears
½ c. diced grapefruit
½ c. cherries
Dash of paprika

Coat bananas with lemon juice; toss all fruits together lightly with fork. Chill. Serve with fruit salad dressing on crisp lettuce. Top with a dash of paprika. Yield: 6 servings.

Mrs. Lydia Roberts, Groesbeck H.S.
Groesbeck, Texas

PEANUT SPREAD-BANANA AND PEAR SALAD

2 bananas
Peanut butter
4 canned pear halves
4 maraschino cherries

Cut bananas lengthwise into halves. Spread cut side of one half with peanut butter; place other half on top sandwich style. Cut into 10 crosswise slices. Arrange 2 pear halves, 2 cherries and 10 banana slices on each salad plate. Garnish with endive. Yield: 2 servings.

Mrs. Helen Alders, Douglass H.S.
Douglass, Texas

SOUR CREAM HAWAIIAN SALAD

1 No. 2 ½ can pears
1 4-oz. bottle maraschino cherries
1 No. 2 ½ can pineapple chunks
1 pt. sour cream
1 can coconut
2 c. miniature marshmallows

Dice pears; halve cherries. Drain pineapple, pears and cherries well; set aside a few cherries for garnish. Blend sour cream, coconut and marshmallows; add fruit. Refrigerate 12 hours. Garnish with cherries. Yield: 8-10 servings.

Mrs. Kathryn Whitten, Hanford H.S.
Hanford, California

TOMORROW'S SALAD

2 well beaten eggs
¼ c. sugar
1 tbsp. vinegar
1 c. heavy cream, whipped
1 lge. can pears, diced
1 lge. can crushed pineapple, drained
1 lge. orange, peeled and diced
1 10 ½-oz. pkg. miniature marshmallows

Combine eggs, sugar and vinegar; cook until thick. Cool. Fold whipped cream into cooled egg sauce; combine with fruit and marshmallows. This salad is even better when made a day ahead. Yield: 12 servings.

Mrs. Betty Addison, Lipan H.S.
Lipan, Texas

Mixed Fruit with Pineapple Salads

TWENTY FOUR-HOUR SALAD

½ c. milk
1 tbsp. sugar
4 egg yolks
½ tsp. salt
1 No. 2 can pears
1 No. 2 can pineapple
1 lb. marshmallows
1 pt. whipping cream
1 No. 2 can Queen Ann cherries
1 c. pecans
2 tbsp. lemon juice

Make custard of milk, sugar, egg yolks and salt, stirring constantly in double boiler until mixture coats a spoon. Cool completely. Cut pears and pineapple into bite-size chunks. Drain fruit completely; add quartered marshmallows. Add custard to whipping cream; gently fold in drained fruits, nuts and lemon juice. Chill 24 hours. Serve in dessert dishes. Yield: 8 servings.

Mrs. Willie B. Pittman Roland, Vivian Jr. H.S.
Vivian, Louisiana

WHIPPED CREAM AND FRUIT

2 envelopes Dream Whip
1 No. 303 can fruit cocktail
1 sm. can crushed pineapple
4 pear halves, chopped
¼ c. maraschino cherries
2 med. bananas
½ c. almonds, walnuts, or pecans

Prepare Dream Whip according to directions on package. Drain fruit cocktail, pineapple, pears and cherries. Fold all ingredients into Dream Whip and chill 30 minutes. Yield: 6 servings.

Mrs. Bobby Dictson, San Jon H.S.
San Jon, New Mexico

PINEAPPLE BOAT

2 fresh pineapples
¼ lb. halved Tokay grapes
½ c. Bing cherries
2 oranges, sectioned
½ c. strawberries
1 banana, quartered

Cut pineapples lengthwise into halves or quarters; trim leaves. Carefully cut fruit away from each portion, leaving wall of fruit about 1/2-inch thick on shell so it will hold its shape. Toss pineapple cubes together with other fruits and sweet French dressing. Refill each pineapple shell with fruit salad mixture. Each pineapple boat is an individual serving. Yield: 4-8 servings.

Mrs. Patricia Mullins, South Fulton H.S.
South Fulton, Tennessee

PINEAPPLE-CHERRY SURPRISE

1 pt. heavy whipping cream
1 tsp. vanilla
Pinch of salt
1 No. 2 can crushed pineapple
1 No. 2 can white cherries, drained
1 c. miniature marshmallows
½ lb. peanut brittle, crushed

Whip cream until thick; add vanilla, salt, pineapple and cherries. Fold in marshmallows and peanut brittle. Chill thoroughly overnight before serving. Yield: 12 servings.

Sarah P. Bowles, Holladay Sch.
Holladay, Tennessee

PINEAPPLE-MINT CUP

1 No. 2 can pineapple, spoon-sized cubes
1 c. halved and seeded Tokay grapes
1 c. ginger ale
½ c. mild white candy mints

Drain pineapple; combine with grapes, ginger ale and mints. Chill. Yield: 6 servings.

Mrs. Garry C. Pittman, Darien H.S.
Darien, Georgia

PINEAPPLE SALAD

½ c. sugar
2 tbsp. flour
2 eggs, beaten well
Salt to taste
1 c. whipping cream or 1 pkg. Dream Whip
1 lge. can pineapple, drained
2 lge. oranges
1 c. chopped nuts
10 sm. marshmallows

Cook mixture of sugar, flour, eggs and salt with reserved pineapple juice in double boiler until thick. Cool. Whip cream and fold into mixture. Pour over fruit, which has been cut into small pieces. Add nuts and marshmallows.

Nellie M. Rice, John Glenn H.S.
New Concord, Ohio

PINEAPPLE SALAD

1 13 ½-oz. can pineapple tidbits
1 ½ tbsp. cornstarch
3 tbsp. sugar
2 sliced bananas
1 c. sm. marshmallows
¼ c. chopped nuts

(Continued on next page)

Drain pineapple; add enough water to juice to make 1 cup liquid. Cook liquid, cornstarch, and sugar until thick and clear. Cool. Add bananas, marshmallows and nuts. Chill. Yield: 6 servings.

Donna Frazier, Wonewoc-Center H.S.
Wonewoc, Wisconsin

QUICK FRUIT DELIGHT SALAD

    1 carton sour cream
    1 c. coconut
    1 c. mandarin oranges, drained
    2 c. chunk pineapple, drained
    2 c. miniature marshmallows
    8 maraschino cherries, cut up
    2 bananas, sliced (opt.)

Combine all ingredients; mix well. Pour into mold or dish. Chill. Yield: 8-10 servings.

Mrs. Doris Balbach, Warren Comm. H.S. No. 205
Warren, Illinois

QUICK FRUIT SALAD

    1 can fruit cocktail, drained
    3 oranges, chopped
    ½ to 1 c. coconut
    1 c. whipped cream
    2 bananas, sliced
    2 apples, chopped
    Toasted nuts
    1 c. miniature marshmallows

Mix all ingredients together; chill in refrigerator. Yield: 8-10 servings.

Kate H. DeGaris, Pell City H.S.
Pell City, Alabama

QUICK SALAD

    2 med. apples, chopped
    2 oranges, cut up
    1 c. raisins
    ½ c. chopped walnuts (opt.)
    Mayonnaise
    Lettuce leaves
    5 or 6 maraschino cherries

Mix apples, oranges, raisins and walnuts; add mayonnaise. Mix well. Serve on lettuce leaves; top with maraschino cherry. Yield: 5-6 servings.

Sara Swanson, Graveraet Jr. H.S.
Marquette, Michigan

SAUCY FRUIT

    ½ c. honey
    3 peeled crushed cardamom seeds
    ½ tsp. salt
    6 mint leaves, crushed
    1 tbsp. lemon juice
    ½ c. sherry
    1 7-oz. bottle Seven-Up
    1 No. 2 can plums, drained and chilled
    1 No. 2 can pineapple chunks, drained and chilled
    1 7-oz. jar mandarin oranges, drained and chilled
    2 bananas, sliced
    Maraschino cherries

Simmer honey, cardamom seeds and salt for 5 minutes; add mint. Cool. Add lemon juice and sherry. Strain; cover and chill. Add Seven-Up and pour mixture over fruit. Other fruits may be substituted for those listed. Yield: 6 servings.

Mrs. Ruth H. Winslow, H. Wilson Thorpe Jr. H.S.
Hampton, Virginia

SHARON'S FRUIT-CHEESE SALAD

    2 c. cubed unpared apples
    1 c. orange sections
    1 ½ c. cubed sharp cheese
    ½ c. chopped dates
    ½ c. chopped walnuts
    1 tsp. grated orange rind
    ½ c. salad dressing

Combine fruit, cheese, dates, nuts and orange rind. Add salad dressing; toss lightly. Yield: 4-6 servings.

Nancy W. Anderson, Hanover-Horton Sch.
Horton, Michigan

SIX-CUP SALAD

    1 c. drained crushed pineapple
    1 c. drained fruit cocktail
    1 c. cottage cheese
    1 c. sour cream
    1 c. shredded coconut
    1 c. miniature marshmallows

Combine all ingredients in a large mixing bowl. Chill. Serve on lettuce leaves as salad or with vanilla wafers as dessert. Yield: 6-8 servings.

Mrs. Judy Frazier, Chester H.S.
Chester, Illinois

AMBROSIA MEDLEY

    1 pt. fresh strawberries, cut in half
    2 c. fresh or canned pineapple tidbits
    2 bananas, sliced

(Continued on next page)

¼ c. chopped dates
1 c. flaked coconut
Confectioners' sugar
¾ c. orange juice

Combine fruits; arrange with coconut in layers with confectioners' sugar, ending with sprinkling of coconut on top. Drizzle with orange juice. Chill. Yield: 6-8 servings.

Mrs. Gladys Schneider, Burlington Sr. H.S.
Burlington, Wisconsin
Mrs. Kay Nemitz, So. Door H.S.
Brussels, Wisconsin

COTTAGE CHEESE WITH FRESH FRUIT

1 tsp. salt
1 tsp. lemon juice
2 c. cottage cheese
¼ c. chopped pecans
Salad greens
1 melon, cut in round slices
2 oranges, sectioned
2 bananas, soaked in lemon or pineapple juice
3 pineapple slices, cut in sections
1 pt. strawberries or fresh sweet cherries

Add salt and lemon juice to cottage cheese; fold in part of chopped pecans. Turn into bowl that has been rinsed in cold water; place in refrigerator to chill. Unmold on large salad plate just before serving; surround with crisp salad greens or lettuce cups filled with melon rounds, orange sections, banana slices, pineapple sections and strawberries. Yield: 6 servings.

Magdalene Beehler, Mt. St. Benedict Academy
Crookston, Minnesota

STRAWBERRY AND PINEAPPLE SALAD

1 ⅓ c. fresh strawberries
½ c. diced fresh pineapple
3 tbsp. sugar
2 tsp. lemon juice
½ c. diced marshmallows
¼ c. whipped cream
3 tbsp. salad dressing

Wash, hull and halve strawberries; add pineapple. Mix sugar and lemon juice with fruit; add marshmallows. Allow to stand 1 hour. Arrange on lettuce. Fold whipped cream into salad dressing and place on top of fruit. Yield: 4 servings.

Mrs. Bettye R. Perry, 5th St. H.S.
West Point, Mississippi

STRAWBERRY SALAD

3 tbsp. strawberry juice
16 lge. marshmallows
1 3-oz. pkg. cream cheese

½ c. cream, whipped
½ c. salad dressing
1 sm. can crushed pineapple, drained
1 c. sliced strawberries

Melt strawberry juice and marshmallows in double boiler. Cool; add cream cheese, cream, salad dressing, pineapple and strawberries. Yield: 8-10 servings.

Mrs. Marion Clark, St. Edward H.S.
St. Edward, Nebraska

SWEET COMBINATION SALAD

1 pkg. whipped topping
1 c. colored miniature marshmallows
1 diced apple
1 chopped banana
1 sm. can fruit cocktail, drained
1 orange, chopped
Nuts (opt.)

Combine all ingredients, reserving small amount of fruit. Garnish with reserved fruit. Serve on lettuce leaf. Yield: 4 servings.

Jan Svingen, Round Lake H.S.
Round Lake, Minnestoa

SWEET FRUIT SALAD

1 sm. can mandarin oranges, drained
1 can pineapple chunks, drained
¾ c. miniature marshmallows
½ c. coarsely chopped nuts
½ c. sour cream or ½ pkg. Dream Whip, prepared

Mix fruits, marshmallows and nuts in bowl; add sour cream and toss gently. Chill and serve. Yield: 4-6 servings.

Mrs. Beverly Burton, Beggs H.S.
Beggs, Oklahoma

TANGY FRUIT SALAD

1 can pineapple tidbits
6 oranges, pared and sectioned
Juice of 1 lemon
½ c. sugar
2 tbsp. cornstarch
3 bananas, sliced

Add pineapple and juice to oranges. Add lemon juice and sugar; let set in refrigerator overnight. Drain juice; thicken with cornstarch and cool. Add oranges and pineapple; place in refrigerator. Add bananas before serving.

Mrs. Dorothy Anderson, Montrose H.S.
Montrose, South Dakota

TANGY OVERNIGHT SALAD

    1 can frozen orange juice concentrate,
        thawed
    ½ c. sugar
    2 tbsp. flour
    ¼ tsp. salt
    1 c. light cream, whipped
    3 13-oz. cans pineapple tidbits, well
        drained
    3 cans mandarin oranges, well drained
    8 maraschino cherries, quartered
    1 c. miniature marshmallows
    ½ c. coarsely chopped nuts

Combine orange juice, sugar, flour and salt
in saucepan. Cook, stirring constantly, over low
heat until thickened. Let cool. Fold in whipped
cream. Combine pineapple, oranges cherries,
marshmallows and nuts in large bowl. Add whipped cream dressing; mix lightly. Chill thoroughly. Yield: 8-10 servings.

Eva Jane Schwartz, Gettysburg Sr. H.S.
Gettysburg, Pennsylvania

TWENTY FOUR-HOUR FRUIT SALAD

    ½ c. pineapple juice
    ½ tsp. dry mustard
    4 egg yolks
    Pinch of salt
    Juice of 1 lemon
    1 c. cream, whipped
    2 c. white cherries, halved
    2 c. diced pineapple
    2 c. diced peaches or mandarin oranges
    2 c. miniature marshmallows

Combine first 4 ingredients in double boiler;
cook to consistency of custard. Remove from heat
and cool; add lemon juice and whipped cream.
Combine fruits and marshmallows; pour in mixture. Pour into bowl or pan. Chill overnight.
Yield: 10-12 servings.

Linda L. Stiller, Neah-Kah-Nie H.S.
Rockaway, Oregon

TOKAY GRAPE SALAD

    ¼ c. sugar
    ½ tsp. vanilla
    ½ pt. cream, whipped
    1 ½ lb. Tokay grapes, cut and seeded
    ⅓ c. miniature marshmallows
    3 bananas, sliced
    6 tbsp. Grape Nuts

Mix sugar and vanilla into whipped cream. Add
remaining ingredients except Grape Nuts; pour
into mold or dish. Refrigerate. Add Grape Nuts
just before serving. Yield: 8 servings.

Annah Simonson, Dawson Pub. Sch.
Dawson, Minnesota

TWENTY FOUR-HOUR SALAD

    2 c. light and dark grapes
    2 c. chunk pineapple
    2 oranges
    1 sm. jar maraschino cherries
    2 c. sm. white marshmallows
    4 tbsp. butter
    ½ c. vinegar
    ½ c. sugar
    4 egg yolks, beaten
    2 c. cream, whipped

Drain fruits; cut fruits and marshmallows into
bite-sized pieces. Melt butter in double boiler;
add vinegar and sugar. Add egg yolks slowly.
Cook over hot water until thick. Cool; add
whipped cream. Pour over fruit. Refrigerate
24 hours; serve on crisp lettuce leaf. Yield: 12-15
servings.

Mrs. Esther Braman, Atlantic Comm. Sch.
Atlantic, Iowa

TWO-PLUS CITRUS FRUIT SALAD

    2 grapefruit
    2 cans pineapple chunks
    2 cans mandarin oranges
    2 sm. cans fruit cocktail
    2 tbsp. (heaping) sour cream
    2 tbsp. (heaping) mayonnaise or salad
        dressing
    2 tbsp. fruit juice
    2 tbsp. powdered sugar

Prepare grapefruit sections in bite-sized pieces.
Drain remaining fruits well. Blend sour cream,
mayonnaise, juice and sugar lightly. Toss gently
with mixed fruits. Serve chilled on crisp lettuce
cups. Yield: 10-12 servings.

Mary A. Campbell, Ft. Necessity H.S.
Ft. Necessity, Louisiana

WALDORF SALAD

    4 med. apples, cored, diced
    1 c. pineapple tidbits or chunks
    1 c. cheddar cheese, cubed
    ½ c. salad dressing or mayonnaise

Combine apples, pineapple and cheese in mixing
bowl; add salad dressing until well-coated. Chill
until serving time. Nuts, raisins and celery may
be added if desired. Yield: 4-6 servings.

Mrs. Betty J. Jones, Les Cheneaux Comm. H.S.
Cedarville, Michigan

TWENTY FOUR-HOUR SALAD

2 eggs
4 tbsp. vinegar
4 tbsp. sugar
2 tbsp. butter
1 pt. cream, whipped
2 c. white cherries, halved
2 c. pineapple, cut into pieces
2 oranges, cut into pieces
1 lge. bag marshmallows, cut into
    pieces
1 c. broken nuts
Maraschino cherries

Beat eggs in saucepan; add vinegar and sugar. Heat, beating constantly, until thick and smooth. Add butter. Set aside and let cool. Add whipped cream. Fold in cherries, pineapple, oranges, marshmallows and nuts. Top with cherries. Chill in refrigerator 24 hours. Other fruits may be substituted for those listed. Yield: 15 servings.

Mrs. Mary N. Davis, No. Shore Sr. H.S.
Houston, Texas

TWENTY FOUR-HOUR SALAD

2 eggs, well beaten
2 tbsp. sugar
2 tbsp. lemon juice
¼ c. fruit juice
1 tbsp. oleo
2 c. fresh mandarin orange sections,
    drained
2 c. diced pineapple, drained
2 c. fruit cocktail, drained
½ lb. sm. marshmallows
½ pt. heavy cream, whipped

Combine eggs, sugar, lemon juice, fruit juice and oleo. Cook over low heat, stirring constantly until thick. Cool. Combine orange sections, pineapple and fruit cocktail; add marshmallows. Fold whipped cream into cooked salad dressing. Add to fruit mixture, blending lightly. Chill in glass bowl 24 hours. Spoon onto lettuce leaves or serve from bowl. Garnish with pecans and maraschino cherries. Yield: 8 servings.

Mrs. Violet Leissner, Furr Jr.-Sr. H.S.
Houston, Texas

TWENTY FOUR-HOUR SALAD

3 beaten egg yolks
2 tbsp. sugar
2 tbsp. vinegar
2 tbsp. pineapple syrup
1 tbsp. butter or margarine
Dash of salt
2 c. drained, canned, pitted white
    cherries
2 c. drained, canned pineapple tidbits
2 pared oranges, cut into pieces, drained
2 c. tiny marshmallows or 16 lge.
    marshmallows, cut into eighths
1 c. heavy cream, whipped

Combine egg yolks, sugar, vinegar, pineapple syrup, butter and salt in top of double boiler; cook over hot, not boiling, water until thick, stirring constantly. Cool. Stir in cherries, pineapple tidbits, orange pieces and marshmallows. Fold in whipped cream. Spoon gently into serving bowl. Chill 24 hours in refrigerator. Trim salad with orange sections, maraschino cherries and green seedless grapes. Tuck in sprigs of mint. Yield: 6-8 servings.

Mrs. Zona Beth Cates, Tempe H.S.
Tempe, Arizona
Mrs. Verna Reynolds, Kinmundy-Alma H.S.
Kinmundy, Illinois

WALDORF SALAD

2 apples
¼ c. miniature marshmallows
¼ c. broken walnuts
2 tbsp. mayonnaise

Cut apples in quarters; core and dice. Combine all ingredients thoroughly. Yield: 3 servings.

Mrs. Harvey Jacobs, Woodmere Jr. H.S. No.
Hewlett, New York

WHIPPED CREAM SALAD

½ c. frozen undiluted orange juice,
    thawed
2 tbsp. sugar
1 egg
Pineapple tidbits juice
½ lb. miniature marshmallows
1 7-oz. can pineapple tidbits
1 can mandarin oranges, drained
1 c. whipped cream

Cook first 4 ingredients slowly until thickened; cool. Add remaining ingredients. Let stand overnight.

Mary L. Vanderbeek, MSD Oregon-Davis H.S.
Grovertown, Indiana

BUSY DAY PEACH SALAD

¼ c. salad dressing
2 tbsp. walnuts, finely chopped
Salad greens
8 peach halves, canned

Arrange salad greens on salad plate or in salad bowl. Place 2 peach halves on each plate. Place salad dressing over peaches. Sprinkle nuts over dressing. Yield: 4 servings.

Marjorie Harris, Greeley H.S.
Greeley, Nebraska

EASY PEACH SALAD

4 canned peach halves
4 lettuce leaves
4 tbsp. mayonnaise
4 tbsp. shredded sharp cheddar cheese

Place each peach half on lettuce leaf. Top each peach with 1 tablespoon mayonnaise. Sprinkle with 1 tablespoon shredded cheese. Chill and serve. Yield: 4 servings.

Mrs. Judy Harrell, Oaktown Jr. H.S.
Oaktown, Indiana

STUFFED PEACH SALAD

1 3-oz. pkg. cream cheese
2 doz. salted almonds, finely chopped
⅛ tsp. salt
¼ tsp. sugar
Dash of paprika
Grated rind of ½ orange
12 canned peach halves
6 lettuce leaves

Blend cream cheese, almonds, salt, sugar, paprika and grated orange rind; form into small balls. Drain peaches; arrange in nests of lettuce. Place a cream cheese ball in hollow of each peach half. Serve with or without dressing. Add cream or orange juice to cream cheese if mixture is too dry. Yield: 6 servings.

Mrs. Leda Callahan, Ysleta H.S.
El Paso, Texas

PEAR BLUSH SALAD

1 c. red cinnamon candies
1 c. Karo red label syrup
1 ½ c. water
6 lge. fresh pears
1 3-oz. pkg. cream cheese
⅓ c. coarsely chopped nuts
Crisp green lettuce

Cook and stir cinnamon candies, Karo syrup and water in saucepan over low heat to dissolve candies. Boil 5 minutes, stirring constantly. Peel and core pears; cut into halves. Simmer pear halves in syrup until tender. Remove from syrup; drain and chill. Soften cream cheese, adding a few drops of milk, if needed. Stir in nuts. Spread flat sides of pear halves with mixture; press together sandwich fashion. Stand on bed of greens. Serve with fruit salad dressing. Yield: 6 servings.

Sister Mary Ignatius, Madonna H.S.
Chicago, Illinois

PEAR-CHEESE SALAD

1 2 ½-oz. can pears
½ to 1 c. grated cheese
½ c. sliced stuffed olives
½ c. chopped pecans
Mayonnaise to moisten

Cut drained pears into bite-sized pieces. Grate cheese; slice olives. Chop pecans. Toss all ingredients together lightly with mayonnaise. Yield: 4-6 servings.

Henryetta Sands, Wichita Falls H.S.
Witchita Falls, Texas

PEAR DELIGHT

Curly endive
8 pear halves
8 tsp. grape jelly
¼ c. chopped walnuts
French dressing

Wash endive; dry with paper towels. Arrange on 4 salad plates. Place 2 pear halves on each plate; place 1 teaspoon jelly on each pear. Sprinkle with nutmeats. Add French dressing. Yield: 4 servings.

Mrs. Beatrice Birchard, Hackettstown H.S.
Hackettstown, New Jersey

FRUIT SALAD

Pineapple juice
1 egg, beaten
2 tbsp. flour
2 tbsp. sugar
1 tbsp. butter
1 can diced pineapple, drained
20 marshmallows, cut fine
¼ lb. Velveeta cheese, cubed

Heat pineapple juice in double boiler; add egg, flour and sugar. Add butter. Cook until slightly thickened; pour over pineapple, marshmallows and cheese. Yield: 4-6 servings.

Marie B. Atkinson, Ben Eielson H.S.
Fairbanks, Alaska

LOVE SALAD

1 sm. can crushed pineapple
1 sm. jar cherries
1 sm. bag miniature marshmallows
1 ½ c. heavy cream
1 tsp. vanilla
½ c. chopped walnuts

Drain pineapple and cherries; combine with marshmallows. Let stand in refrigerator until

(Continued on next page)

any remaining juice is soaked up. Fold in cream and vanilla; mix in walnuts. Serve in lettuce cups.

Mrs. Gaylord N. Webster
Mattanawcook Academy
Lincoln, Maine

PIMENTO CHEESE SALAD

1 sm. jar pimento cheese spread
1 pkg. Dream Whip, whipped
1 ½ c. marshmallows
1 c. drained crushed pineapple
½ c. nut pieces

Combine all ingredients. Chill 1 hour or longer. Serve in lettuce cup. Yield: 8 servings.

Mildred Gates, Claude H.S.
Claude, Texas

PINEAPPLE-CHEESE SALAD

½ c. soft cream cheese
¼ c. mayonnaise
½ lb. miniature marshmallows
½ c. crushed pineapple, well drained
1 c. whipping cream

Cream cheese; add mayonnaise, marshmallows and pineapple. Beat cream until stiff; fold lightly into cheese mixture. Place in mold or large refrigerator tray lined with oiled paper. Chill and serve. Yield: 10-12 servings.

Lydia Branch, Big Sandy Sch.
Big Sandy, Tennessee

PINEAPPLE EASY

1 lge. fresh pineapple
1 pt. marshmallow creme
¼ c. milk
¾ c. coarsely chopped walnuts
Lettuce

Cut unpeeled pineapple in half lengthwise, including green top. Cut each half into thirds, lengthwise. Slice core from center of each piece. Slice peel from fruit with 1 stroke, from bottom to top end. Peel and top should be connected. Cut pineapple into bite-sized pieces, not disturbing position on peel. Dilute marshmallow creme with milk; spoon sauce on pineapple. Sprinkle nuts on sauce. Serve on lettuce.

Mrs. Lindell Stanton, Butte Valley H.S.
Dorris, California

PINEAPPLE-MARSHMALLOW SALAD

1 No. 2 can crushed pineapple
¼ c. sugar
½ tsp. salt
2 tbsp. flour
1 egg
2 tbsp. lemon juice
1 tsp. lemon peel
1 c. whipped Lucky or Dream Whip
¼ lb. marshmallows

Drain pineapple, reserving syrup. Combine sugar, salt and flour in saucepan. Add egg; blend thoroughly. Stir in pineapple syrup. Cook, stirring constantly, until thick and smooth. Remove from heat; add lemon juice and peel. Cover and chill. Whip Lucky Whip and fold into cooked mixture. Fold in marshmallows and pineapple. Chill 4 to 6 hours. Serve in lettuce cups. Maraschino cherries may be added for color.

Mrs. Sharon Altmaier, Pleasanton Pub. Sch.
Pleasanton, Nebraska

QUICK 'N' EASY PINEAPPLE SALAD

8 crisp lettuce leaves
1 No. 2 ½ can minted pineapple chunks
½ c. flaked coconut

Place lettuce leaves on 4 salad plates. Divide pineapple chunks on lettuce. Top with flaked coconut. Top with salad dressing made by combining 1/4 cup prepared salad dressing and 2 tablespoons pineapple juice, if desired.

Mrs. Carlene S. Hack, East Juniata H.S.
Cocolamus, Pennsylvania

TWENTY FOUR-HOUR SALAD

6 egg yolks
2 tbsp. margarine, melted
¾ c. milk
1 tsp. salt
1 tbsp. flour
1 tbsp. sugar
1 lb. miniature marshmallows
3 tbsp. vinegar
2 lge. cans pineapple chunks
1 lge. jar maraschino cherries, chopped
½ lb. blanched almond slivers
1 pt. whipping cream

Combine egg yolks, margarine, milk, salt, flour and sugar. Cook slowly until smooth. Add about 1/4 of the marshmallows; cool. Add vinegar. Add pineapple chunks, cherries and almonds. Fold in remaining marshmallows and whipping cream. Refrigerate overnight. Yield: 12 servings.

Mrs. Eugenia Wilson, Townsend H.S.
Townsend, Tennessee

Congealed
Fruit Salads

CONTENTS ONE PINT
Creamed
cottage
cheese

RECIPE FOR LIME COTTAGE CHEESE SALAD ON PAGE 158

APPLE-CHEESE SALAD

    1 tsp. sugar
    ¼ tsp. salt
    1 pkg. lemon gelatin
    1 c. boiling water
    6 or 8 ice cubes
    1 med. unpeeled red apple, diced
    1 3-oz. pkg. cream cheese, cubed
    ¼ c. chopped nuts

Combine sugar, salt and gelatin; dissolve in boiling water. Add ice; stir until gelatin begins to thicken. Remove unmelted ice; divide gelatin into 2 equal parts. Add apple to half the gelatin; place in 1 quart mold. Chill. Add cream cheese and nuts to remaining gelatin; beat at high speed in electric mixer until light and fluffy, about 4 to 5 minutes. Spoon carefully over clear layer of gelatin; chill until set. Unmold on lettuce; serve with mayonnaise. Yield: 4 servings.

Mrs. Alice Ketcham
Chenango Forks, New York

RED HOT CHERRY JELL-O

    2 c. water
    ¼ c. red cinnamon candies
    1 lge. pkg. cherry Jell-O
    1 can apples

Bring water to boil; add candies. Heat until dissolved. Add Jell-O; stir until dissolved. Add apples. Pour into mold or dish; chill until firm.

Mrs. James J. Sullivan
East Grand Forks Sr. H.S.
East Grand Forks, Minnesota

SPICY APPLE MOLD

    ⅔ c. red cinnamon candies
    1 ½ c. hot water
    3 to 4 med. apples, sliced
    1 pkg. cherry gelatin

Dissolve cinnamon candies in hot water. Add apples; cook until apples are tender. Add gelatin; stir until dissolved. Pour into ring mold; chill until firm. Yield: 6 servings.

Mrs. Diane Bagley, Todd Co. H.S.
Mission, South Dakota

SUMMER CIDER SALAD

    1 envelope gelatin
    ¼ c. cold water
    1 c. boiling cider
    ⅓ c. sugar
    Dash of salt
    ¼ c. lemon juice
    1 apple, finely diced
    2 tbsp. chopped preserved ginger
    ⅓ c. chopped salted peanuts

Soften gelatin in cold water; dissolve in cider. Add sugar, salt and lemon juice; chill until slightly thickened. Add apple, ginger and peanuts; pour into 4 or 6 individual molds. Chill until firm. Unmold; surround with crisp endive. Serve with mayonnaise or salad dressing. Yield: 4-6 servings.

Sister M. Aloysius P. B. V. M.
O'Gorman H.S.
Sioux Falls, South Dakota

APPLESAUCE JELL-O

    2 c. applesauce
    1 tbsp. lemon juice
    Dash of salt
    ½ c. sugar
    3 tbsp. red cinnamon hearts
    1 ½ c. water
    1 pkg. lemon Jell-O
    3 oz. cream cheese
    Milk
    Chopped nuts

Heat applesauce, lemon juice, salt, sugar and cinnamon hearts until candies are melted. Boil water; add Jell-O. Stir until dissolved. Add applesauce mixture to Jell-O; refrigerate in desired pan until firm. Soften cream cheese with small amount of milk; spread on top of salad. Top with chopped nuts.

Lorene A. Hesterberg, Estacada Union H.S.
Estacada, Oregon

APPLESAUCE SALAD

    1 pkg. unflavored gelatin
    ¼ c. cold water
    1 pkg. lemon Jell-O
    2 c. hot water
    ⅓ lb. cinnamon candies
    Applesauce
    1 3-oz. pkg. cream cheese
    ⅓ c. chopped nuts

Soften gelatin in cold water; pour in lemon Jell-O. Add hot water; dissolve. Mix in cinnamon candies; stir until candy is melted. Chill until semi-hardened. Add applesauce. Form cheese into small balls; roll each ball in nuts. Fill molds 1/2 full with gelatin mixture; drop in cheese balls. Fill molds with gelatin. Chill until firm. Yield: 8 servings.

Mrs. Gladys Baldwin, Huff Jr. H.S.
Lincoln Park, Michigan

APPLESAUCE SALAD

2 pkg. lemon Jell-O
½ lb. red cinnamon candy
1 ½ c. applesauce
1 8-oz. pkg. cream cheese, softened
¼ c. chopped nuts

Prepare Jell-O as directed on package, reserving 1 cup boiling water to dissolve cinnamon candy. Add dissolved candy to Jell-O; add applesauce. Fill mold 1/2 full. Chill until partially set. Blend cream cheese and nuts; spread over Jell-O. Top with remaining Jell-O. Chill until firm. Yield: 6-8 servings.

Joan F. Jenkins, Bridgman H.S.
Bridgman, Michigan

CHERRY BLUSH SALAD

2 pkg. cherry gelatin
2 c. hot water
1 c. cold water
2 c. applesauce

Dissolve gelatin in hot water; add cold water. Chill until partially thick. Add applesauce. Place in 1 1/2-quart mold. Yield: 6-8 servings.

Mrs. Gaynelle C. James, Gardner SW H.S.
Gardner, Illinois

CINNAMON SWIRL SALAD

2 3-oz. boxes lemon Jell-O
½ c. red cinnamon candies
3 c. boiling water
2 c. applesauce
1 tbsp. lemon juice
Dash of salt
½ c. coarsely chopped walnuts
2 3-oz. pkg. cream cheese, softened
¼ c. milk
2 tbsp. mayonnaise or salad dressing

Dissolve Jell-O and candies in boiling water; stir in applesauce, lemon juice and salt. Chill until partially set. Fold in nuts. Turn into 8 x 8 x 2-inch pan. Beat together cream cheese, milk and mayonnaise. Spoon over salad; swirl through to marble. Chill until firm. Yield: 8-10 servings.

Mrs. Clifford E. Wheeler
Woodville Attendance Center
Woodville, Mississippi

JELLIED SEVEN-UP SALAD

1 ½ c. applesauce
1 pkg. lime Jell-O
1 sm. bottle Seven-Up

Heat applesauce; add Jell-O. Dissolve Jell-O. Add Seven-Up; mix. Pour into mold; chill. Serve on lettuce leaf. Yield: 6 servings.

Florence Hughes, Toaz Jr. H.S.
Huntington, North Carolina

PINK RIBBON SALAD

¼ c. cinnamon red hots
1 c. boiling water
1 pkg. lemon Jell-O
1 c. applesauce
1 3-oz. pkg. cream cheese
2 tbsp. cream
2 tbsp. mayonnaise

Dissolve red hots in boiling water; pour liquid over lemon Jell-O. Stir to dissolve; add applesauce. Spoon half the mixture into loaf pan; chill until set. Blend cream cheese, cream and mayonnaise; spoon onto Jell-O mixture. Chill until set. Spoon remaining Jell-O mixture over top; chill until set. Cut into slices; serve on frilly lettuce leaves. Yield: 6-8 servings.

Sister M. Rose Catherine Kuehner
St. Mary Grade Sch.
West Point, Iowa

RASPBERRY ASPIC

1 pkg. raspberry gelatin
1 c. boiling water
1 6-oz. can frozen orange juice
1 No. 2 can applesauce

Dissolve gelatin in boiling water in mixing bowl. Add orange juice and applesauce. Stir until well mixed. Pour mixture into mold; place in refrigerator until firm. Unmold; serve on bed of salad greens.

Glenda Sue Smith, Marshall Co. H.S.
Guntersville, Alabama

RED CONGEALED SALAD

1 6-oz. pkg. lemon Jell-O
3 c. hot water
½ c. red hots
2 c. applesauce
2 tbsp. lemon juice
Salt to taste
2 3-oz. pkg. cream cheese
¼ c. milk
2 tbsp. mayonnaise
½ c. chopped walnuts

147

(Continued on next page)

Combine Jell-O, hot water, red hots, applesauce, lemon juice and salt. Stir until dissolved. Set in refrigerator until partially congealed. Cream cheese, milk and mayonnaise with mixer. Mix walnuts with creamed mixture; swirl into Jell-O mixture. Place in molds; chill until firm. Yield: 8-10 servings.

Mrs. Paulita Williams, Cooper H.S.
Cooper, Texas

SEVEN-UP SALAD

    1 No. 303 can applesauce
    2 3-oz. pkg. lime gelatin
    5 ice cubes
    1 12-oz. bottle lemon-lime carbonated
       drink

Heat applesauce; dissolve Jell-O in hot applesauce. Stir in ice cubes until dissolved; chill until partially set. Stir in lemon-lime. Pour into 9 x 13-inch pan. Chill until set. Spread with whipped cream, if desired; garnish with cherries. Yield: 8-10 servings.

Mrs. Michele Haller, Mohawk H.S.
Marcola, Oregon

APRICOT NECTAR SALAD

    2 pkg. orange gelatin
    2 c. boiling water
    3 c. apricot nectar
    1 c. miniature marshmallows
    ½ c. sugar
    2 tbsp. flour
    1 beaten egg
    ½ pt. cream, whipped
    Shredded Longhorn cheese

Dissolve gelatin in boiling water; cool. Add 2 cups apricot nectar; chill until partially set. Add marshmallows; pour into 8 x 12-inch glass dish. Chill until firm. Cook sugar, flour and egg; add 1 cup apricot nectar slowly. Cool; fold in cream. Spread over gelatin; sprinkle with cheese. Chill 6 to 8 hours before serving. Serve on lettuce. Yield: 8-10 servings.

Mrs. Leone Maurer, Herrin H.S.
Herrin, Illinois

APRICOT SALAD

    1 pkg. orange Jell-O
    1 ½ c. boiling water
    1 can peeled apricots
    ½ c. cream, whipped and sweetened
    ¼ c. mayonnaise
    ½ c. chopped nuts

Dissolve Jell-O in water; chill until partially set. Fold in remaining ingredients. Yield: 6-8 servings.

Mrs. Mildred R. Buck, Linden H.S.
Linden, Alabama

APRICOT SALAD

    1 1-lb. can apricots
    1 pkg. lemon gelatin
    Juice of 1 lemon
    Juice of 1 orange
    ½ c. chopped pecans
    1 sm. pkg. cream cheese, cubed

Drain apricots; add water to liquid to equal 1 1/2 cups. Puree apricot pulp. Dissolve gelatin in apricot liquid; add apricots, lemon juice and orange juice. Chill until partially set; add nuts and cheese. Chill until firm; cut with knife dipped in cold water. Yield: 12 servings.

Peggy Thrasher, Nowata H.S.
Nowata, Oklahoma

APRICOT SURPRISE RING

    1 1-lb. 4-oz. can apricot halves
    1 3-oz. pkg. orange gelatin
    ½ c. water
    ⅓ c. sm. curd cottage cheese
    1 c. regular or skim evaporated milk

Drain apricots; reserve syrup. Heat syrup to boiling; dissolve gelatin. Stir in water; cool. Fill apricot halves with cheese. Press 2 halves together; place in 5 1/2-cup ring mold. Stir milk into gelatin; pour over apricots. Chill until firm; unmold and garnish. Yield: 6 servings.

Mrs. Caryl Nelson, Glenwood H.S.
Gleenwood, Minnesota

ORANGE SALAD

    1 pkg. orange Jell-O
    1 c. boiling water
    1 c. apricot juice
    1 c. sweetened whipped cream
    1 c. mashed apricots
    Nuts (opt.)

Dissolve Jell-O in boiling water; add apricot juice. Add cream, apricots and nuts when mixture is slightly thickened. Chill for 1 hour or longer. Serve on lettuce or plain. Oranges and bananas may be added to Jell-O mixture.

Idella Q. Alfron, Woonsocket H.S.
Woonsocket, South Dakota

JEWELED APRICOT MOLD

1 1-lb. can unpeeled apricot halves
3 7-oz. bottles Seven-Up
2 3-oz. pkg. orange gelatin
1 c. sour cream
12 to 14 red maraschino cherries

Drain apricots; reserve 1/3 cup syrup. Heat 2 bottles Seven-Up to boiling; dissolve gelatin. Add remaining bottle Seven-Up and reserved apricot syrup; chill slightly. Measure 2 cups mixture; add sour cream. Blend thoroughly; chill plain orange gelatin and gelatin-cream mixture until partially set. Pour 1/4 cup orange gelatin in 8 1/2-inch ring mold; arrange cherries in apricot halves. Place apricots cut side down in mold; chill until partially set. Add remaining orange gelatin. Chill again until partially set; pour gelatin-cream mixture on top. Chill overnight until firm. Unmold; garnish with salad greens. Yield: 10 servings.

Mrs. Barbara S. Carr, Southside Jr. H.S.
Greenwood, South Carolina

APRICOT SALAD

3 pkg. orange Jell-O
3 c. boiling water
3 c. apricot nectar
1 c. sm. marshmallows
1 c. pecans
1 No. 2 ½ can apricots, cut up
½ c. sugar
2 tbsp. flour
1 egg, well beaten
1 pkg. Dream Whip, whipped

Dissolve Jell-O in boiling water; add 2 cups apricot nectar. Cool. Add marshamallows, nuts and apricots. Chill until set. Combine sugar and flour; add egg and remaining apricot nectar slowly. Cook until thick; fold in Dream Whip. Spread on Jell-O.

Mrs. Frances Eldridge, Central Sr. H.S.
Clifton, Illinois

SPICED APRICOT MOLD

1 No. 202 can apricots
¾ c. apricot juice
¼ c. vinegar
½ c. sugar
12 whole cloves
1 stick cinnamon
1 pkg. orange Jell-O

Simmer apricots, apricot juice, vinegar, sugar and spices until apricots are soft. Remove apricots; strain syrup. Add hot water to equal 2 cups liquid; dissolve Jell-O in liquid. Puree apricots; add. Place in mold; chill until set. Yield: 6 servings.

Mrs. Lewis Frazier, Duakesboro Consl. Sch.
Duakesboro, Kentucky

CINNAMON SALAD

2 pkg. lemon Jell-O
1 c. cinnamon hearts
1 3-oz. pkg. cream cheese
3 tbsp. milk
2 bananas
¼ c. chopped pecans

Dissolve 1 package lemon Jell-O in 1 3/4 cup hot water; add 1/2 cup candy. Stir to dissolve. Strain if candies do not dissolve by the time Jell-O cools. Pour into mold or dish; chill until firm. Soften cream cheese; thin with milk. Spread over congealed layer. Prepare remaining Jell-O as the first; chill until partially set. Add bananas and nuts. Spread over cream cheese layer. Chill until firm.

Lola Schall, York Public Sch.
York, Nebraska

JELL-O DELIGHT

1 pkg. strawberry Jell-O
2 lge. bananas, sliced
1 pkg. Dream Whip
1 sm. jar maraschino cherries

Prepare Jell-O as directed on package; add bananas. Chill until firm. Prepare Dream Whip as directed on package. Place 1 heaping tablespoon Jell-O in stemmed goblet; add layer of Dream Whip. Alternate layers with Dream Whip as last layer; top with cherry. Place in refrigerator until serving time. Yield: 4-6 servings.

Mrs. Selma Meyer, Tennyson Sch.
Tennyson, Indiana

BLACKBERRY SALAD

1 sm. pkg. Jell-O
1 pt. frozen blackberries
1 envelope Dream Whip or whipped cream
½ c. nuts

Prepare Jell-O according to package directions. Add cold berries; separate and mix well. Fold in whipped cream and nuts combined. Place in covered dish to set. Yield: 6 servings.

Mrs. Arva McCarty Knight, Bellevue H.S.
Bellevue, Texas

BLUEBERRY CREAM

1 envelope gelatin
¼ c. cold water
1 c. half and half cream
¾ c. sugar
1 tsp. vanilla

(Continued on next page)

1 c. sour cream
1 sm. pkg. black raspberry Jell-O
1 c. hot water
1 can blueberries

Soak gelatin in cold water. Heat cream and sugar in saucepan; add gelatin, vanilla and sour cream. Pour into molds or 8 x 8-inch pan. Mix Jell-O, hot water and blueberries including juice. When gelatin mixture is almost set, add syrupy Jell-O-blueberry mixture. Yield: 5 servings.

Mrs. Erleen Johnson, Clay H.S.
Oregon, Ohio

DEEP PURPLE SALAD

1 pkg. grape Jell-O
2 c. boiling blueberry liquid plus water
1 can blueberries, drained
1 tbsp. lemon juice
1 c. whipped cream, whipped

Prepare Jell-O using boiling liquid; let partially set. Add blueberries, lemon juice and whipped cream. Chill for 6 hours and serve. Yield: 8-10 servings.

Mrs. Allan P. Cobb, Mosinee H.S.
Mosinee, Wisconsin

RED-WHITE AND BLUE SALAD

2 pkg. raspberry Jell-O
2 c. boiling water
1 envelope unflavored gelatin
1 c. cold water
1 c. half and half
1 c. sugar
8 oz. cream cheese
1 tsp. vanilla
½ c. nutmeats
1 can blueberries
Blueberry juice

Dissolve 1 package raspberry Jell-O in boiling water; pour into 9 x 13-inch pan. Chill until set. Combine unflavored gelatin and cold water; set aside. Combine half and half and sugar; bring to a boil. Remove from heat; add cream cheese and beat until smooth. Add vanilla, nuts and un-flavored gelatin; cool. Pour mixture over chilled layer; chill until set. Drain blueberries; add enough water to juice to equal 2 cups. Heat to boiling; add remaining raspberry Jell-O. Add blueberries. Pour over cheese layer; chill until firm. Yield: 15 servings.

Mrs. Mary Eveland, Irving H.S.
Des Moines, Iowa

BING CHERRY MOLD

1 No. 2 can Bing cherries
1 c. port
1 envelope plain gelatin
1 pkg. cherry gelatin
1 pkg. cream cheese
Cream

Drain cherries; heat 1 cup cherry juice in port. Pour remaining juice over plain gelatin; mix cherry gelatin and plain gelatin together. Dissolve mixed gelatins in hot cherry juice-port mixture. Stir; mix well. Add halved cherries. Place in ring mold or individual molds. Serve with cream cheese softened with cream. Yield: 10 servings.

Mrs. Mary Pinkston Whaley
Tuscaloosa Co. H.S.
Northport, Alabama

BLACK CHERRY DELIGHT

1 can pitted black cherries
1 6-oz. box black cherry Jell-O
1 pkg. cream cheese
1 pkg. Dream Whip
½ c. milk

Drain cherries; reserve juice. Prepare Jell-O according to directions using cherry juice as part of cold liquid. Pour a layer of Jell-O in mold; let solidify. Spread with cream cheese; top with another layer of Jell-O. When solid, frost with Dream Whip beaten with milk. Yield: 12 servings.

Mrs. Helen Winkelman, Triopia Jr. H.S.
Arenzville, Illinois

CHERRY CHRISTMAS SALAD

1 No. 2 can unsweetened pie cherries
¾ c. sugar
1 pkg. lime Jell-O
1 ½ c. boiling water
1 3-oz. pkg. cream cheese
1 c. cream, whipped
1 tbsp. cornstarch
¼ tsp. almond extract
Red food coloring

Simmer cherries and 1/2 cup sugar 5 minutes; cool. Drain; reserve juice. Dissolve Jell-O and remaining sugar in boiling water; cool. Blend Jell-O mixture and cream cheese with mixer; add cherries. Refrigerate. When it begins to set, fold in cream. Pour into mold. Mix 1 cup reserved cherry juice, cornstarch, almond flavoring and red food coloring in saucepan. Stir and cook dressing until thick. Cool. Serve over salad.

Mrs. Joyce Johnson, Ashby H.S.
Ashby, Minnesota

CHERRY-COKE SALAD

1 pkg. cherry Jell-O
¾ c. hot water
½ sm. bottle Coke
1 sm. pkg. cream cheese
1 c. chopped nuts
1 8-oz. can crushed pineapple
½ c. chopped maraschino cherries

Combine Jell-O, hot water and Coke. Cool. Mix in softened cream cheese. Add nuts, pineapple and cherries. Chill and serve. Yield: 4-5 servings.

Donna G. Phillips, Waynoka H.S.
Waynoka, Oklahoma

CHERRY-COKE SALAD

1 pkg. cherry Jell-O
2 8-oz. bottles Coca-Cola
1 c. maraschino cherries, drained
1 c. pecans, chopped

Dissolve Jell-O in 1 bottle Coca-Cola, which has been heated to boiling point. Add remaining bottle of Coca-Cola, which has been chilled, cherries and pecans. Pour into shallow mold and chill until congealed.

Mrs. Betty Addison, Lipan H.S.
Lipan, Texas

CHERRY-SHERRY SALAD

1 can Bing cherries
1 can Royal Anne cherries
2½ c. juice from drained cherries
2 pkg. cherry Jell-O
½ c. sherry wine
Pecans (opt.)

Drain fruit; reserve liquid. Add water if not enough juice. Boil juice; pour over Jell-O. Stir until dissolved. Add sherry, fruit and pecans. Mold until firm. Yield: 8 servings.

Mrs. Peggy Wood, South Park H.S.
Beaumont, Texas

CHERRY-SHERRY-JELL-O SALAD

1 3-oz. pkg. cherry Jell-O
½ c. hot cherry juice
½ c. hot water
½ c. sherry
1 tbsp. lemon juice
1 No. 1 can Bing cherries, pitted and drained
¼ c. slivered almonds
Cream cheese dressing

Dissolve Jell-O in hot cherry juice and water. Add sherry, lemon juice, Bing cherries and almonds. Pour into 8-inch square pan to set. Serve with softened cream cheese dressing.

Mrs. Esther E. Green, Hoover Jr. H.S.
Oklahoma City, Oklahoma

COKE SALAD

1 No. 1 can black pitted cherries
1 No. 1 can pineapple juice
1 pkg. black raspberry Jell-O
1 cold Coca-Cola
1 c. nuts

Drain cherries; reserve fruit. Combine and heat fruit juices; dissolve Jell-O. Add Coke; cool until thick. Mix in fruit and nuts; place in refrigerator to continue setting. Yield: 4-6 servings.

Mrs. Charles Ambrose, Jr., Robert Lee H.S.
Midland, Texas

JELLIED ORANGE QUARTERS

1 No. 303 can pitted black cherries
1 c. cherry juice
1 pkg. cherry gelatin
¼ c. fresh orange juice
3 tbsp. fresh lemon juice
½ c. sherry
½ c. chopped nutmeats
6 bright yellow seedless orange shells

Drain juice from cherries to measure 1 cup. Heat; add gelatin, stirring until dissolved. Combine orange juice, lemon juice and sherry with enough water to make 1 cup liquid; add to gelatin. Chill until slightly thickened; fold in cherries and nuts. Spoon into orange shells; set these in muffin tins to keep shape. Chill until firm. Cut into quarters. Orange juice may be substituted for sherry. Yield: 12 servings.

Harriet Reed, Milltown H.S.
Milltown, Indiana

REFRESHING SALAD

2 c. crushed pineapple
1 pkg. orange gelatin
1 pkg. lemon gelatin
1½ c. ginger ale
Juice of 1 orange
Juice of 1 lemon
2 c. Royal Anne cherries
1 c. chopped nuts

Drain juice from pineapple; heat juice and dissolve gelatin in it. Cool. Add ginger ale, orange

(Continued on next page)

juice and lemon juice; let jell slightly. Add fruit and nuts; mold until firm. Yield: 8-10 servings.

Vivian Pommer, New Monroe Comm. Sch.
Monroe, Iowa

STRUBLE'S CHERRY SALAD

1 c. sour cherries
Red food coloring
1 c. sugar
1 pkg. cherry gelatin
1 pkg. Knox gelatin
1 c. broken pecans
1 tsp. almond flavoring

Drain cherries. Add red food coloring to juice and enough water to make 2 1/2 cups liquid. Add sugar. Heat thoroughly; do not boil. Pour over mixed cherry gelatin and Knox gelatin. Add cherries, nuts and almond flavoring. Chill in 10 x 13 1/2-inch Pyrex dish or molds. Yield: 12 servings.

Mrs. Maxine Bohart, Lake Highlands Jr. H.S.
Dallas, Texas

STUFFED BLACK CHERRY SALAD

1 pkg. black cherry Jell-O
1 c. boiling water
1 No. 303 can black sweet pitted cherries
1 4-oz. pkg. cream cheese
1 4-oz. pkg. whole pecans

Dissolve Jell-O in boiling water. Add 12 ice cubes; let set until of jelly consistency. Drain cherries well. Scoop a portion of cream cheese with each pecan so that cheese covers nut. Stuff each drained cherry; drop into Jell-O, making rows of filled cherries. Let set until firm; cut and serve on lettuce leaves. Yield: 6 servings.

Ruth I. Schwarz, Galesburg Sr. H.S.
Galesburg, Illinois

COFFEE-MINCEMEAT RELISH

1 3-oz. pkg. orange Jell-O
1 tbsp. instant coffee
1 c. boiling water
½ c. cold water
½ c. moist mincemeat
¼ c. chopped nuts

Dissolve Jell-O and coffee in boiling water; add cold water. Chill until thickened. Add mincemeat and nuts. Place in 3-cup mold or individual molds. Chill until firm. Yield: 6 servings.

Mrs. Karen Demko, Evergreen H.S.
Vancouver, Washington

CHRISTMAS JEWEL SALAD

1 pkg. wild cherry Jell-O
2 c. boiling water
¼ c. sugar
½ c. grated orange rind
2 c. fresh cranberries, chopped
½ pt. whipping cream, whipped

Dissolve Jell-O in boiling water; add sugar. Stir until dissolved. Cool until mixture begins to thicken. Fold in half the orange rind, cranberries and whipped cream. Dip 12 small jelly molds in cold water. Spoon in congealed mixture; refrigerate for several hours. Unmold on lettuce, garnish with maraschino cherry and small amount of grated orange.

Mary Maddox, Simonds H.S.
New Brunswick, Canada

CRANBERRY MOLD

1 envelope plain gelatin
2 tbsp. cold water
1 box lemon Jell-O
1 c. boiling water
1 teaspoon salt
3 c. sugar
1 lb. fresh cranberries, ground
½ c. orange juice
3 tbsp. lemon juice
Grated rind of 1 lemon
½ c. chopped nuts

Soak gelatin in cold water for 5 minutes. Dissolve Jell-O in hot water; add salt and sugar. Stir until dissolved. Add cranberries, orange juice, lemon juice, rind and chopped nuts. Stir well. Place in refrigerator until firm. Yield: 12 servings.

Mrs. Kate Strom Berry, Latta H.S.
Latta, South Carolina

CRANBERRY SALAD

1 c. ground cranberries
Grated rind of 1 orange
1 c. ground nuts
1 c. sugar
1 ½ c. water
1 lge. pkg. lemon Jell-O
Few drops of red food coloring

Combine cranberries, rind, nuts and sugar; let set overnight. Boil water; add Jell-O. Stir until dissolved. Chill until partially set; add cranberry mixture. Add food coloring. Chill until firm. Yield: 12 servings.

Willie M. Trotter, Batesburg Leesville H.S.
Batesburg, South Carolina

CRANBERRY SPARKLE SALAD

1 pkg. raspberry gelatin
1 1-lb. can whole cranberry sauce
Grated peel from 1 orange
Salad greens

Prepare gelatin according to directions on package; chill until syrupy. Stir in cranberry sauce and orange peel. Spoon into 8 individual molds. Chill until firm. Unmold on crisp salad greens. Yield: 8 servings.

Mrs. Cele Olson, Eagle Bend H.S.
Eagle Bend, Maine

HOLIDAY CRANBERRY MOLD

2 pkg. cherry gelatin
2 c. sour cream
1 16-oz. can whole cranberry sauce

Prepare gelatin using one-half the amount of water given on package directions. Chill until thickened. Beat in sour cream and cranberry sauce. Pour into 2-quart mold; freeze. Yield: 8 servings.

Mrs. Betty Rassette, Salina Sr. H.S.
Salina, Kansas

FROSTED MELON MOLD

1 melon
1 pkg. fruit gelatin, prepared
1 6-oz. pkg. cream cheese
2 tbsp. milk
Leaf lettuce
French dressing or mayonnaise

Peel whole melon; cut slice from end. Remove seeds. Fill center with fruit gelatin; refrigerate until gelatin is firm. Soften cheese with milk; frost outside of melon with mixture. Serve in slices on crisp lettuce. Garnish with mayonnaise.

Mattie Finney, Vashon H.S.
Burton, Washington

APRICOT-LEMON JELL-O SALAD

1 pkg. lemon Jell-O
1 c. boiling water
1 c. apricot nectar
1 can fruit cocktail

Dissolve Jell-O in boiling water; add apricot nectar. Add fruit cocktail when mixture is partially congealed. Yield: 6 servings.

Mrs. Sam Crow, Hollis H.S.
Hollis, Okalhoma

BUTTERMILK-FRUIT SALAD MOLD

1 envelope Knox gelatin
1 8 ¼-oz. can low-calorie fruit cocktail, drain and reserve liquid
½ c. granulated, imitation sugar
1 tbsp. lemon juice
1 ¼ c. buttermilk
1 tsp. almond extract

Soften gelatin in fruit cocktail liquid; dissolve over hot water. Blend in remaining ingredients. Chill until mixture begins to thicken; fold in fruit cocktail. Spoon into lightly oiled, 2-cup mold. Chill until firm. Yield: 4 servings.

Gladys Fry, Brown Co. H.S.
Mt. Sterling, Illinois

BUTTERMILK-FRUIT MOLD

1 envelope unflavored gelatin
1 8-oz. can fruit cocktail, drain and reserve liquid
½ c. sugar
1 tbsp. lemon juice
1 ¼ c. buttermilk
1 tsp. almond extract

Soften gelatin in 1/2 cup fruit cocktail liquid. Pour into double boiler; dissolve over hot water. Blend in sugar, lemon juice, buttermilk and extract. Fold in fruit cokctail. Spoon into lightly oiled, 2-cup mold. Chill until firm. Yield: 4-5 servings.

Gladys Fry, Brown Co. H.S.
Mt. Sterling, Illinois

COCONUT-FRUIT SALAD

1 3-oz. pkg. lemon Jell-O
1 c. boiling water
Juice and rind of 1 orange and 1 lemon
1 No. 2 ½ can fruit cocktail, drained
⅓ can coconut
2 tbsp. mayonnaise
½ c. chopped nuts

(Continued on next page)

Dissolve Jell-O in boiling water. Combine orange and lemon juices plus enough fruit cocktail juice to make 2/3 cup; add to Jell-O. Congeal slightly. Add remaining ingredients. Pour into mold. Refrigerate until firm. Yield: 8 servings.

Katherine Simons, Cross H.S.
Cross, South Carolina

CONGEALED FRUIT SALAD

    1 pkg. orange Jell-O
    1 c. hot water
    1 can fruit cocktail, drained
    1 sm. bottle cherries
    ½ c. Pet milk, chilled
    ½ c. mayonnaise

Dissolve Jell-O in hot water; add fruit cocktail and cherries. Place in refrigerator until partially congealed. Whip canned milk; add mayonnaise. Fold mixture into fruit Jell-O. Pour into molds. Yield: 8 servings.

Earle H. Vallentine, Edisto Sch.
Cordova, South Carolina

FRUIT COCKTAIL SALAD

    1 box Jell-O, any flavor
    1 envelope Dream Whip, whipped
    1 sm. can fruit cocktail, drained

Prepare Jell-O as directed on box; congeal slightly. Beat Dream Whip into Jell-O, using mixer. Fold in fruit. Chill. Yield: 5 servings.

Mrs. Claire Schultz, Rossville H.S.
Rossville, Illinois

PARTY SALAD MOLD

    1 lge. No. 2 can fruit cocktail, drained
    2 pkg. peach Jell-O
    2 c. boiling water
    1 c. syrup from fruit
    1 pt. sour cream
    1 lge. No. 2 can fruit cocktail, drained

Dissolve Jell-O in boiling water. Stir in fruit cocktail syrup, then sour cream. Congeal slightly. Add fruit cocktail. Pour into mold. Chill until firm. Yield: 8-10 servings.

Mrs. Majorie Townsend, East Deer-Frazer H.S.
Creighton, Pennsylvania

PINEAPPLE-GRAPEFRUIT SALAD

    2 c. pineapple-grapefruit drink
    1 3-oz. pkg. lemon gelatin
    1 1-lb. 14-oz. can fruit cocktail,
      well-drained

Heat pineapple-grapefruit drink to boiling. Add gelatin, stirring until dissolved. Chill slightly. Add fruit cocktail. Chill until set. Yield: 6 servings.

Mary Elizabeth Ball, Waukegan Township H.S.
Waukegan, Illinois

RIBBON SALAD

    1 3-oz. pkg. lemon gelatin
    1 envelope unflavored gelatin
    ¼ c. cold water
    ½ c. fruit cocktail syrup
    1 pt. creamed cottage cheese
    1 1-lb. can fruit cocktail, drained
    1 3-oz. pkg. cherry gelatin

Prepare lemon gelatin according to package directions; pour into 9 x 5 x 3-inch oiled pan. Chill until firm. Soften unflavored gelatin in cold water. Bring fruit cocktail syrup to a boil; remove from heat. Dissolve unflavored gelatin in hot syrup; stir into cottage cheese. Add fruit cocktail; spread evenly over lemon gelatin. Chill until firm. Prepare cherry gelatin according to package directions. Chill until mixture mounds when dropped from spoon. Pour over cheese layer. Chill until firm. Unmold on lettuce. Slice and serve. Yield: 6-8 servings.

Rosetta A. Wheeler, Giles H.S.
Pearisburg, Virginia

GRAPEFRUIT SALAD

    2 grapefruit
    2 3-oz. pkg. lemon Jell-O
    ¾ c. boiling water
    1 tbsp. flour
    3 tbsp. sugar
    1 egg yolk, beaten
    Juice of 1 lemon
    ⅓ c. pineapple juice
    4 marshmallows
    ⅓ pt. cream, whipped
    ⅓ c. chopped nuts

Halve grapefruit; scoop out pulp and juice. Dissolve Jell-O in boiling water. Stir in 3 1/4 cups grapefruit pulp and juice; pour into grapefruit halves to congeal. Cut in quarters. Cook flour, sugar, egg yolk, lemon juice and pineapple juice in double boiler until thickened. Add marshmallows; stir until melted. Cool; fold in cream and nuts. Serve over gelatin. Yield: 8 servings.

Mrs. Pauline S. Slate, Greensville Co. H.S.
Emporia, Virginia

HOLIDAY SALAD MOLD

    1 box grape Jell-O
    1½ c. water
    1 pkg. California figs, cut up
    ½ c. chopped walnuts

Dissolve Jell-O in 1 cup boiling water; add 1/2 cup cold water. Pour into mold. Add figs; let stand until cool and almost set. Add walnuts. Chill until set. Yield: 8 servings.

Ellen Goldstein, Parkside Jr. H.S.
Massapequa, New York

MOLDED CHEESE SALAD

    2 tsp. gelatin
    ¼ c. cold water
    1 c. hot pineapple juice
    1½ c. cottage cheese
    4 tbsp. heavy cream
    Salt and paprika to taste
    1 c. dried prunes, cooked, pitted and
       drained

Soak gelatin in cold water; dissolve with hot pineapple juice. Cool. Mix cottage cheese, cream and seasonings together. Add cheese mixture to thickened gelatin. Cut prunes into small pieces; add to mixture. Mix thoroughly. Pour into wet, cold ring mold. Chill thoroughly. Unmold on a bed of crisp lettuce. Garnish with dressing. Yield: 6-8 servings.

Mickey Schliefert, Plattsmouth H.S.
Plattsmouth, Nebraska

CELESTIAL GOLDEN SALAD

    2 3-oz. pkg. orange Jell-O
    2 c. hot water
    1 11-oz. can mandarin oranges
    1 6-oz. can frozen orange juice
    1 c. ginger ale or Seven-Up

Pour Jell-O into bowl. Blend in hot water; stir until dissolved. Drain oranges, reserving syrup. Stir reserved syrup, orange juice concentrate and ginger ale into Jell-O. Chill until mixture is slightly thicker than consistancy of unbeaten egg white. Mix Jell-O mixture with oranges and turn into 1 1/2-quart oiled mold. Chill until firm. Yield: 10 servings.

Willie Mae Cornwell, Midway H.S.
Waco, Texas

EASY ORANGE SALAD

    1 6-oz. pkg. orange Jell-O
    2 c. boiling water
    1¼ c. cold water
    1 can mandarin oranges
    1 c. grated Velveeta or other cheese

Dissolve Jell-O in boiling water. Add cold water and juice from oranges. Chill until thickened. Add grated cheese and oranges; pour into 9 x 9 x 2-inch pan. Chill 2 hours. Cut into squares and serve on lettuce leaves. Yield: 9 servings.

Mrs. Sue Purcell, New Deal H.S.
New Deal, Texas

LEMON-COCONUT SALAD

    2 pkg. lemon Jell-O
    2 c. hot water
    2 c. cold water
    1 c. whipped cream
    ½ c. chopped walnuts
    ½ c. shredded coconut
    1 can drained mandarin oranges
    1 c. miniature marshmallows

Dissolve Jell-O in hot water; add cold water. Cool until slightly congealed; fold in remaining ingredients. Chill until set. Mandarin orange juice may be substituted for part of cold water. Yield: 10-12 servings.

Mrs. Bonnie Shaw, Clarkfield H.S.
Clarkfield, Minnesota

MANDARIN ORANGE SALAD

    2 pkg. orange Jell-O
    2 c. water
    1 6-oz. can frozen orange juice
    1 can mandarin oranges

Dissolve Jell-O in hot water; cool. Add frozen orange juice; stir to dissolve. Add mandarin oranges and mold. Yield: 6 servings.

Mrs. Kathryn I. Starcher, Sunnyside H.S.
Tucson, Arizona

MOLDED ORANGE JUICE SALAD

    Mandarin orange syrup
    1 pkg. orange, lime or raspberry gelatin
    1 6-oz. can frozen orange juice,
       undiluted
    1 can mandarin oranges, drained
    Sour cream

Measure liquid from oranges; add enough water to equal 1 cup liquid. Boil liquid and add to gelatin. Stir in frozen orange juice. Fold in orange segments when mixture is partially set. Chill until firm. Serve with sour cream. Bananas may be added if desired. Yield: 6-8 servings.

Mary Elizabeth Kloos, Helix H.S.
La Mesa, California

ORANGE CREAM

1 8-oz. pkg. cream cheese
¼ c. sugar
1 c. evaporated milk
1 3-oz. pkg. orange gelatin
1 c. hot water
2 tsp. grated orange rind
2 tbsp. orange juice

Beat cream cheese with sugar until light and smooth; blend in evaporated milk gradually. Dissolve gelatin in hot water; cool slightly. Add to milk mixture gradually; stir in orange rind and juice. Pour into 3 1/2-cup mold. Chill for about 4 hours or until firm. Unmold by dipping mold into hot water for several seconds. Top with whole cranberrry sauce and mandarin oranges. Place in refrigerator until ready to serve. Yield: 4-5 servings.

Mrs. Keith Acker
West Branch-Rose City Area Sch.
West Branch, Michigan

ORANGE DELIGHT

1 sm. box orange gelatin
2 c. orange juice
2 cans mandarin oranges, drained

Mix gelatin according to directions on package, substituting 1 cup hot orange juice and 1 cup cold orange juice for water. Chill until mixture begins to thicken. Add orange sections; continue to chill until firm. Unmold on bed of greens. Yield: 6 servings.

Mrs. Jolene Hartman, Lancaster H.S.
Lancaster, Texas

ORANGE FROSTY DESSERT

1 sm. pkg. orange Jell-O
1 sm. pkg. Dream Whip
1 sm. can mandarin oranges
1 tbsp. mayonnaise

Prepare Jell-O as directed on package; chill until almost set. Whip until mixture foams. Prepare Dream Whip as directed. Drain oranges; combine with Jell-O and Dream Whip. Beat until thoroughly mixed. Pour into individual sherbets or into 8-inch square pan; allow to set until firm. Serve with mayonnaise. Yield: 8 servings.

Dianne Huston, Roseville H.S.
Roseville, Illinois

ORANGE SPECIAL

2 pkg. orange Jell-O
3 sm. cans mandarin oranges, drained
Creamed cottage cheese or whipped
    cream cheese

Dissolve Jell-O in 2 cups hot water; add 1 1/2 cups ice water. Chill until partially set. Fold in orange sections. Chill until firm. Serve topped with creamed cottage cheese. Yield: 12 servings.

Mrs. Imogene Spring, Seymour H.S.
Seymour, Texas

ORANGE TANG SALAD

1 family-size pkg. orange Jell-O
1 c. dry Tang
1 qt. boiling water
2 cans mandarin oranges
2 pkg. prepared Dream Whip
4 c. sm. marshmallows

Dissolve Jell-O and Tang in boiling water; cool to syrup stage. Add oranges and Dream Whip. Stir into Jell-O. Add marshmallows. Chill. Yield: 12 servings.

Mrs. Janice L. Spears, Rockport Fulton H.S.
Rockport, Texas

BUFFET PEACH SALAD

1 3-oz. pkg. orange gelatin
1 c. boiling water
¼ c. peach syrup
¼ c. orange juice
½ c. ginger ale
1 No. 2 ½ can peach halves, drained
¼ c. pecan halves
6 to 8 maraschino cherries

Dissolve gelatin in water; add syrup, orange juice and ginger ale. Chill until slightly thickened. Arrange peach halves in shallow serving bowl. Yield: 6-8 servings.

Mrs. Mary Ann Schroeder, Windthorst H.S.
Windthorst, Texas

PEACHES AND CREAM SALAD

2 c. sliced peaches
3 oz. pkg. lemon gelatin
⅔ c. cream style cottage cheese
½ c. chopped pecans
2 c. heavy cream, whipped

Drain peaches; reserve 1 cup juice. Bring juice to boil in saucepan; add gelatin. Stir until completely dissolved. Cool until slightly thickened. Fold in cheese, peaches and pecans. Fold into cream. Pour into 2-quart mold. Chill for 3 hours. Yield: 8 servings.

LaVerne Stansell, Cary M. Abney Sch.
Waskom, Texas

FRUIT SALAD MOLD

1 12-oz. pkg. frozen or fresh sliced
peaches
1 pkg. orange gelatin
1 c. ginger ale
¼ c. lemon juice
½ c. halved maraschino cherries
¼ c. chopped pecans or walnuts
Lettuce
Dressing

Drain peaches; reserve juice. Heat juice and enough water to make 1 cup. Place gelatin in hot liquid; stir until dissolved. Add ginger ale and lemon juice. Chill until consistency of egg white. Blend in peaches, cherries and nuts. Pour into oiled ring mold. Chill until firm. Serve on bed of lettuce with Dressing.

DRESSING:

1 c. whipped cream
1 c. mayonnaise

Whip cream; blend in mayonnaise. Yield: 6 servings.

Marcelle T. Montminy, Memorial H.S.
Manchester, New Hampshire

SPICED PEACH MOLD

2 pkg. orange Jell-O
1 jar whole spiced peaches, drained
1 8-oz. pkg. cream cheese, room
temperature
½ c. chopped nuts
Mayonnaise
½ c. chopped nuts

Prepare Jell-O according to directions on package. Place in deep square Pyrex dish or individual molds. Chill until partially set. Remove seeds without tearing up peaches. Blend cream cheese and enough mayonnaise to taste; add nuts. Mix well. Stuff peaches with cheese mixture; turn upside-down in Jell-O. Arrange so that it may be cut in squares. Chill until set. Unmold upside down on serving plate. Cut in squares; serve on lettuce leaves. Yield: 8-10 servings.

Mrs. John L. Hansbrough, Magee Attendance Ctr.
Magee, Mississippi

SPICED PEACH SALAD

1 No. 2 can spiced pickled peaches
1 3-oz. pkg. cream cheese
2 tsp. mayonnaise
¼ c. plus 1 tsp. bourbon
¼ c. chopped nuts
½ c. hot water
1 pkg. lemon Jell-O

Drain peaches; reserve 3/4 cup liquid. Remove seeds from peaches. Mash cream cheese; add mayonnaise, 1 teaspoon bourbon and nuts. Stuff peach with cheese mixture. Combine 1/2 cup water with Jell-O. Add remaining bourbon and reserved peach juice. Place stuffed peach in individual molds; cover with Jell-O mixture. Place in refrigerator to congeal. Serve on lettuce leaf. Yield: 6 servings.

Mrs. Stacie O. Houser, Sun Valley H.S.
Monroe, North Carolina

SPICED PEACH SALAD

1 c. water
⅓ c. sugar
1 tsp. whole cloves
1 stick cinnamon
2 tbsp. vinegar
1 No. 2 ½ can whole or sliced peaches
1 3-oz. pkg. orange Jell-O

Boil water, sugar, spices and vinegar. Drain peaches; reserve juice. Add 1 cup juice to spice mixture; boil. Add peaches; boil until peaches are flavored. Add Jell-O. Remove cloves and cinnamon. Chill until set. Yield: 6-8 servings.

Velva Johnson, Adams H.S.
Adams, Minnesota

BLUSHING PEAR SALAD

1 3-oz. pkg. lime gelatin
6 pear halves
Red food coloring
3 tbsp. undiluted frozen limeade
concentrate
3 tbsp. honey
3 tbsp. vegetable oil
½ tsp. celery or poppy seeds

Prepare gelatin as directed on package. Tint pear halves pink with solution of red food coloring and water; arrange cut side down in 9 x 9 x 1 3/4-inch pan. Add gelatin; chill until firm. Combine remaining ingredients; beat with rotary beater until smooth. Serve over gelatin. Yield: 6 servings.

Mrs. J. P. Stanley, Saltillo H.S.
Saltillo, Texas

PEAR-PECAN SALAD

1 No. 2 ½ can pears
1 3-oz. pkg. lemon gelatin
1 8-oz. pkg. cream cheese
1 c. chopped pecans
½ pt. cream, whipped

157

(Continued on next page)

Congealed Pear, Pineapple Salads

Drain pears; reserve 1 cup liquid. Bring juice to boil; remove from heat. Add gelatin; stir until dissolved. Chill until partially set. Place pears in blender or mixer; blend until soupy. Stir in gelatin mixture and nuts; fold in cream. Pour into large mold or 16 individual molds; chill. Serve in slices or unmold on lettuce leaf. Garnish with maraschino cherries if desired. Yield: 12-16 servings.

Mrs. Barbara H. Thompson, Tom Bean H.S.
Tom Bean, Texas

LIME-COTTAGE CHEESE SALAD
    2 3-oz. pkg. lime gelatin
    2 ½ c. boiling water
    1 c. creamed cottage cheese
    1 1-lb. can pear halves, drained and
       diced
    ½ c. whipping cream, whipped

Dissolve gelatin in boiling water. Chill until gelatin begins to t h i c k e n; whip until light and fluffy. Fold in remaining ingredients. Pour into oiled 6-cup mold or 9 x 5 x 3-i n c h loaf pan; chill until firm. Unmold onto crisp salad greens. Yield: 8 servings.

Photograph for this recipe on page 145.

LIME DELIGHT
    1 pkg. lime gelatin
    1 c. hot water
    1 c. pear juice
    ¾ c. sm. curd cottage cheese, drained
    1 c. diced canned pears
    ½ to 1 c. shredded American cheese

Dissolve gelatin in hot water; add pear juice. Chill until slightly thickened; stir in cottage cheese, pears and American cheese. Pour in mold; chill until firm. Yield: 9 servings.

Mrs. James Eckhout, Ansley H.S.
Ansley, Nebraska

PEAR SALAD
    1 c. pear juice
    1 box lime Jell-O
    1 No. 2 ½ can pears
    2 pkg. cream cheese
    3 tbsp. cream
    1 tbsp. salad dressing
    1 c. cream, whipped
    ¼ c. chopped nuts

Heat pear juice; add Jell-O. Stir until dissolved; cool. Sieve pears; blend c r e a m cheese and

cream. Add pears, cheese and salad dressing to gelatin. Fold in cream and nuts. Pour in greased dish; chill till firm. Yield: 12 servings.

Evelyn Van Vleet, Garden City Sr. H.S.
Garden City, Kansas

PEAR SALAD
    1 3-oz. pkg. lime or lemon Jell-O
    1 ⅓ c. pear liquid, heated
    1 8-oz. pkg. cream cheese
    1 No. 2 ½ can pears, diced
    ½ c. nuts
    1 pkg. Dream Whip, whipped

Dissolve gelatin in pear liquid; add cream cheese. Blend with mixer at low speed; chill until slightly thickened. Add pears and nuts. Fold into Dream Whip; Place in ring mold. Chill until set. Garnish with cherries. Yield: 6-8 servings.

Zelda H. Gerstner, Savanna H.S.
Anaheim, California

UNDER THE SEA SALAD
    1 3-oz. pkg. lime or lemon-lime
       gelatin
    ¼ tsp. salt
    1 c. boiling water
    1 1-lb. can pear halves
    1 tbsp. lemon juice
    2 3-oz. pkg. cream cheese
    ⅛ tsp. ginger

Dissolve gelatin and salt in boiling water. Drain pears; add water to syrup to equal 3/4 cup. Dice pears; set aside. Add pear syrup and lemon juice to gelatin; measure 1 1/4 cups into 1-quart mold. Chill until set, but not firm. Soften cheese until creamy; add remaining gelatin gradually. Blend until smooth; add ginger. Chill until very thick; fold in pears. Spoon into mold; chill until firm. Unmold on crisp lettuce. Yield: 8 servings.

Joyce S. Longest, Henrico H.S.
Richmond, Virginia
Mrs. Adrienne Applegate, Atlanta H.S.
Atlanta, Illinois

ANGEL DELIGHT SALAD
    1 sm. can crushed pineapple
    1 pkg. lime gelatin
    1 c. miniature marshmallows
    ¼ c. sugar
    ¼ tsp. salt
    2 tsp. lemon juice
    1 c. boiling water
    1 c. whipping cream, whipped
    ½ c. chopped pecans
    1 c. cottage cheese

(Continued on next page)

Drain pineapple, reserving juice. Dissolve gelatin, marshmallows, sugar and salt in reserved juice, lemon juice and boiling water; chill until firm. Add remaining ingredients to mixture. Chill until set. Two to three drops green food coloring may be added if desired. Yield: 8 servings.

Mrs. Doris W. Sanders, A. S. Johnston H.S.
Austin, Texas

BERNICE'S LIME SALAD

    1 c. boiling water
    1 pkg. lime gelatin
    1 c. miniature marshmallows
    ½ c. cold water
    1 sm. can crushed pineapple
    ½ c. nuts (opt.)
    ½ c. cream, whipped or 1 pkg. Dream
        Whip
    ½ c. cottage cheese

Pour boiling water over gelatin; stir until dissolved. Add marshmallows; stir until soft. Add cold water, pineapple and nuts; fold in whipped cream and cottage cheese. Refrigerate until set. Yield: 6 servings.

Mrs. Stella P. Jones, Coldspring H.S.
Coldspring, Texas

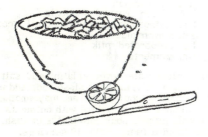

CHEESE AND PINEAPPLE SALAD

    1 tbsp. unflavored gelatin
    ¼ c. cold water
    ¾ c. sugar
    ½ c. pineapple syrup
    1 c. crushed pineapple, drained
    1 c. shredded American cheese
    1 c. heavy cream, whipped

Soften gelatin in cold water. Dissolve sugar in pineapple syrup over low heat; add gelatin, stirring until dissolved. Chill until partially set; add

pineapple and cheese. Fold in whipped cream. Turn into 1-quart mold; chill until firm. Yield: 6-8 servings.

Mrs. Phyllis Rogers, Prattsville H.S.
Prattsville, Arkansas

CHERRY-CREAM SALAD

    1 pkg. cherry Jell-O
    1 jar chopped maraschino cherries
    1 c. chopped nuts
    1 can crushed pineapple
    ½ pt. whipped cream

Prepare Jell-O according to package directions; chill until partially set. Mix cherries, nuts and pineapple with thickened Jell-O; fold in whipped cream. Yield: 8 servings.

Mrs. Jolene Corcoran, Follett H.S.
Follett, Texas

CHERRY-PINEAPPLE DELIGHT

    1 box cherry gelatin
    1 c. boiling water
    1 sm. can crushed pineapple
    1 sm. bottle cherries, halved
    1 c. chopped pecans
    1 sm. pkg. miniature marshmallows
    ½ pt. whipped cream

Dissolve gelatin in boiling water; add juice of pineapple and cherries. Chill until partially set. Fold in pineapple, pecans, cherries and marshmallows; chill about 10 minutes. Fold in whipped cream. Turn into 1-quart mold and refrigerate until firm. Yield: 8-10 servings.

Mrs. Dorothy M. Ham, Brantley Co. H.S.
Nahunta, Georgia

CHRISTMAS DELIGHT

    3 egg yolks, beaten
    2 tbsp. sugar
    2 tbsp. vinegar
    ½ c. milk
    1 pkg. lime gelatin
    ½ c. hot water
    1 No. 1 ½ can chunk pineapple, drained
    1 c. miniature marshmallows
    1 c. pecans, halved

Combine egg yolks, sugar, vinegar and milk. Cook over low heat until to consistency of custard; cool. Dissolve gelatin in hot water; let cool. Add gelatin to custard mixture; boil for 1 minute.

(Continued on next page)

Cool; add pineapple, marshmallows and pecans. Pour into mold; place in refrigerator until set or overnight. Cherries and nuts may be used for garnish. Yield: 8-10 servings.

Lou Olson, Rule H.S.
Rule, Texas

CHRISTMAS RIBBON SALAD

1 pkg. lime Jell-O
1 pkg. cherry Jell-O
1 pkg. lemon Jell-O
¼ c. miniature marshmallows
1 c. crushed pineapple
¼ c. cottage cheese
½ c. mayonnaise
½ c. whipping cream, whipped

Dissolve lime and cherry Jell-O in separate bowls in 1 cup hot water each; add 1 cup cold water to each. Pour cherry Jell-O into 8-inch square Pyrex pan; refrigerate until firm. Dissolve lemon Jell-O in 1 cup hot water; add marshmallows, pineapple, cottage cheese and mayonnaise. Fold in whipped cream. Pour mixture over congealed cherry layer; refrigerate until firm. Pour lime Jell-O over top of congealed lemon layer; chill. Cut in squares; serve on lettuce leaves. Yield: 12-16 servings.

Mrs. A. F. Burnett, Eminence Consol. Sch.
Eminence, Indiana

COKE SALAD

1 can sliced pineapple
1 sm. jar maraschino cherries
1 pkg. cherry Jell-O
2 6-oz. Cokes
2 3-oz. pkg. cream cheese
2 c. finely chopped pecans

Drain and combine pineapple and cherry juice; add Jell-O, beating until Jell-O dissolves. Refrigerate until cool; mix Cokes with Jell-O. Add remaining ingredients. Pour into a mold; chill until firm. Yield: 12 servings.

Andrea Fletcher, Mountain Pine H.S.
Mt. Pine, Arkansas

CONGEALED PINK SALAD

1 pkg. strawberry Jell-O
1 sm. can crushed pineapple
¼ c. chopped nuts
1 c. sm. curd cottage cheese
1 pkg. Dream Whip

Mix Jell-O as directed on package; chill until partially set. Beat Jell-O until frothy; fold in

pineapple, nuts and cottage cheese. Prepare Dream Whip as directed on package; fold into Jell-O mixture. Place in greased mold; refrigerate. Yield: 8 servings.

Mrs. Rama Steen, Caldwell H.S.
Caldwell, Ohio

COTTAGE CHEESE-JELL-O SALAD

1 box orange Jell-O
½ lb. marshmallows, quartered
1 c. crushed pineapple, drained
1 c. cottage cheese
1 c. whipped cream
½ c. salad dressing
1 box lime Jell-O

Dissolve orange Jell-O in 2 cups boiling water; stir in marshmallows. Cool; add pineapple, cottage cheese, cream and salad dressing. Refrigerate until set. Dissolve lime Jell-O according to package directions; pour over congealed layer. Yield: 8 servings.

Mrs. Barbara Deane, Hoxie H.S.
Hoxie, Kansas

COTTAGE CHEESE MOLDED SALAD

1 c. boiling water
1 pkg. lime gelatin
Pinch of salt
Juice of 1 lemon
1 No. 2 can crushed pineapple
1 c. cottage cheese, mashed until smooth
½ c. mayonnaise
1 c. evaporated milk
1 c. nutmeats

Pour boiling water over gelatin; add salt and lemon juice, stirring until dissolved. Add pineapple. Combine cottage cheese, mayonnaise and milk; add to gelatin mixture with nutmeats. Stir until well mixed; pour into molds or dish. Refrigerate until firm. Yield: 10 servings.

Mrs. Janet E. Whetzel, Turner Ashby H.S.
Dayton, Virginia

COTTAGE CHEESE SALAD

1 pkg. lime gelatin
1 c. boiling water
1 c. whipping cream, stiffly beaten
1 c. lge. curd cottage cheese
¼ c. blanched almonds or pecans, cut fine
1 sm. can crushed pineapple, drained
1 sm. bottle maraschino cherries, drained and sliced

(Continued on next page)

Dissolve gelatin in boiling water; cool and let set until slightly thickened. Add remaining ingredients; pour into 8 x 8-inch pan. Chill until firm. Yield: 9 servings.

Mrs. Sandra Sue Riedel, Morland H.S.
Morland, Kansas

Dissolve gelatin in water; add pineapple juice and cheese. Chill until partially set; whip. Add pineapple, cut-up cherries and whipped cream. Pour into 9 x 13-inch pan; refrigerate. Unmold; garnish with reserved cherries. Yield: 12 servings.

Mrs. Sandra E. Olson, Monroe H.S.
St. Paul, Minnesota

COTTAGE SALAD
    ¾ c. boiling water
    ½ c. sugar
    1 pkg. lime gelatin
    1 c. cottage cheese
    ½ c. crushed pineapple
    ½ c. chopped nuts
    ½ c. maraschino cherries
    1 c. evaporated milk

Add boiling water and sugar to gelatin; chill or whip until slightly stiff. Add remaining ingredients. Pour into mold and chill until firm. Yield: 8 servings.

Sister Raomona Ann O.S.F., St. Mary's H.S.
Holly Springs, Mississippi

CREAMY LIME SALAD
    1 sm. box lime Jell-O
    1 8-oz. pkg. cream cheese
    1 c. whipped cream
    1 c. sm. marshmallows
    1 8-oz. can crushed pineapple
    ½ c. diced walnuts

Dissolve Jello-O as directed on box; chill. Beat cream cheese into Jell-O when Jell-O has reached consistency of egg whites. Fold in cream, marshmallows, pineapple and walnuts. Pour into mold and chill until firm. Yield: 8 servings.

Mrs. Elaine R. Tschetter, Bath H.S.
Bath, Michigan

CREAM CHEESE-JELL-O SALAD
    2 c. hot water
    1 pkg. orange Jell-O
    15 marshmallows, cut up
    2 3-oz. pkg. cream cheese, cubed
    1 sm. can crushed pineapple
    1 c. cream, whipped
    ½ c. salad dressing (opt.)
    1 pkg. cherry or lime Jell-O

Add hot water to orange Jell-O; bring to boil. Add marshmallows and cream cheese; remove from heat and stir until almost dissolved. Cool; add pineapple. Add whipped cream and salad dressing. Pour into 9 x 12-inch pan and chill until firm. Prepare remaining Jell-O according to package directions; let cool. Pour over congealed mixture. Yield: 12 servings.

Elaine Banks, Nebraska City H.S.
Nebraska City, Nebraska

EMERALD SALAD
    1 sm. pkg. lime Jell-O
    1 sm. pkg. lemon Jell-O
    2 c. hot water
    1 16-oz. can crushed pineapple
    1 pkg. miniature marshmallows
    1 pt. whipping cream
    1 c. grated sharp cheese

Dissolve Jell-O in hot water. Drain juice from pineapple; add water to measure 2 cups. Add liquid to Jell-O; add pineapple. Pour into 12 x 15-inch pan; refrigerate until partially set. Push marshmallows into partially set Jell-O. Whip cream; sweeten to taste. Spread whip cream over marshallows. Sprinkle grated cheese over whipped cream; refrigerate until set. Yield: 20 servings.

Mrs. Barbara Gilhaus, ABL Comm. Unit #6 H.S.
Broadlands, Illinois

CREAM CHEESE SALAD
    1 pkg. lemon gelatin
    ¾ c. boiling water
    ¾ c. pineapple juice
    6 oz. cream cheese
    1 cup drained crushed pineapple
    1 10-oz. jar maraschino cherries,
      cut up, reserve portion of whole
      cherries for garnish
    1 pt. whipping cream, whipped

FAVORITE FRUIT SALAD
    2 pkg. orange Jell-O
    3 c. hot water
    1 lge. pkg. marshmallows
    1 pkg. cream cheese
    1 c. mayonnaise
    1 No. 2 can crushed pineapple
    1 c. nuts, mashed
    ½ c. whipping cream, whipped

161

(Continued on next page)

Congealed Pineapple Salads

Dissolve Jell-O with 1 cup hot water; cool. Dissolve marshmallows in remaining hot water. Cream cheese. Add mayonnaise, pineapple and nuts. Combine Jell-O and pineapple mixture; fold in whipped cream. Yield: 18 servings.

Mrs. Miriam Bobo Templeton
Hickory Tavern H.S.
Gray Court, South Carolina

FLUFFY LIME MOLD

    1 pkg. lime gelatin
    1 pkg. Dream Whip
    1 c. chopped pecans
    1 lge. can pineapple chunks

Prepare gelatin according to package directions; refrigerate until partially set. Prepare Dream Whip according to package directions; fold into gelatin. Add pecans and pineapple. Crushed pineapple, fruit cocktail or other fruits may be substituted for pineapple chunks. Yield: 4-6 servings.

Mrs. R. L. Burton, Beggs H.S.
Beggs, Oklahoma

FROSTED MINT MOLD

    1 pkg. family-size lime gelatin
    1 c. mint jelly
    2 drops mint flavoring
    Few drops green food coloring (opt.)
    1 20-oz. can crushed pineapple,
        drained
    1 c. sour cream or 1 8-oz. pkg. cream
        cheese

Add water to reserved pineapple juice to make 2 1/2 cups; heat. Dissolve gelatin in hot liquid. Melt jelly and add. Cool; place in refrigerator until slightly thickened. Beat until foamy with rotary beater; add flavoring and food coloring. Fold in pineapple and sour cream. Pour into mold and chill until firm. Garnish with mint leaves. Yield: 10 servings.

Mrs. Grace L. Engelbrecht, Frederick H.S.
Frederick, Maryland

GRATED ALMOND MOUSSE

    1 ½ c. sugar
    2 tbsp. grated orange rind
    2 tbsp. unflavored gelatin
    1 ½ c. water
    ⅓ c. drained pineapple juice
    ⅓ c. lemon juice
    ¾ c. instant nonfat dry milk
    ½ c. drained chopped maraschino
        cherries
    ½ c. drained crushed pineapple
    ½ c. chopped blanched almonds
    Fruit garnish

Mix sugar, orange rind and gelatin in saucepan; stir in water. Heat slowly, stirring constantly, until sugar and gelatin are dissolved. Remove from heat; stir in fruit juices. Cool until partially congealed; add milk, beating until fluffy. Fold in fruits and almonds; pour into mold, rinsed in cold water. Chill until firm. Unmold; garnish with fruit. Yield: 8-10 servings.

Elaine Petrik, South Winneshiek Comm. Sch.
Calmar, Iowa

GOLDEN SALAD

    2 pkg. lemon gelatin
    2 c. hot pineapple juice with water
    1 lge. can sliced pineapple, drained
        and ground
    ½ lb. American cheese, ground
    ¾ c. yellow miniature marshmallows
    Juice of 1 lemon
    2 tbsp. sugar
    1 sm. can milk

Dissolve gelatin in hot liquid mixture; add pineapple, cheese and marshmallows. Chill until slightly thick. Add lemon juice and sugar to milk; whip until stiff. Fold into gelatin mixture; chill until firm. Yield: 6-8 servings.

Mrs. L. O. Freeman, Chickasaw Co. H.S.
Houston, Mississippi

HEAVENLY LIME SALAD

    1 6-oz. pkg. lime flavored gelatin
    2 ¼ c. hot water
    1 8-oz. pkg. cream cheese
    1 c. marshmallows
    1 ½ c. cold water
    ½ c. heavy cream, whipped
    1 No. 2 can crushed pineapple
    1 c. chopped pecans

Dissolve gelatin in 2 cups boiling water in large bowl. Mash cream cheese in small bowl and add to gelatin mixture, stirring until dissolved. Melt marshmallows in remaining 1/4 cup boiling water over low heat. Add to gelatin mixture. Add cold water. Add cream and beat until mixture is smooth. Add fruit and pecans. Pour into lightly greased mold. Chill. Yield: 18-20 servings.

Mrs. Harriet Krause, Pasadena H.S.
Pasadena, Texas

HEAVENLY SALAD

    1 pkg. lime Jell-O
    ½ lb. marshmallows, cut up
    1 No. 2 can crushed pineapple
    1 c. mayonnaise
    2 3-oz. pkg. cream cheese
    1 c. whipping cream, whipped
    1 pkg. cherry Jell-O

162

(Continued on next page)

Dissolve lime Jell-O in 1 cup hot water in double boiler; add marshmallows. Stir until marshmallows are almost completely melted. Remove from heat; add pineapple. Blend mayonnaise and cream cheese; add to Jell-O mixture. Cool; fold in whipped cream. Pour into flat pan; let stand until firm. Dissolve cherry Jell-O in 2 cups hot water; cool. Pour over congealed mixture; let set. Cut into squares. Yield: 20 servings.

Mrs. Wallace Halcomb, Williamsburg H.S.
Williamsburg, Kentucky

LAYERED PINEAPPLE-JELL-O SALAD

    1 pkg. lime Jell-O
    2 c. hot water
    ¾ c. canned pineapple juice
    1 c. drained canned, crushed pineapple
    1 pkg. lemon Jell-O
    ¾ c. cold water
    ½ c. whipping cream
    1 3-oz. pkg. cream cheese

Dissolve lime Jell-O in 1 cup hot water; add pineapple juice and pineapple. Pour into 8 x 8 x 2-inch pan or use large loaf pan or mold. Chill until firm. Dissolve lemon Jell-O in remaining hot water. Add cold water; chill until slightly thickened. Place bowl of lemon Jell-O in larger bowl or ice water; whip Jell-O until fluffy and thick. Whip cream; stir gradually into cream cheese. Whip cream cheese mixture until thick and smooth; fold into Jell-O; pour over congealed pineapple layer. Chill until firm. Cut into 9 squares; serve on crisp salad greens. Yield: 9 servings.

Mrs. Janie A. Stahlecker, Idalia H.S.
Idalia, Colorado

LIME GELATIN SALAD

    2 pkg. lime gelatin
    2 c. boiling water
    1 c. mixed pineapple juice and water
    8 canned pineapple slices, drained
    16 maraschino cherries
    1 c. sm. curd cottage cheese, creamed
    1 tbsp. salad dressing

Dissolve 1 package gelatin in 1 cup boiling water; add mixed pineapple juice and water. Chill until mixture begins to congeal. Arrange pineapple rings and cherries in large ring mold; pour in congealed mixture. Chill until set. Dissolve remaining gelatin in remaining boiling water; cool to room temperature. Stir in cottage cheese and salad dressing. Pour onto congealed layer in mold. Chill until firm. Yield: 8-10 servings.

Mrs. Janet Lightfoot, Niles Sr. H.S.
Niles, Michigan

LEMON SURPRISE SALAD

    1 reg. size lemon gelatin
    1 c. hot water
    1 10-oz. sm. can crushed pineapple, drained
    1 c. cottage cheese
    ½ c. chopped walnuts
    ½ c. chopped maraschino cherries
    ½ c. cream, whipped

Dissolve lemon gelatin in hot water; let stand until firm. Beat with egg beater until foamy; add pineapple, cottage cheese, walnuts and maraschino cherries. Fold in whipped cream; pour into mold. Yield: 6 servings.

Dorothy Pomraning, Big Spring H.S.
Newville, Pennsylvania

LIME CHIFFON SALAD

    1 9-oz. can crushed pineapple
    1 3-oz. pkg. lime gelatin
    1 c. boiling water
    1 c. creamed cottage cheese
    ½ c. mayonnaise
    ¼ c. chopped nuts

Drain pineapple, reserving juice. Dissolve gelatin in boiling water; add reserved juice. Cool until slightly thickened; beat until frothy. Fold in pineapple, cottage cheese, mayonnaise and nuts. Place in 13 x 9-inch pan or mold. Refrigerate until firm. Serve on lettuce or other salad greens. Yield: 6 servings.

Mrs. Mary Ellen Moore, Radford H.S.
Radford, Virginia

LIME CONGEALED SALAD

    1 3-oz. pkg. lime gelatin
    8 lge. marshmallows
    2 c. boiling water
    ½ c. evaporated milk, chilled
    1 No. 1 can crushed pineapple, drained
    ½ c. chopped pecans
    ½ c. diced maraschino cherries
    ½ c. diced Velveeta cheese

Dissolve gelatin and marshmallows in boiling water; chill until firm. Whip milk in large mixing bowl for 2 to 3 minutes; add firm gelatin slowly. Whip until well blended. Stir in pineapple, pecans, cherries and cheese by hand. Chill for several hours or until firm. Yield: 8 servings.

Mrs. Marshall J. King, Gatesville H.S.
Gatesville, Texas

Congealed Pineapple Salads

LIME FREEZE

1 No. 2 can crushed pineapple
2 pkg. lime gelatin
1 c. cream, whipped
¼ c. salad dressing
1 11-oz. pkg. cottage cheese

Drain pineapple, reserving juice; add water to make 2 cups liquid. Bring to boil; add gelatin and 1 cup cold water. Let cool. Add cream, salad dressing, cottage cheese and pineapple to gelatin. Place in refrigerator until firm. Yield: 8 servings.

Kathryn Davison, Hot Springs Co. H.S.
Thermopolis, Wyoming

LIME GELATIN SALAD

1 6-oz. pkg. lime gelatin
2 c. boiling water
1 6-oz. pkg. cream cheese
2 c. milk
1 med. can crushed pineapple

Dissolve gelatin in boiling water. Soften cream cheese with milk; blend with mixer. Add cheese mixture to gelatin mixture; add drained pineapple. Refrigerate until set; cut into squares. Yield: 10-12 servings.

Mrs. Carol Myers, Charlotte Jr.-Sr. H.S.
Rochester, New York

LIME JELL-O MOLD

2 boxes lime Jell-O
1 pkg. Dream Whip
1 med. can crushed pineapple, drained
2 tsp. horseradish

Prepare Jell-O according to instructions on box; chill until firm. Prepare Dream Whip according to package directions. Whip gelatin until frothy; fold in Dream Whip, pineapple and horseradish. Pour into mold; chill until firm. Yield: 12 servings.

Mrs. Helen Renoe, Stephen Decatur H.S.
Decatur, Illinois

LIME JELL-O SALAD

1 3-oz. pkg. lime Jell-O
1 c. hot water
1 3-oz. pkg. cream cheese
⅔ c. evaporated milk
½ c. pineapple juice
2 tbsp. lemon juice
⅛ tsp. salt
1 c. pineapple chunks
½ c. chopped nuts

Dissolve Jell-O in hot water. Soften cream cheese in milk; blend together. Combine all ingredients, except pineapple chunks and nuts. Chill until slightly thickened; add pineapple and nuts. Place in mold; chill until set. Yield: 8 servings.

Mrs. Lucille King, Nazareth H.S.
Nazareth, Texas

LIME JELL-O SALAD

1 3-oz. pkg. lime Jell-O
1 c. boiling water
1 8-oz. pkg. cream cheese
1 sm. can crushed pineapple, drained
½ c. chopped nuts
1 tsp. sugar
1 tsp. vanilla
1 6-oz. bottle Seven-Up chilled

Dissolve Jell-O in water; add cream cheese, mixing until dissolved. Add remaining ingredients; blend. Pour into 6 individual molds or 1-quart mold; chill overnight. Unmold on crisp lettuce. Yield: 6 servings.

Mrs. H. W. Sebern, Cummings Jr. H.S.
Brownsville, Texas

LIME JELL-O SALAD

1 pkg. lime Jell-O
1 c. boiling water
½ pkg. unflavored gelatin
¼ c. cold water
18 lge. marshmallows
1 lge. can crushed pineapple
1 c. cottage cheese
1 c. chopped nuts
1 c. whipped cream

Dissolve Jell-O in boiling water. Soften gelatin in cold water; add to Jell-O. Add marshmallows; heat until dissolved. Cool. Fold pineapple, cottage cheese, nuts and whipped cream into cooled Jell-O mixture. Refrigerate until set. Yield: 8-10 servings.

Mrs. Dixie Strode, Gamaliel H.S.
Gamaliel, Kentucky

LIME JELL-O SALAD

2 pkg. lime Jell-O
2 c. hot water
⅔ c. sugar
1 can coconut
1 sm. can pineapple
1 16-oz. carton cottage cheese
2 c. chopped pecans

(Continued on next page)

Dissolve Jell-O in hot water; add sugar. Chill until Jell-O begins to set; add coconut, pineapple, cottage cheese and pecans. Pour into molds; chill until firm. Yield: 10 servings.

Patricia McCreary, Edinburg Sch.
Carthage, Mississippi

Dissolve gelatin and marshmallows in hot water; refrigerate until mixture begins to set. Add grated cheese, nuts, whipped cream and pineapple; mix well. Chill until firm in mold or pan. Yield: 8 servings.

Mrs. Joan Ellison, Carter H.S.
Carter, Oklahoma

LIME MOLD SALAD

    1 No. 2 can crushed pineapple, drained
    2 sm. pkg. lime Jell-O
    ½ c. sugar
    ¼ lb. miniature marshmallows
    1 pt. cottage cheese
    1 c. whipped cream
    1 c. walnuts or pecans, chopped fine

Combine drained pineapple juice with enough water to equal 2 cups liquid. Heat Jell-O, sugar, marshmallows with liquid in double boiler until marshmallows melt and sugar dissolves. Cool until partially set; add pineapple, cheese, cream and nuts. Pour into mold; refrigerate until set. Yield: 10-12 servings.

Elsie Hadley, Weinert H.S.
Weinert, Texas

LIME PARTY MOLD

    ¼ lb. marshmallows
    1 c. milk
    1 pkg. lime Jell-O
    2 3-oz. pkg. cream cheese
    1 No. 2 can undrained crushed pineapple
    1 c. heavy cream, whipped
    ½ c. mayonnaise

Melt marshmallows and milk over low heat. Pour mixture over Jell-O and stir until dissolved. Stir in cream cheese until cheese dissolves and add pineapple. Cool. Blend in cream and mayonnaise. Chill until firm. Salad is delicious frozen. Yield: 10-12 servings.

Helen M. Mooney, Head Homemaking Dept.
Susquehanna Valley Jr. H.S.
Conklin, New York

LIME PARTY SALAD

    1 pkg. lime gelatin
    20 marshmallows
    1 c. hot water
    1 c. grated cheese
    ½ c. nuts
    1 c. whipped cream
    1 c. crushed pineapple

LIME-PINEAPPLE MOLD

    1 pkg. lime gelatin
    1 c. hot water
    1 8-oz. pkg. cream cheese, softened
    ½ c. pineapple juice
    2 tbsp. lemon juice
    ¼ tsp. salt
    ¼ c. mayonnaise or salad dressing
    1 c. drained crushed pineapple
    ½ c. chopped nuts

Dissolve gelatin in hot water; add to cream cheese gradually, blending until smooth. Add pineapple juice, lemon juice, salt and mayonnaise; chill until slightly thickened. Fold in pineapple and nuts; pour into 1 1/2-quart mold. Chill until firm. Unmold and surround with crisp lettuce. Yield: 8-10 servings.

Mrs. Peggy Hancuff, Hollidaysburg Sr. H.S.
Hollidaysburg, Pennsylvania

LIME-PINEAPPLE SALAD

    1 pkg. lime Jell-O
    1 ⅔ c. boiling water
    1 c. tiny marshmallows
    3 tsp. lemon juice
    1 sm. can crushed pineapple
    ¼ c. broken pecans
    1 c. cottage cheese
    1 c. whipped cream
    Mayonnaise
    6 maraschino cherries

Mix boiling water and Jell-O; add marshmallows, stirring until dissolved. Chill until slightly thickened; add lemon juice, pineapple, pecans, cottage cheese and whipped cream. Pour into oiled molds or pan. Chill until firm. Slice in bars or squares. Serve on lettuce leaves; top with mayonnaise and maraschino cherries. Yield: 6 servings.

Mrs. Edna M. Chandler, Jellico H.S.
Jellico, Tennessee

LIME-PINEAPPLE SALAD

    1 pkg. lime Jell-O
    1 c. boiling water
    1 can crushed, undrained pineapple
    ⅛ tsp. salt
    ½ c. sour cream

(Continued on next page)

Congealed Pineapple Salads

Dissolve Jell-O in hot water. Add pineapple, salt and cream. Congeal. Yield: 6-8 servings.

Mary R. Abney, Bay Springs H.S.
Bay Springs, Mississippi

LIME SALAD

    1 3-oz. pkg. lime Jell-O
    1 3-oz. pkg. cream cheese
    1 c. boiling water
    1 ½ c. crushed undrained pineapple
    ½ c. chopped nuts
    1 tbsp. vinegar
    ½ tsp. salt

Cream dry Jell-O with cream cheese. Add water and stir until completely dissolved. Add pineapple, nuts, vinegar and salt. Pour into 8-inch square Pyrex pan. Yield: 8-10 servings.

Virginia K. Goolsby, Warwick H.S.
Newport News, Virginia

LIME SALAD

    1 pkg. lime gelatin
    1 c. boiling water
    1 c. pineapple juice
    1 4-oz. pkg. cream cheese
    1 No. 2 can crushed pineapple, drained
    ½ pt. whipped cream

Dissolve gelatin in water; add pineapple juice. Chill until firm. Whip until light and foamy. Mash cream cheese; add to pineapple and fold mixture into gelatin. Fold in cream. Chill until firm. Serve with cream-fruit dressing, if desired. Yield: 10 servings.

Delores Vondrak, Elk Point H.S.
Elk Point, South Dakota

LIME SALAD MOLD

    1 3-oz. pkg. lime gelatin
    1 c. boiling water
    ½ c. salad dressing
    ¼ c. light cream
    ¾ tsp. prepared horseradish
    1 8-oz. can crushed pineapple, undrained
    1 c. cottage cheese
    ½ c. chopped walnuts

Dissolve gelatin in water; chill until slightly thickened. Blend salad dressing, cream and horseradish; stir into gelatin. Add remaining ingredients. Spoon into mold and chill. Yield: 6 servings.

Cornelia Gilbert, Oglala Comm. H.S.
Pine Ridge, South Dakota

LIME SNOW SALAD

    1 pkg. lime gelatin
    1 c. boiling water
    12 marshmallows
    1 c. crushed pineapple
    1 c. broken pecans
    1 pt. whipped cream or whipped topping

Dissolve gelatin in boiling water; add marshmallows and dissolve. Let cool. Add pineapple, pecans and whipped cream; pour into 1-quart mold. Chill for several hours. Dip mold into lukewarm water briefly to remove salad. Garnish with fruit slices. Yield: 4 servings.

Mrs. Thelma McClain, Bremond H.S.
Bremond, Texas

LIME-STRAWBERRY SURPRISE

    1 3-oz. pkg. lime gelatin
    1 c. drained crushed pineapple
    ½ c. mayonnaise
    1 8-oz. pkg. cream cheese, softened
    ½ c. chopped nuts
    1 3-oz. pkg. strawberry gelatin

Prepare lime gelatin as directed on package; chill until slightly thickened. Fold in pineapple. Pour into 8-inch square pan; chill until firm. Add mayonnaise gradually to cream cheese; blend well. Add nuts; spread over molded gelatin layer. Chill until firm. Prepare strawberry gelatin; pour over cheese mixture. Chill until firm. Yield: 6-8 servings.

Mrs. Kay Wasmuth, Bellflower H.S.
Bellflower, California

MARY'S GREEN PARTY SALAD

    2 3-oz. pkg. lime gelatin
    2 ½ c. hot water
    1 sm. pkg. cream cheese, cut into sm. pieces
    1 c. sugar
    1 sm. can crushed pineapple
    1 c. chopped pecans
    1 sm. can evaporated milk, chilled and whipped

Dissolve gelatin in boiling water; add cream cheese, stirring until melted. Add sugar, pineapple and chopped pecans. Fold milk into gelatin mixture; turn into mold. Chill until firm. Unmold onto serving plate; garnish with mint leaves or fruit. Yield: 10-12 servings.

Mrs. Wilda Jean Davis, Lumpkin Co. H.S.
Dahlonega, Georgia

MOLDED CHEESE AND PINEAPPLE SALAD

    1 3-oz. pkg. lemon flavored gelatin
    2 c. boiling water
    1 c. whipping cream, whipped
    1 ½ c. cottage cheese
    1 3-oz. pkg. lime flavored gelatin
    1 c. pineapple juice
    1 c. crushed pineapple

Dissolve lemon gelatin in 1 cup boiling water; chill until mixture is consistency of unbeaten egg whites. Beat until light and fluffy; fold in whipped cream. Add cottage cheese; pour into large mold or 9 x 13-inch pan. Dissolve lime gelatin in remaining boiling water; add pineapple juice. Chill until partially set. Add pineapple; pour over congealed lemon layer. Chill until firm. Yield: 10 servings.

Dora C. Fleming, Centerville H.S.
Sand Coulee, Montana

MOLDED PINEAPPLE-GELATIN SALAD

    1 pkg. lemon gelatin
    1 c. boiling water
    ½ c. cold water
    1 pkg. dessert topping mix
    1 lge. pkg. cream cheese
    ¾ c. mayonnaise or salad dressing
    ½ c. miniature marshmallows
    ½ c. walnuts
    1 sm. can crushed pineapple
    6 maraschino cherries, cut up

Dissolve gelatin in boiling water; add cold water. Set aside. Prepare topping mix according to package directions; add cream cheese and mayonnaise, whipping until quite stiff. Add marshmallows, walnuts and pour pineapple into mold; chill. Salad may be tinted with green food coloring, if desired. Yield: 6-8 servings.

Mrs. Janet M. Bowen, Edmeston Central Sch.
Edmeston, New York

NISSEN SALAD

    1 pt. crushed pineapple
    1 c. sugar
    1 envelope unflavored gelatin
    ¼ c. cold water
    ¾ c. chopped nuts
    1 8-oz. pkg. cream cheese
    ½ pt. whipping cream, whipped

Boil pineapple and sugar for 5 minutes. Dissolve gelatin in cold water; pour into hot mixture. Cool until partially set; add chopped nuts. Soften cream cheese; whip until smooth. Add to pineapple mixture; blend well. Fold in whipped cream. Pour into mold; let stand overnight. Garnish with maraschino cherries, if desired.

Mrs. Ray Mofield, Benton H.S.
Benton, Kentucky

ORANGE-CHEESE MOLD

    1 No. 2 ½ can sliced pineapple
    1 pkg. orange Jell-O
    1 8-oz. pkg. cream cheese, softened
    ½ c. fresh orange juice
    2 tbsp. fresh lemon juice

Drain pineapple; measure syrup, adding hot water to measure 1 1/2 cups. Add Jell-O to hot liquid; stir until dissolved. Gradually blend Jell-O into cream cheese; stir in fruit juices. Pour into individual molds; chill until set. Unmold salad on pineapple slices. Garnish with avocado slices, if desired. Yield: 8 servings.

Billie B. Ingram, Sparkman H.S.
Toney, Alabama

ORANGE CONGEALED SALAD

    2 sm. boxes orange gelatin
    2 c. hot water
    1 sm. can crushed pineapple
    1 8-oz. pkg. cream cheese
    2 tbsp. sugar
    2 tbsp. mayonnaise
    ½ c. chopped nuts
    1 pkg. Dream Whip (opt.)

Mix gelatin and hot water; cool. Cream pineapple with cream cheese; add sugar and mayonnaise. Add pineapple mixture and nuts to gelatin mixture; stir. Whip Dream Whip according to package directions; fold into gelatin mixture. Pour into molds; refrigerate until set. Yield: 14 servings.

Joyce Gray, Waynesboro H.S.
Waynesboro, Georgia

ORANGE JELL-O SALAD

    1 3-oz. pkg. orange Jell-O
    1 c. sm. marshmallows
    ½ c. boiling water
    1 sm. can frozen orange juice
    1 sm. can crushed pineapple
    ½ c. chopped pecans
    ½ pt. cream, whipped or 1 pkg. prepared
       Dream Whip

Stir Jell-O and marshmallows in boiling water until dissolved; add orange juice, pineapple and pecans. Fold in whipped cream; chill. Yield: 6 servings.

Theresa K. Pittman, Coopers H.S.
Elm City, North Carolina

OUT OF THIS WORLD SALAD

    2 pkg. lime Jell-O
    1 pkg. marshmallows
    ¾ c. boiling water

167

(Continued on next page)

Congealed Pineapple Salads

1 No. 2 can crushed pineapple
1 c. pecans
1 carton cottage cheese
15 maraschino cherries
½ pt. whipping cream

Dissolve Jell-O and marshmallows in boiling water; add pineapple. Add pecans, cottage cheese and cherries when partially jelled. Whip cream; fold in gelatin mixture. Chill until firm. Yield: 8 servings.

Helen M. Young, William Byrd H.S.
Venton, Virginia

PACIFIC LIME MOLD

1 9-oz. can crushed pineapple
1 3-oz. pkg. lime gelatin
1 c. boiling water
1 c. creamed cottage cheese
½ c. whipping cream, whipped
¼ c. chopped nuts

Drain pineapple; reserve juice. Dissolve gelatin in boiling water; add reserved juice. Chill until slightly thickened; beat until frothy. Fold in pineapple, cottage cheese, whipped cream and nuts. Chill until firm. Yield: 6 servings.

Mrs. Estella Hottel, Dimmitt H.S.
Dimmitt, Texas

PINEAPPLE-CHEESE SALAD

1 pkg. lemon Jell-O
1 c. hot water
1 sm. pkg. cream cheese
1 c. crushed pineapple
½ c. chopped pecans
½ c. chilled evaporated milk
Juice of ½ lemon
2 tbsp. sugar

Dissolve gelatin in water; crumble in cheese. Stir until well mixed. Chill until syrupy or almost firm. Whip gelatin thoroughly; add pineapple and nuts. Whip milk with lemon juice and sugar; fold into Jell-O mixture. Chill thoroughly. Yield: 6-8 servings.

Mrs. Rebecca Anthony, Abernathy H.S.
Abernathy, Texas

PINEAPPLE-CHEESE SALAD

1 3-oz. pkg. lemon Jell-O
2 c. boiling water
2 tbsp. white vinegar
2 tbsp. sugar
1 c. crushed pineapple
1 c. grated cheese
1 c. cream, whipped

Dissolve Jell-O in boiling water; add vinegar and sugar. Chill until syrupy; fold in pineapple, cheese and whipped cream. Pour into 1-quart mold or individual molds; chill until thoroughly set. Unmold on greens. Yield: 6-8 servings.

Mrs. Betty Eggland, South Hamilton Schs.
Jewell, Iowa

PINEAPPLE-CHEESE SALAD

½ c. sugar
Juice of 1 lemon
1 pt. boiling water
1 pkg. lemon gelatin
1 9-oz. can crushed pineapple
¼ c. chopped maraschino cherries
1 c. grated longhorn cheese
½ c. chopped pecans
½ pt. whipping cream, whipped

Add sugar and lemon juice to water; boil for 4 minutes. Add gelatin; cool until partially set. Add pineapple, cherries, cheese and pecans; fold in whipped cream. Pour into mold; chill until set. Serve on lettuce leaf. Yield: 6-8 servings.

Mrs. M. C. Henderson, Ainsworth H.S.
Flint, Michigan

PINEAPPLE-CHEESE SALAD

2 envelopes gelatin
½ c. cold water
1 No. 2 can crushed pineapple
1 c. sugar
Pinch of salt
3 tbsp. lemon juice
1 ½ c. grated sharp cheddar cheese
½ c. stuffed olives, sliced
½ c. chopped pecans
1 can evaporated milk, chilled and
    whipped

Mix gelatin and water; set aside to soak. Combine pineapple and sugar in saucepan; heat to boiling. Remove from heat; add gelatin, salt and lemon juice. Cool; blend in cheese, olives and pecans. Fold whipped milk into pineapple mixture. Place in refrigerator overnight. Yield: 8 servings.

Mrs. Jacquelyn Sanders, Taft H.S.
Taft, Texas

PINEAPPLE-CHEESE SALAD

1 lge. can crushed pineapple
1 c. sugar
Juice of 2 lemons
2 envelopes unflavored gelatin
½ c. cold water
1 c. grated cheese
½ pt. cream, whipped

(Continued on next page)

Combine pineapple, sugar and lemon juice; bring to boil. Add gelatin which has been dissolved in cold water; cool until mixture begins to congeal. Add cheese and whipped cream; mix well. Pour into shallow dish. Refrigerate until firm or overnight. Cut into squares and serve on lettuce leaf. Yield: 8-10 servings.

Jeannette Reynolds, Crowville H.S.
Delhi, Louisiana

Dissolve Jell-O in water; add 1/2 cup reserved pineapple juice. Refrigerate until consistency of egg whites. Place in large mixing bowl; add sour cream and beat well. Add pineapple, nuts and food coloring. Pour into mold and chill until firm. Yield: 6-8 servings.

Barbara E. Wenner, Escambia H.S.
Pensacola, Florida

PINEAPPLE-CHEESE SALAD MOLD

1 envelope unflavored gelatin
¼ c. cold water
1 tbsp. sugar
¼ tsp. salt
½ c. hot water
2 tbsp. lemon juice
1 can crushed pineapple
½ c. cream, whipped
⅔ c. grated American cheese

Soften gelatin in cold water; add sugar, salt and hot water. Stir until sugar and gelatin are dissolved; add lemon juice and pineapple. Cool until slightly thickened; stir in cream and cheese. Turn into mold or pan, rinsed with cold water. Chill until firm. Serve on lettuce leaf. Yield: 6 servings.

Mrs. Annie Rovenka, Riverdale H.S.
Riverdale, North Dakota

PINEAPPLE-LIME SALAD

1 sm. can crushed pineapple
1 pkg. lime gelatin
4 tbsp. mayonnaise
½ pt. sm. curd cottage cheese

Drain pineapple, reserving juice. Heat 1 cup water to boiling; add gelatin, stirring to dissolve. Pour reserved juice into measuring cup. Add mayonnaise and enough water to fill cup 3/4 full. Add pineapple juice-mixture to gelatin; stir well. Chill until syrupy; add cottage cheese and pineapple. Pour into pint mold. Chill. Yield: 5 servings.

Mrs. Elizabeth Skaggs, Cero Gordo H.S.
Cero Gordo, Illinois

PINEAPPLE-LIME SALAD

1 3-oz. pkg. lime Jell-O
1 c. boiling water
½ pt. sour cream
1 No. 2 can crushed pineapple, drained
1 c. chopped nuts
Green food coloring (opt.)

PINEAPPLE-MARSHMALLOW SALAD

1 pkg. unflavored gelatin
¼ c. cold water
¼ c. sugar
1 tbsp. vinegar
1 tsp. vanilla
Juice from pineapple
1 No. 2 or 2 ½ can crushed pineapple, drained
½ lb. diced marshmallows
1 pt. whipped cream

Soften gelatin in cold water. Combine gelatin, sugar, vinegar, vanilla and juice in saucepan. Heat until gelatin is dissolved. Place pineapple and marshmallows in 11 x 8-inch dish. Pour hot mixture over pineapple mixture, stirring until marshmallows begin to soften. Refrigerate until slightly congealed. Whip cream; fold into pineapple mixture. Garnish with maraschino cherries, if desired. Nutmeats may be added, if desired. Chill until set. Yield: 8 servings.

Mrs. Dorothy E. Puryear
Catherine L. Zane Jr. H.S.
Eureka, California

PINEAPPLE-MINT SALAD

1 pkg. lime gelatin
1 c. boiling water
½ c. pineapple juice
½ c. cold water
¼ tsp. mint flavoring
1 c. pineapple, drained and diced

Dissolve gelatin in boiling water; add juice, cold water and flavoring. Cool until syrupy; add pineapple. Pour into mold. Chill until firm. Yield: 4-6 servings.

Gaynelle C. James, Gardner S. W. H.S.
Gardner, Illinois

PINEAPPLE-RASPBERRY SALAD

2 c. water
1 sm. can crushed pineapple, drained
1 pkg. raspberry Jell-O
1 carton whipping cream
1 sm. carton sm. curd cottage cheese

(Continued on next page)

Congealed Pineapple Salads

Bring water to rolling boil; add pineapple and Jell-O. Cool. Whip cream until stiff. Fold cream and cottage cheese into cooled Jell-O mixture. Pour into mold; chill. Yield: 6-8 servings.

Mrs. Elsie Waller, Mt. Enterprise H.S.
Mt. Enterprise, Texas

PINEAPPLE-RASPBERRY SALAD

        2 pkg. raspberry Jell-O
        2 c. hot water
        1 c. pineapple juice with cold water
        1 3-oz. pkg. cream cheese, softened
        ¼ c. mayonnaise
        1 sm. can crushed pineapple, drained
        ¼ c. shredded coconut
        ½ c. chopped pecans

Dissolve Jell-O in hot water; add pineapple juice mixture. Chill until thickened; whip with mixer until light. Mix cream cheese with mayonnaise; combine with Jell-O mixture. Fold in pineapple, coconut and nuts. Pour into mold; chill until set. Yield: 6-8 servings.

Mrs. Peggy Horntrop, Metropolis Comm. H.S.
Metropolis, Illinois

PINEAPPLE SOUFFLE SALAD

        1 pkg. lemon Jell-O
        1 c. water or pineapple juice
        1 lge. can crushed pineapple
        1 lge. pkg. colored marshmallows, cut
          into sm. pieces
        1 pkg. cream cheese
        ½ c. salad dressing
        ½ pt. cream

Dissolve Jell-O in water; cool. Add pineapple and marshmallows. Soften cream cheese; add salad dressing. Whip cream; fold in cheese mixture. Fold cream mixture into pineapple mixture. Pour into mold or refrigerate for 24 hours before serving. One tablespoon lemon juice may be added for more tart flavor. Yield: 6 servings.

Mrs. Gaylord N. Webster
Mattanawcook Academy
Lincoln, Maine

PINEAPPLE SUPREME

        1 pkg. lime or lemon gelatin
        1 sm. can crushed pineapple
        1 c. cottage cheese
        ½ c. chopped nuts

Prepare gelatin as directed on package. Add remaining ingredients. Chill for 1 hour or until firm. Yield: 6 servings.

Mrs. Robert Stone, Clarendon H.S.
Clarendon, Arkansas

PINK DELIGHT

        1 3-oz. pkg. raspberry gelatin
        1 c. boiling water
        1 8-oz. pkg. cream cheese
        1 1-lb. can crushed pineapple
        1 c. broken walnuts

Dissolve gelatin in hot water; blend in cream cheese thoroughly. Add pineapple and walnuts. Refrigerate until set. Yield: 8 servings.

Barsha Elzey, Terra Linda H.S.
San Rafael, California

PINK PARTY SALAD

        1 8½-oz. can crushed pineapple
        ½ c. sugar
        1 3-oz. box cherry Jell-O
        1 8-oz. pkg. cream cheese
        1 can evaporated milk, chilled
        ½ c. nuts

Cook pineapple and sugar together 5 minutes; dissolve Jell-O in mixture. Cool; stir in cream cheese. Beat evaporated milk until stiff; add Jell-O mixture, beating well. Fold in portion of nuts; sprinkle top with remaining nuts. Refrigerate. Yield: 8 servings.

Mrs. Carol Lee Dively, Claysburg-Kimmel H.S.
Claysburg, Pennsylvania

PINK SALAD

        1 3-oz. pkg. cherry Jell-O
        1 c. cold water
        1 c. sugar
        1 c. crushed pineapple
        1 c. whipping cream
        1 c. chopped pecans
        1 c. grated American cheese

Dissolve Jell-O in water. Combine sugar and pineapple in saucepan; heat until sugar is dissolved. Combine pineapple mixture with Jell-O; chill until firm. Whip cream; add pecans, cheese and Jell-O mixture. Whip just enough to thoroughly combine all ingredients. Refrigerate until serving time. Yield: 10 servings.

Mrs. Sunny Stephens, Poteet H.S.
Poteet, Texas

PIQUANT LIME MOLD

        1 No. 2 can crushed pineapple
        1 pkg. lime gelatin
        1 c. boiling water
        12 oz. cottage cheese
        2 tbsp. horseradish

(Continued on next page)

170

Drain pineapple; reserve 7/8 cup juice. Dissolve gelatin in boiling water; stir in reserved juice. Blend in cottage cheese and horseradish. Pour into ring or individual molds; chill until set. Unmold onto lettuce. Garnish with parsley and serve with mayonnaise if desired. Yield: 6-8 servings.

Mrs. C. W. Lutz, Gilboa-Conesville Cen. Sch.
Gilboa, New York

RIBBON SALAD

2 3-oz. pkg. lime gelatin
5 c. hot water
4 c. cold water
1 3-oz. pkg. lemon gelatin
½ c. miniature marshmallows
1 c. pineapple juice
1 8-oz. pkg. cream cheese
1 20-oz. can crushed pineapple
1 c. heavy cream, whipped
1 c. mayonnaise or salad dressing
2 3-oz. pkg. cherry gelatin

Dissolve lime gelatin in 2 cups hot water; add 2 cups cold water. Pour into 14 x 10 x 2-inch pan; chill until partially set. Dissolve lemon gelatin in 1 cup hot water in double boiler; add marshmallows, stirring until melted. Remove from heat; add pineapple juice and cream cheese. Beat until well blended; stir in pineapple. Cool slightly; fold in whipped cream and mayonnaise. Chill until partially set; pour over lime gelatin. Chill. Dissolve cherry gelatin in remaining hot water; add remaining cold water. Chill until syrupy; pour over pineapple layer. Chill until firm. Gelatin flavors may be substituted as desired. Yield: 24 servings.

Mrs. Norbeth Coleman, Carter H.S.
Olive Hill, Kentucky

SEAFOAM LIME SALAD

1 3-oz. pkg. lime gelatin
1 c. boiling water
1 c. drained, crushed pineapple
½ c. pineapple juice
½ c. cold water
Miniature marshmallows
½ c. whipped cream
¾ c. shredded longhorn cheese

Dissolve gelatin in boiling water; add pineapple, juice and cold water. Pour into 9 x 9-inch pan. Add marshmallows until top is well covered. Chill until firm. Spread whipped cream on top; sprinkle with shredded cheese. Yield: 6 servings.

Shari Bolander, Del Norte H.S.
Del Norte, Colorado

SEAFOAM SALAD

3 pkg. lime gelatin
1 pt. cottage cheese
1 8-oz. can crushed pineapple, drained
½ c. chopped walnuts

Prepare gelatin as directed on package; chill until mixture begins to set. Add cottage cheese, pineapple and walnuts. Chill until firm. Juice drained from pineapple may be used as liquid in preparing gelatin if desired. Yield: 16 servings.

Janice Bell, Perris Union H.S.
Perris, California

SEAFOAM SALAD

1 pkg. lime Jell-O
1 ¼ c. boiling water
1 sm. can drained crushed pineapple
1 3-oz. pkg. cream cheese
1 c. nuts, chopped

Dissolve Jello in water. Add pineapple and chill until slightly congealed. Mash cream cheese with little reserved pineapple juice. Mix with Jell-O. Add nuts and congeal. Serve with mayonnaise as a salad or with whipped cream as a dessert. Yield: 8 servings.

Mrs. W. L. Cope, Swansea H.S.
Swansea, South Carolina

SEVEN-UP SALAD

1 pkg. lime Jell-O
1 c. boiling water
1 sm. pkg. cream cheese
1 No. 2 can crushed pineapple, drained
1 6-oz. bottle Seven-Up
¼ c. walnuts, broken

Dissolve Jell-O in boiling water; add cream cheese, mixing until thoroughly blended. Add pineapple, Seven-Up and nuts; mix. Pour into 9 x 13-inch pan; chill until set. Serve on lettuce leaf; garnish with maraschino cherry. Yield: 6 servings.

Betty Jeanne Gragg, Buckhannon-Upshur Sr. H.S.
Buckhannon, West Virginia

SOUR CREAM-PINEAPPLE MOLD

2 sm. pkg. lime gelatin
1 c. boiling water
1 pt. sour cream
1 No. 2 can crushed pineapple
1 sm. bottle drained maraschino cherries

171

(Continued on next page)

Dissolve gelatin in water; add sour cream and beat until well blended with rotary beater. Stir in pineapple and cherries; pour into individual molds or 1 large mold. Yield: 12 servings.

Mrs. Betty Lute, Avon Lake H.S.
Avon Lake, Ohio

Pour mixture into 13 x 9 x 2-inch pan; refrigerate until set. Dissolve cherry Jell-O in remaining boiling water; cool. Pour over congealed mixture; let stand until set. Cut into individual sections; serve with spoonful of mayonnaise or whipped cream, topped with cherry. Yield: 12 servings.

Leeta G. Adolphe, Fort Vancouver H.S.
Vancouver, Washington

SPRING LIME SALAD

    1 3-oz. pkg. lime Jell-O
    1 c. hot water
    1 lb. cottage cheese
    1 c. crushed pineapple
    10 cut marshmallows
    ½ c. cream, whipped

Mix Jell-O with hot water; let stand until partially set. Whip Jell-O; fold in cottage cheese, pineapple and marshmallows. Whip cream; fold into Jell-O mixture. Refrigerate until set. Yield: 8-10 servings.

Jane Hubbell, Bonneville H.S.
Idaho Falls, Idaho

STRAWBERRY-PINEAPPLE DELIGHT

    1 No. 2 can crushed pineapple
    1 box strawberry gelatin
    ½ c. chopped pecans
    1 ½ c. miniature marshmallows
    1 c. cottage cheese
    1 pkg. prepared Dream Whip

Heat crushed pineapple; add gelatin and mix to dissolve. Cool until partially congealed; add pecans, marshmallows, cottage cheese and Dream Whip. Pour into 8 x 8-inch dish. Chill until firm. Yield: 12 servings.

Mrs. Velma Clark, Brimfield H.S.
Brimfield, Illinois

SURPRISE SALAD

    1 3-oz. pkg. lime Jell-O
    3 c. boiling water
    1 c. crushed pineapple
    ½ c. canned milk
    ½ c. mayonnaise
    1 c. cottage cheese
    1 tbsp. horseradish
    ½ c. chopped nuts
    Juice of ½ lemon
    1 3-oz. pkg. cherry Jell-O

Dissolve lime Jell-O in 1 cup boiling water; cool. Add crushed pineapple, milk, mayonnaise, cottage cheese, horseradish, nuts and lemon juice.

SEVEN-UP SALAD

    1 8-oz. bottle Seven-Up
    1 sm. pkg. lime Jell-O
    1 3-oz. pkg. cream cheese
    2 tbsp. hot water
    1 No. 2 can crushed pineapple
    ½ c. chopped pecans

Heat Seven-Up; pour over Jell-O. Stir until dissolved. Mix cream cheese with hot water until smooth. Combine Jell-O mixture and cream cheese mixture; add pineapple and pecans. Chill until firm. Yield: 8 servings.

Mrs. Dickie F. Winn, Tavares H.S.
Tavares, Florida

SURPRISE SALAD

    1 pkg. raspberry Jell-O
    1 c. hot water
    ½ c. sugar
    1 sm. can crushed pineapple
    1 c. grated American cheese or 1 8-oz.
        pkg. cream cheese
    1 c. chopped pecans
    1 c. whipped cream

Dissolve Jell-O in water. Heat sugar and pineapple; add to Jell-O mixture. Cool; add cheese and pecans. Refrigerate until almost set; add whipped cream. Pour into mold; chill. Yield: 8 servings.

Barbara Waybourn, Childress H.S.
Childress, Texas

SWEETHEART SALAD

    1 can crushed pineapple
    ⅓ c. sugar
    Juice from ½ lemon
    1 tbsp. maraschino cherry juice
    1 envelope unflavored gelatin
    ½ c. cold water
    1 8-oz. pkg. cream cheese
    1 8-oz. jar maraschino cherries
    1 c. whipping cream, whipped

Combine pineapple, sugar, lemon juice and cherry juice; bring to boil. Cool. Add gelatin

(Continued on next page)

and cold water; mix. Mash cream cheese; add cherries. Combine cream cheese mixture with pineapple mixture; refrigerate until almost set. Fold in whipped cream.

Mrs. Bernice Neff, Carsonville H.S.
Carsonville, Michigan

over congealed gelatin; refrigerate until set. Dissolve remaining gelatin according to package directions; pour over cream cheese layer. Refrigerate. Cut in squares to serve. Yield: 12 servings.

Linda S. Clark, Jones Jr. H.S.
Marion, Indiana

SWEETHEART SALAD

1 pkg. lemon Jell-O
1 ½ c. hot water
2 c. crushed pineapple, drained
1 pkg. American cheese, grated
2 tbsp. cherry juice
1 c. whipping cream
½ c. sugar
12 maraschino cherries

Dissolve Jell-O in hot water; chill until partially set. Add pineapple, cheese and cherry juice; chill. Whip cream; add sugar. Fold into chilled gelatin; pour into mold. Garnish with cherries. Yield: 6-8 servings.

Lois Pieters, Parrish Jr. H.S.
Salem, Oregon

TERESA'S SALAD

1 8 ½-oz. can crushed pineapple
1 3-oz. pkg. lime gelatin
1 c. boiling water
½ c. chopped celery
½ c. cubed American cheese
½ c. chopped English walnuts or pecans (opt.)

Drain pineapple; reserve juice. Add cold water to reserved juice to make 1 cup liquid. Dissolve gelatin in boiling water; add reserved juice-water mixture. Cool until mixture begins to congeal; stir in remaining ingredients. Chill. Yield: 9 servings.

Mrs. Clara M. Trout, Oakland Comm. Sch.
Oakland, Iowa

THREE-LAYER JELL-O SALAD

2 pkg. lime or cherry gelatin
1 pkg. lemon gelatin
1 pkg. cream cheese
½ pt. whipping cream
1 can crushed pineapple, drained

Dissolve 1 package lime gelatin according to package directions. Pour into 12 x 9-inch glass pan; refrigerate. Dissolve lemon gelatin in 1 cup boiling water. Melt cream cheese, beating occasionally. Let cream cheese cool but not set. Whip cream. Add cream cheese, whipped cream and pineapple to lemon gelatin; mix. Pour mixture

YUM YUM SALAD

2 c. crushed pineapple
½ c. cold water
Juice of 1 lemon
½ c. sugar
1 pkg. lime gelatin
1 c. grated cheese
½ c. nutmeats
1 c. whipped cream

Drain pineapple; reserve juice. Combine reserved juice, water, lemon juice and sugar; bring to boil. Add gelatin and stir until dissolved; cool until mixture begins to set. Add cheese, pineapple, nuts and whipped cream. Pour into greased salad molds and chill until firm. Serve on lettuce. Yield: 6 servings.

Dorothy Shipley McCubbin, Temple Hill Sch.
Glasgow, Kentucky
Mrs. Betty G. Brant
Shanksville-Stoneycreek Sch.
Shanksville, Pennsylvania

GREENGAGE PLUM SALAD

1 1-lb. 4-oz. can greengage plums
1 3-oz. pkg. lemon gelatin
Lemon juice
½ tsp. salt
¾ c. slivered toasted almonds
Crisp lettuce cups
Salad dressing

Drain juice from plums; add water to make 2 cups liquid. Heat to boiling; pour over gelatin. Add small amount lemon juice and salt, stirring to dissolve; cool until thickened. Pour 2 tablespoons gelatin into each of 6 baking cups or individual molds. Chill until firm. Chill remaining gelatin until syrupy. Pit plums and chop; fold with almonds into gelatin. Spoon over clear gelatin in molds. Chill until firm. Serve in lettuce cups with salad dressing. Yield: 6 servings.

Mrs. Mary Esther Rowe, Swartz Creek H.S.
Swartz Creek, Michigan

GREENGAGE PLUM SALAD

1 pkg. lime gelatin
1 ½ c. hot water
½ c. greengage plum juice

(Continued on next page)

⅛ tsp. salt
½ tsp. vinegar
1 can pitted greengage plums
1 3-oz. pkg. cream cheese

Dissolve gelatin in hot water; add plum juice, salt and vinegar. Cool. Place plums in mold; pour half the gelatin mixture over plums. Add remaining gelatin mixture to cream cheese; whip until light. Pour over plum mixture. Chill for several hours. Unmold onto lettuce leaf. Yield: 8 servings.

Emma Lou Leftwich, Mt. Pleasant H.S.
Mt. Pleasant, Texas

RASPBERRY DELIGHT SALAD

1 c. boiling water
1 3-oz. pkg. black raspberry Jell-O
1 10-oz. pkg. frozen raspberries
½ c. canned pineapple juice

Pour boiling water over Jell-O; stir until dissolved. Add raspberries and pineapple juice. Stir until berries are thawed and Jell-O is slightly thickened. Refrigerate until firm. Serve on lettuce leaves. Serve with whipped cream, if desired. Yield: 6 servings.

Mrs. Ann Enriquis, Ysleta H.S.
El Paso, Texas

SPICED GRAPE SALAD

1 can spiced seedless grapes
1 3-oz. pkg. lime Jell-O
1 c. Seven-Up, chilled
½ c. chopped walnuts

Drain liquid from grapes. Bring one cup liquid to a boil; pour over Jell-O to dissolve. Add Seven-Up; cool. Add grapes and nuts.

Lynne Perry, Polson H.S.
Polson, Montana

STRAWBERRY BAVARIAN SALAD

1 3-oz. pkg. strawberry Jell-O
1 c. boiling water
1 10-oz. pkg. frozen strawberries, sliced
½ pt. heavy cream

Dissolve Jell-O in boiling water; break frozen strawberries into Jell-O. Stir until ice is melted; refrigerate 10 minutes. Beat cream until peaks form; fold into Jell-O with rubber spatula. Pour into mold; refrigerate for at least 2 hours. Unmold; garnish with fresh strawberries. Yield: 6-8 servings.

Mrs. Harvey Jacobs, Woodmere Jr. H.S. North Hewlett, New York

STRAWBERRY SALAD GLACE

1 pkg. raspberry or strawberry gelatin
2 3-oz. pkg. cream cheese, softened with milk
½ c. finely chopped nuts
1 pt. strawberries or raspberries, lightly sugared

Prepare gelatin according to package directions; chill until partially set. Shape cream cheese into 12 balls; roll in nuts. Space balls evenly in 10-inch ring mold; cover with layer of strawberries. Pour gelatin over cheese balls and strawberries; chill until set. Unmold; garnish with watercress or lettuce. Yield: 8-10 servings.

Arlene Maisel, Highland Park H.S.
Highland Park, New Jersey

STRAWBERRY SOUFFLE SALAD

1 pkg. frozen strawberries
1 pkg. lemon Jell-O
1 c. hot water
2 tbsp. lemon juice
½ c. mayonnaise
¼ tsp. salt
¼ c. chopped nuts

Thaw strawberries; drain and reserve 1/2 cup juice. Dissolve Jell-O in hot water; add strawberry juice, lemon juice, mayonnaise and salt. Blend well with rotary beater; pour in refrigerator tray. Quick chill 15 or 20 minutes or until firm 1 inch from edge but soft in center. Turn into bowl; whip with rotary until fluffy. Fold in strawberries and chopped nuts; pour into individual molds. Chill until firm. Unmold; garnish with greens and mayonnaise. Yield: 4-6 servings.

Evelyn Van Vleet, Garden City Sr. H.S.
Garden City, Kansas

STRAWBERRY SWIRL

2 tbsp. sugar
2 c. sliced fresh strawberries
1 3-oz. pkg. strawberry gelatin
1 c. boiling water
½ lb. marshmallows
½ c. milk
1 c. cream, whipped

Sprinkle sugar over berries; let stand 30 minutes. Dissolve gelatin in boiling water. Drain strawberries; add water to juice to equal 1 cup. Add to gelatin; chill until partially set. Combine marshmallows and milk; heat, stirring, till marshmallows melt. Add berries to gelatin; swirl in marshmallow mixture. Chill till set; cut into squares. Yield: 9-12 servings.

Ruby Roach, Adair Co. H.S.
Columbia, Kentucky

Congealed Mixed Fruit Salads

RECIPE FOR FRUIT SALAD MOLD ON PAGE 198

AMBROSIA GLOW

1 3-oz. pkg. orange gelatin
1 c. hot water
½ c. sliced bananas
½ c. orange sections
¼ c. shredded coconut
⅔ c. evaporated milk
1 tbsp. lemon juice

Dissolve gelatin in water; chill until slightly thickened and stir in fruit and coconut. Chill evaporated milk in freezer section until crystals form. Whip until stiff. Add lemon juice and whip 1 minute longer. Fold 2 mixtures together. Chill until firm, in mold, if desired. Yield: 4 servings.

Mrs. Deborah Purvis, Soquel H.S.
Soquel, California

APPLESAUCE-PEACH SALAD

1 3-oz. pkg. lemon gelatin
1 ½ c. boiling water
1 c. applesauce
1 pkg. frozen peaches, drained
Lettuce leaves

Mix gelatin and water; stir until dissolved. Add applesauce; chill until partially set. Add peaches; chill until firm. Unmold and serve on lettuce leaves. Two or 3 fresh sliced peaches may be substituted for frozen peaches.

Jacqueline Tuttle, Southampton Jr. H.S.
Southampton, N.Y.

APPLESAUCE SALAD

1 pkg. strawberry Jell-O
1 c. applesauce
1 c. crushed pineapple
1 sm. Seven-Up

Mix Jell-O and applesauce; heat until Jell-O is dissolved. Add pineapple and Seven-up. Pour into molds and chill. Yield: 6-8 servings.

Mrs. Wilma Tucker, Marion H.S.
Marion, Louisiana
Marion, Louisiana

MOLDED APPLESAUCE SALAD

1 lge. fruit punch gelatin
1 can applesauce
1 can crushed pineapple
1 pkg. miniature marshmallows

Dissolve gelatin in 2 cups hot water; add 1 cup cold water. Chill till partially set. Add applesauce and pineapple. Top with marshmallows. Yield: 12 servings.

Mrs. Mark Thomas, East Limestone Sch.
Athens, Alabama

PINK LADY

1 family size pkg. raspberry gelatin
1 c. boiling water
1 c. pineapple juice
½ c. mayonnaise
1 c. applesauce
1 No. 2 can crushed pineapple
1 c. grated process cheese
½ c. halved maraschino cherries
1 c. pecans
½ c. evaporated milk

Dissolve gelatin in water and juice. Add remaining ingredients; mix. Congeal in shallow 2-quart Pyrex dish in refrigerator. Serve with whipped cream as garnish. Yield: 10 servings.

Pauline W. Ball, Austin H.S.
Decatur, Alabama

APRICOT-CHEESE DELIGHT SALAD

1 17-oz. can apricots, drained and chopped fine
1 lge. can crushed pineapple, drained
2 pkg. orange-flavored gelatin
2 c. hot water
1 c. miniature marshmallows
½ c. sugar
3 tbsp. cornstarch
1 egg, well beaten
2 tbsp. butter
1 c. pineapple juice
1 c. whipping cream, whipped
1 c. or less grated cheddar cheese

Drain fruits; reserve juices, keeping separate. Chill fruit. Dissolve gelatin in hot water. Add apricot juice. Fold in apricots, pineapple and marshmallows. Chill until firm. Combine sugar and flour; blend in egg and butter. Add pineapple juice and cook over low heat, stirring constantly until thickened. Let cool thoroughly. Fold in whipped cream; spread over congealed salad. Sprinkle with grated cheese and chill thoroughly. Cut into squares and serve on lettuce. Yield: 12 servings.

Mrs. Rebecca McGaughy, Montevallo H.S.
Montevallo, Alabama

APRICOT-CHEESE SALAD

2 pkg. orange gelatin
2 c. hot water
¾ c. marshmallows
2 c. drained fruit juice
1 med. can crushed pineapple
1 29-oz. can apricots, drained and
    finely chopped
½ c. sugar
3 tbsp. flour
1 egg, slightly beaten
2 tbsp. butter
2 drops almond extract (opt.)
1 c. whipped cream
¾ c. grated cheddar cheese

Dissolve gelatin in hot water; add marshmallows. Stir until dissolved. Cool slightly. Add 1 cup fruit juice, pineapple and apricots. Pour into large mold or individual molds. Combine sugar, flour, egg and remaining juice. Cook over low heat until thick. Add butter and extract. Cool; add whipped cream and cheese. Serve with salad. Yield: 12-15 servings.

Mrs. G. T. Lilly, Murray H.S.
Murray, Kentucky
Judy Cooper, Marissa Twp. H.S.
Marissa, Illinois

APRICOT DELIGHT

1 lge. or 2 sm. pkg. apricot Jell-O
2 c. boiling water
1 No. 2½ can sliced peaches
1 No. 2 can whole apricots, sliced
½ c. mayonnaise
½ c. confectioners' sugar
1 tbsp. orange juice concentrate

Dissolve Jell-O in boiling water; let partially set. Place layer of peaches in bottom of mold; add 1/2 cup Jell-O and peach juice. Add layer of apricots, 1/2 cup Jell-O and apricot juice. Repeat layers. Congeal. Serve on lettuce with dressing made with mayonnaise, confectioners' sugar and orange juice concentrate. Yield: 10 servings.

Mrs. Wade H. Harris, Seagrove H.S.
Seagrove, North Carolina

APRICOT DELIGHT

1 29-oz. can apricots drained and
    chopped
1 29-oz. can chunk pineapple, drained
2 pkg. orange gelatin
2 c. boiling water
2 c. pineapple and apricot juice, combined
¾ c. miniature marshmallows
½ c. sugar
3 tbsp. flour
1 egg
2 tbsp. butter
1 c. whipped cream

Drain fruits; chill. Reserve juice. Dissolve gelatin in boiling water; add 1 cup fruit juice. Chill until partially set. Fold in fruits and marshmallows; chill until firm. Combine sugar and flour; blend in egg. Gradually stir in juice. Cook over low heat until thick; remove from heat. Stir in butter. Cool. Fold in whipped cream; spread over gelatin.

Mrs. Nancy J. Slezak, Seneca Valley H.S.
Harmony, Pennsylvania

APRICOT FRUIT SALAD

1 lge. box apricot Jell-O
2 c. hot water
1½ c. cold water
1 sm. can crushed pineapple
2 bananas, diced
½ c. chopped nuts
1 c. miniature marshmallows
½ c. sugar
2 tbsp. flour
2 tbsp. butter
1 egg
½ c. pineapple juice
1 sm. pkg. cream cheese
1 sm. box Dream Whip

Dissolve Jell-O in hot water; add cold water. Pour into mold; refrigerate until partially set. Add pineapple, bananas, nuts and marshmallows and chill until firm. Make custard by combining sugar, flour, butter, egg and pineapple juice. Stir constantly until thick. Cool. Add cream cheese and blend well. Whip Dream Whip and fold into custard mixture. Spread on top of Jell-O mixture and store in refrigerator. Yield: 12 servings.

Mrs. Vergie Hill, Forest Jr. H.S.
Owensboro, Kentucky

APRICOT JELL-O

2 pkg. orange Jell-O
2 c. boiling water
2 c. pineapple and apricot juice, mixed
1 lge. can apricots, mashed
1 lge. can pineapple, diced
10 marshmallows, cut fine
½ c. sugar
1 beaten egg
2 tsp. (heaping) flour
2 tbsp. butter
1 c. whipped Dream Whip
Grated Parmesan cheese

Prepare Jell-O by dissolving in boiling water; stir in 1 cup juices. Refrigerate until partially set; add fruit and marshmallows. Let chill until

177

(Continued on next page)

firm. Cook next 4 ingredients until thick; cool. Add Dream Whip. Spread on congealed mixture. Sprinkle cheese on top.

Mrs. Gerald Bruner, Valier H.S.
Valier, Montana

APRICOT JELL-O SALAD

2 pkg. apricot or peach Jell-O
2 c. hot water
2 c. cold water
1 No. 2 can crushed pineapple, drained
1 c. miniature marshmallows
2 lge. bananas, diced
½ c. sugar
1 egg, beaten
½ c. pineapple juice
2 tbsp. flour
2 tbsp. butter
1 3-oz. pkg. cream cheese
½ c. whipping cream

Dissolve Jell-O in hot water; add cold water. Fold in pineapple, marshmallows and bananas. Place in refrigerator until firm. Combine sugar, egg, reserved pineapple juice, flour and butter; cook mixture until thickened. Remove and add cream cheese. Allow mixture to cool. Whip cream and fold into cream cheese mixture. Spread over Jell-O mixture. Refrigerate several hours or overnight. Yield: 10-12 servings.

Mrs. Helen Coe, Eastwood H.S.
Perrysburg, Ohio

APRICOT-PINEAPPLE SALAD

2 pkg. orange Jell-O
2 c. boiling water
2 c. cold water
2 c. miniature marshmallows
1 No. 2 can crushed pineapple, well drained
½ c. pineapple juice
½ c. apricot nectar
1 egg, well beaten
½ c. sugar
1 tbsp. flour
1 c. whipping cream, whipped

Dissolve Jell-O in boiling water; add cold water, marshmallows and pineapple. Pour into two 8-inch square pans; let set. Combine remaining ingredients except whipped cream in top of double boiler; cook until thick, stirring. Let cool. Fold in whipped cream. Place on top of chilled Jell-O; let chill before serving. Yield: 18 servings.

Mrs. Lena Law, Mulberry H.S.
Mulberry, Arkansas

APRICOT-JELL-O SALAD

1 qt. canned apricots
1 sm. can crushed pineapple
2 pkg. orange Jell-O
2 c. sm. marshmallows
½ c. sugar
2 ½ tbsp. flour
1 egg, beaten
2 tbsp. margarine
1 c. whipped cream or Cool Whip

Drain juice from fruit; combine juices. Dissolve Jell-O in 2 cups hot water; add 1 cup juice. Cool and let set. Add mashed apricots, pineapple and marshmallows. Place in 9 x 13-inch pan. Mix sugar, flour, 1 cup juice and egg. Cook until thick; add margarine and cool. Add whipped cream. Pour over Jell-O. Yield: 10-15 servings.

Joan L. Haines, Prairie H.S.
Cottonwood, Idaho

APRICOT-JELL-O SALAD

2 pkg. orange Jell-O
2 c. boiling water
¾ c. marshmallows
1 c. fruit juice
1 No. 2 can apricots, cut into pieces
1 No. 2 can crushed pineapple
1 c. fruit juice
½ c. sugar
3 tbsp. flour
1 tbsp. butter
1 egg, beaten
1 c. whipped cream

Dissolve Jell-O in water; add marshmallows, fruit juice, apricots and pineapple. Pour into mold and chill until firm. Cook fruit juice, sugar, flour and butter until thick. Add egg to hot mixture slowly and cook a little more. Add whipped cream when cold. Spread over set Jell-O. Yield: 10-12 servings.

Frances M. Watson, Lake H.S.
Millbury, Ohio

APRICOT-ORANGE SALAD

½ c. sugar
2 envelopes unflavored gelatin
1 ½ c. cold water
1 can frozen orange juice
¼ c. white vinegar
1 1-lb. 14-oz. can apricot halves, drained
1 can mandarin oranges, drained
¾ c. apricot juice

Mix sugar, gelatin and water. Add orange juice; heat to dissolve gelatin. Stir in vinegar, apricot

(Continued on next page)

halves, oranges and apricot juice. Pour into
1 1/2-quart greased mold. Chill until firm. Yield:
6-8 servings.

Alice M. Ford, Central H.S.
Cheyenne, Wyoming

APRICOT-PINEAPPLE MOLD

    1 3-oz. pkg. lemon Jell-O
    1 c. hot water
    ½ c. apricot juice
    ½ c. pineapple juice
    1 c. cottage cheese
    1 c. whipping cream
    ½ c. chopped nuts
    ½ c. maraschino cherries, quartered
    ½ c. cooked or canned apricots, sliced
    ½ c. pineapple cubes, canned

Dissolve Jell-O in water; add fruit juices. Chill
until slightly thickened. Fold in cottage cheese,
whipped cream, nuts and fruits. Pour into oiled
mold and chill until firm. Unmold on crisp salad
greens and garnish with apricot halves, pineapple
cubes and maraschino cherries.

Mrs. Ellen Lamison, Surrattsville Sr. H.S.
Clinton, Maryland

APRICOT-PINEAPPE SALAD

    2 pkg. orange Jell-O
    2 c. juice
    1 ½ c. apricots, drained
    1 ½ c. crushed pineapple, drained
    1 ¾ c. miniature marshmallows
    ½ c. sugar
    3 tbsp. flour
    1 egg, beaten
    2 tbsp. butter
    Salt to taste
    1 c. whipped cream
    ⅔ c. grated cheese

Combine Jell-O with 2 cups water and 1 cup
juice; cool until partially congealed. Add fruit
and marshmallows; let set. Make sauce with
sugar, flour, egg, remaining juice, butter and
salt; cool. Add whipped cream. Spread sauce
over top of set Jell-O. Top sauce with cheese.
Yield: 6 servings.

Anna B. Whitescarver, Flemington H.S.
Flemington, West Virginia

APRICOT AND PINEAPPLE
SALAD

    2 pkg. orange Jell-O
    2 c. hot water
    3 c. pineapple and apricot juice, combined

    1 lge. can crushed pineapple, drained
    1 lge. can apricots, drained
    2 c. sm. marshmallows
    ½ c. sugar
    2 tbsp. flour
    1 well-beaten egg
    2 tbsp. butter

Prepare Jell-O with hot water; add 2 cups juice.
Cool; add fruit. Place in 9 x 12-inch pan; sprinkle
top with marshmallows. Let set. Combine remaining ingredients. Cook until thick. Let cool;
spread on Jell-O. Yield: 12-15 servings.

Mrs. Sharon Lett, Serena H.S.
Serena, Illinois

APRICOT RING MOLD

    1 No. 2 ½ can whole peeled apricots
    2 pkg. apricot or orange gelatin dessert
    1 3-oz. pkg. cream cheese
    1 ½ c. white seedless grapes, halved

Drain juice from apricots; add water to equal
4 cups liquid. Prepare gelatin with liquid. Remove seeds from apricots; replace with 1/2 inch
cubes of cream cheese. Place apricots in 2-quart
ring mold, rinsed in cold water. Pour enough
gelatin mixture over apricots to cover; allow to
set. Add remaining gelatin and grapes. Unmold
on lettuce leaves. Place small container of salad
dressing in center. Yield: 12 servings.

Mrs. Edna Ruth, Watseka Comm. H.S.
Watseka, Illinois

APRICOT SALAD

    2 No. 303 cans whole peeled apricots
    2 3-oz. pkg. orange Jell-O
    1 No. 303 can crushed pineapple
    2 c. miniature marshmallows
    ¾ c. pineapple juice
    2 tbsp. (heaping) flour
    2 tbsp. (heaping) sugar
    2 beaten egg yolks
    2 tbsp. butter
    Dash of salt
    1 ½ pt. sweetened whipped cream
    Grated cheddar cheese

Stone, chop and drain apricots, reserving juice;
add enough water to juice to equal 3 1/2 cups
liquid. Bring liquid to a boil; add Jell-O. Stir
until dissolved. Cool; add drained fruit and
marshmallows. Pour into 9 x 11-inch pan. Congeal. Add pineapple juice slowly to dry ingredients in top of double boiler. Add egg yolks; stir
until thick over hot water. Remove from heat; add
butter. Stir vigorously; cool. Add whipped cream;
spread on Jell-O. Sprinkle with c h e e s e. Yield:
10-12 servings.

Mrs. Jo Ann Baxter, Ringgold H.S.
Ringgold, Georgia

Molded Fruit Salads With Apricots

APRICOT SALAD

1 No. 2 can apricots
1 No. 2 can crushed pineapple
2 sm. pkg. orange Jell-O
2 c. boiling water
2 c. fruit syrup
½ c. white sugar
2 tbsp. flour
1 egg, beaten
1 c. cream, whipped
Grated American cheese

Drain apricots and pineapple; reserve syrup. Dissolve Jell-O in boiling water; add 1 cup reserved syrup. Chill until partially set. Chop apricots; add to Jell-O with pineapple. Chill until firm. Mix sugar and flour; stir in remaining fruit syrup and egg. Cook in double boiler until thick; cool. Fold in whipped cream. Spread over firm gelatin; sprinkle with cheese. Yield: 8 servings.

Bernetha Gillette, Byron H.S.
Byron, Nebraska

APRICOT SALAD

1 lge. can sliced pineapple
1 lge. can apricot halves
1 envelope plain gelatin
1 pkg. apricot Jell-O
½ c. chopped nuts (opt.)
1 c. miniature marshmallows
½ pt. sour cream

Drain fruit juices into saucepan; cut fruit into small pieces. Soak gelatin in 1/2 cup cold water. Bring fruit juices to a boil; pour over Jell-O and soaked gelatin. Stir in nuts, fruits and marshmallows. Mix well; fold in sour cream. Mold in large square glass dish or aluminum pan. Chill. Cut into squares and serve on lettuce. May be molded in individual molds if desired. Yield: 12 servings.

Mrs. Obera Pruitt, Belton-Honea Path H.S.
Belton, South Carolina

APRICOT SALAD WITH TOPPING

1 No. 2½ can peeled apricots
1 No. 2 can crushed pineapple
1 6-oz. pkg. orange Jell-O
2 c. boiling water
2 c. fruit juices
3 tbsp. flour
½ c. sugar
1 beaten egg
2 tbsp. margarine
1 envelope Dream Whip
Grated cheese

Remove seeds from apricots; mash. Reserve juice. Drain pineapple; reserve juice. Dissolve Jell-O in boiling water; add 1 cup mixed juices. Stir fruits into Jell-O. Pour into 13 x 9 x 2-inch pan. Refrigerate until set. Mix flour and sugar; stir in remaining fruit juices and egg. Cook over medium heat until very thick; stir during cooking. Remove from heat; add margarine. Cool completely. Prepare Dream Whip according to directions. Fold into cooked mixture; spread on salad. Sprinkle with grated cheese. Cut into squares. Yield: 12-15 servings.

Linda R. Kennerly, Trinity H.S.
Trinity, North Carolina

FRUIT JELL-O SALAD

2 3-oz. pkg. orange Jell-O
2 c. boiling water
1 No. 2 can apricot
1 No. 2 can pineapple tidbits
1 c. miniature marshmallows
1 egg
2 tbsp. flour
½ c. sugar
1 envelope Dream Whip

Dissolve Jell-O in boiling water; let cool. Drain apricots and pineapple, reserving juice. Add 2 cups fruit juice to Jell-O. Mash apricots; add to Jell-O. Add pineapple and marshmallows. Let Jell-O mixture set. Mix remaining juice with egg, flour and sugar in top of double boiler. Cook until thick; cool. Prepare Dream Whip as directed on package. Fold thickened sauce into Dream Whip and spread on top of set Jell-O. Yield: 10 servings.

Virginia Darnell, Apache H.S.
Apache, Oklahoma

LILLY'S APRICOT SALAD

1 family-size pkg. apricot Jell-O
1 lge. can crushed pineapple, drained
1 c. miniature marshmallows
2 bananas, diced
½ c. chopped nutmeats
2 tbsp. flour
1 egg, beaten
2 tbsp. butter
½ c. pineapple juice
1 3-oz. pkg. cream cheese
1 pkg. Dream Whip, prepared

Mix Jell-O according to package directions; add next 4 ingredients. Let set. Blend flour with egg; add butter. Add pineapple juice; cook until thick over low heat or in top of double boiler. Cool. Add softened cream cheese and Dream Whip to custard mix. Spread on congealed Jell-O. Yield: 12 servings.

Harriet Reed, Milltown H.S.
Milltown, Indiana

180

MOLDED FRUIT SALAD

2 pkg. orange Jell-O
2 c. hot water
2 c. fruit juice
¾ c. marshmallows
1 16-oz. can apricots, drained
1 16-oz. can pineapple chunks, drained
½ c. sugar
3 tbsp. flour
1 egg
2 tbsp. butter
1 c. whipped cream
¾ c. grated cheddar cheese
Lettuce

Dissolve Jell-O in water. Add 1 cup fruit juice, marshmallows, apricots and pineapple; stir until marshmallows are melted. Pour into 13 x 9 x 2-inch dish. Let stand until firm. Cook sugar, flour, egg and remaining fruit juice until thickened. Add butter. Cool and fold in whipped cream. Spread on firm Jell-O mixture. Chill at least 8 hours. Spread cheese on top. Serve on lettuce. Yield: 12 servings.

Mrs. Ruth H. Hebenstreit, Pana Sr. H.S.
Pana, Illinois

PINEAPPLE-APRICOT SALAD

1 No. 2 ½ can apricots, drained and diced
1 No. 2 can crushed pineapple, drained
2 tbsp. butter
4 tbsp. sugar
2 tbsp. cornstarch
2 c. fruit juice
2 eggs, slightly beaten
1 pkg. Dream Whip, well whipped

Prepare Jell-O as directed on package, using 1 cup less water. Chill until slightly set. Fold in fruit; pour into long low 8 x 13-inch dish to set. Cook butter, sugar, cornstarch, eggs and fruit juice over medium heat until thickened. Cool. Spread cooled dressing over Jell-O. Cover with Dream Whip.

Thelma Dellinger, Byng H.S.
Ada, Oklahoma

PINEAPPLE-APRICOT SALAD

1 No. 2 can crushed pineapple
1 lge. can peeled apricots, mashed
2 sm. pkg. orange Jell-O
1 sm. pkg. miniature marshmallows
2 c. fruit juice
½ c. sugar
1 tbsp. flour
1 egg, well beaten
1 c. cream, whipped

Drain fruit; reserve juice. Dissolve Jell-O in 2 1/2 cups boiling water; add marshmallows to

soften. Add 1 cup juice; add fruit. Pour into molds or pan. Let set in refrigerator. Mix sugar, flour, egg and remaining fruit juice. Cook until thick; cool. Add 1 cup whipped cream. Serve with congealed salad. Yield: 8 servings.

Mrs. Virginia Robinson, Blytheville H.S.
Blytheville, Arkansas

SPICED APRICOT SALAD

3 ½ c. apricot halves
¼ tsp. salt
6 inch cinnamon stick
Cloves
2 3-oz. pkg. orange gelatin
1 9-oz. can crushed pineapple
3 tbsp. lemon juice
1 c. seedless green grapes, halved
1 3-oz. pkg. cream cheese
¼ c. chopped walnuts

Drain apricots; reserve syrup. Cut into quarters. Add water to syrup to equal 1 3/4 cup liquid. Add salt, cinnamon and cloves to juice. Simmer 10 minutes. Remove from heat; let stand 10 minutes to steep. Strain juice. Dissolve orange gelatin in hot mixture. Drain pineapple, reserving syrup. Add water to syrup to equal 2 cups liquid. Add to gelatin mixture with lemon juice. Chill until set. Stir in apricots and grapes. Pour into 11 1/2 x 7 1/2 x 1 1/2-inch dish. Chill until firm. Soften cream cheese; mix with pineapple. Spread over gelatin. Sprinkle with walnuts. Cut into 10 or 12 squares; serve on lettuce.

Mrs. Douglas Case, Blissfield H.S.
Blissfield, Michigan

SPICY APRICOT MOLD

1 1-lb. can unpeeled apricot halves, halved
1 8 ¾-oz. can pineapple tidbits
2 tbsp. vinegar
1 tsp. whole cloves
4 inch stick cinnamon
2 to 3 oz. pkg. orange gelatin
¾ c. boiling water
¾ c. apricot nectar
½ c. sour cream

Drain fruits, reserving syrup. Combine syrup; add vinegar and spices. Bring to a boil. Simmer 10 minutes. Strain syrup; add hot water to equal 2 cups. Pour mixture over package orange gelatin; stir till dissolved. Chill until partially set. Fold in apricots and pineapple. Pour into 6-cup mold. Chill until almost firm. Dissolve remaining gelatin in boiling water; stir in apricot nectar. Chill until partially set; whip until fluffy. Swirl in sour cream. Pour over first layer. Chill 8 hours or longer.

Donna G. Bennett
North Kamloops Sr. Secondary Sch.
North Kamloops, British Columbia, Canada

TRI-COLOR FRUIT MOLD

1 No. 2 can apricots
1 3-oz. pkg. orange gelatin
1 3-oz. pkg. lime gelatin
1 c. crushed pineapple and juice
½ c. heavy cream, whipped
1 pkg. strawberry gelatin
1 pt. fresh strawberries
5 to 6 lettuce leaves

Drain and save juice from apricots and puree apricots. Measure juice and add enough water to make 1 3/4 cups. Heat to boiling and add to orange gelatin. Stir until thoroughly dissolved; chill until mixture is slightly congealed. Add puree and pour into round 8 x 9 x 2-inch mold or deep layer cake pan, rinsed with cold water. Chill until firm. Pour 1 cup boiling water over lime gelatin; stir until dissolved. Add pineapple with juice; fold in cream. Pour over firm orange layer in mold. Chill second layer until firm. Pour 1 cup boiling water over strawberry gelatin; stir until dissolved. Chill until slightly congealed. Pick out enough whole berries to fill 3/4 cup. Puree remaining berries; measure pulp and juice. Add water, if necessary, to make 3/4 cup. Combine with gelatin; fold in fruit and pour over 2 layers in mold. Chill until firm. Unmold on chilled, flat serving plate. Garnish with mayonnaise, if desired. Cut into pie-shaped wedges. Place on lettuce leaves. Serve with additional fresh fruits, if desired. Yield: 12-14 servings.

Mrs. Hellen Evans, Adams City H.S.
Commerce City, Colorado

AVOCADO CITRUS SALAD

1 sm. pkg. lime gelatin
1 c. boiling water
2 med. avocados
1 3-oz. pkg. cream cheese
2 tbsp. mayonnaise
2 tbsp. lemon juice
1 tsp. salt
1 tsp. grated onion (opt.)
1 c. grapefruit sections

Dissolve gelatin in boiling water. Chill in refrigerator until thickened. Peel avocados. Mash enough to make 2/3 cup; slice remainder. Mix mashed avocado, softened cream cheese, mayonnaise, lemon juice, salt and grated onion together; combine with thickened gelatin. Add sliced avocados and grapefruit sections; reserve some grapefruit for garnish. Pour into oiled 1-quart mold. Chill until firm. Unmold on salad greens; garnish with grapefruit sections. Yield: 6-8 servings.

Elizabeth Chenoweth, Area Supvr.
Texas Ed. Agency
Corpus Christi, Texas

AVOCADO-ALMOND SALAD

1 pkg. lime Jell-O
½ lb. cottage cheese
1 sm. can crushed pineapple
2 avocados
½ lb. almonds
1 clove of garlic
Mayonnaise
Dash of Worcestershire sauce
1 tsp. lemon juice

Dissolve Jell-O in 1 pint boiling water. When partially set add cottage cheese, pineapple, 1 mashed avocado and almonds sliced in small strips. Pour into individual molds. Chill until firm. Rub mixing bowl with garlic. Mash remaining avocado with fork; add an equal amount of mayonnaise, Worcestershire sauce, and lemon juice. Serve congealed salad on greens with avocado dressing. Yield: 8 servings.

Mrs. Sarah M. Gleason, East Jr. H.S.
East Walpole, Massachusetts

AVOCADO-GRAPEFRUIT SOUFFLE

1 pkg. lime gelatin
1 c. hot water
½ c. cold water
1½ tbsp. lemon juice
½ c. mayonnaise
¼ tsp. salt
2 tbsp. chopped green pepper
1 c. diced grapefruit sections, drained
½ c. mashed avocado pulp

Dissolve gelatin in hot water. Stir in cold water, lemon juice, mayonnaise and salt. Turn into freezing tray. Freeze 15 or 20 minutes or until firm about 1 inch from edge but still soft in center. Turn into bowl; whip with rotary beater until fluffy. Fold in green pepper and fruit. Pour into 1-quart mold; chill until firm, 30 to 60 minutes. Yield: 5-6 servings.

Zona Beth Cates, Tempe H.S.
Tempe, Arizona

AVOCADO-LIME SALAD

1 pkg. lime Jell-O
8 oz. cream cheese
2 avocados
1 sm. can crushed pineapple
1 tsp. mayonnaise

Prepare Jell-O according to directions on box. Soften cream cheese; crush avocados. Mix cheese, avocados, pineapple and mayonnaise with thickened Jell-O; mold. Let set in refrigerator for several hours. Yield: 8 servings.

Mrs. Jolene Corcoran, Follett H.S.
Follett, Texas

AVOCADO SALAD

1 sm. can crushed pineapple
1 pkg. lime gelatin
½ c. whipped cream
2 tbsp. lemon juice
¼ tsp. salt
1 tbsp. mayonnaise
2 ripe avocados, chopped

Drain pineapple; reserve juice. Dissolve gelatin in 1 cup boiling water; add juice from pineapple and let stand in refrigerator until thick. Add pineapple, whipped cream, lemon juice, salt, mayonnaise and avocados. Mix well. Place in refrigerator to congeal. Serve on lettuce, if desired. Yield: 8 servings.

Dorothy Schroeder, Yorktown H.S.
Yorktown, Texas

GRAPEFRUIT AND AVOCADO SALAD

1 pkg. lemon gelatin
1 can grapefruit sections
1 can pimento, chopped
1 avocado, cubed
Salad greens
Mayonnaise

Dissolve gelatin as directed on package; chill. When gelatin begins to thicken, add grapefruit, pimento and avocado. Pour into mold; chill until firm. Serve on salad greens with mayonnaise or dressing. Yield: 6 servings.

Mrs. George M. Ballard, Cumberland Jr. H.S.
Harriman, Tennessee

BANANA-CREAM-GELATIN SALAD

2 3-oz. pkg. strawberry or cherry-
   flavored gelatin
1 ½ c. boiling water
2 c. cold water
1 c. crushed pineapple
¼ c. sugar
2 tbsp. flour
1 egg
1 c. pineapple juice, drained from
   crushed pineapple with water added to
   make 1 c.
3 bananas
½ pt. whipping cream, whipped with 3
   tbsp. sugar and 1 tsp. vanilla
½ c. finely chopped walnuts

Dissolve gelatin in boiling water. Stir in cold water. Chill until slightly thickened. Drain pineapple, reserving juice, and stir drained pineapple into slightly thickened gelatin. Pour into a 9 x 13-inch glass baking dish and chill until firm. Mix together sugar, flour, egg and pineapple juice. Cook until thickened, about 5 minutes. Cool.

Slice bananas over firm gelatin. Spread cooled custard filling over bananas. Top with whipped cream and sprinkle with chopped nuts. Yield: 10 servings.

Patricia A. Severin, Hopewell Memorial Jr. H.S.
Aliquippa, Pennsylvania

BANANA AND PINEAPPLE SALAD

2 pkg. lime Jell-O
2 cans pineapple chunks
2 lge. bananas, sliced
½ c. sugar
2 c. pineapple juice
2 tbsp. flour
2 eggs, beaten
⅛ tsp. salt
1 tbsp. gelatin in ¼ c. cold water
1 c. whipped cream
1 c. grated cheese

Prepare lime Jell-O according to package directions. Chill; add pineapple and bananas. Pour into 9 x 13 x 2-inch pan; chill until firm. Mix sugar, flour, pineapple juice in saucepan; stir in eggs and salt. Cook over low heat until thick. Add softened gelatin to hot mixture. Cool. Fold in whipped cream and cheese. Spread over congealed mixture. Yield: 8 servings.

Sister Anne Beaton, CND, Mabou Consol. Sch.
Mabou, Nova Scotia, Canada

BANANA-PINEAPPLE SALAD

2 sm. boxes lemon Jell-O
4 c. hot water
16 lge. marshmallows
4 sliced bananas
1 No. 2 can crushed pineapple, drained
1 c. pineapple juice
½ c. sugar
2 tbsp. flour
2 tbsp. butter
2 eggs, beaten
1 c. whipped cream
Crushed nuts

Dissolve Jell-O in hot water; stir in marshmallows until melted. Cool. Add bananas and pineapple. Place in 13 x 9-inch pan; refrigerate until firm. Cook pineapple juice, sugar, flour, butter and eggs until thick, stirring constantly. Fold in whipped cream. Spread mixture over salad. Sprinkle with crushed nuts. Refrigerate until ready to serve. Yield: 12 servings.

Mrs. Jill Kaufman, Cullom H.S.
Cullom, Illinois

Molded Mixed Fruit Salads

BLACK WALNUT-MALAGA MOLD

1 3-oz. pkg. lemon Jell-O
2 c. hot water
1 c. crushed pineapple
1 c. Malaga grapes, sliced and seeded
2 raw carrots, ground in chopper or
    blender
½ c. ground black walnut meats or
    English walnuts

Dissolve Jell-O in hot water. Chill Jell-O mixture until syrupy. Add remaining ingredients to Jell-O. Turn into ring or fancy mold; chill until firm. Turn onto lettuce garnished plate. Serve with mayonnaise, if desired. Yield: 8 servings.

Mrs. Doris Schlumpf, Durand Unified Sch.
Durand, Wisconsin

BLUEBERRY JELL-O DELIGHT

1 16-oz. can crushed pineapple,
    drained
1 3-oz. pkg. lemon Jell-O
1 8-oz. pkg. cream cheese
3 tbsp. powdered sugar
¾ c. half and half
½ tsp. vanilla
1 No. 303 can blueberries
1 6-oz. pkg. cherry Jell-O

Drain pineapple, reserving juice, and add hot water to make 1 1/2 cups of liquid. Dissolve lemon Jell-O and chill. Cream together next 4 ingredients. Add to creamed mixture and mix slowly when Jell-O is cooled. Add pineapple and set until firm. Drain blueberries and add enough hot water to juice to make 3 1/2 cups of liquid. Dissolve cherry Jell-O. Refrigerate in mold. Add blueberries and pour over set lemon Jell-O. Yield: 10-12 servings.

Jean Daniels, Excelsior H.S.
Norwalk, California

BLUEBERRY JELL-O SALAD

1 can blueberries, drained
1 pkg. lemon Jell-O
1 c. pineapple juice
2 mashed bananas
1 c. whipped cream
3 tbsp. sugar
Nuts (opt.)

Drain blueberries; reserve juice. Dissolve Jell-O in blueberry juice and pineapple juice. Chill until partially set. Add bananas, cream, blueberries and sugar. Add nuts; pour into mold or dish. Chill until firm. Yield: 4-6 servings.

Mrs. Betty Ambrose, Robert Lee H.S.
Midland, Texas

BLUEBERRY SALAD

1 c. milk
1 c. sugar
1 pkg. unflavored gelatin
¼ c. cold water
1 c. sour cream
1 tsp. vanilla
2 3-oz. pkg. blackberry Jell-O
1 c. boiling water
2 c. blueberry juice
1 c. pineapple juice
2 No. 303 cans blueberries, drained
1 sm. can crushed pineapple, drained
¼ c. sugar

Heat milk; dissolve sugar in milk. Add gelatin softened in cold water. Chill. Add sour cream and vanilla. Pour into 8-cup mold; chill until firm. Dissolve Jell-O in boiling water. Chill until partially thick; add remaining ingredients. Pour onto set gelatin mixture. Refrigerate until firm; unmold and serve. Yield: 8 servings.

Mrs. Carol Rohrbacher, Maumee H.S.
Maumee, Ohio

BLUEBERRY SALAD

1 pkg. raspberry Jell-O
1 c. hot water
1 can blueberries
¼ c. pineapple juice
1 sm. can crushed pineapple, drained
1 pkg. Dream Whip, prepared

Dissolve Jell-O in hot water. Drain blueberries; reserve 3/4 liquid. Add liquid and pineapple juice to Jell-O. Chill until partially set. Fold in blueberries and pineapple. Fold in Dream Whip. Chill until firm. Yield: 6 servings.

Mrs. Lois Lovas, Mayville Pub. Sch.
Mayville, North Dakota

BLUEBERRY SALAD

1 lge. pkg. lemon Jell-O
1 c. boiling water
1 No. 211 can crushed pineapple and juice
1 No. 300 can blueberries and juice
1 tbsp. lemon juice
1 mashed banana
½ pt. whipping cream

Dissolve Jell-O in boiling water. Drain juice from pineapple and blueberries; add enough water to juice to make 2 cups. Add to Jell-O with lemon juice. Allow to thicken slightly; add banana, pineapple and blueberries. Whip cream; fold into Jell-O mixture. Pour in 9 x 13-inch pan or large mold; refrigerate until firm. Serve on lettuce. Yield: 12 servings.

Mrs. Joy Potter, Gehlen Cath. H.S.
Le Mars, Iowa

CONGEALED PINEAPPLE AND BLUEBERRY SALAD

2 envelopes unflavored gelatin
3 ½ c. pineapple juice
1 tbsp. fresh lemon juice
1 c. drained crushed pineapple
1 c. fresh blueberries
Pineapple slices and additional
    blueberries for garnish (opt.)
Mayonnaise

Soften gelatin in 1/2 cup of cold pineapple juice. Heat 1 cup of pineapple juice to boiling point; add gelatin. Stir until melted. Add remaining pineapple juice and lemon juice and chill until the mixture begins to thicken. Fold in pineapple and blueberries. Pour mixture into 1-quart mold or 8 half-cup individual molds. Garnish serving platter with salad greens, pineapple slices and fresh blueberries. Serve with mayonnaise. Yield: 6-8 servings.

Mrs. Ruth Yelvington, Mildred H.S.
Corsicana, Texas

BANANA-CHERRY REGAL SALAD

1 3-oz. pkg. cherry gelatin
2 c. hot water
1 c. pitted Bing cherries, drained
2 bananas, sliced
1 c. miniature marshmallows

Dissolve gelatin in hot water; chill until almost firm. Fold in fruit and marshmallows; pour into 1-quart mold. Chill until firm. Unmold on salad greens. Serve with salad dressing, if desired. Yield: 8 servings.

Mrs. Rogene Moss, Page H.S.
Page, North Dakota

BLACK CHERRY SQUARES

2 1-lb. cans (4 c.) pitted Bing cherries
⅓ c. lemon juice
1 pkg. orange-flavored gelatin
¾ c. broken pecans
⅔ c. sliced stuffed green olives

Drain cherries; add enough syrup to lemon juice to make 1 3/4 cups liquid. Heat; pour over gelatin till dissolved. Chill till partially set. Add cherries, pecans and olives. Pour into 10 x 6 x 1 1/2-inch pan; chill till firm. Cut into squares and serve on lettuce. Chill in individual molds and unmold on pineapple rings, if desired. Yield: 6-8 servings.

Sharon Hoogland, Kendrick H.S.
Kendrick, Idaho

BLACK CHERRY MOLD

1 No. 2 can dark sweet cherries
1 No. 2 can crushed pineapple
2 3-oz. pkg. black cherry gelatin
4 tbsp. powdered sugar
½ tsp. cinnamon
2 tbsp. maraschino cherry juice
1 tbsp. lemon juice
1 c. whipping cream, whipped

Drain juice from cherries and pineapple; add enough water to measure 1 quart. Heat 2 cups of liquid; add gelatin and stir until dissolved. Add remaining 2 cups juice; chill until partially thickened. Pour a layer of gelatin, 1/2 inch deep, into an oiled, ring mold. Add cherries. Fold pineapple into remaining gelatin; pour in mold and chill until firm. Blend together all ingredients except whipped cream; chill for 1 hour. Fold in whipped cream and serve with salad. Yield: 8 servings.

Mrs. Carol Roberts, Auburn H.S.
Auburn, Illinois

BING CHERRY MOLD

1 can pitted Bing cherries
1 envelope or 1 tbsp. gelatin
½ lb. cream cheese
¼ c. pineapple juice
Watercress

Drain cherries, reserving juice. Place cherries in a ring mold. Add enough water to cherry juice to make 2 cups. Place 1/2 cup juice in a saucepan; add gelatin and stir over low heat until gelatin dissolves. Add remaining 1 1/2 cups juice; pour over cherries. Chill until firm. Unmold. Beat cream cheese and pineapple juice until light as whipped cream. Pile into center of ring. Garnish with watercress. Yield: 6 servings.

Sister M. Roseleen, O.S.F., Mt. Assisi Acad.
Pittsburgh, Pennsylvania

CHERRY-COKE SALAD

½ c. water
½ c. sugar
½ can pie cherries and juice
1 pkg. cherry Jell-O
1 8-oz. can crushed pineapple
½ sm. bottle Coca-Cola

Heat water, sugar, cherries and juice to boiling. Stir in Jell-O until dissolved. Cool. Add pineapple and Coca-Cola. Pour into 9 inch square pan. Cut into squares when set. Yield: 9 servings.

Mrs. Charles Peterson, Abilene H.S.
Abilene, Kansas

Molded Fruit Salads With Cherries

CHERRY-COKE SALAD

1 No. 2 can dark sweet cherries, pitted
1 buffet can crushed pineapple
2 pkg. cherry Jell-O
2 6-oz. bottles Coca-Cola
1 c. pecans, chopped (opt.)

Drain fruit. Combine juice with enough water to make 2 cups liquid; bring to boil. Add Jell-O; stir until dissolved and cool. Add Coca-Cola. Let set until begins to thicken. Add cherries, pineapple and nuts. Place in refrigerator until completely jelled. Yield: 8 servings.

Mrs. Mary Lue Tibbitts, Spiro H.S.
Spiro, Oklahoma
Mrs. Edith Solomon, Blair H.S.
Blair, Nebraska

CHERRY JELL-O MOLD

1 No. 2 can sour pitted cherries
¾ c. sugar
1 3-oz. pkg. cherry Jell-O
1 6-oz. can crushed pineapple
½ c. chopped nuts

Bring cherries and sugar to boil; remove from heat. Add Jell-O; stir until dissolved. Cool slightly. Add pineapple and nuts. Pour into mold. Chill until set. Sugar substitute may be used. Yield: 6-8 servings.

Marie Welch, Lookout Jr. H.S.
Chattanooga, Tennessee

CHERRY SALAD

1 pkg. cherry Jell-O
¼ c. sugar
1 ½ c. orange juice
½ c. cherry juice
1 can pie cherries
¼ c. chopped celery
½ c. pecans
¼ c. crushed pineapple

Dissolve Jell-O and sugar in hot juices. When Jell-O begins to thicken, fold in cherries, celery, pecans and pineapple. Chill until set. Yield: 8-10 servings.

Mrs. Laurissa Rawlings, Brady H.S.
Brady, Texas

CHERRY SALAD WITH DRESSING

1 3-oz. box cherry Jell-O
1 ⅓ c. boiling water
1 No. 303 can instant cherry pie filling
1 8-oz. pkg. cream cheese, room temperature

1 sm. can crushed pineapple, drained
2 tbsp. salad dressing
6 tbsp. concentrated frozen orange juice

Dissolve Jell-O in boiling water. Add pie filling; stir. Pour into serving bowl. Let set until firm. Cream the cheese. Add pineapple, salad dressing and orange juice; blend well. Spread on set Jell-O. Sprinkle with chopped nuts, if desired. Yield: 8-10 servings.

Mrs. Marie Mohr, Wayne H.S.
Wayne, Nebraska

CHERRY-SHERRY MOLD

1 pkg. dark cherry Jell-O
2 c. hot water
½ pt. heavy whipping cream
1 tbsp. sugar
1 tbsp. orange juice
1 tbsp. lemon juice
1 tbsp. pineapple juice
¼ c. sherry
1 No. 303 can dark cherries, drained
¾ c. chopped pecans

Prepare Jell-O with hot water. Chill until softly set. Whip cream; fold in sugar, juices and sherry gradually, then fold into Jell-O. Add cherries and nuts. Yield: 8 servings.

Marilyn Butler, Lefors H.S.
Lefors, Texas

CHERRY-SOUR CREAM SALAD

1 No. 2 can dark, sweet pitted cherries
1 sm. can crushed pineapple
1 pkg. cherry flavored gelatin
½ c. broken nuts
½ pt. sour cream

Drain liquid from cherries and pineapple; add enough water to measure 1 1/2 cups. Dissolve gelatin in 1 cup liquid, heated to boiling point. Add remaining 1/2 cup liquid; chill until begins to thicken. Add pineapple and nuts; mix well. Chill until syrupy. Fold in sour cream and cherries. Fill salad molds and chill. Yield: 8 servings.

Ethel F. Johnson, New Brockton H.S.
New Brockton, Alabama

COCA-COLA FRUIT SALAD

1 can black Bing cherries
1 can chunk pineapple
2 pkg. black cherry Jell-O
1 lge. pkg. softened cream cheese
½ c. chopped walnuts
2 cans or 1 lge. bottle Coca-Cola
Pinch of salt

(Continued on next page)

Drain, mix and heat 1 cup juice from cherries and pineapple. Dissolve Jell-O in hot juice. Add cheese and whip to blend. Stir in all remaining ingredients. Chill. Stir to mix when partly set. Pour into 10 x 13-inch pan. Yield: 10 servings.

Mrs. I. M. Klungle, Beecher H.S.
Flint, Michigan

MARY'S FRUIT SALAD

    1 can diced pineapple
    1 can pitted Royal Anne cherries
    1 can mandarin oranges
    1 pkg. Jell-O
    ½ pt. whipping cream
    2 doz. marshmallows, quartered
    1 apple, cored and diced
    1 banana, sliced
    Nuts (opt.)

Drain juice from canned fruits; reserve. Make Jell-O according to package directions, using reserved juice as part of liquid. Allow to cool and congeal. Whip cream; stir into Jell-O. Add marshmallows, fruit and nuts. Allow to set 4 to 8 hours. Garnish with lettuce or may be served in individual portions on lettuce leaf. Yield: 10-12 servings.

Mary L. Scott, Lyman H.S.
Lyman, Nebraska

RED CHERRY SALAD

    1 No. 2 can crushed pineapple
    1 No. 2 can red sour cherries
    Grated rind and juice of 1 lemon and 1
      orange
    2 pkg. cherry Jell-O
    ½ c. sugar
    1 envelope Knox gelatin
    1 c. chopped pecans

Drain fruit; reserve juice. Combine reserved juice with enough lemon and orange juice to measure 3 cups. Heat. Stir in Jell-O and sugar until dissolved. Dissolve gelatin in 1/4 cup cold water; add to hot mixture. Set aside until it begins to congeal, then add fruit and nuts. Yield: 8-12 servings.

Mrs. Margaret W. Lyles, Westminster H.S.
Westminster, South Carolina

TANGY CHERRY SALAD

    1 9-oz. can crushed pineapple
    1 1-lb. can red, sour pitted cherries
    1 pkg. cherry-flavored gelatin

    ¼ c. sugar
    ⅓ c. orange juice
    2 tbsp. lemon juice
    ⅓ c. broken pecans

Drain pineapple, reserving 1/3 cup syrup. Drain cherries; combine syrup with pineapple syrup and enough water to make 1 1/2 cups liquid. Heat to boiling. Add gelatin and sugar; stir until dissolved. Add orange juice and lemon juice. Chill until partially set. Stir in cherries, pineapple and pecans. Chill until set. Unmold. Yield: 8 servings.

Mrs. Carol Hurlbert, Henry H.S.
Henry, South Dakota

CHRISTMAS GARLAND JELL-O

    1 20-oz. can drained pineapple tidbits
    1 3-oz. pkg. red Jell-O
    1 c. hot water
    ¾ c. cold water
    1 med. banana, sliced
    1 3-oz. pkg. lime Jell-O
    1 c. hot water
    1 pkg. Dream Whip, prepared

Drain pineapple; reserve 3/4 cup juice. Dissolve red Jell-O in hot water; add cold water. Chill until syrupy. Fold in banana. Pour into 6-cup ring mold or 9 x 5 x 3-inch pan. Chill until almost firm. Dissolve lime Jell-O in hot water; add reserved pineapple juice. Chill 1/2 cup lime Jell-O until syrupy. Fold 1 cup Dream Whip into syrupy lime Jell-O. Pour over red Jell-O in mold; chill until almost firm. Chill remaining lime Jell-O until syrupy. Fold in pineapple tidbits. Pour over contents of mold; chill. Unmold. Pile remaining Dream Whip into center; garnish with almonds and maraschino cherries. Yield: 8-10 servings.

Mrs. E. Fahlgren, St. James Collegiate
Winnipeg, Manitoba, Canada

CLOUD NINE SALAD

    2 pkg. orange Jell-O
    2 c. boiling water
    2 c. Seven-Up
    1 No. 2 can crushed pineapple, drained
    2 bananas, sliced
    1 ⅓ c. miniature marshmallows
    ½ c. sugar
    2 tbsp. flour
    1 egg, beaten
    1 c. pineapple juice
    2 tbsp. butter
    1 c. heavy cream, whipped
    1 ½ c. grated cheese

Dissolve Jell-O in boiling water. Add Seven-up and chill until mixture begins to congeal. Add drained pineapple, bananas and marshmallows.

(Continued on next page)

Pour into 9 x 13-inch pan; chill until firm. Combine sugar, flour, egg and juice. Cook over low heat, stirring constantly until thick. Remove from heat; add butter. Cool. Whip cream; add to cooked mixture. Pour mixture over congealed salad. Sprinkle top with grated cheese. Chill 3 to 4 hours. Cut into squares and serve on lettuce. Yield: 12 servings.

Sister M. Loretta Cecile, BVM, Alleman H.S.
Rock Island, Illinois

CLUB FRUIT SALAD

1 13-oz. can pineapple tidbits
1 No. 303 can light sweet cherries
1 11-oz. can mandarin oranges
½ c. sugar
3 tbsp. cornstarch
¼ tsp. salt
1 egg, slightly beaten
1 envelope unflavored gelatin
¼ c. lemon juice
1 10-oz. pkg. strawberries, thawed
   and drained
2 c. miniature marshmallows
1 c. cream, whipped

Drain canned fruit, reserving 1/2 cup syrup from each can. Combine sugar, cornstarch and salt. Add reserved syrup. Cook over low heat until thick. Stir small amount fruit sauce into egg. Return to hot mixture; cook 1 minute. Soften gelatin in lemon juice. Add to hot mixture. Stir until dissolved; chill until partially set. Add canned fruit, strawberries and marshmallows. Fold in whipped cream. Place in mold or pan; chill until set. Yield: 10-12 servings.

Mrs. Wesley Rieke, Fairfax H.S.
Fairfax, Minnesota

CLUB SODA-FRUIT SALAD

2 pkg. lemon gelatin
2 c. boiling water
2 c. carbonated soda
1 20-oz. can crushed pineapple
1 c. miniature marshmallows
2 lge. bananas, sliced

Dissolve gelatin in water; stir in soda. Chill until partially set. Drain pineapple; reserve juice. Fold pineapple, marshmallows and bananas into gelatin mixture. Pour into 13 x 7-inch pan; chill until firm.

TOPPING:

½ c. sugar
1 tbsp. flour
1 c. pineapple juice
1 egg, slightly beaten
1 tbsp. butter
1 c. whipping cream, whipped

Combine sugar and flour in saucepan; stir in pineapple juice and egg. Cook over low heat until thick. Remove from heat; stir in butter. Cool. Fold in whipped cream; frost salad. Yield: 12 servings.

Mrs. Herbert Milroy, Belle Center Local
Belle Center, Ohio

COMPANY SALAD

2 pkg. lemon Jell-O
3 c. hot water
1 No. 2 can pineapple, drained
3 bananas, cubed
1 ½ c. miniature marshmallows
½ c. nuts
1 c. pineapple juice
1 ½ tbsp. flour
½ c. sugar
1 egg, beaten
1 c. whipping cream

Dissolve Jell-O in 3 cups hot water; cool. Add pineapple, bananas, marshmallows and nuts. Chill in large flat dish until firm. Heat pineapple juice in top of double boiler. Add flour and sugar to beaten egg. Mix with juice; cook until thick, stirring constantly. Cool. Fold in whipped cream. Spread over gelatin mixture. Sprinkle with additional nuts or shredded cheddar cheese, if desired. Yield: 15 servings.

Mrs. Nadine Kaiser, Hydro H.S.
Hydro, Oklahoma

COMPANY SALAD

2 c. boiling water
2 3-oz. pkg. lemon Jell-O
2 c. cold water
1 No. 2 can crushed pineapple, drained
3 bananas, cubed
1 ½ c. miniature marshmallows
1 egg
½ c. sugar
2 tbsp. flour
½ pt. whipping cream, whipped
American cheese

Mix boiling water with Jell-O; stir until thoroughly dissolved. Add cold water; stir. Drain pineapple; reserve 1 cup juice. Add pineapple, bananas, and marshmallows. Chill until firm. Mix reserved pineapple juice, egg, sugar and flour in saucepan with mixer. Cook over low heat until thick. Cool. Fold cream into cooked custard; spread on top of Jell-O mixture. Grate cheese on top; let set in refrigerator overnight. Yield: 12 servings.

Carolyn Waymack, Dollarway H.S.
Pine Bluff, Arkansas

CHRISTMAS CRANBERRY MOLD

1 pkg. strawberry or cherry Jell-O
1 sm. carton sour cream
1 sm. can crushed pineapple
1 lge. can whole cranberry sauce
½ c. chopped nuts

Dissolve Jell-O in 1 cup hot water; cool. Fold in remaining ingredients. Chill until firm. Yield: 8 servings.

Jenell Rogers, Jenkins H.S.
Savannah, Georgia

CRAN-APPLE SALAD

1 3-oz. pkg. strawberry gelatin
⅛ tsp. salt
1 ¼ c. boiling water
1 1-lb. can jellied cranberry sauce
2 c. finely chopped apples

Dissolve gelatin and salt in boiling water; break cranberry sauce with fork. Add to gelatin; chill until thick. Fold in apples; pour into individual molds or 8 x 8-inch square pan. Chill until firm. Yield: 6-8 servings.

Lois S. Gass, Line Mountain Sr. H.S.
Herndon, Pennsylvania

CRANBERRY BUBBLE

1 pkg. raspberry gelatin
1 pkg. lemon gelatin
1 ½ c. boiling water
1 sm. pkg. frozen raspberries
1 c. cranberry relish
1 c. Bubble-Up

Dissolve gelatin in boiling water; add raspberry and cranberry relish. Chill until syrupy; add Bubble-Up. Chill until firm. Yield: 8-10 servings.

Jill Fox, Falmouth H.S.
Falmouth, Maine

CRANBERRY-CREAM SALAD

1 ½ tbsp. unflavored gelatin
¼ c. cold water
1 1-lb. can whole cranberry sauce
1 tbsp. lemon juice
¼ tsp. salt
2 3-oz. pkg. cream cheese
¾ c. crushed pineapple
½ c. heavy cream, whipped

Place gelatin in custard cup; add cold water. Let set 2 minutes; place cup in pan of boiling water. Heat until gelatin is dissolved. Add to cranberry sauce; stir in lemon juice and salt. Chill until mixture begins to thicken. Stir cream cheese with fork; add pineapple. Stir until well blended; add to cranberry mixture. Fold in whipped cream; pour into 2-quart mold. Chill until firm. Yield: 12 servings.

Freda F. Bennett, Orchard H.S.
Orchard, Nebraska

CRANBERRY DELIGHT

1 pkg. cranberries
1 ½ c. sugar
1 pkg. strawberry Jell-O
1 ½ c. hot water
1 sm. can crushed pineapple
1 c. diced marshmallows
1 c. nuts
½ c. flaked coconut

Grind cranberries; add sugar. Let set overnight. Dissolve Jell-O in hot water; add cranberries, pineapple, marshmallows and nuts. Mix well; pour into molds. Sprinkle with coconut; chill until set. Yield: 8 servings.

Mrs. Margaret Kemp, Mountain View H.S.
Mountain View, Arkansas

CRANBERRY FLUFF

2 c. raw cranberries, ground
3 c. tiny marshmallows
¾ c. sugar
2 c. diced tart apples
½ c. seedless green grapes
½ c. broken walnuts
¼ tsp. salt
1 c. heavy cream, whipped

Combine cranberries, marshmallows and sugar. Cover and chill overnight. Add apples, grapes, walnuts and salt. Fold in cream. Chill. Turn into serving bowl or spoon into individual lettuce cups. Trim with cluster of green grapes, if desired. May be served as luncheon salad or dessert. Yield: 8-10 servings.

Mrs. Hazel Huckaby, Fowler H.S.
Fowler, Colorado

CRANBERRY JEWEL SALAD

1 pkg. raspberry gelatin
1 c. hot water
½ c. cold water
2 c. fresh cranberries
1 orange, quartered and seeds removed
1 c. sugar

189

(Continued on next page)

Dissolve gelatin in hot water; stir to dissolve. Add cold water; cool. Put cranberries and orange through food chopper. Add sugar; mix well. Fold cranberry mixture into congealed mixture. Pour into large mold; chill until firm. Yield: 4-6 servings.

Gail Speron, Dye Jr. H.S.
Flint, Michigan

CRANBERRY MOLD

1 pkg. cherry gelatin
1 ½ c. water
½ lb. cranberries
2 apples
1 orange
¼ c. sugar
4 oz. canned crushed pineapple

Dissolve gelatin in hot water. Grind cranberries, apples and orange. Cover with sugar; let stand 1 hour. Fold fruit into gelatin. Place in mold; chill until firm. Yield: 6 servings.

Ruby V. Beto, Flandreau Indian H.S.
Flandreau, South Dakota

CRANBERRY MOLD

1 3-oz. pkg. orange gelatin
1 1-lb. can whole cranberry sauce
1 7-oz. bottle ginger ale

Combine gelatin and cranberry sauce; heat till almost boiling. Stir until gelatin is dissolved; chill slightly. Stir in ginger ale carefully; pour into mold. Chill till set; unmold. Garnish with salad greens and orange and grapefruit sections. Serve with dressing of equal parts mayonnaise and sour cream. Yield: 6 servings.

Mrs. Virginia Smith, North H.S.
Evansville, Indiana

CRANBERRY MOLD WITH CREAMY ORANGE DRESSING

1 3-oz. pkg. black cherry Jell-O
1 c. hot water
½ c. orange juice
2 tbsp. lemon juice
½ c. drained mandarin oranges
1 ½ c. whole cranberry sauce
1 c. chopped nuts
Creamy Orange Dressing

Dissolve Jell-O in hot water; add orange juice and lemon juice. Chill until slightly thickened; fold in oranges, cranberry sauce and nuts. Pour into 1-quart mold; chill until firm. Unmold; serve on salad greens with Creamy Orange Dressing. Yield: 6 servings.

CREAMY ORANGE DRESSING:

1 3-oz. pkg. cream cheese
2 tbsp. orange juice
1 tbsp. lemon juice
2 tsp. sugar
½ tsp. grated orange rind

Soften cream cheese; blend in orange juice and lemon juice. Add sugar and orange rind; beat until smooth. Yield: 6 servings.

Mrs. Cynthia Agresta, Roseville H.S.
Roseville, Michigan

CRANBERRY MOLDED SALAD

1 1-lb. can whole cranberry sauce
1 c. boiling water
1 3-oz. pkg. strawberry gelatin
1 tbsp. lemon juice
¼ tsp. salt
½ c. mayonnaise
1 apple, diced
¼ c. chopped walnuts

Heat cranberry sauce; strain and reserve liquid. Combine liquid and boiling water; add gelatin, stirring until completely dissolved. Add lemon juice and salt; chill until slightly thickened. Add mayonnaise; beat with rotary beater until fluffy. Fold in cranberries, apples and nuts; stir well. Chill until slightly thickened; pour into mold. Yield: 6 servings.

Mrs. Anita Spalding, Adelphian Acad.
Holly, Michigan

CRANBERRY-NUT MOLD

1 c. hot water
1 pkg. strawberry gelatin
½ c. cold water
1 1-lb. can jellied cranberry sauce
1 sm. banana, diced
¼ c. chopped walnuts
1 3-oz. pkg. cream cheese
¼ c. milk or cream
Dash of salt
¾ c. shredded coconut

Pour hot water over gelatin; stir until dissolved. Add cold water; refrigerate, stirring occasionally, till consistency of unbeaten egg white. Fold sauce, banana and walnuts into gelatin. Pour into 1-quart mold; chill until firm. Soften cream cheese; add milk and salt. Whip smooth with fork; add coconut. Serve over gelatin. Yield: 6 servings.

Mrs. Iris Hendershot
Southern Fulton Jr.-Sr. H.S.
Warfordsburg, Pennsylvania

CRANBERRY-ORANGE MOLD

1 ¼ c. boiling water
1 3-oz. pkg. raspberry gelatin
1 orange, seeded and diced
Rind of 1 orange, colored portion only
1 1-lb. can whole cranberry sauce

Place boiling water and gelatin in blender container; cover and run on low speed until gelatin is dissolved. Add remaining ingredients; cover and run on high speed until orange rind is ground fine. Pour into 1 1/2-quart mold; chill until set. May be made without blender by grating orange rind and grinding cranberry and orange together. Yield: 6 servings.

Mrs. Nancy Hower, Hulett H.S.
Hulett, Wyoming

CRANBERRY-ORANGE SALAD

1 ½ c. cranberry juice cocktail
1 3-oz. pkg. cherry gelatin
¼ tsp. salt
1 10-oz. pkg. frozen cranberry-orange relish
1 tbsp. grated orange rind

Bring cranberry juice cocktail to boil; add gelatin, stirring until dissolved. Add salt, frozen cranberry-orange relish and orange rind; stir until relish is blended. Pour into oiled 3-cup ring mold or individual molds. Yield: 4-6 servings.

Joanne Weber, East H.S.
Green Bay, Wisconsin

CRANBERRY-PEACH SALAD

1 family-sized pkg. peach gelatin
1 ½ c. canned peach slices, drained
1 c. fresh cranberries
½ orange
½ c. sugar

Dissolve gelatin in 2 cups boiling water; add 1 3/4 cups cold water. Chill 2 cups gelatin until slightly thickened; keep remaining gelatin at room temperature. Fold peach slices into chilled gelatin; Turn into 1 1/2-quart mold. Chill until set. Grind cranberries and orange; stir in sugar. Let stand for 15 minutes; stir in reserved gelatin. Pour into mold over peach layer; chill until set. Yield: 10-12 servings.

Mrs. Erma E. Goehring, Harbor Creek H.S.
Harbor Creek, Pennsylvania

CRANBERRY-PINEAPPLE DELIGHT

2 boxes cherry Jell-O
1 ½ c. boiling water
1 c. crushed pineapple
1 c. whole cranberry sauce
1 c. chopped walnuts or pecans (opt.)

Dissolve Jell-O in water; add pineapple, cranberries and nuts. Pour in 9 x 13-inch container; chill until firm. Serve with turkey or chicken. Yield: 10 servings.

Mrs. W. B. Wilkerson, Jr., Aldine Sr. H.S.
Houston, Texas

CRANBERRY-PINEAPPLE TREAT

1 6-oz. pkg. cherry gelatin
2 c. boiling water
1 1-lb. can whole cranberry sauce
1 ½ c. cold water
½ c. chopped walnuts
2 c. drained canned crushed pineapple

Dissolve gelatin in boiling water; blend in cranberry sauce. Add cold water; chill until slightly thickened. Fold in nuts and pineapple; chill until firm. Serve as salad with mayonnaise or as dessert with whipped topping. Yield: 14-15 servings.

Mrs. Iva W. Ammon, Beth-Center Jr. H.S.
Brownsville, Pennsylvania

CRANBERRY-RASPBERRY SALAD

1 3-oz. pkg. lemon gelatin
1 3-oz. pkg. raspberry gelatin
1 ½ c. boiling water
1 10-oz. pkg. frozen raspberries
¼ c. cranberry-orange relish
1 7-oz. bottle lemon-lime carbonated beverage

Dissolve gelatin in boiling water; add frozen raspberries. Break with fork; stir in relish. Add lemon-lime beverage slowly. Pour in 9-inch square pan. Chill until firm. Yield: 9-12 servings.

Mrs. Mildred Snell, Spon.
Austintown-Fitch H.S.
Youngstown, Ohio

CRANBERRY-RASPBERRY SALAD

    2 pkg. raspberry gelatin
    1½ c. boiling water
    ½ c. ginger ale
    Grated rind and juice of 1 lemon
    1 pkg. frozen raspberries
    1 pkg. frozen cranberry-orange relish

Dissolve gelatin in boiling water; add remaining ingredients. Stir to break up frozen fruit. Sets very quickly. Yield: 12 servings.

Myrtle Sellie, Ellis Jr. H.S.
Austin, Minnesota

CRANBERRY RELISH MOLD

    ½ c. cold water
    2 envelopes unflavored gelatin
    ½ c. boiling water
    1¼ c. sugar
    1 orange, sliced and seeded
    3 c. cranberries

Place water in blender; sprinkle with gelatin. Add boiling water; cover and process at low speed until gelatin dissolves. Turn control to high speed; add sugar and orange. Blend until orange is finely chopped; add cranberries. Process until cranberries are finely chopped; turn into 5-cup mold or individual molds. Chill until firm; unmold on orange or pineapple slice. Yield: 8 servings.

Ann M. Greenheck, Riverdale H.S.
Museoda, Wisconsin

CRANBERRY RELISH MOLD

    4 c. cranberries
    2 oranges
    2 tart apples
    1 tsp. salt
    2 c. sugar
    1 family-sized box orange Jell-O
    2 c. boiling water
    1 c. cold water

Grind cranberries, oranges and apples together. Stir in salt and sugar. Dissolve Jell-O in boiling water; add cold water and cranberry mixture. Chill until firm. Serve on lettuce or with favorite topping. Will keep in refrigerator for 2 to 3 weeks. Yield: 8-10 servings.

Mrs. Jean B. Wilson, Charlotte H.S.
Charlotte, Texas

CRANBERRY SALAD

    1 pkg. lemon Jell-O
    ½ c. hot water
    1 c. orange juice
    2 c. fresh ground cranberries
    1 c. ground unpeeled orange
    1 c. sugar
    1 c. chopped nuts

Dissolve Jell-O in hot water; add orange juice. Chill until partially set. Combine cranberries, orange, sugar and nuts; add to Jell-O. Chill until firm. Yield: 8 servings.

Ramona Lawton, Mercer Jr. H.S.
Garden City, Georgia

CRANBERRY SALAD

    1 sm. can crushed pineapple
    1 orange, diced
    1 can cranberry sauce
    1 box strawberry Jell-O
    ½ c. nuts

Drain liquid from pineapple, orange and cranberry sauce; reserve. Dissolve Jell-O in 3/4 cup boiling water; add 3/4 cup reserved juice. Chill until partially set; add pineapple, orange, nuts and cranberry sauce. Mix lightly; chill until firm. Serve. Yield: 6-8 servings.

Mrs. Sam Whitley, Laneville H.S.
Laneville, Texas

CRANBERRY SALAD

    2 pkg. gelatin
    2 c. sugar
    1 lb. raw cranberries
    ½ c. orange juice
    ¼ c. lemon juice
    1 sm. can crushed pineapple
    2 c. chopped pecans
    2 c. miniature marshmallows

Dissolve gelatin in 2 cups cold water. Add 1/2 cup boiling water. Stir until dissolved; add sugar. Run cranberries through food chopper, catching all the juice; add water to juice to equal 1/2 cup. Combine all ingredients; pour into mold. Chill overnight. Serve on lettuce leaf with sour cream dressing. Salad will stay fresh for a week. Freezes well. Yield: 12 servings.

Mrs. Vivian Bain, Brackenridge H.S.
San Antonio, Texas

CRANBERRY SALAD

    1 10-oz. pkg. frozen cranberry and orange
    1 3-oz. pkg. red raspberry gelatin
    1 c. boiling water
    1 9-oz. can crushed pineapple
    ¾ c. chopped pecans

(Continued on next page)

Partially thaw frozen cranberry and orange. Dissolve gelatin in hot water; add fruit and nuts. Place in individual molds or ring mold; chill until firm. Serve with turkey.

Mrs. Orrissa P. Simpson, Reg. Supvr.
Home Ec. Education
State Dept. of Education
Knoxville, Tennessee

CRANBERRY SALAD

2 c. raw cranberries
1 c. sugar
Juice of 1 orange
Juice of 1 lemon
½ c. cold water
1 3-oz. pkg. strawberry Jell-O
Pinch of salt
1 c. pineapple, drained and crushed
1 c. diced celery
1 c. chopped nuts

Boil cranberries, sugar, orange juice and lemon juice over low heat for 10 minutes or until berries pop. Pour cold water over Jell-O; add hot mixture and salt. Cool until syrupy; add pineapple, celery and nuts. Pour into buttered mold; chill until firm. Unmold; serve with turkey and dressing or roast pork. Yield: 8-10 servings.

Mrs. Pauline K. Henslee, Irving H.S.
Irving, Texas

CRANBERRY SALAD MOLD

2 c. sugar
1 c. water
2½ tbsp. gelatin soaked in ½ c. cold water
4 c. raw cranberries, ground
1 med. orange with rind, ground
1 c. chopped celery
1 c. chopped nuts

Cook sugar and water to make thin syrup. Add soaked gelatin; stir until dissolved. Cool. Add remaining ingredients; pour into mold. Chill. Yield: 16 servings.

Mrs. Norine E. Sipe, Goffstown H.S.
Goffstown, New Hampshire

CRANBERRY SOUFFLE SALAD

1 envelope unflavored gelatin
2 tbsp. sugar
¼ tsp. salt
1 c. water
½ c. mayonnaise
2 tbsp. lemon juice
1 tsp. grated lemon rind
1 1-lb. can whole cranberry sauce
1 apple, peeled and diced
1 c. crushed pineapple, drained
½ c. chopped walnuts

Combine gelatin, sugar and salt; add water. Place over low heat, stirring constantly until gelatin is dissolved. Remove from heat; stir in mayonnaise, lemon juice and lemon rind. Blend with rotary beater; chill until slightly thickened. Beat until fluffy; fold in cranberry sauce, apple, pineapple and walnuts. Turn into 4-cup mold or individual molds; chill until firm. Unmold on serving plate. Garnish with salad greens. Yield: 6 servings.

Mrs. Eris Terry, San Perlita H.S.
San Perlita, Texas

CRANBERRY SOUFFLE SALAD

1 envelope unflavored gelatin
2 tbsp. sugar
¼ tsp. salt
1 c. water
½ c. mayonnaise
2 tbsp. lemon juice
1 tsp. grated lemon rind
1 1-lb. can whole cranberry sauce
1 8½-oz. can pineapple tidbits
¼ c. chopped walnuts

Mix gelatin, sugar and salt thoroughly in saucepan; add water. Place over low heat, stirring constantly, until gelatin is dissolved. Remove from heat; stir in mayonnaise, lemon juice and lemon rind. Blend with rotary beater. Pour in refrigerator tray. Quick chill in freezing unit for 10 to 15 minutes or until firm, about 1 inch from edge, but soft in center. Beat until fluffy; fold in remaining ingredients. Turn into 4-cup mold or individual molds. Chill until firm. Unmold on serving plate; garnish with salad greens. Yield: 6 servings.

Kathleen Garrett, Albertville H.S.
Albertville, Alabama

FROSTED CRANBERRY SQUARES

1⅔ c. crushed pineapple
1 6-oz. pkg. lemon gelatin
1 c. ginger ale
2 c. jellied cranberry sauce, drained
1 2-oz. pkg. dessert topping mix
1 8-oz. pkg. cream cheese

Drain pineapple; add water to syrup to equal 1 cup liquid. Heat liquid to a boil; add gelatin and dissolve. Cool; Stir in ginger ale gently. Chill till partly set. Combine cranberry sauce and pineapple; fold into gelatin. Pour into 9 x 9 x 2-inch dish; chill till firm. Prepare topping according to package directions; fold in cream cheese. Spread over gelatin. If desired, toast pecans in butter in 350-degree oven about 10 minutes. Sprinkle over salad. Chill until firm. Yield: 9 servings.

Mrs. Allan P. Cobb
Mosinee H.S.
Mosinee, Wisconsin

JANE'S CRANBERRY SALAD

1 pkg. cherry Jell-O
1 c. hot water
1 c. sugar
Juice of 1 lemon
1 c. pineapple syrup
1 lb. ground cranberries
1 ground orange
½ c. ground nutmeats

Dissolve Jell-O in hot water; add sugar, lemon juice and pineapple juice. Chill until set; add remaining ingredients.

Jane Kolb Woods, Wood Memorial H.S.
Oakland City, Indiana

JELLIED CRANBERRY MOLD

1 pkg. orange gelatin
1 pkg. lemon gelatin
1½ c. boiling water
10 ice cubes
2 c. fresh cranberry sauce
¾ c. crushed pineapple, drained
½ c. chopped nuts

Dissolve gelatin in boiling water; add ice and stir until almost jelled. Break cranberry sauce with fork; add pineapple and nuts. Fold into gelatin; pour in 1 1/2-quart mold. Chill until firm. Yield: 12 servings.

Ellen Webb Massengill, Seminole H.S.
Seminole, Texas

MOLDED CRANBERRY SALAD

1 pkg. raspberry Jell-O
1 c. boiling water
1 can whole cranberry sauce
1 sm. can crushed pineapple
1 orange, ground in food chopper
½ c. walnuts

Dissolve Jell-O in boiling water; chill until partially set. Stir in remaining ingredients; pour into mold. Chill until firm. Serve on lettuce. An attractive salad when made in ring mold and center filled with cottage cheese. Yield: 10 servings.

Mrs. Marie Breyette, Plattsburgh Sr. H.S.
Plattsburgh, New York

MOLDED CRANBERRY AND ORANGE SALAD

4 c. fresh cranberries
2 med. apples, peeled
1 tbsp. grated orange rind
1½ c. diced fresh oranges
2 c. sugar
1 c. chopped pecans
2 envelopes unflavored gelatin
¾ c. cold water

Grind cranberries and apples in food chopper using medium blade; stir in orange rind, oranges, sugar and pecans. Soften gelatin in cold water; place over hot water to melt. Stir into cranberry mixture; pour into 2-quart mold. Chill until firm. Turn onto serving plate; garnish with salad greens. Yield: 6-8 servings.

Mrs. Hal J. Puett, North Cobb H.S.
Acworth, Georgia

MOLDED JELL-O SALAD

2 boxes lime Jell-O
1 No. 2 can crushed pineapple
3 tsp. plain gelatin
1 c. milk
1 c. nuts
2 8-oz. pkg. cream cheese
2 boxes strawberry Jell-O
1 can whole cranberry sauce

Dissolve lime Jell-O in 2 cups boiling water. Add crushed pineapple; mix. Pour into salad mold. Refrigerate until firm. Soak plain gelatin in 1/4 cup cold water; dissolve in hot milk. Add gelatin mixture and nuts to cream cheese; mix until smooth. Spread over lime Jell-O mixture; chill until firm. Dissolve strawberry Jell-O in 2 cups hot water. Add cranberry sauce; mix well. Add mold to form third layer. Refrigerate overnight or until firm. To unmold, set mold in warm water for a little while; turn upside down on large plate or stand. Slice and serve on lettuce. Yield: 20-25 servings.

Mrs. Mallie Venn Steger
Montgomery H.S.
Montgomery, Texas

RASPBERRY-CRANBERRY SALAD

1 3-oz. pkg. raspberry gelatin
1 3-oz. pkg. lemon gelatin
1½ c. boiling water
1 10-oz. pkg. frozen raspberries
1 c. cranberry-orange relish
1 7-oz. bottle Seven-Up

Dissolve gelatin in boiling water; add raspberries and relish. Chill; add Seven-Up gently. Stir carefully; pour into 9 x 9-inch pan. Chill until firm. Serve on lettuce. Yield: 9 servings.

Genevieve Overvaag, Pub. H.S.
Mountain Lake, Minnesota
Mrs. Ray White, Hillsboro H.S.
Nashville, Tennessee

PINEAPPLE-CRANBERRY MOLD

1 No. 2 can crushed pineapple
2 pkg. lemon gelatin
½ c. lemon juice
⅓ c. chopped walnuts
3 tbsp. shredded or chopped orange peel
3 c. whole cranberry sauce

Drain pineapple; add water to juice to equal 1 1/2 cups liquid. Heat liquid to boiling; pour over gelatin. Chill until syrupy; stir in remaining ingredients. Chill until firm. Yield: 8 servings.

Florence T. Shaffer, Berwick Area Sr. H.S.
Berwick, Pennsylvania

PRIZE CHRISTMAS SALAD

1 pkg. raspberry gelatin
1 c. hot water
½ c. cold water
1 orange, cut in chunks
½ c. pineapple chunks
1 can jellied or whole cranberry sauce
¼ c. chopped walnuts

Dissolve gelatin in hot water; add cold water. Chill until partly thickened; fold in orange, pineapple, cranberry sauce and nuts. Chill until firm. Yield: 8-10 servings.

Mrs. Charlene Slack, Santiam H.S.
Mill City, Oregon

RAW CRANBERRY SALAD

2 c. raw cranberries
2 c. sugar
1 unpeeled apple
1 unpeeled orange
2 pkg. lemon gelatin
1 c. boiling water
1 c. chopped nutmeats

Grind cranberries coarsely; cover with sugar. Grind apple and orange; dissolve gelatin in water. Combine all ingredients together; place in mold. Chill until firm. Yield: 6-8 servings.

Mrs. Jane Choate, Welch H.S.
Welch, Oklahoma

SPICY PEACH-CRANBERRY RING

1 No. 2 ½ can peach halves
1 tsp. whole cloves
1 3-in. stick cinnamon
¼ c. vinegar
1 pkg. lemon gelatin
1 c. fresh cranberries
½ unpeeled orange
⅓ c. sugar

1 pkg. cherry gelatin
1 ¾ c. hot water
Lemon Cream Mayonnaise

Drain peaches; add water to syrup to equal 1 3/4 cups. Add cloves, cinnamon and vinegar; simmer, uncovered, 10 minutes. Add peaches; heat slowly 5 minutes. Remove peaches; place cut sides up in 3-quart ring mold. Strain peach syrup; measure and add hot water to equal 1 2/3 cups. Add lemon gelatin, stirring until dissolved; pour over peaches. Refrigerate until almost firm. Grind cranberries and orange; stir in sugar. Dissolve cherry gelatin in hot water; cool. Fold in cranberries and orange; pour over peach layer. Chill until firm; unmold. Fill center with greens; serve with Lemon Cream Mayonnaise. Yield: 10-12 servings.

LEMON CREAM MAYONNAISE:

3 tbsp. lemon juice
3 tbsp. confectioners' sugar
3 tbsp. heavy cream
Dash of salt

Combine all ingredients; blend until smooth.

Ramona deSilva, Fresno H.S.
Fresno, California

SUNSHINE SALAD

1 c. pineapple juice
1 pkg. lemon Jell-O
1 c. crushed pineapple, drained
1 c. sour cream
Few grains of salt
1 tbsp. gelatin
¼ c. cold water
1 15-oz. can cranberry sauce

Heat pineapple juice; pour over Jell-O and stir to dissolve. Rinse ring mold in cold water; spoon pineapple in mold. Pour 1/4 cup Jell-O over pineapple; chill. Beat sour cream with remaining Jell-O; add salt. Pour over pineapple mixture; chill until slightly thickened. Soak gelatin in cold water; heat cranberry sauce. Stir gelatin into cranberry sauce; pour over sour cream mixture. Chill until firm. Turn out carefully on lettuce. Yield: 6-8 servings.

H. H. Johnston, Cornwallis Jr. H.S.
Halifax, Nova Scotia, Canada

DEWEY LEMON SALAD

1 lge. pkg. lemon Jell-O
2 c. boiling water
2 c. Mountain Dew and pineapple juice
1 No. 211 can pineapple tidbits
2 bananas, sliced
2 c. miniature marshmallows
1 can lemon pie filling
1 pkg. Dream Whip, prepared or 1 c. whipped cream

195

(Continued on next page)

Molded Mixed Fruit Salads

Dissolve Jell-O in hot water; add Mountain Dew and pineapple juice. Allow to cool until partially set. Fold in fruit and marshmallows. Fold lemon pie filling into Dream Whip; spread over congealed Jell-O mixture. Chill. Serve on lettuce; top with mayonnaise. Yield: 15 servings.

Genevieve Overvaag, Public H.S.
Mountain Lake, Minnesota

DIVINITY FRUIT SALAD

1 tbsp. gelatin
2 tbsp. lemon juice
4 oz. cream cheese
4 tbsp. sugar
1 c. crushed pineapple, drained
2 c. chopped dates
1 c. heavy cream, whipped
½ c. chopped nuts

Soften gelatin in lemon juice in Pyrex cup. Set cup in pan of boiling water until gelatin dissolves. Combine cream cheese and sugar. Stir in dissolved gelatin; fold in pineapple and dates. Gently fold in whipped cream and nuts. Chill several hours until set. Yield: 8 servings.

Mrs. Beverly McGlamery, Carey H.S.
Carey, Ohio

COOL WHIP SALAD

1 3-oz. pkg. cherry Jell-O
1 3-oz. pkg. cream cheese
1 sm. can pineapple tidbits, drained
1 c. drained fruit cocktail
1 pkg. Cool Whip

Mix Jell-O with 1 1/2 cups boiling water; add softened cream cheese. Mix well. Add pineapple and fruit cocktail. Let chill for about 2 hours or until firm. Spread Cool Whip on top of chilled mixture. Serve on lettuce leaf. Yield: 8 servings.

Mrs. Bonnie Caldwell, Mt. Vernon H.S.
Mt. Vernon, Arkansas

FRUIT COCKTAIL-LEMON JELL-O SALAD

½ c. sugar
1 sm. can crushed pineapple
2 pkg. lemon Jell-O
½ to 1 c. grated cheese
1 No. 2½ can fruit cocktail
½ to 1 c. chopped nuts (opt.)
1 lge. can evaporated milk, chilled

Bring sugar and pineapple to boil. Add Jell-O and 2 cups water. Cool. Add cheese, fruit cocktail and nuts. Whip evaporated milk until stiff; fold into Jell-O mixture. Chill until firm in large ring mold that has been rinsed in cold

water or slightly moistened with salad oil. Serve on salad greens. Yield: 6-8 servings.

Mrs. Wendell Utley, Magnolia Sr. H.S.
Magnolia, Arkansas

FRUIT SALAD SQUARES

½ c. pineapple juice
½ c. white cherry juice
½ c. sugar
3 tbsp. cornstarch
1 3-oz. pkg. lemon gelatin
¼ tsp. salt
½ c. orange juice
2 tbsp. lemon juice
1 slightly beaten egg
1 No. 2 can pineapple pieces
1 1-lb. can pitted halved white cherries or fruit cocktail
1 peeled diced orange
2 c. miniature marshmallows
1 c. heavy cream, whipped
½ c. chopped nuts
12 red maraschino cherries

Combine pineapple juice, cherry juice, sugar, cornstarch, gelatin, salt, orange juice and lemon juice in saucepan. Cook, stirring, until mixture thickens and boils. Cook 2 minutes; add small amount hot mixture to egg; return to remaining hot mixture and cook 1 minute longer. Cool to room temperature. Fold in pineapple pieces, white cherries, orange marshmallows and whipped cream. Pour into 11x7x2-inch dish. Chill until set; cut into squares. Sprinkle with nuts and trim with maraschino cherries. Yield: 12 servings.

Mrs. Loretta Schrowang, Hennepin Jr. H.S.
Hennepin, Illinois

JELL-O DELIGHT

2 pkg. strawberry Jell-O
2 bananas, cut up
½ c. nuts, finely chopped
1 c. miniature marshmallows
1 can fruit cocktail, drained
1 envelope Dream Whip, prepared

Dissolve Jell-O in 2 cups hot water; add 1 cup cold water. Let set. Cut Jell-O into cubes; Mix all ingredients together lightly.

Eleanor Wheeler, Coalinga H.S.
Coalinga, California

MIXED FRUIT CONGEALED SALAD

1 box cherry Jell-O
1 c. hot water

196

(Continued on next page)

1 c. cold fruit juice
1 can fruit cocktail
1 can crushed pineapple
3 bananas
12 marshmallows
½ c. nuts
Maraschino cherries

Dissolve Jell-O in hot water. Add fruit juice; stir in fruit cocktail and crushed pineapple. Dice or slice bananas and add to mixture. Cut marshmallows into pieces with scissors. Add with nuts to fruit mixture. Place in large flat Pyrex dish. Garnish with cherries. This is especially pretty for the Valentine season. Yield: 12 servings.

Mabel Brill, Moorefield H.S.
Moorefield, West Virginia

LEMONAIRE

1 3-oz. pkg. lemon Jell-O
1 c. boiling water
1 c. cold water or fruit juice
2 oranges
Hawaiian fruit cocktail
1 pkg. Dream Whip

Dissolve Jell-O in hot water; add cold water. Let thicken until firm. Cube Jell-O. Dice oranges; add fruit cocktail. Whip Dream Whip; fold into mixture. Yield: 6-8 servings.

Mrs. Elizabeth Doss, Silverton Union H.S.
Silverton, Oregon

PINK DELIGHT SALAD

1 3-oz. pkg. strawberry flavored
   gelatin
1 No. 3 can fruit cocktail
1 11-oz. can mandarin oranges
1 No. 303 can sliced peaches
1 sm. can pineapple tidbits
1 envelope Dream Whip, whipped

Prepare gelatin as directed on package. Allow to set until firm. Beat until frothy. Add well-drained fruit. Prepare Dream Whip as directed on package. Fold into fruit-gelatin mixture. Serve at once, or refrigerate. Yield: 12 servings.

Mrs. Betty Dean, Joaquin H.S.
Joaquin, Texas

PINK LADY CONGEALED FRUIT SALAD

1 pkg. red Jell-O
1 c. hot water or fruit juice
Pineapple, oranges or peaches, drained
   and diced
1 can fruit cocktail, drained
1 c. miniature marshmallows
½ c. chopped nuts

1 pkg. Dream Whip
½ c. chilled milk
¼ c. mayonnaise or cream cheese

Dissolve Jell-O in 1 cup hot liquid. Cool. Add pineapple to fruit cocktail. Add marshmallows and nuts. Combine Dream Whip with milk; add mayonnaise. Chill in oiled molds until firm. Unmold on lettuce. Add salad dressing and garnish. Yield: 10-12 servings.

Mary G. McConnaughhay, Ocala H.S.
Ocala, Florida

FRUIT GELATIN MOLD

1 c. pineapple chunks
1 3-oz. pkg. lemon or strawberry gelatin
1 c. boiling water
2 oranges, diced
1 banana, sliced
1 apple, sliced
½ c. broken nuts

Drain pineapple; reserve liquid. Add enough cold water to liquid to dissolve gelatin in boiling water. Add liquid. Chill until partially set. Add fruits and nuts; chill until firm. Unmold on lettuce. Yield: 6 servings.

Mrs. Dorothy Sue T. Hill, Oberlin H.S.
Oberlin, Louisiana

FRUITED GINGER ALE SALAD

2 3-oz. pkg. orange Jell-O
1 3-oz. pkg. lemon Jell-O
2 c. boiling water
2 c. ginger ale
1 c. pineapple tidbits, drained
1 c. mandarin oranges, drained
1 c. whole strawberries, halved
1 c. blueberries, well-drained
2 c. diced bananas

Dissolve orange and lemon Jell-O in boiling water; add ginger ale. Cool. Add fruit to Jell-O in 9 x 13-inch pan, reserving pineapple and orange juice. Refrigerate until set.

TOPPING:

1 3-oz. pkg. lemon Jell-O
1 ½ c. pineapple and orange juice
¾ c. sugar
1 tsp. vanilla
1 c. sour cream, whipped

Dissolve Jell-O in hot fruit juices. Add sugar, vanilla and sour cream. Mixture is thin. Pour over Jell-O and refrigerate until set. Yield: 15 servings.

Mrs. John Wyant, Newman Grove H.S.
Newman Grove, Nebraska

FRUIT JELL-O SALAD

2 pkg. lemon Jell-O
3 lge. apples, cut fine
3 bananas, cut fine
1 can crushed pineapple
½ c. pineapple juice
¼ c. sugar
1 egg
1 tsp. flour
1 pkg. Dream Whip, prepared

Prepare Jell-O as directed on package; add fruit when Jell-O is partially set. Pour into 9 x 13-inch glass dish. Combine juice, sugar, egg and flour; cook until thick. Cool. Add Dream Whip; spread on top of congealed salad. Yield: 20 servings.

Sister M. Alcantara, O. S. F.
St. Francis de Sales H.S.
Chicago, Illinois

FRUIT SALAD

½ c. hot pineapple juice
1 pkg. lemon gelatin
1 c. cola or ginger ale
1 8-oz. can pineapple chunks
1 8-oz. can spiced grapes
½ c. slivered almonds

Heat pineapple juice and dissolve gelatin. Place in refrigerator until almost firm. Add remaining ingredients; refrigerate until firm. Yield: 4-6 servings.

Lillian Barber, Haines City H.S.
Haines City, Florida

FRUIT SALAD

1 box lemon Jell-O
1 c. boiling water
1 c. pineapple juice
1 banana, diced
2 oranges, diced
½ c. diced pineapple
½ c. nuts, chopped

Dissolve Jell-O in boiling water; add pineapple juice. Set aside to partially set. Add fruit and nuts to Jell-O. Let set. Yield: 6-8 servings.

Mrs. Vanora Fry, Little River H.S.
Little River, Kansas

FRUIT SALAD AMBROSIA

½ c. pineapple tidbits
1 lb. rhubarb
Dash of salt
⅓ c. sugar
1 pkg. lemon gelatin
1 tbsp. lemon juice

Few drops food coloring (opt.)
½ c. Tokay grapes, cut in halves and seeded
Salad greens
Mayonnaise

Drain pineapple; reserve syrup. Clean rhubarb and cut into 1-inch chunks. Combine rhubarb, 2/3 cup reserved pineapple syrup, salt and sugar in saucepan. Cover; cook gently until rhubarb is tender. Add gelatin; stir until dissolved. Stir in lemon juice and food coloring. Partially chill; fold in fruits. Mold. Unmold on salad greens; top with mayonnaise. Yield: 8-10 servings.

Eulyn Dynes, Phillips H.S.
Borger, Texas

FRUIT SALAD MOLD

2 envelopes unflavored gelatin
1 c. cold water
1 6-oz. can frozen orange juice concentrate, kept frozen
1 1-lb. can apricot halves
1 1-lb. can fruit cocktail
1 c. salad dressing
Sliced chicken or turkey and ham

Sprinkle gelatin over water in saucepan. Place over low heat; stir constantly until gelatin dissolves, for 3 to 5 minutes. Remove from heat. Add frozen concentrate; stir until melted. Gradually blend syrup from fruit into salad dressing in mixing bowl; blend into gelatin mixture. Chill until mixture mounds slightly when dropped from spoon. Cut apricot halves in 4 pieces. Add to fruit cocktail and fold into gelatin mixture. Turn into 6-cup mold. Chill until firm. Unmold onto large platter; arrange slices of chicken or turkey and ham on platter. Serve with salad greens. Yield: 8 servings.

Photograph for this recipe on page 175.

FROSTED FRUIT MOLD

1 3-oz. pkg. lime-flavored gelatin
1 c. boiling water
1 7-oz. bottle lemon-lime carbonated beverage
1 8 ¾-oz. can crushed pineapple
1 banana, sliced
¼ c. sugar
1 tbsp. all-purpose flour
1 slightly beaten egg
½ c. whipping cream
¼ c. shredded sharp process American cheese
2 tbsp. grated Parmesan cheese

Dissolve gelatin in boiling water; cool. Add carbonated beverage. Chill until partially set. Drain pineapple, reserving syrup. Fold pineapple and banana into gelatin mixture. Turn into 8 x 8 x 2-inch baking pan. Chill until firm. Combine sugar

(Continued on next page)

and flour in saucepan. Stir in reserved pineapple syrup and egg. Cook and stir over low heat until thickened; chill. Whip cream; fold into egg mixture. Spread over gelatin and sprinkle with cheese. Yield: 6-8 servings.

Pauline Reeves, Emma Sansom Sch.
Gadsden, Alabama
Frances Glinsmann, North-Loup Scotia Sch.
Scotia, Nebraska

FROSTED FRUIT SALAD

    1 3-oz. box lemon Jell-O
    1 3-oz. box orange Jell-O
    2 c. hot water
    1 ½ c. cold water
    Juice of 1 lemon
    1 No. 2 can pineapple, drained
    2 or 3 bananas, diced
    1 c. miniature marshmallows
    2 tbsp. flour
    ½ c. sugar
    1 egg, slightly beaten
    1 c. pineapple juice
    2 tbsp. butter
    1 pkg. Dream Whip

Dissolve Jell-O in hot water; add cold water and lemon juice. Chill until slightly thick. Add pineapple, bananas and marshmallow bits. Pour into 9 x 14-inch Pyrex pan and chill. Combine flour, sugar, egg and pineapple juice in saucepan. Cook until thick. Add 2 tablespoons butter. Let stand until cool and then add Dream Whip, prepared as directed on package. Spread on Jell-O topping. Garnish with nuts. Yield: 24 servings.

Dorethy K. Caudle, Scotland Neck H.S.
Scotland Neck, North Carolina

FROSTED JELL-O DESSERT SALAD

    2 pkg. lemon Jell-O
    2 c. boiling water
    2 sm. bottles Seven-Up
    1 No. 2 can crushed pineapple, drained
    2 lge. bananas, cut into sm. pieces
    2 c. sm. marshmallows
    ½ c. sugar
    2 tbsp. flour
    1 c. pineapple juice
    1 beaten egg
    2 tbsp. butter
    1 c. cream, whipped

Dissolve Jell-O in boiling water; cool. Add Seven-Up. Cool until mixture begins to set. Add pineapple, bananas and marshmallows. Blend sugar and flour; moisten with pineapple juice. Add egg. Cook slowly until thick; stir to prevent sticking. Add butter; cool. Add whipped cream, blending thoroughly. Frost salad with sugar mixture and refrigerate. Yield: 12 servings.

Mrs. Mina F. Robinson, Perry H.S.
Perry, Kansas

FROSTED JELL-O SALAD

    2 pkg. lemon Jell-O
    2 c. boiling water
    2 c. ginger ale
    1 c. miniature marshmallows
    2 lge. bananas, cut up
    1 20-oz. can crushed pineapple
    ½ c. sugar
    2 tbsp. flour
    1 egg, slightly beaten
    1 c. pineapple juice
    2 tbsp. butter
    1 pt. cream, whipped

Mix first 6 ingredients; chill until set. Cook sugar, flour, egg and juice until thick. Add butter; cool. Fold into whipped cream. Spread over chilled salad. Yield: 12 servings.

Naoma Brown, East H.S.
Aurora, Illinois

FROSTED LEMON JELL-O

    1 No. 2 can crushed pineapple
    2 pkg. lemon Jell-O
    2 c. boiling water
    2 c. cold water
    3 bananas, cut up
    16 marshmallows, cut up
    1 sm. jar maraschino cherries, cut up

Drain pineapple; reserve juice. Dissolve Jell-O in boiling water; add cold water. Chill. Pour into 9 x 12-inch pan; add remaining ingredients. Chill until set.

FROSTING:

    Reserved pineapple juice
    ½ c. sugar
    1 beaten egg
    2 tbsp. flour
    2 tbsp. butter
    1 c. whipped cream

Combine first 4 ingredients; cook until thick. Remove from heat; add butter. Cool. Add whipped cream; spread over Jell-O mixture. Chill until firm. Cut into squares; serve on lettuce leaf. Yield: 12 servings.

Carol Jackell, Slayton Pub. Sch.
Slayton, Minnesota

FROSTED SALAD

    2 pkg. lime Jell-O
    1 pkg. lemon Jell-O
    3 c. hot water
    3 c. Seven-Up or Bubble-Up
    1 No. 2 can crushed pineapple, drained
    3 lge. bananas, sliced
    1 ½ c. miniature marshmallows

Dissolve Jell-O in hot water; add Seven-Up. Chill until partially set. Add pineapple and bananas;

(Continued on next page)

pour into oiled 9 x 12-inch pan. Top with marsh-mallows.

FROSTING:

½ c. sugar
2 tbsp. flour
1 c. pineapple juice
1 egg, slightly beaten
2 tbsp. butter
1 c. cream, whipped
1 tbsp. lemon juice
Grated cheese

Combine sugar, flour, pineapple juice and egg; cook over low heat until thickened. Add butter; chill. Fold in cream; add lemon juice. Frost firm Jell-O; sprinkle with cheese.

Mrs. Carol Ludtke, Morton Pub. Sch.
Morton, Minnesota

FROSTED SALAD

1 pkg. lemon gelatin
1 c. boiling water
1 c. carbonated beverage
1 No. 2 can crushed pineapple
½ c. miniature marshmallows
1 lge. banana, cut up
½ c. sugar
2 tbsp. flour
1 egg, slightly beaten
2 tbsp. butter
1 c. whipping cream, whipped

Dissolve gelatin in boiling water; stir in beverage. Chill until partially set. Drain pineapple; reserve juice. Fold pineapple, marshmallows and banana in gelatin. Chill until firm. Combine sugar and flour in saucepan. Slowly stir in reserved pineapple juice plus enough water to make 1 cup. Add egg. Cook over low heat until thick. Remove from heat; add butter. Cool. Fold into cream. Frost gelatin mixture. Yield: 8 servings.

Mrs. Kristin Baier, Jefferson Sr. H.S.
Roanoke, Virginia

FRUIT FESTIVAL SALAD

1 pkg. lime gelatin
⅓ c. pineapple juice
1 drained, canned, crushed pineapple
1½ tsp. unflavored gelatin
1 8-oz. pkg. cream cheese
¼ c. milk
2 pkg. strawberry gelatin
1 1-lb. can whole cranberry sauce

Tear off an 18 inch length of heavy duty foil. Cut lengthwise into 9 x 5-inch strips. Cross strips to line 9 x 5 x 3 inch loaf pan. Prepare lime gelatin according to package directions, using pineapple juice in place of cold water called for. Chill until syrupy; fold in pineapple.

Pour into foil-lined pan. Chill until firm. Combine unflavored gelatin and 2 tablespoons water; heat until clear. Blend in cheese and milk. Pour over lime layer; chill until firm. Prepare strawberry gelatin according to package directions but add only 2 cups of hot water. Stir in cranberry sauce. Chill until syrupy; stir and pour over cheese layer. Chill until firm. Lift out of pan, peel off foil. Garnish with lettuce.

Sister Mary Albertus, S.S.N.D.
Tyler Cath. H.S.
Tyler, Texas

GINGER ALE SALAD

2 tbsp. gelatin
4 tbsp. cold water
½ c. boiling fruit juice
½ c. sugar
⅛ tsp. salt
1 pt. ginger ale
Juice of 1 lemon
½ lb. peeled seeded grapes
1 peeled sliced orange
1 grapefruit in peeled sections
6 slices canned pineapple, cut in pieces
⅛ to ¼ lb. Canton ginger
Lettuce
½ to 1 c. heavy cream, whipped
1 c. Mayonnaise

Soak gelatin in cold water; dissolve in fruit juice. Add sugar, salt, ginger ale and lemon juice; mix thoroughly. Chill until jelly is nearly set. Combine with fruits and ginger. Place salad in wet mold; chill and unmold on lettuce. Add cream to mayonnaise; serve cream-mayonnaise with salad. Yield: 10 servings.

Mrs. Mary F. Yost, Cairo Central Sch.
Cairo, New York

GINGER ALE SALAD

3 pkg. lemon Jell-O
2 c. boiling water
2 c. ginger ale
1 No. 2 can crushed pineapple, drained
1 c. miniature marshmallows
½ c. chopped nuts
½ c. maraschino cherries, cut
4 bananas, cut lengthwise
1 egg, beaten
½ c. sugar
2 tbsp. cornstarch
1 c. pineapple juice
Juice of 1 lemon
1 pkg. Dream Whip
½ c. milk
1 tsp. vanilla
Coconut

Combine Jell-O and boiling water; stir until dissolved. Add ginger ale. Add pineapple, marsh-mallows, nuts and cherries. Place bananas on

(Continued on next page)

bottom of dish; pour Jell-O over bananas. Chill until partially set. Combine egg, sugar, cornstarch, pineapple and lemon juices; cook over low heat until thick and clear. Cool. Combine Dream Whip, milk and vanilla; whip until stiff. Fold cooked mixture into Dream Whip; spread over Jello-O mixture. Sprinkle with coconut.

Mrs. Edith Moy Bryan, Harrisonburg H.S.
Harrisonburg, Virginia

GINGER ALE SALAD

1 pkg. lime gelatin
½ c. boiling water
1 ½ c. ginger ale
¼ c. chopped nuts
¼ c. crystallized ginger
1 c. chopped assorted fruits

Dissolve gelatin in boiling water. Chill; add ginger ale. When slightly thickened, fold in remaining ingredients. Chill until firm.

Mrs. H. D. Haggard, Itasca H.S.
Itasca, Texas

CITRUS DELIGHT

2 pkg. lemon gelatin
2 c. water
2 c. grapefruit juice
1 grapefruit, sectioned
3 oranges, sectioned
1 can chunk pineapple, drained
½ c. salad dressing
2 tbsp. pineapple juice

Prepare gelatin as directed on package, substituting grapefruit juice for water. Chill until almost set; stir in grapefruit sections, orange sections and pineapple chunks. Pour into 6-cup mold; chill. Combine salad dressing and pineapple chunks. Pour into 6-cup mold; chill. Combine salad dressing and pineapple juice. Turn salad out of mold; drizzle dressing over top. Yield: 8 servings.

Kay Wallace, Fairfield H.S.
Leesburg, Ohio

FRUIT DELIGHT

1 ½ tbsp. plain gelatin
¼ c. cold water
1 c. unpeeled apples, cubed
1 c. grapefruit sections, cut into pieces and juice
1 c. orange sections, cut into pieces and juice
1 tbsp. lemon juice
½ c. chopped pecans
½ c. sugar
½ c. boiling water

Soak gelatin in cold water 5 minutes. Add apples to grapefruit and oranges. Add lemon juice and nuts. Dissolve sugar and gelatin in boiling water. Combine with fruit mixture. Pour into mold and chill. Serve on salad greens with or without dressing. Yield: 6-8 servings.

Mrs. Jane Robinson, Quitman H.S.
Quitman, Texas

GRAPEFRUIT SALAD RING

1 6-oz. pkg. orange gelatin
1 ½ c. boiling water
1 6-oz. can frozen orange juice concentrate
1 c. cold water
1 11-oz. can mandarin oranges
1 1-lb. can grapefruit sections, drained and cut into pieces

Dissolve gelatin in boiling water; add orange juice and cold water. Drain oranges, reserving syrup. Add syrup to gelatin mixture. Chill until partially set. Fold in oranges and grapefruit. Pour into ring mold. Chill until set. Yield: 8 servings.

Mrs. Raye S. King, Coleman H.S.
Coleman, Texas

MOLDED GRAPEFRUIT SALAD

1 tbsp. unflavored gelatin
¼ c. cold water
½ c. hot water
½ c. sugar
1 c. diced unpared red apple
2 c. fresh or canned grapefruit segments, undrained
½ c. walnut meats

Soften gelatin in cold water; dissolve in hot water. Add sugar; cool. Add fruit; chill until partially set. Add nutmeats; pour into oiled molds or shallow pan. Chill until firm. Unmold; nest in lettuce. Serve with salad dressing.

Myrta Jean Dorn, Licking Valley Sch.
Newark, Ohio

PINK GRAPEFRUIT SALAD

1 3-oz. pkg. pink grapefruit gelatin
1 c. boiling water
1 11-oz. can mandarin oranges, drained
1 sm. can pineapple tidbits and juice
¾ c. Mountain Dew

Dissolve gelatin in hot water. Cool. Stir in remaining ingredients; pour into mold and chill. Yield: 6-8 servings.

Mrs. Geraldine Marrs Homer Comm. Schs.
Homer, Illinois

PINEAPPLE-GRAPEFRUIT SALAD

    1 1-lb. can grapefruit sections
    1 13-oz. can pineapple chunks
    1 tbsp. sugar
    1 pkg. orange or lemon gelatin

Drain juice from pineapple and grapefruit. Add sugar to juice; boil rapidly for 1 minute. Pour over gelatin; dissolve. Cool. Add grapefruit and pineapple. Pour into large or individual molds. Serve on lettuce with mayonnaise. Yield: 8 servings.

Mrs. Kathryn J. Lumpkin, Randolph Co. H.S.
Wedowee, Alabama

GOLDEN FRUIT SALAD

    2 3-oz. pkg. orange gelatin
    2 c. boiling water
    2 c. cold water
    1 11-oz. can mandarin oranges, drained
    1 8¾-oz. can apricot halves, drained
    1 c. white seedless grapes, fresh or
        canned
    2 lge. bananas, sliced
    6 tbsp. sugar
    2 tbsp. cornstarch
    1 egg, slightly beaten
    1 c. fruit liquid
    2 tbsp. butter
    1 tbsp. lemon juice
    1 c. heavy cream
    1 pkg. Dream Whip, whipped
    ¼ c. grated American cheese

Dissolve gelatin in boiling water; add cold water. Refrigerate until syrupy. Fold fruit into gelatin. Pour into 9 x 5 x 3 or 12 x 7 1/2 x 2-inch pan. Chill until firm. Place sugar and cornstarch in heavy saucepan. Blend in egg and fruit liquid. Cook over low heat, stirring constantly until thickened. Remove from heat; stir in butter and lemon juice. Cool and fold in whipped cream. Spread mixture on congealed salad; top with cheese. Refrigerate for about 1 hour. Yield: 12 servings.

Florence T. Shaffer, Berwick Area Sr. H.S.
Berwick, Pennsylvania

GUMDROP SALAD

    ½ lb. quartered marshmallows
    ½ lb. sm. or lge. quartered gumdrops
    1 No. 2 ½ can drained pineapple, cut into
        sm. pieces
    1 lb. white or red grapes, halved and
        seeded
    ½ c. broken nutmeats
    1 sm. bottle maraschino cherries
    ½ c. sugar
    4 tbsp. flour
    ⅛ tsp. salt
    Juice of 2 lemons
    ¾ c. reserved pineapple juice
    1 tbsp. vinegar
    1 pt. heavy whipping cream, whipped

Combine first 6 ingredients; set aside. Blend sugar and flour and add remaining ingredients except cream. Cook in double boiler until thick and smooth, stirring constantly. Fold in cream and combine with gumdrop-fruit mixture. Pour into flat dish or bowl. Cut into squares. Chill 12 to 24 hours. Freezes well. Yield: 10-12 servings.

Mary Ann Sewalt, Midway H.S.
Henrietta, Texas

HOLIDAY FRUIT MOLD

    2 boxes raspberry Jell-O
    2 c. boiling water
    2 c. cold water
    1 29-oz. jar fruits for salad
    2 bananas, fluted

Dissolve Jell-O in boiling water; add cold water. Drain fruits; add to Jell-O mixture. Slice banana, scored with fork, into fruit and Jell-O mixture. Pour into 2-quart ring mold. Chill until firm. Unmold on wreath of bibb lettuce or other salad greens. Serve with salad dressing or whipped cream. Yield: 10 servings.

Treva L. Kelly, Riverside-Brookfield H.S.
Riverside, Illinois

ICED FRUIT GELATIN SALAD

    2 pkg. lemon gelatin
    2 c. hot water
    Pineapple syrup
    4 oranges, diced
    2 c. pineapple chunks
    3 bananas, sliced
    2 apples, diced
    2 pkg. Dream Whip
    1 8-oz. pkg. cream cheese at room
        temperature
    Chopped walnuts or pecans
    Lettuce

Dissolve gelatin in water. Add enough water to pineapple syrup to make 2 cups. Add to gelatin; chill until partially set. Add fruits; chill until firm in 9 x 12-inch pan. Prepare Dream Whip according to package. Add cream cheese gradually to Dream Whip. Spread on gelatin; sprinkle with nuts. Chill; serve on lettuce. Yield: 12 servings.

Mrs. G. Sue Lacy, Kermit H.S.
Kermit, West Virginia

JELLIED PEACH SALAD

    1 sm. can crushed pineapple
    1 pkg. peach Jell-O
    1 banana, cut up
    10 maraschino cherries, cut up

(Continued on next page)

Drain peaches and pineapple; reserve juice. Add enough water to juice to equal 1 1/2 cups liquid. Heat to boiling point. Dissolve Jell-O in hot liquid. Add remaining ingredients; heat in blender or mixer until well blended. Place in refrigerator to set. Yield: 8 servings.

Virginia Curran, Swope Jr. H.S.
Reno, Nevada

JEWEL SALAD

1 11-oz. can mandarin oranges, drained
1 No. 1 ½ can pineapple chunks, drained
1 3-oz. pkg. orange gelatin
1 3-oz. pkg. lime gelatin
1 3-oz. pkg. raspberry gelatin
3 bananas, sliced
1 pkg. whipped topping mix

Drain oranges and pineapple; reserve juice. Prepare gelatin according to directions on package using liquid drained from fruit and enough water to make 1 1/2 cups for each package. Place each gelatin separately in 8-inch square pan; chill until firm. Prepare whipped topping according to package directions. Cut gelatin into cubes about an inch thick. Fold fruit and gelatin cubes gently into whipped topping. Yield: 20-24 servings.

Mrs. Lester Ewy, Pretty Prairie H.S.
Pretty Prairie, Kansas

LEMON JELL-O SALAD

2 pkg. lemon Jell-O
2 c. boiling water
2 c. ginger ale
2 c. white grapes
2 c. pineapple, diced
Bibb lettuce

Dissolve Jell-O in boiling water. Cool; add remaining ingredients. Chill several hours. Serve on lettuce. Yield: 10 servings.

Mrs. May Schlichtemier Koch, Converse Co. H.S.
Douglas, Wyoming

LEMON-RED HOT SALAD

2 pkg. lemon gelatin
1 pkg. red hot candies
2 c. boiling water
1 No. 303 can applesauce
1 No. 303 can crushed pineapple
Nuts or coconut (opt.)

Dissolve gelatin and red hots in boiling water. Add applesauce and pineapple with juice and nuts. Pour into 2-quart mold. Refrigerate until set. Yield: 12 servings.

Mrs. Marsene B. Ham, Denver City H.S.
Denver City, Texas

LEMON-LIME SALAD

2 c. boiling water
1 pkg. lemon gelatin
1 pkg. lime gelatin
1 c. mayonnaise
1 c. canned milk
2 c. cottage cheese
1 No. 2 can pineapple, drained and cut up
1 to 2 c. nuts
2 or 3 lge. apples, chopped

Pour boiling water over gelatin. Let cool slightly. Fold in remaining ingredients. Place in refrigerator to congeal. Boiling fruit juice may be substituted for part of boiling water. Yield: 10-12 servings.

Mrs. Theresa H. Smith, Northside H.S.
Warner Robins, Georgia

LEMON-STRAWBERRY GEL

1 pkg. lemon gelatin
1 pkg. strawberry gelatin
2 c. boiling water
1 c. miniature marshmallows
1 ½ c. cold water
1 sm. can crushed pineapple, undrained
½ c. nuts, broken
2 med. bananas, sliced

Dissolve gelatins in boiling water. Add marshmallows, stirring to dissolve. Add cold water and let stand until mixture is slightly thickened. Stir in pineapple, nuts and bananas. Chill until firm. Yield: 10-12 servings.

Mrs. Martha B. Wheeler, Le Roy H.S.
Le Roy, Kansas

LIME BUFFET SALAD
WITH BRANDIED FRUITS

Canned fruit
¼ c. brandy
1 6-oz. pkg. lime jelly powder
1 ½ c. boiling water
2 c. cold water
2 tsp. salt
¼ tsp. paprika
½ c. horseradish
3 c. sieved cottage cheese
2 tbsp. mayonnaise
2 tsp. minced onion

(Continued on next page)

Drain canned fruit; place 1 cup or reserved fruit juice in saucepan. Add brandy and bring to a boil. Pour over fruit and let stand overnight. Dissolve jelly p o w d e r in boiling water. Add cold water. Cool. Add salt, paprika, horseradish, cottage cheese, mayonnaise and onion. Beat until smooth. Pour into 6-cup ring mold rinsed with ice water. Chill until firm. Unmold on lettuce greens and decorate with brandied fruits. Yield: 8 servings.

Mrs. E. J. A. Young
Mount Sentinel Secondary Sch.
South Slocan, British Columbia, Canada

CANTALOUPE FRUIT MOLD

      1 pkg. lime gelatin
      ½ c. boiling water
      1 ½ c. ginger ale
      1 c. cantaloupe balls
      ½ c. white grapes, cut in halves
      2 fresh peaches, cut
      ½ c. pineapple, diced
      ½ c. whipped cream
      ½ c. mayonnaise

Dissolve gelatin in boiling w a t e r; cool. Add ginger ale and fruit. Chill in ring mold until fir m. Turn out on shredded lettuce. Make dressing of whipped cream and mayonnaise; s e r v e with salad. Yield: 8 servings.

Marion Clark, St. Edward H.S.
St. Edward, Nebraska

JELLIED FRUIT MEDLEYS

      1 pkg. fruit gelatin
      1 tbsp. lemon juice (opt.)
      1 ½ c. melon balls, Bing cherries and
          green grapes
      Lettuce

Prepare gelatin according to package directions. When partially set, add fruit. Pour into 6 to 8 individual molds. Chill until firm. Unmold on plates; garnish with lettuce. Yield: 6-8 servings.

Joan Balish, Colonia Jr. H.S.
Edison, New York

MOLDED MELON SALAD

      2 3-oz. pkg. lemon gelatin
      1 c. boiling water
      1 6-oz. can frozen lemonade concentrate
      1 c. ginger ale
      1 pkg. frozen melon balls
      2 bananas, sliced
      1 c. seedless grapes
      Lettuce

Dissolve gelatin in boiling water. Add lemonade concentrate; stir to dissolve. Add ginger ale and

partially thawed melon balls. Chill until slightly thickened; fold in remaining ingredients. Pour into a 2 1/2-quart mold. Chill until firm. Unmold and serve on lettuce leaves. Yield: 8-10 servings.

Betsy Blake, Bridgeport H.S.
Bridgeport, Washington

MOLDED AMBROSIA

      1 3-oz. pkg. orange Jell-O
      1 c. boiling water
      1 c. fresh orange juice
      ½ c. sour cream
      2 oranges, peeled and cut into bite-sized
          pieces
      1 c. well-drained pineapple chunks
      ½ c. flaked coconut

Dissolve gelatin in boiling water; add orange juice. Cool until slightly thickened. Fold in sour cream. Add remaining ingredients. Chill until set, at least 2 hours. Yield: 8 servings.

Emma Andreae, Bellows Falls H.S.
Bellows Falls, Vermont

MOLDED FRUIT RING
WITH COTTAGE CHEESE

      1 3-oz. pkg. lime gelatin
      2 c. boiling water
      1 c. seedless green grapes
      1 c. pineapple tidbits, drained
      Cottage cheese
      Paprika or chopped nuts

Dissolve gelatin in boiling water. Cool. Add fruit; pour into ring mold. Chill. Unmold on lettuce-lined plate. Fill center with cottage cheese. Garnish cottage cheese with paprika. Yield: 6-8 servings.

Mary Ann DeVore, Fort Recovery H.S.
Fort Recovery, Ohio

MOLDED FRUIT 'N' NUT SALAD

      1 No. 1 can sliced pineapple
      1 pkg. lemon gelatin
      2 tbsp. lemon juice
      Lettuce cups
      ½ c. raisins
      1 apple, chopped
      1 pkg. English walnuts, chopped

Drain syrup from pineapple and add enough water to measure 1 3/4 cups. Bring to boil and pour over lemon gelatin. Stir until gelatin is dissolved. Add lemon juice. Cool until slightly thickened. Chop pineapple and add to gelatin. Add raisins, apple and nuts. Spoon into individual molds and chill until firm. Unmold in lettuce cups. Yield: 6-7 servings.

Ella S. Harrell, Central H.S.
Victoria, Virginia

MOLDED FRUIT SALAD

1 pkg. lemon gelatin
1 c. hot water
1 c. orange and pineapple syrup
4 slices canned pineapple
2 bananas
8 marshmallows
1 11-oz. can mandarin oranges
¼ c. mayonnaise
½ c. cream, whipped

Dissolve gelatin in hot water; add syrups from fruits. Chill until partially set. Dice pineapple and bananas; quarter marshmallows. Add to thickened gelatin; add orange sections. Stir mayonnaise into whipped cream, blending thoroughly; fold into gelatin mixture. Pour into individual molds; chill until firm. Unmold on lettuce; garnish with maraschino cherries or other fruit in season. Serve with mayonnaise thinned with pineapple juice. Yield: 6 servings.

Darlene M. Pohlman, Priest River Sr. H.S.
Priest River, Idaho

MOLDED GRAPE SUPREME

1 envelope unflavored gelatin
¼ c. cold water
1 c. boiling water
Dash of salt
⅓ c. granulated sugar
1 6-oz. can frozen grape juice
    concentrate
3 tbsp. lemon juice
¾ c. halved seedless grapes
2 diced med. bananas
¼ c. chopped walnuts
Salad greens

Sprinkle gelatin over cold water to soften. Add boiling water, salt and sugar; stir until dissolved. Stir in grape juice and lemon juice. Refrigerate until partially thickened. Fold in fruits and nuts; pour into 6 individual molds. Refrigerate until firm. Serve on salad greens. Yield: 6 servings.

Ruth E. Carlson, Donovan H.S.
Donovan, Illinois

MRS. SWIFT'S SUNSHINE SALAD

1 pkg. lemon gelatin
1 pkg. orange gelatin
2 c. boiling water
1½ c. cold water
1 No. 2 can crushed pineapple, drained
2 bananas, diced
10 marshmallows
Topping

Dissolve both packages of gelatin in boiling water. Add cold water; set in cool place until consistency of unbeaten egg white. Add fruit and marshmallows. Pour into 9 x 15-inch pan. Chill until firm.

TOPPING:

1 egg, beaten
2 tbsp. butter
2 tbsp. flour
1½ c. sugar
1 c. pineapple juice
1 c. heavy cream, whipped
½ c. shredded sharp cheese

Combine egg, butter, flour and sugar in saucepan; add pineapple juice. Mix well. Cook, stirring, over low heat until thickened. Cool. Fold in whipped cream; spread over chilled salad. Sprinkle cheese over top. Yield: 12-15 servings.

Mrs. Eva Padilla, Belen H.S.
Belen, New Mexico

NORTH CAROLINA RIBBON SALAD

1 box raspberry Jell-O
1 c. canned pears, drained
1 c. canned peaches, drained
1 box lime Jell-O
1 8-oz. pkg. cream cheese
1 c. chopped pecans
1 box orange Jell-O
1 c. mandarin oranges, drained
1 c. seedless grapes

Prepare raspberry Jell-O according to package directions but omit 1/4 cup cold water. Add chopped pears and peaches; refrigerate in 9 x 14-inch glass baking dish. Combine lime Jell-O and 1 cup boiling water; dissolve completely. Add cream cheese and mix until dissolved. Add pecans and pour over first congealed layer. Prepare orange Jell-O according to directions but omit 1/4 cup cold water. Add oranges and grapes; refrigerate. Serve when completely congealed. Yield: 8-12 servings.

Georganna B. Rice, McKean H.S.
Wilmington, Delaware

OCTOBER SALAD WITH GINGER-MAYONNAISE DRESSING

1 3-oz. pkg. apple gelatin
2 c. hot water
⅛ tsp. salt
⅓ c. coarsely chopped dates
⅓ c. nuts
1 c. diced unpeeled red apples
1 c. diced unpeeled fresh pears
⅓ c. mayonnaise
⅓ c. sour cream
2 tbsp. chopped candied gingerroot

Dissolve gelatin in hot water. Add salt and dates; chill until mixture is slightly thickened. Fold in nuts and fruit. Pour into 5-cup mold and chill until firm. Mix mayonnaise and sour cream; add gingerroot. Unmold salad on greens and serve with mayonnaise dressing. Yield: 6 servings.

Carolyn Ewan, Arlington H.S.
Arlington Heights, Illinois

DAIRY ORANGE SALAD

    1 c. boiling water
    1 3-oz. pkg. orange gelatin
    2 c. miniature marshmallows
    1 c. frozen orange juice
    ½ c. sugar
    1 3-oz. pkg. cream cheese
    1 c. crushed pineapple
    1 c. cottage cheese
    2 bananas, mashed
    1 c. mandarin orange sections
    ½ pt. cream, whipped

Pour boiling water over gelatin; add marshmallows. Stir until gelatin is dissolved. Defrost orange juice; stir in sugar. Add to gelatin mixture. Cream the cheese; add pineapple. Add to gelatin mixture. Stir cottage cheese, bananas and orange sections into gelatin mixture until well mixed. Fold in whipped cream. Pour into large container; place in refrigerator for at least 3 hours. Yield: 15 servings.

Mrs. Carolyn Jordan, Catoosa H.S.
Catoosa, Oklahoma
Lorene L. Arent, Wausa H.S.
Wausa, Nebraska

EMPRESS ORANGE MOLD

    2 3-oz. pkg. orange gelatin
    2½ c. boiling water
    1 7-oz. bottle ginger ale
    1 c. orange sections
    ½ c. seedless green grapes
    ½ c. mayonnaise
    1 3-oz. pkg. cream cheese
    ¼ c. chopped pecans
    ¼ tsp. nutmeg
    ¼ tsp. cinnamon

Dissolve gelatin in boiling water; add ginger ale. Chill until slightly thickened. Fold orange sections and grapes into gelatin mixture. Spoon a small amount into 1 1/2-quart mold; chill until firm. Gradually add mayonnaise to softened cream cheese; mix until well blended. Stir in nuts and spices; spread over molded gelatin layer. Cover with remaining gelatin mixture; chill until firm. Top with additional mayonnaise. Yield: 6 servings.

Mrs. Effie G. Hoyle, Warwick H.S.
Newport News, Virginia

FRUIT SALAD

    1 pkg. orange gelatin
    1 pkg. lemon gelatin
    1 c. boiling water
    1 No. 2 can crushed pineapple
    3 cans mandarin orange slices
    1 sm. pkg. marshmallows
    1 pt. whipping cream, whipped
    1 c. salad dressing plus 1 tsp. prepared
      mustard
    Grated sharp cheese

Dissolve gelatins in boiling water. Add with fruit juices; mix well. Pour into 13 x 9-inch shallow dish; top with marshmallows. Congeal. Fold salad dressing and mustard into whipped cream. Top congealed salad with whipped cream dressing. Sprinkle with grated cheese. Yield: 12-15 servings.

Mrs. Anona Moore, Alvin Jr. H.S.
Alvin, Texas

HEAVENLY ORANGE FLUFF

    2 pkg. orange gelatin
    2 c. boiling water
    1 sm. can concentrated frozen orange
      juice
    2 cans mandarin oranges, drained
    1 lge. can crushed pineapple, not
      drained
    Lemon Topping

Dissolve gelatin in boiling water; add frozen orange juice, undiluted. Add orange sections and pineapple. Mix well; pour into molds. Congeal. When set, cover with Lemon Topping.

LEMON TOPPING:

    1 c. milk
    1 pkg. instant lemon pudding
    ½ pt. whipping cream

Add milk to pudding; beat with rotary beater until thick. Whip cream; fold into pudding. Yield: 12 servings.

Mrs. Eleanor Puckett, North Mecklenburg H.S.
Huntersville, North Carolina

IMPERIAL ORANGE DESSERT SALAD

    2 envelopes unflavored gelatin
    1 c. water
    2 tbsp. grated orange rind
    1 c. fresh orange juice
    2 c. buttermilk
    ¼ c. sugar
    1 tsp. vanilla extract
    Green grapes
    Low-calorie mandarin orange sections

Soften gelatin in water and dissolve over low heat; set aside. Mix orange rind, juice, buttermilk, sugar and vanilla together. Add dissolved gelatin to orange juice mixture. Pour into 1-quart mold and chill until set. Unmold; decorate with grapes and mandarin orange sections. Yield: 6 servings.

Mrs. Doris Schnurrenberger, Sycamore H.S.
Cincinnati, Ohio

MARSHMALLOW PINEAPPLE FLUFF

1 lge. can crushed pineapple
32 lge. marshmallows, quartered
1 pkg. unflavored gelatin
1 c. cold milk
1 c. chopped nuts
1 can mandarin orange sections (opt.)
1 carton whipped cream

Pour pineapple into dish with marshmallows. Let stand, covered, overnight. Soften gelatin in milk; heat to dissolve gelatin. Mix with pineapple and marshmallows. Add nuts and orange sections. Fold in whipped cream. Chill until firm. Yield: 10 servings.

Jacquie Eddleman, Dongola H.S.
Dongola, Illinois

MANDARIN ORANGE SALAD

2 c. orange juice
1 pkg. orange gelatin
¼ lb. sm. marshmallows
2 tbsp. lemon juice
1 sm. pkg. cream cheese
1 can mandarin oranges
1 c. pineapple tidbits
¼ c. sliced almonds

Heat orange juice. Dissolve gelatin in 1/4 of the hot juice; dissolve marshmallows in remaining hot juice. Mix together. Add lemon juice; cool. When almost thick, beat with mixer. Beat in softened cream cheese. Fold in oranges and pineapple; chill. Garnish with almonds. Yield: 8 servings.

Jane Craig, Sonoma Valley H.S.
Sonoma, California

MANDARIN ORANGE SALAD

2 cans mandarin oranges
1 pkg. lemon gelatin
1 pkg. orange gelatin
2 lge. cans frozen orange juice, undiluted
1 tall can crushed pineapple
½ to ¾ c. ground pecans or almonds (opt.)
Sour cream

Drain oranges. Heat drained juice to boiling; dissolve gelatins. Add frozen orange juice; mix well. Add pineapple, orange sections and nuts. Mold in 9 x 13-inch Pyrex dish. Cut in squares to serve. Serve with sour cream. Yield: 10-12 servings.

Mrs. Almeda B. Thomas, Maynard H.S.
Maynard, Arkansas

ORANGE-BLACK WALNUT SALAD

1 pkg. orange gelatin
1 c. hot water
½ c. cold water
½ pt. whipping cream or Dream Whip
1 sm. can crushed pineapple, drained
1 sm. can mandarin oranges, drained
½ c. black walnuts

Dissolve gelatin in hot water; add cold water. Chill until partially set. Whip cream. Combine pineapple, oranges and gelatin with electric mixer. Fold in nuts and whipped cream. Yield: 8 servings.

Judith A. Anderson, Tuscola H.S.
Tuscola, Illinois

ORANGE FLUFF

3 pkg. orange Jell-O
2 c. boiling water
2 c. cold water
1 No. 2 can crushed pineapple, drained
1 c. whipping cream, whipped
½ pkg. miniature marshmallows
1 can mandarin oranges
Maraschino cherries (opt.)

Mix Jell-O and boiling water together. Add cold water and 1 cup juice from pineapple. Let stand until thick and syrupy. Beat well with mixer; fold in whipping cream, pineapple and marshmallows. Arrange oranges in mold; add Jell-O filling and refrigerate. Arrange orange slices and cherries around mold, if desired. Yield: 8 servings.

Mrs. Videllia M. Peters, Goodridge H.S.
Goodridge, Minnesota

ORANGE-GRAPEFRUIT MOLDED RING

2 3-oz. pkg. orange Jell-O
1 ½ c. boiling water
1 6-oz. can orange juice concentrate
1 c. cold water
1 11-oz. can mandarin oranges, drained
1 16-oz. can grapefruit sections, drained and cut into sm. pieces
1 c. pineapple chunks (opt.)

Dissolve Jell-O in hot water. Add orange juice concentrate and cold water. Add drained juice from mandarin oranges. Chill until partially set. Fold in oranges and grapefruit sections. Pour into mold and let set until firm. Serve with small dish of salad dressing in center of ring. Add pineapple chunks if desired. Yield: 10-12 servings.

Mrs. Ivell Halseide, Culbertson H.S.
Culbertson, Montana

Molded Fruit Salads With Oranges

ORANGE-GRAPEFRUIT SALAD RING

2 3-oz. pkg. orange gelatin
1½ c. boiling water
1 6-oz. can frozen orange juice concentrate, thawed
1 c. cold water
1 11-oz. can mandarin oranges
1 1-lb. can grapefruit sections, drained and cut into pieces

Dissolve gelatin in boiling water; add orange juice concentrate and cold water. Drain oranges, reserving syrup. Add syrup to gelatin mixture. Chill until partially set. Fold in oranges and grapefruit. Pour into 6 1/2-cup ring mold. Chill until set. Unmold; serve with mayonnaise or salad dressing. Yield: 8-10 servings.

Mrs. Margarette Weeks, Highland Jr. H.S.
Highland, California

ORANGE-MARSHMALLOW SALAD

1 3-oz. pkg. orange gelatin
1 3-oz. pkg. lemon gelatin
2 c. boiling water
2 11-oz. cans mandarin oranges
1 13-oz. can pineapple tidbits
1 c. chopped pecans
2 c. miniature marshmallows

Mix gelatins; dissolve in boiling water. Drain oranges and pineapple; add cold water to combined juices to make 2 cups. Stir into slightly cooled gelatin. Add orange segments, pineapple, pecans and marshmallows. Pour into 9 x 9 x 2-inch pan; chill until firm. Yield: 12 servings.

Linda Lee West, Hooks H.S.
Hooks, Texas

ORANGE SALAD

2 3-oz. pkg. orange gelatin
1½ c. boiling water
1 sm. can frozen orange juice
1 No. 211 can crushed pineapple
1 sm. can mandarin oranges
1 pkg. lemon pie filling (not instant)
½ c. whipping cream
Grated cheese

Dissolve gelatin in boiling water; add frozen orange juice. Drain juice from pineapple and oranges. Add sufficient water to make 1 1/2 cups liquid; add to gelatin mixture. When gelatin is syrupy, add fruit. Pour into 9 x 13-inch pan; refrigerate overnight. Make lemon pie filling as directed; cool. Whip cream; fold into pudding. Spread on top of gelatin mixture; sprinkle with grated cheese. Yield: 15 servings.

Becky Bahnsen, Reed City H.S.
Reed City, Michigan

ORANGE-PINEAPPLE SNOW

1 20-oz. can crushed or chunk pineapple
1 pkg. lemon Jell-O
Juice from 1 lemon
1 c. sour cream
1 c. tiny marshmallows
1 tbsp. grated orange peel
1 c. orange slices, quartered

Drain pineapple; reserve juice. Add enough water to make 1 cup. Add Jell-O. Heat until Jell-O is dissolved. Add lemon juice. Chill until partially set. Fold in remaining ingredients. Place in mold. Chill until firm. Yield: 8 servings.

Mrs. John Fullmer, Waupaca H.S.
Waupaca, Wisconsin

ORANGE SALAD

1 can mandarin oranges
1 sm. can crushed pineapple
1 c. miniature marshmallows
1 3-oz. pkg. cream cheese
1 box orange Jell-O
½ pt. whipping cream, whipped

Drain juice from oranges and pineapple. Add water to make 2 cups; heat. Add marshmallows, cheese and Jell-O; cool. Add fruit and whipped cream. Chill several hours. Yield: 8 servings.

Mrs. Nancye H. Shannon, Greenbrier H.S.
Greenbrier, Tennessee

ORANGE VELVET SALAD

½ c. sugar
3 envelopes plain gelatin
⅔ c. boiling water
1 6-oz. can frozen orange juice
12 ice cubes
1 can mandarin orange sections, drained
1 can pineapple chunks, drained

Place sugar and gelatin in blender container; cover and run on low speed until mixed. Add boiling water; run on low for 1 minute. Add frozen orange juice; run on low for 1 minute. Add ice cubes 1 at a time; blend on high speed until each is completely liquefied before adding another. Quickly pour into 1-quart mold. Chill. Unmold on lettuce; serve with mandarin oranges and pineapple. Yield: 8-10 servings.

Mrs. Frances Daniel, Gwinnett Co. Voc. H.S.
Lawrenceville, Georgia

TANGERINE MOLDED SALAD

1 pkg. orange gelatin
1 sm. can crushed pineapple, undrained
1 can seedless grapes, drained
1 3-oz. can frozen orange juice, undiluted
1 can mandarin oranges, drained

208

(Continued on next page)

Soften gelatin in 1 cup hot water. Mix all ingredients; pour into small mold. For large ring mold, double recipe using still only 1 can orange juice. Yield: 4 servings.

Mrs. Martha M. Reichle, Cardston H.S.
Cardston, Alberta, Canada

WHITE SALAD

2 envelopes unflavored gelatin
½ c. cold, unsweetened pineapple juice
1 ½ c. hot pineapple juice
½ c. sugar
Juice of 1 lemon
1 c. milk or thin cream
1 c. heavy cream, whipped
1 tsp. almond extract
Lettuce or other greens
1 banana, sliced
1 can mandarin orange sections
Maraschino cherries

Soften gelatin in cold pineapple juice. Add hot juice, sugar and lemon juice; stir until dissolved. Cool; add milk. Mixture looks curdled at this point. Chill until partially set. Fold in whipped cream and extract. Pour into a 1 1/2-quart ring mold. Chill until firm. Unmold on large plate. Fill center with lettuce, banana slices and some of the orange sections. Garnish outer edge with 5 clusters of orange sections placed on lettuce; complete garnish with a few cherries. Yield: 8 servings.

Mrs. Marie Larson, Cokato H.S.
Cokato, Minnesota

PACIFIC LIME MOLD

1 pkg. lime Jell-O
1 c. boiling water
1 9-oz. can crushed pineapple
1 c. mashed bananas
2 tbsp. lemon juice
½ c. mayonnaise
¼ c. chopped nuts

Dissolve Jell-O in boiling water; add juice from pineapple. Chill until slightly thick. Beat until frothy. Fold in remaining ingredients. Chill in 1 1/2-quart mold. Yield: 6 servings.

Mrs. Carol Erickson, North Jr. H.S.
Hopkins, Minnesota

PARTY SALAD WITH TOPPING

3 pkg. lemon Jell-O
3 c. boiling water
1 ½ c. crushed pineapple
3 bananas, diced
1 c. red apple, diced

Dissolve Jell-O in water; add pineapple. Pour into mold and place in refrigerator; add bananas and apple when partially set.

TOPPING:

1 c. pineapple juice
Juice of 1 lemon
2 tbsp. cornstarch
½ c. sugar
2 eggs, beaten
1 pkg. Dream Whip

Cook all ingredients except Dream Whip in double boiler until thick; cool. Add Dream Whip, prepared according to directions on package. Serve over salad. Yield: 12-18 servings.

Mildred Burris, Delta Sch.
Delta, Ohio

LAYERED FRUIT SALAD

1 3-oz. pkg. cream cheese
1 8-oz. can crushed pineapple
1 pkg. lime Jell-O
6 pear halves, canned
1 pkg. orange Jell-O
1 sm. can mandarin orange slices

Soften cream cheese at room temperature. Drain pineapple, reserving juice to use in Jell-O. Dissolve lime Jell-O in 1 cup boiling water. Measure pineapple juice and add water to make 1 cup. Add to lime Jell-O. Arrange pear halves in bottom of large mold. Pour about 1/3 of lime Jell-O over pears and refrigerate to set. Mix remaining lime Jell-O with cream cheese, beating with egg beater until smooth. Add pineapple and pour over firm Jell-O. Dissolve orange Jell-O in 1 cup boiling water. Drain mandarin orange slices. Measure juice and add water to make 1 cup. Stir into dissolved orange Jell-O. Let Jell-O set; Mix in mandarin slices and pour over thoroughly set cream cheese layer. Refrigerate 4 to 6 hours before serving. Yield: 12 servings.

Elizabeth S. Yocom, Owen J. Roberts H.S.
Pottstown, Pennsylvania

FROSTED JELL-O SALAD

1 pkg. orange gelatin
1 pkg. lemon gelatin
1 No. 2 can crushed pineapple, drained
1 c. cubed pears
1 c. milk
¼ lb. Velveeta cheese
1 pkg. unflavored gelatin

Dissolve orange and lemon gelatins in 2 cups hot water. Drain pineapple and pears; add water, if necessary, to combined juices to make 2 cups liquid. Add to orange-lemon gelatin. When gelatin begins to set, add pineapple and pears. Let set until solid. Dissolve unflavored gelatin in a small amount of the milk. Heat remaining milk; melt

209

(Continued on next page)

cheese in another pan. Combine warm milk, unflavored gelatin and cheese; cool. Pour over firm fruit gelatin mixture. Yield: 12 servings.

Mrs. Vester Collins, Coweta Sch.
Coweta, Oklahoma

SEAFOAM SALAD

1 c. pear juice
1 pkg. lime Jell-O
1 lge. pkg. cream cheese
Milk
1 lge. can pears
1 flat can crushed pineapple
1 pkg. Dream Whip

Heat pear juice; pour over Jell-O. Mash cheese with small amount milk; add to hot Jell-O mixture. Mash pears with fork. Add to Jell-O mixture. Add crushed pineapple. Let set until mixture partially thickens. Beat Dream Whip, fold into Jell-O mixture. Chill until firmly set in 7 1/2 x 12-inch pan. Yield: 12 servings.

Mrs. Viola Johnson, Karnes City H.S.
Karnes City, Texas

PINEAPPLE-CHEESE SALAD

1 pkg. lemon gelatin
1 c. boiling water
1 c. cold water
3 bananas, sliced
1 c. miniature marshmallows
¼ c. sugar
1 ½ tbsp. cornstarch
1 8 ½-oz. can crushed pineapple
½ c. heavy cream
½ c. shredded, longhorn cheddar cheese

Dissolve gelatin in boiling water; add cold water. Chill until syrupy. Stir in bananas and marshmallows. Pour into oblong glass salad dish; chill until set. Mix sugar and cornstarch; add to pineapple. Cook over medium heat, stirring constantly, until thickened. Cool. Whip cream; fold into cooled pineapple mixture with half the shredded cheese. Spread mixture on congealed lemon gelatin. Sprinkle cheese on top. Chill overnight. Yield: 15 servings.

Mrs. Edward McCoy, Booneville H.S.
Booneville, Mississippi

PINEAPPLE-ORANGE-BANANA SALAD

1 pkg. orange gelatin
1 pkg. lemon gelatin
1 ½ c. boiling water
1 ½ c. sm. marshmallows
2 c. cold water
1 No. 2 can crushed pineapple, drained
1 banana, mashed fine
Juice of 1 lemon

Dissolve gelatin in boiling water; add marshmallows. Stir until marshmallows are almost melted. Add cold water, pineapple, banana and lemon juice. Chill until firm.

TOPPING:

2 tbsp. flour
½ c. sugar
1 c. pineapple juice
1 egg, well beaten
Juice of ½ lemon
1 pkg. Dream Whip, prepared

Mix flour, sugar and pineapple juice; add egg and lemon juice. Cook over low heat until thick; cool. Fold Dream Whip into sauce. Refrigerate. Yield: 8-12 servings.

Mrs. D. J. Dear, Stringer H.S.
Stringer, Mississippi

PINEAPPLE-CREAM SALAD

2 boxes lemon Jell-O
2 c. boiling water
1 4-oz. can crushed pineapple
½ lb. marshmallows, cut up
3 bananas, sliced
¾ c. cream, whipped
1 c. pineapple juice
½ c. sugar
2 tbsp. butter
2 tbsp. flour
1 egg
½ c. chopped pecans

Mix Jell-O with hot water; cool. Add pineapple, marshmallows and bananas. Pour into 9 x 13-inch pan; let set in refrigerator. Place pineapple juice, sugar, butter, flour and egg in top of double boiler. Cook until thick; cool. Add whipped cream; fold in. Frost set Jell-O with cream mixture. Cut; serve while cold. Yield: 12-15 servings.

Sheryl K. Jordan, Colby H.S.
Colby, Kansas

CHEESE-RASPBERRY MOLD

1 pkg. lemon gelatin
3 c. hot water
¼ c. lemon juice
1 8-oz. pkg. cream cheese
1 9-oz. can crushed pineapple
1 pkg. raspberry gelatin
½ c. seeded Tokay grapes, cut in halves
½ c. chopped walnuts

Dissolve lemon gelatin in 1 1/2 cups hot water; stir in 2 tablespoons lemon juice. Whip cream cheese; gradually add hot lemon gelatin, beating until smooth. Chill until mixture begins to thicken. Beat until fluffy; pour into 6-cup mold. Chill until firm. Drain pineapple; measure 1/4 cup pineapple syrup. Add syrup to remaining hot

(Continued on next page)

water. Add raspberry gelatin; stir until dissolved. Add remaining lemon juice; chill until syrupy. Stir in pineapple, grapes and walnuts. Spoon over lemon-cheese layer in mold. Chill until firm. Unmold on serving plate; garnish with salad greens, additional grapes and apple slices. Yield: 8-10 servings.

Mrs. Margaret A. Rossander, Westmoor H.S.
Daly City, California

CONGEALED RASPBERRY-SOUR CREAM SALAD

    ½ pt. sour cream
    1 c. miniature marshmallows
    2 pkg. raspberry Jell-O
    2 c. boiling water
    2 10-oz. pkg. frozen raspberries
    1 No. 303 can applesauce

Mix sour cream and marshmallows. Dissolve Jell-O in hot water. Add raspberries and applesauce mixing well. Pour into 8 or 9-inch square pan. Chill until firm. Spread with marshmallow mixture. Yield: 12-16 servings.

Mrs. Hazel I. Coatsworth, Pueblo H.S.
Tucson, Arizona

HEAVENLY RASPBERRY SALAD

    1 3-oz. pkg. lemon gelatin
    1 c. water and pineapple juice, heated
    1 ½ c. diced marshmallows
    1 8-oz. pkg. cream cheese, cut up
    1 c. salad dressing
    ½ pt. whipping cream, whipped
    2 ½ c. crushed pineapple
    2 c. water
    2 3-oz. pkg. raspberry gelatin
    1 pkg. from raspberries, thawed

Dissolve lemon gelatin in heated liquid. Pour over marshmallows and cream cheese. Blend with rotary beater; cool. Add salad dressing and whipped cream. Fold in crushed pineapple. Pour into 9 x 9 x 1-inch pan. Chill until firm. Dissolve raspberry gelatin in 2 cups boiling water; add berries. Cool. Spoon onto lemon gelatin mixture. Refrigerate until set. Cut into squares. Serve on lettuce. Yield: 6-8 servings.

Mrs. Douglas Case, Blissfield H.S.
Blissfield, Michigan

QUICK RASPBERRY-APPLESAUCE SALAD

    1 box red raspberry Jell-O
    1 c. hot water
    1 box frozen raspberries
    1 303 can applesauce

Dissolve Jell-O in hot water; add remaining ingredients. Pour into 9 x 5 x 3-inch pan. Chill until firm. Serve. Yield: 6 servings.

Jane E. Spangler, Shippensburg Area Sr. H.S.
Shippensburg, Pennsylvania
Joyce Harter, Pella Comm.
Pella, Iowa

RASPBERRY-APPLESAUCE MOLD

    ½ pkg. miniature marshmallows
    ¾ carton cultured cream
    2 pkg. raspberry Jell-O
    2 c. boiling water
    2 pkg. frozen raspberries
    2 c. applesauce

Combine marshmallows and cream. Let stand for 24 hours to dissolve marshmallows. Dissolve Jell-O in boiling water; add raspberries and applesauce. Stir well. Pour into mold. Frost with marshmallow mixture. Yield: 8-10 servings.

Mrs. Karen Williams, Perham H.S.
Perham, Minnesota

RASPBERRY-APPLESAUCE SALAD

    1 3-oz. pkg. raspberry Jell-O
    1 c. boiling water
    1 10-oz. pkg. frozen raspberries
    1 c. applesauce
    1 c. sour cream
    2 c. miniature marshmallows

Dissolve Jell-O in boiling water; add raspberries and applesauce. Pour into 8-inch cake pan. Chill until firm. Combine sour cream and marshmallows. Pour over Jell-O mixture. Cut into squares. Serve on bed of lettuce. Delicious with pork. Yield: 8 servings.

Mrs. Gary Jurgenson, Fremont Sr. H.S.
Fremont, Nebraska

RASPBERRY DELIGHT

    1 c. miniature marshmallows
    1 lge. carton sour cream
    1 lge. pkg. raspberry gelatin
    1 c. applesauce
    1 lge. pkg. frozen raspberries, thawed

Combine marshmallows and sour cream; let stand 24 to 36 hours to dissolve marshmallows. Stir occasionally. Dissolve gelatin in 1 cup hot water; stir in applesauce and raspberries. Place in refrigerator until congealed. Cut into squares; dot with marshmallow mixture. Yield: 10-12 servings.

Mrs. Eleanor Roberts, Benton Consol. H.S.
Benton, Illinois

RASPBERRY MOLDED SALAD

½ c. miniature marshmallows
½ c. sour cream
1 lge. pkg. raspberry Jell-O
1 ½ c. hot water
1 c. applesauce
2 pkg. frozen raspberries, thawed

Combine marshmallows and sour cream. Let stand for 24 hours to dissolve marshmallows. Dissolve Jell-O in hot water; add applesauce and raspberries. Refrigerate until congealed. Dot each serving with marshmallows mixture. Yield: 15 servings.

Mrs. Eleanor Roberts, Benton Consol. H.S.
Benton, Illinois

RASPBERRY SALAD

1 pkg. raspberry Jell-O
1 3-oz. pkg. cream cheese,
  well-beaten
¼ c. mayonnaise
1 diced banana
¼ c. nuts
½ c. coconut
1 sm. can crushed pineapple,
  well-drained

Prepare Jell-O as directed on package. Chill until slightly thickened. Combine cheese and mayonnaise; pour into Jell-O. Add remaining ingredients. Pour into mold. Chill. Yield: 8 servings.

Ruth Bailey, Jonesboro H.S.
Jonesboro, Tennessee

RASPBERRY TANG SALAD

1 pkg. raspberry Jell-O
½ c. boiling water
¼ c. salad dressing
1 3-oz. pkg. cream cheese
1 8 ½-oz. can crushed pineapple
1 banana, diced
¼ c. shredded coconut
½ c. pecans, chopped
1 c. cream, whipped

Dissolve Jell-O in boiling water; set aside. Gradually add salad dressing to cream cheese, creaming until well blended. Slowly, add Jell-O to cheese mixture, mixing until smooth. Chill until slightly congealed; add pineapple, banana, coconut and pecans. Fold in whipped cream. Pour into mold. Chill until firm. Unmold on nest of watercress or lettuce. Serve. Yield: 8-10 servings.

Frances Bolles, Keene H.S.
Keene, New Hampshire

RASPBERRY SALAD

3 c. hot water
3 6-oz. pkg. frozen raspberries
3 3-oz. pkg. raspberry Jell-O
1 No. 303 can drained, crushed pineapple
3 cubed bananas
¾ c. chopped walnuts
1 pt. sour cream

Dissolve Jell-O in hot water. Add raspberries, then remaining ingredients except sour cream. Pour half of Jell-O mixture into 3-quart mold, follow with layer of sour cream, then remaining Jell-O. Chill until firm. Yield: 20-24 servings.

Mrs. Thelma Leigh, Quincy Jr.-Sr. H.S.
Quincy, California

RASPBERRY SWEET TREAT

2 pkg. raspberry Jell-O
1 ½ c. boiling water
2 or 3 mashed bananas
1 can crushed pineapple
2 sm. boxes frozen raspberries
12-oz. sour cream

Dissolve Jell-O in boiling water. Allow to set for 5 minutes. Combine bananas, pineapple and raspberries; add Jell-O. Pour half of mixture into mold; chill. When mixture is firm, spread sour cream across top. Pour remaining Jell-O mixture over sour cream. Yield: 12 servings.

Mrs. William D. Bowen, Parsons Jr. H.S.
Parsons, Kansas

RIBBON SALAD

1 6-oz. pkg. raspberry gelatin
1 ½ c. boiling water
2 10-oz. pkg. frozen raspberries
1 13 ½-oz. can crushed pineapple,
  undrained
¼ tsp. salt
1 pt. sour cream

Dissolve gelatin in boiling water; add raspberries, pineapple and salt. Pour 1 1/2 cups gelatin into 6-cup ring mold; chill quickly until firm. Keep remaining gelatin at room temperature. Carefully spread 1 cup sour cream over chilled gelatin; spoon half of remaining gelatin over top. Chill until firm. Spread remaining sour cream; top with remaining gelatin. Chill several hours or overnight. Unmold onto serving plate. Garnish with crisp salad greens. Yield: 8-10 servings.

Marian S. Russell, Northwestern H.S.
Hyattsville, Maryland

VIVIAN'S HOLIDAY SALAD

    1 box raspberry Jell-O
    1 box lemon Jell-O
    2 c. boiling water
    1 10-oz. pkg. frozen raspberries
    1 14-oz. jar cranberry-orange relish
    1 7-oz. bottle lemon-lime soft drink

Dissolve Jell-O in water; add frozen raspberries and relish. Chill till cold; add soft drink slowly with bottle on rim of bowl. Stir with up and down motion. Chill until partially set; pour into 6-cup mold. Chill until set; unmold on bed of lettuce or other salad greens. Yield: 10 servings.

Agnes Kowitz Boulger
Bradley-Bourbonnaise Comm. H.S.
Bradley, Illinois

SALAD APPLE RING

    1 pkg. apple-flavored gelatin
    Dash of salt
    1 c. hot water
    2 tbsp. lemon juice
    1 7-oz. bottle lemon-lime carbonated
      beverage, well-chilled
    1 unpared, tart red apple
    ½ c. halved, seedless green grapes

Dissolve gelatin and salt in hot water; cool to room temperature. Add lemon juice. Pour lemon-lime beverage carefully down side of bowl; stir gently with up and down motion. Chill until partially set. Core apple; slice very thin. Add apple and grapes to gelatin mixture, stirring gently with up and down motion. Pour into 1-quart mold or ring mold. Chill until firm. Serve on salad greens. Yield: 6 servings.

Helen Janis Hale, Somerset H.S.
Somerset, Kentucky

SALLY'S PINK SALAD

    1 pkg. strawberry Jell-O
    1 c. boiling water
    1 sm. can crushed pineapple with liquid
    2 sm. or 1 lge. orange, cut into bits
    1 apple, finely chopped (opt.)
    ½ to 1 c. finely cut pecans
    1 c. coconut
    2 tbsp. mayonnaise

Mix Jell-O and boiling water; add pineapple, orange, apple, pecans, coconut and mayonnaise. Mix together until mayonnaise is thoroughly blended. Yield: 6-8 servings.

Mrs. Sarah W. Huebner, Area Adv.
Home Econ. Ed. and Sch. Food Serv.
Norristown, Pennsylvania

SEVEN-UP JELL-O

    1 family-sized pkg. lemon Jell-O
    1 c. boiling water
    1 c. cold water
    1 12-oz. bottle Seven-Up
    3 bananas, cut up
    1 7-oz. can crushed pineapple
    1 10-oz. pkg. miniature marshmallows
    1 c. pineapple juice
    ¼ c. sugar
    1 tbsp. flour
    1 beaten egg
    2 tbsp. butter
    1 c. whipped cream or substitute

Dissolve Jell-O in boiling water; add cold water and Seven-Up. Add bananas and pineapple. Pour marshmallows on top. Place in refrigerator until firm. Mix pineapple juice, sugar, flour and egg in saucepan; cook until mixture thickens. Add butter; remove from heat. Cool. Add whipped cream. Spread on set Jell-O mixture. Refrigerate. Yield: 10 servings.

Mrs. Dorothy Beeler, Beaver City H.S.
Beaver City, Nebraska

SEVEN-UP SALAD

    1 20-oz. can pineapple chunks
    2 pkg. lemon Jell-O
    2 c. hot water
    2 c. Seven-Up
    2 bananas, sliced
    1 c. miniature marshmallows
    5 tbsp. flour
    ½ c. sugar
    Salt to taste
    2 beaten eggs
    1 c. cream, whipped or 1 pkg. Lucky
      Whip
    Nuts or grated cheese

Drain pineapple; reserve juice. Dissolve Jell-O in hot water. Cool. Add Seven-Up, pineapple chunks, bananas and marshmallows. Pour into 9 x 13-inch cake pan; place in refrigerator to set. Combine flour, sugar and salt in saucepan. Add enough water to reserved juice to make 1 cup liquid. Add juice and eggs to flour mixture; cook until thick. Cool. Fold in cream; spread over set Jell-O. Sprinkle with nuts. Refrigerate. Yield: 12 servings.

Gudrun Harstad, Sr. H.S.
Detroit Lakes, Minnesota

CHERRY-BERRY-CHEESE SALAD

    1 family-size pkg. cherry gelatin
    2 c. boiling water
    1 10-oz. pkg. frozen strawberries
    1 lge. can crushed pineapple, drained
    1 3-oz. pkg. cream cheese
    Mayonnaise
    ½ c. chopped pecans

(Continued on next page)

Molded Fruit Salads With Strawberries

Dissolve gelatin in boiling water; add frozen strawberries and pineapple. Pour half the mixture into 9 x 12-inch dish; chill until firm. Soften cream cheese with small amount mayonnaise; spread over congealed mixture. Sprinkle cheese with chopped pecans; pour in remaining gelatin mixture. Chill until firm. Cut into squares and serve on lettuce leaf. Yield: 8-10 servings.

Mrs. Sondra Allen, Hughes Springs Jr. H.S.
Hughes Springs, Texas

DELUXE STRAWBERRY-CREAM SALAD

    2 c. boiling water
    2 3-oz. pkg. strawberry gelatin
    2 10-oz. pkg. frozen sliced strawberries
    1 13 ½-oz. can crushed pineapple
    1 c. canned pears, diced
    1 ripe banana, diced
    1 c. sour cream

Add hot water to gelatin and dissolve; add frozen strawberries and stir occasionally until dissolved. Add fruits; stir well. Pour half the mixture into 8 x 8 x 2-inch pan; chill until firm. Spread evenly with sour cream. Pour on remaining gelatin mixture; chill until firm. Top each serving with spoonful sour cream if desired. Yield: 9 servings.

Freda Enoch, Shelby Sr. H.S.
Shelby, Ohio

FILLED STRAWBERRY SALAD

    1 6-oz. pkg. strawberry gelatin
    2 c. boiling water
    2 10-oz. boxes frozen strawberries
    3 bananas, mashed
    1 No. 303 can crushed pineapple
    1 12-oz. carton sour cream

Dissolve gelatin in boiling water; add frozen strawberries, bananas and pineapple. Pour half the mixture into 9 x 13 x 2-inch pan; chill until firm. Spread sour cream over congealed mixture; add remaining gelatin mixture. Refrigerate until firm. Yield: 18 servings.

Barbara Johnson, Otis H.S.
Otis, Colorado

MOLDED STRAWBERRY SALAD

    2 3-oz. pkg. strawberry gelatin
    2 c. hot water
    2 med. bananas, diced
    1 No. 2 can pineapple wedges and juice
    2 c. chopped pecans
    2 10-oz. pkg. frozen strawberries, thawed
    ½ pt. sour cream

Combine 1 package gelatin with 1 cup hot water; stir until dissolved. Chill until partially set. Mix remaining gelatin and water; cool at room temperature. Add half the bananas, pineapple wedges, pecans and strawberries to first mixture. Mix thoroughly; pour into 13 x 9 1/2 x 2-inch glass dish. Return mixture to refrigerator; chill until firm. Spread sour cream over congealed mixture. Add remaining fruit and nuts to second gelatin mixture; mix thoroughly. Pour over sour cream. Chill until firm. Yield: 12 servings.

Mrs. Elaine M. Free, Irving H.S.
Irving, Texas

STRAWBERRY-CREAM CHEESE SALAD

    1 pkg. raspberry gelatin
    1 c. boiling water
    1 pkg. frozen strawberries and juice
    1 can crushed pineapple, undrained
    1 sm. pkg. cream cheese
    ½ c. diced pecans

Mix gelatin with boiling water; add strawberries and pineapple. Refrigerate. Form cream cheese into small balls; roll each in diced pecans. Place cheese balls in individual molds; add thickened gelatin. Chill until firm. Yield: 6 servings.

Mrs. J. Ralph Kemp, Henry Grady H.S.
Atlanta, Georgia

STRAWBERRY AND CREAM SQUARES

    2 pkg. strawberry gelatin
    2 c. boiling water
    2 10-oz. pkg. frozen strawberries
    1 13 ½-oz. can crushed pineapple
    2 lge. ripe bananas, finely diced
    1 c. sour cream

Dissolve gelatin in boiling water; add berries, stirring occasionally until thawed. Add pineapple and bananas. Pour half the mixture into 8 x 8 x 2-inch pan; chill until firm. Spoon layer sour cream evenly over chilled gelatin; pour on remaining gelatin. Chill until firm. Cut into squares and serve on lettuce ruffles. Garnish each square with dollop of sour cream and whole strawberry split in half from top almost to bottom. Yield: 12 servings.

Mrs. Marjorie Ankney
Berlin-Brothersvalley Jt. Sch.
Berlin, Pennsylvania
Mrs. Murradell Travis
Stephen F. Austin Jr. H.S.
Garland, Texas
Nadine Kaiser, Hydro Public Sch.
Hydro, Oklahoma

STRAWBERRY-CREAM SUPREME

    3 3-oz. pkg. strawberry gelatin
    2 c. boiling water
    2 c. cold water
    2 10-oz. pkg. frozen strawberries,
       partially thawed
    3 ripe bananas, mashed
    1 6-oz. can crushed pineapple, drained
    ½ pt. sour cream, softened

Dissolve gelatin in boiling water; add cold water. Stir in strawberries until completely thawed; add bananas and pineapple. Pour half the mixture into moistened 8 x 12-inch pan; refrigerate until firm. Spread congealed mixture with sour cream; pour remaining gelatin mixture over sour cream. Chill for several hours or overnight. Cut into squares and serve on lettuce. Yield: 12 servings.

Sister M. John Vianney, SS.C.M., Andrean H.S.
Gary, Indiana

STRAWBERRY DELIGHT

    1 can crushed pineapple
    1 pkg. frozen strawberries
    1 pkg. strawberry gelatin
    1 pkg. Dream Whip, prepared
    1 c. miniature marshmallows

Drain juice from pineapple and strawberries; reserve 1 cup. Prepare gelatin according to directions on package, substituting reserved juice for cold water. Chill until firm; beat well. Fold in Dream Whip; add pineapple, marshmallows and strawberries. Pour into mold; chill until firm. Yield: 6-8 servings.

Mrs. Elizabeth Potts, Lott H.S.
Lott, Texas

STRAWBERRY JELL-O SALAD

    2 3-oz. boxes strawberry Jell-O
    1 ½ c. hot water
    1 10-oz. box frozen strawberries
    2 bananas, mashed
    1 No. 2 can crushed pineapple and juice
    ½ pt. sour cream

Dissolve Jell-O in hot water; add frozen berries. Add bananas and pineapple, mixing thoroughly. Divide mixture into 2 equal portions; place 1 portion in 13 1/2 x 9 1/2-inch dish or salad mold. Chill until firm. Spread evenly with sour cream. Add remaining portion Jell-O mixture; chill until firm. Yield: 16 servings.

Jane E. Lindeman, Jefferson Local Sch.
West Jefferson, Ohio

STRAWBERRY JELL-O SALAD

    1 lge. box strawberry Jell-O
    1 c. boiling water
    1 1 lb. 14-oz. can crushed pineapple
    2 bananas, mashed
    2 10-oz. boxes frozen strawberries,
       partially thawed
    ½ pt. sour cream

Dissolve Jell-O in boiling water; add crushed pineapple. Chill until partially set; add bananas and strawberries. Pour half the mixture into dish; chill until firm. Spread sour cream over congealed mixture; let set until partially firm. Add remaining Jell-O mixtures; chill until firm. Yield: 8-10 servings.

Mrs. Martha Wilson, St. Joseph Ogden H.S.
St. Joseph, Illinois

STRAWBERRY-NUT SALAD

    2 pkg. strawberry gelatin
    1 c. boiling water
    2 10-oz. pkg. frozen sliced strawberries,
       thawed
    2 ½ c. crushed pineapple, drained
    3 bananas, mashed
    1 c. chopped walnuts
    1 pt. sour cream

Dissolve gelatin in water; fold in fruits and nuts. Pour half the mixture in 12 x 8 x 2-inch dish; chill until set. Cover with sour cream. Gently spoon on remaining mixture; chill until firm. Yield: 12 servings.

Helen Phillips, Evergreen H.S.
Metamora, Ohio

STRAWBERRY-NUT SALAD

    1 family-size pkg. strawberry gelatin
    1 c. boiling water
    3 bananas, mashed
    2 10-oz. pkg. frozen strawberries
    1 sm. can crushed pineapple
    1 c. chopped nuts
    1 pt. sour cream

Combine gelatin and boiling water; stir until gelatin is dissolved. Fold in bananas, strawberries, pineapple and nuts. Pour half the mixture into 12 x 8 x 2-inch dish; refrigerate until firm. Spread sour cream evenly over congealed mixture; add remaining gelatin mixture. Refrigerate until firm; cut into squares and serve. Yield: 24 servings.

Mrs. Louise H. Griner, Baker H.S.
Columbus, Georgia

Molded Mixed Fruit Salads

STRAWBERRY SALAD

2 3-oz. pkg. strawberry gelatin
1 ½ c. boiling water
2 10-oz. pkg. frozen strawberries
1 c. crushed pineapple, drained
½ c. nuts, chopped
2 lge. bananas, mashed
1 c. sour cream

Dissolve gelatin in water. Combine remaining ingredients except sour cream; add to gelatin. Pour half the gelatin mixture into mold; chill until set. Spread sour cream evenly over firm gelatin; spoon in remaining gelatin. Chill. Yield: 12-15 servings.

Mrs. Anne Lennebacker
Cherry Valley Central Sch.
Cherry Valley, New York

STRAWBERRY SALAD

2 pkg. strawberry gelatin
2 ½ c. boiling water
1 lge. pkg. frozen strawberries
1 c. pineapple juice
2 bananas, mashed
1 No. 2 can pineapple tidbits
1 c. sour cream

Dissolve gelatin in boiling water; add frozen strawberries and pineapple juice. Chill until partially firm; add bananas and pineapple. Place 1/2 of the mixture in 7 1/2 x 11 1/2-inch pan; chill until firm. Add sour cream, spreading smoothly. Add remaining gelatin mixture; chill until firm. Yield: 12 servings.

Carol J. Henderson, Shelby Public Sch.
Shelby, Nebraska

STRAWBERRY SOUR CREAM SALAD

2 6-oz. pkg. strawberry gelatin
3 c. hot water
1 16-oz. pkg. frozen strawberries
1 8-oz. can crushed pineapple, undrained
2 c. cold water
3 lge. bananas, mashed
½ c. chopped walnuts
1 pt. sour cream

Dissolve gelatin in hot water; add frozen strawberries, stirring until dissolved. Add crushed pineapple and cold water. Pour half the mixture into 13 x 9 x 2-inch pan or 2 1-quart molds; cool. Add half the bananas and walnuts; refrigerate until firm. Spread sour cream evenly over congealed mixture; pour in remaining gelatin mixture. Add remaining bananas and walnuts; chill until firm. Cut into squares and serve on lettuce leaves. Yield: 16-20 servings.

Mary E. Steele, Central H.S.
Auburn, New York

STRAWBERRY-SOUR CREAM SALAD

2 boxes strawberry gelatin
2 c. boiling water
1 c. drained crushed pineapple
2 pkg. frozen strawberries
1 c. sour cream

Dissolve gelatin in hot water; add pineapple and strawberries. Pour half the mixture into bowl; chill until firm. Add sour cream over congealed mixture; add remaining gelatin mixture over sour cream. Chill until firm. Yield: 12 servings.

Mrs. Elden Brunet, Oakdale H.S.
Oakdale, Louisiana

SWEETHEART SALAD

1 6-oz. pkg. strawberry gelatin
2 ½ c. water
1 10-oz. pkg. frozen strawberries
1 c. crushed pineapple
1 c. chopped nuts (opt.)
1 pkg. Dream Whip
½ c. and 1 tbsp. milk
1 8-oz. pkg. cream cheese

Dissolve gelatin in water; let set until slightly firm. Add strawberries, pineapple and nuts; pour into 9 x 13-inch pan. Chill until firm. Combine Dream Whip, milk and cream cheese; place on chilled mixture. Refrigerate until serving time. Yield: 12 servings.

Mrs. Betty D. Pastorius, German Jr.-Sr. H.S.
McClellandtown, Pennsylvania

RUSSIAN SALAD

1 pkg. lime Jell-O
¾ c. boiling water
3 oz. cream cheese
24 sm. marshmallows
½ c. pineapple juice
½ c. milk
½ c. crushed pineapple
⅓ c. salad dressing
¾ c. diced bananas
1 tsp. lemon juice
1 c. nuts

Dissolve Jell-O in boiling water; add cream cheese and marshmallows. Place over heat in double boiler; stir until marshmallows are melted and mixture is smooth. Add pineapple juice and milk. Cool. Add pineapple, salad dressing, bananas, lemon juice and nuts. Chill until firm. Yield: 10-12 servings.

Mrs. Josephine P. Clark, Fairview H.S.
Fairview, Tennessee

Vegetable Salads

RECIPE FOR CAESAR SALAD ON PAGE 221

ARTICHOKE-ALMOND SALAD

4 c. salad greens, washed and torn into
bite-sized pieces
1 1-lb. can artichoke hearts, chilled
and drained
½ c. chopped salted almonds
3 scallions chopped, include some tops
½ c. salad oil
¼ c. red wine vinegar
¼ tsp. dry mustard
¼ tsp. salt
⅛ tsp. pepper
Pinch of sugar

Chill greens. Place in salad bowl with artichoke hearts, almonds and scallions. Combine remaining ingredients. Shake until well
blended. Pour enough dressing over salad mixture to coat leaves; toss well. Yield: 6 servings.

Mrs. Jewel Hoogstoel, Endwell Jr. H.S.
Endwell, New York

ARTICHOKE SALAD

½ lge. head lettuce
1 6-oz. jar marinated artichoke hearts
Salt to taste
Freshly ground pepper to taste
Italian salad dressing

Combine all ingredients, using enough dressing
to coat greens well. Yield: 4-6 servings.

Mrs. Peggy Wood, South Park H.S.
Beaumont, Texas

ARTICHOKES VINAIGRETTE

1 ⅓ c. Italian dressing
⅔ c. chopped dill pickle
⅔ c. chopped onion
⅔ c. chopped green pepper
2 tbsp. pimento
2 hard-cooked eggs, chopped
2 10-oz. pkg. frozen artichoke hearts,
cooked
Crisp lettuce

Combine dressing, pickle, onion, pepper, pimento and eggs. Marinate artichoke hearts in
dressing mixture. Chill until serving time. Serve
on crisp lettuce. Yield: 8-10 servings.

Sande J. Speck, Watertown Sr. H.S.
Watertown, Minnesota

BEAN SALAD

1 can beans
1 sm. can pimento, cut into sm. pieces
½ c. celery
½ c. onion
⅓ c. salad oil
⅔ c. vinegar
¾ c. sugar

Combine all ingredients; chill for 24 hours
before serving. Yield: 6-8 servings.

Sarah Elizabeth Yarbrough, Hawkins Jr. Sr. HS
Hattiesburg, Mississippi

BEAN SALAD

1 can cut wax beans, drained
1 can green beans, drained
1 can kidney beans, drained
1 med. onion, chopped
¾ c. vinegar
¼ c. sugar
1 tsp. salt
½ tsp. pepper
1 sm. bottle stuffed olives
½ c. salad oil

Combine beans and onion. Heat vinegar and
sugar; pour over bean mixture. Add salt, pepper, olives and salad oil. Chill in refrigerator
for 24 hours. Serve on lettuce. Yield: 12 servings.

Oleta Hayden, Milford H.S.
Milford, Texas

BEAN SALAD

⅔ c. vinegar
1 c. sugar
⅓ c. salad oil
1 can green beans
1 can yellow wax beans
1 can kidney beans
1 green pepper, diced
1 tbsp. minced onion
¼ c. olives, diced

Combine all ingredients; let stand overnight in
refrigerator. Drain well before serving. Yield:
12 servings.

Oleta Hayden, Milford H.S.
Milford, Texas

BEAN SALAD

1 No. 303 can green beans, drained
1 No. 303 can wax beans, drained
1 No. 303 can red kidney beans, drained
½ c. onion, minced
½ c. green pepper, minced
½ c. salad oil
½ c. cider or plain vinegar
¾ c. sugar
½ tsp. pepper
1 tsp. salt

Mix first 5 ingredients; set aside. Mix remaining ingredients; heat until sugar is dissolved.

(Continued on next page)

Cool slightly; pour over vegetable mixture. Marinate overnight or longer. Yield: 8 servings.

Mrs. Guy Mitchell, Chataigneir H.S.
Chataigneir, Louisiana
Mrs. Ruth Severson, Huntley H.S.
Huntley, Illinois

BEAN SALAD

   1 can green beans
   1 can lima beans
   1 can wax beans
   1 can kidney beans
   1 can chick peas
   1 lge. onion, sliced
   1 c. celery, sliced
   1 green pepper, sliced
   1 1/4 c. sugar
   1 1/4 c. vinegar
   1 1/4 c. water

Drain canned vegetables well; combine. Add onion, celery and green pepper. Combine sugar, vinegar and water; beat until sugar dissolves. Cool; toss with vegetable mixture. Let stand overnight. Yield: 25 servings.

Mrs. Pauline Camp, Hunter Jr. H.S.
Detroit, Michigan

DIETETIC FIVE-BEAN SALAD

   1 c. green onions, chopped
   1 c. celery, chopped
   1 1/2 c. sugar or 3 tbsp. Sucaryl
   1 c. vinegar
   1/4 c. oil
   Salt and pepper to taste
   1 No. 303 can green beans, drained
   1 No. 303 can yellow beans, drained
   1 No. 303 can lima beans, drained
   1 No. 303 can kidney beans, drained
   1 No. 303 can chick peas, drained

Combine all ingredients in large bowl; cover. Chill 5 to 6 hours or overnight. Salad will keep several days. Flavor improves if prepared 24 hours before serving. Yield: 20-25 servings.

Mrs. Ruth Tompkins, Fitzgerald H.S.
Warren, Michigan

EASY PICKLED GREEN BEANS

   1 can green beans, drained
   Sweet pickle juice to cover

Cover beans with pickle juice in jar or other tightly covered container. Refrigerate at least 24 hours before serving. Keeps well indefinitely. Fresh onion rings may be substituted for, or combined with green beans.

Janet White Stafford, Hanover Comm. H.S.
Hanover, Illinois

GREEN BEAN SALAD

   1 No. 2 can green whole beans
   1/4 tsp. salt
   1/4 c. chopped pimento
   1 c. French dressing

Drain green beans; sprinkle salt and chopped pimento over beans. Pour French dressing over beans. Let stand for 20 minutes. Yield: 4 servings.

Mrs. Ruby Tepher, Booker T. Washington Sch.
Houston, Texas

GREEN BEAN SALAD
MEDITERRANEAN

   1 9-oz. pkg. frozen French-cut green
     beans, thawed
   1 med. onion, thinly sliced and separated
     into rings
   1 3-oz. can broiled sliced mushrooms,
     drained
   1/3 c. Italian salad dressing
   1/4 tsp. salt
   Dash of freshly ground pepper
   2 med. tomatoes, cut into wedges

Pour boiling water over beans; let stand about 5 minutes. Drain thoroughly; place in salad bowl with onion rings and mushrooms. Combine salad dressing, salt, and pepper. Add to bean mixture; toss. Marinate in refrigerator at least 2 hours, tossing occasionally. Arrange tomato wedges on salad just before serving. Top with bacon bits before serving for added flavor. Yield: 4-6 servings.

Thelma P. Peoples, E. A. Poe Intermediate Sch.
Annandale, Virginia

GREEN BEANS WITH
TANGY DRESSING

   1/2 tsp. finely cut garlic
   3/4 tsp. salt
   2 tbsp. wine vinegar
   3 tbsp. salad oil
   Dash of pepper
   1 can cut green beans, drained and
     chilled
   1/4 c. thinly sliced onion

Place garlic on waxed paper; add salt. Mash with flat side of knife until well blended. Place jar with vinegar oil and pepper; cover. Shake well and chill. Combine beans and onions. Shake dressing well; add to bean mixture. Place on bed of lettuce. Will keep well in refrigerator for several days. Yield: 4-5 servings.

Mrs. Mary Esther Rowe, Swartz Creek H.S.
Swartz Creek, Michigan

PICKLED GREEN BEANS

2 cans French-style green beans
2 med. onions, sliced thin
½ c. water
1 c. sugar
¼ c. salad oil
Garlic to taste
1 c. apple cider vinegar

Layer beans and onions in casserole. Combine remaining ingredients; pour over bean mixture. Cover; place in refrigerator overnight. Pour off sauce before serving. Yield: 8 servings.

Margrett J. Hughey, Eustace H.S.
Eustace, Texas

TOMATO-BEAN COMBO

½ c. sour cream
¼ c. Italian salad dressing
1 1-lb. can cut green beans, drained
2 med. tomatoes, cut into wedges
¼ c. finely chopped onion

Combine sour cream and Italian dressing thoroughly. Add beans, tomatoes, onions; mix well. Chill 2 to 3 hours. Yield: 6 servings.

Mrs. Billie Nowlin, Rising Star H.S.
Rising Star, Texas
Beulah G. Mounger, Morganza H.S.
Morganza, Louisiana
Mrs. Lee Iris Britton, Buhler H.S.
Hutchinson, Kansas

JIFFY BEAN SALAD

1 can drained kidney beans
1 can drained wax beans
1 can drained Blue Lake cut green beans
1 med. onion, sliced into rings
½ bottle oil and vinegar dressing

Combine all ingredients at least 4 hours before serving. Salad keeps well in refrigerator for several days.

Rita Rummelsburg, South Side Jr. H.S.
Rockville Centre, New York

KIDNEY BEAN SALAD

¼ c. vinegar
3 tbsp. olive oil
¼ tsp. oregano
¼ tsp. salt
1 fresh onion, chopped
¼ c. chopped celery
1 can kidney beans, drained

Combine all ingredients except beans; add to beans. Chill.

Madeline M. Thomas, Appomattox H.S.
Appomattox, Virginia

KIDNEY BEAN SALAD

2 c. drained cooked kidney beans
¼ c. sliced celery
¼ c. diced green pepper
¼ c. diced onion, white or green
¼ c. mayonnaise thinned with sm. amount
    of lemon juice
¼ c. diced cucumber
¼ c. grated carrot
2 hard-cooked eggs, diced
1 tsp. salt

Mix all ingredients lightly in bowl; chill thoroughly. Serve on salad greens. Yield: 4-6 servings.

Mrs. Myra Garrison, Nebraska Sch. for the Deaf
Omaha, Nebraska

MARINATED BEAN SALAD

1 1-lb. can cut green beans, drained
1 1-lb. can wax beans, drained
1 1-lb. can kidney beans, drained
½ c. chopped green pepper
½ c. onion rings
¾ c. sugar
⅓ c. Italian dressing
⅔ c. vinegar
1 tsp. pepper
1 tsp. salt

Combine beans, green pepper and onion rings. Combine remaining ingredients; pour over bean mixture. Refrigerate overnight in glass bowl. Pour off liquid just before serving. Yield: 10-12 servings.

Pearl Robinson, Ahrens Trade H.S.
Louisville, Kentucky

SPICY BEAN SALAD

1 14-oz. can green beans
1 14-oz. can yellow wax beans
1 can kidney beans
1 Bermuda onion, sliced into rings
Chopped parsley
1 green pepper, chopped
½ c. white sugar
½ c. salad oil
½ c. vinegar
½ tsp. celery seed
½ tsp. dillseed

Combine beans, onion, small amount of parsley and green pepper. Combine sugar, oil, vinegar and seasoning; pour over bean mixture. Let stand overnight; drain. Serve on lettuce. Garnish with hard-cooked egg slices. Yield: 6-8 servings.

Mrs. N. S. Thomson, St. Mary's Sch.
Lethbridge, Alberta, Canada

SWEET-SOUR BEAN SALAD

1 can yellow wax beans
1 can green beans
1 can kidney beans
1 c. sugar
¾ c. vinegar
¾ c. salad oil
2 tsp. salt
1 c. green pepper, diced
1 c. diced onion
Dash of pepper

Drain beans well. Mix all ingredients. Marinate 5 to 6 hours, preferably overnight. Drain before serving. Dressing can be used again, if refrigerated.

Mrs. Charlotte Hunt, J. Watson Bailey
Kingston, New York

THREE-BEAN SALAD

1 No. 2 can wax beans
1 No. 2 can red kidney beans
1 No. 2 can green beans
1 lge. white onion, cut into rings
⅓ c. salad oil
¾ c. white vinegar
¾ c. sugar
1 tsp. salt
1 tsp. pepper

Drain beans well; mix with onion rings. Combine oil, vinegar, sugar, salt and pepper; pour over bean mixture. Marinate in refrigerator overnight. Yield: 6 servings.

Alice B. Carlton, Madison Jr. H.S.
Tampa, Florida

WAX BEAN SALAD BOWL

2 10-oz. pkg. frozen French-style wax beans
1 tbsp. minced onion
1 tsp. salt
2 tbsp. salad oil
1 tbsp. sugar
¼ c. wine vinegar
¼ c. cold water
⅛ tsp. pepper
Red onion slices

Cook beans according to directions on package; do not overcook. Drain and cool. Combine remaining ingredients, reserving onion slices for garnish; toss lightly with beans. Chill 5 to 6 hours. Arrange in lettuce-lined bowl; top with slices of red onion. Yield: 6 servings.

Mrs. Miriam B. Templeton, Hickory Tavern H.S.
Gray Court, South Carolina

BELGIAN ENDIVE SALAD

4 heads endive
4 tbsp. olive oil
1 tbsp. wine vinegar
½ tsp. salt
⅛ tsp. freshly ground pepper
Dijon mustard

Break leaves from endive. Wash in cold water; shake out. Dry thoroughly in clean towel. Refrigerate until ready to use. Combine remaining ingredients. Place leaves in wooden salad bowl. Season with dressing immediately before serving. Toss gently until leaves are shiny and coated with dressing. Yield: 4 servings.

Betty Berk, Othello H.S.
Othello, Washington

CAESAR SALAD

½ c. plus 2 tbsp. salad oil
1 garlic clove, minced
2 c. bread cubes
1 lge. head romaine, chilled
1 lge. head lettuce, chilled
¼ c. grated Parmesan cheese
¼ c. crumbled bleu cheese
¼ c. lemon juice
¼ tsp. Tabasco sauce
¾ tsp. salt
¼ tsp. dry mustard
1 egg

Heat 2 tablespoons oil in skillet with garlic. Add bread cubes and heat until lightly browned. Remove. Tear romaine and lettuce into bite-sized pieces into salad bowl. Sprinkle with cheese. Combine remaining salad oil, lemon juice, Tabasco, salt and dry mustard; beat or shake to blend. Pour over salad greens; toss lightly. Break raw egg into greens; toss lightly until egg particles disappear. Add croutons; toss. Yield: 6 servings.

Photograph for this recipe on page 217.

CAESAR SALAD

3 to 4 peeled cloves of garlic
1 c. olive oil
4 heads crisp romaine lettuce
½ c. salad oil
1 tbsp. Worcestershire sauce
Salt and pepper to taste
¾ to 1 c. grated Romanello or other hard cheese
1 raw egg
Juice and pulp of 3 lemons

Chop garlic; add to olive oil and cover for 3 to 4 hours. Tear lettuce into large salad bowl; add 1/4 cup garlic-olive oil and salad oil. Sprinkle with Worcestershire sauce, salt, pepper and cheese. Break egg into greens; sprinkle lemon

(Continued on next page)

juice and pulp over all ingredients. Toss and mix thoroughly until no trace of egg is left. Add croutons; toss lightly and serve. Croutons may be dipped into garlic-flavored oil before adding to salad. Yield: 8 servings.

Mary Fitch, Summerland Secondary Sch.
Summerland, B.C., Canada

CAESAR SALAD

    3 or 4 cloves of garlic
    1 c. olive oil
    2 c. crisp croutons
    ½ c. unseasoned salad oil
    ½ c. Parmesan cheese, grated
    ¼ c. blue cheese, broken
    3 qt. salad greens
    1 tbsp. Worcestershire sauce
    ½ tsp. dry mustard
    Salt and pepper to taste
    2 hard-cooked eggs, chopped
    ½ c. fresh lemon juice

Cut garlic into olive oil. Let stand several hours at room temperature. Prepare croutons by placing tiny bread cubes in slow oven until browned; set aside. Pour unseasoned salad oil, Parmesan cheese and blue cheese over salad greens; add Worcestershire sauce, mustard, salt and pepper. Scatter eggs over greens and add lemon juice. Toss thoroughly so salad greens are combined with other ingredients. Dip croutons into garlic-flavored oil. Toss with salad and serve at once, while croutons are crunchy. Yield: 6-8 servings.

Mrs. Mary Lowe Perkins, A. T. Johnson H.S.
Montross, Virginia

TRULY CAESAR SALAD AND DRESSING

    1 lge. head romaine or iceberg lettuce, cut
    6 radishes, sliced thinly
    1 sm. cucumber, cubed
    ½ c. cheddar cheese croutons
    ½ c. cubed sharp cheddar cheese

Place all ingredients in chilled salad bowl. Toss lightly.

TRULY CAESAR DRESSING:

    Juice of 1 ½ lemons
    ¼ c. olive oil
    ½ tsp. pepper
    1 tsp. Worcestershire sauce
    ½ tsp. salt
    ½ tsp. garlic powder
    1 beaten egg
    ½ c. grated Parmesan cheese

Place all ingredients in jar; cover and shake well. Pour over salad at serving time and toss

lightly. Add cheddar cheese croutons. Serve cold over salad. Yield: 6 servings.

Mrs. Gertrude Wilson, Nahant Jr. H.S.
Nahant, Massachusetts

CABBAGE-BELL PEPPER SALAD

    2 c. shredded cabbage
    ⅔ c. chopped green peppers
    2 hard-cooked eggs, yolks and whites chopped separately
    ¼ tsp. salt
    ¼ tsp. garlic salt
    ¼ c. finely chopped onion
    4 tbsp. mayonnaise

Mix cabbage, peppers and onions together. Mix egg yolks and seasonings with mayonnaise. Add egg whites to cabbage mixture; add mayonnaise mixture and blend. Serve cold. Yield: 6-8 servings.

Frances Y. Wise, Quitaque H.S.
Quitaque, Texas

CABBAGE WITH COTTAGE CHEESE DRESSING

    2 c. finely sliced cabbage
    ½ c. chopped celery (opt.)
    ½ c. cottage cheese
    ½ c. salad dressing

Mix cabbage and celery. Blend cottage cheese and salad dressing; add to cabbage mixture. Mix until dressing is well distributed. Serve in bowls or on lettuce. Yield: 4 servings.

Mrs. Laura Anderson, Sutherlin H.S.
Sutherlin, Oregon

PICCADILLY CIRCUS SALAD

    ½ tsp. dried dillweed
    ¼ tsp. salt
    Dash of pepper
    ¼ tsp. dry mustard
    2 tbsp. vinegar
    ¼ c. salad oil
    ¼ c. evaporated milk
    2 ½ to 3 c. finely cut cabbage
    4 med. tomatoes, peeled and chilled
    4 lettuce leaves

Measure seasonings, vinegar, salad oil and evaporated milk into small jar with tight lid. Cover tightly; shake until dressing is creamy and smooth. Pour over cabbage in bowl; mix lightly. Cover and chill. Core tomatoes when ready to serve; place core side down on cutting board. Cut tomato through almost to bottom in 6 or 8 sections. Place tomato on lettuce leaf on each salad plate. Spread sections apart; fill with dill coleslaw. Yield: 4 servings.

Requa K. Spears, Mullins H.S.
Pikeville, Kentucky

DIET SAUERKRAUT SALAD

2 c. sauerkraut, drained
½ c. diced green pepper
1 c. diced celery
½ c. chopped onion
Red pepper for color, if desired
Artificial sweetener equal to 1 c. sugar
2 tbsp. cooking oil
¼ c. vinegar
¼ tsp. salt

Mix all ingredients together; chill before serving. Salad keeps well for several days in the refrigerator. Yield: 10 servings.

Gudrun Harstad, Sr. H.S.
Detroit Lakes, Minnesota

HOT KRAUT SALAD

5 slices bacon
1 bunch green onions, sliced
1 lge. green pepper, diced
1 No. 2 ½ can sauerkraut, drained
1 sm. can tomatoes with green chilies

Fry bacon until crisp; remove from pan. Saute onions and green pepper in bacon fat. Combine sauerkraut and tomatoes with green chilies; add onions and pepper to sauerkraut mixture. Mix well. Place in serving dish; garnish with crumbled bacon. Yield: 4 servings.

Sue Kidd, Crockett Jr. H.S.
Odessa, Texas

KRAUT SALAD

1 No. 303 can sauerkraut
1 med. onion, finely sliced
1 sm. can pimento
2 c. celery, chopped
½ c. sugar

Cut up sauerkraut with kitchen scissors. Add remaining ingredients; mix well. Let stand at least 2 hours in refrigerator. Salad keeps well in refrigerator for several days. Yield: 6 servings.

Mary Ann Van Leeuwen, Fredonia Jr. H.S.
Fredonia, Kansas

SAUERKRAUT SALAD

1 lge. can kraut, drained well
1 c. diced celery
1 c. diced green pepper
1 lge. onion, diced
½ c. vinegar
½ c. salad oil
1 ¼ c. sugar

Combine all ingredients; mix well. Let stand for 1 hour. Salad may be kept in refrigerator several days. Yield: 8-10 servings.

Mrs. Ann W. Stewart, McClain H.S.
Greenfield, Ohio

SAUERKRAUT SALAD

1 No. 2 can sauerkraut
½ c. chopped onions
½ c. chopped celery
½ c. green peppers
1 c. sugar
¼ c. vinegar

Drain sauerkraut well; rinse several times. Add onions, celery and green pepper. Blend sugar and vinegar; pour over the sauerkraut mixture. Salad keeps well in refrigerator. Recipe may be doubled. Yield: 6-8 servings.

Mrs. Beverly Haas, Elgin H.S.
Elgin, North Dakota
Mrs. Vera Joyner Shaddix
Leverett's Chapel ISD Sch.
Overton, Texas

SAUERKRAUT SALAD

1 No. 2 ½ can sauerkraut
1 c. finely chopped celery
1 sm. onion, grated
1 chopped green pepper
1 chopped pimento
¾ c. sugar

Drain sauerkraut. Add all remaining ingredients to sauerkraut; mix lightly. Refrigerate for 24 hours before serving. Salad will keep 2 weeks, if refrigerated. Yield: 8 servings.

Mrs. Merle Twesme, Arcadia H.S.
Arcadia, Wisconsin

SOUTHERN RELISH SALAD

1 No. 2 ½ can sauerkraut
1 c. celery, chopped fine
1 onion, minced
1 green pepper, chopped
1 sm. can pimento, chopped
1 ¼ c. salad oil
1 ⅓ c. vinegar
1 ½ c. sugar

Wash and rinse sauerkraut; drain well. Combine chopped ingredients; add sauerkraut. Mix oil, vinegar and sugar until sugar is dissolved;

223

(Continued on next page)

pour over vegetable mixture. Let stand in refrigerator several hours before serving. Salad keeps well in refrigerator, well covered, for several days. Yield: 8 servings.

Louise S. Barton, Herrin H.S.
Herrin, Illinois

SEVEN-DAY SALAD

    2 lb. cabbage, shredded
    ½ c. chopped green peppers
    ½ c. chopped green onions
    1 c. sugar
    1 tsp. salt
    ½ c. salad oil
    ½ c. vinegar
    1 tsp. celery seed

Combine cabbage, peppers and onions; sprinkle with sugar and salt. Let stand for 1 hour; drain off some of liquid. Combine oil, vinegar and celery seed; pour over cabbage mixture. Small jar of pimento may be added for color, if desired.

Mrs. Freda Brisman, Commerce H.S.
Commerce, Oklahoma

CARROT COLESLAW

    2 c. finely chopped cabbage
    2 c. shredded carrots
    2 tsp. minced onion
    ¼ c. chopped green pepper
    1 tsp. salt
    ¼ tsp. pepper
    ¾ c. sour cream
    2 tbsp. vinegar
    1 tbsp. sugar
    ¼ c. cream cheese

Combine cabbage, carrots, onion, green pepper, salt and pepper in separate bowl; blend together remaining ingredients. Toss sour cream mixture with cabbage mixture. Chill and serve. Yield: 6 servings.

Mrs. Paula Disterhaupt, Glenwood Sr. H.S.
Glenwood, Iowa

CABBAGE-PEPPER SLAW

    4 c. shredded cabbage
    ½ c. chopped green pepper
    1 tsp. salt
    ⅛ tsp. white pepper
    2 tbsp. sugar
    1 tsp. celery seed
    2 tbsp. tarragon vinegar
    1 tsp. prepared mustard
    ½ c. salad dressing

Combine vegetables, salt, pepper, sugar and celery seed. Combine vinegar, mustard and salad dressing; add to vegetable mixture. Mix thoroughly. Yield: 6 servings.

Laura Howell, Ashley Township H.S.
Ashley, Illinois
Mrs. Charlene Hyde, Senatobia City Sch.
Senatobia, Mississippi
Mrs. James D. Wolf, Leigh H.S.
San Jose, California

CABBAGE SLAW AND DRESSING

    1 lge. head cabbage, shredded
    1 lge. onion, chopped fine
    6 stalks celery, cut into sm. pieces
    1 lge. green pepper, shredded (opt.)
    1 tsp. mustard seed
    1 tsp. celery seed
    2 c. white sugar
    1 tsp. salt
    ½ c. vinegar
    Green food coloring to taste

Combine vegetables; add mustard and celery seeds. Combine remaining ingredients thoroughly; pour over cabbage mixture. Place salad in glass or plastic container. Salad will keep fresh for several weeks in refrigerator. Yield: 10-15 servings.

Mrs. Helen Knudson, Lyle H.S.
Lyle, Minnesota

CALICO COLESLAW

    ¾ c. mayonnaise
    2 tbsp. grated onion
    ½ tsp. salt
    4 tbsp. sugar
    2 tbsp. vinegar
    ½ tsp. pepper
    ½ tsp. celery seed
    1 med. head white cabbage, shredded
    1 c. red cabbage, shredded
    ½ c. celery, diced
    ½ c. carrots, shredded

Combine mayonnaise, onion, salt, sugar, vinegar, pepper and celery seed. Cover; refrigerate until serving time. Combine cabbage, celery and carrots; add enough mayonnaise mixture to coat. Yield: 8 servings.

Mrs. Loretta Stock, Murdock Consolidated H.S.
Murdock, Nebraska

COLESLAW

    1 med. head cabbage
    2 med. onions
    1 green pepper

224

(Continued on next page)

¾ c. sugar
½ c. salad oil
½ c. apple cider vinegar
1 tsp. celery seed
1 tsp. dry mustard
1 tbsp. sugar
1 tbsp. salt

Grind cabbage, onions and pepper together. Cover with sugar; set aside. Mix oil, vinegar, celery seed, mustard, salt and sugar; bring to a boil. Pour over slaw while hot. Chill for 6 hours before serving. Yield: 8 servings.

Jane Ellison, Penelope H.S.
Penelope, Texas

COOKED CABBAGE SLAW

1 med. head cabbage, chopped or grated
1 tsp. salt
1 tsp. sugar
2 tbsp. melted lard or meat drippings
1 tbsp. butter
1 c. sweet or sour cream
1 tbsp. (or more) vinegar

Place cabbage in cooker with salt, sugar, lard and small amount of water; cook until tender. Drain; add butter. Remove from heat; add cream and vinegar. Yield: 6-8 servings.

Mrs. Norma Womble, Broadway H.S.
Broadway, North Carolina

COLESLAW WITH BACON DRESSING

4 slices bacon, cut into ½-in. pieces
1 sm. onion, finely chopped
1 tsp. salt
1 tsp. sugar
1 tsp. celery seed
2 tbsp. vinegar
¼ c. mayonnaise
1 sm. head cabbage, shredded
¼ c. chopped pimento
1 green pepper, finely chopped

Cook bacon with onion in heavy skillet; add salt, sugar, celery seed, vinegar and mayonnaise. Stir well. Combine cabbage, pimento and green pepper in bowl; add hot mixture. Mix lightly. Serve at once or chill and serve cold. Yield: 4 servings.

Carolyn Wayman, Mooreland H.S.
Mooreland, Oklahoma

DILLED CABBAGE SLAW

3 c. coarsely chopped cabbage
1 med. carrot
1 sm. onion
Juice from dill pickles

Combine all ingredients in blender container; cover vegetables with pickle juice. Shred in blender until as fine as desired. Drain off excess liquid. Yield: 4-6 servings.

Mrs. Laurena Ward, Ashford H.S.
Ashford, Alabama

CONVENIENT COLESLAW

1 med. head cabbage, shredded
1 med. onion, shredded
1 sm. green pepper, chopped
1 tsp. (heaping) salt
1 ½ c. boiling water
1 c. vinegar
1 c. sugar
1 tsp. mustard seed
1 tsp. celery seed
½ sm. can pimento

Mix vegetables with salt in large bowl; pour boiling water over mixture. Cover; let stand 1 hour. Squeeze moisture from cabbage mixture; mix in remaining ingredients. Chill before serving. Salad will keep 2 to 3 weeks in refrigerator. Yield: 8-10 servings.

Mrs. Rosemary Patton, Rosiclare H.S.
Rosiclare, Illinois

EASY SLAW

1 head cabbage, shredded
1 onion, sliced and separated into rings
½ green pepper, cut into strips
¼ c. vinegar
¼ c. salad oil
¼ c. sugar

Combine vegetables. Mix vinegar, oil and sugar; pour over vegetables, mixing well. Refrigerate 3 hours or longer before serving. Yield: 8-10 servings.

Mrs. Joyce Kaplan, Drew H.S.
Drew, Mississippi

Coleslaw

GERMAN SLAW

1 lge. head cabbage, shredded into long
   strips
1 lge. onion, sliced thin
¾ c. plus 2 tbsp. sugar
1 c. vinegar
¾ c. salad oil
1 tbsp. salt
1 tsp. celery seed
1 tsp. dry mustard
2 tsp. sugar

Mix cabbage, onion and sugar; let stand 5 to 10 minutes. Mix remaining ingredients; bring to a boil. Pour over cabbage mixture; place in container with tight lid. Store in refrigerator for 24 hours. Yield: 12-15 servings.

Dorothy Jarrett, Keota H.S.
Keota, Oklahoma

GREEN COLESLAW

2 c. finely shredded cabbage
½ c. chopped fresh parsley or ¼ c.
   parsley flakes
½ c. chopped onion or chives
Chopped green pepper (opt.)
1 tsp. salt
2 tbsp. salad oil
3 tbsp. red wine vinegar
½ tsp. celery seed
3 tbsp. sugar

Combine vegetables. Combine remaining ingredients; mix well. Toss vegetables with dressing mixture just before serving. Garnish with green pepper rings and thinly sliced radishes, if desired. Yield: 6 servings.

Mrs. Joan Nayes, Jamestown Jr. H.S.
Jamestown, North Dakota

PENNSYLVANIA-DUTCH HOT CABBAGE SLAW

6 slices bacon
2 tbsp. flour
⅓ c. sugar
½ tsp. salt
⅛ tsp. pepper
1 tsp. mustard, dry
1 egg, beaten
1 ½ c. milk
2 tbsp. vinegar
2 ½ to 3 c. cabbage, finely shredded

Fry bacon until crisp; remove from pan. Mix flour and sugar with seasonings; add to bacon fat. Mix egg with milk; add to flour mixture. Cook until thick; stir in vinegar. Remove from heat; mix with cabbage. Sprinkle crumbled bacon over top; serve hot. Yield: 6 servings.

Carol Lammert, Calvert Sr. H.S.
Prince Frederick, Maryland

GLORIFIED CABBAGE SLAW

3 c. shredded, crisp cabbage
3 med. carrots, shredded
⅔ c. shredded or flake coconut
½ tsp. salt
½ c. (about) mayonnaise with 1 tbsp.
   sugar added

Place cabbage, carrots, coconut and salt in mixing bowl; mix well. Add mayonnaise mixture; toss well. Serve. Yield: 6 servings.

Sister M. Constancea, O.S.B., LeBlond H.S.
St. Joseph, Missouri

PEANUT CRUNCH SLAW

4 c. shredded cabbage
1 c. finely cut celery
½ c. sour cream
½ c. mayonnaise
1 tsp. salt
¼ c. chopped green onions
¼ c. chopped green peppers
½ c. chopped cucumber
1 tbsp. butter
½ c. salted peanuts, chopped
2 tbsp. Parmesan cheese

Toss cabbage and celery together; chill. Mix sour cream, mayonnaise, salt, onions, green peppers and cucumber; chill. Melt butter in small skillet just before serving; add peanuts and heat until lightly browned. Immediately stir in cheese. Toss chilled vegetables with mayonnaise mixture. Sprinkle peanut mixture on top. Yield: 6-8 servings.

Mrs. Marvin Henning, Glasco H.S.
Glasco, Kansas

REFRIGERATOR COLESLAW

1 lge. head cabbage, chopped fine
1 onion, chopped fine
3 to 4 stalks celery, chopped fine
1 green pepper, chopped fine
1 c. vinegar
1 c. sugar
1 tsp. turmeric
¼ tsp. salt
1 tsp. mustard seed

Combine cabbage, onion, celery and pepper. Combine vinegar, sugar, turmeric, salt and mustard seed; simmer for 5 minutes. Remove from heat; pour over cabbage mixture. Stir. Refrigerate for 3 hours before serving. Mixture may be kept for 1 week, refrigerated. Yield: 12-15 servings.

Barbara D. Ayers, Phil Campbell H.S.
Phil Campbell, Alabama

SOUTHERN SLAW

1 ½ c. shredded cabbage
2 tbsp. grated carrots
½ tsp. garlic salt
½ c. salad dressing
3 tbsp. sugar
1 tbsp. cream or milk

Place cabbage and carrots in bowl. Sprinkle with garlic salt; let stand 5 minutes. Blend salad dressing, sugar and cream together. Pour salad dressing mixture over cabbage mixture; mix well. Refrigerate until serving time. Do not keep in refrigerator more than 24 hours. Yield: 4 servings.

Mrs. Linda Cherry, Griggsville H.S.
Griggsville, Illinois

TWENTY-FOUR HOUR SLAW

2 c. sugar
2 c. water
2 c. white vinegar
2 tbsp. mustard seed
1 tsp. salt
3 lb. grated cabbage
1 med. onion, finely chopped
1 sm. can pimento, chopped
1 med. green pepper, chopped

Heat sugar, water, vinegar, mustard seed and salt to boiling; set aside to cool. Place cabbage, onion, pimento and green pepper into gallon jar; pour cooled liquid over mixture. Cover and refrigerate. Salad may be kept several days or weeks in refrigerator. Do not substitute for white vinegar in recipe or ingredients will be discolored. Yield: 25 servings.

Jean M. Bonknight, Clinton H.S.
Clinton, South Carolina

WINTER VEGETABLE SALAD

1 c. shredded cabbage
½ c. diced celery
1 tsp. scraped onion
Salt and pepper to taste
½ tsp. sugar
1 c. well-drained canned tomatoes, chopped
1 tbsp. vinegar
3 tbsp. salad oil

Combine cabbage, celery, onion, salt, pepper, sugar and tomatoes. Sprinkle with vinegar and salad oil; toss lightly. Chill before serving. Yield: 4 servings.

Mrs. Betty J. Jones, Les Cheneaux Comm. Schs.
Cedarville, Michigan

CARROT AND COTTAGE CHEESE SALAD

6 med. carrots
4 tbsp. lemon juice
1 tsp. garlic salt
1 tsp. onion salt
1 pt. cottage cheese
4 tbsp. mayonnaise

Grate carrots into large mixing bowl. Sprinkle with lemon juice; stir in seasonings. Blend in cottage cheese. Heap on lettuce leaf or garnish in salad bowl. Yield: 6 servings.

Mrs. Ronnie Watson, Johnston Jr. H.S.
Houston, Texas

GYPSY SALAD

2 lge. carrots, grated
2 tbsp. hamburger relish
1 tbsp. mayonnaise
Salt and pepper to taste

Combine all ingredients; serve on bed of lettuce. Yield: 3 servings.

Mrs. Helen E. Stanford, Union H.S.
Union, Oregon

CARTWHEEL SALAD

1 c. soft pimento cheese
6 to 8 olives, chopped
¼ c. chopped nuts
3 med. green peppers, stem and seeds removed
¼ c. French dressing
6 to 8 lettuce leaves

Mix cheese, olives and nuts together; stuff peppers with cheese mixture. Chill. Slice stuffed peppers into thin sections; serve with French dressing on lettuce. Yield: 6-8 servings.

Mrs. Ina C. Hooper, Elizabeth H.S.
Elizabeth, Louisiana

CAULIFLOWER BERMUDA SALAD BOWL

1 head cauliflower
4 med.-sized tomatoes
1 med.-sized head lettuce
1 c. mild cheddar cheese, grated
1 c. French dressing

Separate cauliflower into flowerets; slice thinly crosswise. Add tomatoes and lettuce in bite-sized pieces. Add cheese. Pour dressing over; toss lightly. Yield: 12-15 servings.

Mrs. Ruby K. Halbert, Ranger H.S.
Ranger, Texas

CHRISTMAS SALAD VINAIGRETTE

1 c. oil
⅓ c. cider vinegar
1½ tsp. sugar
1 tsp. salt
½ tsp. garlic salt
2 tbsp. minced green onion
2 tbsp. minced green pepper
2 tbsp. parsley
⅛ tsp. cayenne pepper
4 c. cooked Brussels sprouts
1 c. halved cherry tomatoes
Romaine lettuce

Combine first 9 ingredients; mix well. Chill Brussels sprouts and tomatoes in marinade for at least 1 hour, stirring several times. Spoon sprouts into serving bowl; mound tomatoes in center. Arrange romaine lettuce around edges. Yield: 4-6 servings.

Judith Wright, Humboldt H.S.
St. Paul, Minnesota

COMBINATION VEGETABLE SALAD

½ head lettuce, chopped
1 tbsp. minced onion
¼ c. chopped green pepper
2 to 3 med. tomatoes, cut in chunks
¼ c. diced celery
Salt to taste
Dash of pepper
French dressing

Toss vegetables; add salt, pepper and French dressing. Serve while crisp and fresh. Yield: 6 servings.

Effie Lois Greene, Potts Camp H.S.
Potts Camp, Mississippi

CORN SALAD

2 cans whole kernel corn, drained
¾ c. diced unpared cucumber
¼ c. diced onion
2 sm. tomatoes, chopped
¼ c. sour cream
2 tbsp. mayonnaise
1 tbsp. vinegar
½ tsp. salt
¼ tsp. dry mustard
¼ tsp. celery seed

Combine corn, cucumber, onion and tomatoes. Blend remaining ingredients; add to vegetables, tossing gently just to coat vegetables. Chill thoroughly. Spoon into lettuce cups. Yield: 6-8 servings.

Doris S. Poindexter, Sumner Comm. Sch.
Sumner, Iowa

SPANISH SALAD

6 lge. fresh whole tomatoes, pulp removed
1 c. whole kernel corn
1 sm. green pepper, chopped
1 tsp. vinegar
1 sm. onion, chopped
Salt and pepper to taste
Mayonnaise

Cut top of tomato in small pieces; mix with remaining ingredients. Place mixture in tomatoes. Serve on lettuce leaf. Dot with mayonnaise; sprinkle with paprika. Yield: 6 servings.

Mrs. Fernette Honaker, Menaul Presb. H.S.
Albuquerque, New Mexico

CUCUMBERS A LA KINDLER

2 lge. cucumbers, peeled and thinly sliced
1½ tsp. salt
1 c. sour cream
2 tbsp. lemon juice
1 tbsp. minced onion
2 tbsp. chopped dill pickle
¼ tsp. sugar
Dash of pepper
3 radishes, thinly sliced
1½ tsp. finely chopped parsley

Toss cucumbers lightly with 1 teaspoon salt; refrigerate until well chilled. Combine sour cream, lemon juice, remaining salt, onion, dill pickle, sugar, pepper and radishes. Reserve 1/2 cup sour cream mixture for garnish. Toss cucumbers with remaining sour cream mixture; refrigerate. Arrange cucumbers in bed of lettuce. Garnish with reserved sour cream mixture; sprinkle with parsley. Yield: 6 servings.

Mrs. Gertrude Wilson, Nahant Jr. H.S.
Nahant, Massachusetts

CUCUMBER SALAD

2 tbsp. vinegar
½ c. buttermilk
½ c. mayonnaise
4 med. cucumbers, thinly sliced
1 sm. onion, grated
Salt to taste
Parsley flakes
Paprika

Combine vinegar, buttermilk and mayonnaise; add cucumbers and onion. Season with salt and parsley flakes; toss lightly. Sprinkle with paprika. Sour cream may be substituted for buttermilk and mayonnaise. Yield: 6 servings.

Mrs. Emma R. Everett, Covington H.S.
Covington, Louisiana

CUCUMBERS AND ONIONS IN YOGURT

1 tsp. minced dill (opt.)
½ c. yogurt
½ c. sour cream
1 c. sliced cucumber
1 c. sliced onion

Combine dill, yogurt and sour cream; pour over cucumber and onions. Marinate for at least 2 hours. Yield: 4 servings.

LaBerta W. Bowler, Virgin Valley H.S.
Mesquite, Nevada

CUCUMBER SALAD

3 c. diced cucumbers
1 c. crumbled saltine crackers
Mayonnaise

Combine cucumbers and crackers; moisten well with mayonnaise. Serve immediately to preserve crispness. Yield: 4 servings.

Mary E. Finley, Baker Co. H.S.
MacClenny, Florida

CUCUMBER SLICES

½ c. butter or margarine, softened
2 c. grated cheddar cheese
1 lb. bacon, cooked and crumbled
4 tbsp. milk
1 tsp. garlic salt
1 tsp. Worcestershire sauce
1 med.-sized unpared cucumber, cut into 3 cylinders

Blend butter, cheese, bacon, milk, garlic salt and Worcestershire sauce. Scoop out centers of cucumber cylinders, leaving 1/4-inch shell; fill with cheese mixture. Chill 2 to 3 hours; cut in 1/2-inch slices to serve.

Mrs. Emilie E. Mugnani, Jamestown Area H.S.
Jamestown, Pennsylvania

CUCUMBERS IN SOUR CREAM

4 tsp. sugar
3 tsp. salt
½ tsp. pepper
2 tbsp. lemon juice
¾ c. sour cream
2 med. onions, sliced
1 qt. sliced pared cucumber

Blend sugar, salt, pepper and lemon juice into sour cream; fold into onions and cucumbers. Garnish with watercress. Yield: 8 servings.

Mrs. Eileen Olson, Siren H.S.
Siren, Wisconsin

CUCUMBER SLICES IN SOUR CREAM

2 cucumbers, pared, scored, sliced thin
1 tsp. salt
½ c. sour cream
1 tbsp. vinegar
2 drops Tabasco sauce
2 tsp. chopped chives
1 tsp. dillseed
Dash of pepper

Sprinkle cucumbers with salt; let stand at least 30 minutes. Press out moisture. Combine remaining ingredients; pour over cucumbers. Chill well before serving. Yield: 6 servings.

Mickey F. Olsen, New Underwood H.S.
New Underwood, South Dakota

DANDELION SALAD

1 lb. dandelion greens
4 slices bacon, cubed
¼ c. butter
½ c. (scant) cream
2 eggs, beaten
1 tsp. salt
Dash of paprika and pepper
1 tbsp. sugar
4 tbsp. vinegar

Wash and prepare dandelion as lettuce; roll in cloth. Pat dry. Fry bacon; scoop out pieces. Drop over dandelion. Place butter and cream in skillet; melt over low heat. Combine eggs, salt, paprika, pepper, sugar and vinegar. Mix with cream mixture. Pour into skillet; increase heat. Cook until mixture becomes thick like custard. Remove from fire; pour over dandelions. Stir thoroughly. Yield: 6 servings.

Mrs. Dorothy Z. Norton, Midland Jr.-Sr. H.S.
Midland, Pennsylvania

EGGPLANT SALAD

1 med. eggplant, unpared
2 green onions, chopped
3 med. fresh tomatoes, cut in cubes
¼ c. cider vinegar
3 tbsp. salad oil
1 ½ tsp. salt
Freshly ground pepper to taste
½ tsp. sugar

Place eggplant on baking sheet. Bake in 375-degree oven for about 45 minutes or until tender when pierced with fork. Cool; peel. Chill in refrigerator. Cut into cubes; mix with onion, tomatoes, vinegar, salad oil, salt, pepper and sugar. Chill for several hours to marinate vegetables. Serve on lettuce. Yield: 4-6 servings.

Mrs. Kathleen Barnes, Lawrence Cen. H.S.
Lawrence, Indiana

DOUBLE OLIVE SALAD

1 c. diagonally sliced raw carrots
1 c. thinly-sliced radishes
1 c. thinly-sliced celery
1 ½ c. sliced, pitted ripe olives
1 ½ c. sliced stuffed olives
1 head iceberg lettuce
2 tbsp. capers
2 tbsp. snipped parsley
6 tbsp. salad oil
¼ c. lemon juice

Wrap carrots, radishes, celery and olives in aluminum foil; refrigerate for several hours. Tear lettuce into bite-sized pieces; refrigerate. Place vegetables and olives in large bowl. Combine capers, parsley, oil and lemon juice in jar; shake or mix well. Pour over vegetables mixture; toss lightly. Serve immediately. Yield: 8 servings.

Mary Piraino, Tuley H.S.
Chicago, Illinois

MAKE AHEAD CUCUMBER-WALNUT SALAD BOWL

⅔ c. salad oil
¼ c. wine vinegar
1 tbsp. finely grated onion
2 tsp. dry mustard
1 ½ tsp. salt
2 lge. cucumbers, peeled, thinly sliced
6 c. torn crisp lettuce
1 c. finely chopped walnuts, toasted

Combine salad oil, vinegar, onion, mustard and salt; shake well. Pour half over cucumbers; cover and chill at least 2 hours. Drain well; combine with lettuce and walnuts. Toss with remaining dressing; serve immediately. Yield: 6 servings.

Mrs. Mary J. Higgins, Marietta H.S.
Marietta, Georgia

GREEN SALAD

1 head lettuce, torn into bite-sized
   pieces
⅓ c. coarsely broken walnuts
¼ c. grated Parmesan cheese
¼ c. salad oil
3 tbsp. V-8 juice
1 tbsp. lemon juice
1 tsp. grated onion
¼ tsp. salt
¼ tsp. black pepper
¼ tsp. sugar
¼ tsp. dried sweet basil, crumbled

Place lettuce in salad bowl; add walnuts and cheese. Combine remaining ingredients; pour over salad. Toss; serve at once. Yield: 3 servings.

Bonnie Wentworth, North Charleston H.S.
North Charleston, South Carolina

IMPERIAL SALAD

¼ c. sugar
1 tsp. Worcestershire sauce
1 tsp. salt
¼ tsp. pepper
¼ tsp. garlic salt
1 tsp. prepared mustard
¼ c. cider vinegar
3 strips bacon, cooked in 4 tbsp. salad
   oil
1 lge. head lettuce
½ lge. onion, diced

Combine first 7 ingredients in measuring cup; add water to fill cup. Break lettuce into large bowl; add onion. Stir contents of cup; combine with fried bacon and oil. Heat; do not boil. Pour over salad. Serve immediately. Yield: 4 servings.

Sister M. Aloysius, PBVM, O'Gorman H.S.
Sioux Falls, South Dakota

ARTICHOKE SALAD

1 can Italian green beans
1 pkg. frozen broccoli
1 jar marinated artichoke hearts
Green Goddess dressing
Pimentos

Drain beans. Cook, drain and chill broccoli. Drain artichoke hearts. Combine vegetables; mix lightly with dressing. Decorate with pimento. Yield: 4 servings.

Jan Genetti, Natrona Co. H.S.
Casper, Wyoming

BEAN AND BACON SALAD

1 pkg. frozen green beans
¼ c. cider vinegar
¼ c. water
¼ c. sugar
1 c. cooked cauliflowerets, drained
1 tbsp. chopped pimento
4 green onions, sliced
½ c. diced celery
8 slices crisp diced bacon
Hot Sweet-Sour Dressing

Cook the beans and drain; stir in vinegar, water, sugar and let marinate 2 to 3 hours. Drain beans and add cauliflowerets, pimento, onions, celery and bacon. Toss with hot Sweet-Sour Dressing. Serve in crisp lettuce cups.

SWEET-SOUR DRESSING:

1 tbsp. brown sugar
2 tbsp. bacon drippings
2 tbsp. vinegar
½ tsp. salt

(Continued on next page)

Combine brown sugar, bacon drippings, vinegar and salt; heat over low heat until flavors blend. Yield: 8 servings.

Carolyn Ewan, Arlington H.S.
Arlington Heights, Illinois

BEAN AND PEA SALAD

1 can pork and beans
1 can drained peas
1 c. finely chopped celery
1 minced onion
Salad dressing

Remove pork from beans; drain beans. Add peas, celery and onion. Mix with salad dressing. Chill. Yield: 6-8 servings.

Mrs. Vera J. Martin, Eleva-Strum Cen. Sch.
Strum, Wisconsin

BEAN SALAD

1 can chick peas
1 can red kidney beans
1 can cut green beans
1 can cut yellow beans
1 c. shredded onions
½ c. chopped green pepper
½ c. salad oil
½ c. vinegar
½ c. sugar
¾ tsp. salt

Combine all ingredients in large mixing bowl; cover. Let stand in refrigerator at least 2 hours; will keep for several days. Yield: 12 servings.

Betty E. Cuneo, Williamson Jr.-Sr. H.S.
Tioga, Pennsylvania

BEST SALAD BOWL

2 c. torn head lettuce
2 c. torn endive
2 c. torn romaine lettuce
6 tbsp. mayonnaise
1 med. red onion, thinly sliced
3 tsp. sugar
¾ tsp. salt
1 No. 303 can cooked peas, drained
Freshly ground pepper
1 c. julienne strips natural Swiss cheese
6 slices bacon, crisp-cooked and
   crumbled

Place 1/3 of the greens in bowl; dot with mayonnaise. Top with 1/3 of the onion slices; sprinkle with 1 teaspoon sugar. Dash with 1/4 teaspoon

salt and pepper. Add 1/3 of the peas and cheese. Repeat layers, seasoning each. Do not toss. Cover; chill 2 hours. Just before serving, top with bacon and toss. Yield: 6 servings.

Mrs. Dolores C. Gaska, Kennedy Jr. H.S.
St. Clair Shores, Michigan

CALICO SALAD

1 1-lb. can cut green beans, drained
1 1-lb. jar sliced carrots, drained
1 12-oz. can whole kernel vacuum
   packed golden corn
2 tbsp. chopped onion
Celery Seed Dressing

Combine vegetables. Toss with Celery Seed Dressing. Chill in covered container several hours or overnight. Serve on salad greens.

CELERY SEED DRESSING:

½ c. brown sugar
⅓ c. cider vinegar
1 tbsp. salt
2 tsp. celery seed
¼ tsp. ground turmeric
Dash of pepper

Combine all ingredients. Yield: 6-8 servings.

Barbara Jackson, Charles H. Milby H.S.
Houston, Texas

CANNED VEGETABLE SALAD

1 No. 303 can baby limas
1 No. 303 can baby peas
1 No. 303 can French-style green beans
½ c. chopped onion
1 c. chopped celery
1 c. chopped pimento
½ c. slivered almonds
1 tsp. salt
½ c. vinegar
½ c. sugar
½ c. salad oil
½ tsp. mustard seed
½ tsp. celery seed
½ tsp. paprika

Combine first 8 ingredients; mix well and drain. Mix vinegar, sugar, oil, mustard seed, celery seed and paprika; combine with vegetable mixture. Chill 4 hours before serving. Yield: 10-12 servings.

Lucille S. Brown, Narrows H.S.
Narrows, Virginia

CALIFORNIA GREEN SALAD

    1 c. sour cream
    1 tsp. Worcestershire sauce
    ¼ tsp. garlic salt
    ⅛ tsp. black pepper, coarsely ground
    Dash of cayenne pepper
    ½ head iceberg lettuce
    ½ head romaine lettuce
    4 tomatoes, sliced thin
    1 cucumber, sliced thin
    2 scallions, chopped
    4 slices bacon, fried crisp
    2 eggs, hard-cooked

Combine sour cream, Worcestershire sauce, garlic salt, black pepper and cayenne pepper. Mix well. Break up lettuce; add tomatoes, cucumbers and scallions. Toss with dressing. Arrange on salad plates. Garnish with crumbled bacon and hard-cooked eggs, diced or halved.

Susan Holbrook, Blackford H.S.
San Jose, California

CHRISTMAS DELIGHT

    1 c. raw cauliflowerets
    1 c. raw broccoli flowerets
    2 c. quartered tomatoes
    Mayonnaise or boiled dressing
    Lettuce

Mix and toss ingredients with mayonnaise. Place in salad bowl lined with lettuce leaves. Yield: 4 servings.

Mrs. Leita Askew, George McDougall H.S.
Airdrie, Alberta, Canada

CURRY SALAD

    ½ tsp. beef-flavored gravy base
    ¼ c. hot water
    1 c. mayonnaise
    1 clove garlic, minced
    1 tbsp. curry powder
    ¼ tsp. Worcestershire sauce
    6 to 8 drops bottled hot pepper sauce
    6 c. torn mixed salad greens
    4 c. torn spinach
    1 1-lb. can artichoke hearts, chilled,
        drained and halved
    ¼ c. radish slices

Stir together gravy base and hot water; blend into mayonnaise. Stir in garlic, curry and Worcestershire sauce; add hot pepper sauce. Chill several hours or overnight. Combine mixed greens, spinach, artichoke hearts and radish slices in large salad bowl. Add dressing and toss. Yield: 8 servings.

Mrs. Virginia Taylor, Dierks H.S.
Dierks, Arkansas

DELUXE ARTICHOKES
AND HEARTS OF PALM SALAD

    Pinch each of tarragon, thyme and
        basil leaves
    ½ tsp. salt
    2 tbsp. tarragon white wine vinegar
    ⅓ c. good olive oil
    1 tbsp. Dijon-style mustard
    ½ tsp. ground pepper
    Clove of garlic, crushed
    1 16-oz. can hearts of palm
    1 6-oz. jar marinated artichokes or
        1 lge. can plain artichokes
    3 c. torn romaine or Bibb lettuce
    2 c. torn iceberg lettuce

Soak tarragon, thyme and basil leaves in wine vinegar for 1 hour. Dissolve salt in seasoned vinegar. Add the olive oil, mustard, pepper and garlic. Shake well; refrigerate. Drain hearts of palm; slice into 1/4-inch slices. Slice artichokes into small pieces. Combine hearts of palm and artichokes with romaine and iceberg lettuce. Place greens in large wooden salad bowl. Toss with dressing just prior to serving. Each leaf should glisten with dressing but not be soggy. Yield: 6-8 servings.

Ruby A. Lesch, Wayzata Jr. H.S.
Wayzata, Minnesota

DO AHEAD
SALADE PROVENCE

    2 lge. heads lettuce
    1 pkg. fresh spinach
    2 sm. cans pitted ripe olives
    2 6-oz. jars marinated artichoke hearts
    1 8-oz. bottle herb dressing

Wash and core lettuce and spinach. Wrap in paper towels to dry. Remove spinach stems. Tear greens into bite-sized pieces and place in plastic bags. Refrigerate until serving time. Place 1 can of olives, 1 jar of artichoke hearts and half the dressing in 1 bag. Place remaining olives, artichoke hearts and dressing in other bag. Close bags tightly and shake vigorously until greens are well coated. Pour into large salad bowl. Yield: 12 servings.

Mrs. Carolyn Harris, Campolindo H.S.
Moraga, California

ENDIVE AND BEET SALAD

    4 heads of endive
    1 cooked beet, sliced thin
    2 tsp. finely chopped parsley
    2 tsp. finely chopped tarragon
    2 tsp. finely chopped chervil
    ½ tsp. salt
    ⅛ tsp. freshly ground pepper
    3 tbsp. olive oil
    1 ½ tbsp. wine vinegar

(Continued on next page)

Wash endive, keeping heads intact. Shake well; dry thoroughly in towel. Cut endive in quarters lengthwise, then into pieces about 2 inches long. Place in wooden salad bowl. Add beet. Sprinkle with parsley, tarragon and chervil. Just before serving, sprinkle salad with salt and pepper. Pour olive oil over salad, mixing well to coat. Add wine vinegar; mix thoroughly. Yield: 4 servings.

Betty Berk, Othello H.S.
Othello, Washington

GALETTE

1 clove of garlic, minced
¼ c. wine vinegar
¾ c. olive oil
Salt to taste
1 bunch celery, cut into ¼ inch slices
1 cucumber, cut into chunks
1 green pepper, cut into chunks
1 bunch scallions, cut into chunks
1 bag radishes, cut into chunks
1 med.-sized Spanish or red onion, sliced
3 med. or 2 lge. tomatoes, cut into chunks
Oregano
Bleu cheese, grated

Mince garlic; add vinegar, oil and salt. Shake or mix well. Set aside. Combine all vegetables in salad bowl; sprinkle top of vegetable mixture with light covering of oregano. Sprinkle bleu cheese over top of vegetable mixture. Pour oil and vinegar mixture over entire surface; toss lightly. Avocado may be added, if desired. Yield: 8-10 servings.

Dorothy O. Marotta, Pleasantville H.S.
Pleasantville, N. Y.

GARDEN SALAD

½ head lettuce
3 med. tomatoes
1 med. cucumber
½ c. chopped celery
¼ c. chopped onion
1 sm. can shoestring potatoes
4 tbsp. mayonnaise
1 tbsp. mustard
1 tbsp. vinegar
1 tbsp. sugar
½ c. cream

Shred lettuce and cut up tomatoes and cucumber. Combine all vegetables, except potatoes. Combine last 5 ingredients for dressing. Pour over vegetables when well blended and toss lightly. Refrigerate. Mix in potatoes just before serving. Yield: 6 servings.

Margaret Holland, Brainerd H.S.
Brainerd, Minnesota

GAZPACHO

6 tbsp. Italian dressing
1 c. tomato juice
1 tsp. salt
⅛ tsp. pepper
6 med. ripe tomatoes, peeled and diced
1 lge. cucumber, peeled and diced
1 med. onion, minced
1 green pepper, finely chopped
Croutons

Combine dressing, tomato juice, salt and pepper. Pour over lightly tossed vegetables in large bowl. Refrigerate until well chilled. Serve in bowls; top with croutons. Yield: 6-8 servings.

Nita Thompson, Tornillo H.S.
Tornillo, Texas

GOLDEN SALAD

1½ c. shredded cabbage
1 c. grated carrots
½ c. grated sharp cheddar cheese
2 tbsp. lemon juice
½ tsp. salt
Salad dressing or mayonnaise
Lettuce leaves
Paprika

Mix cabbage, carrots and cheese. Add lemon juice, salt and dressing to moisten. Serve on lettuce leaves; garnish with paprika. Yield: 4 servings.

Roberta S. Priestley, Brigham Young U Lab. Sch.
Provo, Utah

GREEK SALAD

1 head lettuce, torn into small pieces
1 c. celery, cut up
½ c. radishes, sliced
½ c. green peppers, cut into rings
1 c. sm. stuffed olives
3 tbsp. olive oil
2 tbsp. vinegar
2 buttons garlic
¼ tsp. salt
¼ tsp. paprika
¼ tsp. pepper
12 finger pieces Feta cheese

Combine first 4 ingredients; add olives. Combine oil, vinegar, garlic, salt, paprika and pepper; mix well. Pour over greens; toss. Remove garlic. Place in large salad bowl. Top with Feta cheese. Yield: 6 servings.

Mrs. Imogene F. Abernathie
Williamsville Co. #15 H.S.
Williamsville, Illinois

Mixed Vegetable Salads

GREEN BEAN SALAD

1 can Blue Lake green beans, whole
1 can English peas
1 sm. can pimento
1 bell pepper
¾ to 1 ½ c. celery, diced
2 or 3 sm. onions, cut into rings
1 c. sugar
¾ c. vinegar
Salt to taste
½ c. Wesson oil

Drain beans and peas. Add chopped pimento, pepper, celery and onion rings. Heat sugar and vinegar until sugar dissolves. Cool. Add salt and Wesson oil. Pour over vegetables. Marinate for 24 hours. Drain before serving. Will keep for several days. Yield: 10 servings.

Sandra King, Dist. Supvr.
Home Ec. Ed.
Montevallo, Alabama
Mrs. Mary B. Mills, Vina H.S.
Vina, Alabama

GREEN SALAD

½ head lettuce
¼ bunch endive
2 tomatoes
2 stalks celery, cut into pieces
6 radishes, sliced
3 green onions, chopped
½ green pepper, sliced
¼ c. salad dressing

Break lettuce into bowl; tear endive into small pieces. Arrange remaining vegetables on top. Pour dressing over; toss lightly. Yield: 6 servings.

Elaine M. Krick, Jefferson H.S.
Alexandria, Minnesota

HARDY COMBINATION SALAD

¼ head green lettuce, torn
¼ c. red onion, slices
¼ c. sweet relish
¼ c. sliced pickled beets
¼ c. chopped celery
1 tomato, cut in bite sizes
¼ c. vinegar
¼ c. salad oil
½ tsp. salt
Pepper to taste
Garlic salt to taste

Combine lettuce, onion, relish, beets, celery and tomato; chill. Combine vinegar, oil, salt, pepper and garlic salt in jar; shake well. Serve over vegetable mixture. Yield: 6 servings.

Mrs. Ernestine O. Clark
M. L. Kirkpatrick Jr. H.S.
Fort Worth, Texas

HEARTY GREEN VEGETABLE SALAD

2 pkg. frozen French-style green beans
2 pkg. frozen baby lima beans
2 pkg. frozen green peas
1 sm. onion, chopped fine
½ c. (or more) mayonnaise
Salt and pepper to taste

Cook and drain each cooked vegetable separately; combine with onion and mayonnaise. Mix lightly. Chill. Serve in bowl lined with lettuce. Yield: 8 servings.

Jane Washburn, Hudson Falls Sr. H.S.
Hudson Falls, New York

HOT VEGETABLE SALAD

¾ c. sugar
1 c. Wesson oil
⅔ c. vinegar
1 tsp. salt
½ tsp. pepper
1 8-oz. can butter beans
1 8-oz. can snap beans
1 8-oz. can English peas
½ c. chopped celery
1 bell pepper, chopped
1 sliced Italian onion
1 sm. pimento, sliced

Combine sugar, oil, vinegar, salt and pepper; bring to a boil. Drain liquid from butter beans, snap beans and English peas; add to celery, bell pepper, onion and pimento. Pour boiling all-vinegar mixture over combined vegetables. Yield: 6-8 servings.

Sara G. McInnis, Evergreen H.S.
Evergreen, Alabama

INTERNATIONAL SALAD

1 lge. head lettuce
1 head red cabbage
6 carrots
6 lge. pieces celery
12 radishes
1 green pepper
1 cucumber
1 bunch spring onions
1 sm. cauliflower
1 No. 2 can garbanzo beans
1 bottle Wishbone Italian dressing

Tear lettuce into bite-sized pieces. Cut red cabbage into thin strips. Slice carrots into thin horizontal discs. Cut celery into bite-sized pieces. Cut radishes into thin horizontal discs. Cut pepper, cucumber and onions into bite-sized pieces and break cauliflower into small flowerets. Drain garbanzo beans. Toss all ingredients, except dressing, to mix well. Add dressing just before serving. Yield: 18 servings.

Nancye H. Shannon, Greenbrier H.S.
Greenbrier, Tennessee

ITALIAN VEGTABLE SALAD

1 diced tomato
½ c. diced celery
⅓ c. shredded carrots
1 tbsp. finely chopped onion
¼ c. sliced black olives
3 sliced red radishes
½ head of lettuce, torn in sm. pieces
¼ c. olive oil
1 tbsp. flavored vinegar
2 tsp. sugar
1 tsp. salt

Combine prepared vegetables in salad bowl. Combine oil, vinegar, sugar and salt in a shaker or bowl; mix. Just before serving pour dressing over salad and toss. Yield: 4 servings.

Mrs. Alice Jean Camigliano, Youngsville H.S.
Youngsville, Pennsylvania

JULIENNE SALAD BOWL

1 c. cooked or canned green beans, julienne-style
1 c. fresh cooked or raw carrots, julienne-style
1 c. fresh cooked or canned peas
¼ c. French dressing
½ bunch endive

Chill all ingredients. Combine vegetables in salad bowl; add dressing. Cover; place in re-frigerator to marinate 30 minutes. Add endive torn into bite-size pieces; toss lightly and serve. Yield: 4 servings.

Naomi M. Vaught, Manatee H.S.
Bradenton, Florida

KRAUT SALAD

1 No. 2½ can kraut
1 No. 2 can bean sprouts
2 c. diced celery
2 c. diced onion
1 c. diced mango
2 c. sugar
½ c. vinegar

Drain kraut and bean sprouts. Add vegetables and mix together. Heat sugar and vinegar until sugar is dissolved and pour over vegetables. Stir again and let stand overnight in refriger-ator. Serve. Yield: 12 servings.

Mrs. Forrest A. Stewart, Salem Comm. H.S.
Salem, Illinois

MARINATED MIXED VEGETABLES

1 can whole green beans
1 can wax beans
1 can English peas
4 sticks chopped celery
3 sm. onions, cut in rings
1 jar pimento, chopped
1 bell pepper, cut in rings
1 c. vinegar
1 c. sugar
1 tsp. salt
½ c. Wesson Oil
Black pepper to taste
Paprika

Drain canned vegetables; add fresh vegetables. Mix vinegar, sugar, salt, oil, black pepper and paprika; pour over vegetables. Stir to mix. Store in refrigerator for 24 hours. Drain; serve with lettuce as a salad or plain as a vegetable. Will keep several days. Yield: 8 servings.

Minnie Van W. Stuart, Livingston H.S.
Livingston, Alabama

MARINATED VEGETABLE MEDLEY

1 No. 303 can French-style green beans, drained
1 No. 303 can tiny English peas, drained
½ green pepper, diced
1 sm. white onion, chopped
2 pieces celery, chopped
1 or 2 pimentos, chopped
Salt to taste
½ c. salad oil
⅔ c. (scant) sugar
¼ tsp. paprika
⅓ c. vinegar
⅓ c. water

Place vegetables into bowl in layers; salt as desired. Mix oil, sugar, paprika, vinegar and water; stir until sugar dissolves. Pour mix-ture over vegetables. Marinate for 24 hours; drain before serving. Yield: 8 servings.

Mrs. Nancy Bomar, Trezevant H.S.
Memphis, Tennessee

MEDITERRANEAN SALAD

1 15-oz. can cut green beans
1 sm. head cauliflower
1 10-oz. pkg. frozen artichoke hearts
1 c. olive oil
½ c. wine vinegar
2 lge. cloves of garlic, crushed
1 tsp. salt
2½ qt. salad greens
4 oz. pitted ripe olives.
1 red onion, cut into rings
3 tomatoes, diced
2 hard-cooked eggs, sliced
12 oz. luncheon meats, slivered

Drain and rinse green beans. Cut cauliflower into flowerets and cook in boiling salted water 3 minutes or until almost tender. Cook arti-choke hearts as directed on package. Combine oil, vinegar, garlic and salt. Marinate green beans, cauliflower and artichokes in separate

235

(Continued on next page)

bowls in 3 to 4 tablespoons dressing mixture each. Chill 1 hour. Break salad greens into bite-sized pieces. Place greens in large salad bowl; toss with remaining dressing. Arrange marinated vegetables, olives, onion, tomatoes, eggs and luncheon meat in rows on top of greens. Yield: 8 servings.

Linda Porter, Porter H.S.
Maryville, Tennessee

MIXED BEAN SALAD

1 can garbanzo beans
1 can string beans
1 can kidney beans
1 pkg. Italian dressing mix or vinegar
   and oil dressing
3 tbsp. Bacos or crisp fried bacon,
   crumbled

Place beans in salad bowl; pour dressing over beans. Let stand in refrigerator for a couple of hours or overnight. Add bacon bits shortly before serving to add a crunchy texture. Celery and onions may be added, if desired. Yield: 6-8 servings.

Saralee Dinelli, Homemaking Ed.
Dept. of Ed.
Sacramento, California

MIXED VEGETABLE SALAD

1 10-oz. pkg. frozen mixed vegetables
1 No. 303 can red kidney beans,
   drained and washed
½ c. celery
1 onion, chopped
2 green peppers, chopped

Cook mixed vegetables as directed on package. Drain; cool. Combine with remaining ingredients.

DRESSING:

½ c. sugar
½ c. vinegar
1 tbsp. flour
1 tbsp. prepared mustard

Combine all ingredients; cook until thickened. Cool. Pour over vegetables. Yield: 8 servings.

Mrs. Pat Vaughan, Fairfield H.S.
Fairfield, Illinois

PICKLED BEAN SALAD

1 16-oz. can diagonal-cut green beans,
   drained
1 2½-oz. jar sliced mushrooms, drained
½ c. Italian-style salad dressing
1 8¼-oz. can sliced beets
1 bunch leaf lettuce
Grated Parmesan cheese

Combine beans and mushrooms; toss with salad dressing. Refrigerate several hours until chilled through. Chill beets. Arrange lettuce in salad bowl. Drain marinated beans and mushrooms; add to salad bowl. Drain beets; arrange around outside edge of salad. Sprinkle with cheese. Yield: 5 servings.

Myrtle Knutson, Fairview Jr. H.S.
St. Paul, Minnesota

PIEMONT ITALIAN SALAD

1 head shredded lettuce
1 can julienne cut green beens,
   drained
1 can shredded beets, drained
1 can asparagus tips, drained
½ c. salad oil
½ c. red wine
1 tsp. salt
Dash of pepper

Arrange lettuce, green beans, beets and asparagus in layers on platter, starting with lettuce and ending with asparagus tips. Combine next ingredients. Pour over salad just before serving. Yield: 10-12 servings.

Sharon Doke, Weed H.S.
Weed, California

SPECIAL SALAD

½ lge. head lettuce, washed and drained
¼ c. sliced radishes
¼ c. minced green pepper
¼ c. diced carrots
¼ c. celery
4 slices bacon, fried and crumbled
½ c. grated cheese
Salad dressing to taste

Break lettuce into small pieces with hands. Combine lettuce, radishes, green pepper, carrots, celery, bacon and cheese. Add enough dressing to taste. Yield: 6 servings.

Mrs. Betty Jones, Les Cheneaux Comm. Sch.
Cedarville, Michigan

SPINACH SALAD

1 c. salad oil
½ c. dark vinegar
¾ c. sugar
2 tsp. salt
⅓ c. catsup
2 bags spinach, torn
2 c. water chestnuts, diced
1 c. bean sprouts, drained
1 Bermuda onion, sliced
4 hard-cooked eggs, chopped
½ lb. bacon, crisp-cooked, drained and crumbled

Combine oil, vinegar, sugar, salt and catsup; mix in blender or shake in bottle. Combine remaining ingredients; toss with dressing. Yield: 12 servings.

Mrs. Helen Orlyk, Cen. H.S.
Grand Rapids, Michigan

TURNIP AND CARROT SLAW

¼ c. mayonnaise
½ tsp. salt
⅛ tsp. pepper
¼ tsp. dry mustard
¼ c. sweet pickle, chopped
1 ½ c. carrots, grated
3 c. turnips, grated

Prepare dressing of mayonnaise, salt, pepper, dry mustard and pickle. Toss carrots, turnips and dressing lightly. Serve on lettuce. For variation use same amount of turnips and carrots; add 6 tablespoons crushed pineapple with juice, 2 teaspoons lemon juice, 3/4 cup dairy sour cream, 2 tablespoons finely chopped green pepper. Prepare dressing of sour cream, lemon juice, crushed pineapple, chopped green pepper. Toss carrots and turnips and dressing together lightly. Serve on lettuce.

Mrs. Minta Palmer, Johnston H.S.
Austin, Texas

TOMATO-CUCUMBER SALAD

4 tomatoes, peeled and diced
1 lge. cucumber, peeled and diced
¼ c. mayonnaise
2 tbsp. vinegar
Salt and pepper to taste

Combine all ingredients; toss lightly. Serve on leaf lettuce. Yield: 4 servings.

Mrs. Virginia B. Collie, Tunstall H.S.
Dry Fork, Virginia

VEGETABLE COUPE

1 head cauliflower
1 head lettuce
1 c. wax beans
1 c. green beans
1 c. salad oil
1 c. vinegar

Break cauliflower into small pieces. Break lettuce into bite-sized pieces. Mix lettuce, wax beans, green beans and cauliflower together. Mix oil and vinegar together. Pour over vegetables and let stand about 4 hours.

Mrs. Kathy Hufstedler, Pampa H.S.
Pampa, Texas

TOMATO AND CUCUMBER SALAD

3 med.-sized tomatoes, sliced
Salt to taste
⅓ c. vegetable oil
1 ½ tsp. vinegar
¼ tsp. oregano
1 med.-sized cucumber, diced
2 tbsp. mayonnaise
¼ tsp. dillseed
¼ tsp. salt

Place tomatoes in bowl in layers. Salt each layer. Pour oil, vinegar and oregano over top. Allow to stand for at least 1 hour in refrigerator. Place cucumber in mayonnaise, dillseed and salt mixture. Allow to stand for at least 1 hour in refrigerator. Place cucumber in small bowl; drain mixture from tomatoes. Arrange tomatoes around cucumber. Yield: 6 servings.

Mrs. Shirley Holmes, Camas Jr. H.S.
Camas, Washington

VEGETABLE SALAD

½ c. chopped ripe olives
½ c. cubed cooked carrots
1 c. diced celery
1 c. cooked peas
1 sm. mild onion, grated
French dressing
Salt and pepper
Lettuce
Mayonnaise

Chill first 5 ingredients; toss together lightly, adding enough French dressing to coat thoroughly. Chill 30 minutes; season to taste with salt and pepper. Serve in lettuce cups. Garnish with mayonnaise. Yield: 6 servings.

Mrs. Mary S. Hines, George C. Wallace H.S.
Clayton, Alabama

VEGETABLE SALAD

4 10-oz. pkg. frozen lima beans
4 10-oz. pkg. frozen whole kernel
   corn
2 tbsp. minced onion
½ c. sliced pimento
2 qt. diced celery
2 c. French dressing
Lettuce

Cook lima beans and corn separately as directed
on packages; drain and cool. Add onion, pimento,
celery and French dressing; mix well. Chill
thoroughly. Serve on crisp lettuce. Yield: 32
servings.

Mrs. Willie Ruth Atchley, Lanier H.S.
Maryville, Tennessee

VEGETABLES UNIQUE

1 lge. can chow mein vegetables with
   mushrooms
1 can French-style green beans
1 can tiny English peas
2 cans water chestnuts, sliced thin
1 sm. can pimentos, cut in strips
2 raw carrots, coarsely diced
1 ½ c. chopped celery
1 grated onion
Salt and pepper to taste
1 c. sugar
¾ c. vinegar

Drain all canned vegetables; add fresh vegetables. Mix well. Add salt, pepper, sugar and
vinegar; mix well. Store in covered glass container in refrigerator. Let stand 24 hours before
serving; will keep in refrigerator for 10-14 days.
Yield: 20-25 servings.

Mrs. J. Fred Jones, Ridge Road Jr. H.S.
North Little Rock, Arkansas

WINTER SALAD BOWL

4 cooked cauliflowerets
½ c. cooked beets, cut into strips
½ c. cooked green beans, cut into
   strips
½ c. cooked carrots, cut into strips
½ c. cooked peas
Lemon French dressing
1 sm. head lettuce
3 oz. Swiss cheese

Marinate cooked vegetables separately in French
dressing; chill for 1 hour. Drain vegetables; reserve marinade. Shred lettuce into salad bowl;
toss with enough reserved dressing to coat.
Arrange cauliflowerets in center of bowl;
group remaining vegetables around cauliflower.
Sprinkle with grated cheese. Yield: 6 servings.

Mrs. Alice McKelvie, Sandy Creek H.S.
Fairfield, Nebraska

OLD-FASHIONED SALAD

1 c. light cream
2 tsp. sugar
½ c. vinegar
½ tsp. salt
2 med. heads lettuce, cut into bite-sized
   pieces
½ c. chopped onion

Combine cream, sugar, vinegar and salt. Chill.
Toss with lettuce and onion just before serving. Yield: 8-10 servings.

Jessye P. MacKay, Pollock H.S.
Pollock, South Dakota

CHICK PEA SALAD

1 can chick peas
1 sm. onion, sliced and diced
⅓ c. salad oil
½ c. vinegar
1 tsp. sugar
½ tsp. salt
Few grains of pepper
½ tsp. celery seed
1 tsp. dillweed or dillseed

Combine all ingredients. Cover. Place in refrigerator overnight. May be stored indefinitely.
Yield: 8 servings.

Mrs. Doris Gustafson, Brethren H.S.
Brethren, Michigan

COUNTRY PEA SALAD

1 No. 303 can sweet peas
2 tbsp. minced onion
¼ c. minced celery
½ c. cheddar cheese cubes
½ c. broken pecan pieces
2 hard-boiled eggs
¼ tsp. salt
⅛ tsp. pepper
½ c. mayonnaise

Combine peas, onion, celery, cheese and pecans.
Chop eggs; add to salad mixture. Season with
salt and pepper. Add mayonnaise. Toss lightly.
Serve on lettuce leaf; garnish with parsley.
Yield: 6 servings.

Lena McMillan, O'lney H.S.
Clarita, Oklahoma

HERBED PEA SALAD

4 c. fresh or 2 10-oz. pkg. frozen peas
1 c. thinly sliced celery
¼ c. salad oil

(Continued on next page)

2 tbsp. lemon juice
¾ tsp. dillweed
¼ tsp. basil
½ tsp. salt
Dash of pepper
Lettuce
1 hard-boiled egg, sliced

Cook peas, until tender; drain well, reserving 1/3 cup liquid. Combine peas and reserved liquid. Add celery, oil, lemon juice and seasoning. Chill several hours or overnight. Serve in lettuce-lined bowl or lettuce cup. Garnish with egg slices. Yield: 6 servings.

Mrs. Carol Wisnewshi, Stratford H.S.
Stratford, Wisconsin

PEA AND CHEESE SALAD

1 lge. onion, sliced
2 tbsp. cooking oil
½ tsp. powdered ginger
½ tsp. salt
1 10-oz. box frozen peas, partially
    thawed
½ lb. mozzarella cheese, cubed
4 lettuce cup leaves
Chopped fresh mint

Saute onion in oil until golden. Add ginger, salt and peas. Cook 2 minutes over low flame or until peas are tender. Stir in mozzarella cheese. Serve in lettuce cups. Garnish with chopped mint. Yield: 4 servings.

Mrs. Oscar L. Villarreal, United H.S.
Laredo, Texas

PEAS AND PEANUT SALAD

1 8-oz. can peas
½ c. salted Spanish peanuts
⅓ c. mayonnaise

Combine all ingredients. Chill 30 minutes to 1 hour. Serve on lettuce leaf. Yield: 4 servings.

Mrs. Mary Hartz, Holly Sr. H.S.
Holly, Michigan

PEA SALAD

1 No. 303 can sm. English peas, drained
¼ lb. sharp cheddar cheese, cut in ¼-in.
    cubes
2 tbsp. minced onion
¼ c. minced olives
Dressing

Combine all ingredients. Add enough dressing to hold mixture together. Let set several hours for flavors to blend.

DRESSING:

½ c. sugar
1 tsp. salt
1 tsp. mustard, powdered or prepared
⅛ tsp. white pepper
4 eggs
½ c. apple cider vinegar

Combine sugar, salt, mustard, pepper. Beat eggs with rotary or electric beater; gradually add sugar mixture. Add vinegar. Cook in double boiler over simmering water until mixture thickens to consistency of mayonnaise. Cool. Excellent as dressing of Waldorf or cabbage salads. Yield: 6 servings.

Mrs. Virginia Pope, Lake View H.S.
San Angelo, Texas

PEA SALAD

1 No. 2 can English peas, drained
4 hard-boiled eggs, diced
2 tbsp. onion, minced
4 tbsp. sweet relish
2 tbsp. sugar
2 tbsp. salad dressing

Place peas in 1-quart bowl. Add remaining ingredients. Toss lightly. Chill several hours. Yield: 6 servings.

Norma Weaver, Lone Grove Sch.
Lone Grove, Oklahoma

PEPPER AND ONION SALAD

2 lge. green peppers, core removed
2 lge. sweet onions, separated into rings
Crisp lettuce, torn into bite-sized
    pieces
Salad dressing

Cut pepper into rings; place with onions on lettuce. Add enough salad dressing to coat leaves. Yield: 4-6 servings.

Mrs. Elizabeth M. Turner, Algood Jr. H.S.
Algood, Tennessee

CREAMY POTATO SALAD

4 c. sliced warm potatoes
½ tsp. salt
⅛ tsp. pepper
2 tsp. grated onion

(Continued on next page)

½ c. garlic salad dressing
¼ c. chopped celery
¼ c. diced cucumber
½ pt. sour cream
¼ c. mayonnaise

Combine potatoes, salt, pepper, onion and half the salad dressing in bowl; stir well and chill. Combine celery, cucumber, sour cream and mayonnaise in separate bowls; stir in remaining salad dressing. Chill. Combine mixtures before serving. Yield: 8 servings.

Gail Finkelstein, Lindenhurst Jr. H.S.
Lindenhurst, New York

CREAMY POTATO SALAD

7 c. sliced boiled potatoes
⅓ c. chopped chives
1 tsp. salt
⅛ tsp. pepper
1 tbsp. grated onion
1 c. garlic salad dressing
¼ c. chopped celery
½ c. diced cucumber
½ pt. sour cream
½ c. mayonnaise

Combine potatoes, chives, salt, pepper, onion and 1/2 cup salad dressing in large bowl; stir well and chill. Combine celery, cucumber, sour cream and mayonnaise in separate bowl; stir in remaining salad dressing. Chill. Combine mayonnaise and potato mixtures before serving. Garnish with salad greens, parsley, radishes and additional chopped chives, if desired. Yield: 8 servings.

Alfrena Herman, Alton H.S.
Alton, Kansas

CURRIED POTATO SALAD

1 tbsp. lemon juice
1 tbsp. vinegar
2 tbsp. salad oil
2½ tsp. salt
¼ tsp. pepper
2 tsp. curry powder
4 c. diced cooked potatoes
1½ c. diced celery
⅔ c. diced green pepper
⅔ c. diced onion
2 hard-cooked eggs, diced
⅔ c. mayonnaise

Combine first 6 ingredients; pour over diced potatoes in large bowl. Cover and marinate for 1 to 2 hours. Add remaining ingredients just before serving; mix lightly. Serve on lettuce; garnish with paprika. Yield: 6-8 servings.

Mrs. Mabel McClure, New Bremen H.S.
New Bremen, Ohio

GOURMET POTATO SALAD

4 lge. potatoes, cooked
4 hard-cooked eggs, sliced
½ c. minced onions
¼ c. parsley
½ c. melted butter
¼ c. tarragon vinegar
½ c. cultured sour cream
Salt and pepper to taste

Peel and cube potatoes while warm; add remaining ingredients. Pack salad into ring mold and chill. Unmold onto lettuce-lined plate. Yield: 8 servings.

Mrs. Diane Caviezel, Enumclaw Jr. H.S.
Enumclaw, Washington

GERMAN POTATO SALAD

5 med. potatoes
4 strips bacon, diced
¼ c. chopped onion
1 tbsp. flour
2 tsp. salt
1¼ tbsp. sugar
¼ tsp. black pepper
⅔ c. vinegar
⅓ c. water

Simmer potatoes in jackets until tender; peel and slice thinly. Fry bacon until crisp; add onion and cook for 1 minute. Blend in flour, salt, sugar and pepper; stir in vinegar and water. Cook for 10 minutes, stirring occasionally. Pour bacon mixture over warm potatoes. Serve warm. Yield: 8 servings.

Mrs. Wanda La Rochelle, Odem H.S.
Odem, Texas

GERMAN POTATO SALAD

8 med. potatoes
1 lge. onion, sliced
2 green peppers, sliced
Sweet pickles
Olives
1 c. cooking oil
1 c. vinegar
3 tbsp. sugar
1 tsp. mustard
1 tsp. celery salt

Cook potatoes in jackets in salted water; remove and slice thinly. Arrange layer of potatoes in container; add sliced onion, pepper, pickles and olives. Heat remaining ingredients for dressing; pour over potatoes while very hot. Cool. Chill overnight. Yield: 6 servings.

Mrs. Sundra M. Ingram, Lineville H.S.
Lineville, Alabama

GERMAN POTATO SALAD WITH LEMON JUICE

6 potatoes, cooked
2 tbsp. vinegar
Juice of ½ lemon
4 tbsp. cooking oil
¼ c. chopped onion
⅓ c. chopped pickles
Salt and pepper to taste
Mayonnaise

Peel and slice potatoes into large bowl; add remaining ingredients. Garnish with sliced hard-cooked eggs, if desired. Yield: 8-10 servings.

Evangelena L. Barber, Salvda H.S.
Salvda, North Carolina

HOT GERMAN POTATO SALAD

6 baking potatoes
⅓ c. vinegar
2 tsp. salt
¼ tsp. pepper
1 lb. bacon, chopped
6 eggs
2 tbsp. bacon fat
¾ c. chopped green onions or ½ c. chopped onions

Cook potatoes in boiling water; peel and dice. Add vinegar and seasonings. Fry bacon until crisp. Cook eggs for 4 minutes. Combine potatoes, bacon, fat, soft-cooked eggs and chopped onions; mix well. Serve hot salad on bed of lettuce with large frankfurters. Yield: 8 servings.

Esta Newman, Bluffs H.S.
Bluffs, Illinois

HOT POTATO SALAD

½ c. chopped celery
2 pimentos, chopped
2 tbsp. chopped onion
¼ c. chopped pickles
2 hard-cooked eggs, chopped
¼ c. prepared mustard
2 c. hot instant potatoes
⅓ c. salad dressing

Add celery, pimentos, onion, pickles, eggs and mustard to hot potatoes in large bowl; add dressing and mix well. Serve hot. Yield: 6 servings.

Mrs. Ida Mae Fair, Matador H.S.
Matador, Texas

HOT POTATO SALAD

6 med. potatoes, boiled in jackets
6 to 8 slices bacon
¾ c. chopped onion
1½ to 2 tbsp. flour
1 to 2 tbsp. sugar
1½ tsp. salt
½ tsp. celery salt
½ tsp. celery seeds
Dash of pepper
¾ c. water
⅓ c. vinegar

Peel potatoes while hot; slice thinly or cube. Set aside. Fry bacon slowly in skillet; drain. Saute onion in bacon drippings until golden brown; blend in flour, sugar, salt, celery salt and celery seeds and pepper. Cook over low heat, stirring constantly, until smooth and bubbly; remove from heat. Stir in water and vinegar; heat to boiling, stirring constantly. Boil for 1 minute. Stir in potatoes and bacon carefully. Remove from heat and serve hot. Yield: 6-8 servings.

V. K. Tchir, Camrose Composite H.S.
Camros, Alberta, Canada

PERKY POTATO SALAD

¾ c. salad dressing
⅓ c. milk
2 tbsp. vinegar
3 tbsp. sugar
1 tbsp. prepared mustard
1 tsp. salt
¼ tsp. pepper
4 med. potatoes, cooked, cooled and cubed
2 hard-cooked eggs, diced
1 sm. onion, diced
4 sm. sweet pickles, diced

Combine first 7 ingredients; mix well. Refrigerate. Combine remaining ingredients in large bowl; add chilled dressing and mix thoroughly. Garnish with paprika. Refrigerate until time to serve. Yield: 6 servings.

Phyllis A. Stephens, Cody H.S.
Cody, Wyoming

POTATO SALAD

6 c. diced cooked potatoes
½ c. snipped scallions
1 tsp. celery seed
1½ tsp. salt
Dash of pepper
½ pt. sour cream
½ c. salad dressing
½ c. vinegar
1 tsp. mustard
¼ c. chopped green pepper
1 tbsp. grated carrot
3 hard-cooked eggs

(Continued on next page)

Potato Salads

Mix potatoes, scallions, celery seed, salt, pepper and chopped egg whites in large bowl; toss lightly. Blend together sour cream, salad dressing, vinegar, mustard, green pepper, carrot and chopped egg yolks; add to potato mixture and chill. Garnish with wedges of hard-cooked eggs, sliced olives, tomato wedges or sliced pickles. Yield: 6-8 servings.

Mrs. Jane Savidge Jerreris
No. Burlington Co. Reg. H.S.
Columbus, New Jersey

POTATO SALAD

    4 c. cubed cold boiled potatoes
    1 tbsp. finely chopped onion
    ½ tsp. salt
    Dash of pepper
    ¼ c. French dressing
    ½ c. salad dressing or mayonnaise
    2 hard-cooked eggs, chopped
    Minced pimento
    Minced parsley

Place potatoes and onion in bowl; sprinkle with salt and pepper. Mix lightly with French dressing. Chill for 1 to 2 hours. Add salad dressing and toss lightly; blend in eggs. Mix in small amount minced pimento and parsley for color. Add salad dressing and toss lightly; blend in eggs. Mix in small amount minced pimento and parsley for color. Add additional seasoning and dressing to taste, if desired. Serve in bowl or on platter surrounded with salad greens, tomato sections, slices or wedges of hard-cooked eggs or cucumber sticks. Garnish with paprika. Yield: 6 servings.

Margaret Lieb, USD #377
Effingham, Kansas

POTATO SALAD WITH BACON

    4 slices bacon, diced
    2 tbsp. sugar
    1 tbsp. sugar
    ¼ tsp. seasoned pepper
    1 tsp. prepared mustard
    ½ tsp. celery seed
    ⅓ c. vinegar
    1 lge. onion, chopped
    6 lge. potatoes, cooked, peeled and diced

Heat pressure saucepan; add bacon and cook until brown. Drain off almost all drippings. Combine remaining ingredients except potatoes; stir into fat. Add potatoes and mix well. Close over securely; pressure for 5 minutes. Reduce pressure immediately. Serve hot or cold. Yield: 6 servings.

Mrs. Aleen Hartman, Manderson-Hyattville H.S.
Manderson, Wyoming

POTATO SALAD

    3 to 4 potatoes, cooked and diced
    2 hard-cooked eggs, chopped coarsely
    ½ c. diced celery
    1 ½ tbsp. chopped onion
    1 tsp. salt
    ⅛ tsp. pepper
    2 to 3 tbsp. salad dressing

Place potatoes in mixing bowl; add chopped eggs and remaining ingredients. Mix thoroughly. Chill before serving. Serve on bed of salad greens. Yield: 4 servings.

Sister Mary Annunciata, South Cath. H.S.
Hartford, Connecticut

POTATO SALAD

    1 ½ tsp. flour
    ½ c. sugar
    1 tsp. dry mustard
    2 eggs
    ½ c. vinegar
    1 ½ c. water
    2 tbsp. butter
    ½ c. salad dressing (opt.)
    Dash of celery seed (opt.)
    Paprika (opt.)
    8 med. potatoes, cooked and chopped
    4 hard-cooked eggs, diced
    1 onion, chopped
    1 c. diced celery
    1 ½ tsp. salt
    3 sm. pickles, chopped

Mix first 3 ingredients; add eggs, vinegar and water. Melt butter; add dressing mixture. Cook until thickened; cool. Add salad dressing, celery seed and paprika. Combine remaining ingredients in large bowl; add dressing mixture. Yield: 12 servings.

Mrs. Jacqueline H. Spang, Cornwall Middle Sch.
Cornwall, Pennsylvania

POTATO SALAD

    6 c. cubed boiled potatoes, cold
    2 tbsp. chopped onion
    ¼ c. chopped cucumber pickle
    2 hard-boiled eggs, chopped
    1 tsp. prepared mustard
    ½ tsp. salt
    ⅛ tsp. pepper
    ¾ c. mayonnaise

Combine potatoes, onion, pickle, eggs and mustard in large bowl; sprinkle with salt and pepper and toss lightly. Add mayonnaise and toss well. Chill. Serve on platter surrounded with salad greens or sliced tomatoes. Garnish with paprika. Yield: 6 servings.

Mrs. David Crawford, Myrtle Attendance Ctr.
Myrtle, Mississippi

POTATO SALAD CAKE

Diced potatoes
Diced celery
Minced onion
Mayonnaise
Seasonings
Hard-cooked eggs

Combine all ingredients, reserving yolks of hard-cooked eggs. Line springform or fruit-cake pan with aluminum foil or waxed paper; press in potato salad. Cover tightly; store in refrigerator for s e v e r a l hours or overnight. Remove salad from pan. Prepare egg paste with reserved yolks as you would for deviled eggs. Place egg paste into cake decorator; decorate top of potato salad. Garnish with olive or radish slices. Yield: 15-20 servings.

Sister M. John Vianney, SSCM, Andrean H.S.
Gary, Indiana

POTATO SALAD WITH CARROT

4 potatoes, cooked and cubed
2 tbsp. grated onion
1 carrot, grated
½ c. chopped celery
1 tsp. salt
2 sweet pickles, chopped
¼ c. mayonnaise
2 tbsp. sweet pickle juice
4 lettuce leaves

Combine all ingredients except lettuce; place in large bowl and mix carefully. Chill overnight. Arrange on lettuce leaves. Serve immediately. Yield: 4 servings.

Barbara Powers, Benson Union H.S.
Benson, Arizona

POTATO SALAD WITH A FLAVOR

4 boiled potatoes, diced
1 lge. onion, diced
1 cucumber, diced (opt.)
5 hard-cooked eggs, diced
½ tsp. garlic powder
1 ½ tbsp. prepared mustard
3 tbsp. mayonnaise
3 tbsp. sandwich relish spread
2 to 3 tbsp. lemon juice

Combine all ingredients in large bowl; mix well. Chill until serving time. Yield: 6 servings.

Mrs. Helen E. Stanford, Union H.S.
Union, Oregon

POTATO SALAD WITH COOKED DRESSING

2 ½ to 3 lb. cooked and peeled potatoes, cubed
2 med. carrots, shredded
1 med. green pepper, chopped
1 med. onion, chopped
½ c. chopped celery
2 hard-boiled eggs, finely chopped
1 c. chopped sweet cucumber pickle
Cooked Salad Dressing

Place potatoes in large bowl. Mix next 6 ingredients. Add cooked salad dressing; toss lightly. Chill for 6 to 8 hours. Serve on lettuce.

COOKED SALAD DRESSING:

3 eggs, beaten
½ c. wine vinegar
¼ c. water
2 tbsp. sugar
1 tsp. salt
1 tsp. pepper
1 tsp. paprika
1 tsp. celery salt
2 tbsp. prepared mustard
½ c. mayonnaise

Mix all ingredients except mustard and mayonnaise; beat until smooth. Cook over medium heat, stirring constantly, until mixture thickens. Cool; add mayonnaise and mustard. Yield: 18 servings.

Jeri Bosserman, Drewry Mason Sch.
Ridgeway, Virginia

SLOVAK POTATO SALAD

6 to 8 sm. new potatoes
1 lge. sweet onion, sliced
¼ c. vinegar
¾ c. cooking oil
Salt and pepper to taste
1 tsp. paprika

Cook potatoes in jackets; peel and slice while warm. Place potatoes in bowl; add onion. Combine vinegar, oil, salt and pepper in small saucepan; bring to boil. Pour over potatoes; toss lightly. Garnish with paprika. Yield: 6 servings.

Mrs. Lois Maxiah, Estee Jr. High Sch.
Gloversville, New York

RIPE OLIVE-POTATO SALAD

3 tbsp. salad oil
1 tbsp. vinegar
1 ½ tsp. salt
⅛ tsp. black pepper
2 c. diced boiled potatoes
1 c. ripe olives

(Continued on next page)

2 hard-cooked eggs, diced
1 c. sliced celery or diced cucumber
¼ c. diced dill pickle
¼ c. diced pimento
⅓ c. mayonnaise
1 tsp. grated onion

Blend oil, vinegar, salt and pepper; pour over potatoes in large bowl. Toss lightly; cool thoroughly. Cut olives from pits into large pieces. Combine potatoes, olives, eggs, celery, pickle and pimento. Blend mayonnaise and onion; mix lightly into salad. Chill thoroughly. Yield: 4-6 servings.

Mrs. Anne Strychar, Lamont H.S.
Lamont, Alberta, Canada

POTATO SALAD ROLL

3 c. thick mashed potatoes
½ tsp. salt
Dash of white pepper
Dry mustard
3 hard-boiled eggs, chopped
¼ c. chopped celery
⅓ c. chopped onions
¼ c. pickle relish, drained
½ c. mayonnaise or salad dressing
¼ c. thick sour cream
1 tbsp. vinegar or lemon juice
Pimento strips

Season potatoes with salt, pepper and dash of dry mustard; roll or pat out on cloth. Mix eggs, celery, onions, pickle relish, mayonnaise, sour cream, vinegar and dash of mustard; spread mixture over potatoes. Add pimento strips. Roll up and wrap in cloth. Chill for 1 hour. Cut into 1-inch slices; garnish with parsley or olives. Yield: 8 servings.

Katharine Rigby, Starr-Washington Sch.
Union Furnace, Ohio

SOUR CREAM-POTATO SALAD

7 med. potatoes, cooked, peeled and diced
⅓ c. diced onion
4 hard-cooked eggs, diced
¾ c. chopped celery
¾ c. pickle relish or chopped sweet pickles
⅓ c. mayonnaise
¾ c. sour cream
Salt to taste
1 tsp. mustard
2 tbsp. sugar
2 tbsp. (about) pickle juice

Combine potatoes, onion, eggs and celery in large bowl; add pickle relish and mix lightly. Mix together mayonnaise, sour cream, salt, mustard,

sugar and pickle juice; add to potato mixture, mixing lightly. Yield: 8 servings.

Mrs. Sara Sprunger
Paulding Exempted Village Sch.
Paulding, Ohio

WEDDING RING MOLDED POTATO SALAD

10 to 12 new red potatoes
1 c. finely chopped celery
¾ c. finely diced cucumber
6 hard-boiled eggs, chopped
4 c. mayonnaise
2 tsp. prepared mustard
2 tbsp. grated onion
1 ½ tsp. salt
1 c. sliced, black pitted olives or stuffed green olives
¼ c. grated carrot
½ bunch parsley sprigs

Boil potatoes in jackets in salted water until done; cool, peel and dice. Add celery, cucumber and eggs; toss lightly with 2 forks. Mix 3 cups mayonnaise, mustard, onion and salt; add to mixture. Pack firmly in large bowl; chill for several hours or overnight. Unmold salad onto large round platter; frost top with remaining mayonnaise. Circle base of salad with ring of sliced olives and grated carrot. Surround with parsley sprigs. Yield: 10-12 servings.

Mrs. Gloriann Martinson Katabi
Watsonville H.S.
Watsonville, California

SWEET POTATO SALAD

½ c. sugar
¼ c. butter
4 c. sweet potatoes, cooked
½ c. pecans
½ c. coconut
¾ c. marshmallows
¼ c. raisins (opt.)

Add sugar and butter to potatoes while warm; mash potatoes and set aside to cool. Combine remaining ingredients; add to potato mixture in bowl. Chill before serving. Top salad with whipped cream or fold in whipped cream before serving, if desired. Yield: 10-12 servings.

Mrs. Linda Frank, Sam Houston H.S.
Arlington, Texas

RAW BROCCOLI SALAD

1 bunch tender broccoli
Salt and pepper to taste
⅓ c. salad oil

(Continued on next page)

2 tbsp. lemon juice
4 ripe tomatoes
⅓ c. sour cream
1 tsp. prepared mustard
4 to 6 lettuce cups

Wash broccoli, cutting off flowerets; chop flowerets fine. Reserve stalk for later use. Sprinkle with salt, pepper, oil and lemon juice. Mix well; chill for 30 minutes or longer. Peel tomatoes; cut in half. Squeeze out most of seeds. Cut up into cubes; add to broccoli. Add sour cream blended with mustard. Mix well; serve in lettuce cups. Yield: 4-6 servings.

Mrs. Anne Bailey, Santa Monica H.S.
Santa Monica, California

SESAME SEED SALAD

1 head lettuce, torn into sm. pieces
1 tsp. toasted sesame seed
1 tsp. Romano cheese
Italian dressing

Sprinkle lettuce with sesame seed and Romano cheese. Add dressing; toss until each lettuce leaf is covered. Yield: 6 servings.

Mrs. Wana Miller, Trenton H.S.
Trenton, Texas

FAIRY TOADSTOOLS FOR BUFFET

Spinach or green salad
Hard-boiled eggs
Sm. tomatoes, halved
Mayonnaise

Make bed of spinach; stand eggs on ends. Top with tomato caps; fleck with mayonnaise.

Sue Daye, William Floyd Sch.
Mastic Beach, New York

FRESH SPINACH SALAD

4 c. fresh spinach
¼ c. chopped onion
¼ c. diced celery
4 hard-cooked eggs, sliced
¼ c. oil
2 tbsp. tarragon vinegar
1 ½ tsp. salt
¼ tsp. pepper
Dash of garlic salt

Wash spinach; drain. Tear into bite-sized pieces; add onions, celery and eggs. Toss lightly; chill. Combine remaining ingredients in jar; shake vigorously. Serve over greens.

Margaret Holland, Washington H.S.
Brainerd, Minnesota

FRESH SPINACH SALAD

2 lb. fresh young spinach
1 lge. Spanish onion
⅓ c. lemon juice
⅔ c. salad oil
¾ tsp. salt
½ tsp. coarsely ground pepper

Wash spinach leaves in cold water; drain thoroughly. Break into large wooden bowl. Slice onion in thin rings; place on top of spinach. Combine lemon juice, oil and seasonings in jar; shake well. Pour over spinach and onion; toss lightly. Yield: 8 servings.

Mrs. Dorothy Huchro, Keene Cen. Sch.
Keene Valley, New York

RAW SPINACH

1 lb. spinach
8 slices crisp bacon, crumbled
6 green onions, sliced
4 hard-cooked eggs, chopped
1 clove of garlic, cut
½ c. oil
½ tsp. salt
3 tbsp. lemon juice
¼ c. vinegar

Wash spinach; break leaves into bite-sized pieces. Toss with bacon, onions and eggs. Cover; refrigerate about 2 hours. Marinate garlic in salad oil at least 1 hour. Remove garlic; discard. Combine salt, lemon juice and vinegar; beat in oil. Pour over salad. Toss well. Serve immediately. Yield: 8-10 servings.

Mrs. Erleen Johnson, Clay H.S.
Oregon, Ohio

SPINACH YOU'LL LOVE

1 lb. fresh spinach
½ c. water
3 strips bacon
Salt and pepper to taste
¼ c. vinegar

Clean spinach; add water. Cover; cook for 4 minutes. Remove lid; cook until completely wilted and done. Drain. Fry bacon until crisp; drain on paper towel. Cool; crumble into spinach. Add salt, pepper and vinegar. Serve piping hot. Canned or frozen spinach may be substituted. Yield: 4 servings.

Mrs. Connie McClure, Nimitz Jr. H.S.
San Antonio, Texas

SPINACH-LETTUCE-BACON SALAD

    6 strips bacon, diced
    4 c. young spinach, torn in bite-sized
      pieces
    2 c. lettuce, torn in bite-sized pieces
    2 finely chopped hard-cooked eggs
    ⅓ c. salad dressing

Fry bacon until crisp; drain. Place spinach and lettuce in bowl. Sprinkle with bacon and eggs. Add salad dressing; toss lightly. Yield: 8 servings.

Marie K. Jaspers, Pomeroy H.S.
Pomeroy, Washington

TOSSED GREEN SALAD

    1 sm. head lettuce
    ¼ lb. uncooked spinach
    ⅛ lb. chicory
    1 bunch watercress
    2 scallions, minced
    1 clove of garlic, cut
    ¼ c. French dressing
    Salt and pepper to taste

Wash greens well; drain. Chill for 30 minutes; wrap in towel to dry. Rub salad bowl with garlic; allow shreds to remain in bowl. Tear or cut greens into salad bowl; add dressing. Season with salt and pepper; toss with fork until greens are coated with dressing. Yield: 4 servings.

Huquette Levesque, Atholville Composite H.S.
Atholville, New Brunswick, Canada

WILTED LEAF SALAD

    1 pkg. leaf spinach
    1 or 2 bunches onions, chopped
    6 slices bacon
    ½ c. Italian salad dressing

Wash spinach in cold water; place in wooden salad bowl. Add onions; blend with forks. Fry bacon; drain and crumble. Add to spinach and onion. Heat salad dressing; pour over salad. Toss until greens are well saturated. Serve immediately. Yield: 4-6 servings.

Sue Evelyn Smith, Victoria H.S.
Victoria, Texas

BUFFET STUFFED TOMATOES

    5 hard-cooked eggs, chopped
    ¾ c. chopped celery
    ¼ c. mayonnaise
    2 tbsp. coarsely chopped parsley
    1 tsp. salt

    ½ tsp. prepared mustard
    ⅛ tsp. pepper
    4 tomatoes
    Salad greens

Combine all ingredients except tomatoes and greens. Remove stem ends from tomatoes; scoop out pulp. Fill tomatoes with the egg salad mixture; place on salad greens. If desired, garnish with corn chips. Yield: 4 servings.

Mrs. Esther Williams, Pocatello H.S.
Pocatello, Idaho

GARLIC-LETTUCE SALAD

    1 clove of garlic
    ½ tsp. lemon juice
    ½ head lettuce
    2 med. tomatoes
    Salt to taste

Peel garlic; chop finely in bottom of salad bowl. Add lemon juice. Break lettuce in bite-sized pieces; add tomatoes cut in wedges. Toss lightly. Serve in individual salad bowls. Yield: 4 servings.

Mrs. Coleman Goodwin, Lowndes Co. H.S.
Fort Deposit, Alabama

HELGA'S GERMAN TOMATO SALAD

    4 med. ripe tomatoes
    2 slender cucumbers
    1 sm. onion, purple or white
    Salt
    Black pepper, coarsely ground
    3 tbsp. salad oil
    3 tbsp. wine vinegar

Wash and dry tomatoes. Peel if desired; slice. Peel cucumbers; score with a fork and slice. Peel onion; slice very thin. Place tomato slices in large flat bowl; place 1 slice onion on each tomato slice. Top with 1 slice cucumber. Sprinkle with salt; grind pepper over them. Spread salad oil over slices, then vinegar. Repeat until all tomatoes, cucumbers and onions are used. Marinate 10 minutes before serving. Yield: 6 servings.

Mrs. Bette D. Jenness
Linesville-Conneaut-Summit Joint Sch.
Linesville, Pennsylvania

MARINATED SLICED TOMATOES

    3 peeled tomatoes, sliced
    ¼ c. minced white onion
    ¼ c. Parmesan salad dressing

(Continued on next page)

Place tomatoes in flat dish; sprinkle onion on top. Cover with Parmesan salad dressing. Chill 1 hour and 30 minutes to 2 hours. Serve with marinade. Yield: 4 servings.

Emily Daniel, Talbot Co. Sch.
Talbotton, Georgia

ITALIAN TOMATOES

3 med. fresh tomatoes
¼ tsp. salt
⅛ tsp. black pepper
3 tbsp. butter or margarine
½ tsp. Italian seasoning
1 c. soft bread crumbs
1 tbsp. grated Parmesan cheese

Cut tomatoes into halves. Sprinkle with salt and black pepper; set aside. Melt butter; add Italian seasoning. Mix well. Stir in bread crumbs and cheese; blend thoroughly. Spoon mixture onto cut sides of tomatoes. Place under broiler for 5 minutes 4 inches from heat source. Serve as an accompaniment or as a meat garnish. Yield: 6 servings.

Mrs. George A. Miller, Milan H.S.
Milan, Ohio

STUFFED TOMATO SALAD

½ c. chopped celery
¼ c. chopped green pepper
¼ c. chopped onion
¾ c. salad dressing or mayonnaise
6 med. tomatoes
½ head lettuce

Mix celery, green pepper and onion with salad dressing. Blanch tomatoes; cut into tomato roses, making about six petals. Stuff tomatoes with filling; place on lettuce leaf. Yield: 6 servings.

Mrs. Fay G. Whittaker, Michel Jr. H.S.
Biloxi, Mississippi

TASTY TOMATO SALAD

1 lge. can tomatoes
2 c. saltine crackers
1 egg, diced
2 tbsp. chopped celery
1 tsp. salt
¼ tsp. pepper
1 tbsp. mayonnaise

Drain tomatoes well; add finely crushed crackers. Add egg, celery, salt and pepper; mix lightly. Add mayonnaise; mix slightly. Chill and serve on lettuce. Yield: 4 servings.

Mrs. Brooksie Rentz, Brookland-Cayce H.S.
Cayce, South Carolina

TOMATO AND GREEN PEPPER SALAD

2 lge. tomatoes, diced
1 lge. green pepper, diced
1 med. onion, diced
¼ lge. box crackers, crumbled
Salt and pepper to taste
1 tsp. celery salt
2 tbsp. (heaping) mayonnaise

Combine all ingredients; toss lightly. Serve. Yield: 5 servings.

Cynthia Weddle, Brock H.S.
Brock, Nebraska

TOMATO ROSE SALAD

6 med. firm tomatoes
9 oz. cream cheese
Milk
6 hard-cooked egg yolks
Watercress or lettuce
French dressing

Peel and chill tomatoes. Soften cream cheese slightly with milk. Form 2 rows of petals on each tomato by pressing level teaspoons of softened cheese against side of tomato, then drawing teaspoon down with a curving motion. Sprinkle each tomato center with hard-cooked egg yolk pressed through a strainer. Serve on crisp watercress or lettuce with French dressing. Yield: 6 servings.

Mrs. Odessa H. Bieschke, Carthage H.S.
Carthage, Indiana

TOMATOES STUFFED WITH GUACAMOLE

3 lge. ripe avocados, peeled and seeded
2 tsp. lemon juice
Salt and pepper to taste
1 pt. lge. curd cottage cheese
1 green onion, chopped
1½ tbsp. (about) chili sauce
6 lge. tomatoes
Lettuce leaves
Paprika
6 pitted black olives

Mash avocados until very creamy; add lemon juice, salt, pepper, cottage cheese, green onion and chili sauce. Blend well. Blanch tomatoes and remove skin. Place tomatoes on end; cut into eighths, slicing almost to bottom, resembling flowers. Spread petals gently. Arrange tomatoes on lettuce leaves. Fill each with guacamole. Sprinkle paprika on top. Garnish with black olives. Yield: 6 servings.

Mrs. Judith Hernandez, Alchesay H.S.
Whiteriver, Arizona

Tomato Lettuce Salads

TOSSED SALAD SANS TOMATOES

½ to 1 head lettuce
10 to 15 stuffed olives, chopped
½ to 1 med. onion, chopped
2 raw carrots, peeled and sliced
2 stalks celery, sliced
¼ to ½ c. salad dressing
2 to 3 tbsp. olive juice
⅛ tsp. garlic salt
½ tsp. salt and pepper

Break lettuce into salad bowl; add olives, onion, carrots and celery. Mix salad dressing with olive juice and seasoning. Toss salad lightly with dressing. Yield: 4-6 servings.

Mrs. Blanche Farrell, Indian Lake Cen. Sch.
Indian Lake, New York

WILTED LEAF LETTUCE SALAD

¼ c. pork drippings
1 tbsp. chopped onion
3 tbsp. vinegar
1 tbsp. water
½ tsp. salt
½ tsp. sugar
1 med. head lettuce, broken into pieces
1 hard-cooked egg, diced

Heat drippings in small frying pan; add onion. Cook until golden, stirring 2 or 3 times. Add vinegar, water, salt and sugar; heat to rolling boil. Combine lettuce and egg; toss with dressing. Yield: 6-8 servings.

Patricia Irvin, Wells H.S.
Wells, Minnesota

HOT LETTUCE

4 strips bacon, diced
1 tbsp. flour
1 ½ tbsp. sugar
⅛ tsp. salt
Dash of pepper
⅛ tsp. dry mustard
1 egg, beaten
½ c. milk
2 tbsp. vinegar
Shredded lettuce or endive
Chopped onion

Fry bacon; stir in flour, sugar, salt, pepper and mustard. Combine egg, milk and vinegar; add to bacon and seasonings. Cook until thickened; pour immediately over lettuce and onion. Yield: 4 servings.

Mrs. Marion R. Hessler, Gov. Mifflin Sr. H.S.
Shillington, Pennsylvania

WILTED LETTUCE SALAD

3 slices bacon, diced
1 egg, slightly beaten
¼ c. vinegar
1 sm. onion, finely chopped
1 tsp. sugar
1 tsp. salt
1 tsp. pepper
1 tsp. paprika
Lettuce
1 or 2 hard-cooked eggs, diced

Fry bacon until crisp; remove from pan. Combine egg, vinegar, onion and seasonings; add to bacon drippings. Cook over low heat, stirring constantly, for about 5 minutes or until thickened and smooth; cool. Break lettuce into salad bowl; add bacon and eggs. Toss salad lightly with dressing until ingredients are well mixed. Serve at once. Yield: 4 servings.

Barbara A. West, Cradock H.S.
Portsmouth, Virginia

WILTED GREENS

4 or 5 slices bacon
2 tbsp. melted butter
¼ c. mild vinegar
1 tsp. grated onion
1 tsp. sugar
1 head lettuce, separated
Shredded cabbage, dandelion, young spinach leaves or other greens
2 hard-cooked eggs, sliced

Saute bacon until crisp; remove from pan. Drain; crumble in small pieces. Heat butter; add vinegar, bacon, onion and sugar. Pour over greens Serve at once on warm plates; garnish with eggs. Yield: 4 servings.

Janice Kindler, Grand Rapids H.S.
Grand Rapids, Ohio

WILTED LETTUCE SALAD

6 slices bacon, diced
1 lge. head lettuce, torn into bite-sized pieces
2 green onions, chopped
½ c. bacon drippings
¼ c. vinegar
¼ c. sugar
½ tsp. salt

Fry bacon until crisp; set aside. Combine lettuce and onions; sprinkle with bacon. Heat bacon drippings, vinegar, sugar and salt; pour over lettuce. Toss lightly; serve immediately. Yield: 6 servings.

Margaret Poling, Berrien Springs H.S.
Berrien Springs, Michigan

RECIPE FOR KRAUT LOAF SUPREME ON PAGE 253

Congealed Vegetable Salads

ASPARAGUS MOLD

1 c. hot asparagus liquid
1 tbsp. gelatin, dissolved in ¼ c. cold
  water
½ c. mayonnaise
½ c. cream, whipped
1 tsp. salt
2 tbsp. lemon juice
1 can all-green asparagus
1 c. shelled blanched almonds, chopped

Pour hot liquid over dissolved gelatin. Fold in mayonnaise, whipped cream, salt and lemon juice when partially set. Add asparagus and almonds. Pour into mold and congeal. Serve with additional mayonnaise whipped with small amount additional lemon juice. Yield: 12 servings.

Mrs. Eddie Hilou, Cayuga H.S.
Cayuga, Texas

MARY LEE'S FAVORITE SALAD

¾ c. sugar
½ c. wine vinegar
½ tsp. salt
2 envelopes gelatin
1 med. can all-green asparagus,
  mashed fine
1 c. finely cut celery
1 sm. can pimento, chopped
½ c. chopped nuts (opt.)
1 tsp. (scant) grated or finely chopped
  onion (opt.)

Heat 1/2 cup water, sugar, vinegar and salt to a boil. Melt gelatin in 1/2 cup cold water; add to hot mixture. Chill until partially set. Combine asparagus, celery, pimento, nuts and onion. Add to gelatin. Chill until firm. Yield: 8-10 servings.

Mary Lee Hartley, Criso Co. H.S.
Cordele, Georgia

ASPARAGUS SOUP SALAD

1 sm. pkg. lime Jell-O
½ c. hot water
1 c. cream of asparagus soup
½ c. mayonnaise
1 tbsp. vinegar
1 tsp. grated onion
Dash of pepper
¾ c. shredded cucumber, drained well
½ c. celery, chopped fine
1 tbsp. chopped parsley

Mix Jell-O and water in saucepan. Add soup gradually. Heat, stirring until Jell-O dissolves. Add mayonnaise, vinegar, onion and pepper. Beat with electric mixer until smooth. Chill until partially set. Fold in cucumber, celery and parsley. Chill. Yield: 8 servings.

Mrs. Raye L. Evers, McGregor H.S.
McGregor, Texas

BEET RING

1 3-oz. pkg. lemon gelatin
2 c. beet juice
Juice of 1 lemon
1 1-lb. can shoestring beets
⅛ tsp. salt
4 tbsp. prepared horseradish

Dissolve gelatin in 1 cup hot beet juice; add remaining juice and lemon juice. Chill until thick. Add beets, salt and horseradish. Pour into oiled 1-quart ring mold; chill until firm. Unmold; serve on lettuce. Surround with sliced cucumbers. Yield: 6-8 servings.

Mrs. Anne Stalter, Riverside Park Jr. H.S.
Springfield, Vermont

CONGEALED ASPARAGUS SALAD

1 pkg. unflavored gelatin
½ c. cold water
1 c. hot asparagus liquid
½ tsp. salt
¼ c. sugar
¼ c. lemon juice
½ c. chopped celery
½ c. chopped green pepper
1 4-oz. jar pimento, cut into strips
1 No. 2 can asparagus

Soften gelatin in cold water. Dissolve thoroughly in hot liquid. Add salt, sugar and lemon juice; stir until dissolved. Fold celery, pepper and pimento into partially congealed gelatin. Arrange asparagus in ring mold. Pour mixture over asparagus. Chill until firm. Yield: 8 servings.

Annette Braswell, Monroe Area H.S.
Monroe, Georgia

BEET SALAD

1 pkg. cherry Jell-O
1 can shoestring beets
¼ c. (scant) vinegar
½ c. sugar
5 to 6 whole cloves
1 pkg. cherry Jell-O
Mayonnaise
2 hard-boiled eggs, grated

Drain liquid from beets into measuring cup; add vinegar and enough water to make 2 cups liquid. Add sugar and cloves. Simmer gently for 10 minutes; do not reduce quantity below 2 cups. Remove cloves; add Jell-O. Cool. Add beets. Pour into individual molds. Chill until set. Top servings with 1 teaspoon mayonnaise; sprinkle egg on top. Yield: 7 servings.

Mrs. Norma Macri, Kellogg Jr. H.S.
Kellogg, Idaho

BEET SALAD

1 1-lb. can shoestring beets
1 3-oz. pkg. lemon gelatin
¼ c. sugar
¼ c. vinegar
1 tbsp. horseradish

Drain beets; measure juice. Add water to make 1 1/2 cups liquid. Bring liquid to boil; remove from heat. Add gelatin, sugar, vinegar and horseradish, stirring until gelatin and sugar have dissolved. Add beets. Turn into 1-quart mold. Chill until firm. Yield: 4-6 servings.

Mrs. Madie Oliver, Centerville Sch.
Groveton, Texas

BEET VELVET SALAD

1 pkg. lemon gelatin
1 c. hot water
1 can diced beets, minced fine
½ pt. thick sour cream
1 tbsp. lemon juice
1 tsp. grated onion
Salt and pepper to taste

Dissolve gelatin in hot water; stir in beets. Add sour cream; blend well. Add remaining ingredients. Pour into large mold; chill until firm. Unmold on crisp salad greens. Yield: 6 servings.

Mrs. Ruth Gill, Tuloso-Midway H.S.
Corpus Christi, Texas

TART RED BEET SALAD

1 pkg. cherry gelatin
1 ¾ c. hot liquid, including juice from beets
2 tbsp. sugar
2 tbsp. vinegar
⅛ tsp. cloves
1 No. 303 can shredded beets

Dissolve gelatin in hot liquid. Add sugar, vinegar and cloves; chill. Add beets. Mix well. Chill; serve.

Dianne Smith, Bay Dist. H.S.
Kearny, Arizona

BEST BEET SALAD

1 envelope red gelatin
¼ c. cold water
¼ c. sugar
½ tsp. salt
1 c. hot water
¼ c. vinegar
1 tbsp. lemon juice
1 c. diced cooked beets
1 c. finely chopped celery
2 tbsp. horseradish

Soften gelatin in cold water; add sugar, salt and hot water. Add vinegar, lemon juice, beets, celery and horseradish. Pour into greased mold; refrigerate until set. Unmold; serve with sour cream dressing.

Mary H. Dyke, Gardiner Area H.S.
Gardiner, Maine

MOLDED BEETS

1 3-oz. pkg. lemon gelatin
1 tbsp. lemon juice
1 tbsp. horseradish
½ tsp. salt
Pinch of white pepper
1 ½ c. julienne beets
¼ c. sliced stuffed olives

Prepare gelatin according to package directions, using only 1 3/4 cups water. Add lemon juice, horseradish, salt and pepper; stir well. Cool until partially set. Fold in beets and olives; place in 3 to 4-cup mold. Serve with sour cream dressing. Yield: 6-8 servings.

Mrs. Ethel M. Poley, Narrows Burg Central
Narrowsburg, New York

MOLDED BEET SALAD

1 pkg. lemon Jell-O
1 c. beet juice, hot
2 tsp. lemon juice
1 tsp. grated lemon rind
1 tsp. salt
1 tbsp. finely diced onion
1 tbsp. horseradish
1 c. chopped cooked beets
¼ c. coarsely grated carrots
¼ c. diced celery
½ c. cold water

Dissolve Jell-O in hot beet juice; add lemon juice, lemon rind, salt, onion and horseradish. Mix well. Add beets, carrots and celery. Add cold water; mix. Pour into ring mold; chill until firm. Serve on endive; garnish with sour cream. Yield: 6 servings.

Barbara Mac Ritchie, Northville Cen. Sch.
Northville, New York

COLESLAW SOUFFLE SALAD

    1 3-oz. pkg. lemon gelatin
    1 ¼ c. hot water
    1 ½ tbsp. vinegar
    ⅓ c. mayonnaise
    Dash of salt
    Dash of black pepper
    1 ½ c. chopped cabbage
    1 ½ tsp. chopped onion
    1 ½ tbsp. chopped green pepper
    1 ½ tbsp. chopped pimento
    ¼ tsp. celery seed

Combine gelatin and hot water. Combine vinegar, mayonnaise, salt and pepper; add to gelatin mixture. Chill until partially congealed. Beat until fluffy. Add remaining ingredients. Pour into mold or pan. Chill until firm. Yield: 5 servings.

Mrs. E. R. Moss, Biggersville H.S.
Corinth, Mississippi

COLESLAW PERFECTION SALAD

    1 pkg. lemon gelatin
    1 c. hot water
    ½ c. mayonnaise
    1 c. cold water
    2 tbsp. vinegar
    ¼ tsp. salt
    1 ½ c. finely shredded cabbage
    ½ c. radish slices
    ½ c. diced celery
    2 tbsp. diced green pepper
    1 tbsp. diced onion

Dissolve gelatin in hot water. Blend in mayonnaise, cold water, vinegar and salt. Chill mixture until partially set; beat until fluffy. Add cabbage, radish slices, celery, green pepper and onion. Pour into individual molds. Chill until set. Yield: 8 servings.

Karen Quam, Central Jr. H.S.
Alexandria, Minnesota
Mrs. Margaret Egolf, Armstrong Township H.S.
Armstrong, Illinois

COLESLAW SALAD

    1 3-oz. pkg. lemon Jell-O
    1 c. hot water
    ½ c. cold water
    2 tbsp. vinegar
    ½ c. salad dressing
    ¼ tsp. salt
    ⅛ tsp. pepper
    2 c. chopped cabbage
    1 tbsp. chopped onion
    2 tbsp. chopped celery

Dissolve Jell-O in hot water. Add cold water and vinegar. Allow to set until gelatin is consistency of thick molasses. Whip with beaters until gelatin is fluffy. Add salad dressing and seasonings. Beat to combine well. Fold cabbage, onion and celery into gelatin mixture. Chill. Yield: 8 servings.

Katherine Rempel, Skenna Secondary Sch.
Terrace, British Columbia, Canada

CONGEALED SLAW

    8 c. shredded cabbage
    ½ c. chopped onion
    1 c. chopped green pepper
    1 envelope unflavored gelatin
    ⅔ c. sugar
    ⅔ c. vinegar
    2 tsp. celery seed
    1 ½ tsp. salt
    ¼ tsp. pepper
    ⅔ c. salad oil

Mix cabbage, onion and green pepper; sprinkle with 1/2 cup cold water. Set in refrigerator to chill. Soften gelatin in 1/4 cup cold water. Mix sugar, vinegar, celery seed, salt and pepper in saucepan. Bring to a boil. Remove from heat; stir in softened gelatin. Cool until slightly thickened; beat well. Gradually beat in salad oil. Drain vegetables; pour dressing over top. Mix slightly until all vegetables are coated with dressing. May be served immediately or kept a week in refrigerator. Grated carrots and apples may be added, if desired. Yield: 16 servings.

Mrs. Ruth N. Powell, Asheboro Jr. H.S.
Asheboro, North Carolina

MOLDED COLESLAW RING

    1 envelope unflavored gelatin
    1 c. milk
    ⅔ c. mayonnaise
    1 tsp. prepared mustard
    1 ½ tsp. grated onion
    1 ½ tsp. celery seed
    1 tsp. salt
    ⅓ c. light cream
    1 ½ c. finely shredded cabbage
    ½ c. finely shredded carrots

Sprinkle gelatin over 1/2 cup milk in measuring cup; let stand 5 minutes to soften. Set in pan of boiling water. Heat, stirring to dissolve gelatin. Let cool slightly. Combine mayonnaise, mustard, onion, celery seed and salt in large bowl. Mix well. Stir in cream, remaining milk and gelatin mixture gradually. Refrigerate until consistency of unbeaten egg white, about 45 minutes. Fold in cabbage and carrots. Refrigerate 2 hours. Yield: 5 servings.

Mrs. Mary C. McClincy, Western H.S.
Las Vegas, Nevada

KRAUT LOAF SUPREME

3 envelopes unflavored gelatin
1 ½ c. cold water
4 c. chicken bouillon or broth
1 tbsp. instant minced onion
½ tsp. celery seed
2 c. sauerkraut, drained and chopped
1 tbsp. lemon juice
½ tsp. salt
¼ tsp. pepper
½ tsp. Worcestershire sauce
2 c. cubed cooked chicken or 2 6-oz. cans
1 4-oz. can Vienna sausages, sliced
¾ c. chopped green pepper

Sprinkle gelatin from 1 envelope on 1 cup water in saucepan. Dissolve gelatin over low heat, stirring constantly. Remove from heat; stir in 1 cup bouillon, 1 teaspoon onion and half the celery seed. Chill to consistency of unbeaten egg white. Fold in kraut and turn into 9 x 5 x 3-inch loaf pan. Chill until almost firm. Meanwhile, sprinkle remaining gelatin on remaining water. Dissolve gelatin over low heat, stirring constantly. Remove from heat; stir in lemon juice, remaining bouillon and seasonings. Chill to consistency of unbeaten egg white. Fold in chicken, sausages and green pepper. Pour on almost-firm kraut layer and chill until firm. Unmold on bed of lettuce; garnish with radishes, green pepper and parsley, if desired.

Photograph for this recipe on page 249.

PERFECTION SALAD

1 3-oz. pkg. lemon gelatin
1 c. boiling water
1 c. pineapple juice
1 tbsp. lemon juice
1 c. cabbage, diced fine
2 med. carrots, diced fine

Mix gelatin and water until gelatin is dissolved. Add pineapple juice and lemon juice. Empty into bowl; chill until partially set. Stir and add vegetables. Pour into mold; chill until firm. Yield: 6 servings.

Mrs. Katherine McIlquham, Senior H.S.
Chippewa Falls, Wisconsin

SEAFOAM COLESLAW

1 pkg. lime-flavored gelatin
¾ tsp. salt
1 c. hot water
¾ c. cold water
⅔ c. mayonnaise
2 tbsp. vinegar
2 to 3 tsp. grated onion
¾ tsp. celery seed
2 c. finely shredded cabbage, chopped

Dissolve gelatin and salt in hot water. Add cold water, mayonnaise, vinegar, onion and celery seed. Beat with rotary beater to blend. Chill until slightly thickened. Fold in cabbage. Pour into a 3-cup mold or 6 individual molds. Chill until firm. Yield: 6 servings.

Arlene Lenort, Pine Island H.S.
Pine Island, Minnesota
Ruth Wiggins, Merritt H.S.
Merritt, Michigan

STAY CRISP SLAW

8 c. cabbage, shredded with knife
2 carrots, shredded
1 green pepper, cut into thin strips
½ c. chopped onion
¾ c. cold water
1 envelope unflavored gelatin
⅔ c. sugar
⅔ c. vinegar
2 tsp. celery seeds
1 ½ tsp. salt
¼ tsp. black pepper
⅔ c. salad oil

Mix cabbage, carrots, green pepper and onion; sprinkle with 1/2 cup cold water. Chill. Soften gelatin in 1/4 cup cold water. Mix sugar, vinegar, celery seeds, salt and pepper in saucepan; bring to a boil. Stir in softened gelatin. Cool until slightly thickened; beat well. Gradually beat in salad oil. Drain vegetables; pour dressing over top. Mix lightly until all vegetables are coated with dressing. May be served immediately or stored in refrigerator. Stir just before serving to separate pieces. Yield: 8 servings.

Anna Louise Baker, Pine Hill H.S.
Pine Hill, Alabama
Mrs. Delia McClurg, Merino H.S.
Merino, Colorado

THREE-POINT SALAD

1 pkg. lemon gelatin
2 c. warm water
1 tsp. celery salt
3 tbsp. vinegar
2 tbsp. tomato catsup
1 c. shredded cabbage

Dissolve gelatin in warm water. Add celery salt, vinegar and catsup. Chill until slightly congealed; add cabbage. Chill until firm. Serve on crisp lettuce and garnish with mayonnaise.

Margaret Henderson, Walters H.S.
Walters, Oklahoma

TWENTY-FOUR HOUR VEGETABLE SALAD

2 lb. cabbage, shredded
1 green pepper, diced
1 carrot, grated
½ onion, grated
1 ½ tsp. gelatin
2 tbsp. cold water
¾ c. sugar
½ c. vinegar
½ tsp. celery seed
½ tsp. salt
⅛ tsp. pepper
½ c. salad oil

Combine vegetables in cellophane bag; place in refrigerator. Dissolve gelatin in cold water. Heat sugar and vinegar to boiling point; cool slightly. Add gelatin to vinegar. Chill until consistency of cream. Add remaining ingredients; mix in well-drained vegetables. Refrigerate for 24 hours. Yield: 8-10 servings.

Mary Ann Carlson, Kaukauna H.S.
Kaukauna, Wisconsin

CREAMY PIMENTO SALAD

1 pkg. lemon Jell-O
1 ½ c. warm water
½ tsp. salt
½ tsp. vinegar
½ c. milk
¼ tsp. paprika
1 tsp. minced onion
½ c. mayonnaise
½ c. grated cheese
½ c. finely chopped pimento

Dissolve Jell-O in warm water; add salt and vinegar. Chill until slightly thickened. Combine milk, paprika, onion and mayonnaise; blend well. Beat into Jell-O. Fold in cheese and pimento. Yield: 6 servings.

Willie Hawkins, Lovelady H.S.
Lovelady, Texas

CUCUMBER CREME SALAD

1 pkg. lime Jell-O
¾ c. boiling water
1 cucumber
1 c. sm. curd cottage cheese
1 c. salad dressing

Dissolve Jell-O in boiling water. Hollow out cucumber; grate shell. Combine cottage cheese and salad dressing; add grated cucumber. Add cottage cheese mixture to Jell-O; pour into 1-quart mold. Yield: 8 servings.

Mrs. Ethyl Dahler, Central H.S.
La Crosse, Wisconsin

BRIDE'S SALAD

1 3-oz. pkg. lime gelatin
1 c. warm water
1 c. grated cucumber
1 tsp. vinegar
1 tsp. minced onion
⅛ tsp. cayenne
½ tsp. salt
1 3-oz. pkg. cream cheese, softened
¼ c. chopped green pepper
1 c. diced celery

Dissolve gelatin in warm water; add cucumber, vinegar, onion, cayenne and salt. Chill until slightly thickened; add half the gelatin mixture to cream cheese. Fold in green pepper and celery. Place in large mold or individual molds. Chill until firm; add remaining gelatin mixture. Chill until firm. Unmold; serve on lettuce leaves. Yield: 8 servings.

Mrs. Lucile Gans, Abraham Lincoln H.S.
San Jose, California

CUCUMBER SALAD

1 pkg. lime Jell-O
1 c. hot water
1 med. cucumber
1 sm. onion
1 tsp. lemon juice
1 c. mayonnaise

Dissolve Jell-O in hot water. Grate cucumber and onion; mix with lemon juice and mayonnaise. Stir until smooth. Add to dissolved Jell-O; mix. Pour into mold to congeal. Yield: 8 servings.

Mrs. Joyce Gray, Waynesboro H.S.
Waynesboro, Georgia

LIME CUCUMBER SALAD

1 pkg. lime gelatin
1 c. boiling water
½ c. cold water
1 tbsp. vinegar
½ c. salad dressing
Dash of salt
1 tsp. grated onion
1 cucumber, grated

Dissolve gelatin in boiling water; mix well. Add cold water, vinegar, salad dressing and salt; beat well. Let set until partly congealed. Beat until fluffy. Squeeze water from cucumber; add onion and cucumber. Pour into 4-cup mold.

Vivian Delene, Barage H.S.
Baraga, Michigan

LIME CUCUMBER SALAD

1 pkg. lime Jell-O
1 c. boiling water
½ c. cold water
4 or 5 drops green food coloring
2 tbsp. vinegar
1 tbsp. lemon juice
¾ c. finely chopped cucumber
¼ c. finely chopped onion
⅓ c. mayonnaise

Dissolve Jell-O in boiling water; add cold water and green food coloring. Let stand until slightly thickened. Mix together vinegar, lemon juice, cucumber, onion and mayonnaise; stir into Jell-O. Chill until firm. Yield: 4-6 servings.

Dora R. Wray, Brookland Jr. H.S.
Richmond, Virginia

ST. PATRICK'S MOLD

1½ c. boiling water
1 pkg. lime gelatin
½ c. Miracle Whip
½ c. finely chopped onion
½ c. finely chopped celery
1 c. chopped cucumber

Pour boiling water over gelatin; stir until dissolved. Cool. Beat in Miracle Whip; fold in onion, celery and cucumber. Pour into oiled mold. Chill. Yield: 6 servings.

Mrs. Myrtle Mary Nicholson
Eastglen Composite H.S.
Edmonton, Alberta, Canada

JELLIED SPRING SALAD

1 tbsp. gelatin
¼ c. cold water
1½ c. hot water
1 tbsp. lemon juice
1 tbsp. vinegar
1 tsp. salt
1 c. diced cucumber
1 c. chopped celery
½ c. sliced green onion
½ c. sliced radishes
Lettuce
Mayonnaise

Soften gelatin in cold water; dissolve in hot water. Add lemon juice, vinegar and salt; chill until partially set. Add remaining ingredients. Pour into individual molds. Chill until firm. Unmold and serve on lettuce cup with mayonnaise.

Mrs. Jean Bauer, Hilda Sch.
Hilda, Alberta, Canada

FRESH SPINACH SALAD

1 pkg. lemon gelatin
1½ c. water
1 tbsp. vinegar
Dash of salt
1 c. cottage cheese
1 c. chopped fresh spinach
½ c. chopped celery
½ c. diced cucumber
½ c. mayonnaise or salad dressing
Sm. amount of grated onion (opt.)

Dissolve gelatin in water; add vinegar and salt. Chill until slightly thickened; whip until fluffy. Fold in remaining ingredients; pour into 8 x 8-inch pan. Chill until firm. Yield: 8-9 servings.

Mrs. Edgar W. Hermann, Franklin Jr. H.S.
Cedar Rapids, Iowa

MOLDED CUCUMBER SALAD

2 3-oz. pkg. lime gelatin
1½ c. boiling water
⅓ c. lemon juice
2 c. sour cream
2 c. chopped cucumber
¼ c. finely chopped onion
Salad greens
Mayonnaise

Dissolve gelatin in boiling water; add lemon juice. Chill until gelatin starts to thicken. Stir in sour cream, cucumber and onion. Pour into 8 individual molds or 6-cup mold; chill until firm. Unmold onto salad greens; serve with mayonnaise. Yield: 8 servings.

Helen S. Wilson, Miller H.S.
Hemlock, Ohio

JELLIED OLIVE SALAD

3 tbsp. unflavored gelatin
¾ c. cold water
½ c. mild vinegar
½ c. lemon juice
2½ c. boiling water
¾ c. sugar
1 tsp. salt
½ c. thinly sliced, stuffed olives
2 c. finely chopped celery
½ c. finely chopped nuts

Soak gelatin in cold water for 5 minutes; add vinegar, lemon juice, boiling water, sugar and salt. Cool until slightly thickened; add olives, celery and nuts. Dip mold in cold water; pour in gelatin. Chill until set. Serve on lettuce with mayonnaise. Yield: 8-10 servings.

Alice M. Ford, Central H.S.
Cheyenne, Wyoming

Congealed Mixed Vegetable Salads

CHEESE-SOUP SALAD

1 can condensed tomato soup
6 to 8 oz. cream or cottage cheese
1 tbsp. butter
⅓ tsp. salt
1 tbsp. onion juice
1 ½ tbsp. gelatin
¼ c. cold water
½ c. mayonnaise
1 c. chopped celery
1 c. chopped cucumber
½ c. sliced radishes
½ c. green onions, part of tops included

Heat soup; add cheese, butter, salt and onion juice. Soften gelatin in cold water; add to soup. Cool until partly set; fold in mayonnaise, celery, cucumber, radishes and onions. Chill until firm. Yield: 8-10 servings.

Helen Firkus, Neenah H.S.
Neenah, Wisconsin

CRUNCHY SALAD

1 pkg. lime Jell-O
1 c. grated cabbage
1 c. grated carrots
½ c. finely chopped celery

Prepare Jell-O according to package directions. Pour into 1 1/2 quart mold or loaf pan; chill until partially set. Mix cabbage, carrots and celery. Press vegetables into Jell-O. Chill until firm. Unmold; serve on lettuce. Yield: 8 servings.

Mrs. Altanette Autry, Woodsboro H.S.
Woodsboro, Texas

GOLDEN SURPRISE SALAD

1 pkg. lime Jell-O
2 c. boiling water
1 ¾ c. cold water
1 pkg. orange or lemon Jell-O
½ c. salad dressing
Dash of salt
3 med. carrots, shredded
¼ c. chopped cucumber
½ c. chopped celery

Dissolve lime Jell-O in 1 cup boiling water; add 3/4 cup cold water. Chill until syrupy. Dissolve orange Jell-O in remaining boiling water; add remaining cold water. Chill until syrupy. Add salad dressing to lime Jell-O; whip until smooth. Pour into individual molds or 2 x 6 x 10-inch pan; chill until set. Add remaining ingredients to orange Jell-O; pour over lime mixture. Chill until set. Cut into servings; place on lettuce. Garnish with salad dressing. Yield: 8-10 servings.

Mrs. J. Fred Jones, Ridgeroad Jr. H.S.
North Little Rock, Arkansas

LIME DELIGHT

1 pkg. lime gelatin
1 c. hot water
1 c. cold water
½ c. grated carrot
½ c. finely chopped cabbage
¼ c. finely chopped celery
1 tbsp. grated onion
Lettuce leaves

Dissolve gelatin in hot water; add cold water. Place in refrigerator until slightly thickened. Add vegetables; stir until evenly distributed. Pour mixture into mold; chill until firm. Unmold on bed of lettuce leaves. Garnish with carrot curls and radish roses. Serve with mayonnaise or salad dressing, if desired. Yield: 6 servings.

Mrs. Ruth G. Kuchler, Adirondack Cen.
Boonville, New York

ORIENTAL SALAD

1 lge. pkg. lemon gelatin
2 c. boiling water
2 c. cold water
3 tbsp. soy sauce
Dash of pepper
2 tsp. grated onion
1 c. grated carrots
1 c. thinly sliced celery
1 c. bean sprouts

Dissolve gelatin in boiling water; add cold water, soy sauce, pepper and onion. Chill until thickened. Fold in carrots, celery and bean sprouts. Pour into individual molds or 1 1/2-quart mold. Chill until firm. Unmold; serve with mayonnaise or salad dressing, if desired. Yield: 10-12 servings.

Mary Sullivan Debevec, Chisholm Sr. H.S.
Chisholm, Minnesota

PICTURE PRETTY SALAD

2 pkg. lemon Jell-O
2 c. boiling water
1 ½ c. cold water
5 tbsp. vinegar
½ c. thinly sliced radishes
½ c. celery slices
½ c. coarsly chopped nuts
½ c. grated carrots
½ c. chopped sweet pickle
1 c. sm. garden peas
½ tsp. salt

Dissolve Jell-O in boiling water; add cold water and vinegar. Chill until partially set. Add remaining ingredients. Pour into individual molds or large mold. Chill until set. Serve on salad greens. Top with favorite dressing; sprinkle with paprika. Yield: 12-14 servings.

Mrs. Gordon Louis Moore, Sidney Lanier H.S.
San Antonio, Texas

TASTE OF SPRING

3 pkg. lime Jell-O
2 ¼ c. hot water
¾ c. lemon juice
½ tsp. onion powder
3 c. mayonnaise
1 c. grated cabbage
1 c. grated carrots
½ c. grated radishes
½ c. grated cucumbers

Dissolve Jell-O in hot water; add lemon juice and onion powder. Chill until partially set. Fold in mayonnaise and vegetables. Pour into pans or molds. Chill until firm. Yield: 18-20 servings.

Kay Ann Mees, Brandon-Valley Jr. H.S.
Brandon, South Dakota

VEGETABLE SALAD LOAF

1 3-oz. pkg. lemon gelatin
¼ tsp. salt
1 c. canned green beans
½ c. grated carrot
1 ½ c. hot water
1 tbsp. vinegar
1 c. chopped raw cauliflower
¼ c. chopped celery

Dissolve gelatin in hot water. Pour half the mixture into loaf pan; chill until firm. Combine remaining ingredients; pour onto chilled mixture. Chill until firm, about 2 hours. Yield: 8 servings.

Mrs. Alice Blakeney, Runge H.S.
Runge, Texas

VEGETABLE SALAD LOAF

2 pkg. lemon gelatin
3 ½ c. hot water
½ tsp. salt
2 tbsp. vinegar
1 No. 2 can tiny whole green beans
9 pimento strips
3 cooked carrots, sliced
1 sm. head cooked cauliflower, broken in flowerets
½ c. diced cooked celery
6 radishes, sliced

Dissolve gelatin in hot water; add salt and vinegar. Pour half of gelatin mixture into 8 x 8 x 2-inch pan; chill until partially set. Arrange 9 bundles of 6 to 8 green beans, circled with pimento strips, in rows over gelatin mixture. Chill until firm. Combine remaining gelatin with remaining vegetables; pour over first layer. Chill until firm. Unmold; cut into squares with bundle for each serving. Yield: 9 servings.

Janice Sapp, Bartlett Jr. H.S.
Savannah, Georgia

NEIGHBORLY SALAD

1 box lemon Jell-O
1 sm. bottle sliced stuffed olives
1 c. chopped pecans
½ c. diced celery

Prepare Jell-O according to package directions; chill until slightly thickened. Fold in olives, pecans and celery; chill until firm. Cut into squares; serve on lettuce leaf. Top with mayonnaise and dash of paprika. Yield: 10 servings.

Joyce Herndon, Madill H.S.
Madill, Oklahoma

ONION SALAD

1 3-oz. pkg. lime or lemon Jell-O
1 ½ c. boiling water
½ pt. whipping cream
½ c. finely chopped sweet onion
1 3-oz. pkg. cream cheese
1 c. mayonnaise

Dissolve Jell-O in boiling water; chill until slightly thickened adding onion, cheese and mayonnaise. Fold into Jell-O; pour in 8 x 8-inch dish. Yield: 8-10 servings.

Bernice Ehrenhart, Hinsdale Cen. Sch.
Hinsdale, Illinois

QUICK TOMATO ASPIC

1 3-oz. lemon gelatin
1 c. boiling water
½ c. cold water
½ c. catsup
1 tbsp. vinegar

Dissolve gelatin in boiling water; add cold water, catsup and vinegar. Mix well; place in refrigerator until firm. Serve with salad dressing. Yield: 8-10 servings.

Mrs. Carol Canada, Colcord H.S.
Colcord, Oklahoma

TOMATO ASPIC

1 pkg. lemon gelatin
1 can tomato soup
½ c. water

Prepare gelatin according to package directions. Add tomato soup and water; chill until firm. Yield: 6 servings.

Mrs. Mary McKinney
Thornton Fractional North
Calumet City, Illinois

TOMATO ASPIC

1 ½ tbsp. gelatin
2 c. tomato juice
¼ c. vinegar
1 tbsp. sugar
1 bay leaf
½ tsp. salt
⅛ tsp. cayenne
1 sm. onion, minced
Juice of 1 lemon

Soak gelatin in 1/4 cup cold water for 10 minutes. Combine remaining ingredients; bring to boil. Strain; add gelatin. Pour into lightly greased mold; chill until set. Chopped celery or cooked peas may be added.

Mrs. Lena Bell Moore, Bd. of Education
Vegreville Composite H.S.
Vegreville, Alberta, Canada

TOMATO JELLY

1 tbsp. gelatin
¼ c. cold water
2 c. tomato juice
¼ tsp. salt
Dash of pepper
1 stalk celery
4 tsp. grated onion
1 tbsp. vinegar
1 tbsp. lemon juice

Soak gelatin in cold water. Simmer tomato juice, salt, pepper, celery and onion for 10 minutes; strain. Add vinegar and lemon juice; pour into mold. Yield: 4-6 servings.

Roberta S. Priestley
Brigham Young U Lab. Sch.
Provo, Utah

TOMATO ASPIC SALAD

4 c. tomato juice
⅓ c. chopped onion
¼ c. chopped celery leaves
2 tbsp. brown sugar
1 tsp. salt
2 sm. bay leaves
4 whole cloves
2 envelopes unflavored gelatin
3 tbsp. lemon juice
1 c. chopped celery

Combine 2 cups tomato juice, celery leaves, sugar, salt, bay leaves and cloves. Simmer, uncovered, 5 minutes; strain. Soften gelatin in 1 cup cold tomato juice; dissolve in small amount of hot tomato juice. Add remaining tomato juice and lemon juice; chill until partially set. Add celery; pour into 5-cup ring mold. Chill until firm. Yield: 8-10 servings.

Marion Popham, Charleston H.S.
Charleston, Illinois

TOMATO JELLY SALAD

1 can tomatoes
1 slice onion
1 tsp. salt
Dash of cayenne
3 c. tomato juice
2 envelopes gelatin
½ c. cold water
1 c. chopped celery
1 sm. can pimentos
½ c. chopped stuffed olives
½ c. pecans

Combine tomatoes and onion; simmer 10 minutes. Strain; add salt, cayenne and tomato juice. Heat to boiling. Soak gelatin in cold water; add boiling juice and stir. Cool until slightly thickened; add celery, pimentos, olives and pecans. Chill until firm. Serve on lettuce with mayonnaise.

Madeline M. Thomas, Appomattox H.S.
Appomattox, Virginia

TOMATO-VEGETABLE ASPIC

1 envelope unflavored gelatin
2 c. tomato juice
1 tbsp. grated onion
1 tsp. salt
¾ c. finely shredded cabbage
¼ c. chopped celery

Soften gelatin in 1/4 cup cold tomato juice. Heat remaining tomato juice to full boil; add onion, salt and gelatin. Stir until gelatin dissolves; chill until slightly thickened. Fold in cabbage and celery; mold as desired. Chill until firm; unmold on salad greens. Yield: 5-6 servings.

Azalee S. Bowlin, Dacusville Sch.
Easley, South Carolina
Naomi M. Vaught, Manotee H.S.
Bradenton, Florida

YUMMY SALAD

1 3-oz. pkg. Jell-O
1 c. hot water
⅓ lb. cottage cheese
½ c. milk
1 carrot, grated
⅓ c. salad dressing
1 sm. onion, cut fine
¼ c. celery, cut fine (opt.)

Dissolve Jell-O in hot water; add remaining ingredients. Pour into mold; stir occasionally before completely set. Unmold on layer of lettuce. Yield: 6 servings.

Rosalie Wentzell, Wm. E. Hay Composite H.S.
Stettler, Alberta, Canada

Combination Fruit & Vegetable Salads

RECIPE FOR KITCHEN SUPPER SALAD ON PAGE 262

APPLE-SPINACH SALAD

1 c. fresh spinach leaves
1 lge. apple, unpared, cored and diced
1 c. grated cabbage (opt.)
⅓ c. chopped celery
Mayonnaise or salad dressing

Wash spinach; tear into bite-sized pieces. Place in large bowl; add apple, cabbage and celery. Add dressing and toss lightly, just until blended. Yield: 6 servings.

Mrs. Virginia Sheely, Littlestown Jr.-Sr. H.S. Littlestown, Pennsylvania

APPLE WONDER SALAD

¼ c. milk
¼ c. crunchy peanut butter
1 c. mayonnaise
3 c. cubed apples
1 c. sliced celery
½ c. seedless grapes
4 to 6 leaves of lettuce
¼ c. salted roasted peanuts (opt.)

Add milk to peanut butter gradually; mix until well blended. Stir in mayonnaise; mix well. Combine apples, celery, grapes and enough peanut butter dressing to moisten; toss lightly. Serve on lettuce leaf; top with additional dressing if desired. Sprinkle with roasted peanuts. Yield: 4-6 servings.

Mrs. Kay Fulton, Farmington H.S. Farmington, Arkansas

CINNAMON-APPLE SALAD

6 tart apples
1 c. red cinnamon candies
2 c. water
½ c. salad dressing
1 c. miniature marshmallows
½ c. finely chopped celery
1 c. seedless raisins
⅓ c. chopped pecans

Pare and core apples. Cook candies in water until dissolved; add apples. Simmer until tender, turning frequently. Chill thoroughly in syrup, turning to color evenly. Drain; place on salad greens. Combine remaining ingredients; stuff centers of apples with mixture. Top with favorite fruit garnish. Yield: 6 servings.

Mrs. Glendis Painter, Boaz H.S. Boaz, Alabama

FRENCH APPLE SALAD

3 Delicious apples
1 c. diced celery

¼ c. stuffed olives, sliced
¼ c. diced cucumber
¼ c. French dressing
Endive or lettuce
2 c. cottage cheese
½ c. cashews, chopped
Mayonnaise

Wash, dry and dice unpeeled apples; add celery, olives, cucumber and French dressing. Toss. Arrange endive or shredded lettuce on salad plates; place 1/3 cup cottage cheese on endive. Top with apple salad; sprinkle with cashews. Top with swirl of mayonnaise. Yield: 6 servings.

Mrs. LeNora Hudson, Oklahoma Sch. for Deaf Sulphur, Oklahoma

LETTUCE-APPLE SALAD

¼ c. mayonnaise
2 tbsp. milk
1 tsp. sugar
½ tsp. salt
1 qt. chopped lettuce
2 red apples, cored and diced

Mix together mayonnaise, milk, sugar and salt; add to lettuce and apples. Chill until ready to serve. Yield: 4-6 servings.

Phoebe Stout, Stephen Decatur Sch. Berlin, Maryland

AVOCADO-CABBAGE SALAD

3 c. shredded red cabbage
1 med. avocado, diced
1 c. white seedless grape halves
¼ c. chopped nuts
¼ c. poppy seed dressing

Combine all ingredients except dressing. Refrigerate until ready to serve. Add dressing just before serving. Yield: 6 servings.

Wilma Gould, Gorham H.S. Rowland Heights, California

AVOCADO SALAD

1 lge. avocado, peeled
2 sm. oranges, peeled
1 sm. head lettuce, torn into bite-sized pieces
½ c. diced American cheese
1 sm. onion, sliced into rings
½ c. salad dressing
2 tbsp. sugar

Combine all ingredients except dressing and sugar in large bowl; toss lightly. Combine salad

(Continued on next page)

dressing and sugar in small bowl; chill. Pour dressing mixture over salad when ready to serve. Yield: 4 servings.

Mrs. Linda Wells Cherry, Griggsville H.S.
Griggsville, Illinois

AVOCADO SALAD

3 med. avocados
1 tbsp. minced onion
1 tsp. chili powder
½ tsp. salt
1 lge. ripe tomato, cut up
½ c. French dressing

Mash avocados with onion, chili powder and salt. Add tomato and French dressing; mix until smooth. Serve chilled on shredded lettuce. Yield: 6 servings.

Mrs. Charlotte Smithson, Tivy H.S.
Kerrville, Texas

CAULIFLOWER WITH GUACAMOLE SAUCE

1 lge. cauliflower
1 lge. avocado
¼ c. mayonnaise
1 tsp. Worcestershire sauce
¼ tsp. onion salt
¼ tsp. garlic powder
2 drops green food coloring

Cook cauliflower in boiling salted water about 20 minutes or until tender; drain. Combine avocado with mayonnaise; press through sieve. Add Worcestershire sauce, onion salt, garlic powder and food coloring. Chill Guacamole and cauliflower. Place cauliflower on serving dish; garnish with lettuce, tomatoes, cucumbers and olives. Spoon Guacamole over cauliflower; serve chilled. Yield: 6 servings.

Betty Sue Mann, Colmesneil H.S.
Colmesneil, Texas

COLOR THROUGHOUT

1 head romaine lettuce
1 buffet can mandarin oranges, drained
1 red Bermuda onion, sliced in rings
1 med. avocado, sliced
½ bottle Kraft Creamy French Dressing

Tear lettuce in large bowl; add oranges, onion and avocado. Toss with dressing. Yield: 6 servings.

Mrs. James D. Wolfe, Leigh H.S.
San Jose, California

FRITO SALAD

¼ lb. Velveeta cheese
2 tbsp. evaporated milk
½ head lettuce, torn into pieces
2 tomatoes, cut up
1 lge. ripe avocado, cut up
1 sm. onion, cut up
1 med. pkg. Fritos

Melt cheese in double boiler; add milk. Stir until blended and smooth; set aside. Combine lettuce, tomatoes, avocado and onion; add Fritos and toss gently. Pour warm cheese mixture over salad; toss until covered with cheese. Serve immediately. Do not substitute for Velveeta cheese or evaporated milk. Yield: 6 servings.

Mrs. Joyce Burlison, Westwood H.S.
Palestine, Texas

GUACAMOLE

4 well-ripened avocados
1 whole grated onion
Juice of 1 lge. lemon
1 tbsp. mayonnaise
Salt and pepper to taste

Mash avocados; add remaining ingredients. Serve on shredded lettuce with tortillas or use as dip. Yield: 8 servings.

Mrs. Ruby W. Harkey, San Saba H.S.
San Saba, Texas

GUACAMOLE

1 sm. tomato, chopped fine
1 sm. onion, chopped fine
1 sm. dried red pepper, chopped fine
6 pitted avocados, chopped fine
2½ tsp. salt
2 tsp. lemon juice
2 tbsp. mayonnaise
1 tsp. salad oil
4 drops Tabasco

Combine all ingredients. Serve in wooden bowl or on shredded lettuce. Yield: 8 servings.

Janice C. Wilkes, Bay Co. H.S.
Panama City, Florida

GUACAMOLE SALAD

2 ripe avocados
2½ tbsp. lemon juice
¼ tsp. garlic salt
2 tbsp. grated onion
½ tsp. salt
¼ tsp. coarse pepper
2 to 4 tbsp. chopped, canned green chilies

(Continued on next page)

Avocado-Vegetable Salads

Place avocados in blender; mix. Add remaining ingredients and blend. Chill. Serve with corn or potato chips.

Mrs. Hazel Jacobsen, Highland H.S.
Ault, Colorado

KITCHEN SUPPER SALAD

8 hard-cooked eggs
¼ c. salad dressing
1 tbsp. chili sauce
¾ tsp. seasoned salt
⅛ tsp. chili powder
3 avocados
Lemon juice
1 qt. potato salad
Lettuce

Shell eggs and cut crosswise into halves; remove yolks and mash with fork or put through sieve. Mix with salad dressing, chili sauce, seasoned salt and chili powder. Fill half the egg whites with mixture, mounding high. Reserve remaining egg whites for use in potato salad. Cut avocados lengthwise into thirds; remove seeds and skin. Sprinkle fruit with lemon juice. Spoon potato salad into center of lettuce-lined platter. Slice 1 avocado section and garnish salad. Arrange remaining 8 avocado sections around salad. Place stuffed eggs in avocado sections. Serve at once. Yield: 8 servings.

Photograph for this recipe on page 259.

MEXICAN FLAG SALAD

5 tender ears of sweet corn
2 egg yolks
Vinegar
Salt and pepper to taste
½ c. salad oil
5 pomegranates
5 avocados, sliced

Boil corn until tender; scrape off kernels. Make mayonnaise by beating egg yolks, vinegar, salt and pepper; beat in oil slowly. Combine mayonnaise with corn kernels and place in salad dish. Surround with ring each of pomegranate seeds and avocado slices to represent colors of Mexican Flag. Yield: 6 servings.

Anita Smith, Edinburg H.S.
Edinburg, Texas

ORANGE-AVOCADO TOSS

1 med. head lettuce, torn in bite-sized pieces
1 sm. cucumber, thinly sliced
1 avocado, seeded, peeled and sliced
1 11-oz. can mandarin orange sections, drained
2 tbsp. sliced green onion

½ tsp. grated orange peel
¼ c. orange juice
½ c. salad oil
2 tbsp. sugar
2 tbsp. red wine vinegar
1 tbsp. lemon juice
¼ tsp. salt

Combine lettuce, cucumber, avocado, mandarin orange sections and onion in large salad bowl. Combine orange peel, juice, salad oil, sugar, vinegar, lemon juice and salt in screw-top jar; cover tightly and shake well. Pour over salad just before serving; toss lightly. Yield: 8 servings.

Mrs. Paula E. Compton, Custer Co. H.S.
Miles City, Montana

SPICY AVOCADO SALAD

1 head lettuce, torn into sm. pieces
1 avocado, sliced
2 tbsp. salad oil
2 tbsp. cider or tarragon vinegar
1 clove of garlic, crushed

Toss together lettuce pieces and avocado slices in bowl; pour in combined salad oil, vinegar and garlic. Toss to mix well. Chill before serving. Yield: 8 servings.

Mrs. Ruth Riffe, Hobart, H.S.
Hobart, Oklahoma

TOMATO-AVOCADO SALAD

2 lge. tomatoes, cut into eighths
¼ c. French dressing
1 avocado, peeled and sliced
1 sm. cucumber, sliced
1 head lettuce, broken into bite-sized pieces

Marinate tomato sections in French dressing in bowl in refrigerator for about 5 minutes; add avocado, cucumber and lettuce. Toss well. Yield: 4 servings.

Mrs. Naomi Hofacket, Canton H.S.
Canton, Oklahoma

VIP TOSSED SALAD

1 clove of garlic, sliced
1 tsp. salt
2 tbsp. lemon juice
¼ tsp. sugar
¼ tsp. pepper
⅛ tsp. celery seed
½ tsp. paprika
¾ tsp. dry mustard
5 tbsp. salad oil
1 clove of garlic

(Continued on next page)

262

1 med. head lettuce
½ head romaine
Watercress
½ avocado, peeled and diced
1 c. raw cauliflower
1 tomato, peeled and sliced
½ c. slivered toasted almonds

Mash sliced garlic in salt; blend in lemon juice, sugar, pepper, celery seed, paprika and mustard. Add oil. Pour into jar; shake well and chill. Rub salad bowl with garlic. Tear greens into bowl; add avocado, cauliflower, tomato and almonds. Pour chilled dressing over all; toss well. Yield: 4 servings.

Mrs. Eleanor Ray, Elderton H.S.
Elderton, Pennsylvania

WESTERN TOSSED SALAD

2 cloves of garlic, peeled and sliced
2 tsp. salt
¼ c. lemon juice
½ tsp. sugar
½ tsp. pepper
¼ tsp. celery seeds
1 tsp. paprika
1½ tsp. dry mustard
10 tbsp. salad oil
2 med. heads lettuce
2 bunches watercress or 1 sm. bunch
   romaine
1 clove of garlic, peeled
1½ c. very tiny raw cauliflowerets
1 c. toasted blanched almonds, sliced
1 very ripe avocado, cut into pieces
2 tomatoes, peeled and sliced

Mash slices garlic with salt; add lemon juice, sugar, pepper, celery seeds, paprika and mustard. Blend well. Add oil; pour into jar and shake well. Chill. Wash lettuce and watercress; dry well and tear into pieces. Chill greens and all vegetables. Rub salad bowl well with clove of garlic. Add prepared greens, cauliflowerets, almonds, avocado and tomatoes; add chilled dressing and toss well. Add bits of cheddar or Roquefort cheese, grated raw carrot, or chopped hard-boiled egg if desired. Yield: 8 servings.

Sister Mary Benedict Beehler, O.S.B
Mount St. Benedict Academy
Crookston, Minnesota

BANANA-CELERY-CHEESE SALAD

1 lb. cheddar cheese, diced
1 bunch celery, chopped into bite-sized
   pieces
4 lge. bananas, diced
½ c. mayonnaise

Mix cheese, celery, bananas and mayonnaise. Serve with light meal. Yield: 8-10 servings.

Mrs. Dorothy Marie Jarrett, Keota H.S.
Keota, Oklahoma

BEAN SPROUT SALAD

1 c. bean sprouts, fresh if possible
¼ c. diced Jerusalem artichokes
½ c. pineapple chunks
1 tsp. soy sauce
½ tsp. curry powder
1 c. mayonnaise
¼ c. toasted almonds

Combine bean sprouts, artichokes and pineapple. Blend soy sauce and curry with mayonnaise; mix through salad. Arrange salad in lettuce-lined bowl. Sprinkle toasted almonds over top. Yield: 6 servings.

LaBerta W. Bowler, Virgin Valley H.S.
Mesquite, Nevada

BEAN WALDORF SALAD

1 tbsp. lemon juice
1 red apple, diced
1 1-lb. can pork and beans with
   tomato sauce
1 tbsp. mayonnaise
½ c. chopped celery
¼ c. chopped walnuts

Sprinkle lemon juice over apple to prevent browning. Add remaining ingredients; mix lightly. Chill; serve in crisp lettuce cups. Yield: 4 servings.

Eileen H. MacDonald, Jenifer Jr. H.S.
Lewiston, Idaho

APPLE-PINEAPPLE SLAW

2 unpared tart apples, diced
3 c. shredded cabbage
1 sm. can crushed pineapple, drained
1 c. miniature marshmallows
⅔ c. mayonnaise or salad dressing
1 tsp. salt
Lettuce

Combine all ingredients; serve on lettuce leaf. Yield: 8-10 servings.

Cleo Codas, Northern H.S.
Durham, North Carolina

CABBAGE SALAD

2 beaten eggs
1 c. pineapple juice
3 tbsp. vinegar
1 c. salad marshmallows
1 tbsp. flour
½ c. whipped cream or Dream Whip
4 c. cabbage, chopped
2 c. crushed pineapple, drained
1 c. nuts

(Continued on next page)

Cook eggs, pineapple juice, vinegar and marsh-mallows until marshmallows dissolve; add flour. Remove from heat; cool. Fold in whipped cream. Combine cabbage and pineapple; add dressing and nuts. Chill until ready to serve. Yield: 8 to 10 servings.

Mary Lloyd Faulkner, Manville H.S.
Manville, New Jersey

BIRD'S NEST SALAD

    3 hard-boiled eggs, diced
    2 c. shredded cabbage
    1 c. shredded carrots
    ½ c. crushed pineapple
    ½ c. raisins (opt.)
    2 tbsp. chopped celery
    1 tbsp. chopped onion
    1 tbsp. sweet relish
    ⅔ c. mayonnaise
    ½ c. shredded cheese
    Salt and pepper to taste
    10 hard-boiled quail eggs

Combine all ingredients except quail eggs; chill. Place quail eggs on top before serving. Yield: 8-10 servings.

Virginia B. Habito, Kennedy Comm. Sch.
Kennedy, Minnesota

BLENDER SLAW

    ¼ head cabbage, cut in chunks
    ½ med. carrot, sliced
    ½ unpared red apple, quartered

Combine all ingredients; place in blender. Cover with cold water; blend on low speed 5 seconds or until ingredients have gone through blades once. Drain; add favorite dressing. Grated cheese and raisins may be added with dressing. Yield: 4 servings.

Mrs. Jean Head, Etowah H.S.
Attala, Alabama

COCONUT-PINEAPPLE SLAW

    1 c. shredded cabbage
    1 c. shredded carrots
    1 9-oz. can drained crushed pineapple
    ¼ c. broken nuts
    ¼ c. flaked coconut
    ¼ c. mayonnaise
    ½ tsp. salt
    1 tbsp. sugar

Combine all ingredients; toss lightly. Serve at once. Yield: 4-6 servings.

Mrs. Caryl Nelson, Glenwood H.S.
Glenwood, Minnesota

FRESH APPLE SLAW

    3 c. finely shredded cabbage
    4 ½ c. thinly sliced, cored, unpared
      red apples
    ¼ c. chopped green pepper
    1 cucumber, chopped
    1 c. sour cream
    3 tbsp. lemon juice
    2 tbsp. mayonnaise
    1 tbsp. sugar
    1 tsp. salt
    ⅛ tsp. pepper

Lightly toss all ingredients in large bowl until well combined. Refrigerate at least 1 hour before serving. Yield: 8 servings.

Mrs. Louella R. Pence, Macon H.S.
Macon, Illinois

FRUIT SLAW

    3 c. shredded cabbage
    1 c. miniature marshmallows
    1 8-oz. can pineapple tidbits, drained
    1 c. chopped walnuts
    2 med. apples, chopped
    1 c. Miracle Whip salad dressing
    ½ c. pineapple juice

Combine cabbage, marshmallows, pineapple, nuts and apples; blend salad dressing and pine-apple juice. Toss salad with dressing; garnish with banana slices and maraschino cherries. Yield: 8 servings.

Phyllis A. Stephens, Cody H.S.
Cody, Wyoming

FRUITED COLESLAW

    3 c. shredded crisp cabbage
    1 c. pineapple tidbits, drained
    1 c. mandarin oranges, drained
    1 c. diced unpared apples
    ½ c. cut maraschino cherries
    ½ c. mayonnaise

(Continued on next page)

Combine first 5 ingredients; toss lightly with mayonnaise. Serve in bowl lined with lettuce; garnish with apple wedges. Yield: 6 servings.

Patricia Rovey, Buckeye Union H.S.
Buckeye, Arizona

FRUITED SLAW

1 tbsp. honey
¼ c. salad dressing
½ c. yogurt
2 tsp. lemon juice
½ tsp. salt
Dash of white pepper
4 c. shredded cabbage
2 minced green onions
¼ tsp. celery seed
¼ tsp. mustard seed
1 11-oz. can drained mandarin oranges
½ c. diced unpeeled red apple
½ c. unsalted roasted peanuts

Combine first 6 ingredients; toss cabbage, onions, celery seed and mustard seed with dressing. Fold in oranges, apple and peanuts. Garnish with orange sections. Yield: 4-6 servings.

Mrs. Beth Porter, Washington H.S.
Fremont, California

GRAPE SLAW
WITH BANANA DRESSING

¼ c. mayonnaise
2 tsp. prepared mustard
2 tbsp. lemon juice
2 med. ripe bananas, sliced
4 c. finely shredded green cabbage, packed
2 tsp. salt
White pepper to taste
2 c. seedless grapes, halved

Combine mayonnaise, mustard and lemon juice; blend in bananas. Add cabbage; sprinkle with salt and pepper. Mix well; fold in grapes. Salad may be served immediately or chilled for several hours or overnight. Yield: 6 servings.

Arlene Maisel, Highland Park H.S.
Highland Park, New Jersey

JEWELED CABBAGE SLAW

½ med. head cabbage, shredded
1 8-oz. can pineapple tidbits, drained
2 unpeeled Jonathan apples, diced
½ c. diced celery
¼ c. black walnuts
½ tsp. salt
½ c. cream, whipped
½ c. mayonnaise

Combine cabbage, pineapple, apples, celery and nuts in large bowl; sprinkle with salt. Blend cream and mayonnaise; pour over salad. Mix gently; serve in lettuce cups. Yield: 8 servings.

Mrs. Doris W. Larke, Peoria H.S.
Peoria, Illinois

NAPA VALLEY COLESLAW

12 c. finely shredded green cabbage
1 c. seedless or pitted white grapes
1 c. chopped, unpeeled red apple
1 c. sour cream
3 tbsp. lemon juice
½ tsp. salt
3 tbsp. sugar
1 tsp. celery seeds

Combine cabbage, grapes and apple in large bowl. Blend sour cream and remaining ingredients; pour over cabbage mixture. Toss to blend; chill at least 1 hour. Garnish chilled serving bowl with lettuce and unpeeled apple slices. Yield: 12 servings.

Mrs. Charles R. Thompson, Tom Bean Rural H.S.
Tom Bean, Texas

PINEAPPLE COLESLAW

2 c. chopped cabbage
¼ tsp. salt
1 tbsp. sugar
⅛ tsp. celery
⅓ c. sour cream
3 tbsp. vinegar
½ c. drained pineapple

Combine all ingredients; toss to blend. May be served immediately or chilled in covered dish until serving time. Yield: 4 servings.

Biffiel Glenn, Skiatook Sch.
Skiatook, Oklahoma

PRINCE'S CABBAGE

3 c. shredded cabbage
½ c. broken walnuts
2 or 3 unpeeled apples, diced
½ c. pineapple tidbits
⅓ c. raisins
2 tbsp. sugar
¾ c. (about) mayonnaise

Combine all ingredients; toss to blend. Chill until ready to serve; garnish with apple slices. Yield: 8 servings.

Mrs. Beverly A. Reed, Stamford Central Sch.
Stamford, New York

PINEAPPLE SLAW WITH ROQUEFORT DRESSING

4 c. shredded green cabbage
1 lge. carrot, pared and shredded
½ c. sliced radishes
½ c. slivered green pepper
1 c. drained pineapple tidbits
¾ c. buttermilk
¾ c. mayonnaise
⅓ c. crumbled Roquefort cheese
½ tsp. celery seed
Salt to taste

Toss cabbage, carrot, radishes, green pepper and pineapple together. Beat remaining ingredients together; add to cabbage mixture. Toss to distribute dressing. Yield: 6-8 servings.

Beth Seaver, Doland H.S.
Doland, South Dakota

RED CABBAGE SALAD

1 sm. head red cabbage, shredded
1 sm. can pineapple, drained
1 sm. pkg. marshmallows
2 tbsp. Miracle Whip salad dressing
2 tbsp. sugar

Combine cabbage, pineapple and marshmallows; blend Miracle Whip and sugar. Pour dressing over salad; toss well. Serve on lettuce cups. Yield: 6-8 servings.

Stella Unruh, Paola H.S.
Paola, Kansas

VEGETABLE SALAD

2 c. finely chopped cabbage
½ c. chopped celery
½ c. diced apple
¼ c. diced green pepper
½ tsp. salt
2 tbsp. sugar
2 tbsp. vinegar
¾ c. whipped cream, whipped

Soak cabbage in ice water until well chilled; drain. Add celery, apple, green pepper and salt. Add sugar and vinegar to cream; chill. Pour over vegetables; serve immediately. Yield: 6 servings.

Mrs. Ida Mae Fair, Matador H.S.
Matador, Texas

BLACK-EYED SALAD

4 med. carrots, grated
1 15-oz. can pineapple tidbits, drained
½ c. plumped raisins
¼ c. combined lemon and pineapple
 juice

Combine all ingredients; toss lightly. Yield: 6 servings.

Mrs. Marilyn O. Duigou, Drumheller Jr. H.S.
Drumheller, Alberta, Canada

CARROT AND DATE SALAD

5 to 6 med. carrots
1 c. dates, cut up
1 c. crushed pineapple, drained
1 c. sour cream

Grind carrots in food grinder or grate; add dates, pineapple and sour cream. Let stand in refrigerator 1 hour to blend. Serve on lettuce leaf. Yield: 8 servings.

Mrs. Leona Winters, Heppner H.S.
Heppner, Oregon

CARROT-PINEAPPLE SALAD

2 c. finely chopped carrots
½ c. crushed pineapple
½ c. evaporated milk
2 tbsp. sugar
Dash of salt

Combine all ingredients; chill before serving. Yield: 6 servings.

Janie O. Sutton, Deweyville Sch.
Deweyville, Texas

CARROT-RAISINS AND NUT SALAD

4 lge. carrots, grated
½ c. seedless raisins
½ c. coarsely chopped pecans or peanuts
¾ tsp. salt
Freshly ground pepper to taste
2 tsp. grated lemon peel
1 tbsp. lemon juice
1 c. sour cream

Combine all ingredients except sour cream; cover with sour cream. Yield: 4 servings.

Mrs. Hilda Lee, Cedartown H.S.
Cedartown, Georgia

CARROT-RAISIN SALAD

½ c. light or dark raisins
1 lge. orange, cubed
1½ c. grated carrots
¼ c. mayonnaise
1 tbsp. fresh, frozen or bottled lemon
 juice
1 tsp. sugar
¼ tsp. salt
Lettuce

(Continued on next page)

Cover raisins with boiling water; let stand 5 minutes. Drain; cool. Combine raisins, orange and carrots. Blend mayonnaise with lemon juice, sugar and salt. Toss with carrot mixture; serve on lettuce. Yield: 4 servings.

Mrs. Juanita Willis, Carlsbad Sr. H.S.
Carlsbad, New Mexico

CARROT SALAD

2 c. grated carrots
½ c. seedless raisins
Salad dressing

Combine all ingredients; serve on lettuce. Yield: 4 servings.

Mrs. Elane F. McCarriar, Hayti H.S.
Hayti, South Dakota

COCONUT-CARROT SALAD

1 c. Angel Flake coconut
1 ½ c. shredded carrots
¼ c. seedless raisins
2 tbsp. lemon juice
½ tsp. ground ginger
¼ c. mayonnaise

Combine all ingredients; mix well. Chill; serve on lettuce with mayonnaise. Yield: 4-5 servings.

Gail Speron, Dye Jr. H.S.
Flint, Michigan

CRANBERRY DELIGHT SALAD

1 lb. cranberries
2 c. sugar
½ c. diced celery
1 c. chopped pecans
1 ½ c. miniature marshmallows
½ pt. whipping cream, whipped

Grind cranberries; cover with sugar, mix and let stand overnight. Add celery, pecans and marshmallows about 1 hour before serving; mix well. Fold in whipped cream; refrigerate. Serve as desired. Yield: 8 servings.

Estel L. Simmons, Norte Vista H.S.
Riverside, California

CRANBERRY SALAD

1 qt. cranberries
1 ½ c. sugar
2 tbsp. gelatin
½ c. orange juice
1 c. finely chopped celery
1 c. diced unpeeled apples
1 c. chopped nuts

Grind cranberries, using fine blade; add sugar. Mix and let stand for at least 1 hour, stirring occasionally. Soften gelatin in orange juice for 5 minutes; stir over hot water until dissolved. Mix gelatin mixture with cranberries, celery, apples and nuts. Place ingredients in individual molds or flat dish, rinsed in cold water. Chill in refrigerator until set. Unmold or cut into squares. Serve on crisp lettuce leaf with mayonnaise, if desired. Marshmallows may be added to salad. Yield: 8 servings.

Mrs. Paulita Williams, Cooper H.S.
Cooper, Texas

CRUNCHY WALDORF SALAD

2 c. diced apples, unpeeled
1 c. seedless grapes
1 c. diced celery
½ c. chopped nuts
½ c. mayonnaise
6 lettuce cups

Gently combine all ingredients except lettuce. Chill until serving time. Serve in lettuce cups. Yield: 6 servings.

Mrs. Shelly Langley, Coppell H.S.
Coppell, Texas

DREAM FRUIT SALAD

2 apples, diced
2 bananas, sliced
½ c. raisins, softened in warm water
⅔ c. diced celery
½ c. pecans, chopped
1 c. sm. marshmallows
¼ c. salad dressing
½ c. cream, milk or fruit juice
2 tbsp. sugar
1 tbsp. lemon juice

Combine fruits, celery, nuts and marshmallows. Combine salad dressing, cream, sugar and lemon juice; add to fruit mixture. Toss gently. Yield: 10-12 servings.

Ethel Spradling, Bixby H.S.
Bixby, Oklahoma

FANCY WALDORF SALAD

1 lge. red apple
½ c. raisins
½ c. sliced celery
½ c. chopped pineapple
6 to 8 mandarin oranges
¼ c. chopped walnuts or pecans (opt.)
4 tbsp. salad dressing
3 tbsp. pineapple juice
¼ tsp. salt
1 tsp. sugar or honey
Grated American cheese

(Continued on next page)

Dice apple into large bowl; add raisins, celery, pineapple, oranges, and chopped nuts. Toss well. Combine remaining ingredients for dressing; add to fruit mixture, tossing well. Serve on lettuce cups; garnish with grated cheese. Yield: 4 servings.

Virginia Burchette, Wicomico Sr. H.S.
Salisbury, Maryland

EASY WALDORF SALAD

2 c. diced apples
1 c. diced celery
1 c. seedless grapes
½ c. chopped nuts
½ c. mayonnaise
6 lettuce leaves

Combine apples, celery, grapes, nuts and mayonnaise. Chill until serving time. Serve on lettuce leaves. Yield: 6 servings.

Mrs. Sharol J. Wilkes
McColl-Fletcher Memorial H.S.
McColl, South Carolina

FRESH SALAD

1 c. diced celery
1 c. diced apple
2 c. lettuce, torn into bite-sized pieces
½ c. salad dressing
2 tbsp. milk
1 tbsp. sugar

Place celery, apple and lettuce in salad bowl. Beat salad dressing and milk until creamy. Sprinkle sugar over mixture in salad bowl. Add dressing just before serving time; toss until food is well coated. Yield: 6 servings.

Mary Ella Porter, Como-Pickton H.S.
Como, Texas

FRUIT AND CHEESE SALAD

12 med. tomato slices
8 lettuce leaves
12 tbsp. cottage cheese
8 dried prunes, cooked without sugar
Chopped chives, watercress or parsley
Zero Salad Dressing

Place 3 slices tomato on plate containing 2 lettuce leaves; top with 3 tablespoons cottage cheese. Place 2 pitted prunes on side of plate. Garnish with chives. Repeat for 4 servings. Serve with Zero Salad Dressing.

ZERO SALAD DRESSING:

½ c. tomato juice
2 tbsp. lemon juice
1 tbsp. finely chopped onion
Salt and pepper to taste

Combine all ingredients in jar; cover and shake well. Yield: 4 servings.

Huquette Levesque, Atholville Composite H.S.
Atholville, New Brunswick, Canada

FRUIT CHEF SALAD

1 med. head lettuce
1 c. cottage cheese
1 c. diced canned pineapple
1 apple, unpared, diced
¼ c. raisins
¼ c. broken nuts
3 to 4 tbsp. French dressing

Break lettuce into bite-sized pieces in bowl; add cottage cheese, fruits and nuts. Add dressing just before serving; toss lightly. Yield: 4-6 servings.

Mrs. Elizabeth M. Turner, Algood Jr. H.S.
Algood, Tennessee

JEWEL'S WALDORF SALAD

2 c. apple, diced
Orange juice or other fruit juice
¾ c. celery, diced
¼ c. nutmeats
½ c. salad dressing
Lettuce or endive

Dip diced apples in orange juice. Combine all ingredients; serve on lettuce. Yield: 4 servings.

Jewel Babb, West Side Sch.
Heber Springs, Arkansas

LETTUCE-FRUIT STIR UP

1 med. head lettuce
1 No. 303 can fruit cocktail, drained
1 to 2 tbsp. mayonnaise

Cut lettuce up into large bowl; add fruit cocktail and mayonnaise. Chill until serving time. Yield: 8-10 servings.

Mary Ann Devore, Fort Recovery H.S.
Fort Recovery, Ohio

MEXICALI SALAD RING

½ c. coarsely chopped onion
¼ c. chopped parsley
¼ c. salad oil
2 tbsp. cider vinegar
1 tsp. sugar
½ tsp. salt
Lettuce
1 1-lb. can red kidney beans, drained
1 11-oz. can mandarin oranges, drained

(Continued on next page)

Toss onion with parsley in small bowl; set aside. Mix salad oil, vinegar, sugar and salt in cup. Line shallow serving bowl with lettuce; spoon in beans in ring around edge. Place mandarin oranges next to beans; pile onion mixture in center. Drizzle oil mixture over ingredients; toss lightly. Yield: 6 servings.

Mrs. J. Sigurdson, Hastings Jr. H.S.
Winnipeg, Manitoba, Canada

MY FRUIT SALAD

    2 c. diced apples, unpeeled
    1 c. diced celery
    1 c. miniature marshmallows
    1 c. chopped English walnuts
    ¼ c. chopped red candied cherries
    1 c. diced canned pineapple
    ¼ tsp. salt
    ½ c. mayonnaise
    ¼ c. grated coconut

Toss apples, celery, marshmallows, nuts, cherries and pineapple together; add salt and mayonnaise. Mix well. Place in lettuce cups; sprinkle with coconut. Yield: 4 servings.

Mrs. Irene Alexander, DuPont H.S.
Belle, West Virginia

ALMOND-ORANGE SALAD

    1 head lettuce, shredded
    2 c. finely chopped celery
    2 tbsp. minced parsley
    4 green onions, chopped
    2 cans mandarin oranges, drained
    1 tsp. salt
    Dash of pepper
    ½ tsp. Worcestershire sauce
    ¼ c. sugar
    ½ c. tarragon vinegar
    ¼ c. salad oil
    ½ c. slivered toasted almonds

Mix and chill vegetables and oranges in bowl. Mix next 6 ingredients; chill. Combine vegetable and dressing mixtures just before serving. Top with almonds. Yield: 10 servings.

Nancy L. Smithson, Laramie Sr. H.S.
Laramie, Wyoming

LETTUCE MANDARIN SALAD

    1 head lettuce, washed
    1 lge. onion, sliced into rings
    2 11-oz. cans mandarin oranges
    ⅓ c. water
    ½ c. sugar
    ½ c. vinegar
    Salt and pepper to taste

Break lettuce into small pieces in salad bowl; add onion. Drain oranges; reserve juice. Add oranges to bowl. Combine reserved juice with remaining ingredients. Add to salad. Chill and serve. Yield: 8 servings.

Mrs. Roger Gammel, North Sr. H.S.
North St. Paul, Minnesota

MANDARIN ORANGE SALAD

    2 11-oz. cans mandarin oranges
    1 c. sliced celery
    ¼ flaked coconut
    2 tbsp. creamy fruit or slaw dresssing

Combine oranges, celery and coconut. Toss with dressing. Serve on chilled crisp lettuce. Yield: 4-6 servings.

Mrs. Pat Wolf, Leigh H.S.
San Jose, California

MANDARIN ORANGE AND ARTICHOKE HEART SALAD

    ½ head lettuce, washed
    3 tbsp. wine vinegar
    1 c. drained mandarin oranges
    1 6-oz. jar marinated artichoke
      hearts, including oil

Break lettuce into bite-sized pieces; place in salad bowl. Add remaining ingredients; toss salad, blending well. Serve immediately. Yield: 6 servings.

Betty Harvey, Edgemont H.S.
Scarsdale, New York

MANDARIN SALAD

    1 can mandarin oranges
    1 c. raisins
    1 head lettuce
    1 c. chopped celery
    1 c. grated carrots
    ⅓ c. mayonnaise

Drain oranges; reserve juice. Boil raisins for 1 minute in reserved juice; drain and cool. Combine lettuce, celery and carrots in bowl; add raisins and oranges. Toss well; chill. Add mayonnaise just before serving. Yield: 4 servings.

Mrs. Mary Reid, Lord Byng Secondary Sch.
Vancouver, British Columbia, Canada

ORANGE-ONION COMBINATION

    1 orange, peeled
    Lettuce leaves
    ½ onion, cut into rings

(Continued on next page)

Slice oranges crosswise. Place lettuce leaves on salad plate; top with orange slices and onion ring. Yield: 1 serving.

JoAnn Greenman, Herscher H.S.
Herscher, Illinois

ORANGE AND ONION SALAD

3 white onions, peeled and sliced
3 oranges, peeled and sliced
French dressing

Arrange onions and oranges in bowl; cover with French dressing. Cover and marinate for about 7 to 8 hours. Drain; arrange on bed of salad greens to serve. Yield: 6 servings.

Mrs. Bonnie Morris, Throckmorton H.S.
Throckmorton, Texas

ORANGE WALDORF SALAD

2 c. chopped unpeeled apples
1 tbsp. lemon juice
½ c. diced celery
3 med. oranges, sectioned
¼ c. chopped pecans
½ c. mayonnaise

Sprinkle apple with lemon juice; combine apple, celery, oranges, pecans and mayonnaise. Toss lightly; chill before serving. Serve in lettuce cups; garnish with red maraschino cherry. Yield: 6 servings.

Mrs. Variel Garner, Moody H.S.
Moody, Texas

ONE-TWO-THREE

3 tbsp. French dressing
3 tbsp. Miracle Whip
1 med. onion, diced
2 dill pickles, diced
4 tart apples, peeled and diced

Combine French and Miracle Whip dressings; add remaining ingredients. Chill before serving. Yield: 3-4 servings.

Ella Bang, Yankton Sr. H.S.
Yankton, South Dakota

PEA SALAD

½ c. mayonnaise
1 No. 2 can early garden green peas, drained
1 can pineapple tidbits, drained
½ c. cheese cubes

Add mayonnaise to peas, pineapple and cheese; toss lightly. Place in casserole. Chill before serving. Yield: 4-6 servings.

Laura Howell, Ashley Township H.S.
Ashley, Illinois

ENGLISH PEA SALAD

1 No. 2 can English peas
3 hard-boiled eggs, diced
1 c. diced American cheese
¼ c. chopped, green sweet peppers
½ c. diced sweet pickle
1 Winesap apple, diced
2 tbsp. diced pimento
Dash of white pepper
½ c. mayonnaise

Combine all ingredients in casserole; mix thoroughly. Chill before serving. Yield: 10 servings.

Evia C. Arnold, Rio Vista H.S.
Rio Vista, Texas

PINEAPPLE-BEET SALAD

1 c. drained julienne beets
1 c. drained pineapple chunks
1 c. miniature marshmallows
½ to 1 c. whipped cream

Combine beets, pineapple and marshmallows in bowl. Fold in whipped cream. Chill and serve. Yield: 6 servings.

Linda Stiller, Neah-Kah-Nie H.S.
Rockaway, Oregon

SPICY SALAD

1 14-oz. jar spiced apple rings, cut into sm. pieces
½ c. walnuts, broken
1 c. celery, sliced
½ c. diced dates
¼ c. salad dressing
1 tbsp. lemon juice

Combine apple rings, walnuts, celery and dates. Combine salad dressing and lemon juice. Serve apple mixture on lettuce leaves; top with salad dressing mixture. One cup seedless green grapes, 1/2 cup raisins or 1 cup fresh diced pineapple may be substituted for dates. Yield: 6 servings.

Mrs. Dianne Rader, Rich Central H.S.
Olympia Fields, Illinois

SWEET SALAD

¾ c. salad dressing
2 tbsp. sugar
½ c. flaked coconut
½ c. pineapple tidbits, drained
3 c. bite-sized iceberg lettuce
½ c. miniature marshmallows
1 seedless orange, sectioned and cut
    into bite-sized pieces

Combine salad dressing and sugar; set aside. Combine remaining ingredients in salad bowl; add dressing and toss. Yield: 4-6 servings.

Mrs. Virginia F. Darling, Olivet H.S.
Olivet, Michigan

SWEDISH SALAD

1 No. 2½ can chunk pineapple, drained
2 sm. cans mandarin oranges, drained
1 lb. green grapes
1 c. blanched almonds, slivered
¾ lb. miniature marshmallows
1 tsp. salt
2 tbsp. water
2 eggs
2 tbsp. lemon juice
½ pt. whipped cream
1 c. sliced celery

Combine pineapple, oranges, grapes, almonds and marshmallows. Mix salt, water, eggs and lemon juice. Cook in double boiler until thick. Add to fruit mixture. Let stand 24 hours. Fold in whipped cream and celery just before serving. Yield: 8-10 servings.

Mrs. Beverly Wruck, Clintonville Sr. H.S.
Clintonville, Wisconsin

SWEDISH SALAD BOWL

1 8-oz. can pineapple tidbits
1 tart apple, chopped
1 stalk celery, chopped
5 tomatoes, cut into wedges
½ cucumber, cut into strips
2 egg yolks
1 hard-cooked egg yolk, mashed
¼ tsp. prepared mustard
1 tbsp. vinegar
1 c. whipped cream
½ head lettuce, shredded

Drain pineapple; reserve juice. Combine pineapple, apple, celery, tomatoes and cucumber in large bowl; set aside. Mix egg yolks with reserved juice; cook over low heat until thick, stirring constantly. Cool; add mashed egg yolk mixed with mustard and vinegar. Fold in whipped cream. Combine with pineapple mixture. Chill. Add lettuce just before serving. Yield: 8 servings.

Mrs. Scott Willock, Alexander H.S.
Albany, Ohio

WALDORF

2 tbsp. flour
2 tbsp. sugar
1 egg
1 c. pineapple juice
1 c. cream, whipped
6 apples, peeled or unpeeled
1 c. celery, diced
1 c. English walnuts or pecans
3 bananas, diced
6 slices pineapple, cut into ¼-in. pieces

Combine flour, sugar and egg; beat until light. Add pineapple juice; cook until thick. Cool; fold in whipped cream, apples, celery, nuts, bananas and pineapple. Yield: 20 servings.

Mrs. Wretha W. Simms, Beth Center Jr. H.S.
Brownsville, Pennsylvania

WALDORF SALAD

6 tart red apples, cut into long thin strips
Lemon water
2 oz. English walnuts, shaved into fine
    pieces, or pecans, chopped
4 celery hearts, cut into long thin strips
Whipped cream dressing or salad
    dressing
Lettuce

Dip apple strips into lemon water. Combine walnuts, apples and celery with enough dressing to moisten; heap on lettuce on salad plates. Yield: 6 servings.

Mrs. J.E. Proctor, Dilley H.S.
Dilley, Texas

WALDORF SALAD

9 apples, diced
1 sm. bunch celery, diced
½ c. raisins
¼ c. nutmeats, broken
1 c. water
½ c. vinegar
1 tbsp. butter
½ c. sugar
2 tbsp. cornstarch

Combine apples, celery, raisins and nutmeats. Combine remaining ingredients; cook until thickened. Cool; pour over celery mixture. Chill and serve. Yield: 15 servings.

Mrs. Mabel Brill, Moorefield H.S.
Moorefield, West Virginia

WALDORF SALAD

3 c. diced apples
1 ½ c. chopped celery
⅔ c. broken nuts
½ c. mayonnaise

Combine ingredients; chill thoroughly. Serve on crisp lettuce. Yield: 8 servings.

Mrs. John McAdams, Rosedale H.S.
Rosedale, Mississippi

WALDORF SALAD

2 c. diced unpeeled apples
1 c. chopped celery
1 c. finely chopped dates
2 tbsp. sugar
½ tsp. salt
½ c. (about) mayonnaise

Combine all ingredients; mix gently until blended. Serve on lettuce; garnish with paprika. Yield: 6-8 servings.

Sister M. Maurice, R.S.M., Mercy H.S.
Baltimore, Maryland

WALDORF SPIRAL SALAD

6 red apples
⅓ c. lemon juice
4 c. cold water
1 c. celery, diced
½ c. seedless raisins
1 c. miniature marshmallows
1 c. pineapple chunks
1 sm. jar maraschino cherries
¼ c. mayonnaise
¼ c. whipped cream
½ c. walnuts, coarsely chopped
6 lettuce cups

Pare apples very thick, being sure each paring is long and unbroken. Add 3 tablespoons lemon juice to cold water; drop in parings to keep color bright. Core pared apples and dice fine; sprinkle with remaining lemon juice. Combine apples, celery, raisins, marshmallows, pineapple chunks, cherries and mayonnaise; fold in whipped cream. Add nuts before serving. Curl each paring into cup shape on lettuce; fill with salad. Yield: 6 servings.

Shirley Ann Boddie, Calvin H.S.
Calvin, Louisiana

WALDORF SUPREME

2 c. red apple, cubed
Dash of salt
½ c. pineapple juice
1 c. chopped celery
Pecans
½ to ¾ c. mayonnaise
1 banana

Sprinkle apple with salt; add juice and stir. Allow to stand for 15 minutes. Drain and reserve juice. Add celery, pecans and mayonnaise; stir. Slice banana into reserved juice; drain. Fold bananas into apple mixture lightly. Serve on crisp lettuce leaf; garnish with maraschino cherries and nuts. Yield: 6 servings.

Mary E. Lash, Paramount Sr. H.S.
Paramount, California

WINTER TOSSED SALAD

1 head iceberg lettuce
½ sm. head curly endive or other salad green
1 red onion, cut into rings
4 oranges, sectioned
Juice of 1 lemon
¼ tsp. garlic salt
1 tbsp. grated Parmesan cheese
2 tbsp. light salad oil
Salt and pepper to taste

Toss vegetables and oranges together in large bowl. Combine remaining ingredients; pour over salad. Mix well and serve. Yield: 8 servings.

Mrs. Doris W. Larke, Peoria H.S.
Peoria, Illinois

ANGEL SALAD

2 pkg. lime gelatin
2 c. hot water
2 or 3 pkg. cream cheese
1 sm. can crushed pineapple, drained
1 2-oz. jar pimentos, chopped
1 c. diced celery
1 c. chopped pecans
½ pt. whipped cream

Dissolve gelatin in hot water; cool. Blend cream cheese; add pineapple, pimentos, celery and pecans. Fold into gelatin; refrigerate until thick but not firm. Fold in cream. Rinse mold in cold water; pour in gelatin. Chill until firm. Yield: 12 servings.

Nancy B. Tyler, W.E. Boswell Sch.
Saginaw, Texas

APPLE-CINNAMON MOLDED SALAD

¼ to ½ c. cinnamon candies
1 lge. pkg. cherry Jell-O
1 No. 303 can applesauce
1 8-oz. pkg. cream cheese, softened
½ c. mayonnaise
½ c. chopped pecans
½ c. finely chopped celery

272

(Continued on next page)

Combine 1 cup water and candies; heat to boiling point. Simmer until candies are melted. Add Jell-O; stir until dissolved. Add applesuace and 1 cup cold water. Pour half the mixture into ring mold. Chill until firm. Beat cream cheese and mayonnaise together until smooth. Add nuts and celery. Spoon over Jell-O mixture. Pour remaining applesauce-Jell-O mixture over cheese. Refrigerate until firm. May double recipe in large cake pan and frost with cheese mixture. Yield: 12 servings.

Mrs. Geraldine Ramsay, U.S.D. 219
Minneola, Kansas

APPLE RED SALAD

1 3-oz. pkg. cherry-flavored gelatin
⅓ c. cinnamon-flavored hard candies, crushed
1 c. boiling water
1 c. cold water
1 ⅓ c. chopped Delicious apples
⅓ c. chopped celery
½ c. chopped nuts
1 3-oz. pkg. cream cheese
Salad greens

Dissolve gelatin and candies in boiling water; stir in cold water. Chill until thick and syrupy. Combine apples, celery and 1/3 cup chopped nuts. Fold into gelatin mixture. Turn into a 1 1/2-quart ring mold or individual molds. Chill until firm. Cut cheese into 6 to 8 cubes; shape into balls. Roll in remaining chopped nuts. Garnish salad with cheese balls and salad greens. Yield: 8-10 servings.

Esther Moorhead, Berryhill H.S.
Tulsa, Oklahoma

CELERY-APPLE SALAD

1 3-oz. pkg. cherry gelatin
1 c. hot water
¼ c. red cinnamon candies
½ c. boiling water
1 c. chopped pared apples
1 c. chopped celery
½ c. chopped walnuts

Dissolve gelatin in hot water. Add cinnamon candies to boiling water; stir to dissolve. Pour cinnamon candy liquid into measuring cup; add enough water to make 1 cup liquid. Add dissolved gelatin; cool until partially set. Add remaining ingredients; pour into 1-quart melon mold or 6 individual molds. Chill until firm. Serve on crisp lettuce.

Patricia Rovey, Buckeye Union H.S.
Buckeye, Arizona
Mrs. Marian Webb, O.E. Bell Jr. H.S.
Idaho Falls, Idaho

APPLE SURPRISE SALAD

1 pkg. raspberry Jell-O
1 c. boiling water
1 c. fruit juice
1 ½ c. diced apples
1 ½ c. chopped celery
1 ½ c. crushed pineapple
½ c. chopped dates
¼ c. chopped nuts
2 tbsp. mayonnaise
½ c. whipping cream, whipped

Dissolve Jell-O in boiling water; add fruit juice. Cool until almost jelled. Combine apples, celery, pineapple, dates, nuts and mayonnaise. Fold into whipped cream. Add fruit-whipped cream mixture to Jell-O. Place in mold and chill until firm. Yield: 6 servings.

Mrs. A.V. Clark, Westminster Jr. H.S.
Westminster, Maryland

CINNAMON-APPLE SALAD

⅔ c. cinnamon candies
1 c. hot water
1 pkg. strawberry Jell-O
½ c. sweetened applesauce
1 8-oz. pkg. cream cheese
½ c. chopped nuts
½ c. chopped celery
½ c. mayonnaise

Cook cinnamon candies in hot water until dissolved. Add Jell-O; stir until dissolved. Add applesauce. Stir. Pour 1/2 of the mixture into 8 x 8-inch pan; let set until firm in refrigerator. Blend cheese, nuts, celery and mayonnaise. Spread cheese mixture on top of congealed mixture. Pour in remaining apple mixture and set in refrigerator until firm. Serve on lettuce leaves. Yield: 8 servings.

Elizabeth Sacker, Edgewood H.S.
Atce, New Jersey

JELLIED APPLE-BEET-CELERY SALAD

1 envelope dietetic lemon gelatin
¾ c. hot water
¼ c. beet juice
3 drops of red food coloring
¼ tbsp. vinegar
½ tsp. salt
Dash of pepper
½ c. diced canned beets
¼ c. celery, chopped
1 med. apple, peeled, cored and diced

Dissolve gelatin in hot water; stir in beet juice, food coloring, vinegar, salt and pepper. Cool; stir in beets, celery and apple. Pour into molds; chill until firm. Yield: 3 servings.

Janis Diane Hefner, Turrell H.S.
Turrell, Arkansas

APPLESAUCE-CHEESE SALAD

¾ c. boiling water
1 ½ c. canned thick applesauce
1 pkg. lime-flavored gelatin dessert
Salad greens
2 c. cottage cheese
½ c. diced celery
¼ c. mayonnaise
¼ c. chopped pecans (opt.)
Salt and pepper to taste
Dash of paprika

Combine water and applesauce; bring to a boil, stirring. Pour over gelatin; stir until gelatin is dissolved. Pour into 6 individual ring molds, rinsed in cold water. Chill until set. Unmold on bed of salad greens. Combine cottage cheese, celery, mayonnaise, nuts, salt and pepper. Pile into center of molds. Top with paprika. Serve with additional mayonnaise. Yield: 6 servings.

Blanche Portwood, State Supvr.
Home Ec. Ed.
Oklahoma City, Oklahoma

APPLESAUCE-CHEESE SALAD

1 c. hot water
⅔ c. sm. cinnamon candies
1 3-oz. pkg. raspberry gelatin
1 ½ c. sweetened applesauce
1 8-oz. pkg. cream cheese, at room temperature
½ c. chopped nuts
½ c. finely cut celery
½ c. salad dressing

Pour hot water over cinnamon candies; stir to dissolve. Add gelatin; stir until completely dissolved. Add applesauce. Pour half the mixture into 8 x 8 x 2-inch pan. Chill. Blend cream cheese, nuts and celery together; add salad dressing. Spread in layer over firm apple mixture. Pour on remaining apple mixture; chill until firm. Unmold; garnish with small bunches of grapes. Yield: 6 servings.

Mrs. Louis Ivanish, Malta H.S.
Malta, Montana

RED HOT-APPLESAUCE SALAD

1 pkg. lemon gelatin
⅔ c. red hots
1 c. boiling water
1 ½ c. applesauce
½ c. mayonnaise
1 8-oz. pkg. cream cheese
1 c. chopped pecans
½ c. diced celery

Dissolve gelatin and candies in boiling water; add applesauce. Pour 1/2 of the mixture into flat 9-inch square dish or ring mold. Chill. Spread mayonnaise, cream cheese, nuts and celery, mixed over chilled gelatin. Add remaining gelatin and chill until firm. Serve in squares or unmolded on lettuce leaves.

Mrs. Jacquetta Finley, Goddard H.S.
Roswell, New Mexico

RED HOTS AND APPLESAUCE SALAD

⅓ c. red hots
1 c. boiling water
1 pkg. lemon, raspberry or cherry Jell-O
¾ c. cold water
1 c. applesauce
1 c. chopped celery
1 c. chopped English walnuts

Dissolve red hots in boiling water; bring to boil. Add Jell-O and dissolve. Remove from heat; add cold water. Chill until mixture begins to jell. Add applesauce, celery and walnuts. Chill until firm.

Mrs. Janie A. Stahlecker, Idalia H.S.
Idalia, Colorado

APRICOT-LIME SALAD

1 1-lb. can peeled whole apricots, halved
Apricot juice
1 3-oz. pkg. lime-flavored gelatin
1 c. cream-style cottage cheese
½ c. chopped celery
½ c. chopped pecans
2 tbsp. lemon juice
½ c. evaporated milk, chilled for whipping

Place apricot halves in bottom of 6-cup ring mold. Cut any remaining apricots into pieces and set aside. Add enough water to apricot juice to equal 1 cup liquid. Heat to boiling point. Pour mixture over gelatin and stir until dissolved. Chill gelatin until consistency of unbeaten egg white. Stir in cottage cheese, celery, pecans, lemon juice and apricot pieces. Whip chilled milk until stiff and holds peak. Fold into chilled gelatin mixture lightly but thoroughly. Spoon mixture into ring mold carefully. Chill until firm, about 2 hours. Yield: 8 servings.

Mrs. Alice Blakeney, Runge H.S.
Runge, Texas

AVOCADO CHIFFON SALAD

2 pkg. lime Jell-O
3 c. boiling water
1 8-oz. pkg. cream cheese, creamed
4 lge. avocados, peeled and mashed
½ c. celery, cut fine
½ green pepper, chopped fine
½ sm. onion, chopped fine

(Continued on next page)

1 c. chopped pecans
1 c. mayonnaise
1 tsp. tarragon vinegar
Salt to taste
1 sm. jar Miracle Whip salad dressing
1 sm. jar Brockles dressing (opt.)
1 sm. carton sour cream

Dissolve Jell-O in boiling water. Mix next 9 ingredients in order given. Combine with gelatin. Place in ring mold or oblong dish. Chill overnight. Combine remaining ingredients for dressing. Serve with salad. One envelope unflavored gelatin may be added to help keep mixture firm. Yield: 15-18 servings.

Mrs. Martha Harkey, Crystal City H.S.
Crystal City, Texas

AVOCADO MOUSSE WITH MAYONNAISE

½ tsp. dry mustard
½ tsp. sugar
1½ tsp. salt
Dash of cayenne
1 egg yolk
1 tbsp. vinegar
¾ c. olive oil
1 tbsp. lemon juice
1 tbsp. hot water
3 c. avocado pulp
Dash of onion juice
2 tsp. Worcestershire sauce
½ tbsp. gelatin, soaked in ½ c. cold
   water
½ c. boiling water
½ c. heavy cream, whipped

Sift mustard, sugar, 1/2 teaspoon salt and cayenne into deep bowl. Stir in egg yolk and vinegar. Beat in 3 teaspoons olive oil, 1 drop at a time. Beat in remaining olive oil, 1 teaspoon at a time, until thick. Stir in lemon juice; add hot water to preserve mayonnaise. Mix remaining ingredients with mayonnaise; pour into cold water-rinsed molds. Chill. Yield: 4-6 servings.

Niva J. Reddick, Largo Sr. H.S.
Largo, Florida

AVOCADO-PECAN SALAD

2 pkg. lime gelatin
2 c. boiling water
1 c. sour cream
1 c. mayonnaise
2 c. pecans, broken
1⅓ c. avocado, mashed
2 tsp. onion, minced
2 tsp. celery, minced
1 c. green pepper, chopped
1 tsp. salt

Dissolve gelatin in boiling water. Refrigerate until gelatin reaches consistency of egg white. Whip until foamy. Beat in sour cream and may-

onnaise. Blend thoroughly. Fold in remaining ingredients. Refrigerate until firm. Yield: 12 servings.

Rachel Brewster, Pottsboro H.S.
Pottsboro, Texas

AVOCADO SALAD

2 3-oz. pkg. lime Jell-O
2 c. boiling water
1 8-oz. pkg. cream cheese
1 c. salad dressing
2 lge. avocados, mashed
1½ tsp. grated onion
1 c. finely chopped celery
½ tsp. garlic powder
1 tsp. salt
¼ tsp. red or black pepper
Stuffed olives (opt.)

Dissolve gelatin in boiling water. Pour into pan; chill until thickened. Cream cream cheese, salad dressing and avocados together. Fold in creamed mixture; chill. Fold in remaining ingredients. Turn into molds and chill until firm. Garnish with olives. Yield: 8 servings.

Katie Smith, Clute Jr. H.S.
Clute, Texas

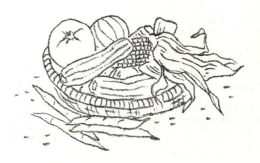

AVOCADO SUPREME

1 pkg. lime Jell-O
1 c. boiling water
½ c. cream
½ c. mayonnaise
1 lge. or 2 sm. avocados
Pinch of salt
Pinch of dry mustard
1 tbsp. minced onion
1 c. finely chopped celery

(Continued on next page)

Congealed Avocado-Vegetable Salads

Dissolve lime Jell-O in boiling water. Chill. Beat cream; add mayonnaise. Mash avocodos with fork or blender; add salt and mustard to pulp. Mix pulp with cream and mayonnaise mixture; add to partially set Jell-O. Add onion and celery. Chill until set. Yield: 6-8 servings.

Mrs. Janine Petaja, Powell Co. H.S.
Deer Lodge, Montana

CALIFORNIA MOLDED CHRISTMAS SALAD

1 pkg. lemon or lime gelatin
1 avocado, diced
1 sm. jar sm. pearl onions
2 tbsp. chopped pimento

Prepare gelatin according to package directions; chill until syrupy. Add avocado, onions and pimento. Mix well. Pour into mold. Chill until firm. Yield: 6 servings.

Mrs. Miriam Toth, Castro Valley H.S.
Castro Valley, California

FIESTA GUACAMOLD

2 envelopes unflavored gelatin
½ c. cold water
½ c. boiling water
2 lge. avocados, peeled, pitted and sliced
2 onion slices, halved
3 tbsp. lemon juice
1 c. sour cream
1 ½ tsp. salt
1 tsp. chili powder
¼ tsp. Tabasco sauce

Sprinkle gelatin over cold water in blender; let stand. Add boiling water to gelatin; cover and blend at low speed until gelatin dissolves. Turn blender control to highest speed; add remaining ingredients. Blend until smooth. Pour into 4-cup mold or bowl and refrigerate until firm, 4 hours or longer. Unmold by dipping mold in hot water. Place mold on platter with cooked shrimp, sliced tomatoes, ripe olives or any desired vegetables. Yield: 8 servings.

Mrs. Isabel M. Booher, East Jr. H.S.
Nashville, Tennessee

GREEN AVOCADO MOUSSE

½ c. water
½ c. muscatel wine
1 3-oz. lime-flavored gelatin
¼ c. mayonnaise
¼ c. celery
½ c. heavy cream, whipped
1 tbsp. lime juice
1 c. finely diced avocado
1 tbsp. grated or minced green pepper

Salt to taste
Salad greens
Pimento star

Heat water and wine to simmering; remove from heat. Stir in gelatin until dissolved. Chill until syrupy. Blend in mayonnaise, celery, cream, lime juice, avocado, green pepper and salt. Pour into lightly greased 1-quart mold. Chill until firm. Unmold on serving dish lined with salad greens. Decorate with pimento. Yield: 6 servings.

Mary Elizabeth Kloos, Helix H.S.
La Mesa, California

JELLIED AVOCADO SALAD

1 6-oz. pkg. lime or lemon-flavored Jell-O
2 c. boiling water
Salt and pepper to taste
2 avocados, mashed
1 12-oz. pkg. cream cheese
1 pimento, diced
1 green pepper, chopped
1 sm. onion, diced
2 c. celery, diced
1 c. mayonnaise

Prepare Jell-O in boiling water. Cool. Add salt and pepper. Add remaining ingredients to partially jelled Jell-O. Place in a 9 x 12-inch pan. Serve on lettuce leaf. Yield: 15 servings.

Mabel Moorhouse, Belen H.S.
Belen, New Mexico

QUICK AVOCADO SALAD

2 3-oz. pkg. lemon-flavored gelatin
3 c. boiling water
2 tbsp. chili sauce
¼ tbsp. Tabasco or green chili sauce
2 7¾-oz. cans frozen avocado dip or 1 ½ c. mashed avocado
¼ c. lemon juice
¼ c. finely chopped green onion
Chopped celery
Crisp salad greens
Salad dressing

Dissolve gelatin in 2 cups boiling water. Pour into melon mold; let set. Dissolve remaining gelatin in remaining boiling water. Stir in chili sauce and Tabasco. Chill until slightly syrupy. Blend avocado dip with lemon juice. Stir in onion and celery. Pour on top of lemon gelatin; let set. Unmold on bed of salad greens. Serve with desired dressing. Garnish with cherry tomatoes and black olives.

May M. Rorick, The Dalles Sr. H.S.
The Dalles, Oregon

BEET SALAD

1 pkg. red Jell-O
1 c. boiling water
½ c. pineapple juice
1 tbsp. sugar
3 tbsp. lemon juice
1 c. canned shoestring beets
1 c. celery, chopped fine
1 c. crushed pineapple

Dissolve Jell-O in boiling water and pineapple juice; cool. Add sugar, lemon juice and remaining ingredients. Mold in refrigerator and serve with mayonnaise. Yield: 6 servings.

Carolyn Whitley, Morgantown Jr. H.S.
Natchez, Mississippi

CARROT SALAD

1 pkg. orange Jell-O
1 c. boiling water
2 lge. carrots, grated
1 c. raisins

Mix Jell-O with boiling water; add carrots and raisins. Pour into mold. Serve on lettuce leaf with dip of salad dressing. Yield: 8 servings.

Mrs. Agnes Smith, McKinney H.S.
McKinney, Kentucky

CARROT AND PINEAPPLE SALAD

1 sm. can crushed pineapple
1 pkg. lime Jell-O
1 pkg. lemon Jell-O
1 c. grated carrots
1 c. chopped celery

Drain juice from pineapple; use as part of liquid for Jell-O. Prepare Jell-O according to package directions. Chill until slightly thickened. Add carrots, celery and pineapple; mix well. Pour into mold; refrigerate until firm. Yield: 10-12 servings.

Mrs. Eunice S. Tate, Malvern Sr. H.S.
Malvern, Arkansas

CARROT-PINEAPPLE SUNSHINE

1 pkg. lemon Jell-O
1 tbsp. lemon juice
1 6-oz. can crushed pineapple
2 carrots, shredded

Mix Jell-O according to package directions; mix in lemon juice, pineapple and carrots. Chill until set. Yield: 4-8 servings.

Mrs. Peggy Munter, Moore Jr. H.S.
Doraman, Oklahoma

COMPLEXION SALAD

1 pkg. lime Jell-O
2 tbsp. lemon juice
1 ½ c. grated carrots
1 ¼ c. well-drained canned crushed pineapple

Prepare Jell-O according to package directions; add lemon juice. Chill until partially set; add carrots and pineapple. Let partially set again; pour into 8 x 2 1/2-inch ring mold or 8 to 10 individual molds. Chill until firm. Unmold on large chop plate or individual salad plates. Garnish with crisp lettuce, curly endive or lacy watercress. Serve with mayonnaise and whipped cream dressing. Yield: 8-10 servings.

Mrs. Gail Hale, Shongaloo H.S.
Shongaloo, Louisiana

PINEAPPLE-CARROT MOLD

2 pkg. lemon gelatin
2 c. boiling water
2 c. pineapple juice and cold water
½ tsp. vinegar
1 No. 303 can crushed pineapple
4 med. carrots, shredded

Dissolve gelatin in boiling water; add pineapple juice mixture. Chill until partially set; stir in vinegar, pineapple and carrots well. Pour into mold or decorative bowl. Yield: 8 servings.

Mrs. J. R. Stover, Pierce Jr. H.S.
Tampa, Florida

PINEAPPLE AND CARROT MOLD

1 1-lb. can crushed pineapple, well drained
1 pkg. lemon gelatin
½ c. sugar
¼ tsp. salt
2 tbsp. lemon juice
1 c. finely grated carrots
1 c. cream, whipped

Drain pineapple; measure juice and add water to equal 1 1/2 cups liquid. Heat; add gelatin. Stir until dissolved; add sugar, salt and lemon juice. Chill until slightly thickened; fold in pineapple, carrots and whipped cream. Pour into lightly oiled 8-inch ring mold, 1 1/2-quart mold or individual molds; Chill until firm. Unmold; garnish with watercress or parsley. Yield: 8 servings.

Mary B. Konefal, New York Avenue Jr. H.S.
Smithtown, New York

BING CHERRY SALAD

2 pkg. dark cherry Jell-O
1 c. boiling water
1 No. 2 can Bing cherries and juice
1 c. carbonated grape drink
½ c. chopped celery
½ c. pecans, coarsely chopped
8 pecan halves
½ c. whipped cream

Dissolve Jell-O in boiling water; cool partially. Combine remaining ingredients except pecan halves and whipped cream. Mix thoroughly with Jell-O. Pour into mold or into individual molds. Chill until congealed. Unmold; garnish with whipped cream and pecan halves.

Mrs. Thelma L. Graper, Consultant
Dept. of Education
Lansing, Michigan

BLACK CHERRY SALAD

1 lge. can black cherries, chopped
1 box raspberry gelatin
½ c. diced pineapple
½ c. blanched almonds
¼ c. grated carrots

Drain cherries; reserve juice. Prepare gelatin according to package directions, using reserved juice as part of liquid. Add remaining ingredients; pour in individual molds. Chill until firm. Unmold; serve with mayonnaise on lettuce or other greens. Yield: 12 servings.

Mary P. Light, Kingsville H.S.
Kingsville, Texas

BLACK CHERRY WALDORF SALAD

1 pkg. black cherry gelatin
1 c. boiling water
¾ c. cold water
½ c. diced apples
½ c. diced banana
¼ c. chopped celery
½ c. chopped walnuts
3 tbsp. sour cream

Dissolve gelatin in boiling water. Add cold water. Chill until mixture is thick. Fold in remaining ingredients. Spoon into 1-quart mold or 8-inch square pan. Chill until firm. Unmold. Serve on lettuce leaf and garnish with additional sour cream.

Sister Helene Michael, St. Mary Sch.
Westfield, Massachusetts

CHERRY DELIGHT SALAD

1 pkg. cherry Jell-O
1 pkg. lemon Jell-O
1 c. boiling water

1 can chilled Milnot
1 c. finely chopped nuts
1 c. finely cut celery
1 No. 303 can crushed pineapple, undrained

Dissolve Jell-O in boiling water; cool until thick and syrupy. Whip Milnot until stiff; fold in Jell-O and then nuts, celery and pineapple. Pour into large loaf pan; chill until firm. Cut in squares; garnish with salad dressing and maraschino cherries. Yield: 15-20 servings.

Mrs. Margaret McIntosh, Lostant H.S.
Lostant, Illinois

CHERRY MOLD

1 1-lb. can pitted Bing cherries
2 tbsp. lemon juice
1 3-oz. pkg. cherry gelatin
12 lge. pecan halves
1 c. diced celery
½ c. stuffed green olives, sliced

Drain cherries; reserve syrup. Combine cherry syrup and lemon juice; add water to make 2 cups liquid. Bring liquid to boil; remove from heat. Stir in gelatin until dissolved. Arrange pecan halves in 1-quart ring mold. Add enough gelatin mixture so that pecans barely float. Chill until set. Chill remaining gelatin mixture until thick; fold in cherries, celery and olives. Pour into mold; chill until firm. Yield: 8 servings.

Mrs. Marilyn Ehlers, Tuttle H.S.
Tuttle, Oklahoma

CHERRY WALDORF SALAD

1 pkg. black cherry or cherry gelatin
Dash of salt
1 c. boiling water
¾ c. cold water
½ c. diced apples
½ c. diced banana
¼ c. celery, chopped

Dissolve gelatin and salt in boiling water; add cold water. Chill until thick; fold in remaining ingredients. Pour into 1-quart mold, 8-inch square pan, or individual molds. Chill until firm; unmold. Yield: 6 servings.

Mrs. Judy R. Moon, Stuart H.S.
Stuart, Virginia

CONGEALED CHEESE SURPRISE

1 pkg. lemon gelatin
1 c. hot water
1 4-oz. pkg. cream cheese
1 c. combined pineapple juice and water
1 sm. can crushed pineapple, drained
1 c. diced celery
1 c. chopped nuts
1 carrot, grated (opt.)

(Continued on next page)

Dissolve gelatin in hot water; add cheese and stir until melted. Add pineapple juice and water. Fold in remaining ingredients; chill until firm. Yield: 6 servings.

Mrs. Effie G. Hoyle, Warwick H.S.
Newport News, Virginia

CONGEALED LIME SALAD

1 pkg. lime Jell-O
1 c. shredded cabbage
1 c. diced apples
½ c. chopped celery
½ c. crushed pineapple
½ c. nuts

Prepare Jell-O according to package directions. Add remaining ingredients; place in salad mold. Unmold on bed of lettuce; serve with any desired dressing. Yield: 6 servings.

Mildred H. Morris, Reeltown H.S.
Notasulga, Alabama

CONGEALED SALAD

1 pkg. lime Jell-O
1 sm. can crushed pineapple
1 8-oz. lge. pkg. Philadelphia cream cheese
1 c. finely chopped celery
1 c. chopped pecans

Dissolve Jell-O in 1 cup hot water. Drain pineapple juice and use juice for second cup of liquid. Set in refrigerator to jell. While that is in refrigerator, cream together Philadelphia cream cheese and crushed pineapple. Add celery, nuts, mix thoroughly until whitish looking. Return to container. Put in refrigerator and congeal.

Dorothy Jones, Durant H.S.
Durant, Mississippi

COTTAGE CHEESE-PINEAPPLE SALAD

1 sm. pkg. lime Jell-O
1 c. boiling water
1 c. condensed milk
1 c. cottage cheese
1 No. 2½ can crushed pineapple
¼ c. chopped celery
½ c. chopped nuts

Dissolve Jell-O in boiling water; stir in milk cottage cheese, pineapple, celery and nuts, 1 at a time. Pour into decorative mold or 10 x 6-inch dish. Refrigerate till firm. Serve on lettuce. Yield: 6 servings.

Mrs. Eleanor Ray, Elderton H.S.
Elderton, Pennsylvania

AUTUMN FRUIT SALAD

2 3-oz. pkg. lemon gelatin
2 c. hot water
1½ c. cold water
1 8-oz. can crushed pineapple
1 1-lb. can whole cranberry sauce, chilled
2 apples, cut in sm. pieces
1 c. diced celery
Salad greens

Dissolve gelatin in hot water; add cold water and pineapple. Chill. When mixture starts to thicken add cranberry sauce, apples and celery. Pour into 12 x 7 1/2-inch pan. Chill until firm. Serve on greens. Yield: 8-10 servings.

Mrs. Margretta Frey, Hanover Sr. H.S.
Hanover, Pennsylvania

CHRISTMAS CRANBERRY BELLS

2 3-oz. boxes Jell-O
2 c. ground cranberries
1 c. sugar
1 c. crushed pineapple, drained
1½ c. diced celery
1 c. chopped nuts

Prepare Jell-O as directed on package. Grind cranberries; add sugar, pineapple, celery and nuts. Add prepared Jell-O and pour into individual bell, wreath or star molds. Chill until firm. Unmold, serve on lettuce leaf with following dressing.

DRESSING:

1 tbsp. butter
2 tbsp. sugar
6 tbsp. pineapple juice
2 well-beaten eggs
⅔ c. whipped cream

Melt butter; add sugar, pineapple juice and eggs. Cook and stir over medium heat until dressing coats spoon. Remove from heat. Chill. Add whipped cream. Dressing may be arranged as ribbon on bell or wreath. Yield: 10-12 servings.

Mrs. Thelma Stone, Hopewell-Loudon H.S.
Bascom, Ohio

CONGEALED CRANBERRY SALAD

2 boxes cherry gelatin
2 c. sugar
1 lb. cranberries
1 orange, peeled
1 orange, unpeeled
2 apples, diced
½ c. celery
Pecans or walnuts
1 sm. can crushed pineapple

Prepare gelatin as directed on package; add sugar. Stir to dissolve. Grind cranberries and

279

(Continued on next page)

oranges; add apples, celery and nuts. Combine all ingredients; pour into mold. Allow to congeal thoroughly. To unmold, dip mold into warm water a few seconds. Yield: 15 servings.

Evelyn B. Willey, Gates Co. H.S.
Gatesville, North Carolina

COOKED CRANBERRY SALAD

    2 c. raw cranberries
    1 c. sugar
    Juice of 1 orange
    Juice of 1 lemon
    1 3-oz. pkg. strawberry gelatin
    ½ c. water
    Pinch of salt
    1 c. drained crushed pineapple

Cook cranberries, sugar, orange juice and lemon juice over low heat for 10 minutes. Soften gelatin in water. Add cranberry mixture to gelatin; add salt. Cool until syrupy but not set. Add pineapple. Pour into buttered or oiled mold. Diced celery or chopped nuts may be substituted for all or part of the pineapple. Yield: 8 servings.

Mrs. Pauline K. Henslee, Irving H.S.
Irving, Texas

CRANBERRY-APPLE SALAD

    1 lb. cranberries
    Rind and juice of orange
    2 ¼ c. sugar
    2 pkg. red gelatin
    2 ¾ c. hot water
    1 c. pecans, chopped fine
    1 c. celery, chopped fine
    1 lge. or 2 sm. apples, chopped fine

Grind cranberries; add grated orange rind. Squeeze orange juice into cranberries; add sugar. Let stand at least 1 hour. Mix gelatin with water; when cool add all other ingredients. Let stand until it begins to harden; pour into mold. Yield: 10 servings.

Janice Sapp, Bartlett Jr. H.S.
Savannah, Georgia

CRANBERRY CUPS

    1 9-oz. can crushed pineapple
    1 No. 2 ½ can pineapple slices
    1 pkg. cherry gelatin
    ¼ c. sugar
    1 tbsp. lemon juice
    1 c. ground fresh cranberries
    1 sm. unpared orange, quartered, seeded
       and ground
    1 c. chopped celery
    ½ c. broken California walnuts
    Lettuce
    Mayonnaise

Drain both cans of pineapple, reserving syrup. Combine gelatin and sugar in saucepan. Add water to reserved syrup to make 2 cups; add to gelatin mixture. Heat and stir until gelatin and sugar dissolve; add lemon juice. Chill till partially set. Add ground fruits, crushed pineapple, celery and nuts. Pour into individual molds. Chill till firm. Unmold on pineapple rings placed on lettuce. Top with dollops of mayonnaise and tiny lettuce leaves, if desired. Yield: 8-9 servings.

Mrs. Joyce Boyer, Unified Dist. 237 Sch.
Smith Center, Kansas

CRANBERRY-APPLE SALAD

    1 pkg. strawberry gelatin
    1 c. boiling water
    1 No. 2 can whole cranberry sauce
    2 red apples, diced
    ½ c. chopped nuts
    ½ c. diced celery
    1 whole orange including peel, chopped
       in blender

Dissolve gelatin in water; stir in cranberry sauce. Chill until partially set. Add remaining ingredients. Chill until set. Serve garnished with orange segments.

Nanette H. Fisher, El Segundo H.S.
El Segundo, California

CRANBERRY-CREAM SALAD

    1 3-oz. pkg. cherry gelatin
    3 tbsp. sugar
    1 c. boiling water
    1 8-oz. can whole cranberry sauce
    ⅓ c. chopped celery
    ⅓ c. chopped walnuts
    1 c. dairy sour cream
    Lettuce leaves

Dissolve gelatin and sugar in water; add cranberry sauce. Chill until thickened but not firm. Add remaining ingredients except lettuce. Pour into 8-inch square pan; chill until firm. Cut in squares and serve on lettuce. Yield: 6 servings.

Mrs. Jenevieve Klug, Barnesville H.S.
Barnesville, Minnesota

CRANBERRY DELIGHT

    1 pkg. cranberry-orange gelatin
    1 c. boiling water
    1 1-lb. can whole or jellied cranberry
       sauce
    ½ c. cold water or pineapple juice
    1 orange, peeled and sectioned
    ½ c. crushed pineapple, drained
    ½ c. chopped celery
    ½ c. chopped walnuts
    Sour cream or mayonnaise
    Salad greens

(Continued on next page)

Dissolve gelatin in hot water; add cranberry sauce and stir until well blended. Add cold water; chill until partially thickened. Cut orange segments into halves. Fold orange, pineapple, celery and walnuts into thickened gelatin mixture. Pour into mold; chill until firm. Turn out on chilled plate; serve with sour cream. Garnish with crisp greens. Yield: 8 servings.

Naomi Wetzel, Delta H.S.
Clarksburg, California

CRANBERRY FRUIT SALAD MOLD

1 pkg. cherry gelatin
1 c. boiling water
1 ½ oranges
1 c. finely diced celery
1 1-lb. can jellied cranberry sauce

Dissolve gelatin in boiling water. Chill until it begins to thicken. Peel oranges; cut into eighths. Remove seeds and membrane. Put orange skins through food grinder; cut orange slices in small pieces. Crush cranberry sauce with fork; add orange and celery. Mix thoroughly. Fold mixture into thickened gelatin; pour into 1-quart mold or individual molds. Chill until firm. Serve in lettuce cup. Yield: 6-8 servings.

Mrs. Virginia S. McEwen, Coosa Co. H.S.
Rockford, Alabama

CRANBERRY-JELL-O SALAD

2 pkg. orange Jell-O
2 c. boiling water
1 c. nuts, chopped
1 can cranberry sauce, mashed well
1 c. chopped celery (about)
Marshmallows

Mix Jell-O and boiling water until Jell-O is thoroughly dissolved. Add remaining ingredients except marshmallows; mix well. Place in 8 1/2 x 13 1/4-inch Pyrex baking dish for chilling. Add pinches of marshmallows to top of decorations. Place in refrigerator overnight. Yield: 12 servings.

Mrs. Edith Donaldson, Gadsden H.S.
Anthony, New Mexico

CRANBERRY MOLD

1 sm. pkg. cherry gelatin
1 c. hot water
¾ c. sugar
1 tbsp. lemon juice
1 tbsp. plain gelatin
1 c. pineapple juice
1 c. ground raw cranberries
1 orange and rind, ground fine

1 c. crushed pineapple, drained
1 c. chopped celery
½ c. chopped pecans

Dissolve cherry gelatin in hot water; add sugar and lemon juice. Soften plain gelatin in pineapple juice; dissolve over hot water. Combine pineapple juice with cherry gelatin mixture. Chill until partially set; add remaining ingredients. Pour into ring mold. To serve, unmold on lettuce.

Pauline Brown, Lone Wolf H.S.
Lone Wolf, Oklahoma

CRANBERRY-ORANGE SALAD

1 tsp. gelatin
2 tbsp. water
1 pkg. cherry Jell-O
¾ c. hot water
1 tbsp. lemon juice
1 c. pineapple juice
1 c. ground raw cranberries
1 orange, ground
¾ c. sugar
1 c. crushed pineapple
1 c. chopped celery
½ c. chopped pecans
Lettuce
Mayonnaise

Soften plain gelatin in water. Dissolve Jell-O in hot water; add softened plain gelatin, lemon juice and pineapple juice. Stir; chill until partially set. Mix cranberries and orange with the sugar and crushed pineapple. When Jell-O is partially set, add all ingredients except lettuce and mayonnaise. Pour into mold. Chill until set. Unmold onto platter trimmed with lettuce leaves; garnish with mayonnaise. Yield: 10-12 servings.

Faye Nakatsui, Picture Butte H.S.
Picture Butte, Alberta, Canada

CRANBERRY-PINEAPPLE SALAD

1 lb. cranberries
4 pkg. cherry gelatin
2 whole oranges, ground
2 No. 2 cans crushed pineapple
4 c. hot water or pineapple juice
1 c. chopped celery
1 c. chopped nuts
2 c. sugar or more

Grind cranberries in food chopper. Mix all ingredients together. Chill until set. Yield: 25 servings.

Mrs. Lula S. Patrick, Monticello H.S.
Monticello, Kentucky

CRANBERRY RELISH

1 lb. cranberries, ground
2 c. sugar
2 3-oz. pkg. raspberry gelatin
2 c. hot water
1 c. chopped walnuts
1 c. celery cut in sm. pieces

Mix cranberries and sugar; let stand overnight in refrigerator. Mix gelatin and water; cool. Add cranberry mixture, nuts and celery. Chill until firm. Yield: 12 servings.

Mrs. Evelyn Hansen, Dundee H.S.
Dundee, Michigan

CRANBERRY RING

4 c. whole cranberries, ground
1 whole orange rind, ground
2 c. sugar
2 pkg. red gelatin
3 c. boiling water
1 c. dark grapes
1 c. crushed pineapple
1 c. celery, diced fine
1 c. chopped nuts

Combine cranberries and orange with sugar. Let stand about 2 hours. Dissolve gelatin in boiling water; refrigerate until thick. Add remaining ingredients; pour into mold. Yield: 15-20 servings.

Mrs. Joyce Clendennen, Tivy H.S.
Kerrville, Texas

CRANBERRY RING MOLD

1 9-oz. can crushed pineapple
1 3-oz. pkg. cherry gelatin
1 c. sugar
1 c. ground fresh cranberries
1 c. chopped celery
1 orange, ground, seeds removed
½ c. chopped walnuts

Drain pineapple, reserving syrup. Add water to pineapple syrup to make 1/2 cup. Dissolve gelatin and sugar in 1 cup hot water; add reserved syrup. Chill until partially set. Add pineapple and remaining ingredients. Pour into 5-cup ring mold; chill until firmly set. Unmold; trim with curly endive. Yield: 8-10 servings.

Lynda Lee Thorpe, Franklin H.S.
Franklin, Virginia

CRANBERRY SALAD

1 qt. cranberries
1 c. water
2 c. sugar
15 lge. marshmallows

1 pkg. raspberry or lemon gelatin
1 c. diced celery
1 c. diced raw apples
1 c. pecan meats

Boil cranberries, water and sugar together until cranberries are soft. While mixture is hot, whip in marshmallows and gelatin. Let mixture cool; add celery, apples and nuts. Chill 24 hours before serving; will keep for days. Yield: 10-12 servings.

Marianne Estes, La Mirada H.S.
La Mirada, California

CRANBEERRY SALAD

1 c. sugar
2 c. cranberries, ground
½ c. celery, diced
½ c. orange juice
½ c. walnuts
1 pkg. raspberry gelatin

Sprinkle sugar over cranberries; add celery, orange juice and walnuts. Let stand 1 hour. Dissolve gelatin in 1 cup boiling water; add cranberry mixture. Pour into large mold or individual molds. Yield: 6-8 servings.

Mrs. Barbara S. Miller, Fremont H.S.
Sunny Vale California

CRANBERRY SALAD

2 c. fresh cranberries
1 ¼ c. water
1 c. sugar
1 3-oz. pkg. cherry gelatin
¾ c. diced celery
½ c. chopped nuts

Cook cranberries in water until soft; add sugar and cook 5 minutes more. Pour over gelatin; stir until gelatin is dissolved. Chill. When partially set, add celery and nuts; pour into desired mold. Yield: 8 servings.

Mrs. Jean C. Farmer, Amphitheater H.S.
Tucson, Arizona

CRANBERRY SALAD

1 c. jellied cranberry sauce
1 pkg. black cherry gelatin
1 c. boiling water
1 c. celery chopped very fine
1 c. peeled chopped apple
1 c. ground pecans

Mash cranberry sauce until thin. Dissolve gelatin in boiling water; stir thoroughly. Add to cranberry sauce. Mix well; place in refrigerator until mixture begins to jell. Stir in celery, apples and

(Continued on next page)

pecans; blend evenly. Turn into 9 x 12-inch glass dish rinsed with cold water. Chill in refrigerator several hours or overnight, covered with clear plastic. Yield: 16-18 servings.

Mrs. Mildred R. Bowles, Mooreville H.S.
Mooreville, Mississippi

CRANBERRY SALAD

1 lb. cranberries
2 c. sugar
1 c. nuts, chopped
2 c. diced marshmallows
1 c. diced celery
1 pkg. cherry gelatin
½ c. water
1 pt. cream, whipped

Grind cranberries; add sugar. Let stand overnight. Add nuts, marshmallows and celery. Dissolve gelatin in hot water. Cool until syrupy. Mix all ingredients except cream. Fold in whipped cream. Yield: 12 servings.

Mrs. Vanora Fry, Little River H.S.
Little River, Kansas

CRANBERRY SALAD SQUARES

1 pkg. black cherry gelatin
¾ c. very hot water
1 lb. can whole cranberry sauce
¼ c. ginger ale
1 c. chopped apples
½ c. chopped celery
Lettuce
Sour cream
Ground cinnamon

Dissolve gelatin in hot water. Stir in cranberry sauce and ginger ale. Pour into mold. Chill to soft gel; add apples and celery. Chill until firm. Cut into squares; serve on lettuce. Garnish with commercial sour cream mixed with a dash of cinnamon. Yield: 4-6 servings.

Mrs. M. Bodtker, Henry Wise Wood Sch.
Calgary, Alberta, Canada

CRANBERRY SALAD
WITH TART DRESSING

1 sm. pkg. strawberry gelatin
1 c. boiling water
1 c. cranberry sauce
½ c. apples, chopped
½ c. celery, chopped
¼ c. nuts, chopped
Dressing

Dissolve gelatin in boiling water. Add cranberry sauce; whip until gelatin dissolves. Cool; add apples, celery and nuts. Chill. Serve in squares on bed of seedless grapes or lettuce with dressing.

DRESSING:

½ c. sugar
1 tsp. dry mustard
1 tsp. salt
¼ onion, grated
⅓ c. vinegar
1 c. salad oil
1 tbsp. celery seed

Mix together sugar, mustard, salt and onion; add a small amount of the vinegar. Mix thoroughly. Add remaining vinegar and oil alternately; beat well. Add celery seed. Cover and refrigerate. Yield: 12 servings.

Mrs. Earl Ellis, New Summerfield H.S.
New Summerfield, Texas

CRANBERRY SAUCE SALAD

2 3-oz. pkg. cherry gelatin
1 c. boiling water
1 c. cold water
1 lb. can whole cranberry sauce
1 c. chopped celery
1 c. chopped nuts

Dissolve gelatin in boiling water; add cold water. Chill until thick but not set. Stir in cranberry sauce, celery and nuts. Pour into 1 1/2-quart mold. Chill until firm. Unmold. Yield: 8 servings.

Mrs. Ruth A. Schaffner
Cochrane-Fountain City H.S.
Fountain City, Wisconsin

CRANBERRY-WALNUT SALAD

1 c. raw cranberries, ground
1 c. sugar
1 pkg. lemon gelatin
1 c. hot water
1 c. pineapple juice
1 c. drained crushed pineapple
½ c. chopped walnuts
1 c. chopped celery

Grind cranberries; combine with sugar. Dissolve gelatin in hot water; add pineapple juice. Chill until partially set. Add cranberry mixture, pineapple, walnuts and celery. Pour into mold. Chill until firm. Yield: 6 servings.

Mrs. Nancy Putney, Sunapee Cen. Sch.
Sunapee, New Hampshire

CRISP CRANBERRY SALAD

2 envelopes plain gelatin
4 tbsp. cold water
3 c. boiling water
4 tbsp. vinegar
½ tsp. salt
½ c. sugar

283

(Continued on next page)

2 c. ground cranberries
1 c. diced celery
1 c. chopped nuts
1 c. diced orange sections
Lettuce
Mayonnaise

Soften gelatin in cold water 5 minutes. Add boiling water; stir until dissolved. Add vinegar, salt and sugar; chill. When slightly thickened, fold in cranberries, celery, nuts and orange. Turn into molds; chill. Serve on crisp lettuce with mayonnaise garnish. Yield: 12 servings.

Mrs. Frances E. Griffith, Brunswick H.S.
Lawrenceville, Virginia

CRUNCHY CRANBERRY SALAD

1 c. sugar
1 c. raw cranberries, ground
1 pkg. lemon gelatin
½ c. boiling water
½ c. orange juice
2 tbsp. grated orange rind
9 oz. crushed pineapple
½ c. pecans
1 c. chopped celery

Mix sugar and berries together; let stand several hours. Add gelatin to boiling water, stirring until dissolved. Stir in orange juice and remaining ingredients. Pour into mold; chill. Yield: 8 servings.

Mrs. Clyda Phillips, Star City H.S.
Star City, Arkansas

HOLIDAY CRANBERRY SALAD

1 lb. cranberries
1 ¾ c. water
2 pkg. red gelatin
½ c. sugar
1 c. seeded grapes, halved
1 c. diced celery
1 lge. can crushed pineapple
1 c. whipping cream
16 lge. marshmallows
1 3-oz. pkg. cream cheese

Wash cranberries; cook in water until skins pop. Simmer for 5 minutes; beat to partially break up cranberries. Add gelatin and sugar; stir until dissolved. Cool; add grapes, celery and pineapple. Pour into ring mold or 8 x 8-inch pan. Chill. Cut up marshmallows and break cream cheese into bowl; pour cream over this. Let stand overnight; whip mixture before serving. For Christmas salad, tint the dressing green. Yield: 10 servings.

Mrs. Vera Keller, Wellington H.S.
Wellington, Illinois

JELLIED CRANBERRY SALAD

4 c. cranberries
2 c. water
½ tsp. salt
2 tbsp. gelatin
1 c. fruit juice
1 ½ c. white sugar
¾ c. chopped celery, pineapple or grapes

Cook cranberries in water until they pop; add salt. Soften gelatin in fruit juice. Add sugar to cranberries; simmer a few minutes. Pour over gelatin; stir to dissolve. Chill. When partially set, fold in celery. Chill 3 to 4 hours. Unmold on endive or lettuce. Yield: 6 servings.

Isabel Chipman, Queen Elizabeth H.S.
Halifax, Nova Scotia, Canada

JELLIED CRANBERRY SALAD

1 pkg. lemon gelatin
1 c. boiling water
1 c. canned cranberry sauce
1 c. diced celery
½ c. drained crushed pineapple
½ c. chopped nutmeats

Dissolve gelatin in boiling water; add cranberry sauce. Beat until smooth; chill. When slightly thickened, fold in celery, pineapple and nuts. Turn into molds and chill. Serve on lettuce cups. Yield: 8 servings.

Margaret Hambleton, Lake Weir H.S.
Summerfield, Florida

MOLDED CRANBERRY PARTY SALAD

1 c. sugar
2 c. fresh cranberries
1 6-oz. pkg. orange, pineapple gelatin
1 c. ginger ale
2 tbsp. lemon juice
1 c. crushed pineapple
½ c. chopped nuts
1 c. chopped celery

Combine 1 cup water, sugar and cranberries in saucepan; bring just to a boil. Remove from heat; cover and cool for about 5 minutes. Combine 1 cup boiling water and gelatin; stir until gelatin dissolves. Add ginger ale, cranberry mixture and lemon juice. Chill until thickened. Fold in remaining ingredients. Pour into 1 1/2-quart mold or individual molds. Chill until firm. Yield: 6-8 servings.

LaVerne Stansell, Cary M. Agney Sch.
Waskom, Texas

JELLIED FRUIT SALAD

1 pkg. lime gelatin
1 c. boiling pineapple juice
⅔ c. crushed pineapple
⅔ c. celery, cut fine
12 lge. marshmallows, cut fine
⅔ c. diced apples
½ c. boiled salad dressing
½ c. cream, whipped

Dissolve gelatin in pineapple juice. Chill until as thick as unbeaten egg white; add remaining ingredients. Pour into greased molds; chill until firm. Unmold on crisp iceberg lettuce. Serve with salad dressing folded into whipped cream. Garnish with cheese apples. Yield: 6-8 servings.

Teresa MacIsaac, Central Sch.
Sydney, Nova Scotia, Canada

MOLDED CRANBERRY SALAD

2 ½ c. sugar
2 ½ tbsp. gelatin
1 lb. cranberries
1 med. orange
1 c. diced celery
1 c. chopped nutmeats

Boil sugar and 1 cup water to syrup about 5 minutes. Soak gelatin in 1/2 cup water until soft. Add to hot syrup; stir until dissolved. Cool. Grind cranberries and orange with medium blade of food chopper. Add all ingredients to cooled syrup; pour into 1 large mold or individual molds. Let stand several hours before serving. Yield: 10-12 servings.

Frances L. Rice, Litton Sr. H.S.
Nashville, Tennessee

MOLDED CRANBERRY WALDORFS

1 pt. bottle cranberry juice cocktail
1 pkg. lemon gelatin
¼ tsp. salt
1 c. chopped unpared apple
½ c. chopped celery
¾ c. broken walnuts
Lettuce
Mayonnaise

Heat 1 cup cranberry juice cocktail just to boiling; dissolve gelatin. Add remaining juice and salt. Chill until partially set. Stir in apple, celery and nuts. Pour into 6 individual molds. Chill until firm. Serve on lettuce leaf; garnish with mayonnaise. Yield: 6 servings.

Mrs. Elizabeth C. Wilson, Greensboro H.S.
Greensboro, Alabama

MOLDED CRANBERRY SALAD

2 3-oz. pkg. cherry gelatin
1 c. boiling water
1 c. cold water
1 1-lb. can whole cranberry sauce
1 c. chopped celery
½ c. chopped nuts

Dissolve gelatin in boiling water; add cold water. Chill until thick but not set. Stir in cranberry sauce, celery and nuts. Pour into 1 1/2-quart mold. Chill until firm. Unmold. Yield: 8 servings.

Mrs. Delores Weir, Starbuck H.S.
Starbuck, Minnesota

RAW CRANBERRY APPLE SALAD

1 pkg. strawberry Jell-O
½ c. hot water
1 c. sugar
1 c. chopped cranberries
1 c. chopped tart apples
1 c. chopped celery
¼ to ½ c. chopped pecans

Dissolve Jell-O in hot water; add sugar and cranberries. Cool slightly. Add remaining ingredients. Chill. Serve on lettuce. Yield: 6 servings.

Mrs. Jean Sneezby, Ysleta H.S.
El Paso, Texas

NUTTED CRANBERRY SALAD

1 lb. cranberries
2 ½ c. water
2 c. sugar
2 3-oz. pkg. cherry gelatin
1 ½ c. diced celery
1 c. diced apples
1 c. chopped nuts

Cook cranberries in water until soft. Add sugar; cook 4 to 5 minutes longer. Pour over gelatin; stir. Cool. Add celery, apples and nuts. Refrigerate until set. Yield: 12 servings.

Mrs. Carole Fisher, Martinsville H.S.
Martinsville, Indiana

RAW CRANBERRY SALAD

2 c. chopped raw cranberries
1 c. sugar
1 pkg. lemon Jell-O
1 c. hot water
½ c. nutmeats
2 c. diced apples
2 or 3 pieces of chopped celery

(Continued on next page)

Cover cranberries with sugar; let stand for several hours or overnight. Drain berries; reserve juice. Mix Jell-O and hot water; add reserved juice from cranberries. When Jell-O is cool, add cranberries and remaining ingredients. Place in mold; chill in refrigerator until set. Can be kept for several days. Yield: 6-8 servings.

Lillian Thompson, Salina H.S.
Salina, Oklahoma

Grind raw cranberries and orange; set aside. Cook sugar and 1/2 cup water to soft ball stage. Remove from heat and pour over cranberry mixture; mix thoroughly. Dissolve gelatin in 1 cup boiling water; add to cranberry mixture. Add apples, celery and nuts. Pour into mold; chill. Yield: 8 servings.

Ann Good, Inola H.S.
Inola, Oklahoma

TANGY CRANBERRY SALAD

    1 6-oz. pkg. lemon gelatin
    1 c. boiling water
    1 c. pineapple syrup
    1 c. ground cranberries
    1 c. ground celery
    1 c. crushed pineapple
    1 c. sugar
    ½ c. pecans, chopped

Dissolve gelatin in water. Add pineapple syrup; partially jell. Combine cranberries and celery; add pineapple, sugar and pecans. Add to gelatin mixture and complete jelling process. Yield: 12-15 servings.

Mrs. Nelson R. Allen, Catlettsburg H.S.
Catlettsburg, Kentucky

WALDORF CRANBERRY MOLD

    1 pkg. cranberry-orange gelatin
    1 c. boiling water
    1 c. orange juice
    1 c. chopped apples
    ½ c. chopped celery
    ¼ c. broken walnut meats
    1 8-oz. can mandarin oranges

Dissolve gelatin in boiling water. Add orange juice; chill until partially set. Stir in apples, celery and nuts. Pour into 6 individual molds or 1 large mold. Serve on lettuce bed; garnish with mandarin oranges. A small bunch of seedless grapes may be substituted for oranges. Yield: 6 servings.

Mrs. Barbara Potterton, Illing Jr. H.S.
Manchester, Connecticut

THANKSGIVING DAY SURPRISE

    1 3-oz. pkg. cherry gelatin
    1 ½ c. hot water
    ¾ c. sugar
    1 c. raw cranberries
    ¼ orange
    ½ c. diced celery
    ½ c. chopped apples
    ¼ c. walnuts

Combine gelatin, hot water and 1/4 cup sugar in bowl; stir until gelatin and sugar dissolve. Cool. Put cranberries, orange and remaining sugar through food chopper; let mixture set for an hour. Add celery, apples and nuts to cranberries; pour cranberry mixture into gelatin. Place in mold; let set until firm. Yield: 10 servings.

Janice Kay Freeland, Delleurne Sch.
Delleurne, Alberta, Canada

CREAM CHEESE SALAD

    1 c. crushed pineapple
    1 pkg. lemon gelatin
    1 sm. pkg. Philadelphia cream cheese
    1 c. diced celery
    1 c. pecans
    ¼ tsp. salt
    ½ pt. cream, whipped

Drain pineapple; heat juice. Add gelatin; stir to dissolve. Add cream cheese; stir until melted. Fold in remaining ingredients; place in refrigerator overnight. Yield: 8 servings.

Betty Porter, Oilton H.S.
Oilton, Oklahoma

STARS AND BARS

    2 c. raw cranberries
    ½ orange
    1 c. sugar
    1 sm. pkg. cherry gelatin
    1 c. chopped apples
    1 c. chopped celery
    ½ c. chopped nuts

CREAM CHEESE SALAD

    1 pkg. lime Jell-O
    1 c. boiling water
    1 sm. can crushed pineapple, undrained
    ½ c. finely chopped nuts
    ½ c. finely chopped celery
    1 pkg. Philadelphia cream cheese
    1 c. chopped marshmallows (opt.)

(Continued on next page)

Dissolve Jell-O in boiling water; chill until syrupy. Whip until fluffy. Add remaining ingredients in order given. Chill until firm. Yield: 8-10 servings.

Glenda L. Nybo, Richmond H.S.
Richmond, Michigan

CREAMY WALDORF SALAD MOLD

1 3-oz. pkg. lime flavored gelatin
6 to 8 thin, unpeeled red apple slices
1 c. diced unpeeled red apples
¾ c. diced celery
1 c. chopped walnuts
2 tbsp. mayonnaise
½ c. whipping cream

Prepare gelatin according to package directions. Arrange apple slices in pattern in bottom of 6-cup mold. Spoon in enough gelatin to anchor apple slices; chill until set. Add additional gelatin to depth of about 1 inch. Chill until almost set. Chill remaining gelatin until consistency of unbeaten egg white. Combine diced apples, celery, walnuts and mayonnaise. Whip cream; fold into apple mixture. Fold chilled gelatin into apple mixture. Spoon into mold or top of clear gelatin layer. Chill until set. Unmold. Surround with crisp salad greens. Makes 8 servings.

Mrs. Hal. J. Puett, North Cobb H.S.
Acworth, Georgia

CRUNCHY LIME MOLDED SALAD

1 pkg. lime gelatin
1 sm. can crushed pineapple, drained
2 c. miniature marshmallows
1 c. finely diced celery
¾ c. walnuts or pecans
1 c. whipped cream or Dream Whip

Make gelatin according to package directions. When partially set, fold in remaining ingredients and chill until firm. This may be garnished with whipped cream, if desired. Pineapple juice may be used as part of liquid for gelatin. Yield: 8-10 servings.

Mrs. James Huelskamp, Bedford H.S.
Bedford, Iowa

CRYSTAL SALAD

1 pkg. lemon or lime gelatin
1 ¼ c. hot water
½ c. pineapple juice
½ c. cream, whipped
¼ c. salad dressing
½ c. diced celery
½ c. diced pineapple
½ c. unpeeled diced apple
6 marshmallows, cut fine

Dissolve gelatin in hot water; add pineapple juice. Chill until slightly thickened. Blend cream and salad dressing. Combine all ingredients; chill until firm. Yield: 6 servings.

Mrs. Lucille Sylvester, Central H.S.
Crookston, Minnesota

DARN GOOD SALAD

2 pkg. lemon Jell-O
1 3-oz. pkg. cream cheese
2 c. boiling water
12 lge. marshmallows
1 c. grated carrots
1 c. coconut
1 c. crushed pineapple
1 c. chopped nuts
½ pt. whipped cream or 1 pkg. Dream Whip

Mix Jell-O and cream cheese together; add water and stir until dissolved. Add marshmallows and stir until dissolved. When nearly set, add carrots, coconut, pineapple and nuts. Fold in whipped cream. Pour into mold. Salad may be frozen, if desired. Yield: 16 servings.

Mrs. Edwina Deffebach, DeSoto H.S.
DeSoto, Texas

DILL SALAD

1 envelope gelatin
¾ c. pineapple juice
¼ c. dill pickle juice
¼ c. pimento juice
¼ c. vinegar
1 c. sugar
¼ tsp. salt
1 sm. can sliced pineapple
1 c. slivered almonds
½ c. chopped pimentos
2 lge. dill pickles, chopped

Soak gelatin in 1/2 cup cold water. Combine pineapple juice, dill pickle juice, pimento juice, vinegar, sugar and salt. Heat; pour over gelatin. Chill; add remaining ingredients. Pour into mold; chill until firm. Serve with favorite dressing. Yield: 4-6 servings.

Flo Perry Brame, Lake Air Jr. H.S.
Waco, Texas

EMERALD SALAD

2 pkg. lime gelatin
2 c. boiling water
1 c. cold water
6 grated carrots
1 c. celery, chopped
1 c. crushed pineapple
2 unpeeled apples, finely chopped

287

(Continued on next page)

Dissolve gelatin in boiling water; add cold water. Add remaining ingredients; pour into greased mold. Chill until firm. Serve on salad greens. Yield: 6-8 servings.

Mrs. Catherine R. Trotter, Independence H.S.
Independence, Louisiana

FIESTA SALAD

1 c. hot water
1 c. sm. marshmallows
1 3-oz. pkg. lime Jell-O
1 c. grated cabbage
1 c. crushed pineapple
½ c. chopped walnuts
1 c. mayonnaise
1 c. whipped cream

Pour water over marshmallows and Jell-O and stir until dissolved. Add cabbage, pineapple, walnuts and mayonnaise. Add whipped cream when mixture starts to set and pour in 8 x 8-inch square pan or mold of equivalent size. Yield: 6 servings.

Mrs. Christine Lawrence, Williamsport H.S.
Williamsport, Indiana

FRUIT-NUT-CHEESE MOLD

1 No. 2 can or 2½ c. crushed pineapple
1 pkg. lime gelatin
2 3-oz. pkg. cream cheese
⅓ c. chopped pimento
1 c. heavy cream, whipped
1 c. diced celery
1 c. chopped California walnuts

Heat pineapple to boiling; add gelatin. Stir to dissolve; chill till partially set. Soften cream cheese; stir in pimento. Add to gelatin mixture; blend. Fold in whipped cream, celery and nuts; pour into 1 1/2-quart mold or individual molds. Chill until firm; serve with assorted fruits. Yield: 6-8 servings.

Mrs. Margaret W. McCormick
St. Pauls City Sch.
St. Pauls, North Carolina

FROSTED LIME-NUT SALAD

1 c. boiling water
1 pkg. lime gelatin
1 No. 2 can crushed pineapple, undrained
1 c. cottage cheese
1 tsp. lemon juice
½ c. diced celery
1 tbsp. chopped pimento
½ c. chopped nuts
1 3-oz. pkg. cream cheese
1 tbsp. mayonnaise

Pour boiling water over gelatin; stir until dissolved. Chill until slightly thickened. Add pineapple, cottage cheese, celery, pimento and nuts; pour into 8 x 8 x 2-inch pan. Chill until firm. Combine cream cheese, mayonnaise and lemon juice; frost gelatin. Yield: 4-6 servings.

Thelma McClain, Bremond H.S.
Bremond, Texas

FROSTED LIME SALAD

1 pkg. lime gelatin
1 c. boiling water
1 c. crushed pineapple
½ c. finely chopped celery
1 c. sm. curd cottage cheese
½ c. chopped walnuts
1 3-oz. pkg. cream cheese
1 tbsp. mayonnaise
1 tsp. lemon juice

Dissolve gelatin in boiling water; cool until slightly thickened. Stir in pineapple, celery, cottage cheese and walnuts. Pour into 8-inch square pan rinsed in cold water; chill until firm. Unmold on bed of lettuce or greens. Blend cream cheese, mayonnaise and lemon juice until smooth; frost salad. Cut into squares for serving. Yield: 8 servings.

Julia A. Walter, Jupiter Jr.-Sr. H.S.
Jupiter, Florida

FROSTED VEGETABLE SALAD

1 3-oz. pkg. lime gelatin
1½ c. cabbage, finely shredded
1 c. carrots, finely shredded
½ c. grated pineapple
3 tsp. minced onion
1 c. mayonnaise
½ c. pickle relish
1 lb. cottage cheese
1 tsp. salt
½ tsp. pepper
¼ c. sugar

Prepare gelatin according to package directions. Cool mixture until syrupy. Combine remaining ingredients and stir into gelatin. Chill in refrigerator.

FROSTING:

1 c. sour cream
½ lb. cheese
1 tsp. horseradish
1 tsp. minced onion
1 tsp. Worcestershire sauce
Dash of salt and pepper

Combine all ingredients; spread on congealed salad. Garnish with parsley and paprika, if desired. Yield: 8-10 servings.

Mary Kay Labbe, Eastern Jr. H.S.
Silver Spring, Maryland

GELATIN DELIGHT

1 lge. pkg. orange or lime Jell-O
½ c. grated carrots
½ c. crushed pineapple
¼ c. mayonnaise
½ c. grated cheese

Mix Jell-O according to directions on package and place in attractive dish. Add carrots and pineapple. Refrigerate until firm. Spread mayonnaise on top of gelatin; sprinkle cheese on top. Yield: 6-8 servings.

Mrs. Sue Reynolds, Copan H.S.
Copan, Oklahoma

GLORIFIED PERFECTION SALAD

1 8-9 oz. can crushed pineapple
2 pkg. lemon Jell-O
¼ c. vinegar
¼ tsp. salt
1 c. cultured sour cream
1 ½ c. shredded cabbage
1 ½ c. shredded carrots
½ c. celery

Drain pineapple; add water to syrup to make 3 cups liquid. Heat 1 1/2 cups of liquid to boiling point. Dissolve Jell-O in boiling water in large bowl; add remaining 1 1/2 cups of juice, vinegar and salt. Chill until mixture starts to thicken. Fold in sour cream, cabbage, carrots and celery. Pour into 6 1/2-cup mold. Refrigerate.

Naomi Stone, Staples H.S.
Staples, Minnesota

GOLDEN GLOW GELATIN SALAD

¾ c. plus 2 tbsp. pineapple juice
¾ c. plus 2 tbsp. water
½ tsp. salt
1 pkg. lemon gelatin
2 c. grated raw carrots
1 c. canned crushed pineapple
½ c. chopped pecans
Lettuce
Mayonnaise

Combine pineapple juice, water and salt; bring to a boil. Dissolve gelatin in hot liquid. Chill until partially set. Add carrots, pineapple and pecans. Rinse mold in cold water; pour in salad. Chill until firm; unmold on lettuce. Serve with mayonnaise. Yield: 8-10 servings.

Janice A. Kindler, Grand Rapids, H.S.
Grand Rapids, Ohio

GOLDEN GLOW SALAD

1 pkg. orange Jell-O
1 sm. can crushed pineapple
1 c. shredded carrots

Prepare Jell-O as directed on package, substituting pineapple juice from drained pineapple for 1 cup cold water. Chill until partially set. Add pineapple and carrots. Chill for 5 to 6 hours before unmolding. Yield: 8 servings.

Sharon Petry, DuQuoin H.S.
DuQuoin Illinois

GOLDEN GLOW SALAD

1 pkg. lemon gelatin
½ tsp. salt
1 ½ c. hot water
⅔ c. drained, crushed canned pineapple
⅓ c. pineapple juice
1 tbsp. lemon juice or vinegar
1 c. coarsely grated carrots
⅓ c. chopped pecans

Dissolve gelatin and salt in hot water; add pineapple and juices. Chill until slightly thickened; fold in carrots and pecans. Pour into 1-quart mold; chill until firm. Unmold on crisp lettuce; garnish with mayonnaise, if desired. Yield: 6 servings.

Janice Smithson, Wasco Union H.S.
Wasco, California

GOLDEN GLOW SALAD

1 box lemon gelatin
1 c. ground carrots
1 c. crushed pineapple, drained
Mayonnaise or cream dressing

Prepare gelatin according to package directions, substituting reserved pineapple juice for equal amount of water. Stir in carrots and pineapple. Pour into individual molds and chill until set. Serve with mayonnaise or cream dressing. Yield: 5-6 servings.

Mildred Bolin, S and S Consolidated H.S.
Sadler, Texas

GOLDEN SALAD

1 pkg. lemon gelatin
1 c. hot pineapple juice
1 orange, peeled and quartered
2 med. carrots, washed and coarsely cut
1 c. crushed pineapple

Place first 3 ingredients in blender. Cover; blend 20 seconds. Add carrots and pineapple; cover and blend for 5 seconds, or until carrots are finely chopped. Pour into oiled salad mold or individual molds and chill until firm. Serve on crisp salad greens with mayonnaise. Yield: 6 servings.

Carolyn Wayman, Mooreland Sch.
Mooreland, Oklahoma

GOLDEN GLOW SALAD

3 3-oz. pkg. orange-pineapple Jell-O
    or orange Jell-O
¾ tsp. salt
3 c. boiling water
1 13-oz. can pineapple tidbits
2 tsp. lemon juice
2 c. mandarin oranges, chopped
½ c. chopped pecans
2 c. chopped celery
Sour cream
Maraschino cherry

Dissolve Jell-O and salt in water. Drain pine-apple, measuring syrup; add water to make 1 1/2 cups. Stir syrup and lemon juice into gelatin. Chill until thick. Fold in fruit, nuts and celery. Chill until firm; unmold on lettuce leaves. Top with sour cream and maraschino cherry. Yield: 12 servings.

Louise Hall, Amador Co. H.S.
Sutter Creek, California

GOOSEBERRY SALAD

1 No. 2 can sweetened gooseberries
⅔ c. sugar
2 pkg. lemon-lime Jell-O
3 c. water
1 c. celery, sliced
½ c. nuts, chopped
½ c. cheese, grated

Drain juice from gooseberries; heat juice with sugar. Dissolve Jell-O in hot juice. Add water and gooseberries. Cool until syrupy. Add remaining ingredients and cool until set. Yield: 8-10 serv-ings.

Mrs. Jean Searcy, Silver Lake H.S.
Silver Lake, Kansas

GRANDMA PAYNE'S
GOOD GOOD SALAD

1 pkg. lemon Jell-O
2 c. boiling water
1 ⅓ pkg. Philadelphia cream cheese
1 sm. can crushed pineapple
¼ c. water
⅓ c. mayonnaise
½ tsp. vanilla
1 pkg. Dream Whip
½ c. cold milk
½ c. celery, chopped fine
½ c. walnuts
1 pkg. orange Jell-O
1 c. orange juice

Dissolve lemon Jell-O in 1 cup boiling water; add cream cheese, pineapple, water and mayonnaise. Cool. Beat vanilla, Dream Whip and milk until thick; fold into pineapple and cream cheese mix-ture. Add celery and walnuts; refrigerate over-night or until set. Dissolve orange Jell-O in

remaining boiling water; add orange juice. Cool; pour over congealed mixture. Chill until firm. Yield: 9-12 servings.

Luella P. Gresslin, Robert A. Millikan Sr. H.S.
Long Beach, California

GRAPEFRUIT ASPIC

2 envelopes gelatin
1 c. cold water
1 c. boiling water
3 tbsp. lemon juice
¾ c. sugar
3 lge. grapefruit, peeled and sectioned
¾ c. tender celery, chopped
½ c. blanched almonds, chopped (opt.)

Soak gelatin in cold water. Add boiling water to dissolve gelatin. Add lemon juice and sugar. Chill until partially set. Reserve grapefruit juice; add juice and grapefruit to gelatin mixture. Chop and add celery and almonds. Chill until firm. Yield: 8 servings.

Lucy H. Dunn, Jerome Sr. H.S.
Jerome, Idaho

GRAPEFRUIT CRUNCH SALAD

1 pkg. lemon jelly powder
1 c. hot water
1 tbsp. vinegar
¼ tsp. salt
2 c. grapefruit sections
½ c. diced celery
¼ c. slivered almonds

Dissolve jelly powder in hot water; add vinegar and salt. Drain grapefruit, reserving syrup. Add water to syrup to make 1 cup; add to jelly powder. Chill until partially set. Stir in grape-fruit, celery and almonds. Turn into 1-quart mold. Chill until firm. Yield: 6 servings.

Mrs. M. E. Hughes, C. Fulton Sr. H.S.
Vernon, British Columbia, Canada

LIME-GRAPEFRUIT SALAD

1 No. 2 can grapefruit sections
1 pkg. lime gelatin
2 tbsp. lemon juice
¼ tsp. salt
½ c. broken nutmeats
1 c. cold evaporated milk
½ c. sliced celery

Drain syrup from grapefruit, reserving syrup; add water to make 1 1/4 cups. Heat; add gelatin and stir until dissolved. Add lemon juice and salt.

(Continued on next page)

Chill until partially set; stir in nuts, milk, celery and grapefruit. Pour into 5-cup mold; chill until firm. Yield: 6-8 servings.

Mrs. Joy L. Manson
Parishville-Hopkinton Central Sch.
Parishville, New York

Heat carrot juice; add gelatin. Stir until dissolved; chill until slightly thickened. Fold in remaining ingredients; pour into 1-quart mold. Chill until firm. Unmold on lettuce base; serve with mayonnaise. Yield: 8 servings.

Mrs. Virginia Verrill, Rangeley H.S.
Rangeley, Maine

GREEN DINNER SALAD

1 pkg. lemon gelatin
1 c. boiling water
1 ½ c. crushed pineapple
½ c. chopped pimento
½ c. cream, whipped
1 3-oz. pkg. cream cheese
1 c. chopped celery
½ c. chopped nuts

Dissolve gelatin in boiling water; add cheese and stir until dissolved. Add pineapple; chill until slightly thickened. Add remaining ingredients; chill until firm.

Janet Bromert, Akron Comm. Sch.
Akron, Iowa

HEAVENLY ORANGE SALAD

1 pkg. orange Jell-O
1 sm. pkg. cream cheese, softened
12 to 14 lge. marshmallows
2 c. boiling water
1 c. crushed pineapple, drained
1 c. grated carrots
1 c. whipping cream, whipped

Place Jell-O, cream cheese and marshmallows into bowl. Add boiling water; dissolve completely. Chill until set. Whip slightly with mixer; Add pineapple and carrots. Fold in whipped cream. Place in salad bowl or mold; chill until firm. Garnish; serve. Yield: 8-10 servings.

Mrs. Joan Hollinger, Oltman Jr. H.S.
St. Paul Park, Minnesota

GREEN SALAD

½ c. cold water
1 envelope unflavored gelatin
½ c. sugar
¼ tsp. salt
½ c. hot water
¼ c. mild vinegar
Green food coloring
½ c. stuffed olives
½ c. sliced pineapple, cut up
½ c. sm. sweet cucumber pickle, sliced thin
½ c. blanched almonds or other nuts, chopped

Pour cold water in bowl; sprinkle gelatin on top of water. Add sugar, salt, and hot water; stir until dissolved. Add vinegar and food coloring; cool. Chill until partially set; add remaining ingredients. Turn into individual molds; chill until firm. Unmold on lettuce. Yield: 6 servings.

Margaret H. Peden, Hoke Co. H.S.
Raeford, North Carolina

JELLIED ORANGE WALDORF

1 3-oz. pkg. lemon gelatin
1 c. boiling water
½ c. cold water
½ c. salad dressing
1 c. diced apples
½ c. orange slices or sections
½ c. diced celery
½ c. coarsely chopped pecans
1 tsp. grated orange rind

Dissolve gelatin in boiling water; stir in cold water. Gradually add gelatin to salad dressing, mixing well until blended. Chill until slightly thickened; fold in apples, oranges, celery, nuts and orange rind. Pour into 1-quart mold; chill until firm. Unmold. Surround with curly endive, if desired. Yield: 6 servings.

Mrs. Dixie E. Stafford
Nueces Canyon Consolidated Indep. Schs.
Barksdale, Texas
Mrs. Iris Kocmak, Two Hills H.S.
Two Hills, Alberta, Canada

HARVEST GOLD SALAD

1 12-oz. can carrot juice
1 pkg. lemon gelatin
⅔ c. shredded cabbage
⅓ c. chopped green pepper
⅓ c. chopped onion
1 tbsp. horseradish
¼ tsp. salt
1 c. undrained crushed pineapple

JUNE SALAD

1 No. 2 can crushed pineapple
2 pkg. Philadelphia cream cheese
1 box lemon Jell-O
1 c. diced celery
½ c. chopped California walnuts
⅛ tsp. salt
1 sm. can pimentos, chopped
1 can heavy cream, whipped

291

(Continued on next page)

Drain pineapple; heat juice. Blend with cream cheese; beat until smooth. Press through sieve; cool. Prepare Jell-O according to package directions; stir in cheese mixture. Add pineapple, celery, walnuts, salt and pimentos; chill until slightly thickened. Fold in cream; place in square or oblong pan. Chill until firm. Cut into squares; serve on crisp lettuce. Yield: 16 servings.

Mrs. Elizabeth B. Miller
Conneaut Valley Merged H.S.
Conneautville, Pennsylvania

LEMON-LIME FRUIT WHIP

1 1 lb. 1-oz. can fruit cocktail
1 3-oz. pkg. lemon gelatin
1 3-oz. pkg. lime gelatin
⅓ c. mayonnaise
½ c. finely chopped celery
¼ c. chopped walnuts
⅔ c. evaporated milk
1 tbsp. lemon juice

Drain fruit cocktail; reserve syrup. Add enough water to syrup to make 2 cups. Heat to boiling; pour into gelatin in mixing bowl; blend well. Chill until syrupy. Add mayonnaise, celery, walnuts and fruit cocktail. Chill evaporated milk in refrigerator tray until soft ice crystals form, 10 to 15 minutes. Whip until stiff; add lemon juice. Whip very stiff. Fold into gelatin mixture. Spoon into 6-cup mold. Chill until firm, about 2 hours. Yield: 6 servings.

Mrs. Julia Ausmus, Wynn H.S.
Duff, Tennessee

LIME-COTTAGE CHEESE SALAD

1 pkg. lime gelatin
1 c. boiling water
½ c. pineapple juice
1 tbsp. lemon juice
1 c. diced pineapple
¼ c. chopped green pepper
½ c. chopped celery
¼ c. chopped pecan meats
⅛ tsp. salt
1 c. cottage cheese
½ c. mayonnaise
½ c. whipping cream

Dissolve gelatin in boiling water; add pineapple juice and lemon juice. Chill until slightly thickened. Combine pineapple, green pepper, celery, pecan meats, salt, cottage cheese and mayonnaise; add to gelatin. Whip cream until stiff; fold into other ingredients. Turn into mold rinsed in cold water; chill until firm. Unmold; garnish with salad greens. Yield: 6 servings.

Patricia M. O'Brien, Duchesne Acad.
Omaha, Nebraska

LIME-CHEESE SALAD

2 3-oz. pkg. lime Jell-O
2 c. boiling water
1 8-oz. pkg. cream cheese
36 miniature marshmallows
Juice of 1 lemon
1 sm. can crushed pineapple
1 c. finely cut celery
1 c. chopped nuts
1 c. cream, whipped

Dissolve Jell-O in boiling water. Add cheese, marshmallows and lemon juice. Whip until well blended; cool. Add pineapple, celery and nuts; fold in cream. Turn into mold; chill until firm. Yield: 8 servings.

Mrs. Alma C. McGimsey, Nebo H.S.
Nebo, North Carolina

LIME DELIGHT

2 pkg. lime Jell-O
1 c. cubed celery
1 c. crushed pineapple, well drained
1 qt. ice cream

Dissolve Jell-O in 2 cups hot water; cool slightly. Whip in ice cream, 1 spoonful at a time. Fold in celery and pineapple. Place in 2-quart mold or bowl; chill until set, 1 hour to 1 hour and 30 minutes. Yield: 4-6 servings.

Mrs. Sandra V. Ziegler, Sparland H.S.
Sparland, Illinois

LIME DELIGHT

2 pkg. lime Jell-O
1 No. 211 can crushed pineapple, drained
1 3-oz. pkg. cream cheese
1 c. diced celery
½ c. nuts
1 sm. jar maraschino cherries
1 pkg. Dream Whip

Dissolve Jell-O in 2 cups boiling water; cool until slightly thickened. Add remaining ingredients except Dream Whip. Prepare Dream Whip according to package directions; fold into Jell-O. Yield: 4 servings.

Mrs. Raenn Larsen, Story City Comm. H.S.
Story City, Iowa

LIME DELIGHT SALAD

1 pkg. lime Jell-O
1 c. boiling water
1 c. finely chopped marshmallows
2 c. crushed pineapple
½ c. chopped walnuts
1 c. mayonnaise
1 c. finely chopped cabbage
1 c. heavy cream, whipped

(Continued on next page)

Dissolve Jell-O in boiling water; add marsh-mallows, stirring until melted. Drain pineapple; stir juice into Jell-O. Chill until slightly thickened; whip. Combine remaining ingredients; fold into gelatin mixture. Pour into 2-quart mold; chill until set. Yield: 12 servings.

Mrs. Roberta Sundberg, Nooksack Valley H.S.
Nooksack, Washington

LIME SALAD

    1 pkg. lime gelatin
    1 3-oz. pkg. cream cheese
    1 c. boiling water
    1 9-oz. can crushed pineapple, undrained
    ½ c. finely chopped celery

Cream gelatin and cream cheese until smooth; add boiling water. Cool until slightly set; add pineapple and celery. Yield: 5-6 servings.

Mrs. Judith W. Arnold, Shaler Jr. H.S.
Glensboro, Pennsylvania

LIME VELVET

    1 No. 2 can crushed pineapple
    1 pkg. lime Jell-O
    1 3-oz. pkg. cream cheese
    ½ pt. cream, whipped
    1 c. finely chopped celery
    ½ c. chopped nuts

Drain pineapple; heat juice. Add Jell-O and cream cheese; beat until cheese is melted. Cool; fold in cream, celery, nuts and pineapple. Pour into 13 x 9-inch pan; chill until firm. Cut into squares; place on lettuce. Top with whipped cream; serve. Yield: 12 servings.

Mrs. Mary White, Cale H.S.
Cale, Arkansas

LOW-CALORIE LIME SALAD

    1 pkg. lime gelatin
    2 c. boiling, dietetic pineapple juice
    1 c. dietetic pineapple chunks
    1 c. grated carrots
    1 c. miniature marshmallows

Mix gelatin with juice; chill until partially set. Add pineapple, carrots and marshmallows; chill until firm. Serve on lettuce leaf. Yield: 9 servings.

Clara W. Grimes, Payson H.S.
Payson, Arizona

MERRY CHRISTMAS SALAD

    1 pkg. lime gelatin
    1 c. boiling water
    1 No. 2 can crushed pineapple
    1 c. sm. curd cottage cheese
    ½ c. finely sliced celery
    1 tbsp. chopped pimento
    ½ c. chopped walnuts
    Jellied cranberry sauce
    6 walnuts, halved
    1 3-oz. pkg. cream cheese
    1 tbsp. mayonnaise
    1 tsp. lemon juice
    Maraschino cherries

Dissolve gelatin in boiling water; cool till syrupy. Stir in pineapple, cottage cheese, celery, pimento and walnuts. Turn into round 8 or 9-inch cake pan lined with waxed paper. Chill till firm; turn out on waxed paper. Cut into 6 wedges; nest on lettuce. Cut squares of cranberry sauce for base; top with walnut halves. Blend cream cheese, mayonnaise and lemon juice; frost gelatin. Top with cherries. Yield: 6 servings.

Mrs. Elizabeth Lehew, Coloma Jr. H.S.
Coloma, Michigan
Mrs. Betty Pastorius, German Jr.-Sr. H.S.
McClellandtown, Pennsylvania
Mrs. Virginia Marquett, Milford H.S.
Milford, Ohio

MIDAS' DELIGHT

    1 pkg. orange Jell-O
    3 shredded carrots
    1 grated orange rind
    ¼ lb. grated cheddar cheese
    Lettuce leaves

Prepare Jell-O according to directions on package. Chill until slightly thick; stir in remaining ingredients. Pour into 8 x 8-inch pan; chill. Cut into 4-inch squares; serve on lettuce leaves. Yield: 4 servings.

Mrs. Judith G. Blankenship, Merkel H.S.
Merkel, Texas

MOLDED CINNAMON CANDY SALAD

    1 ½ c. boiling water
    ½ c. red cinnamon candies
    1 pkg. cherry Jell-O
    ½ c. cold water
    1 apple, cut up
    ½ c. celery, cut up
    ⅓ c. slivered almonds or chopped pecans

Pour 1/2 cup boiling water over cinnamon candies; stir until dissolved. Set aside. Pour remaining boiling water over cherry Jell-O; stir until dissolved. Add cold water. Add dissolved cinnamon candies; cool. Add apple, celery and nuts. Pour into 1-quart mold. Chill.

Mrs. Ethel D. Finley, Montgomery Blair H.S.
Silver Spring, Maryland

MOLDED FRUIT SUPREME

    1 pkg. red jelly powder
    ½ c. boiling water
    1 c. pineapple juice
    1 10-oz. can pineapple chunks
    1 8-oz. pkg. cream cheese, diced
    2 apples, chopped
    2 oranges, chopped
    1 c. chopped celery
    1 c. chopped nuts
    1 c. whipped cream or prepared topping
      mix

Dissolve jelly powder in boiling water; add pineapple juice. Chill till nearly firm; add cream cheese, apples, oranges, celery and nuts. Fold in whipped cream; chill for 24 hours. Scoop into glass serving dishes; top with whipped cream. Yield: 12 servings.

Mrs. Margaret E. Thompson
Fruitvale Jr. Secondary
Fruitvale, British Columbia, Canada

MOLDED GARDEN SALAD

    1 tbsp. gelatin
    ⅔ c. milk
    1 c. salad dressing
    ⅓ c. catsup
    1 tbsp. prepared mustard
    1 c. cabbage, shredded
    ½ c. seedless raisins
    ½ c. carrots, grated
    ½ c. celery, chopped
    ¼ c. green pepper, chopped
    ½ c. julienne turnips (opt.)

Soften gelatin in milk; dissolve over hot water. Mix in salad dressing, catsup and mustard. Add cabbage and remaining ingredients. Pour into 1-quart ring mold or individual molds. Chill until firm. Serve on lettuce leaf. Yield: 6-8 servings.

Shirley Hooks, Piggott H.S.
Piggott, Arkansas

MOLDED WALDORF SALAD

    1 pkg. lemon Jell-O
    1 c. hot water
    ¼ tsp. salt
    2 tsp. vinegar
    1 c. apples, cut up
    ¼ c. walnuts, cut up
    ¾ c. celery, cut up
    ¼ c. mayonnaise
    1 3-oz. pkg. cream cheese
    Milk

Dissolve Jell-O in hot water; add salt and vinegar. Chill until partially congealed; add apples, walnuts, celery and mayonnaise. Chill. Thin

cream cheese with milk; add additional nuts, if desired. Serve as dressing. Yield: 8 servings.

Hilda G. Rohlf, Tallmadge H.S.
Tallmadge, Ohio

ORANGE-PINEAPPLE SALAD

    1 pkg. orange gelatin
    1 c. hot water
    1 6-oz. can concentrated frozen orange
      juice
    1 sm. can crushed pineapple
    Shredded carrots

Dissolve gelatin in hot water; add orange juice. Cool; add pineapple and carrots. Place in molds; refrigerate until firm.

Geraldine M. Scott, Randolph H.S.
Randolph, Massachusetts

ORANGE-PINEAPPLE SALAD

    1 sm. pkg. orange or lemon Jell-O
    1 sm. can crushed pineapple
    3 or 4 grated carrots

Make Jell-O according to package directions; add pineapple and carrots. Chill until firm. Yield: 4 servings.

Ann Hoit, Ousley Jr. H.S.
Arlington, Texas

PACIFIC LIME SALAD

    1 c. pineapple juice
    1 box lime Jell-O
    1 3-oz. pkg. cream cheese, softened
    1 c. evaporated milk
    1 No. 2 can crushed pineapple, drained
    ½ c. broken pecans
    1 c. chopped celery
    1 tsp. horseradish

Heat pineapple juice to boiling; dissolve Jell-O. Chill until slightly thickened; whip with egg beater. Blend cream cheese and milk; fold into Jell-O. Add pineapple, pecans, celery and horseradish; chill until firm. Yield: 12 servings.

Mrs. Helen J. Watson, Lakeview H.S.
Winter Garden, Florida

PARADISE SALAD

    1 box lime Jell-O
    1 3-oz. pkg. cream cheese
    2 c. boiling water
    ½ c. chopped celery

(Continued on next page)

½ c. chopped pecans
1 sm. can crushed pineapple
2 tbsp. chopped pimento
½ pt. cream, whipped

Combine Jell-O and cream cheese; add boiling water. Stir until cheese and Jell-O are dissolved; add celery, pecans, pineapple and pimento. Chill until slightly thickened; fold in whipped cream. Pour into lightly oiled 10 x 10-inch glass dish; chill until firm. Cut into squares; serve on lettuce. Yield: 8-10 servings.

Kit C. Moore, Fort Stockton H.S.
Fort Stockton, Texas

PARTY SALAD

2 pkg. lime gelatin
2 c. boiling water
2 c. sm. marshmallows
2 c. grated cabbage
1 c. chopped nuts
2 9-oz. cans crushed pineapple, drained
1 pt. whipping cream
½ c. mayonnaise

Dissolve gelatin in boiling water; add marshmallows. Stir until melted. Let stand until slightly thickened. Add cabbage, nuts and pineapple. Whip cream; add mayonnaise. Fold into gelatin mixture; chill until firm. Yield: 12-16 servings.

Mrs. Dallas Sturlaugson, Maddock H.S.
Maddock, North Dakota

BRILLIANT DECEMBER SALAD

1 pkg. cherry Jell-O
1 c. boiling water
¼ c. red cinnamon candies
1 c. hot peach juice
1 c. canned peaches, diced
½ c. pared chopped apples
½ c. chopped celery
½ c. broken walnuts

Dissolve Jell-O in boiling water. Heat candies and peach juice to boiling point, adding water, if necessary. Mix Jell-O and candy juice; cool to room temperature. Chill until partially congealed, stirring once while chilling. Fold in peaches, apples, celery and walnuts. Place in Pyrex dish. Chill until firm. Serve on lettuce. Yield: 6 servings.

Mrs. Betty Jean Flocco, West Allegheny Sr. H.S.
Imperial, Pennsylvania

GINGER ALE SALAD

1 3-oz. pkg. lime Jell-O
1 c. hot water or juice from fruit
1 c. ginger ale
¼ c. chopped celery
¼ c. chopped nuts
1 c. sweetened peaches or fruit cocktail, drained
½ c. whipping cream, whipped
½ c. mayonnaise

Dissolve Jell-O in hot water; add ginger ale. Chill until slightly thickened. Fold in celery, nuts and fruit. Pour into mold; chill until firm. Unmold on crisp salad greens; serve with dressing of 1/2 whipped cream and mayonnaise. Yield: 4 servings.

Ethel Spradling, Bixby H.S.
Bixby, Oklahoma

GINGER ALE SALAD

1 pkg. lime Jell-O
1 c. hot water
1 c. ginger ale
¼ c. chopped celery
¼ c. chopped nuts
1 c. sweetened peaches

Dissolve Jell-O in hot water; add ginger ale. Chill until slightly thickened. Fold in celery, nuts and peaches. Place in mold; chill until firm. Serve on crisp salad greens; top with mayonnaise. Yield: 6 servings.

Helen Reesor, Colon Comm. Sch.
Colon, Michigan

LIME SALAD

1 box lime Jell-O
1 c. hot water
1 c. Seven-Up
⅓ c. diced celery
⅓ c. chopped pecans
1 sm. can sliced peaches

Dissolve Jell-O in hot water; add Seven-Up. Chill until slightly thickened. Add celery and pecans. Pour into square Pyrex pan. Arrange peaches on top of salad. Chill until firm. Yield: 6-8 servings.

Mrs. Elsie Waller, Mt. Enterprise H.S.
Mt. Enterprise, Texas

PEACH CHIFFON DELIGHT

1 buffet sized can sliced peaches
1 3-oz. pkg. peach gelatin
¾ c. cold water

(Continued on next page)

⅓ c. powdered milk crystals
⅓ c. sliced celery
⅓ c. chopped walnuts
Mayonnaise

Drain juice from peaches. Add enough water to make 3/4 cup. Bring to boil; dissolve gelatin in hot liquid. Add cold water. Chill until syrupy. Sprinkle milk crystals over gelatin; beat with electric mixer until very foamy. Fold in peaches, celery and nuts. Pour into individual gelatin molds. Chill for 4 or 5 hours. Serve on bed of lettuce. Garnish with mayonnaise. Yield: 6 servings.

Mrs. Lindell Stanton, Butte Valley H.S.
Dorris, California

PEACH HALO SALAD

¾ c. peach syrup
1 tbsp. gelatin
3 tbsp. lemon juice
2 3-oz. pkg. cream cheese
½ c. mayonnasie
¼ tsp. salt
1 tsp. horseradish
½ c. evaporated milk
1 ½ c. canned cling peach slices
½ c. celery, finely chopped
½ c. chopped maraschino cherries

Heat peach syrup in saucepan. Soften gelatin in lemon juice; dissolve in hot syrup. Cool. Soften cream cheese with fork; blend in mayonnaise, salt, horseradish and gelatin mixture. Whip evaporated milk until ice crystals form; whip until fluffy. Fold into gelatin-cream cheese mixture; fold in peach slices, celery and cherries. Pour into 8-inch ring mold; chill until firm. Unmold and garnish with additional peach slices and cherries if desired. Yield: 8 servings.

Diana Sanders Moniz, James Monroe H.S.
Sepulveda, California

PERFECTION SALAD

2 tsp. Knox gelatin
¼ c. cold water
1 sm. can crushed pineapple
1 pkg. lemon Jell-O
2 3-oz. pkg. Philadelphia cream cheese
½ c. chopped celery
½ c. chopped nuts
Pinch of salt
1 sm. can pimento, chopped
½ pt. cream, whipped

Soak Knox gelatin in water. Drain pineapple; add water to juice to equal 2 cups liquid. Heat liquid to boiling; add gelatin and Jell-O. Stir until dissolved. Add cream cheese; stir until melted. Add pineapple, celery, nuts, salt and pimento. Chill; fold in whipped cream. Pour in molds; chill until firm. Top with mayonnaise, if desired. Yield: 8 servings.

Mrs. Bettye R. Perry, Fifth St. H.S.
West Point, Mississippi

PINEAPPLE-CHEESE MOLD

1 1-lb. 4 ½-oz. can crushed pineapple
1 3-oz. pkg. lime Jell-O
1 c. boiling water
1 c. evaporated milk
1 c. cottage cheese
½ c. mayonnaise
¼ c. chopped celery
¼ c. chopped nuts (opt.)

Drain pineapple; set aside. Dissolve Jell-O in boiling water; stir in remaining ingredients. Pour into 1-quart mold; chill until firm. Unmold; garnish with mandarin orange sections and maraschino cherries. Yield: 8 servings.

Mary H. West, Damascus H.S.
Damascus, Maryland

PINEAPPLE-CHEESE SALAD

2 3-oz. pkg. orange gelatin
3 c. boiling water
4 tbsp. mayonnaise
1 8-oz. pkg. cream cheese
1 No. 2 can crushed pineapple
2 med. carrots, finely grated

Dissolve gelatin in boiling water; chill until slightly thickened. Beat mayonnaise and cream cheese until smooth. Combine all ingredients; chill until firm. Yield: 6-8 servings.

Velma Martin, Fuller H.S.
Little Rock, Arkansas

PINEAPPLE-CREAM CHEESE SALAD

1 8-oz. pkg. cream cheese, softened
½ c. pineapple juice
1 3-oz. pkg. lime Jell-o
1½ c. hot water
½ c. chopped celery
½ c. crushed pineapple
1 c. chopped nuts

Combine cream cheese and pineapple juice; beat until smooth. Dissolve Jell-O in hot water; add cheese mixture. Chill until partially set; add celery, pineapple and nuts. Pour into mold; chill until firm.

Megan Jones, Cowichan Sr. H.S.
Duncan, British Columbia, Canada

PINEAPPLE-CREAM CHEESE SALAD

2 sm. or 1 lge. pkg. lime Jell-O
2 c. hot water
1 c. cold water
1 lge. pkg. cream cheese, softened
1 tbsp. mayonnaise
1 c. finely chopped celery
1 lge. can crushed pineapple

(Continued on next page)

Dissolve Jell-O in hot water; add cold water. Stir in cream cheese and mayonnaise. Add celery and pineapple; chill until slightly thickened. Stir; chill until firm. Serve on lettuce leaf and top with mayonnaise. Yield: 10 servings.

Hilda Harmon, Crowley H.S.
Crowley, Louisiana

PINEAPPLE DELIGHT

1 No. 2 can crushed pineapple
1 pkg. lime or lemon Jell-O
1 3-oz. pkg. cream cheese, softened
½ c. celery, cut fine
½ c. walnuts, cut fine
1 c. cream, whipped
Red and green cherries

Drain pineapple; bring pineapple juice to boil. Pour over Jell-O; stir well. Add cream cheese; cool. Add remaining ingredients; pour in mold or 8 x 8-inch pan. Chill until firm. Yield: 8 servings.

Mrs. Jeanne Olmstead, Lewiston Public Sch.
Lewiston, Minnesota

PINEAPPLE-LIME SALAD

1 No. 2 can crushed pineapple
1 pkg. lime gelatin
1 3-oz. pkg. cream cheese, cut up
1 c. finely chopped celery
1 c. cream, whipped or 1 pkg. dessert
   topping, whipped
1 c. nuts, chopped

Heat pineapple; dissolve gelatin in pineapple. Add cheese to hot gelatin; stir until almost smooth. Cool; add celery, nuts and whipped cream. Place in loaf pan or flat pan; chill until firm. Cut into squares or slices to serve. Yield: 12 servings.

Mrs. Ruth Riffe, Hobart H.S.
Hobart, Oklahoma

PINEAPPLE RELISH SALAD

1 c. pineapple juice
1 c. water
1 pkg. lime Jell-O
1 tbsp. vinegar
¾ c. sweet pickles, finely chopped
3 slices canned pineapple
1 cucumber, diced
½ c. stuffed olives, finely chopped

Heat pineapple juice and water until boiling; dissolve Jell-O. Add vinegar; chill until slightly thickened. Add remaining ingredients; pour into individual molds. Chill until firm. Unmold on lettuce; serve with mayonnaise. Yield: 8 servings.

Mrs. Norma M. Womble, Broadway H.S.
Broadway, North Carolina

RAISIN SUNSHINE SALAD

⅔ c. seedless raisins
1 pkg. lemon gelatin
1 ¼ c. hot water
2 tbsp. lemon juice
1 c. undrained crushed pineapple
¼ tsp. salt
1 ½ tsp. grated carrot

Rinse raisins; cover with water. Boil 5 minutes; cool and drain. Dissolve gelatin in hot water; add lemon juice, pineapple and salt. Cool until slightly thickened; fold in raisins and carrot. Turn into individual molds or 8-inch square pan; chill until firm. Unmold; serve on salad greens. Yield: 6 servings.

Mrs. Flora Harmon, Hope H.S.
Hope, Arkansas

RUBY SALAD

1 8-oz. can diced beets
1 7-oz. can crushed pineapple
1 tsp. vinegar
1 tsp. horseradish
1 pkg. lemon gelatin

Drain beets and pineapple into measuring cup; add vinegar and horseradish. Add enough water to liquid to make 1 3/4 cups. Heat liquid; add gelatin. Stir until dissolved. Chill until slightly thickened. Stir in beets and pineapple. Chill until firm. Yield: 8 servings.

Mrs. Deborah Purvis, Soquel H.S.
Soquel, California

SALAD DELIGHT

1 pkg. lemon or lime Jell-O
1 pkg. cream cheese, broken in pieces
1 c. celery, chopped fine
1 c. carrots, chopped fine
1 c. crushed pineapple
1 c. whipped cream

Dissolve Jell-O in 1 cup boiling water; add cheese. Stir until cheese is melted. Cool. Add remaining ingredients. Refrigerate until firm. Yield: 8 servings.

Mrs. Lena Bell Moore
Vegreville Composite H.S.
Vegreville, Alberta, Canada

SUNSHINE SALAD

    1 box lemon Jell-O
    3 shredded carrots
    1 can pineapple tidbits
    ½ c. walnut pieces

Prepare Jell-O according to package directions, substituting juice from pineapple for an equal amount of water. Add carrots, pineapple and walnuts; stir lightly. Refrigerate until firm. Yield: 8 servings.

Mrs. Lorraine Fennemore, Mem. H.S.
East Paterson, New Jersey

SUNSHINE SALAD

    1 pkg. lemon gelatin
    ½ c. pineapple tidbits
    ½ c. Malaga grapes, seeded and cut up
    ½ c. walnut meats, cut up
    ½ c. shredded carrots

Prepare gelatin according to package directions; add remaining ingredients. Pour into ring mold; chill until firm. Serve, unmolded, with favorite dressing. Yield: 6 servings.

Mrs. Mildred K. Hencle, Port Byron Central
Port Byron, New York

SUNSHINE SALAD

    1 c. boiling water
    1 pkg. lemon gelatin
    ½ c. ice water
    1 9-oz. can crushed pineapple
    Pinch of salt
    2 med. carrots, grated

Pour boiling water over gelatin; stir until dissolved. Add ice water, pineapple and salt; chill until slightly thickened. Add carrots; pour into 8-inch square pan. Chill until firm; cut in squares. Serve on crisp lettuce with mayonnaise. Yield: 6 servings.

Sallie Friedl, Montcalm H.S.
Montcalm, West Virginia

VEGETABLE-FRUIT SALAD

    1 box lime Jell-O
    1 tbsp. vinegar
    ½ c. sliced olives
    ½ c. chopped apple
    ½ c. shredded cabbage
    ½ c. chopped walnuts

Mix Jell-O according to package directions. Add remaining ingredients; chill until firm. Serve on lettuce leaf. Yield: 6 servings.

Linda Schilling, Wayne-Goshen H.S.
Waynesfield, Ohio

TOMATO COCKTAIL SALAD

    1 10-oz. can tomato cocktail
    1 pkg. lemon Jell-O
    1 8¼-oz. can crushed pineapple

Heat tomato cocktail; add Jell-O. Stir until dissolved; cool. Add pineapple. Chill until firm. Serve on lettuce with mayonnaise. Excellent with roast beef. Yield: 6 servings.

Emily A. Paulus, Kalani H.S.
Honolulu, Hawaii

WALDORF SALAD

    1 envelope unflavored gelatin
    ⅓ c. sugar
    ½ tsp. salt
    1 ½ c. water
    ¼ c. vinegar or lemon juice
    2 c. diced tart apples
    ½ c. diced celery
    ¼ c. chopped pecans or walnuts

Mix gelatin, sugar and salt thoroughly in small saucepan. Add 1/2 cup water. Place over low heat, stirring constantly until gelatin is dissolved. Remove from heat; stir in remaining water and vinegar. Chill mixture to unbeaten egg white consistency. Fold in apples, celery and nuts. Turn into a 4-cup mold or individual molds. Chill until firm. Unmold by dipping mold in warm water to depth of the gelatin. Loosen around edge with tip of paring knife. Place serving dish on mold; turn upside-down. Shake, holding serving dish tightly to mold. Garnish with fruit. Yield: 6 servings.

Mrs. Ray Sartor, Pine Grove H.S.
Ripley, Mississippi
Marion Francone, Caruthers H.S.
Caruthers, California

YUM YUM SALAD

    1 No. 2 can crushed pineapple
    ⅔ c. sugar
    1 box lemon Jell-O
    1 8-oz. pkg. cream cheese
    1 c. celery, chopped fine
    1 c. chopped apples
    ½ c. chopped pecan meats
    1 pkg. Dream Whip

Combine pineapple and sugar; cook for 3 minutes. Add Jell-O and cream cheese; stir until completely mixed. Cool until mixture begins to congeal; add celery, apples and nuts. Prepare Dream Whip according to directions on package, omitting vanilla flavoring; fold into Jell-O mixture. Pour into 12 x 7 1/2 x 2-inch pan; chill for 6 hours. Yield: 12 servings.

Mrs. Juanita B. Ullmann, Fort Frye H.S.
Beverly, Ohio

Meat and Poultry Salads

RECIPE FOR TURKEY-TOMATO SALAD ON PAGE 321

BEEF SALAD

½ lb. cooked roast beef
2 tbsp. chopped onion
4 tbsp. chopped pickle
2 tbsp. chopped celery
½ c. salad dressing
Salt and pepper to taste

Grind beef in food grinder; add remaining ingredients, mixing thoroughly. May be used as sandwich filling or to stuff tomatoes. Yield: 3-4 servings.

Catharine Butterfield, Manchester H.S.
Manchester, Michigan

CALIFORNIA SPROUTS-BEEF-MACARONI SALAD

1 tbsp. salt
3 qt. boiling water
2 c. elbow macaroni
1 10-oz. pkg. frozen Brussels sprouts
1 c. cooked corned beef strips
1 med. onion, chopped
¼ c. canned pimentos, sliced
½ c. mayonnaise
1 tbsp. prepared horseradish
1 tbsp. sugar
3 tbsp. vinegar

Add salt to rapidly boiling water. Gradually add macaroni so that water continues to boil. Cook, uncovered, stirring occasionally, until tender. Drain in colander. Rinse with cold water; drain. Cook Brussels sprouts as directed on package. Drain. Combine macaroni, Brussels sprouts, corned beef, onion and pimentos; toss lightly, but thoroughly. Chill. Combine remaining ingredients; mix well. Arrange macaroni mixture on bed of crisp lettuce, if desired. Top with mayonnaise mixture.

Photograph for this recipe on inside back cover.

CORNED BEEF SALAD

1 3-oz. pkg. lemon Jell-O
1 ¾ c. hot water
3 hard-cooked eggs, cut up
2 tbsp. vinegar
½ can corned beef
1 c. celery
1 c. Miracle Whip salad dressing
1 sm. onion, chopped
1 sm. green pepper, chopped

Dissolve Jell-O in hot water; cool. Add remaining ingredients and chill. Serve with pickled peaches, potato chips and hot bread. Yield: 6 servings.

Willie Mae Cornwell, Midway Sch.
Waco, Texas

CORNED BEEF

2 c. boiling water
1 pkg. prepared aspic
3 c. ground corned beef
6 tbsp. mayonnaise
½ tsp. Worcestershire sauce
4 hard-boiled eggs, chopped
1 c. shredded cabbage
1 c. carrot sticks (marinated in French dressing)
5 sm., unpeeled scored cucumbers

Add boiling water to aspic; cool in refrigerator. Add corned beef, mayonnaise, Worcestershire sauce and eggs; pour into ring mold. Chill until set. Turn out on platter; fill center with marinated cabbage and carrots. Garnish with cucumbers. Serve with mayonnaise. Yield: 6-8 servings.

Mrs. Earl W. Ellis, New Summerfield H.S.
New Summerfield, Texas

CORNED BEEF SALAD

1 pkg. Jell-O
1 ¾ c. hot water
1 tsp. salt
¾ c. salad dressing
1 12-oz. can corned beef
3 hard-cooked eggs
1 c. celery
⅓ c. chopped green pepper
1 tbsp. sweet pickle
1 tbsp. pimento
1 tbsp. chopped or grated onion

Dissolve Jell-O in hot water; chill until slightly thickened. Add remaining ingredients. Yield: 8-10 servings.

Mrs. Margaret Bumpas, West H.S.
Wichita, Kansas

CORNED BEEF SALAD MOLD

1 envelope unflavored gelatin
¼ c. cold water
1 ½ c. boiling tomato juice
2 tsp. lemon juice
½ tsp. salt
1 12-oz. can corned beef, crumbled
½ c. chopped celery
½ c. chopped cucumber
1 tbsp. chopped onion
1 c. mayonnaise

Soften gelatin in cold water; dissolve in tomato juice. Add lemon juice and salt; chill until partially set. Fold in remaining ingredients. Chill until firm in 8 1/2 x 4 1/2 x 2 1/2-inch loaf pan. Unmold; serve with deviled eggs. Yield: 8 servings.

Mary Sullivan Debevec, Chisholm Sr. H.S.
Chisholm, Minnesota

DECEPTION SALAD

1 pkg. plain gelatin
⅓ c. cold water
1 beef bouillon cube
1 c. boiling water
1 12-oz. can chilled corned beef, cubed
3 hard-cooked eggs, sliced or chopped
2 tbsp. green pepper, coarsely chopped
2 tbsp. onion, finely chopped
1 c. cooked salad dressing

Dissolve gelatin in cold water. Add bouillon cube to boiling water; stir in gelatin. Cool; add corned beef, eggs, vegetables and salad dressing. Pour into 8-inch ring mold; refrigerate until firm. Unmold onto lettuce; garnish with radish roses. Yield: 8 servings.

Mrs. Barbara Potterton, Illing Jr. H.S.
Manchester, Connecticut

CORNED BEEF SALAD

2 pkg. lemon Jell-O
3 c. boiling water
1 c. salad dressing
2 c. diced celery
1 green pepper, finely chopped
1 med. onion, finely chopped
1 12-oz. can corned beef, ground

Dissolve Jell-O in boiling water; chill until syrupy. Add salad dressing; mix well. Add celery, green pepper, onion and corned beef. Pour into 13 x 9-inch pan. Chill until firm. Yield: 12 servings.

Carol Brent, Holton H.S.
Holton, Kansas

MEAL IN A MOLD

1 pkg. lemon gelatin
1 c. boiling water
1 c. mayonnaise
1 sm. onion, grated
1 c. celery, sliced
1 pkg. chipped corned beef
3 hard-cooked eggs, chopped

Dissolve gelatin in water; cool. Beat in mayonnaise and remaining ingredients. Pour into mold; refrigerate for 3 hours or until firm. Yield: 6 servings.

Mrs. Ruth Kardox, Marlington H.S.
Alliance, Ohio

GREENS 'N' DRIED BEEF DRESSING

¼ lb. dried beef
¼ c. butter
½ c. onion, diced

½ tsp. salt
1 tsp. sugar
¼ tsp. celery seed
2 tbsp. vinegar
¼ c. mayonnaise
6 c. mixed greens

Rinse dried beef in hot water; drain well. Mix remaining ingredients except greens in small saucepan. Bring to a boil; add dried beef. Pour over greens; toss lightly. Yield: 4-6 servings.

Mrs. Helen H. Norris, Pageland H.S.
Pageland, South Carolina

TACO SALAD

1 head lettuce, shredded
½ c. grated cheddar cheese
1 med. onion, chopped
1 10-oz. can stewed tomatoes
1 lb. ground beef
¼ c. taco sauce
1 6-oz. pkg. corn chips

Place lettuce, cheese and onion in salad bowl. Drain tomatoes well, reserving juice. Add tomatoes to salad mixture. Brown ground beef, crumbling with fork; pour off fat. Add reserved juice and taco sauce to meat; simmer for 5 minutes. Add meat mixture and corn chips to salad. Toss lightly; serve at once. Yield: 6 servings.

Marianne Estes, La Mirada H.S.
La Mirada, California

MEXICAN SALAD

1 lb. ground beef
½ c. chopped onion
2 c. kidney beans, drained
½ c. French dressing
½ c. water
1 tbsp. chili powder
4 c. shredded lettuce
½ c. sliced green onions
2 c. sharp cheddar cheese

Brown ground beef and onion; cook until tender. Stir in kidney beans, French dressing, water and chili powder; simmer 15 minutes. Combine lettuce, onions, meat sauce and 1 1/2 cups cheese; toss lightly. Sprinkle with remaining cheese. Serve with crisp tortillas, if desired. Yield: 4-6 servings.

Mrs. John E. Hillhouse, Mathiston H.S.
Mathiston, Mississippi

ORIENTAL BEEF

2 c. cooked beef, cubed
2 c. cooked red kidney beans
¼ c. diced red pimento

301

(Continued on next page)

1 c. diced celery
½ c. diced onions
2 c. bean sprouts marinated in French
  dressing
Soy sauce to taste
Salt and pepper to taste
½ c. mayonnaise

Combine ingredients in order given; mix thoroughly in salad bowl. Serve as luncheon meal or as dinner salad course. Yield: 10 servings.

Mrs. Earl W. Ellis, New Summerfield H.S.
New Summerfield, Texas

SUMMER BEEF SALAD

1 lb. cold roast beef, trimmed and cubed
2 apples, diced
2 stalks celery, diced
4 shallots, finely chopped
1 sm. clove of garlic, finely chopped
4 tbsp. finely chopped parsley
6 to 8 tbsp. olive oil
2 to 3 tbsp. wine vinegar
Salt and freshly ground black pepper
  to taste

Combine beef, apples and celery with shallots, garlic and parsley in salad bowl. Combine remaining ingredients; season meat mixture to taste with dressing mixture. Yield: 4-6 servings.

Lea Elizabeth Comeau, Eastern Shore Dist. H.S.
Musquodoboit Harbour, Nova Scotia, Canada

HEARTY MEAT SALAD

1 c. chopped celery
1 c. chopped apples
1 ½ c. shredded carrots
1 c. cooked peas
1 green pepper, chopped
2 c. leftover meat
1 c. mayonnaise

Mix all ingredients; season to taste. Serve on lettuce or in tomato cups. Yield: 8 servings.

Freda F. Bennett, Orchard H.S.
Orchard, Nebraska

HOT SALAD TO TOP WAFFLES

1 8-oz. jar prepared cheddar cheese
1 8-oz. can string beans, French or
  regular cut, drained
1 can prepared meat, diced

Melt cheese in top of double boiler or in saucepan over low heat. Add beans and meat. Heat

thoroughly. Serve piping hot on waffles. May be served as salad, hot vegetable or main dish salad. Yield: 4 servings.

Stephanie Preston Heatwole
Mark Twain Intermediate Sch.
Alexandria, Virginia

JELLIED MEAT SALAD

1 tbsp. gelatin
¼ c. cold water
1 ½ c. hot stock
2 tbsp. lemon juice
¼ tsp. salt
1 c. diced meat
½ c. chopped vegetable (peas, celery,
  carrots)
2 tbsp. green pepper, shredded

Soften gelatin in cold water for 10 minutes. Bring stock to a boil; remove from heat. Add softened gelatin, lemon juice and salt; stir until gelatin dissolves. Cool; refrigerate until consistency of unbeaten egg whites. Fold in meat and vegetables. Turn into loaf pan or individual molds; refrigerate for 5 to 6 hours or until firm. Unmold; serve on salad greens. Garnish with mayonnaise. Use 2 bouillon cubes in 1 1/2 cups hot water or canned consomme if stock is not available. Yield: 6 servings.

Mrs. Nancy W. Grammer
Ripley, Tennessee
Mrs. Paul Nickerson, Barrington Municipal H.S.
Barrington Passage, Nova Scotia, Canada

BACON 'N' VEGETABLE SALAD

½ lb. sliced bacon, cut into 1-in. pieces
1 10-oz. pkg. frozen mixed vegetables
2 c. torn lettuce
½ c. chopped celery
2 green onions, sliced crosswise
1 ½ tbsp. vinegar
2 hard cooked eggs, sliced

Panfry bacon until crisp. Drain on absorbent paper. Reserve 2 tablespoons bacon drippings for dressing. Cook mixed vegetables according to directions on package. Combine bacon, mixed vegetables, lettuce, celery and onions. Mix vinegar into reserved bacon drippings in skillet. Heat until flavors are blended. Pour over vegetable mixture and toss lightly. Garnish with eggs. Yield: 4 servings.

Glenda L. Nybo, Richmond H.S.
Richmond, Michigan

CHEF'S SALAD

1 c. diced boiled ham or beef
2 diced hard-boiled eggs
½ c. diced celery

(Continued on next page)

1 diced boiled potato
½ sm. onion, diced
Dressing

Toss ingredients together lightly with fork. Dressing may be thinned with pickle vinegar, poured over or marinated. Yield: 6-8 servings.

Mrs. Dony R. Baker, McLean H.S.
McLean, Texas

CHEF'S SALAD

8 c. mixed greens, cut into 1-in. pieces
1 c. celery, diced
1 c. cooked ham, cut into strips
2 hard-cooked eggs, finely chopped
2 tbsp. parsley, finely chopped
4 tomatoes, cut into wedges
1 c. garlic or French dressing

Chill all ingredients. Combine greens, celery, ham, eggs, parsley and tomatoes; toss. Add dressing; toss again. Yield: 12 servings.

Mrs. Betty Porter, Oilton H.S.
Oilton, Oklahoma

CHEF'S SALAD

8 c. 1-in. pieces mixed greens
1 c. diced celery
1 c. cooked ham strips
2 hard-cooked eggs, chopped fine
2 tbsp. finely chopped parsley
4 tomatoes, cut into wedges
1 c. garlic or plain French dressing

Have all ingredients chilled. Toss greens with celery, ham, eggs, parsley and tomato wedges. Add dressing and toss again. Yield: 12 servings.

Sara Nell Dober, Effingham Co. H.S.
Springfield, Georgia

CHEF'S SALAD HAWAIIANA

2 c. drained pineapple chunks
2 tbsp. chopped dill pickle
2 tbsp. chopped green onion
1 c. cubed ham
1 c. cubed cheddar or Swiss cheese
½ to ¾ c. French dressing

Toss all ingredients together. Serve on lettuce leaves. Yield: 4 servings.

Mrs. Rebecca Burns Drone, College Grove H.S.
College Grove, Tennessee

SPICY HAM AND POTATO SALAD RING

1 ½ c. diced, cooked ham
2 tbsp. minced onion
½ c. mayonnaise or salad dressing
½ c. chili sauce
1 tsp. horseradish
2 tsp. prepared mustard
¼ tsp. Tabasco
1 envelope unflavored gelatin
½ c. water
Potato Salad

Combine ham, onion, mayonnaise, chili sauce, horseradish, mustard and Tabasco; set aside. Sprinkle gelatin on water to soften; place over low heat and stir until dissolved. Remove from heat and blend into meat mixture. Turn into a 6-cup ring mold; chill until almost firm. Top with Potato Salad; chill until firm.

POTATO SALAD:

2 c. diced cooked potatoes
1 c. diced celery
1 sm. onion, minced
2 tbsp. finely chopped green pepper
½ c. mayonnaise or salad dressing
1 tbsp. vinegar
1 ¼ tsp. salt
⅛ tsp. pepper
1 envelope unflavored gelatin
½ c. water

Combine potatoes, celery, onion, green pepper, mayonnaise, vinegar, salt and pepper. Sprinkle gelatin on water to soften. Place over low heat and stir until gelatin is dissolved. Remove from heat and blend into potato mixture. Unmold on serving plate and garnish with salad greens and wedges of tomato. Yield: 8 servings.

Mrs. Alice Hansberger, Canton Sr. H.S.
Canton, Illinois

PARTY HAM RING

1 envelope unflavored gelatin
¼ c. cold water
¾ c. boiling water
1 c. sour cream
½ c. mayonnaise or salad dressing
3 tbsp. vinegar
¼ tsp. salt
Dash of pepper
1 ½ c. diced cooked or canned ham
1 c. celery slices
¼ c. chopped green pepper
3 tbsp. chopped green onions

Soften gelatin in cold water; dissolve in boiling water. Blend in sour cream, mayonnaise, vinegar, salt and pepper. Chill until partially set; whip until fluffy. Fold in remaining ingredients; pour into 5 1/2 cup ring mold. Chill until firm. Yield: 5-6 servings.

Mrs. Joyce Boyer, Unified Dist. 237
Smith Center, Kansas

HAM MOUSSE

1 tbsp. unflavored gelatin
¼ c. cold water
¼ c. vinegar
2 c. finely cubed ham
1 c. finely diced celery
1 tbsp. sugar
1 tbsp. pickle relish
1 tsp. mustard
½ c. heavy cream, whipped

Soften gelatin in cold water and vinegar; dissolve over boiling water. Stir in ham, celery, sugar, relish and mustard. Fold in whipped cream. Turn into mold and chill until set. Unmold and garnish with watercress. Serve with Easy Horseradish Sauce.

EASY HORSERADISH SAUCE:

3 tbsp. well drained horseradish
½ tsp. salt
½ c. whipping cream, whipped

Fold horseradish and salt into cream. Yield: 6 servings.

Mrs. Elvi Salmela, Hudson H.S.
Hudson, Massachusetts

MOLDED POTATO SALAD

6 c. cold cooked potatoes, cubed
1 c. diced onions
½ c. chopped celery
½ c. chopped parsley
1 ½ tsp. salt
¼ tsp. pepper
8 slices cooked ham
2 pkg. unflavored gelatin
½ c. water
1 ½ c. salad dressing

Combine first 6 ingredients in large bowl. Line baking dish with slices of cooked ham. Combine gelatin in water; heat to dissolve. Combine potato mixture and gelatin with salad dressing. Press over ham. Refrigerate to set. Turn out onto platter; garnish with watercress. Slice to serve. Yield: 16 servings.

Mrs. Elizabeth W. Knape, Douglas Sr. H.S.
Douglas, Arizona

FAVORITE SUPPER SALAD

1 sm. head cabbage
1 green pepper
1 med. onion
½ lb. cooked ham
½ lb. American cheese
French Dressing

Shred cabbage. Chop green pepper and onion. Cut ham and cheese into thin strips. Combine all ingredients and chill. Toss lightly with French dressing just before serving. Garnish with green pepper rings and stuffed olives. Yield: 8 servings.

Mrs. Wilma A. Horton, Harrold H.S.
Harrold, Texas

HAM 'N' POTATO SALAD

1 ½ c. diced cooked ham
¼ c. chili sauce
1 tbsp. finely chopped onion
2 tsp. prepared mustard
1 tsp. horseradish
1 envelope unflavored gelatin
½ c. water
1 c. mayonnaise
2 c. diced cooked potatoes
½ c. diced celery
2 tbsp. finely chopped green pepper
2 tsp. vinegar
1 tsp. salt
⅛ tsp. pepper

Combine ham, chili sauce, onion, mustard and horseradish. Soften gelatin in water; cook and stir until gelatin is dissolved. Stir 1/4 cup of gelatin mixture into 1/2 cup mayonnaise; add to ham mixture and mix well. Turn into 10 x 5 x 1 1/2-inch baking dish; chill until almost set. Keep remaining gelatin at room temperature. Combine potatoes, celery, green pepper, vinegar, salt and pepper. Stir remaining 1/4 cup gelatin mixture into remaining 1/2 cup mayonnaise; add to potato mixture and mix well. Spoon onto ham layer; chill until firm. Yield: 8-10 servings.

Mrs. Eleanor Tedford, Wiggins H.S.
Wiggins, Colorado

SPRING VEGETABLE SALAD

1 6-oz. pkg. lemon, lime or orange gelatin
1 tsp. salt
1 ½ c. boiling water
¾ c. cold water
3 tbsp. vinegar
4 tsp. grated onion
Dash of pepper
¼ c. thinly chopped green pepper (opt.)
2 tbsp. diced pimento
¾ c. finely chopped celery
¾ c. diced tomato
½ c. thinly sliced radishes
1 c. thinly shredded lettuce
½ c. slivered cooked ham
½ c. slivered Swiss cheese

Dissolve gelatin and salt in boiling water. Add cold water, vinegar, onion and pepper. Chill until thick and syrupy. Fold in remaining vegetables, ham and cheese. Pour into mold. Chill

(Continued on next page)

until firm. Unmold onto tray. Garnish with lettuce and additional vegetables if desired. Yield: 8 servings.

Mrs. Jacqueline H. Spang, Cornwall Middle Sch.
Cornwall, Pennsylvania

FRESH CABBAGE AND HAM SALAD

3 c. finely shredded cabbage
1 c. slivered cooked ham
2 tbsp. finely chopped fresh onion
¼ c. finely chopped fresh parsley
2 tsp. caraway seeds
¼ tsp. salt
⅛ tsp. pepper
3 tbsp. mayonnaise
1 tsp. cider vinegar
Head of lettuce
Radishes for garnish

Combine cabbage, ham, onion, parsley, seasonings, mayonnaise and vinegar in salad bowl. Toss lightly. Serve on lettuce. Garnish with radishes. Yield: 6 servings.

Mrs. George A. Miller, Milan H.S.
Milan, Ohio

HAM AND RICE SALAD

1 ½ c. mayonnaise
¼ tsp. pepper
1 tsp. salt
2 tbsp. lemon juice
2 tsp. grated onion
2 tsp. mustard
2 ½ c. cooked rice, cooled
3 c. diced cooked ham
2 c. drained pineapple tidbits
2 c. diced celery

Combine mayonnaise, pepper, salt, lemon juice, onion and mustard in a bowl. Mix well and refrigerate. Combine rice, ham, pineapple and celery. Toss mayonnaise mixture and rice mixture together just before serving. Serve on lettuce leaves. Yield: 8 servings.

Mrs. Paula Disterhaupt, Glenwood Sr. H.S.
Glenwood, Iowa

HAM-CHEESE-GREEN PEPPER SALAD

1 c. ground cooked ham
1 c. finely cut celery
6 oz. cream cheese
¼ c. chopped parsley
Salt to taste
3 med. sized green peppers

Mix ham, celery, cheese and parsley together thoroughly. Add salt. Pack the mixture into peppers and chill. Slice and serve on lettuce leaves with French dressing.

Mrs. Patsy Stinger, McCulloch Jr. H.S.
Marion, Indiana

HAM SALAD

2 c. cubed ham
¼ c. cubed celery
1 c. lettuce
2 lge. tomatoes, sliced
1 c. romaine
1 pt. lge. curd cottage cheese
3 hard-cooked eggs, sliced
1 c. sour cream
⅓ c. catsup

Mix ham and celery together. Layer lettuce, tomatoes, romaine, cottage cheese, ham mixture and eggs in glass salad bowl. Chill. Mix sour cream and catsup together for dressing. Garnish or place slices of ham around top.

Mrs. Carol Naig, Kerkhoven H.S.
Kerkhoven, Minnesota

HAM AND SPAGHETTI SALAD

8 oz. pkg. spiral spaghetti
1 doz. hard cooked eggs
1 No. 303 can peas or 1 pkg. frozen peas, uncooked
1 No. 303 can pineapple tidbits, drained
1 ¼ lb. ready-to-eat ham, cubed
¼ c. pimento
½ c. finely chopped onion
2 c. diced celery
1 pt. Miracle Whip
1 ½ tbsp. prepared mustard
1 ½ tbsp. sugar
½ tsp. salt
1 3-oz. pkg. cashew nuts

Mix first 8 ingredients together. Combine Miracle Whip, mustard, sugar and salt; blend into spaghetti mixture. Let stand for 12 to 24 hours. Add nuts just before serving. Yield: 10 servings.

Annah Simonson, Dawson Public Sch.
Dawson, Minnesota

HAM SALAD

      12 oz. canned chopped ham
      2 pimentos
      4 sweet pickles
      ½ sm. onion
      3 hard-cooked eggs
      12 oz. canned chopped ham
      2 tsp. mustard
      4 tbsp. salad dressing
      Pepper to taste

Grind pimentos, pickles, onion, eggs and ham in a food chopper. Add mustard and salad dressing. Season with pepper. Mix thoroughly. Yield: 4-6 servings.

Mrs. Betty Ambrose, Robert Lee H.S.
Midland, Texas

HOT POTATO AND HAM SALAD

      1 c. diced cooked ham
      ½ c. chopped onion
      1 tbsp. butter
      1 c. cream of celery soup
      ½ c. sour cream
      ¼ tsp. caraway seed
      ⅛ tsp. pepper
      3 c. cubed cooked potatoes
      1 tbsp. chopped parsley

Cook ham and onion in butter until onion is tender. Blend in soup, sour cream, caraway and pepper. Add potatoes and heat. Stir lightly. Garnish with parsley. Yield: 4 servings.

Mrs. Patricia Hartronft, Dill City H.S.
Dill City, Oklahoma

HAM AND THREE-BEAN SALAD

      1 lb. cooked ham
      1 11-oz. can kidney beans, drained
          and rinsed
      1 8-oz. can cut green beans, drained
      1 8-oz. can cut yellow beans, drained
      ½ c. chopped green pepper
      ¼ c. sliced onion
      ¾ tsp. salt
      ¾ c. salad oil
      ½ c. vinegar
      ¼ tsp. pepper

Cut meat into bite-sized pieces; combine with vegetables in large bowl. Mix salt, salad oil, vinegar and pepper. Pour over meat and vegetable mixture and toss well. Chill several hours, stirring occasionally. Yield: 4 servings.

Mrs. James Stratico, R. W. Emerson Sch.
Yonkers, New York

MACARONI AND HAM SALAD

      1 ½ c. macaroni
      1 ½ c. diced cooked ham
      1 c. shredded carrots
      1 c. thinly sliced celery
      ¼ c. thinly sliced green onion tops
      1 sm. clove of garlic, crushed (opt.)
      ½ tsp. salt
      ⅛ tsp. pepper
      ½ c. salad dressing or mayonnaise

Cook macaroni in boiling salted water until tender. Drain and run cold water through macaroni to cool and separate pieces, then drain thoroughly. Combine macaroni, ham and vegetables and toss lightly. Chill. Sprinkle with salt and pepper. Add salad dressing and toss to coat pieces. Serve on lettuce and garnish with hard-cooked or deviled eggs and tomato wedges. Yield: 6 servings.

Mrs. Pat M. Paxton
Hugh McRoberts Jr. Sec. Sch.
Richmond, British Columbia, Canada

JOLLY FULL TOMATO PIE

      4 firm lge. tomatoes
      2 c. cooked cubed ham
      1 c. chopped lettuce
      1 med. green onion, minced
      1 c. cubed American cheese
      ½ c. mayonnaise
      2 tbsp. butter or margarine, melted
      1 c. bread crumbs

Cut across top of tomato and scoop out insides, being careful not to tear sides. Cut up tomato insides; combine with ham. Add lettuce, onion, cheese and mayonnaise; mix well and fill tomato cups. Place on cookie sheet. Combine butter and bread crumbs; spoon onto filled tomatoes. Place under broiler until bread crumbs are browned. Yield: 4 servings.

Alene Sanciar, Lumberton H.S.
Lumberton, Mississippi

MACARONI SUPRISE

      1 7-oz. pkg. macaroni, cooked
      1 c. cubed sharp cheese
      1 tbsp. chopped onion
      ½ c. chopped celery
      1 tsp. (or more) salt
      1 to 1 ½ c. cubed ham or canned meat
      1 can drained kidney beans
      ¼ c. pickle relish
      ¾ c. mayonnaise

Combine all ingredients; mix well. Chill until serving time. Garnish with sliced egg, radishes or green pepper.

Mrs. Beverly A. Reed, Stamford Central Sch.
Stamford, New York

MACARONI-MEAT SALAD

1 16-oz. pkg. macaroni
¼ c. vinegar
2 c. diced ham
¼ c. chopped pimento
1 c. chopped celery
¼ c. grated onion
2 tsp. salt
½ tsp. pepper
½ c. mayonnaise
Lettuce leaves
1 tomato

Cook macaroni and drain. Pour vinegar over macaroni; allow to stand for 10 minutes. Toss macaroni and all remaining ingredients together except lettuce and tomato. Pile salad on crisp lettuce leaves and garnish with tomato wedges. Yield: 8 servings.

Maxine King, Unity H.S.
Mendon, Illinois

MAIN DISH SALAD

1 head iceburg lettuce
3 med. tomatoes
1 med. cucumber (opt.)
1 med. green pepper (opt.)
1 med. onion (opt.)
1 pkg. radishes, (opt.)
1 lb. process cheese, cubed
½ lb. diced ham, prepared meat or turkey

Chop and toss all ingredients together except cheese and ham. Sprinkle cheese and ham over top. Serve with favorite dressing. Yield: 6 servings.

Stephanie Preston Heatwole
Mark Twain Intermediate Sch.
Alexandria, Virginia

PATIO SALAD

1 pkg. sm. frozen green peas
½ tsp. salt
1 ½ c. water
1 ⅓ c. Minute rice
¾ c. mayonnaise
½ c. chopped dill pickle
1 tsp. grated onion
1 c. slivered cooked ham or tuna
1 c. slivered Swiss cheese

Add peas to salted water in saucepan; cover and bring to full boil quickly. Add Minute rice; stir with fork to moisten all rice. Cover; remove from heat and let stand 13 minutes. Add mayonnaise, pickle and onion; mix with fork. Chill. Add ham and cheese before serving. Yield: 6 servings.

Mrs. Gloria Gallion, Gordon H.S.
Gordon, Nebraska

SUPPER SALAD

1 ½ c. diced cooked ham, pork, veal or turkey
½ c. diced cooked potatoes
½ c. sliced cooked carrots
½ c. each cooked peas and green lima beans
½ c. cooked green beans, cut in ½-in. lengths
1 c. French dressing
½ c. chopped sweet pickles
2 hard-cooked eggs, chopped
¾ c. mayonnaise
Salt, pepper and paprika to taste
Crisp salad greens

Place ham, potatoes, carrots, peas, lima beans and green beans in a bowl; pour French dressing over all and toss lightly. Chill for at least 1 hour. Add pickles, eggs and mayonnaise just before serving. Mix lightly. Season to taste with salt, pepper and paprika. Serve on crisp greens. Yield: 6 servings.

Mrs. Kathleen Barnes, Lawrence Cen. H.S.
Lawrence, Indiana

WHOLE MEAL SALAD BOWL

1 clove of garlic (opt.)
½ c. salad oil
2 tbsp. vinegar
¾ tsp. salt
⅛ tsp. pepper
½ tsp. dry mustard
¼ tsp. paprika
½ head lettuce, broken into 1 ½-in. chunks
2 tbsp. chopped green pepper
½ c. sliced celery
½ c. thinly sliced raw cauliflowerets
1 hard-cooked egg, cut in eighths
1 c. cooked asparagus tips
½ lb. baked ham or salami, cut julienne style

Have all salad ingredients chilled. Rub inside of salad bowl with cut surface of garlic, then discard garlic. Pour salad oil and vinegar into bowl; stir to blend. Add seasonings; beat with fork until well mixed. Combine remaining ingredients in order listed. Toss lightly until each piece is coated with dressing. Serve immediately. Yield: 6-8 servings.

Sister M. Benedict, St. Joseph's Academy
Crookston, Minnesota

PORK SALAD

2 c. cubed cooked pork
1 c. diced pared apples
1 ½ c. chopped celery
1 tsp. minced onion
¼ c. minced parsley
¼ c. chopped green pepper
1 tsp. salt

307

(Continued on next page)

¼ c. cooked salad dressing
¼ c. mayonnaise
¼ c. sour cream
1 tbsp. lemon juice
Crisp salad greens
1 can jellied cranberry sauce

Combine pork, apples, celery, onion, parsley and green pepper. Blend together salt, salad dressing, mayonnaise, sour cream and lemon juice. Mix dressing lightly with meat and vegetables. Serve on crisp salad greens. Garnish with slices of jellied cranberry sauce. Yield: 4 servings.

Sister M. Benedict, St. Joseph's Academy
Crookston, Minnesota

UPSIDE-DOWN BOLOGNA SALAD

1 lb. bologna slices
1 8-oz. pkg. elbow macaroni, cooked
¼ lb. cubed sharp cheese
1 c. chopped celery
½ c. sliced ripe olives
¼ c. diced onion
2 tbsp. minced pimento
2 tbsp. minced parsley
¾ c. mayonnaise
1 tbsp. vinegar
2 tsp. mustard
1 tsp. salt
⅛ tsp. pepper

Line a 1 1/2-quart mixing bowl with bologna slices, overlapping. Cut remaining slices into thin strips; combine with macaroni, cheese, celery, olives, onion, pimento and parsley. Blend remaining ingredients. Combine with macaroni mixture, mixing thoroughly. Spoon into bologna lined bowl. Chill. Invert salad onto platter. Garnish with greens. Yield: 6-8 servings.

Ruth Royer, Warrior Run Area Sch.
Turbotville, Pennsylvania

EASY PICNIC SALAD

1 ⅓ c. Minute rice
2 tsp. salt
1 ⅓ c. boiling water
1 to 1 ¼ c. mayonnaise
2 tsp. grated onion
⅛ tsp. pepper
1 lb. bologna, cut into cubes
1 c. grated raw carrots
¼ c. diced pimento
1 to 1 ½ c. cooked peas

Add rice and 1/2 teaspoon salt to boiling water in saucepan. Stir until moistened. Cover; remove from heat. Let stand 5 minutes. Fluff with fork. Cool. Combine mayonnaise, onion, 1 1/2 teaspoons salt and pepper; set aside. Combine remaining ingredients; mix with mayonnaise mixture. Add rice and stir lightly with fork. Chill. Serve on crisp lettuce if desired. Yield: 8 cups.

Frances Rodriguez, Espanola H.S.
Espanola, New Mexico

CHEF'S SALAD

Strips of tongue or ham
Swiss cheese and chicken or turkey
Sliced cucumbers
Hard-boiled eggs, quartered
Radish roses
Assorted greens
Salt
Freshly ground pepper
French dressing

Place ingredients in separate dishes so that guests may combine as desired. Other ingredients such as anchovies, red onion rings, small sardines, green and ripe olives, cauliflowerets and artichoke hearts may be used.

Marion Compton, Crestwood H.S.
Dearborn Heights, Michigan

KRAUT AND FRANKFURTER SALAD

1 lb. frankfurters, chilled
1 1-lb. 13-oz. can sauerkraut, chilled
  and drained
1 sm. onion, peeled and minced
¼ c. green pepper, chopped
¾ c. raw carrots, grated
⅓ c. chili sauce
⅔ c. mayonnaise

Cut frankfurters into diagonal slices about 1/2 inch long; place in large bowl. Add sauerkraut, onion, green pepper and carrots. Blend chili sauce with mayonnaise in small bowl. Pour over frankfurter mixture; toss, mixing well. Cover; refrigerate. Shortly before serving, line salad bowl with greens; pile frankfurter mixture lightly on top. Yield: 6 servings.

Marjorie Bough, Edwardsville Jr. H.S.
Edwardsville, Illinois

APPLE BALL SALAD

4 pared tart apples
1 tbsp. lemon juice
1 c. luncheon meat, canned
½ c. diced celery
2 tbsp. top milk
¼ c. salad dressing

Make balls from apples using a melon-baller. Sprinkle with lemon juice. Combine with luncheon meat and celery. Blend milk and salad dressing; add to apple mixture. Garnish with apple wedges and sprig of parsley. Yield: 4-5 servings.

Mrs. Leanne Fried, Steele H.S.
Steele, North Dakota

CABBAGE SLAW

3 c. shredded cabbage
½ c. chopped salad olives
1 bell pepper, shredded
1 sm. onion, shredded
1 c. chopped luncheon meat, corned
    beef or cooked ham
½ c. sour cream
½ c. mayonnaise

Combine cabbage, olives, pepper, onion and meat. Mix thoroughly. Combine sour cream and mayonnaise; add to cabbage mixture. Toss lightly. Yield: 8 servings.

Mrs. Helen Alders, Douglass H.S.
Douglass, Texas

HEARTY SUPPER SALAD

3 c. cooked elbow macaroni
1 12-oz. can luncheon meat, cut into
    strips
¾ c. diced green pepper
¾ c. thinly sliced green onion
½ c. chopped dill pickle
1 c. diced celery
1 ½ c. lge. curd cottage cheese
¼ c. diced pimento
1 ½ c. mayonnaise or salad dressing
2 ½ tbsp. cider vinegar
¼ tsp. salt
½ tsp. pepper

Combine macaroni, luncheon meat, green pepper, onion, pickle, celery, cottage cheese and pimento in large bowl. Combine mayonnaise, vinegar, salt and pepper; add to macaroni mixture. Mix well. Chill. Serve in lettuce cups if desired. Yield: 6-8 servings.

Mrs. Barbara Sech, Northridge Sr. H.S.
Dayton, Ohio

MAKES A MEAL SALAD

¼ c. lemon juice
1 c. undiluted evaporated milk
¼ c. salad dressing
1 tsp. salt
⅛ tsp. pepper
¼ tsp. crushed dillweed
⅛ tsp. celery seed
2 tbsp. pickle relish
1 12-oz. can diced luncheon meat or
    tuna
2 tbsp. chopped pimento
3 c. cooked drained salad macaroni
1 c. sliced celery
¾ c. finely chopped onion
1 c. well-drained peas and carrots

Pour lemon juice into milk; stir until thickened. Add salad dressing, salt, pepper, dill, celery seed and relish. Combine remaining ingredients in large bowl. Pour milk dressing over macaroni mixture. Toss lightly until blended. Chill thoroughly.

Mrs. Thelma R. Scott, Weirgate H.S.
Burkeville, Texas

POTATO PLUS SALAD

2 c. cubed potatoes
1 c. cubed luncheon meat
1 c. cubed sharp cheese
1 c. chopped celery
2 tbsp. finely grated onion
Salt and fresh ground black pepper
¾ c. salad dressing diluted with sweet
    pickle vinegar

Combine all ingredients. This salad improves if chilled for several hours. Yield: 8 servings.

Pauline B. Commer, Crowder H.S.
Crowder, Mississippi

PREM MEAT LOAF

1 c. tomato juice
1 pkg. gelatin
1 tbsp. water
1 can Prem, ground
½ c. ground green pepper and parsley
½ c. salad dressing
Onion or onion salt

Heat tomato juice; pour over gelatin. Combine all the ingredients. Pour into loaf tin. Chill.

Audrey B. Quigley, Millard H.S.
Fillmore, Utah

TASTY LUNCHEON SALAD

1 12-oz. can luncheon meat
3 hard-boiled eggs
1 pimento
2 sweet pickles
1 sm. onion
Salad dressing to moisten

Combine and grind meat, eggs, pimento, pickles and onion. Add salad dressing. Serve in scoops on fresh spinach leaves. Yield: 4 servings.

Diane E. Bush, North Syracuse H.S.
North Syracuse, New York

SALADE JACQUES

1 lb. endive, cut into ¾-in. lengths
5 tbsp. each raisins, walnuts or pecans,
   halved Greek olives, diced cheddar
   cheese, peeled chopped apple
3 to 4 tbsp. salami, chopped
1 tbsp. minced onion
½ c. olive oil
¼ c. vinegar
½ tsp. each dry mustard and
   Worcestershire sauce
Salt and black pepper to taste

Combine first six ingredients. Toss well. Combine remaining ingredients. Add just enough dressing to salad mixture to coat thoroughly. Toss. Yield: 4-6 servings.

Mrs. Alice Hansberger, Canton Sr. H.S.
Canton, Illinois

VIENNA 'D MACARONI SALAD

1 8-oz. pkg. elbow or salad macaroni
1 c. chopped celery
1 c. chopped sweet pickles
2 tbsp. grated onion
1 5-oz. can Vienna sausage, thinly
   sliced
1 c. mayonnaise
2 tbsp. pickle juice
1 tsp. salt
¼ tsp. pepper
3 to 6 deviled eggs

Cook macaroni until tender. Drain. Blanch in cold water; drain thoroughly. Combine with celery, pickles, onion and sausage. Blend mayonnaise with pickle juice, salt and pepper. Add to macaroni mixture. Chill. Heap Vienna'd Macaroni onto salad greens in center of large serving plate. Arrange sausage in spokes over top. Place deviled eggs around the salad. Yield: 6 servings.

Mrs. Ella Adair, Bryce Valley H.S.
Tropic, Utah

VIENNA 'D MACARONI SALAD

1 8-oz. pkg. macaroni, cooked and
   drained
1 c. chopped celery
1 c. chopped sweet pickles
2 tbsp. grated onion
1 c. mayonnaise or salad dressing
2 tbsp. pickle juice
1 tsp. salt
¼ tsp. pepper
2 cans Vienna sausage, chilled

Combine macaroni with celery, pickles and onion. Blend mayonnaise with pickle juice; combine with macaroni mixture. Season with salt and pepper. Slice one can sausage, add to salad. Chill

thoroughly. Arrange salad on salad greens; arrange remaining sausage in spokes over top. Garnish with deviled or sliced eggs. Yield: 6 servings.

Mrs. Helen M. Godwin, Northwest Guilford H.S.
Greensboro, North Carolina

ALGOOD'S CHICKEN SALAD

3 c. cubed cooked chicken
1 ½ c. diced celery
1 tsp. salt
3 hard-cooked eggs, quartered
3 sweet pickles
Mayonnaise
Leaf lettuce

Combine chicken, celery, salt, eggs and pickles. Moisten with mayonnaise; serve on lettuce leaves. Garnish with additional slices of eggs, olives or pickles. Yield: 8 servings.

Mrs. Elizabeth M. Turner, Algood Jr. H.S.
Algood, Tennessee

ALL IN ONE CHICKEN SALAD

3 tbsp. lemon juice
1 c. diced cooked chicken
½ c. finely diced apple
½ c. chopped ripe olives
½ c. diced celery
2 tbsp. mayonnaise thinned with 2 tbsp.
   sweet or sour cream

Sprinkle lemon juice over chicken and apple, mixing lightly. Combine remaining ingredients, using only enough mayonnaise mixture to moisten. Add chicken and apple; toss together lightly. Serve cold with mayonnaise. Yield: 4 servings.

Mrs. Annie R. Gonzales, Prescott Jr. H.S.
Baton Rouge, Louisiana

CALIFORNIA CHICKEN SALAD

1 c. diced cooked chicken
½ c. chopped ripe olives
Juice of 1 lemon
2 tbsp. mayonnaise
2 tbsp. cream
½ c. diced apples
½ c. chopped celery

Marinate chicken and olives in lemon juice; chill. Combine mayonnaise and cream mixture. Add apples, celery and mayonnaise mixture to chicken mixture; toss gently. Serve on lettuce leaves. Yield: 4-6 servings.

Mrs. Mae Van Citters, Sault Ste. Marie H.S.
Sault Ste. Marie, Michigan

CELESTIAL CHICKEN SALAD

4 c. diced cooked chicken
2 c. diced celery
1 4½-oz. jar whole mushrooms,
   drained
½ c. pecan or almond halves, toasted
½ c. pineapple chunks
1 c. mayonnaise
1 c. sour cream
1½ tsp. salt
2 tbsp. lemon juice

Combine chicken, celery, mushrooms, pecans and pineapple in large bowl. Blend mayonnaise, sour cream, salt and lemon juice; add to chicken mixture, tossing lightly to mix. Chill thoroughly. Serve in crisp lettuce cups or omit pineapple chunks and serve on pineapple slice. Yield: 6-8 servings.

Mrs. LaVera Kraig, Monroe Jr. H.S.
Aberdeen, South Dakota

CHEF'S SALAD

1 head lettuce, torn into small pieces
½ c. chopped celery
½ c. chopped pepper
¼ c. chopped onion (opt.)
Radishes, sliced thin
½ c. diced cold chicken or turkey
¼ to ½ c. cubed cheese
2 tomatoes, cut up
Salad dressing
Strips of dill pickle
1 hard-boiled egg, quartered

Combine lettuce, celery, bell pepper, onion, radishes, meat, cheese and tomatoes; toss, using any desired dressing. Garnish with pickle and egg. Yield: 2-6 servings.

Mildred H. Morris, Reeltown H.S.
Notasulga, Alabama

CHICKEN CHOW MEIN SALAD

1 c. shredded raw carrots
¼ c. minced onion
2 c. finely chopped chicken or tuna,
   well drained
1 c. diced celery
¾ c. salad dressing
½ tsp. mustard
Cream
Chinese noodles or shoestring potatoes

Combine first 6 ingredients; add enough cream to moisten. Toss lightly; chill. Add Chinese noodles. Serve on lettuce cup. Yield: 12 servings.

Lois Schommer, Twin Valley H.S.
Twin Valley, Minnesota

CHICKEN COLESLAW

1 c. shredded red cabbage
½ c. crumbled cauliflower
¼ c. chopped celery
1 c. shredded cabbage
½ c. grated carrots
1 c. chopped chicken
Favorite salad dressing

Combine all ingredients. Garnish with crisp parsley. Yield: 4-6 servings.

Laura J. Collins, Indianola H.S.
Indianola, Oklahoma

CHICKEN-FRUIT SALAD

2 c. cut-up cooked chicken
1 c. sliced celery
1 c. green seedless grapes
1 tbsp. lemon juice
½ c. mayonnaise

Combine chicken, celery, grapes and lemon juice; chill. Fold in mayonnaise before serving. Serve on lettuce. Yield: 6 servings.

Mrs. Susan Wilson, Centerburg H.S.
Centerburg, Ohio

CHICKEN SALAD

2 c. cooked chicken, diced
⅓ c. French dressing
1 c. celery, diced
½ c. almonds, slivered
½ c. pimento olives
½ c. mayonnaise

Marinate chicken in French dressing for 2 hours in refrigerator. Add remaining ingredients; mix lightly to combine. Serve on crisp lettuce. Yield: 6 servings.

Marjorie Harris, Greeley H.S.
Greeley, Nebraska

CHICKEN SALAD

2 c. diced cooked chicken
1 c. diced celery
½ c. diced cucumbers
1 hard-boiled egg, chopped
1 tsp. finely chopped onion
1 tbsp. finely chopped pickles
Salt and pepper to taste
½ c. mayonnaise

Mix all ingredients; chill. Serve on crisp lettuce; garnish with mayonnaise and sliced olives. Yield: 4 servings.

Mrs. L. Podealuk, Hillcrest Jr. H.S.
Edmonton, Alberta, Canada

CHICKEN SALAD

2 c. cooked chicken, cut in lge. chunks
1 No. 1 can peas
⅓ c. ripe pitted olives, sliced
⅔ c. celery, diced
1 tbsp. lemon juice
3 hard-cooked eggs, cut in chunks
½ c. sweet pickles, chopped
½ c. broken pecans
⅛ tsp. pepper
1 tsp. salt
⅓ c. mayonnaise

Combine all ingredients; toss lightly. Chill. Yield: 6 servings.

Mrs. Beverly Witt, Williston H.S.
Williston, North Dakota

CHICKEN SALAD

1 c. cooked chicken, cut into lge. chunks
½ c. celery, cut into ¼-inch pieces
1½ tsp. lemon juice
Salt and pepper to taste
¼ c. mayonnaise
1 to 2 hard-cooked eggs, cut up
¼ c. finely broken crisp bacon

Toss chicken, celery, lemon juice, salt and pepper; mix in mayonnaise. Carefully fold in eggs. Chill thoroughly. Serve in tomato cups or drained pineapple or avocado slices on salad greens. Sprinkle with crisp bacon. Yield: 2 servings.

Mrs. Nellie C. Shymko, Willingdon Sch.
Willingdon, Alta, Canada

CHICKEN SALAD DELUXE

2 to 3 lb. broiler-fryer chicken, cooked
    cubed and chilled
½ c. thinly sliced celery
½ c. drained mandarin oranges
1 c. drained pineapple cubes
½ c. quartered maraschino cherries,
    red, green or both
2 bananas, sliced
¼ c. mayonnaise
¼ c. sour cream
½ tsp. lemon juice
1 tsp. sugar
½ tsp. rum flavoring, if desired

Combine chicken, celery, oranges, pineapple, maraschino cherries and bananas. Combine mayonnaise, sour cream, lemon juice and sugar. Pour over chicken mixture; toss gently. Chill thoroughly. Line salad bowl with hearts of lettuce; fill with chicken salad. Garnish with additional fruit, if desired. Yield: 8 servings.

Sister Clotilda, S.N.D., Julienne H.S.
Dayton, Ohio

CHICKEN SALAD

3 c. diced cooked chicken
1½ c. diced celery
1 c. salted peanuts, ground or chopped
1 tbsp. lemon juice
½ tsp. salt
½ c. mayonnaise
Crisp lettuce

Mix chicken, celery and peanuts in large bowl. Blend lemon juice, salt and mayonnaise together. Pour dressing over chicken mixture; toss. Chill well. Line salad bowl with lettuce; pile salad in center. Garnish with tomato wedges, cucumber slices or stuffed olives. Serve chilled. Yield: 6 servings.

Nita Thompson, Tornillo H.S.
Tornillo, Texas

CHICKEN SALAD WITH APPLES

⅔ c. raisins
2 c. cold cooked diced chicken
1 c. diced celery
½ c. chopped nuts
⅔ c. diced apples
½ c. diced pineapple
⅔ c. mayonnaise

Steam raisins until plump; combine with chicken, celery, nuts, apples and pineapple. Moisten with mayonnaise, mixing lightly with 2 forks. Serve in crisp lettuce cups. Yield: 6 servings.

Mrs. Doris Gruber, Walsh H.S.
Walsh, Colorado

CHICKEN SALAD EXTRAORDINARY

4½ c. water
3 2-lb. broiler-fryers, cut into pieces
1 stalk celery and leaves
1 med. onion, sliced
2 bay leaves
6 whole cloves
1 tbsp. monosodium glutamate
3 c. thinly sliced celery
Salt to taste
¾ c. slivered almonds
⅓ c. chopped green onions
¾ c. mayonnaise
¾ c. sour cream
3 tsp. lemon juice

Combine first 8 ingredients, using 1 tablespoon salt, in large kettle; cover. Simmer until tender. Remove skin and bones from chicken; chop chicken to make 6 cups. Add celery, almonds, green onions and 3/4 teaspoon salt. Toss lightly. Combine mayonnaise, sour cream and lemon juice; pour over salad. Toss to mix well. Refrigerate until serving time. Yield: 10 servings.

Mrs. Karen Demko, Evergreen H.S.
Vancouver, Washington

CHICKEN SALAD DELIGHT

2 c. cooked chicken, diced
3 hard-cooked eggs, chopped
1 c. celery, chopped
¼ c. slivered and salted toasted almonds
2 tbsp. sweet pickle, chopped
½ tsp. salt
1 tsp. onion juice
½ c. mayonnaise

Combine all ingredients; toss lightly. Place in refrigerator; chill for several hours. Pile high in lettuce cups. Serve immediately. Yield: 4-6 servings.

Violet Franklin, Cocke Co. H.S.
Newport, Tennessee

CHICKEN SALAD

2 c. cut-up cooked chicken
1 c. white grapes, cut in half
½ c. celery, cut fine
½ c. slivered almonds
1 c. sliced pineapple
½ c. salad dressing

Mix chicken, grapes, celery, almonds and pineapple together. Add salad dressing; toss lightly. Yield: 6 servings.

Mrs. Phyllis C. Pratt, Canaseraga Central Sch.
Canaseraga, New York

CHICKEN SALAD ROYALE

12 lb. white meat chicken, cut up
2 bay leaves
1 med. onion
2 carrots
3 tsp. salt
¾ c. French dressing
1 tsp. MSG
½ tsp. white pepper
2 green peppers, chopped
1 c. stuffed olives, sliced
2 ½ c. mayonnaise
1 No. 2 ½ can pineapple wedges, drained
2 c. toasted almonds
50 sprigs of parsley

Place first 5 ingredients in large saucepan; add enough water to cover. Cover; cook until tender. Cool; dice chicken. Combine with French dressing; marinate for at least 1 hour or overnight. Combine with remaining ingredients except parsley; chill. Serve in lettuce cups; garnish with parsley. Yield: 50 servings.

Mary Ann Kline, Central Union H.S.
El Centro, California

CHICKEN SALAD WITH GRAPES

2 c. cooked chicken, cubed
1 c. seeded white grapes
French dressing
⅓ c. slivered almonds
½ c. mayonnaise
Lettuce

Mix together chicken and grapes; add enough French dressing to moisten. Chill. Stir in almonds and mayonnaise before serving. Place in lettuce cups. Serve with cranberry salad. Yield: 8 servings.

Mrs. Virginia S. McEwen, Coosa Co. H.S.
Rockford, Alabama

CHICKEN SALAD WITH SHOESTRING POTATOES

2 c. chicken, turkey or tuna
½ c. celery, chopped
¼ c. green pepper, chopped
¼ c. raw carrot, chopped
2 tbsp. onion, chopped
½ c. black pitted olives, chopped
¾ c. mayonnaise
¼ c. cream
2 ½ c. or 1 No. 2 can shoestring potatoes

Mix all ingredients, except shoestring potatoes. Toss with potatoes just before serving. Serve in lettuce cups. Yield: 4 servings.

Mrs. Linda L. Carriere, Alvarado H.S.
Alvarado, Minnesota

CHICKEN SALAD SPECIAL

1 ½ c. coarsely diced cooked chicken
1 c. diced celery
¼ c. mayonnaise
2 tbsp. chopped sweet pickles
1 ½ tbsp. lemon juice
Salt and pepper to taste

Lightly toss all ingredients. Chill. Serve on crisp lettuce. Yield: 5 servings.

Rosalind P. R. Fisher, Harriot Curtis Collegiate
St. Anthony, Newfoundland, Canada

CHICKEN SALAD SUPERB

2 ½ c. cubed cooked chicken
1 c. diced celery
1 c. diced apple
1 c. halved seedless grapes
Salad dressing
Lettuce leaves or cantaloupe halves

313

(Continued on next page)

Chicken Salads

Combine chicken, celery, fruit and enough salad dressing to moisten; toss lightly. Chill. Serve on lettuce or in cantaloupe halves. Yield: 6 servings.

Mrs. Ronald Haney, Wallace Co. H.S.
Sharon Springs, Kansas

CHICKEN SALAD SUPREME

2 ½ c. diced cold chicken
1 c. celery, chopped fine
1 c. sliced white grapes
½ c. shredded almonds, browned
2 tbsp. minced parsley
1 tsp. salt
1 c. mayonnaise
½ c. whipping cream, whipped

Combine all ingredients. Serve in lettuce cups with thin slices of chicken on top. Garnish with sliced stuffed olives or chopped ripe olives. Yield: 8 servings.

Mary A. Hugus, Fairless H.S.
Navarre, Ohio

CHICKEN SALAD SUPREME

3 c. diced chicken, cooked
1 c. finely diced celery
2 tbsp. chopped pimento
2 tbsp. minced green pepper
½ c. mayonnaise
1 ½ tsp. lemon juice
2 tbsp. thin cream

Combine ingredients; serve on lettuce with crackers or croutons. Yield: 6-8 servings.

Hilda Harman, Smithville H.S.
Smithville, Mississippi

CHICKEN-VEGETABLE SALAD IN TOMATO ROSETTE

1 ½ c. cubed chicken
¼ c. cooked peas
¼ c. cooked sm. carrot cubes
½ c. finely cut celery
1 c. whipped cream
½ c. mayonnaise
1 tsp. lemon juice
Salt and pepper to taste
4 tomatoes, medium size
Lettuce leaves

Mix chicken, vegetables, whipped cream and mayonnaise together; stir in lemon juice and seasoning. Cut stem from tomato; quarter tomato by

cutting almost through to base. Halve the quarters, making 8 pieces. Place tomato cup on lettuce leaf; fill with salad mixture. Yield: 4 servings.

Marjory Fuller, Seitz Jr. H.S.
Riverview, Michigan

CHINESE CHICKEN SALAD

3 c. diced cooked chicken
1 c. drained canned bean sprouts
1 ½ c. sliced celery
⅛ tsp. pepper
½ c. French dressing
2 tbsp. soy sauce
¾ c. mayonnaise
Salad greens
Ripe olives

Mix first 5 ingredients; chill. Blend soy sauce and mayonnaise. Stir into chicken mixture; serve on greens with garnish of olives. Yield: 4-6 servings.

Carol Nissen, Park Sr. H.S.
St. Paul Park, Minnesota

CHIP-CHICKEN SALAD

1 ½ c. chicken or 5-oz. boned chicken
½ c. chopped celery
½ c. chopped green pepper
2 tsp. minced green onion
⅓ c. mayonnaise
3 hard-cooked eggs
1 c. crushed potato chips or corn chips

Toss all ingredients except chips; chill. Toss in chips; serve on crisp lettuce. Yield: 4 servings.

Myrta Jean Dorn, Licking Valley H.S.
Newark, Ohio

CHOPPED CHICKEN SALAD

2 c. (packed) chopped cooked chicken, dark and light meat
1 tbsp. finely minced onion
1 tbsp. finely diced green pepper
8 to 12 sliced Spanish olives
½ c. salad dressing
Salt and pepper to taste
¼ c. chopped celery

Combine all ingredients; mix thoroughly. Chill thoroughly before serving. Spoon into lettuce cups; sprinkle with paprika. May be used as sandwich filling. Yield: 4-5 servings.

Mrs. Barbara Berndt, Montello, H.S.
Montello, Wisconsin

314

CLINE'S CHICKEN SALAD

2 c. diced cooked chicken
French dressing
2 c. diced celery
Salt to taste
Pepper to taste
⅔ c. mayonnaise
Lettuce
2 hard-cooked eggs, quartered

Marinate chicken in French dressing in refrigerator for about 2 hours. Drain thoroughly; toss together all ingredients except lettuce and eggs. Season to taste. Pile on lettuce. Garnish with mayonnaise and eggs. Yield: 4 servings.

Shirley Cline, Rugby H.S.
Rugby, North Dakota

COMPANY CHICKEN SALAD

1 c. cream, whipped
¾ c. salad dressing
1 tsp. lemon juice
Salt to taste
4 c. cooked chicken, cubed
5 hard-cooked eggs, sliced
3 tbsp. chopped sweet pickle
1 c. celery, diced
¾ c. slivered almonds toasted

Combine whipped cream, salad dressing, lemon juice and salt. Combine remaining ingredients; place in large bowl. Toss lightly with dressing. Serve in lettuce cup with crispy crackers or potato chips. Yield: 6-8 servings.

Dianne Strope, South Clay Comm. Sch.
Gillett Grove, Iowa

CHICKEN-ALMOND MOLD

1 envelope unflavored gelatin, dissolved
in ¼ c. cold water
½ c. green grapes, cut in half
½ c. toasted shredded almonds
1 c. whipped cream
1 c. mayonnaise
1 ½ c. cooked diced chicken
Honeydew melon, peeled and sliced
crosswise
Pineapple slices

Mix all ingredients except honeydew and pineapple. Place in medium-sized paper cups to mold. Unmold chicken over pineapple on melon slices. Yield: 6 servings.

Mrs. Nancy Simonton, Wade Hampton H.S.
Greenville, South Carolina

COMPANY SALAD

¼ head lettuce, shredded
1 8-oz. can chicken, cut up
3 green onions, chopped
½ c. almonds, blanched and chopped
¼ c. mayonnaise or favorite salad
dressing
Lettuce leaves

Mix lettuce, chicken, green onions and almonds; add mayonnaise. Place individual servings on lettuce leaves. Yield: 4-6 servings.

Mrs. Margaret E. Thompson, Fruitvale Jr. Sec.
Fruitvale, British Columbia, Canada

CHICKEN IN ASPIC

2 envelopes unflavored gelatin
2 c. cold water
2 10 ½-oz. cans condensed consomme
½ tsp. salt
4 tbsp. lemon juice
2 c. diced cooked chicken
1 c. mixed cooked vegetables
½ c. chopped celery
4 tbsp. chopped green pepper
4 tbsp. chopped pimento

Sprinkle gelatin on 1 cup cold water in saucepan to soften. Place over low heat, stirring constantly, until gelatin is dissolved. Remove from heat; add remaining cold water, consomme, salt and lemon juice. Chill until mixture is consistency of unbeaten egg white. Fold in chicken, vegetables, celery, green pepper and pimento. Turn into 6-cup mold or individual molds. Chill until firm. Unmold on crisp spinach greens. Top with toasted almonds. Serve with cranberry sauce.

Mrs. Elvera M. Raff, Longford H.S.
Longford, Kansas

CHICKEN-CRANBERRY SALAD

1 tbsp. plain gelatin
¼ c. cold water
¼ c. pineapple juice
1 1-lb. can whole cranberry sauce
1 c. cooked diced chicken
¾ c. pineapple tidbits
¼ c. diced celery
¼ c. chopped nuts
Crisp salad greens
Mayonnaise

Soften gelatin in cold water. Place pineapple juice and cranberry sauce in pan and bring to boiling point. Add gelatin; stir until dissolved. Chill until partially thickened. Fold in chicken, pineapple, celery and nuts. Turn into large mold. Chill until firm. Serve on salad greens with mayonnaise. Yield: 6-8 servings.

Sister M. Aloysius PEVM, O'Gorman H.S.
Sioux Falls, South Dakota

CHICKEN-CRANBERRY LAYERS

2 envelopes unflavored gelatin
1 1-lb. can whole cranberry sauce
1 9-oz. can crushed pineapple
4 tbsp. lemon juice
1 c. mayonnaise
½ tsp. salt
2 c. diced cooked chicken
½ c. diced celery
2 tbsp. chopped parsley

Soften 1 envelope gelatin in 1/4 cup cold water. Dissolve over hot water. Add cranberry sauce, pineapple and 1 tablespoon lemon juice. Pour into 10 x 6 x 1 1/2-inch baking dish or loaf pan. Chill until firm. Soften remaining gelatin in 1/4 cup cold water. Dissolve over hot water. Blend in mayonnaise, 1/2 cup cold water, remaining lemon juice and salt. Add chicken, celery and parsley. Pour over congealed layer and chill until firm. Cut into squares; invert each square on salad greens. Top with mayonnaise and walnut halves. Yield: 6-8 servings.

Esther D. Horstmann, Van Antwerp Jr. H.S.
Schenectady, New York

CHICKEN MOUSSE

1 pkg. lemon gelatin
½ tsp. salt
1 ¾ c. chicken broth
Dash of cayenne pepper
2 tbsp. vinegar
⅓ c. whipping cream
⅓ c. mayonnaise
1 c. diced cooked chicken
1 c. finely diced celery
1 tbsp. chopped pimento

Dissolve gelatin and salt in boiling broth; add cayenne and vinegar; chill until thick. Whip cream; fold cream and mayonnaise into gelatin, blending well. Fold in remaining ingredients. Pour into 1-quart mold or individual molds. Chill until firm. Yield: 4 servings.

Barbara L. Nelson
Vincent Massey Collegiate Sch.
Winnipeg, Manitoba, Canada

CHICKEN MOUSSE

1 envelope unflavored gelatin
1 ½ c. chicken broth
1 tbsp. onion juice
1 ¼ c. diced cooked chicken
2 tbsp. chopped celery
1 tbsp. chopped stuffed olives
1 c. heavy cream, whipped

Sprinkle gelatin on half the chicken broth to soften. Place over low heat; stir until gelatin is dissolved. Remove from heat; stir in remaining chicken broth and onion juice. Chill mixture to consistency of unbeaten egg white. Fold in chicken, celery, olives and whipped cream. Turn into 4-cup mold and chill until firm. Unmold on serving plate; garnish with watercress and radish roses. Yield: 6 servings.

Mrs. Cecile Herscher, Union H.S.
Dowagiac, Michigan

CHICKEN AND SOUR CREAM MOLD

2 envelopes unflavored gelatin
2 ½ c. chicken broth
2 tbsp. grated onion
1 tsp. salt
Dash of pepper
2 c. cooked diced chicken
½ c. toasted slivered almonds
½ c. sliced black olives
2 c. sour cream

Sprinkle gelatin on 1 cup chicken broth to soften. Place over low heat and stir until gelatin is dissolved. Remove from heat; stir in remaining chicken broth, onion, salt and pepper. Chill to unbeaten egg white consistency. Fold in chicken, almonds, olives and sour cream. Turn into 6-cup mold; chill until firm. Unmold on serving plate; garnish with salad greens. Yield: 8 servings.

Mrs. John L. Hansbrough, Magee Attendance Ctr.
Magee, Mississippi

CHICKEN-SPICED FRUIT SALAD

6 whole cloves
1 ½ c. water
1 pkg. lemon Jell-O
¾ c. peach pickle juice
2 c. diced pickle peaches
½ c. chopped nuts
¼ c. white raisins
2 tbsp. plain gelatin
1 c. chicken stock
2 c. chopped chicken
1 c. Miracle Whip
1 8-oz. can sm. peas with juice
Dash of red pepper and salt
1 c. slivered almonds
1 tbsp. capers
2 tbsp. India relish

Boil cloves in water 5 minutes; strain. Dissolve Jell-O in 1 cup clove water and peach pickle juice. Chill. Add peaches, nuts and raisins when mixture is slightly thickened. Pour into mold and chill until set. Soak gelatin in 1/2 cup chicken stock. Boil remaining stock and dissolve gelatin with stock. Add remaining ingredients. Run hot spoon over fruit layer; pour chicken mixture into mold. Chill until firm. Yield: 12-16 servings.

Reba L. Miller, Gaylesville H.S.
Gaylesville, Alabama

JELLIED CHICKEN ALMOND

1 envelope unflavored gelatin
¼ c. cold water
1 c. mayonnaise
1 c. heavy cream, whipped
½ tsp. salt
1 ½ c. diced cooked chicken
¾ c. chopped almonds
¾ c. halved green seedless grapes

Soften gelatin in cold water; dissolve over hot water. Cool slightly; combine with mayonnaise, whipped cream and salt. Fold in chicken, almonds and grapes. Spoon into 6 to 8 individual molds; chill until firm. Unmold on lettuce.

Donna C. Alexander, Winterboro H.S.
Alpine, Alabama
Mrs. Elizabeth C. Wilson, Greensboro H.S.
Greensboro, Alabama

JELLIED CHICKEN SALAD

1 tbsp. gelatin
¼ c. cold water
¾ c. salad dressing
1 sm. can chicken, jelly removed
½ c. celery, chopped
Salt and paprika to taste

Soak gelatin in cold water; dissolve over hot water. Add to dressing. Fold in chicken and celery. Add seasonings. Mold as desired and chill. Yield: 4 servings.

Mrs. W. H. Livingstone, Middleton Reg. H.S.
Middleton, Nova Scotia, Canada

MOLDED CHICKEN SALAD

1 lge. hen
4 hard-boiled eggs, chopped
1 c. finely cut celery
1 c. blanched almonds, cut fine
1 c. tiny green peas, drained
1 envelope plain gelatin
2 c. chicken broth
1 pt. mayonnaise
1 sm. grated onion

Boil hen until meat falls from bone. Chop chicken. Mix with eggs, celery, almonds and peas. Dissolve gelatin in 1/4 cup cold water. Add to hot chicken broth. Dissolve gelatin; cool. Add remaining ingredients. Pour into mold and chill until firm. Yield: 15 servings.

Mrs. Alma C. McGimsey, Nebo H.S.
Nebo, North Carolina

CURRIED CHICKEN AND FRUIT SALAD

½ c. mayonnaise or cooked salad dressing
1 tbsp. chopped preserved ginger
2 tsp. curry powder
1 tsp. grated onion
½ tsp. salt
½ c. heavy cream, whipped
3 c. cubed cooked chicken or turkey
¼ c. bottled oil and vinegar dressing
2 c. fresh pineapple, cut into 1-inch chunks
1 1-lb. 4 ½-oz. can pineapple chunks, drained
1 ½ c. diced pared apple
1 ½ c. seedless green grapes
¼ c. chutney
¼ c. chopped green pepper
Crisp lettuce

Combine mayonnaise, ginger, curry, onion and salt; mix until well blended. Fold in cream just until combined. Refrigerate, covered until needed. Combine chicken and dressing; toss until well coated. Refrigerate, covered, for at least 2 hours. Add pineapple, apple, grapes, chutney and green pepper to chicken; mix well. Gently fold in curry mayonnaise until well blended. Refrigerate, covered, until chilled, about 2 hours. Arrange lettuce leaves on platter; mound salad in center. Garnish with watercress, if desired. Yield: 6-8 servings.

Mrs. Lucille Murray, Power H.S.
Power, Montana

CURRIED CHICKEN SALAD

3 c. cubed chicken
1 ½ c. sliced celery
½ c. mayonnaise
¼ c. sour cream
1 tsp. salt
⅛ tsp. onion salt
Juice of 1 lemon
1 to 3 tbsp. curry powder
Toasted almonds

Combine chicken and celery. Mix mayonnaise and sour cream; add salt, onion salt, lemon juice and curry powder. Combine with chicken mixture. Serve on large platter or individual plates; garnish with toasted almonds. Yield: 4 servings.

Mrs. George Schwartz, Fort Lee H.S.
Fort Lee, New Jersey

DELICIOUS CHICKEN SALAD

1 chicken, cooked and boned
1 ½ c. chopped celery
⅓ to ½ c. chopped pickle
¼ c. chopped green pepper
1 sm. can mushrooms
6 to 8 hard-cooked eggs, chopped
1 ½ c. cooked frozen peas
Onion, salt and pepper to taste
Mayonnaise

Combine first 8 ingredients; add enough mayonnaise to moisten. Chill well. Serve on lettuce cup or on ring of lime Jell-O. Yield: 15 servings.

Mrs. Kathryn Leischner
Deland-Weldon Sr. H.S.
Deland Illinois

FAVORITE MEAT SALAD

12 oz. minced chicken, turkey, luncheon
    meat, tuna or salmon
¼ c. minced pickles
3 boiled minced eggs
½ c. minced celery
½ c. minced apple (opt.)
¼ c. pimento
¾ c. salad dressing
Salt and pepper to taste

Combine all ingredients; toss lightly. Serve on lettuce leaf or use for sandwich filling. Yield: 6-8 servings.

Mrs. Corrie Parker, Linville H.S.
Linville, Louisiana

HEARTY CHEF'S SALAD

1 head lettuce, torn into bite-sized pieces
½ bunch endive, torn into bite-sized
    pieces
½ c. chopped green onion
½ c. sliced celery
1 c. julienne strips cold cooked chicken,
    ham or beef
1 c. julienne strips cheddar cheese
1 2-oz. can fillets of anchovy
¾ c. French dressing
1 tbsp. capers

Toss greens with onion, celery, meat, cheese and anchovies, reserving few strips of meat and cheese for garnish. Toss with dressing just before serving. Garnish with strips of meat, cheese and capers. Yield: 4 servings.

Emily L. Minnichsoffer, Turtle Lake H.S.
Turtle Lake, Wisconsin

FRUITED CHICKEN DELIGHT

1 can boned chicken
¼ c. orange sections
¼ c. seedlees grapes
1 tbsp. chopped onion
2 tbsp. chopped celery
3 tbsp. sour cream
⅛ tsp. crushed rosemary
Toasted slivered almonds

Combine all ingredients in bowl except almonds; toss lightly. Chill. Serve on crisp salad greens; top with almonds. Yield: 2 servings.

Mrs. Patricia Hartronft, Dill City H.S.
Dill City, Oklahoma

BAKED CHICKEN SALAD

2 c. cut-up chicken
2 c. thinly sliced celery
½ c. chopped toasted almonds or peanuts
2 tsp. grated onion
1 tsp. salt
¾ c. mayonnaise
¼ tsp. poultry seasoning
½ c. grated cheese
1 c. finely crushed potato chips

Combine all ingredients except cheese and potato chips. Pile lightly in casserole or individual baking dishes. Sprinkle with cheese and potato chips. Bake 30 minutes at 350 degrees. Yield: 6-8 servings.

Eunice F. Lewis, Indian River H.S.
Chesapeake, Virginia

BAKED CHICKEN SALAD

2 c. cubed chicken
1 ½ c. chopped celery
1 c. toasted bread cubes
½ c. chopped blanched almonds
2 tsp. grated onion
½ tsp. salt
2 tbsp. lemon juice
1 c. mayonnaise
½ c. grated cheese

Mix together first 8 ingredients. Pile lightly in casserole. Bake at 450 degrees for approximately 10 minutes or until bubbly. Remove; add grated cheese. Return to oven and bake until cheese melts. Chicken, turkey, tuna or salmon may be substituted for chicken. Yield: 6 servings.

Mrs. Janet E. Whetzel, Turner Ashly H.S.
Dayton, Virginia

HOLIDAY CHICKEN SALAD

2 c. cut-up cooked chicken
1 c. sliced celery
½ c. toasted almonds
1 tbsp. lemon juice
½ c. mayonnaise
6 thick slices cranberry sauce
6 lettuce leaves

Combine chicken, celery, almonds and lemon juice. Chill. Add mayonnaise before serving. Serve on cranberry sauce on lettuce. Yield: 6 servings.

Mrs. Camille R. Cambier, Western Beaver H.S.
Industry, Pennsylvania

HOT CHICKEN SALAD

2 c. cooked diced chicken
1 c. sliced celery
1 c. cooked green peas
½ c. mayonnaise
2 tbsp. shredded onion
1 c. crushed potato chips

Combine all ingredients except potato chips. Place mixture in buttered 1 1/2 or 2-quart baking dish. Bake in 350 degree oven for 25 minutes. Top casserole with potato chips; return to oven for 5 minutes. Serve hot. Yield: 6 servings.

Mrs. Frederick L. Blanford, Lincoln Comm. H.S.
Lincoln, Illinois

HOT CHICKEN SALAD

2 c. cubed cooked chicken
2 c. chopped celery
½ c. slivered toasted almonds
2 tsp. chopped onion
1 c. salad dressing
2 tbsp. lemon juice
½ tsp. salt
½ c. shredded American cheese
1 c. crushed potato chips

Combine all ingredients except cheese and potato chips. Toss lightly. Place in individual baking dishes. Sprinkle with potato chips; top with cheese. Bake in 400 degree oven for 10 minutes. Yield: 4-6 servings.

Mrs. Beverly McGlamery, Carey H.S.
Carey, Ohio

HOT CHICKEN SALAD

2 c. cold diced chicken
2 c. diced celery
½ tsp. salt

2 tsp. grated onion
2 tbsp. lemon juice
1 c. mayonnaise
4 hard cooked eggs, chopped
½ c. grated cheese
1 c. crushed potato chips or buttered
   bread crumbs

Toss everything together except potato chips. Place in casserole or baking dish. Bake 10 to 15 minutes in 450-degree oven. Garnish with potato chips. Yield: 10 servings.

Betty M. Shuler, Narbonne H.S.
Harbor City, California

HOT CHICKEN SALAD

2 c. cooked chicken, cubed
2 c. chopped celery
½ c. toasted almonds
1 tsp. salt
2 tbsp. grated onion
2 tbsp. lemon juice
1 c. salad dressing
1 jar pimento
½ c. grated cheese
1 c. potato chips

Combine first 8 ingredients; mix lightly. Place in greased casserole. Sprinkle with cheese and chips. Bake at 450 degrees for 10 minutes. May be prepared ahead and baked when desired. Yield: 6 servings.

Mrs. Jeanne Clark, Bentley H.S.
Flint, Michigan

HOT CHICKEN SALAD SUPREME

2 c. cooked chicken, cut into chunks
2 c. chopped celery
3 tbsp. minced onion
3 tbsp. juice
½ tsp. salt
½ tsp. black pepper
½ c. pecans
¾ c. mayonnaise
1 sm. can sliced mushrooms
1 can cream of chicken soup
1 bag potato chips, crushed

Mix all ingredients except the soup and potato chips. Place in 2-quart casserole. Pour soup over top without mixing. Top with potato chips. Bake at 300 degrees for 30 minutes. Yield: 6-8 servings.

Mrs. Nancye H. Shannon, Greenbrier H.S.
Greenbrier, Tennessee

OVEN CHICKEN SALAD

2 c. cubed cooked chicken
2 c. thinly sliced celery
1 c. toasted bread cubes
½ c. chopped toasted almonds
½ tsp. salt
2 tsp. grated onion
1 c. mayonnaise
2 tbsp. lemon juice
½ c. grated cheese
1 c. toasted bread crumbs

Combine first 8 ingredients; pile lightly into individual baking dishes. Sprinkle with cheese and bread crumbs. Bake at 450 degrees until mixture is bubbly, about 10 to 15 minutes. Yield: 6 servings.

Margaret Lieb, USD #377
Effingham, Kansas

CHICKEN-RICE SALAD

2 c. cut-up chicken
2 c. cooked rice
1 c. celery, cut up
¼ c. chopped green pepper
3 tbsp. chopped pimento
2 tbsp. chopped onion
¼ c. slivered almonds
¾ tsp. salt
½ tsp. curry powder
Dash of pepper
1 tbsp. oil
1 tbsp. vinegar
¾ c. mayonnaise

Combine all ingredients. Chill for several hours. Garnish with lettuce and slivers of pimento. Yield: 8 servings.

Mrs. Virginia Cavellier, North Jr. H.S.
Watertown, New York

MARY'S CHICKEN SALAD

4 c. cooked, diced chicken
1 green pepper, minced
1 c. chopped celery
2 c. diced pineapple
2 c. white grapes, halved
1 c. almonds
¾ c. mayonnaise
¼ c. cream
Salt and pepper to taste
2 tbsp. vinegar
1 tsp. minced onion

Combine chicken, green pepper, celery, pineapple, grapes and almonds; chill. Combine mayonnaise, cream, salt, pepper, vinegar and onion; chill. Blend both mixtures together lightly just before serving. Yield: 12 servings.

Mary Virginia Wood, Bluestone Sch.
Skipwith, Virginia

CURRIED CHICKEN SALAD

¾ c. precooked rice
½ c. chopped red apple
¾ c. cubed, boned chicken
¼ c. toasted slivered almonds
1½ tsp. grated onion
⅓ c. mayonnaise
2 tbsp. cream
1 tbsp. lemon juice
½ tsp. curry powder
¼ tsp. salt
¼ tsp. sugar

Cook rice in small saucepan according to label directions; cool to room temperature. Combine with apple, chicken, almonds and onion in medium-sized bowl. Blend remaining ingredients in cup; stir into rice mixture. Chill. Garnish with sliced red apple. Yield: 4 servings.

Mrs. Fred Staszewski, Edwin Parr Composite
Athabasca, Alberta, Canada

PARTY CHICKEN SALAD

2 c. diced chicken or turkey
2 tbsp. lemon juice
½ tsp. salt
1 c. diced celery
1 c. seedless green grapes
2 hard-cooked eggs, chopped
¼ c. slivered almonds
½ c. salad dressing

Mix chicken, lemon juice and salt; chill 2 hours or longer. Add celery, grapes, eggs and almonds. Add salad dressing; mix thoroughly. Chill. Serve on lettuce leaf or other greens. Yield: 8 servings.

Mrs. Leola Becker, Hustisford H.S.
Hustisford, Wisconsin
Berma F. Doty, Towns Co. H.S.
Hiawassee, Georgia

WALDORF CHICKEN SALAD

3 c. diced cooked chicken
1 c. diced celery
½ c. mayonnaise
2 tbsp. wine vinegar
1 tsp. salt
1 c. diced apples
½ c. chopped nuts

Combine all ingredients; mix well. Chill until serving time. Turkey may be substituted for chicken. Yield: 6 servings.

Mrs. David Hetrick, Cardinal Stritch H.S.
Oregon, Ohio

GOBBLER SALAD

1 ½ tbsp. gelatin
2 c. cold water
½ tsp. salt
Dash of pepper
Dash of paprika
¾ c. chopped celery
1 ½ c. chopped cooked turkey
1 c. cold cooked rice
¼ c. pecans, chopped
¼ c. broken stuffed olives
1 tbsp. pickle relish
⅔ c. mayonnaise
½ c. sour cream

Soften gelatin in cold water. Set in pan of boiling water and stir until dissolved. Stir in salt, pepper and paprika. Place celery, turkey and rice in mixing bowl. Add pecans and olives to turkey. Stir in pickle relish. Pour gelatin mixture into blender or mixing bowl. Add mayonnaise and sour cream. Beat until well-blended and smooth, fold into turkey mixture. Place in 8 x 8 x 2-inch cake pan. Chill until firm. Serve on crisp greens. Yield: 8 servings.

Mrs. Barbara Knowlton, Wellman H.S.
Wellman, Texas

HOT TURKEY SALAD

2 c. cubed cooked turkey
2 c. sliced celery
1 c. mayonnaise
½ c. chopped toasted almonds
2 tbsp. lemon juice
2 tsp. grated onion
½ tsp. salt
½ c. grated American cheese
1 c. crushed potato chips

Combine all ingredients, except cheese and potato chips. Toss lightly. Pile lightly into individual bowls or custard cups. Sprinkle with cheese and potato chips. Bake at 450 degrees for 10 minutes. Yield: 5-6 servings.

Betty Rogers, West Holt H.S.
Atkinson, Nebraska
Diane S. Emigh, Springfield, Jr. H.S.
Springfield, Oregon

TURKEY-WALNUT SALAD

½ c. walnuts
½ c. mayonnaise
1 tbsp. lemon juice
1 tsp. horseradish
½ tsp. grated onion
Salt and pepper to taste
2 c. diced cooked turkey or chicken
2 c. sliced celery
3 tbsp. diced pimento or diced green
  pepper
Salad greens

Place walnuts in shallow pan in 300-degree oven for about 15 minutes. Cool and chop coarsely. Combine mayonnaise, lemon juice, horseradish, onion and seasonings. Add walnuts, turkey, celery and pimento. Place in bowl; chill. Serve on salad greens. Yield: 4-6 servings.

Mrs. Myra Garrison, Nebraska Sch. for the Deaf
Omaha, Nebraska

TURKEY-FRUIT SALAD

1 c. diced turkey
1 c. chopped pineapple
1 c. chopped apple
½ c. chopped orange
1 lge. banana, sliced
½ c. grapes, sliced
½ c. walnuts, chopped
½ c. mayonnaise
¼ c. orange or pineapple juice
2 tsp. sugar

Combine first 7 ingredients; chill. Combine remaining ingredients. Chill. Add dressing to turkey mixture. Yield: 4 servings.

Doris Henlick, Big Fork H.S.
Big Fork, Montana

TURKEY-TOMATO SALAD

1 c. sour cream
¼ c. mayonnaise or salad dressing
2 tbsp. lemon juice
1 tsp. sugar
½ tsp. curry powder
½ tsp. paprika
½ tsp. dry mustard
½ tsp. salt
2 c. diced cooked turkey or chicken
2 c. sliced celery
2 hard-cooked eggs, chopped
½ c. sliced almonds, toasted
6 to 8 lge. tomatoes, chilled

Combine sour cream, mayonnaise and seasonings; mix well. Combine turkey, celery, eggs and almonds; add dressing and mix lightly to coat ingredients well. Chill several hours before serving. Cut tomatoes in sixths 3/4 way through. Fill with salad mixture. Yield: 6-8 servings.

Photograph for this recipe on page 299.

AFTER THANKSGIVING SALAD

1 ½ c. chopped leftover turkey
⅓ c. mayonnaise
½ c. chopped celery
⅓ c. chopped sweet pickles
⅓ c. chopped apple, unpeeled

Mix turkey with remaining ingredients; serve. Makes tasty sandwich filling. Yield: 6 servings.

Mrs. Judy Elmore, Mowat Jr. H.S.
Lynn Haven, Florida

MEAT SALAD

2 c. cubed cooked turkey, chicken or ham
¼ c. French dressing
1 c. diced celery
2 hard-boiled eggs, cut up
2 tbsp. chopped onion
2 tbsp. chopped pimento
2 tbsp. chopped green pepper
Salt to taste
Lettuce

Marinate meat in French dressing for 15 minutes. Drain; combine with other ingredients except lettuce. Toss lightly. Serve on lettuce. Yield: 4 servings.

Effie Lois Greene, Potts Camp H.S.
Potts Camp, Mississippi

TURKEY-FRUIT SALAD

4 c. chopped cooked turkey
1 c. pineapple tidbits
1 c. chopped walnuts
1 c. seedless grapes
1 c. chopped apple
1 ½ c. mayonnaise

Combine all ingredients. Refrigerate before serving. Yield: 8 servings.

Mrs. Marjorie De Leva, Pacific H.S.
San Bernardino, California

TURKEY-GREEN GRAPE SALAD

1 ½ c. diced cooked turkey
1 c. thinly sliced celery
Green seedless grapes
½ c. mayonnaise
Salt and pepper to taste
Greens

Combine turkey, celery, 1/2 cup grapes and mayonnaise. Season and toss lightly. Serve on greens and trim with small bunch of grapes.

Can be served in avocado halves brushed with lemon juice. Yield: 6 servings.

Kathleen Burchett, Flatswoods H.S.
Jonesville, Virginia

CHEF'S SALAD

½ head lettuce, torn into bite-sized pieces
¼ bunch romaine or endive, torn into bite-sized pieces
¼ c. chopped green onion
¼ c. sliced celery
¼ c. julienne strips cold cooked beef, ham, tongue, luncheon meat
¼ c. julienne strips cold cooked chicken or turkey
½ c. julienne strips Swiss cheese
Fillets of anchovy (opt.)
¼ c. mayonnaise
2 tbsp. French dressing
4 ripe olives
1 hard-cooked egg, sliced

Toss greens with onion, celery, meat, chicken, cheese and anchovies, reserving few strips of meat, chicken and cheese for garnish. Combine mayonnaise and French dressing; toss salad with dressing just before serving. Garnish with reserved julienne strips, ripe olives and hard-cooked egg. Yield: 2 servings.

Mrs. Nellie C. Shymko, Willingdon Sch.
Willingdon, Alberta, Canada

ISLEY'S SALAD SUPREME

Lettuce
¼ head purple cabbage
4 to 5 shredded carrots
2 to 4 slices each, cold turkey, ham and cheese
3 tomato wedges
3 boiled egg wedges
Olives

Slice 1 medium head lettuce and shred cabbage and carrots. Chill. Place in lettuce cups. Add turkey, ham, cheese, tomato wedges and egg wedges. Top with olives.

BUTTERMILK DRESSING:

1 c. mayonnaise
1 c. catsup
2 c. buttermilk
Salt and pepper to taste
1 tsp. garlic oil

Mix mayonnaise, catsup, buttermilk, salt, pepper and garlic oil. Refrigerate. Serve over salad. Yield: 6-8 servings.

Mrs. Joy Isley, Paradise Valley H.S.
Phoenix, Arizona

Seafood Salads

RECIPE FOR SOUTH AFRICAN SALAD ON PAGE 343

CAULIFLOWER SALAD

1 med. cauliflower
¼ head lettuce
½ c. sliced, pitted ripe olives
7 anchovy fillets, cut in pieces
1 tbsp. sliced green onion
1 tbsp. capers
1 tsp. salt
Dash of pepper
3 tbsp. salad oil or olive oil
1 tbsp. wine vinegar

Break cauliflower into small flowerettes; cook 2 to 3 minutes in boiling salted water. Drain and chill. Tear lettuce into bite-sized pieces; add remaining ingredients. Toss lightly; chill at least 30 minutes before serving. Recipe may be doubled. Yield: 6 servings.

Sande J. Speck, Watertown Sr. High
Watertown, Minnesota
Shirley Bonomo, Spring Valley H.S.
Spring Valley, Wisconsin

CAESAR SALAD

2 stalks celery
1 sm. onion
2 cloves of garlic
3 egg yolks
1 c. olive oil
1 c. Wesson oil or any salad oil
¼ c. Dusseldorf mustard
1 tube anchovy paste
1 tbsp. Accent
½ tbsp. freshly ground pepper
5 drops Tabasco sauce
¼ c. wine vinegar

Grind celery, onion and garlic; set aside. Beat egg yolks until thick and light; add remaining ingredients, 1 at a time, in order given. Beat in mixture; chill. Serve on crisp greens; garnish with toasted bread cubes. Yield: 3 cups dressing.

Helen Tirkuis, Neenah Sr. High
Neenah, Wisconsin

CAESAR SALAD

1 clove garlic
½ c. salad oil
½ head lettuce
½ bunch curly endive
1 c. croutons
1 2-oz. can anchovy fillets
3 or 4 tomatoes, diced
1 beaten egg
1 tbsp. Worcestershire sauce
¼ c. lemon juice
½ tsp. pepper
½ tsp. salt
½ c. grated Parmesan cheese

Mash garlic; add to salad oil. Break lettuce into large wooden salad bowl. Tear endive; add croutons, anchovies and tomatoes. Strain oil; pour over vegetables. Combine remaining ingredients; beat well. Pour over salad; toss lightly. Yield: 4-6 servings.

Sister Mary Benedict Beehler, OSB
Mount St. Benedict Academy
Crookston, Minnesota

GOURMET SALAD

2 c. coarsely chopped lettuce
1 c. coarsely chopped cabbage
¾ c. coarsely chopped watercress
¾ c. coarsely chopped spinach
½ c. chopped chives
3 tbsp. chopped anchovy
3 tbsp. crumbled bleu cheese
6 tbsp. bleu cheese salad dressing

Combine all ingredients; toss lightly. Yield: 8 servings.

Martha R. Phillips, Kennett H.S.
Conway, New Hampshire

ITALIAN TOSSED SALAD

1 head romaine
1 bunch leaf lettuce
2 tomatoes, cut in wedges
½ c. celery slices
½ c. diced green pepper
½ c. radish slices
¼ c. sliced green onions
1 2-oz. can anchovies, chopped
3 tbsp. olive oil
2 tbsp. tarragon vinegar
2 tbsp. chopped parsley
¾ tsp. salt
Dash of freshly ground pepper
½ tsp. whole basil

Tear romaine and leaf lettuce in bite-sized pieces; place in salad bowl. Arrange vegetables and anchovies over lettuce. Sprinkle with oil, vinegar, parsley and seasonings. Toss lightly. Yield: 6-8 servings.

LaVonne Reinartz, Preston H.S.
Preston, Minnesota

LOUISE'S CAESAR SALAD

Salt
1 clove of garlic
1 tsp. dry mustard
1 tbsp. lemon juice
Liquid hot pepper sauce to taste
3 tbsp. olive oil
3 bunches romaine
1 tbsp. grated Parmesan cheese

(Continued on next page)

1 can anchovies, chopped
1 1-minute egg
½ c. croutons

Sprinkle bottom of wooden salad bowl with salt; rub with garlic. Add mustard, lemon juice and pepper sauce; stir with wooden spoon until salt dissolves. Add olive oil; stir until blended. Wash romaine; dry with paper towel. Tear leaves into bite-sized pieces; add to salad bowl. Sprinkle with Parmesan cheese; add anchovies. Break egg over salad; sprinkle with croutons. Mix gently but thoroughly. Yield: 6 servings.

Mrs. C. W. Hord, Cen. H.S.
Murfreesboro, Tennessee

PIMIENTO-ANCHOVY APPETIZER

½ head lettuce
2 3-oz. cans anchovy fillets, drained
1 6-oz. jar pimentos, drained
4 tbsp. salad oil
2 tbsp. wine vinegar
¼ tsp. pepper
1 tsp. salt
2 hard-cooked eggs, sliced

Wash lettuce; separate and chill. Chill anchovies and pimentos. Combine salad oil, vinegar, pepper and salt; chill. Arrange eggs, pimentos and anchovies on bed of lettuce; cover with dressing. Yield: 4 servings.

Mrs. Olga M. Browner, Wantagh H.S.
Wantagh, New York

TOSSED SALAD WITH BLUE CHEESE

1 head lettuce
2 tomatoes, chopped
1 sm. can anchovies, chopped
1 sm. cucumber, sliced
5 or 6 green onions, chopped
1 sm. green pepper, chopped
1 can green beans
Salt, pepper, garlic salt to taste
Blue cheese
Vinegar and oil dressing

Break lettuce into bite-sized pieces; add tomatoes, anchovies, cucumber, onions, green pepper and beans. Season to taste; crumble cheese over top. Add dressing; marinate until ready to serve. Yield: 6-8 servings.

Mrs. Hazel C. Jacobsen, Highland H.S.
Ault, Connecticut

CURRIED COD SALAD

1 tbsp. lemon juice
1 unpeeled red apple, diced
1 c. diced celery and leaves
½ c. raisins
½ c. chopped onions
1 lb. cooked salt cod
1 ½ tsp. curry powder
½ c. salad dressing

Sprinkle lemon juice over apple. Combine apple, celery, raisins and onions; add cod. Blend curry powder with salad dressing. Combine with fish mixture; toss lightly. Yield: 6-8 servings.

Rosalind P. R. Fisher, Harriot Curtis Collegiate
St. Anthony, Newfoundland, Canada

MOCK LOBSTER SALAD

3 lb. haddock
1 onion, sliced
1 ¼ to 1 ½ c. mayonnaise
1 c. chili sauce
1 ½ c. catsup
Salt and pepper to taste
1 lge. onion, grated fine
3 or 4 stalks celery, cut in chunks
1 2-oz. jar pimento
1 sm. lemon
Paprika

Steam haddock with sliced onion for 15 minutes. Break into large pieces; cool. Mix mayonnaise, chili sauce, catsup, salt and pepper; toss haddock in mayonnaise mixture. Add grated onion, celery and pimento; arrange on lettuce leaves. Squeeze lemon over top; sprinkle with paprika.

Mrs. Emily X. McGuigan, Portsmouth H.S.
Portsmouth, Rhode Island

SEAFOOD SALAD

2 tsp. lemon juice
1 tbsp. minced onion
2 c. diced celery
1 c. cooked macaroni
Salt and pepper to taste
3 or 4 tbsp. mayonnaise or to taste
2 c. flaked cooked haddock, crab meat or shrimp

(Continued on next page)

Mix all ingredients except seafood and mayonnaise; taste for seasoning. Add mayonnaise and seafood. Toss lightly; garnish with lettuce, hard-cooked eggs, olives or pickles. Yield: 6-8 servings.

Dr. Virginia Moses, Northwood H.S.
Silver Spring, Maryland

HALIBUT SALAD

    2½ c. cold halibut, flaked
    French dressing
    1 cucumber, cubed
    1 tsp. salt
    ⅛ tsp. pepper
    1 tbsp. chopped onion
    Salad dressing

Marinate halibut in French dressing; chill 1 hour. Add cucumber, salt, pepper and onion; add salad dressing to moisten. Serve on crisp lettuce; garnish with red and green peppers. Yield: 6 servings.

Catherine Mordan, Millville H.S.
Millville, Pennsylvania

HAWAIIAN HALIBUT SALAD

    2 lb. or 4 c. cooked halibut
    ½ c. diced celery
    ½ c. toasted almond halves
    ¼ c. diced green pepper
    1 c. canned pineapple chunks, drained
    ¾ c. mayonnaise
    1½ tsp. curry powder
    2 tbsp. shredded coconut

Break halibut into bite-sized chunks; combine with celery, almonds, green pepper and pineapple chunks. Blend mayonnaise and curry powder; toss with halibut mixture. Sprinkle with shredded coconut. Yield: 6 servings.

Mrs. Pat M. Paxton
Hugh McRoberts, Jr. Sec. Sch.
Richmond, British Columbia, Canada

SALADE VINEGARED

    2 lge. boiled potatoes, peeled and diced
    2 or 3 cooked beets, diced
    2 or 3 apples, grated
    3 hard-cooked eggs, chopped
    ½ herring, finely chopped
    ¼ c. sour cream
    ¼ c. mayonnaise
    ¾ c. olive oil
    ¼ c. vinegar
    ¼ tsp. salt
    ¼ tsp. pepper

Combine first 5 ingredients in large salad bowl; toss to blend. Combine sour cream and mayonnaise; beat in remaining ingredients. Toss salad with dressing; serve immediately. Yield: 4-6 servings.

Mrs. Alice Hansberger, Canton Sr. High
Canton, Illinois

SWEDISH HERRING SALAD

    1 1-lb. jar herring in wine vinegar
    2 c. cubed cooked potatoes
    1 c. pared cubed apples
    ¼ c. chopped sweet pickles
    1 c. cubed cooked beets, chilled
    1 hard-cooked egg, finely chopped
    1 tbsp. minced parsley
    1 tbsp. chopped capers

Cut herring into pieces; place in large mixing bowl. Add remaining contents of herring, potatoes, apples and sweet pickle; blend. Chill; add beets. Place in serving bowl; garnish with egg, parsley and capers. Yield: 12 servings.

Mrs. Nancy Kores, Coronado H.S.
Scottsdale, Arizona

BASIC SEAFOOD SALAD

    1 head lettuce, coarsely shredded
    ⅓ c. celery, chopped
    ⅓ c. green pepper, slivered
    1 tbsp. parsley, chopped
    1 tbsp. chives or green onion, chopped
    ⅔ c. cucumber, cubed
    ⅓ to ½ c. mayonnaise
    Few drops of Tabasco
    1 tsp. lemon juice
    2 hard-cooked eggs, cut into wedges
    2 tomatoes, cut into wedges
    1 pt. salmon, coarsely broken

Combine lettuce, celery, green pepper, chives and cucumber in wooden bowl. Mix mayonnaise with Tabasco and lemon juice; add to vegetable mixture and toss. Add eggs, tomatoes and seafood; toss once lightly. Serve with hot cheese biscuits. Crab, shrimp or mixed seafood may be substituted for salmon. Yield: 6 servings.

Mrs. W. R. White, Claremont Sr. Secondary Sch.
Victoria, British Columbia, Canada

CANADIAN SALMON MOLD

    2 tbsp. unflavored gelatin
    ½ c. cold water
    1 c. hot chicken bouillon
    1 c. mayonnaise
    3 tbsp. chili sauce
    2 tbsp. lemon juice
    1 tbsp. finely chopped onion

(Continued on next page)

½ tsp. Worcestershire sauce
½ tsp. Accent
Salt and pepper to taste
1 c. finely diced celery
½ c. sliced stuffed olives
1 c. cooked salmon, flaked

Soften gelatin in cold water; dissolve in hot chicken bouillon. Cool slightly; add slowly to mayonnaise, blending after each addition. Add chili sauce, lemon juice, onion, Worcestershire sauce, Accent, salt and pepper; chill until partially set. Combine celery, olives and salmon; add to chilled mixture. Turn into oiled 5-cup mold; chill until firm. Unmold on crisp greens. Serve with dressing. Yield: 8 servings.

Gladys Neilsen, Centreville Reg. Sch.
Centreville, New Brunswick, Canada

JELLIED SALMON SALAD

1 tbsp. gelatin
¼ c. cold water
2 c. flaked salmon
2 tbsp. chopped pickle
2 tbsp. chopped celery tops
½ c. diced celery
½ tsp. salt
Few grains cayenne
1 c. mayonnaise

Soak gelatin in cold water for 5 minutes; dissolve over boiling water. Add remaining ingredients; mix well. Pour into 1-quart mold; chill. Serve on greens. Garnish. Yield: 4-6 servings.

Mrs. E. Fahlgren, St. James Collegiate
Winnipeg, Manitoba, Canada

MOLDED SALMON SALAD

1 tbsp. gelatin
¼ c. cold water
2 egg yolks
1 tsp. salt
1 tsp. dry mustard
Dash of paprika
¾ c. milk
2 ½ tbsp. lemon juice
2 tbsp. butter
2 c. cooked or canned salmon, flaked
½ c. chopped celery

Soften gelatin in cold water. Beat egg yolks; add salt, mustard, paprika, milk, lemon juice and butter. Cook in double boiler until mixture thickens. Add softened gelatin; stir well to dissolve. Add salmon and celery. Pour into 3-cup fish-shaped mold; chill until firm. Unmold on lettuce. Garnish with olive slices, carrot and celery curls. Yield: 6 servings.

Teresa MacIsaac, Cen. Sch.
Sydney, Nova Scotia, Canada

JELLIED SALMON SALAD

1 3-oz. pkg. lemon gelatin
1 c. boiling water
1 c. cold water
2 tbsp. vinegar
2 7½-oz. cans salmon
½ c. chopped celery
2 tbsp. chopped green pepper
2 tbsp. chopped pimento
1 tbsp. grated onion

Dissolve gelatin in boiling water; stir in cold water and vinegar. Chill until slightly thickened; fold in remaining ingredients. Pour into individual molds; chill until firm. Serve on salad greens. Yield: 8 servings.

Mrs. C. L. Herscher, Union H.S.
Donvagiac, Michigan

SALMON MOUSSE

2 envelopes unflavored gelatin
½ c. cold water
½ c. vinegar
4 c. flaked salmon
2 c. finely chopped celery
2 tbsp. sugar
2 tbsp. pickle relish
2 tsp. mustard
1 c. whipping cream, whipped
2 ½ tsp. salt

Soften gelatin in cold water and vinegar; dissolve over boiling water. Stir in salmon, celery, sugar, relish and mustard; fold in whipping cream. Chill in fish-shaped mold until set. Yield: 8-12 servings.

Mrs. Linda Magauson, Hyre Sr. High
Akron, Ohio

REAL COOL FISH SALAD

1 lb. can salmon or tuna
½ c. hard-boiled eggs
1 4-oz. pkg. cream cheese
¼ c. butter or margarine
1 tbsp. grated onion
1 tsp. lemon juice
½ c. chopped celery
½ c. chopped green pepper
Pimentos and olives

Combine and blend all ingredients except pimentos and olives. Pack mixture into slightly oiled 3-cup mold. Chill for 2 or 3 hours. Decorate with pimentos and olives. Border with lettuce and radish roses. Serve as salad or spread. Yield: 6 servings.

Lona W. Capshaw, Hermitage Springs Sch.
Red Boiling Springs, Tennessee

SALMON SALAD

1 pkg. shell macaroni
1 can salmon, drained and flaked
1 can English peas, drained
½ c. chopped celery
½ c. onion, chopped
Salt and pepper to taste
Mayonnaise

Cook macaroni in salted water; drain and chill. Combine all ingredients except mayonnaise with chilled macaroni. Add enough mayonnaise to moisten. Chill; serve on lettuce loaf. Yield: 6 servings.

Mrs. Nell P. Stevers, Indianola H.S.
Indianola, Mississippi

MACARONI-SALMON SALAD

2 c. boiled cooled macaroni
1 c. diced cucumber
1 8-oz. can salmon, flaked
1 tbsp. grated onion
1 tbsp. minced parsley
¾ c. mayonnaise
½ tsp. salt
¼ tsp. pepper

Combine all ingredients; toss together until blended. Serve on lettuce. Garnish with chopped parsley and paprika, if desired. One and one-half cubed, leftover cooked meat may be used in place of salmon. Yield: 4-6 servings.

Maureen Hackett, Stanley Reg. H.S.
Stanley, New Brunswick, Canada

MOM'S SALMON SALAD

3 c. finely chopped cabbage
1 c. chopped peanuts, freshly shelled
1 sm. bottle diced sweet pickles
1 tall can red salmon, drained and
   flaked
Mayonnaise

Mix cabbage, peanuts and sweet pickles thoroughly with salmon; add enough mayonnaise to moisten. Serve on lettuce leaf. Yield: 6 servings.

Mrs. Winifred Iverson, Riggs Sr. H.S.
Pierre, South Dakota

SALMON-APPLE SALAD

1 can salmon, flaked and boned
1 c. diced celery
2 hard-cooked eggs, chopped
½ c. chopped red apple
¼ tsp. rosemary
¼ tsp. savory
Salt to taste
Mayonnaise

Combine salmon, celery, eggs, apple, spices and salt; add enough mayonnaise to moisten. Serve on salad greens with crackers. Yield: 6 servings.

Mrs. Mary Cullison, New London Sr. H.S.
New London, Iowa

SALMON PARTY BALL

1 1-lb. can red salmon, drained, boned
   and skinned
1 8-oz. pkg. cream cheese
1 tbsp. lemon juice
2 tsp. grated onion
1 tsp. prepared horseradish
¼ tsp. salt
¼ tsp. liquid smoke (opt.)
3 tbsp. snipped parsley (opt.)

Combine salmon, cream cheese, lemon juice, onion, horseradish, salt and liquid smoke; mix thoroughly. Chill several hours. Shape into ball; roll in parsley. Chill. Serve with assorted crackers. Keep for at least 3 weeks in refrigerator.

Betty Otteson, Pearl City H.S.
Pearl City, Illinois

SALMON-PEA SALAD

¼ c. mayonnaise
1 ½ tsp. lemon juice
½ tsp. seasoned salt
2 canned pimentos, diced
1 sm. onion, finely chopped
2 hard-cooked eggs, coarsely chopped
1 8-oz. can peas, drained
1 7 ¾-oz. can salmon, drained and
   broken into bite-sized pieces
Lettuce

Mix mayonnaise, lemon juice, seasoned salt, pimentos and onion; add eggs, peas and salmon, mixing lightly. Chill. Serve in lettuce-lined bowl. Yield: 4 servings.

Sharon Stephen, Apache H.S.
Apache, Oklahoma

SALMON SALAD

3 c. finely shredded cabbage
Salt and pepper to taste
1 tbsp. sugar
1 tbsp. vinegar
2 tbsp. cooking oil
1 1-lb. can salmon, drained and
   broken up pickles
2 hard-cooked eggs
½ c. mayonnaise
1 tbsp. catsup
1 tsp. steak sauce
¼ tsp. dry mustard
2 green onions, minced
4 sm. sweet pickles, sliced

(Continued on next page)

Soak cabbage in ice water and ice cubes for 20 minutes; drain and dry on towel. Place in bowl; sprinkle with salt, pepper and sugar. Add vinegar and oil. Drain. Place salmon in bowl; add pickles, eggs, mayonnaise, catsup, steak sauce, mustard and onions. Salt and pepper to taste. Combine with cabbage mixture; mix well. Yield: 6-8 servings.

Cynthia Weddle, Brock H.S.
Brock, Nebraska

SALMON SALAD

1 1-lb. can salmon, drained and flaked
½ c. chopped celery
½ c. chopped sweet pickle
2 tbsp. chopped green pepper
½ tsp. salt
1 tbsp. lemon juice
⅓ c. mayonnaise

Combine all ingredients. Chill. Yield: 4 servings.

Mrs. Mary M. Radford, Waverly H.S.
Waverly, Ohio

SALMON SALAD

2 c. canned red salmon, chilled and flaked
½ c. thinly sliced celery
2 tbsp. diced sweet pickles
2 tsp. grated onion
2 c. finely crushed potato chips
¾ c. mayonnaise
2 tbsp. lemon juice

Combine salmon, celery, pickles, onion and potato chips. Mix the mayonnaise and lemon juice; blend into seafood mixture. Serve with crisp lettuce. Yield: 4-6 servings.

Christina Black, Upper Dauphin Area H.S.
Elizabethville, Pennsylvania

SALMON SALAD

1 c. cold, boiled flaked salmon, fresh or canned
1 c. shredded cabbage or chopped celery
Mayonnaise
Lettuce leaves

Combine salmon and cabbage. Serve with mayonnaise on lettuce leaves. Yield: 4 servings.

Mrs. Ann Hoit, Ousley Jr. H.S.
Arlington, Texas

SARDINE SALAD APPETIZER

Chicory
1 can sardines, boned and cleaned
2 tbsp. chopped onion
2 tbsp. chopped parsley
4 ripe olives
4 pickled beets, sliced
4 pickled eggs, sliced

Arrange chicory on 4 salad plates; place sardines in center of each. Sprinkle with chopped onion and parsley; top each with olive. Surround with border of overlapping slices of beets and eggs. Serve with French dressing.

Alice P. Lynum, Jerusalem Ave. Jr. H.S.
North Bellmine, New York

SEA REEF SALAD

1 16-oz. can liza or 2 c. other canned fish, drained and flaked
2 hard-cooked eggs, chopped
½ c. diced ripe olives
½ c. sliced toasted almonds
1 tbsp. unflavored gelatin
¼ c. cold water
1 c. mayonnaise or salad dressing
1 c. sour cream
1 tbsp. grated onion
¾ tsp. salt
2 tbsp. lemon juice
½ c. chopped parsley
½ c. chopped lettuce
3 tomatoes, quartered
⅓ to ½ c. chopped green peppers
2 tbsp. chopped onion

Combine first 4 ingredients; soak gelatin in cold water for 5 minutes. Dissolve over hot water. Stir into mayonnaise. Add sour cream, grated onion, salt, lemon juice and parsley; combine with fish mixture. Place in ring mold; chill until firm. Unmold on lettuce; fill center with tomatoes, green peppers and chopped onion. Serve with mayonnaise. Yield: 6 servings.

Mrs. J. Ralph Kemp, Henry Grady H.S.
Atlanta, Georgia

CHILI-TUNA SALAD

1 family-sized can tuna
1 med. apple, diced
1 sm. onion
1 med. dill pickle
2 oz. chopped, green chili peppers
⅓ to ½ c. mayonnaise

Combine all ingredients; toss to blend. Serve as sandwich spread or as salad. Yield: 4 servings.

Mrs. Bobby Dictson, San Jon H.S.
San Jon, New Mexico

BETTY'S TUNA SALAD

2 hard-cooked eggs
1 6-oz. can light tuna, drained and
flaked
¼ c. chopped green olives
¼ c. chopped pickles
½ c. mayonnaise

Cool, peel and chop eggs finely; add tuna, olives, pickles and mayonnaise. Blend well; serve in sandwiches, tomato cups, as appetizers on bread squares, or as a main dish salad. Yield: 4 servings.

Mrs. Betty Jones, Les Cheneaux Comm. Schs.
Cedarville, Mich.

CARROT-TUNA SALAD

1 c. grated carrot
1 c. diced celery
2 hard-cooked eggs, sliced
1 tsp. grated onion
2 cans tuna or chicken
½ pt. mayonnaise
1 No. 2 ½ can shoestring potatoes

Combine all ingredients except potatoes; chill 1 hour. Add potatoes; serve on greens. Garnish with wedges of tomato and eggs.

Mrs. Judith Anderson, Stillwater Sr. H.S.
Stillwater, Minnesota

COLD EGG-TUNA SALAD

1 7-oz. can tuna, undrained
½ c. celery, diced
1 sm. onion, finely chopped
½ tsp. curry powder
⅓ c. mayonnaise
6 hard-cooked eggs, shelled
Parsley
Tomatoes

Mash tuna; mix with celery, onion and celery powder. Blend in 1/2 cup mayonnaise. Place in mound in middle of large round platter. Surround with eggs. Top each with 1 teaspoon mayonnaise and tuft of parsley. Quarter as many tomatoes as you like and place between eggs. Yield: 6 servings.

Mrs. Myrtle Mary Nicholson
Eislglen Composite H.S.
Edmonton, Alberta, Canada

CHICKEN GUMBO SALAD

1 pkg. lemon Jell-O
2 tbsp. vinegar
½ c. boiling water

Dash of salt
1 can chicken gumbo soup
1 can tuna, washed and drained
½ c. whipped cream
½ c. Miracle Whip dressing
2 tbsp. green pepper
1 tbsp. pimento
1 tbsp. onion
2 tbsp. celery
Chopped nuts
Sliced olives

Combine first 5 ingredients; add tuna. Chill; add remaining ingredients. Place in salad mold; chill until firm. Yield: 10 servings.

Darlene Moss, Soda Springs H.S.
Soda Springs, Idaho

MOLDED STAR SALAD

1 pkg. lemon Jell-O
½ c. boiling water
1 can tuna
1 can chicken gumbo soup
2 tbsp. green pepper
1 tbsp. chopped onion
2 tbsp. chopped celery
½ c. cream or ½ c. salad dressing and
evaporated milk

Dissolve Jell-O in boiling water; fold in remaining ingredients. Pour into star or other salad mold; chill until firm. Serve on lettuce. Yield: 8 servings.

Mrs. Renee R. Porter, American Fork H.S.
American Fork, Utah

MOLDED TUNA SALAD

2 tbsp. Knox gelatin
½ c. cold water
1 can tomato soup
2 sm. pkg. cream cheese
1 c. mayonnaise
½ c. finely chopped celery
¼ c. finely chopped onion
½ sm. clove of garlic, crushed
1 can tuna
Juice of ½ lemon
½ c. green pepper, finely chopped
½ c. chopped olives
½ c. chopped nuts
4 chopped eggs

Soak gelatin in cold water. Bring tomato soup to boiling point; stir in cream cheese until smooth. Add gelatin; cool. Fold in remaining ingredients; chill until firm. Yield: 8 servings.

Hilda Harmon, Crowley H.S.
Crowley, Louisiana

MOLDED TUNA SALAD

1 envelope plain gelatin
1 c. mayonnaise
1 7-oz. can tuna, flaked
2 hard-boiled eggs, chopped
½ c. olives, sliced
1 2-oz. jar pimentos, chopped
Dash of salt and pepper
1 tsp. Worcestershire sauce

Soak gelatin in 1/4 cup cold water 5 minutes; melt over hot water. Add mayonnaise; blend well. Add remaining ingredients; place in 5-ounce individual molds, rinsed in cold water. Chill until firm; unmold on lettuce leaf. Top with mayonnaise and paprika; garnish with tomato wedges and parsley.

Elizabeth Curry, Marianna H.S.
Marianna, Florida

MOLDED TUNA SALAD

1 3-oz. pkg. lemon, lemon-lime, or lime gelatin
¼ tsp. salt
1 c. boiling water
¾ c. cold water
1 tbsp. lemon juice
½ c. mayonnaise
1 tsp. grated onion
½ c. chopped cucumber
1 7-oz. can tuna, drained and flaked
¼ c. sliced stuffed olives
2 tbsp. chopped pimento

Dissolve gelatin and salt in boiling water; blend in cold water, lemon juice, mayonnaise and onion. Chill until very thick; fold in remaining ingredients. Pour into 1-quart mold or serving bowl; chill until firm. Unmold on crisp salad greens; serve with additional mayonnaise, if desired. Yield: 4 cups.

Mrs. Margaret Raburn, Cen. H.S.
Marlow, Oklahoma

SUPPER JELL-O

1 pkg. lemon Jell-O
1 c. hot water
½ tsp. salt
1 tbsp. grated onion
½ c. whipped cream
½ c. mayonnaise
3 hard-boiled eggs, chopped
3 tbsp. chopped pimento
½ green pepper, chopped
1½ c. chopped celery
½ c. walnuts, chopped
1 can tuna, shrimp or chicken, chopped

Dissolve Jell-O in hot water; add salt and onion. Chill until slightly thickened. Combine remaining ingredients; fold into gelatin. Place in square pan; chill until firm. Cut into servings; place on lettuce leaf. Yield: 8 servings.

Mrs. Gretchen Ryan, Armour Pub. Sch.
Armour, South Dakota

TUNA-APPLE SALAD

1 pkg. celery gelatin
1 c. boiling water
1 tbsp. lemon juice
7 to 10 ice cubes
1 c. finely chopped apples
½ c. grated, sharp cheddar cheese
1 7-oz. can flaked drained tuna
¼ c. coarsely chopped nuts
¼ c. diced celery
½ tsp. salt
1 pkg. lemon lime or mixed fruit gelatin

Dissolve celery gelatin in boiling water; add lemon juice and ice cubes. Stir until thickened, about 3 minutes; remove unmelted ice. Add apples, cheese, tuna, nuts, celery and salt. Spoon into 2-quart mold. Chill until set but not firm. Prepare lemon gelatin according to package directions. Chill until very thick; beat with electric beater until doubles in volume. Spoon into mold; chill until firm. Unmold; garnish. Serve with salad dressing. Yield: 6 servings.

Mrs. Patricia Webb, Forestville Cen. Sch.
Forestville, New York

TUNA TURNOVER

4 envelopes unflavored gelatin
1 c. cold water
4½ c. tomato juice
2 tsp. grated onion
1 tsp. salt
6 tbsp. lemon juice
2 tsp. sugar
2 cans grated tuna
2 hard-cooked eggs, chopped
1 c. celery, chopped fine
½ c. stuffed olives
1 c. mayonnaise

Soften gelatin in cold water; heat 2 cups tomato juice to boiling. Add gelatin; stir until dissolved. Stir in onion, salt, lemon juice and Worcestershire sauce. Divide mixture in half; stir sugar and remaining tomato juice into first half; pour into 9 x 9 x 2-inch pan. Chill until almost firm. Add remaining ingredients to remaining gelatin mixture; gently spoon over clear layer. Chill until firm; unmold on lettuce. Garnish with lemon slices and black olives. Yield: 12 servings.

Mrs. Lois P. Cowley, Caldwell Sr. H.S.
Caldwell, Idaho

Congealed Tuna Salads

TUNA ASPIC MOLD

1st layer

    2 pkg. unflavored gelatin
    2 c. tomato juice
    1 tsp. grated onion

Soften 1 package gelatin in 1/4 cup tomato juice; dissolve over hot water. Stir in remaining tomato juice and onion; pour into 1 1/2-quart ring mold. Chill until firm.

2nd layer

    1 pkg. unflavored gelatin
    ½ c. cold water
    1 c. salad dressing
    2 tbsp. lemon juice
    Dash of salt and pepper
    1 7-oz. can flaked tuna, drained
    ½ c. sliced celery
    2 tbsp. chopped pimento
    ¼ c. chopped green pepper

Soften remaining gelatin in cold water; dissolve over hot water. Cool; stir in salad dressing, lemon juice and seasonings. Chill until slightly thickened; fold in tuna, celery, pimento and green pepper. Pour over molded layer; chill until firm. Turn out carefully on bed of shredded lettuce; place parsley in center of mold. Yield: 6 servings.

Rosalie Wentzell
William E. Hay Composite H.S.
Stettler, Alberta, Canada

TUNA MOLD

    1 envelope unflavored gelatin
    1 ¾ c. milk
    2 egg yolks
    1 tsp. salt
    Dash of pepper
    1 can tuna, drained and flaked
    1 tsp. prepared mustard
    2 tbsp. lemon juice
    ½ c. chopped celery
    2 tbsp. finely chopped pimento
    Cooked marinated green peas

Soften gelatin in 1/2 cup milk. Beat egg yolks; add remaining milk, salt and pepper together. Add to gelatin; place over low heat, stirring constantly until gelatin is dissolved, about 5 minutes. Remove from heat; chill until slightly thickened. Combine tuna, mustard, lemon juice, celery and pimento. Fold into gelatin mixture. Turn into 3-cup ring mold or individual molds; chill until firm. Unmold on serving plate, garnish with salad greens. Fill center with peas. Yield: 4 servings.

Mrs. Florence W. Ponder, Magee Jr. H.S.
Magee, Mississippi
Mrs. Hazel Seaton, Twiggs Co. H.S.
Danville, Georgia

TUNA-CELERY MOLD

    1 envelope unflavored gelatin
    ½ c. cold water
    1 can cream of celery soup
    ¼ c. mayonnaise
    1 tbsp. lemon juice
    1 7-oz. can tuna, drained and flaked
    ¼ c. chopped celery
    2 tbsp. chopped green pepper
    1 tbsp. chopped pimento

Soften gelatin in cold water; stir over boiling water until dissolved. Blend soup, mayonnaise and lemon juice; stir in gelatin. Chill until slightly thickened; fold in tuna, celery, green pepper and pimento. Pour into 3-cup mold; chill until firm. Yield: 4 servings.

Mrs. Sam Crow, Hollis H.S.
Hollis, Oklahoma

TUNA GUMBO SALAD

    1 pkg. lemon jelly powder
    ½ c. boiling water
    1 can chicken gumbo soup
    ½ c. finely diced celery
    ¼ c. finely chopped onion
    1 can flaked tuna
    ½ c. mayonnaise
    ½ c. cream, whipped

Dissolve jelly powder in boiling water; add soup. Chill until slightly thickened; add celery, onion and tuna. Fold in mayonnaise and whipped cream; pour into 6 individual molds or 1-quart mold. Yield: 4-6 servings.

Mrs. Margaret McPherson, Branton Jr. H.S.
Calgary, Alberta, Canada

TUNA MOLD

    1 tbsp. gelatin
    ½ c. cold water
    2 tbsp. lemon juice
    1 can tuna
    ½ c. chopped celery
    ¼ c. chopped bell pepper
    ¾ c. mayonnaise
    ½ tsp. paprika
    1 tbsp. chopped parsley

Add gelatin to cold water; dissolve over hot water. Add remaining ingredients; mix well. Pour into individual molds or loaf pan; chill until firm. Yield: 6 servings.

Mrs. Rush Valentine, Starkville H.S.
Starkville, Mississippi

TUNA SALAD

1 pkg. lime Jell-O
¾ c. mayonnaise
1 c. chopped celery
½ c. chopped sweet pickles
1 c. peas
1 c. tuna

Prepare Jell-O as directed on package; chill until firm. Whip in electric mixer; blend in mayonnaise. Fold in remaining ingredients; chill until firm. Serve in squares. A nice luncheon salad. Yield: 5-6 servings.

Mrs. Eddith M. Davis, Bowie H.S.
El Paso, Texas

CRACKER CRISP SALAD

1 qt. greens
½ c. mayonnaise
1 tbsp. vinegar
¼ tsp. Worcestershire sauce
1 clove of garlic, crushed
¾ tsp. salt
2 tomatoes, cut into chunks
1 7-oz. can tuna or chicken, broken into chunks
6 radishes, sliced
1 c. sm. cheese crackers

Tear greens into bite-sized pieces; refrigerate until crisp. Combine mayonnaise, vinegar, Worcestershire sauce, garlic and salt; chill. Add tomatoes and tuna to greens; toss. Add radishes and crackers; pour in dressing. Toss lightly. Garnish with crackers. Yield: 4-6 servings.

Mrs. Madie Oliver, Centerville Sch.
Groveton, Texas

CRISPY TUNA SALAD

1 No. ½ can tuna
4 ½ tbsp. sweet pickle
1 ½ tbsp. minced onion
½ c. mayonnaise
1 ½ tbsp. lemon juice
1 ½ c. crisp shredded cabbage
1 sm. pkg. potato chips, crushed

Combine tuna, pickle, onion, mayonnaise and lemon juice; chill in covered dish. Add cabbage; toss. Add half the potato chips; toss. Heap in lettuce-lined bowl; sprinkle with remaining potato chips. Garnish with tomato wedges. Yield: 6 servings.

Ethel Spradling, Bixby H.S.
Bixby, Oklahoma

CRISP TUNA SALAD

1 7-oz. can chunk tuna, drained
½ c. diced celery
⅓ c. chopped sweet pickles
⅓ c. broken pecans
½ c. diced apples
¼ c. salad dressing or mayonnaise

Combine all ingredients except salad dressing; chill. Add salad dressing; toss gently. Spoon on lettuce leaves. Yield: 4 servings.

Joyce M. Graham, Grundy Co. H.S.
Tracy City, Tennessee

CRUNCHY TUNA SALAD

1 med. can tuna
1 c. chopped celery
1 c. shredded carrots
2 tbsp. minced onion
½ c. Miracle Whip salad dressing
½ c. cream, whipped
2 c. shoestring potatoes

Pour boiling water over tuna; drain well. Cool; add celery, carrots and onion. Blend salad dressing and whipped cream; add to tuna mixture. Stir in potatoes; serve immediately on crisp bed of lettuce. Yield: 6 servings.

Karen Jodock, Kellogg Sr. H.S.
St. Paul, Minnesota

CURRIED PINEAPPLE-TUNA SALAD

1 tbsp. curry powder
¼ c. cider vinegar
2 tbsp. sugar
1 clove of garlic
2 med. pineapples
4 cans tuna in vegetable oil, drained
1 sm. onion, chopped
1 c. celery, sliced diagonally
1 med. green pepper, slivered
2 c. mayonnaise
1 tsp. salt
¼ tsp. pepper

Heat curry powder, vinegar, sugar and garlic; cool. Cut pineapples lengthwise, leaving stem on. Remove meat from shell; dice. Combine pineapple cubes and tuna with seasonings; chill. Add vegetables, mayonnaise, salt and pepper. Pile into pineapple shells; garnish with chopped nuts, raisins and coconut. Yield: 8 servings.

Barbara Gaylor
Supv., Home Ec. and Family Life Ed.
Michigan Dept. of Ed.
Lansing, Michigan

FRIDAY SUPPER SALAD

2 7½-oz. cans tuna, drained and
   flaked
2 tbsp. lemon juice
¼ tsp. seasoned pepper
1 14-oz. can lima beans, drained
¼ c. bottled French dressing
6 c. broken salad greens
4 slices Muenster cheese, cut in strips
12 pitted ripe olives, quartered

Toss tuna lightly with lemon juice and seasoned
pepper; toss lima beans with French dressing
in separate bowl. Chill both to season and blend
flavors. Place greens in large serving bowl;
pile tuna, lima beans, cheese and olives in rows,
spoke fashion, on top. Garnish with pimento
strips and cashew nuts, if desired; toss. Yield:
6-8 servings.

Mrs. E. J. A. Young, Mt. Sentinel Secondary Sch.
South Slocan, British Columbia, Canada

HIGH NUTRITION-
LOW CALORIE
SEAFOOD DELIGHT

1 can low calorie diet tuna
2 tbsp. vinegar
2 tbsp. low calorie diet salad dressing
3 shredded carrots
1 green pepper, chopped fine
1 ½ c. chopped celery
Salt, pepper and garlic salt to taste
Peeled boiled shrimp
Hard-cooked egg wedges
Tomato wedges
Parsley

Place first 3 ingredients in blender or mixer;
cream thoroughly. Toss with next 4 ingredients.
Garnish with shrimp, egg wedges, tomato wedges
and parsley, if desired. Yield: 6 servings.

Mrs. Elaine T. Carol, Alamo Heights H.S.
San Antonio, Texas

CHOPSTICK TUNA SALAD

1 can condensed cream of mushroom
   soup
¼ c. water
1 3-oz. can chow mein noodles
1 can tuna
1 c. sliced celery
½ c. salted toasted cashews
¼ c. chopped onion
Dash of pepper
1 can mandarin oranges

Blend soup and water; add 1 cup noodles and
remaining ingredients. Toss lightly; place in ungreased 10 x 6 x 1 1/2-inch baking dish. Sprinkle

with remaining noodles. Bake for 15 minutes or
until heated. Garnish with orange slices. Yield:
4-6 servings.

Kathryn Davison, Hot Springs Co. H.S.
Thermopolis, Wyoming

HOT TUNA SALAD

1 c. tuna
1 c. thinly sliced celery
1 c. toasted bread cubes
½ c. mayonnaise
1 tbsp. lemon juice
1 tsp. grated onion
¼ tsp. salt
¼ c. grated cheese

Preheat oven to 450 degrees. Combine all ingredients except cheese and 1/2 cup bread cubes;
pile lightly into individual baking dishes or 1-
quart casserole. Sprinkle with cheese and reserved bread cubes. Bake 10 to 15 minutes or
until bubbly. Yield: 3-4 servings.

Mrs. Douglas Gunn, East Haven Jr. H.S.
East Haven, Connecticut

HOT TUNA SALAD

2 cans drained flaked tuna
2 c. diced celery
⅔ c. salad dressing
½ c. toasted slivered almonds
1 tbsp. lemon juice
¼ c. chopped olives
2 tsp. grated onion
¼ tsp. celery salt
¼ tsp. salt
1 tbsp. melted butter
1 ¼ c. Corn Chex, crushed

Preheat oven to 350 degrees. Combine first 9
ingredients; toss lightly. Place in 8-inch casserole. Bake 10 minutes. Stir butter into Corn
Chex; sprinkle over casserole. Bake 10 minutes
longer or until browned. Yield: 6 servings.

Mrs. Myra D. Sorensen, Richfield H.S.
Richfield, Utah

MACARONI AND TUNA SALAD

2 pkg. elbow or shell macaroni, cooked
4 hard-boiled eggs
4 pieces celery, diced
½ green pepper, diced
3 tomatoes, cut up
1 med. onion, diced
2 cans chunk tuna
1 can peas (opt.)
Salt and pepper to taste
Mayonnaise to moisten

(Continued on next page)

Combine ingredients; chill. An excellent salad for luncheon, party or pot-luck. Yield: 8-10 servings.

Margaret Ide, George Rogers Clark Sch.
Whiting, Indiana

MACARONI-TUNA SALAD

    1 c. salad macaroni
    ½ c. mayonnaise
    1 tbsp. Worcestershire sauce
    1 tbsp. lemon juice
    ½ tsp. salt
    ⅛ tsp. pepper
    1 c. peas, drained
    1 c. diced celery
    ½ c. diced onion
    ½ c. cubed cheese
    1 sm. jar chopped pimento
    1 tbsp. chopped parsley
    ½ c. diced green pepper
    2 diced boiled eggs
    1 lge. can tuna

Cook macaroni; rinse in cold water. Mix together mayonnaise, Worcestershire sauce, lemon juice, salt and pepper; add remaining ingredients; chill 2 to 3 hours. Garnish with stuffed olives. Yield: 6 servings.

Viola Gracey, Travis Jr. H.S.
Snyder, Texas

NEPTUNE SALAD

    1 can tuna, flaked
    ½ c. chopped onion
    ½ c. chopped celery
    ¼ c. chopped bell pepper
    ¼ c. chopped radishes
    ¼ c. chopped cucumber
    1 lge. tomato
    1 ½ c. cooked macaroni
    1 c. mayonnaise
    ½ tsp. salt
    ¼ tsp. pepper

Combine tuna, onion, celery, bell pepper, radishes, cucumber and tomato; add to macaroni. Fold in mayonnaise, salt and pepper; chill. Serve on lettuce. Yield: 4 servings.

Donna C. Alexander, Winterboro H.S.
Alpine, Alabama

PASTA-TUNA SALAD

    2 c. macaroni
    1 qt. water
    ½ tsp. salt
    1 8-oz. can tuna
    1 stalk celery

    1 c. chopped lettuce
    ¼ tsp. salt
    ¼ c. grated cheddar cheese
    Salad dressing

Place macaroni, water and salt in large pot; cook until tender. Drain; wash in warm running water. Drain well. Flake tuna; pour hot water over tuna to remove oil. Add remaining ingredients, using just enough salad dressing to moisten; toss well. Serve on lettuce cup with sliced tomato, pickle or other garnish. Yield: 4-6 servings.

Mrs. Laura Lloyd, Petitcodiac Regional Sch.
Petitcodiac, New Brunswick, Canada

TUNA-MACA SALAD

    1 ½ c. mayonnaise
    ½ c. sweet pickle relish
    2 tbsp. catsup
    1 sm. can tuna
    ½ lb. macaroni, cooked
    4 hard-cooked eggs

Combine mayonnaise, pickle relish, catsup, tuna and macaroni. Dice 3 eggs; add to salad. Slice remaining egg; garnish salad. Serve chilled. Yield: 4 servings.

Georggian Rice, McKean H.S.
Wilmington, Delaware

TUNA-MACARONI SALAD

    1 c. elbow macaroni
    ¼ c. French dressing
    1 7-oz. can chunk style tuna, drained
    ½ c. diced green pepper
    ½ c. diced cucumber
    ¼ c. sliced radishes
    1 tsp. onion salt
    ⅛ tsp. pepper
    3 tbsp. lemon juice
    ¼ c. sour cream

Cook macaroni according to package directions; drain well. Toss with French dressing; refrigerate, covered, 2 to 3 hours. Add remaining ingredients. Toss. Refrigerate at least 1 hour; serve garnished with salad greens. Yield: 4 servings.

Mrs. Ella McDaniel, Granite H.S.
Granite, Oklahoma

TUNA SALAD SUPREME

1 c. macaroni
1 c. chopped, celery
1 can tuna, drained
1 can peas, drained
1 can diced drained carrots
6 tbsp. green pepper
Salt and pepper to taste
Mayonnaise
2 hard-cooked eggs, sliced

Cook macaroni in small amount of water; drain and cool. Combine all ingredients except eggs, using only enough mayonnaise to moisten. Garnish with egg slices. Yield: 8 servings.

Mrs. Pat Allen, Bath H.S.
Bath, New Brunswick, Canada

SUMMER SALAD

1 pkg. Kraft macaroni and cheese
   dinner
1 7-oz. can tuna
1 c. Thousand Island salad dressing
1 c. diced cucumber
1 c. shredded carrots
⅓ c. sliced, stuffed green olives
¼ c. chopped onion
Dash of pepper
4 green peppers

Prepare macaroni and cheese dinner according to package directions. Drain and flake tuna. Combine all ingredients except green peppers; mix lightly. Chill. Cut green peppers in half lengthwise; fill with salad. Yield: 8 servings.

Mrs. Patti Butler, Del Valle H.S.
Del Valle, Texas

MARY'S TUNA SALAD

2 c. canned chunk-style tuna or cleaned
   cooked shrimp
1 c. celery, sliced diagonally
1 tbsp. minced onion (opt.)
2 tbsp. lemon juice or vinegar
½ tsp. salt
¼ tsp. pepper
½ tsp. dry mustard
½ c. salad dressing or mayonnaise
1 tsp. Worcestershire sauce
Dash of Tabasco sauce
Salad greens

Toss all ingredients except salad greens. Serve on salad greens. Garnish with radish roses. May be served in avocado halves or on tomato slices. Yield: 6 servings.

Mrs. Juliet W. Jenkins, Mayewood Sch.
Sumter, South Carolina

MASTERPIECE TUNA SALAD

3 hard-cooked eggs
Salt
Pepper
Dry mustard
Mayonnaise
3 6½ or 7-oz. cans tuna in vegetable
   oil
1 med. head cauliflower, separated
   into flowerets
1 pt. cherry tomatoes
1 red pepper, halved and seeded
1 cucumber, sliced
Olives, ripe and green
Carrot curls
Parsley
Avocado Salad Dressing

Shell eggs; halve lengthwise. Mash yolks and season with salt, pepper and dry mustard; stir in enough mayonnaise to moisten. Refill whites. Arrange tuna in middle of platter or tray and surround with vegetables and eggs. Serve with Avocado Salad Dressing. Yield: 6 servings.

AVOCADO SALAD DRESSING:

1 lge. ripe avocado
2 tbsp. lemon juice
2 tbsp. chopped red pepper
2 tsp. minced onion
½ tsp. salt
¼ tsp. Tabasco
2 tbsp. sour cream

Peel and pit avocado; mash and sprinkle with lemon juice. Stir in remaining ingredients until well blended. Cover tightly. Chill in refrigerator until ready to serve. Serve with Masterpiece Tuna Salad. Yield: 1 cup.

Photograph for this recipe on cover.

QUICK AND EASY TUNA SALAD

1 can tuna, drained and flaked
½ c. diced celery
2 tbsp. sweet pickle relish
¼ c. mayonnaise
Lettuce

Combine tuna, celery and relish. Add mayonnaise and toss lightly. Serve on lettuce. Yield: 4-5 servings.

Anne W. Morgan, Lancaster Jr. H.S.
Lancaster, New Hampshire

QUICK TUNA SALAD

1 can tuna
2 hard-cooked eggs
¼ c. diced sweet pickles
½ c. mayonnaise

Combine all ingredients; serve on toast or in tomato half. Yield: 4-6 servings.

Janet Hethmon, Zeigler-Royalton Jr. H.S.
Royalton, Illinois

SEAFOOD SALAD

1 ½ c. tuna or shrimp
2 tsp. lemon juice
1 ½ tsp. chopped onion
1 ½ c. chopped celery
3 tbsp. chopped green pepper
¼ tsp. salt
⅓ c. mayonnaise

Drain oil or liquid from seafood; place in mixing bowl. Flake into small pieces; add lemon juice, onion, celery, green pepper, salt and mayonnaise to moisten. Toss; serve on lettuce with dressing. Yield: 6 servings.

Sammie Lee Pounds
New Site Attendance Center
New Site, Mississippi

SHOOTING STARS

5 tomatoes
1 7-oz. can flaked tuna, drained
½ c. finely sliced celery
⅓ c. mayonnaise
¼ tsp. salt
Dash of pepper
2 tbsp. green relish or green pepper
Lettuce
Paprika

Remove stem end of each tomato and make four cuts down sides, but not through bottom. Scoop out pulp; refill cavity with next 6 ingredients, which have been combined thoroughly. Place on lettuce leaf and sprinkle with paprika. Yield: 5 servings.

Mrs. Marilyn O. Duigou, Drumheller Jr. H.S.
Drumheller, Alberta, Canada

TOMATO SANDWICH SALAD

Lettuce leaf
1 tomato, sliced in thirds
2 oz. flaked tuna or cottage cheese
1 tbsp. mayonnaise
1 tsp. chopped pickle
½ stalk celery, diced
Salt and pepper to taste

Place lettuce on small plate; place 1 tomato slice on lettuce. Combine remaining ingredients; place half the mixture on tomato slice. Cover with second tomato slice; add remaining tuna mixture. Top with remaining tomato slice; garnish with parsley sprig. Chill; serve. Yield: 1 serving.

Mrs. Mabel I. Rogers, Central Jr. Secondary Sch.
Dawson Creek, British Columbia, Canada

TUNA-BANANA SALAD

1 c. sliced bananas
½ c. drained pineapple
1 7-oz. can tuna, flaked
½ c. diced celery
2 tbsp. chopped gherkins
½ tsp. salt
2 tbsp. mayonnaise or French dressing

Combine bananas and pineapple; add tuna, celery, gherkins and salt. Toss lightly with salad dressing; arrange in lettuce cups. Garnish with black olives. Yield: 4 servings.

Mrs. Mary Puchalik
MacDonald H.S.
Edmonton, Alberta, Canada

TUNA DELIGHT

1 sm. can tuna, drained and flaked
2 hard-boiled eggs
¼ c. chopped celery
2 tbsp. bell pepper
1 to 2 tbsp. sweet cubed pickles
¼ c. mayonnaise or salad dressing
Lettuce

Combine all ingredients, except lettuce and toss until coated with dressing. Heat on lettuce leaf. Yield: 4 servings.

Marie S. Welch, Lookout Jr. H.S.
Chattanooga, Tennessee

TUNA SALAD

1 12 ½-oz. can tuna
1 3-oz. pkg. cream cheese, softened
¼ c. chopped nuts
¼ c. chopped celery
1 tbsp. chopped pimento
2 tbsp. grated carrot
2 tbsp. cubed cheddar cheese
1 can chow mein noodles

Empty tuna into colander; hold under running cold water to rinse. Drain; add cream cheese, nuts, celery, pimento, carrot and cheddar cheese. Serve on chow mein noodles. Yield: 6 servings.

Mrs. Saralu C. Jenkins, Clarkston H.S.
Clarkston, Georgia

TUNA-EGG SALAD

1 sm. can tuna, drained
¼ c. salad dressing
¼ c. sweet pickle relish
2 hard-cooked eggs, chopped

Combine all ingredients; blend well. Yield: 4 servings.

Gwen Morgenstern, New Lexington H.S.
New Lexington, Ohio

Tuna Salads

TUNA SALAD

2 6½ or 7-oz. cans tuna, drained
   and flaked
1 c. diced celery
Dash of lemon juice
1 tsp. finely chopped onion
½ tsp. salt
⅛ tsp. pepper
½ c. finely chopped green pepper
½ c. sweet pickle relish
½ c. mayonnaise

Combine first 8 ingredients; add mayonnaise.
Toss until salad is evenly coated; serve on lettuce. Yield: 8 servings.

Mrs. Dolores Parks, R. B. Worthy H.S.
Saltville, Virginia

TUNA SALAD

1 6½-oz. can tuna
2 hard-cooked eggs
¼ c. chopped pickles
1 med. apple, chopped
⅓ c. salad dressing
¼ c. chopped pecans

Combine all ingredients in large bowl; chill 30
minutes. Serve on lettuce. Yield: 4 servings.

Sandra Walters, Frisco H.S.
Frisco, Texas

TUNA SALAD

2 6½ or 7-oz. cans tuna
½ c. mayonnaise or salad dressing
1 c. chopped celery
2 tbsp. chopped sweet pickle
2 tbsp. chopped onion
½ tsp. salt
Dash of pepper
Lettuce
3 hard-cooked eggs, peeled and sliced

Drain tuna; break into large pieces. Combine all
ingredients except lettuce and egg. Serve on lettuce; garnish with egg slices. Yield: 6 servings.

Alice Ann Walter, Twisp H.S.
Twisp, Washington

TUNA SALAD

1 lge. can flaked tuna
¼ c. chopped pickle
¼ c. chopped celery
1 tbsp. lemon juice
½ tsp. salt
1 tsp. minced onion (opt.)
2 hard-cooked eggs, chopped
½ c. mayonnaise

Combine all ingredients; mix well. Serve on lettuce with crackers or chips. Yield: 4 servings.

Mary B. Lewis, Gilbert H. S.
Gilbert, South Carolina

TUNA SALAD WITH PEAS

2 cans tuna
1 No. 2 can peas
2 c. diced celery
1 green pepper, diced
1 tbsp. lemon juice
1 tbsp. diced onion
1 c. mayonnaise
1 lge. can chow mein noodles

Combine all ingredients except noodles; chill.
Add noodles; serve. Yield: 8 servings.

Carol Jeckell, Slayton Pub. Sch.
Slayton, Minnesota

TUNA-TOMATO FLOWER CUPS

1 7-oz. can tuna
2 hard-cooked eggs, chopped
½ c. celery, chopped
¼ c. stuffed olives, chopped
⅓ c. sweet pickles, chopped
½ c. mayonnaise or salad dressing
Dash of salt and pepper
1 sm. clove of garlic, minced
6 med. tomatoes
Lettuce

Combine all ingredients except tomatoes and
lettuce; chill. Cut tomatoes partially through into
8 wedges; place on lettuce and spread apart
lightly. Spoon tuna mixture into center of wedges.
Yield: 6 servings.

Mrs. D. J. Dear, Stringer H.S.
Stringer, Mississippi

TUNA-TOMATO SALAD

2 6½-oz. cans chunk tuna
½ tsp. oregano
Mayonnaise
1 tsp. mustard
1 lge. dill pickle, chopped
6 lge. tomatoes
Lettuce

Drain tuna; flake into bowl. Sprinkle with oregano; add mayonnaise to moisten. Blend in
mustard and dill pickle. Arrange lettuce on plate;
cut tomatoes and spread into flowers. Place tuna
salad in tomatoes; garnish with radish roses.
Yield: 6 servings.

Darlene Heilmann, McFarland H.S.
McFarland, California

TUNA-TOMATO STARS

1 6 ½ or 7-oz. can tuna
2 hard-cooked eggs, chopped
¼ c. chopped sweet pickle
¼ c. finely chopped onion
2 tbsp. diced pimento
¼ tsp. salt
Dash of pepper
½ c. salad dressing
4 med. tomatoes

Break tuna in chunks; sprinkle with lemon juice. Combine with remaining ingredients except tomatoes; mix gently and chill. Cut tomatoes; mix gently and chill. Cut tomatoes partially through in 6 equal sections; spread apart. Fill with tuna salad; top with carrot curl. Yield: 4 servings.

Mrs. Marian Webb, O. E. Bell Jr. H.S.
Idaho Falls, Idaho

TUNA SUPREME

½ c. mayonnaise
1 tbsp. vinegar
2 tbsp. light cream
1 sm. clove of garlic, crushed
2 6 ½ or 7-oz. cans tuna, drained and chunked
1 c. sliced celery
½ c. diced green pepper
1 5-oz. can water chestnuts, sliced
⅓ c. thinly sliced green onions
¼ c. diced pimento
½ c. sliced, pitted ripe olives
1 3-oz. can Chinese noodles

Blend mayonnaise, vinegar, cream and garlic; add remaining ingredients except noodles. Toss lightly until salad is coated with dressing; chill. Add noodles; mix quickly. Serve immediately on crisp greens. Yield: 6 servings.

Mrs. Phyllis Greene McAfee
Old Rochester Regional H.S.
Mattapoisett, Massachusetts

TUNA-VEGETABLE SALAD

2 7-oz. cans tuna, drained and flaked
¼ head cubed lettuce
1 lge. cubed tomato
¼ c. chopped celery
¼ c. chopped green pepper
¼ c. chopped onion
¼ c. mayonnaise
3 boiled eggs, cubed
Salt and pepper to taste

Combine all ingredients; serve immediately. Yield: 6 servings.

Mrs. Marian Campbell, Destrehan H.S.
Destrehan, Louisiana

SHOESTRING SALAD

1 c. diced celery
1 c. shredded carrots
2 tbsp. chopped onion
½ c. mayonnaise
2 tbsp. milk (opt.)
1 c. cooked tuna, shrimp, salmon or chicken
3 to 4 c. shoestring potatoes

Combine celery, carrots, onion, mayonnaise and milk; let stand to blend. Add tuna and potatoes. Yield: 4-6 servings.

Sharon A. Anderson, Fosston H.S.
Fosston, Minnesota
Fae M. Briggs, Gary H.S.
Gary, South Dakota

VIRGINIA SALAD

1 can chunk tuna
1 8-oz. can pineapple chunks, drained
1 ½ c. diced celery
½ c. cashew nuts
¼ c. salad dressing
Salt to taste
1 can chow mein noodles

Combine first 6 ingredients; chill well. Add noodles; stir. Serve in lettuce cups. Yield: 6 servings.

Nancy M. Riley, Waterford H.S.
Waterford, Ohio

FISH IN THE OCEAN

2 envelopes unflavored gelatin
1 ¾ c. tomato juice
1 tbsp. steak sauce
¼ c. cold water
1 c. sour cream
¾ c. mayonnaise
¼ c. each diced celery, onion, green pepper
1 tbsp. diced pimento
1 tsp. each lemon rind, lemon juice
1 7 ¾-oz. can flaked salmon
1 7-oz. can flaked tuna

Add 1 envelope gelatin to tomato juice in saucepan; let stand 5 minutes. Add steak sauce; heat, stirring constantly, until gelatin is dissolved. Remove from heat and stir in remaining tomato juice. Pour into 2-quart fish-shaped mold; chill until set but still slightly sticky on surface. Add remaining gelatin to cold water in saucepan; let stand 5 minutes. Heat, stirring constantly until gelatin is dissolved; remove from heat. Cool; add all remaining ingredients, stirring lightly to blend. Place in mold on top of firm tomato layer; chill until set. Unmold on lettuce; garnish with deviled eggs. Yield: 8 servings.

Sister Anne Beaton, CNS
Mabou Consolidated Sch.
Mabou, Nova Scotia, Canada

HERBED KIDNEY BEAN AND TUNA SALAD

1 1-lb. can red kidney beans, drained
1 7½-oz. can chunk tuna fish, drained
6 to 8 anchovy fillets, quartered
1 c. sliced celery
2 tbsp. minced onion
1 sm. clove garlic, minced
¼ tsp. ground black pepper
1½ tsp. salt
1½ tsp. basil leaves
½ tsp. thyme
1 tsp. vinegar
½ c. mayonnaise
1 head Boston lettuce
6 to 8 tomato wedges

Combine all ingredients except lettuce and tomato wedges. Mix lightly to prevent breaking up tuna fish too much. Chill mixture for 1 hour. Arrange lettuce leaves on salad or luncheon plates at serving time. Spoon chilled mixture onto salad leaves; garnish with tomato wedges. Yield: 6-8 servings.

Ursula Wagner, Lakeshore Jr. H.S.
Shreveport, Louisiana

TUNA AND SALMON MOLD

2 envelopes unflavored gelatin
1 tbsp. steak sauce
1¾ c. canned tomato juice
Water
¾ c. mayonnaise
1 c. dairy sour cream
1 tsp. grated lemon rind
⅓ c. chopped stuffed olives
1 green onion, chopped
1½ c. diced celery
1 7-oz. can each salmon and tuna
Salt and pepper to taste
Fresh dill
Lemon wedge
Paprika

Mix 1 envelope of gelatin with steak sauce and 3/4 cup of tomato juice; heat, stirring to dissolve gelatin. Add remaining tomato juice; remaining gelatin in 1/2 cup water; dissolve over hot water. Stir in mayonnaise and sour cream; add lemon rind, olives, onion, celery, salmon and tuna. Season to taste with dill and lemon wedges generously sprinkled with paprika. Yield: 6 servings.

Carol Nisson, Park Sr. H.S.
St. Paul Park, Minnesota

SALADE NICOISE

½ c. olive oil
¼ c. salad oil
¾ c. red-wine vinegar
1 tsp. sugar
¾ tsp. salt
¼ tsp. cracked pepper
1 lb. fresh green beans, trimmed
    and washed or 2 9-oz. pkg. frozen
    whole green beans

1 med. red onion, thinly sliced
2 med. tomatoes, cut in wedges
½ c. pitted ripe olives
1 2-oz. cans anchovy fillets
2 7-oz. cans solid pack tuna, drained
    and broken into chunks
2 hard-cooked eggs, sliced

Combine oils, vinegar, sugar, salt and pepper in jar with tight-fitting lid; shake vigorously until ingredients are well combined. Cook beans in small amount of boiling salted water, covered, 17 to 20 minutes or just until tender; drain well. Turn into shallow dish; add 1/2 cup dressing mixture, tossing until beans are well coated. Refrigerate beans, covered. Refrigerate remaining dressing and salad ingredients until well chilled, at least 2 hours. Turn beans into salad bowl. Add all except a few onion slices, tomato wedges, olives and anchovy fillets; toss gently. Add tuna and eggs; toss again. Garnish with reserved onion, tomato, olives and anchovy. Drizzle remaining dressing over all. Yield: 6 servings.

Mrs. Lucille Murray, Power H.S.
Power, Montana

ARTICHOKE-CRAB SALAD

1 c. cooked crab
1 c. cooked artichoke
1 tbsp. chopped chives
1 tbsp. chopped parsley
½ c. heavy cream, whipped
½ tsp. celery seed
Salt and black pepper
2 tbsp. lemon juice
½ c. mayonnaise

Combine all ingredients except mayonnaise and lemon juice. Combine mayonnaise and lemon juice. Fold both mixtures together. Chill. Yield: 6 servings.

Mrs. Anne Beatty Ransing, Ada Merritt Jr. H.S.
Miami, Florida

CRAB MEAT IMPERIAL

1 clove of garlic, cut
2 c. frozen or canned crab meat, cooked
    and flaked
Celery
1 c. finely chopped green pepper
1 tsp. grated onion
¼ c. French dressing
½ tsp. curry powder
1 c. mayonnaise
Capers
Hard-boiled egg wedges

Rub bowl with garlic. Combine crab meat, celery, green pepper, onion and French dressing. Marinate. Remove from marinade 1 hour before serving. Add curry to mayonnaise; toss with crab meat mixture. Garnish with capers and egg wedges. Yield: 8 servings.

Lucille S. Pantel, Fallsburgh Central Sch.
Fallsburgh, New York

CRAB SALAD

1 lb. crab meat
1 c. celery
2 tbsp. chopped pickle
2 hard-cooked eggs, chopped fine
½ c. mayonnaise
Salt and pepper to taste

Combine all ingredients, mixing well. Chill. Serve on lettuce leaf with crackers. Yield: 6 servings.

Mrs. Martha B. Godwin, Windsor H.S.
Windsor, Virginia

CRAB LUNCHEON SALAD

1 7½-oz. can crab meat, well-drained
    and flaked
½ c. sliced celery
2 tbsp. sliced ripe olives
1 tbsp. sliced green onion
1 med. Persian melon or 2 small
    cantaloupes, well chilled
¼ tsp. monosodium glutamate
Dash of pepper
½ c. mayonnaise or salad dressing
3 hard-boiled eggs, sliced

Combine crab meat, celery, olives, onion, salt, monosodium glutamate and pepper. Fold in mayonnaise and 2 eggs. Chill. Remove top third of melon using sawtooth cut. Remove seeds. Loosen meat from rind using grapefruit knife or large sharp-edged spoon. Slice melon meat into sections for serving with salad. Sprinkle inside of melon with lemon juice; fill with crab salad. Garnish with egg slices. Yield: 4 servings.

Cora Elizabeth Fairbanks
Rockport Jr.-Sr. H.S.
Rockport, Massachusetts

CRAB AND CHEESE MOLD

1 tbsp. gelatin
¼ c. cold water
1 can tomato soup
1 c. cottage cheese
½ c. mayonnaise
½ c. cream, whipped
⅓ c. chopped green pepper
⅓ c. chopped celery
⅓ c. chopped onion
1 sm. cucumber, diced
1 c. crab meat

Soak gelatin in cold water. Heat soup; dissolve gelatin in soup. Beat in cottage cheese. Cool. Fold in remaining ingredients. Place in wet ring-mold or individual molds. Chill until set. Serve on lettuce with mayonnaise. Yield: 10-12 servings.

Mrs. Mary M. Lund, Arlington Jr. H.S.
Arlington, Washington

CRAB-TOMATO ROSES

1 lb. crab meat, regular or back fin
1 c. chopped celery
1 tbsp. minced onion
¼ c. chopped green pepper
Juice of ½ lemon
1 tsp. salt
½ tsp. pepper
½ c. (about) mayonnaise
1 tbsp. prepared mustard
4 to 6 tomatoes

Combine crab meat, celery, onion and green pepper in bowl. Sprinkle with lemon juice. Season with salt and pepper. Mix mayonnaise with mustard; add to salad mixture. Toss lightly. Refrigerate. Prepare tomatoes by cutting partially through from top to stem end into 8 sections. Pull sections down in petal formation. Arrange on lettuce or greens. Fill with crab salad. Top with pepper ring or egg slice. Tuna, shrimp or chicken may be substituted. If chicken is used, eliminate lemon juice and add 1/2 chopped pickle. Yield: 4-6 servings.

Mrs. Dorothy A. Foster, Mathews H.S.
Mathews, Virginia

CRAB-LEMON JELL-O

2 pkg. lemon Jell-O
4 c. tomato juice, heated
1 tsp. horseradish
1 tbsp. lemon juice
1 can crab meat
1 avocado, diced

Dissolve Jell-O in tomato juice. Add horseradish and lemon juice. Chill until slightly thickened. Fold in crab meat and avocado. Yield: 10 servings.

Freda H. Montgomery, Central Union H.S.
Fresno, California

CRAB MEAT SALAD

2 tbsp. unflavored gelatin
¼ c. cold water
2 3-oz. pkg. cream cheese
1 can cream of mushroom soup
1 c. mayonnaise
1 sm. grated onion
1 tbsp. Worcestershire sauce
½ tsp. salt
1 c. crab meat
1 c. chopped celery
1 can cranberry sauce, 1 can ripe
    olives for garnish, if desired

Soften gelatin in cold water. Combine remaining ingredients in double boiler over hot water. Heat. Add gelatin; stir until dissolved. Mold. Chill. Yield: 4 servings.

Mrs. Maurine M. Perkins, Lake Arthur H.S.
Lake Arthur, Louisiana

DUAL TONE CRAB SALAD
MOUSSE:

1 6 ½-oz. can crab meat, drained
1 tbsp. gelatin
¼ c. cold milk
¼ c. hot milk
1 ½ tsp. grated onion
¼ tsp. salt
1 c. whipping cream, whipped

Separate crab meat. Soften gelatin in cold milk; dissolve in hot milk. Chill until partially set. Beat until foamy. Add crab meat, grated onion and salt; mix thoroughly. Fold in whipped cream. Pour into individual molds, filling two-thirds full or use 6-cup mold. Chill.

ASPIC:

1 tbsp. gelatin
½ c. cold tomato juice
1 ½ c. hot tomato juice
¼ tsp. salt
½ c. chopped celery
2 tsp. vinegar

Soften gelatin in cold tomato juice; dissolve in hot tomato juice. Add salt. Chill until partially set. Stir in celery and vinegar, mixing well. Pour over firm mousse; continue chilling until firmly set. Unmold on crisp lettuce. Garnish with cucumber slices. Serve with Thousand Island dressing. Yield: 6 servings.

Helen Krueger, Prince Rupert Sr. Sec. Sch.
Prince Rupert, British Columbia, Canada

MOLDED CRAB MEAT SALAD

2 c. crab meat
1 envelope gelatin
½ c. cold water
½ c. boiling water
2 tbsp. sweet pickle, finely chopped
½ c. celery, finely chopped
⅓ c. vinegar
½ c. mayonnaise
½ c. catsup

Remove cartilage from crab meat. Soften gelatin in cold water. Add boiling water, stirring until gelatin is dissolved. Add remaining ingredients. Season to taste. Mix well. Pour into individual molds or large mold rinsed with cold water. Chill until firm. Unmold on bed of crisp lettuce. Garnish with ripe olives, deviled eggs and tomato slices. Yield: 4-6 servings.

Mrs. Thelma M. Ash, George Wythe Jr. H.S.
Hampton, Virginia

TOMATO ASPIC-
CRAB MEAT SALAD

1 pkg. lemon-flavored gelatin
1 ⅔ c. tomato juice
¼ c. vinegar
1 tsp. onion juice

⅛ tsp. white pepper
⅛ tsp. cloves
½ tsp. salt
¼ tsp. paprika
1 c. crab meat
¾ c. diced celery
¼ c. sliced ripe olives

Dissolve gelatin in hot tomato juice; add vinegar and remaining seasonings. Cool until gelatin is consistency of unbeaten egg white. Add crab meat, celery and olives. Pour into individual molds and chill. Unmold on lettuce and garnish with small amount mayonnaise, if desired. Yield: 6-8 servings.

Mrs. B. W. Canfield, Lompoc Sr. H.S.
Lompoc, California

DOCTOR ZIEMER'S
CRAB MEAT SALAD

1 c. stuffed Spanish olives, finely chopped
1 c. sweet pickles, finely chopped
1 c. mayonnaise
1 lb. crab meat
3 lge. tomatoes, halved

Combine olives, pickles and mayonnaise. Fold in crab meat. Serve on tomato halves. Yield: 6 servings.

Mrs. Dorothy Z. Norton, Midland Jr.-Sr. H.S.
Midland, Pennsylvania

HOT CRAB MEAT AVOCADO

1 7 ½-oz. can crab meat, drained
⅓ c. chopped celery
3 hard-boiled eggs, chopped
2 tbsp. chopped pimento
1 tbsp. chopped onion
Salt
½ c. mayonnaise
3 or 4 unpeeled avocados, halved lenthwise
Lemon juice
3 tbsp. dry bread crumbs
1 tsp. butter, melted
2 tbsp. slivered almonds

Heat oven to 400 degrees. Mix crab meat, celery, eggs, pimento, onion, 1/2 teaspoon salt and mayonnaise. Brush cut surfaces of avocados with lemon juice and sprinkle with salt; fill with crab meat mixture. Toss bread crumbs with butter; spoon over crab meat mixture. Place in shallow baking dish. Bake, uncovered, 10 minutes. Sprinkle almonds over crumb topping. Bake 5 minutes longer or until filling is hot and bubbly. Serve at once. Yield: 6-8 servings.

Ruth Torpey, Sewanhaka H.S.
Floral Park, New York

FLANKED CRAB SALAD

1 8-oz. can crab meat, flaked or 1 c. chilled, cooked, fresh crab meat, flaked
2 med. diced, fresh tomatoes
¾ c. diced celery
½ tsp. ground marjoram
⅛ tsp. instant garlic powder
⅛ tsp. ground black pepper or ¼ tsp. lemon pepper
1 ¼ tsp. salt
2 tsp. sugar
1 tbsp. salad oil
1 tbsp. cider vinegar
2 tbsp. mayonnaise

Place crab meat in bowl. Combine with tomatoes and celery. Blend marjoram, garlic powder, pepper, salt and sugar; sprinkle over salad mixture. Combine salad oil, vinegar and mayonnaise. Pour over salad; toss lightly. Serve on bed of head lettuce. Yield: 5 servings.

Sister May Albertus, S.S.N.D., Tyler Cath. H.S.
Tyler, Texas

HOT CRAB MEAT SALAD

½ c. butter
⅔ c. sifted flour
2 ⅔ c. milk
2 c. flaked crab meat
1 lge. stalk celery, diced
⅓ green pepper, minced
1 lge. pimento, minced
⅓ c. blanched almonds, quartered
4 hard-boiled eggs, cut-up
2 tsp. salt
Bread crumbs

Combine all ingredients. Pour into buttered 12 x 7 1/2 x 2-inch baking dish. Sprinkle with buttered, fine, dry bread crumbs. Bake at 350 degrees for 35 minutes. Serve hot placed in crisp lettuce cups topped with chopped sweet pickles and mayonnaise. Yield: 8 servings.

Virginia Stewart, Spanish Fork H.S.
Spanish Fork, Utah

HOT CRAB MEAT SALAD

2 c. flaked, cooked crab meat
1 c. chopped celery
⅓ green pepper, chopped
1 lge. pimento, chopped
⅓ c. chopped blanched almonds
¼ c. mild vinegar
¼ c. butter
½ c. flour
1 tsp. dry mustard
⅛ tsp. paprika
1 tsp. salt
1 c. milk
2 egg yolks, slightly beaten

Marinate crab meat, celery, green pepper, pimento and almonds in vinegar for 2 hours. Heat oven to 425 degrees. Melt butter in saucepan. Blend in flour, mustard, paprika and salt. Cook over low heat until mixture is smooth and bubbly. Remove from heat; stir in milk. Bring to boil; boil 1 minute, stirring constantly. Remove from heat. Stir into egg yolks. Combine with marinated ingredients. Pile lightly into 8 individual baking dishes or an oblong baking dish, 12 x 8-inch. Bake 12 to 15 minutes or until bubbly. Yield: 8 servings.

Mrs. Deborah Longbothum, Mifflinburg H.S.
Mifflinburg, Pennsylvania

ISLAND DELIGHT

4 pineapples
1 lb. cooked lobster meat
1 tsp. lemon juice
⅛ tsp. salt
¼ tsp. pepper
½ tsp. curry powder
¼ tsp. Beau Monde
¼ c. diced celery
¼ c. sour cream
¼ c. mayonnaise
1 avocado

Halve pineapples; scoop out centers and reserve for other dishes. Mix lobster, lemon juice, salt, pepper, curry powder and Beau Monde; add celery, sour cream and mayonnaise. Fill pineapple shells. Peel avocado; slice lengthwise. Arrange crescent slices of avocado on top of lobster mixture. Serve with tart dressing. Yield: 4 servings.

Mrs. Deborah O. Rice, Horace Greeley H.S.
Chappaqua, New York

SOUTH AFRICAN SALAD

6 4-oz. South African rock lobster tails
2 lb. potatoes
½ c. diced onion
1 tsp. salt
¼ tsp. white pepper
1 ½ c. mayonnaise
¼ c. heavy cream

Drop frozen lobster tails into boiling salted water. When water reboils, lower heat and simmer 5 minutes. Drain immediately and drench with cold water. Cut away thin underside membrane and remove meat from shells. Chill. Boil potatoes; drain and peel. While still warm, cut in cubes in bottom of large bowl. Add onion, salt and pepper immediately. Mix mayonnaise with cream until smooth. Pour over potatoes and onions and leave in a thick top layer. Cool, then chill. At serving time, cut chilled lobster into bite-sized pieces; add to potato bowl and toss together until all ingredients are well blended. Yield: 6 servings.

Photograph for this recipe on page 323.

SCALLOP SALAD

    ¾ lb. cooked scallops, chopped and
        chilled
    3 tbsp. chopped onion
    ½ c. chopped celery
    ½ c. chopped cucumber
    ⅓ c. sliced radishes
    ½ c. French dressing
    ½ tsp. salt
    Dash of pepper
    Lettuce
    Tomato wedges

Combine all ingredients except lettuce and tomatoes. Serve on lettuce. Garnish with tomato
wedges. Yield: 6 servings.

N. Young, McNicoll Park Jr. Sec. Sch.
Penticton, British Columbia, Canada

CHICK-PEA SALAD

    2 tbsp. corn oil
    2 c. canned shrimp
    4 tbsp. lemon juice
    2 c. cooked chick-peas
    2 tbsp. grated onion
    ½ c. chopped celery
    ¼ c. diced pimento
    1 tsp. salt
    Dash of pepper
    ½ tsp. monosodium glutamate
    ¾ c. salad dressing
    Salad greens

Heat oil in skillet. Toss shrimp in oil for 2 minutes; drain on absorbent paper. Sprinkle with
lemon juice; chill. Toss chick-peas in hot oil for
3 minutes. Remove and cool. Combine next 7
ingredients with chick-peas. Serve on crisp salad
greens with shrimp. Yield: 6-8 servings.

Mrs. H. Singh, Revelstoke Sec. Sch.
Revelstoke, British Columbia, Canada

AVOCADO GELATIN
WITH SHRIMP DRESSING

    3 lge. avocados, mashed
    1 pkg. lime gelatin
    1 pkg. lemon gelatin
    ½ tsp. salt
    2 tbsp. grated onion
    1 tbsp. grated green pepper
    ¾ c. mayonnaise

Prepare gelatins with 2 cups boiling water and 1
cup cold water. Add avocados to gelatin. Add remaining ingredients; chill until firm.

SHRIMP DRESSING:

    1 c. sour cream
    2 tbsp. Worcestershire sauce
    1 tbsp. lemon juice
    1 tbsp. grated onion

    Dash of Tabasco sauce
    1 tsp. salt
    ½ lb. shrimp, cleaned, cooked and halved

Mix all ingredients together. Serve with avocado.
Yield: 4-6 Servings.

Elynore J. Wilson, Calumet H.S.
Chicago, Illinois

BARBECUE SALAD

    1 pkg. lemon or orange Jell-O
    1 ¼ c. hot water
    1 8-oz. can tomato sauce
    1 ½ tbsp. vinegar
    ½ tsp. salt
    Dash of pepper
    Salad greens
    Cold cooked shrimp

Dissolve Jell-O in hot water. Add remaining ingredients except salad greens and shrimp.
Blend. Pour into individual molds. Chill until
firm. Unmold and serve on crisp salad greens.
Place shrimp around Jell-O. Quartered hard-
cooked eggs may be placed on lettuce, if desired.
Yield: 4-6 servings.

Mrs. Beverly A. Reed, Stamford Cen. Sch.
Stamford, New York

CORAL AND JADE SALAD

    2 pkg. lime Jell-O
    3 c. boiling water
    1 ½ lb. cottage cheese
    1 tbsp. minced onion
    1 tbsp. plus 1 tsp. lemon juice
    ¼ c. horseradish
    2 tbsp. mayonnaise
    1 ½ c. cooked shrimp
    1 c. diced celery
    Salt and pepper to taste
    Thousand Island dressing to taste

Dissolve Jell-O in boiling water; chill. Beat
with rotary beater until light. Stir in cottage
cheese, onion, 1 tablespoon lemon juice, horseradish and mayonnaise. Pour into ring mold,
rinsed in cold water. Chill until set. Combine
remaining ingredients. Turn mold onto serving
plate; fill center with shrimp salad. Garnish
with lemon, sliced cucumbers, whole shrimp
and greens. Yield: 12 servings.

Margaret W. Clanton, Drewry Mason H.S.
Ridgeway, Virginia

IN THE PINK SHRIMP SALAD

    1 can frozen condensed cream of
        shrimp soup
    1 3-oz. pkg. cream cheese

344

(Continued on next page)

1 envelope unflavored gelatin
½ c. cold water
1 c. chopped celery
¼ c. sliced stuffed olives
¼ c. toasted almonds

Thaw soup completely; blend with cream cheese. Soften gelatin in cold water. Set gelatin in pan of hot water until mixture is dissolved. Blend soup, celery and remaining ingredients. Pour into greased molds. Chill until firm. Unmold and serve on crisp salad greens. Yield: 4-6 servings.

Mrs. Georgia Waters Scott, Clarksville H.S.
Clarksville, Texas

2 tsp. prepared horseradish
2 tsp. Worcestershire sauce
1 tsp. salt
½ tsp. celery salt
1 7-oz. bottle Seven-Up
1 lb. cooked shrimp

Soften gelatin in water. Add bouillon cube. Heat tomato juice to boiling; stir into gelatin until dissolved. Add horseradish, Worcestershire sauce, salt and celery salt. Cool slightly. Add 7-Up; pour half the mixture into 2-quart mold. Place in refrigerator until firm, arranging shrimp on top; add remaining mixture. Chill until firm. Garnish with shrimp. Yield: 8-10 servings.

Sister Rose Marie, Sacred Heart H.S.
East Grand Forks, Minnesota

SENATE SALAD

1 pkg. plain gelatin
¼ c. water
1 c. hot water
1 tsp. salt
½ tsp. garlic salt
⅛ tsp. pepper
¼ c. lemon juice
¾ c. cooked shrimp
1 9-oz. pkg. frozen artichoke hearts
1 grapefruit, sectioned
2 tomatoes, cut into wedges
½ c. sliced ripe olives
3 qt. salad greens
Creamy Blue Cheese Dressing

Soften gelatin in cold water; dissolve in hot water. Add salt, garlic salt, pepper and lemon juice. Pour into 8 x 4-inch loaf pan; chill until slightly thickened. Set shrimp in thickened gelatin about 1/4-inch apart. Chill until firm. Cut into 1-inch squares. Cook artichoke hearts as directed on package; drain and chill. Layer remaining salad ingredients in serving bowl; add artichoke hearts and arrange shrimp squares on top. Serve with Creamy Blue Cheese Dressing.

CREAMY BLUE CHEESE DRESSING:

1 envelope garlic dressing mix
½ c. sour cream
¼ c. chopped sm. green onions, stems and bulbs
½ c. crumbled blue cheese

Prepare garlic dressing mix as directed on envelope. Gradually add sour cream, onions and bleu cheese. Mix well. Yield: 12 servings.

Mrs. Mary Westfoll, Colusa H.S.
Colusa, California

SHRIMP ASPIC RING

2 pkg. unflavored gelatin
½ c. water
1 cube beef bouillon
2 c. tomato juice

SHRIMP-CHILI MOLD

1 envelope unflavored gelatin
1 ½ tbsp. sugar
½ tsp. salt
¼ tsp. black pepper
1 ¼ c. water
¼ c. lemon juice
¼ c. chili sauce
2 c. chopped cooked shrimp
2 tbsp. sweet pickle relish

Mix gelatin, sugar, salt and pepper thoroughly in small saucepan. Add water. Place over low heat, stirring constantly until gelatin is dissolved. Remove from heat and stir in lemon juice and chili sauce. Chill to unbeaten egg white consistency. Fold in shrimp and pickle relish. Turn into 3-cup mold and chill until firm. Unmold on serving platter and garnish with salad greens. Yield: 6 servings.

Mrs. Eris Terry, San Perlita H.S.
San Perlita, Texas

SHRIMP SALAD

1 3-oz. pkg. lemon Jell-O
1 c. boiling water
½ c. chili sauce
1 tbsp. vinegar
2 tsp. horseradish
2 tsp. Worcestershire sauce
Dash of Tabasco
1 sm. can shrimp
Diced celery
Diced cucumber

Dissolve Jell-O in boiling water. Add chili sauce, vinegar, horseradish, Worcestershire sauce and Tabasco. Chill. Add shrimp, celery and cucumber. Chill until set. Yield: 4 servings.

Mrs. Katherine DeKay, Alameda Jr. H.S.
Pocatello, Idaho

SHRIMP-TOMATO ASPIC

1 pkg. lemon-flavored gelatin
1 c. hot water
1 6-oz. can tomato sauce
1 sm. can shrimp or 1 c. leftover
  diced meat
¾ c. diced celery
¼ c. diced green onions

Dissolve gelatin in hot water. Stir until gelatin is completely dissolved. Add the tomato sauce; set aside until mixture begins to gel. Add remaining ingredients all at once and refrigerate. Yield: 4-6 servings.

Mrs. Kay Powers, Foothill H.S.
Bakersfield, California

SHRIMP-TOMATO MOLD

1 envelope unflavored gelatin
½ c. cold V-8 juice
1¼ c. hot V-8 juice
½ tsp. salt
1 tsp. horseradish
1 tbsp. lemon juice
½ c. diced celery
2 tbsp. diced green pepper
1 c. cooked or canned shrimp

Soften gelatin in cold V-8 juice. Add hot V-8 juice and stir until dissolved. Add salt, horseradish and lemon juice. Chill until consistency of unbeaten egg whites. Stir in remaining ingredients. Chill until firm. Unmold on lettuce; garnish with mayonnaise and parsley. Yield: 6 servings.

Mrs. Helen J. Watson, Lakeview H.S.
Winter Garden, Florida

TOMATO-SHRIMP
SUPPER SALAD

2 envelopes unflavored gelatin
½ c. cold water
2 1-lb. cans stewed tomatoes, cut into
  lge. pieces
2 tbsp. vinegar
1 tbsp. horseradish
½ tsp. salt
1 4½-oz. can med. shrimp, deveined
Salad greens
2 17-oz. cans peas, drained, (opt.)
Sliced cucumbers (opt.)

Soften gelatin in cold water. Combine tomatoes, vinegar, horseradish and salt. Heat to boiling. Add gelatin; stir until dissolved. Cool. Arrange shrimp around bottom of ring mold. Carefully pour in tomato mixture. Chill for 4 hours. Unmold on greens; fill center with peas. Garnish with cucumber slices. Yield: 6-8 servings.

Mary Jane Bertrand, Blackfoot H.S.
Blackfoot, Idaho

TOMATO ASPIC SALAD

2 pkg. gelatin
½ c. water
2 c. tomato juice
1 tsp. Worcestershire sauce
Dash of Tabasco sauce
1 tsp. lemon juice
¼ c. chopped onion
¼ c. chopped celery
¼ c. chopped green pepper (opt.)
1 can shrimp

Soften gelatin in water. Add remaining liquid ingredients except lemon juice. Bring to a boil. Cool. Add lemon juice; stir. Refrigerate until partially set. Add vegetables and shrimp. Pour into lightly oiled mold. Chill until set. Yield: 6 servings.

Reynola Pakusich, Sedro Woolley H.S.
Sedro Woolley, Washington

TOMATO-SHRIMP SALAD

2 cans tomato soup
1 c. water
2 pkg. lemon Jell-O
1 can shrimp, drained
1 green pepper, chopped
1 c. celery, chopped

Heat tomato soup and water to boiling point; add Jell-O. Chill until slightly thickened. Add shrimp, green pepper and celery. Pour into mold and let set. Yield: 8 servings.

Mrs. Delia McClurg, Merino H.S.
Merino, Colorado

TOMATO ASPIC WITH SHRIMP

1 pkg. lemon gelatin
1 c. hot water
1 can condensed tomato soup
2 tbsp. vinegar
1 tbsp. minced onion
1 tbsp. prepared horseradish
1 4½ or 5-oz. can shrimp, drained

(Continued on next page)

Dissolve gelatin in hot water. Stir in soup, vinegar, onion and horseradish. Let chill until partially thickened. Pour small amount gelatin into mold; tilt to coat. Arrange part of shrimp in mold to make pattern. Chill quickly until firm. Combine remaining shrimp with remaining gelatin mixture; pour into mold. Chill until firm. Unmold on lettuce. Serve with mayonnaise or cucumber-sour cream sauce. Yield: 6-8 servings.

Mrs. Ann Hohman, Juniata Valley H.S.
Alexandria, Pennsylvania

CURRIED SHRIMP SALAD

1 c. cooked shrimp
1 c. cooked shell macaroni
½ c. diced red apple
¼ c. chopped celery
2 tbsp. chopped sweet pickle
½ tsp. curry powder
Salt and pepper to taste
¼ c. mayonnaise
Lettuce cups

Combine shrimp, macaroni, apple, celery and pickle. Add curry, salt and pepper to mayonnaise. Combine with shrimp mixture. Marinate for 1 hour or longer. Serve on lettuce cups. Yield: 4 servings.

H. M. Campbell, Esquiimalt Jr. Sec. Sch.
Victoria, British Columbia, Canada

MAIN DISH SHRIMP SALAD

2 c. cold cooked macaroni
2 cans shrimp, drained
2 hard-cooked eggs, chopped
1 c. cold cooked peas
¼ c. chopped green pepper
2 tbsp. chopped pimento
1 tbsp. chopped onion
¼ c. chopped ripe olives
Salad dressing
Salt and pepper to taste
Lettuce leaves
1 sliced hard-cooked egg

Combine macaroni, shrimp, chopped eggs, peas, green pepper, pimento, onion and olives. Moisten with salad dressing; season. Serve on lettuce leaves. Garnish with egg slices and tomato quarters. Yield: 8 servings.

Mary H. Dyke, Gardiner Area H.S.
Gardiner, Maine

SHRIMP AND ELBOW MACARONI

4 lb. shrimp, steamed in salted water
for 15 minutes

3 lb. elbow macaroni, cooked, drained
and iced
1 onion, chopped fine
1 bunch celery, chopped fine
1 med. jar mayonnaise
Catsup to taste

Chill shrimp. Mix with macaroni, onion and celery. Add dressing made with mayonnaise and catsup. Yield: 6 servings.

Mrs. Louise E. Keller, Rabun Co. H.S.
Clayton, Georgia

QUICK SHRIMP SALAD

2 c. chopped boiled shrimp
2 hard-cooked eggs, chopped
¼ c. chopped sweet pickle
1 tbsp. minced green onion
1 tsp. mustard
⅓ c. mayonnaise
1¼ c. chopped celery
¼ c. chopped bell pepper (opt.)

Mix all ingredients together lightly. Season to taste. Yield: 4 servings.

Mrs. Gerald Richard, Grand Lake H.S.
Lake Charles, Louisiana

SHOESTRING SALAD

½ head lettuce
1 carrot, grated
2 stalks celery, diced
1 tbsp. grated onion or 2 or 3 fresh
green onions, cut up
1 can shrimp, drained and rinsed in
cold water
2 tbsp. salad dressing
1 pkg. or can shoestring potatoes

Combine first 5 ingredients. Toss with salad dressing; add potatoes and toss lightly. Additional lettuce may be added to serve more. Yield: 6-8 servings.

Mrs. Helen A. Alberda, Manhattan H.S.
Manhattan, Montana

SHRIMP APPETIZER SALAD

16 8-oz. glasses ready-to-serve
shrimp cocktail
12 c. finely shredded lettuce
1 c. salad dressing
4 tbsp. sweet pickle relish

Drain juice from shrimp. Place lettuce into 16 serving dishes; spoon shrimp on top of lettuce. Blend salad dressing and relish. Serve separately to spoon over shrimp. Reserve any remaining cocktail juice to season stew or use in sandwich spread. Yield: 16 servings.

Judith Dickson, Simonds Jr. H.W.
Saint John, New Brunswick, Canada

GREEN GODDESS SALAD

½ head romaine
1 bunch leaf lettuce
1 c. cooked cleaned shrimp
1 stalk French endive, sliced
3 med. tomatoes, chopped
½ c. julienne-style cooked beets, drained and chilled
½ c. Green Goddess dressing

Break up romaine and leaf lettuce into bite-sized pieces. Place on 6 to 8 salad plates. Arrange chilled shrimp, endive, tomatoes and beets on top. Spoon dressing over mixture. Yield: 6-8 servings.

Mrs. Ruby R. Helm, North Clay H.S.
Louisville, Illinois

SHRIMP COCKTAIL SALAD

Lettuce
¾ lb. cooked shrimp
Cocktail sauce
Lemon wedges

Arrange lettuce leaves in cocktail glasses. Place shrimp on lettuce; cover with cocktail sauce. Garnish with lemon wedges. Yield: 6 servings.

Alice Ann Walter, Twisp H.S.
Twisp, Washington

SHRIMP SALAD

1 c. chopped shrimp, crab meat or tuna
1 c. diced celery
1 c. lettuce hearts, cut into sm. pieces
1 tsp. lemon juice
1 tsp. finely minced onion
Salt and paprika to taste
Mayonnaise

Mix all ingredients except mayonnaise lightly. Chill thoroughly. Drain and toss together with enough mayonnaise to moisten just before serving. Serve on crisp lettuce. Garnish with tomato sections, lemon wedges, hard-cooked egg slices and ripe olives. Yield: 4 servings.

Riette Godbout, Ecole Secondaire Vanier
New Brunswick, Canada

SHRIMP SALAD

1 lb. shrimp, cooked and diced
2 stalks celery, cut fine
1 sm. white onion, minced
2 hard-boiled eggs, diced
2 tbsp. lemon juice
Salt and pepper to taste
⅓ c. mayonnaise

Combine all ingredients. Mix well. Serve in lettuce cups. Yield: 6 servings.

Jeannette Reynolds, Crowville H.S.
Crowville, Louisiana

SHRIMP SALAD CRUNCH

2 cans shrimp
1 c. cut-up celery
1 c. slivered raw carrots
1 tsp. diced onion
1 c. mayonnaise
1 sm. can shoestring potatoes, crumbled

Mix shrimp, celery, carrots, onion and mayonnaise together. Refrigerate for 2 hours. Add potatoes to serve. Salad may be stretched by adding 2 cups cooked macaroni shells. Yield: 6 servings.

Mrs. Margaret Morgan, Austin H.S.
Austin, Minnesota

SHRIMP SALAD DELUXE

1 7-oz. can shoestring potatoes
1 4½-oz. can shrimp
¼ c. onion, chopped
1 c. raw carrots, grated or cut into strips
1 c. celery, cut fine

Mix all ingredients together. Moisten with salad dressing just before serving. Yield: 8 servings.

Mrs. Karen Williams, Perham H.S.
Perham, Minnesota

SHRIMP SALAD SUPREME

1 lb. shrimp, boiled, cleaned and chopped
½ c. celery, diced
¼ c. olives, chopped
¼ c. pickles, chopped
¼ c. green pepper, chopped
2 tbsp. pimento, chopped
2 hard-cooked eggs, chopped
2 tbsp. onions, chopped
½ c. mayonnaise
Salt and pepper to taste
4 lettuce cups
Potato chips
Small sweet cucumber pickles
Tomato wedges
Whole shrimp

Combine chopped shrimp, celery, olives, pickles, green peppers, pimento, eggs, onions, mayonnaise, salt and pepper. Toss lightly. Arrange in lettuce cups. Garnish with potato chips, whole cucumber pickles, tomato wedges and whole shrimp. Yield: 4 servings.

Shirley Ann Boddie, Calvin H.S.
Calvin, Louisiana

SHRIMP AND TOMATO SALAD

5 ¾-oz. can wet-pack shrimp, cleaned
1 firm head lettuce
2 hard-cooked eggs, sliced
½ med. cucumber, pared and sliced
¼ c. finely chopped celery
¼ c. finely chopped green pepper
2 lge. or 4 sm. tomatoes, quartered
French Dressing

Wash shrimp quickly in cold water. Cut lettuce into 4 crosswise slices; arrange on salad plates. Combine shrimp, eggs, cucumber, celery and green pepper. Heap lightly onto lettuce. Garnish with tomato wedges. Pour dressing over salads. Serve immediately. Three-fourths pound fresh, cooked, cleaned shrimp may be substituted for canned. Yield: 4 servings.

Lois Clarchick, Plum Sr. H.S.
Pittsburgh, Pennsylvania

BAKED SEAFOOD SALAD

¾ lb. cooked cleaned shrimp
1 c. flaked fresh or canned crab meat
½ c. chopped green pepper
¼ c. minced onion
1 c. sliced celery
1 c. mayonnaise
1 tsp. Worcestershire sauce
½ tsp. salt
¼ tsp. pepper
½ c. fresh bread crumbs
1 tbsp. melted butter

Heat oven to 350 degrees. Split shrimp lengthwise; add crab meat, green pepper, onion, celery, mayonnaise, Worcestershire sauce, salt and pepper. Spread in 8-inch square casserole. Toss crumbs with butter; sprinkle over salad. Bake, uncovered, 30 minutes or until brown. Garnish with parsley and lemon sections. Yield: 4 servings.

Mrs. Dorothy M. Hardin, Lebanon Comm. H.S.
Lebanon, Illinois

BAKED SEAFOOD SALAD

1 c. cooked crab meat
1 c. cooked shrimp
¾ c. finely chopped green pepper
¼ c. finely chopped onion
1 c. celery
1 c. mayonnaise
1 tsp. Worcestershire sauce
¼ c. butter, melted
½ c. toasted bread crumbs

Flake crab meat; combine crab meat and shrimp. Add green pepper, onion and celery to crab meat and shrimp. Add mayonnaise and Worcestershire sauce; mix well. Place on seafood shells or in buttered 1 1/2-quart casserole; cover with melted butter and sprinkle with toasted crumbs.

Bake at 350 degrees for 35 to 40 minutes. Yield: 6-8 Servings.

Elizabeth Barush, Brockport H.S.
Brockport, New York

BAKED SEAFOOD SALAD

1 10 or 12-oz. pkg. frozen peeled, deveined shrimp
1 6 ½-oz. can crab meat, flaked and picked over
1 ½ c. finely chopped celery
½ c. finely chopped green pepper
¼ c. finely chopped onion
1 c. mayonnaise
1 tsp. Worcestershire sauce
½ tsp. salt
1 ½ c. crushed potato chips
½ tsp. paprika
2 tbsp. butter

Drop shrimp into boiling salted water and cook until pink, about 1 minute after water returns to boil. If shrimp are large, cut into half-inch pieces. Combine with crab, celery, pepper and onion. Mix mayonnaise with Worcestershire sauce and salt; fold into salad mixture. Spread in buttered 2-quart casserole or 6 individual baking dishes. Bake at 400 degrees for 10 minutes. Blend potato chips with paprika; sprinkle with mixture. Dot with butter. Bake 10 minutes more or until browned. Yield: 6 servings.

Mrs. Zona Beth Cates, Tempe H.S.
Tempe, Arizona

HOT SEAFOOD SALAD

1 7 ½-oz. can crab meat
1 5-oz. can med. shrimp
¾ c. diced celery
1 sm. onion, diced
1 5-oz. can water chestnuts
1 sm. can sliced mushrooms
½ tsp. Tabasco sauce
2 hard-cooked eggs
2 tbsp. lemon juice
1 tsp. Accent
1 tsp. salt
¼ tsp. dry mustard
1 tsp. Worcestershire sauce
1 c. mayonnaise
10 Ritz crackers

Mix all ingredients, except Ritz crackers, adding mayonnaise last. Place in 1 1/2-quart baking dish. Crush Ritz crackers; sprinkle on top. Bake 25 to 30 minutes at 350 degrees. Yield: 6 servings.

Mrs. Carol Erickson, North Jr. H.S.
Hopkins, Minnesota

HOT SEAFOOD SALAD

1 can crab meat
2 cans shrimp
1 lge. can mushrooms
4 hard-cooked eggs, diced
¼ c. chopped green pepper
1 med. onion, chopped
2 cans water chestnuts, sliced thin
2 cans cream of chicken soup
2 tbsp. Worcestershire sauce
1 tsp. salt
Buttered crumbs
Toasted almonds

Mix all ingredients except crumbs and almonds together. Just before putting in oven cover with crumbs. Bake at 350 degrees for 20 to 30 minutes. Top with toasted almonds. Yield: 6 servings.

Mrs. Beverly Witt, Williston H.S.
Williston, North Dakota

MACARONI-SEAFOOD SALAD

Garlic
½ lb. cooked shell macaroni
1 lb. boiled shrimp
1 can white crab meat
1 clove garlic
12 olives, finely chopped
½ c. finely chopped parsley
Mayonnaise
Lettuce leaves

Chill all ingredients thoroughly. Rub well-chilled bowl generously with garlic. Cut shrimp into pieces. Mix all remaining ingredients except mayonnaise and lettuce. Add mayonnaise; toss lightly. Serve cold on lettuce. Yield: 6 servings.

Mrs. Catherine R. Trotter, Independence H.S.
Independence, Louisiana

SWEDISH WEST COAST SALAD

1 lb. mushrooms
Lemon juice
1 lb. cooked shrimp
1 ½ c. crab meat
1 c. canned asparagus, cut up
1 c. sliced celery
1 c. cooked peas
1 sm. head lettuce, shredded
Garlic
Dressing
Sliced hard-cooked eggs
3 tomatoes, peeled and sliced

Clean mushrooms; slice lengthwise. Sprinkle with a few drops lemon juice; place in covered bowl in refrigerator. Peel shrimp; leave whole or cut lengthwise. Dice crab meat; place with shrimp in refrigerator. Half an hour before serving, assemble all ingredients; place in layers in salad bowl rubbed with garlic. Pour Dressing over all; toss lightly. Garnish with eggs and tomatoes. Chill until ready to serve.

DRESSING:

1 clove garlic, crushed
4 tbsp. vinegar
8 tbsp. salad oil
1 ¼ tsp. salt
1 tsp. paprika
Dash of pepper

Place all ingredients in jar; cover and shake well until blended.

Mrs. Barbara Newton, Hudson Falls Sr. H.S.
Hudson Falls, New York

SEAFOOD POTPOURRI

1 6 ½ or 7-oz. can tuna
1 6 ½-oz. can crab meat
1 5-oz. can shrimp
2 tbsp. French dressing
1 c. diced cucumbers
2 tbsp. chopped radishes
1 tbsp. capers
2 tbsp. lemon juice
½ c. mayonnaise
Salt, pepper and paprika to taste

Flake tuna and crab meat. Devein shrimp; mix with tuna and crab meat. Add French dressing; chill 15 minutes. Add remaining ingredients; toss lightly. Serve in crisp lettuce cups. Yield: 6 servings.

Linda Gail Pack, Pisgah H.S.
Cantos, North Carolina

SEAFOOD SALAD SUPREME

1 6 ½-oz. can crab meat
1 7-oz. can shrimp
1 6-oz. can lobster
1 7-oz. can tuna
1 head lettuce, shredded
1 c. diced celery
½ c. chopped walnuts
⅓ c. sliced radishes
¼ c. sliced green onions
1 med. ripe avocado
3 tbsp. lemon juice
1 c. mayonnaise
¼ c. cream
Salt and pepper to taste
3 hard-cooked eggs, finely diced

Drain and remove bony tissues from crab meat, shrimp, lobster and tuna. Cut shrimp into bite-sized pieces; separate tuna into small chunks. Combine meats in bowl; chill in refrigerator. Combine lettuce, celery, walnuts, radishes and onions in another bowl. Peel and dice avocado; sprinkle with lemon juice. Toss lightly to coat pieces thoroughly; add to vegetable bowl. Chill in refrigerator at least 1 hour. Mix mayonnaise, cream, salt and pepper. To serve, combine contents of meat bowl and vegetable bowl; add mayonnaise dressing and eggs. Toss lightly. Serve in lettuce cups.

Virginia St. John, Vance Jr. H.S.
Bristol, Tennessee

Party and Foreign Salads

RECIPE FOR AEGEAN SALAD BOWL WITH GREEN GODDESS DRESSING ON PAGE 373

Party Congealed Salads

BLACKBERRY SALAD

½ c. sugar
¼ c. butter, melted
2 c. crushed graham crackers
1 c. boiling water
1 pkg. raspberry Jell-O
2 c. ice cream
1 No. 2 can blackberry pie mix
1 tbsp. lemon juice

Combine sugar, butter and crumbs; line bottom of 8 x 8-inch pan, reserving 1/4 cup crumb mixture for topping. Add boiling water to Jell-O; dissolve. Add ice cream; stir until blended. Chill until partially set. Add berry mixture and lemon juice; stir. Pour into lined pan. Add reserved crackers to garnish. Chill and serve. Yield: 9 servings.

Mrs. Helen Swanson, Ayrshire Consol. Sch.
Ayrshire, Iowa

BROKEN GLASS TORTE

24 graham crackers, crushed
½ c. sugar
1 stick margarine, softened
1 box lime gelatin
1 box orange gelatin
1 box cherry gelatin
1 c. pineapple juice
1 envelope unflavored gelatin
¼ c. water
1 pt. whipping cream
½ c. sugar
1 tsp. vanilla

Combine graham crackers and sugar. Cut margarine into crumb mixture; line bottom of 13 x 9 x 2-inch pan. Save 1/2 crumb mixture for topping. Use 1 1/2 cups hot water to each box of flavored gelatin. Prepare gelatin in separate square pans. Let set; cut into small cubes. Heat pineapple juice; add unflavored gelatin that has been softened in 1/4 cup water. Cool. Whip cream; add sugar and vanilla. Pour into cooled pineapple juice. Fold gelatin cubes into cream mixture; place on crust in pan. Top with remaining crumbs; chill overnight. Yield: 16 servings.

Patricia A. Bennett, East Sr. H.S.
Nashville, Tennessee

CHERRY-CREAM HEART

¼ c. cold orange juice
1 envelope unflavored gelatin
¼ c. hot orange juice
Dash of salt
½ c. dairy sour cream
2 8-oz. pkg. cream cheese, cubed
¾ c. sugar
1 tbsp. cornstarch
1 1-lb. can pitted sour red cherries with juice
2 tbsp. frozen orange juice concentrate

Place cold orange juice and gelatin in blender container until gelatin is moistened; add hot orange juice. Cover; run on low speed about 1 minute or until gelatin is dissolved. Add salt, sour cream and cream cheese; cover. Run on speed 5 for 2 minutes or until smooth. Stop blender during processing, if necessary, and push ingredients toward blades with rubber spatula. Pour into oiled 1-quart heart-shaped mold or other 1-quart mold. Chill until firm. Combine sugar and cornstarch in saucepan; add cherries and orange juice concentrate. Cook, stirring constantly, until mixture boils and thickens; chill. Unmold cheese mixture when ready to serve; top with cherry sauce. Yield: 8 servings.

Peggy J. Studer, Crest Sr. H.S.
Colony, Kansas

MILLIKAN'S VERY SPECIAL CHERRY DESSERT SALAD

1 ½ c. crushed graham crackers
3 tbsp. sugar
⅓ c. butter
⅛ tsp. salt
1 c. powdered sugar
1 3-oz. pkg. cream cheese
1 pkg. Dream Whip
½ c. cold milk
1 tsp. vanilla
¼ c. chopped walnuts
2 tbsp. cherry mixture
1 pkg. unflavored gelatin
1 can cherry pie mix

Beat crackers, sugar and butter with electric beater; pat into 9-inch square pan. Bake for 3 to 5 minutes at 350 degrees. Chill. Thoroughly cream salt, powdered sugar and cream cheese with electric beater; chill. Whip Dream Whip, cold milk and vanilla until thick; add walnuts. Chill. Combine powdered sugar mixture and whipped cream mixture. Carefully place on chilled graham cracker crust. Dissolve gelatin in 2 tablespoons cherry mixture; add to cherry pie mix. Carefully place cherry pie mixture over Dream Whip mixture. Chill until thoroughly set. Yield: 9 servings.

Luella P. Grisslin, Robert A. Millikan Sr. H.S.
Long Beach, California

CHINESE CUSTARD SALAD

3 ½ tbsp. gelatin
1 c. cold water
⅓ c. sugar
6 c. boiling water
1 can condensed milk
1 can evaporated milk
3 tbsp. almond extract

(Continued on next page)

352

Soften gelatin in cold water; add softened gelatin and sugar to boiling water. Stir until sugar is dissolved; add condensed milk, evaporated milk and almond extract. Stir thoroughly; pour into sherbet glasses. Chill. Yield: 6-8 servings.

Mrs. Margery Sadler, Scranton H.S.
Scranton, Kansas

CHRISTMAS TREE SALADS

1 envelope unflavored gelatin
¼ c. cold water
1 1-lb. can jellied cranberry sauce, crushed with fork
1 c. finely shredded cabbage
¼ c. diced celery
½ c. chopped walnuts

Place gelatin in custard cup; add cold water. Let stand for 2 minutes. Place cup with gelatin in pan of boiling water; heat until dissolved. Mix with cranberry sauce, cabbage, celery and nuts. Spoon into cone-shaped paper cups supported in small glasses. Chill until firm. Invert on lettuce; peel off paper cups. Trim with softened cream cheese. Yield: 4 to 6 servings.

Virginia Stewart, Spanish Fork H.S.
Spanish Fork, Utah

CHRYSANTHEMUM SALAD

4 c. chopped cooked chicken
1 ½ c. diced celery
2 tbsp. lemon juice
1 tsp. salt
Dash of pepper
¾ c. mayonnaise
Fritos or other corn chips
1 hard-cooked egg yolk, sieved

Combine chicken and celery. Stir lemon juice, salt and pepper into mayonnaise; toss lightly with chicken. Mound salad on plate. Place corn chips around salad to form petals. Sprinkle sieved egg yolk on top. Yield: 6-8 servings.

Mrs. Alice Kester, Dawson H.S.
Welch, Texas

CITRUS SHERBET RING

1 lge. grapefruit
1 3-oz. pkg. lime gelatin
½ pt. lime sherbet
2 tbsp. chopped pecans

Section grapefruit; reserve juice. Set aside fruit sections. Add enough water to juice to make 1 1/4 cups. Add gelatin; cook and stir until gelatin is dissolved. Stir in sherbet; chill until partially set. Fold in grapefruit sections and nuts; turn into 3-cup mold. Chill until firm. Yield: 5 servings.

Mrs. Kathleen K. Horne, Powell Valley H.S.
Big Stone Gap, Virginia
Mrs. Irene Struble, Fairview H.S.
Sherwood, Ohio

CRANBERRY HEART SALAD

1 can cranberry sauce
1 pkg. cream cheese
Milk
Lettuce leaves

Remove both top and bottom of cranberry sauce; push out carefully onto plate or cutting board. Cut into 1/2 inch slices; cut heart from each slice with heart-shaped cookie cutter. Place on lettuce leaf. Beat cream cheese with enough milk to make it light and fluffy. Make border of cream cheese around edge of cranberry hearts, using pastry tube. Yield: 5-6 servings.

Mrs. Virginia S. McEwen, Coosa Co. H.S.
Rockford, Alabama

FROZEN LIME-FRUIT CREAM

1 1-lb. can fruit cocktail
1 pkg. lime pudding and pie filling
¾ c. sugar
1 egg
1 c. heavy cream, whipped
½ c. chopped coconut
15 ladyfingers

Drain fruit cocktail, reserving liquid. Set 1/4 cup of fruit aside for garnish. Add enough water to fruit liquid to make 2 1/4 cups. Combine pudding, sugar, 1/4 cup fruit liquid and egg in saucepan; stir in remaining 2 cups of fruit liquid. Cook, stirring, over medium heat until mixture comes to a boil; cool 5 minutes, stirring twice. Chill for 1 hour; fold in whipped cream and coconut. Stir in fruit; pour into 8 x 4-inch waxed paper-lined loaf pan. Freeze until firm. Serve in sherbet glasses with ladyfingers. Top with additional coconut and reserved fruit cocktail. Yield: 10 servings.

Kate Hodges DeGaris, Pell City H.S.
Pell City, Alabama

LEMON SALAD

1 pkg. lemon pie filling or 1 can Wilderness lemon or Apricot pie mix

(Continued on next page)

¼ c. lemon juice
1 c. cream, whipped
1 c. drained fruit cocktail
1 to 2 c. miniature marshmallows

Prepare lemon pie filling according to package directions; add lemon juice. Fold in whipped cream; add fruit cocktail and marshmallows. Chill and serve. Yield: 6-8 servings.

Mrs. V. J. Martin, Eleva-Strum Central Sch. Strum, Wisconsin

ORANGE DELIGHT

3 boxes orange Jell-O
3 c. orange sherbet
1 lge. box Dream Whip
1 can fruit cocktail, drained
1 c. coconut
1 c. chopped pecans
1 c. miniature marshmallows

Add 3 cups hot water to Jell-O; stir in sherbet. Chill in refrigerator. Prepare Dream Whip according to directions on package. Stir fruit cocktail, coconut, pecans and marshmallows into Dream Whip; spread on top of Jell-O. Refrigerate until ready to serve. Yield: 12 servings.

Marianne Estes, La Mirada H.S.
La Mirada, California

MOLDED SALADS

1 pkg. Jell-O
1 pt. ice cream
1 can fruit cocktail, drained
1 8-oz. pkg. cream cheese

Dissolve Jell-O in 1 cup boiling water. Beat ice cream and cream cheese with mixer. Add Jell-O to cream cheese mixture. Add fruit cocktail to Jell-O mixture; pour into mold. Refrigerate for 1 hour. Yield: 6-8 servings.

Mrs. Marion Woodward, Redford Union Sr. H.S.
Detroit, Michigan

WHIP AND CHILL
FRUIT SALAD

2 pkg. vanilla Whip 'n Chill
1 8-oz. pkg. cream cheese
1 can fruit cocktail or crushed pineapple

Prepare Whip 'n Chill according to directions on package, substituting juice from fruit cocktail for 1/2 cup water. Blend cream cheese with Whip 'n Chill. Add fruit; refrigerator for 1 hour. Yield: 6 servings.

Mrs. Linda H. Malloy, Elizabeth Cobb Jr. H.S.
Tallahassee, Florida

FRUIT WHIP

2 egg whites or ½ c. heavy cream
1 c. fruit pulp
¼ to ½ c. sugar
2 tsp. lemon juice

Beat egg whites until softly rounded peaks are formed; carefully fold in fruit pulp, sugar and lemon juice to retain lightness. Place in individual serving dishes; chill. Serve cold. Use grated raw apples, apricot pulp, crushed bananas, berries, drained crushed pineapple, sectioned oranges or any other fruit you may desire. Yield: 4 servings.

Mrs. Margie Walters, Caverna Independent
Cave City, Kentucky

HEAVENLY FRUIT FLUFF

1 lb. marshmallows
1 c. hot coffee
1 pt. whipping cream, whipped
½ c. maraschino cherries, cut into halves
1 c. chopped dates
½ c. chopped nuts
Graham crackers, crushed

Melt marshmallows in coffee in double boiler. Cool; add remaining ingredients except crumbs. Line 9 x 13-inch pan with graham crackers; pour filling in pan. Top with more crushed crackers. Chill; cut into servings. Serve cold. Yield: 12-15 servings.

Sheryl Kay Jordan, Colby H.S.
Colby, Kansas

ICE CREAM CONGEALED
SALAD

1 c. boiling water
1 pkg. strawberry gelatin
1 pkg. lemon gelatin
1 sm. pkg. cream cheese, softened
1 qt. vanilla ice cream
1 c. cold water
1 flat can crushed pineapple

Pour boiling water over gelatin; stir until dissolved. Add cream cheese; stir until nearly dissolved. Stir in ice cream, water and pineapple; chill. Chopped nuts, fresh or frozen strawberries may be added, if desired. Yield: 6-8 servings.

Mrs. Allene McDougall, Luling H.S.
Luling, Texas

JELL-O DELIGHT

1 pkg. lime Jell-O
1 pkg. strawberry Jell-O
1 pkg. orange Jell-O

(Continued on next page)

3 c. hot water
3 c. cold water
1 ½ c. chopped pecans
1 pt. sour cream
24 squares graham crackers, crushed

Dissolve gelatins in hot water, separately. Stir 1 cup cold water into each bowl. Chill in separate bowls until firm. Beat each Jell-O with electric mixer until in small chunks. Fold all Jell-O together; add nuts and sour cream. Fold. Add 1/3 of crumbs to Jell-O mixture. Place 1/3 of crumbs on bottom of large dessert bowl. Pour in Jell-O mixture; top with remaining crumbs. Refrigerate. Yield: 12 servings.

Mrs. Judith Hernandez, Alchesay H.S.
Whiteriver, Arizona

LEMON BISQUE

1 13-oz. can evaporated milk
1 3-oz. pkg. lemon Jell-O
1 ¼ c. boiling water
2 to 3 tbsp. sugar
Dash of salt
3 tbsp. lemon juice
Grated rind of 1 lemon
2 ½ c. vanilla wafers, crushed

Thoroughly chill milk. Dissolve Jell-O in boiling water; add sugar, salt, lemon juice and rind. Place in refrigerator until slightly congealed. Beat milk in large mixing bowl until stiff. Whip Jell-O mixture into milk. Spread half the crumbs in large Pyrex dish or 2 pie plates. Pour mixture over it; place remaining crumbs on top. Chill. Yield: 10-12 servings.

Mrs. Betty Brawley, Piner Jr. H.S.
Sherman, Texas

LEMON SOUFFLE

1 pkg. unflavored gelatin
¼ c. water
4 eggs, separated
1 c. sugar
1 tsp. vanilla
Rind of 1 lemon
⅓ c. lemon juice
½ pt. whipping cream

Soften gelatin in water; melt over hot water. Beat egg yolks and sugar; add vanilla, softened gelatin and lemon rind and juice. Beat egg whites; add to gelatin mixture. Whip cream; fold into gelatin mixture. Chill. Serve on lettuce, if desired. Yield: 8 servings.

Mrs. Laura Webb, Imperial Jr. H.S.
Ontario, California

LIME HALO

4 c. miniature marshmallows
¼ c. fresh lime juice
1 tsp. grated lime rind
Few drops of green food coloring
1 c. heavy cream, whipped
1 8-in. meringue shell

Melt 3 cups marshmallows with lime juice in double boiler; stir until smooth. Add lime rind and food coloring; mix well. Chill until thickened; mix until well blended. Fold in whipped cream and remaining marshmallows. Spoon into meringue shell; chill. Yield: 10-12 servings.

Mrs. Jo Helen Akims, Lexington H.S.
Lexington, Tennessee

LOVE FLOWER

1 lge. ripe tomato, peeled and sliced thick
Lettuce leaves
Hard-boiled egg
Cream cheese, softened
Red and green peppers, chopped

Place slice of tomato on bed of lettuce. Arrange white of egg, cut in fine strips, in petal fashion on top of tomato. Pipe a rosette of cream cheese in center to hold petals together; place slice of egg yolk on top of cheese. Sprinkle yolk with red and green peppers; garnish between the white petals with short strips of green peppers. Serve with French dressing. Yield: 1 serving.

Ouida M. Shows, Theodore H.S.
Theodore, Alabama

MELON SALAD

1 ripe cantaloupe
1 pt. or 1 qt. vanilla ice cream
Whipping cream, whipped

Pare and core cantaloupe; fill cantaloupe with ice cream. Slice crosswise of melon; top each serving with whipped cream. Yield: 6 servings.

Mrs. Glendis Painter, Boaz H.S.
Boaz, Alabama

AMBROSIA FRUIT CUPS

6 oranges
2 red Delicious apples, sliced
1 8-oz. can pineapple tidbits
1 pear
1 c. coconut, flaked
½ c. confectioners' sugar

Slice off top third of oranges; also slice bottom to make orange level. Section fruit, using a grapefruit knife, out of lower part of oranges. Remove membrane with spoon. Refrigerate. Combine remaining ingredients with sugar, mixing well. Chill. Spoon into orange cups; garnish with coconut or orange sherbet. Serve. Yield: 6 servings.

Mrs. Barbara Walker Hammerberg
Hortonville H.S.
Hortonville, Wisconsin

ANGEL PARFAIT

1 c. sugar
¾ c. water
3 egg whites, stiffly beaten
1 pt. whipped cream
¾ to 1 c. pecans or walnuts
¾ c. candied cherries, cut
¾ c. candied pineapple, cut
1 ½ c. tiny marshmallows, white or
    colored
1 tsp. vanilla or almond flavoring

Cook sugar and water together until it spins a thread; pour over egg whites, blending together. Cool. Add whipped cream carefully. Fold in nuts, cherries, pineapple, marshmallows and flavoring. Place in tray or shallow pan; freeze until ready to use. Yield: 8-10 servings.

Mrs. Helen H. Coleman, Virginia Sr. H.S.
Bristol, Virginia

GLAZED HOLIDAY SALAD

1 can apricot pie filling
1 can mandarin oranges
½ lb. green grapes, washed and halved
3 bananas, sliced
6 oz. miniature marshmallows

Combine pie filling, oranges and grapes; refrigerate for about 1 hour. Add bananas and marshmallows just before serving. Garnish with whipped cream, if desired. Variations may be made by adding crushed pineapple, chopped walnuts, coconut or maraschino cherries. Yield: 10 servings.

Judy A. Ritari, Lewiston H.S.
Lewiston, Minnesota

HEAVENLY HASH

¼ lb. marshmallows
1 c. drained pineapple tidbits
½ c. drained apricot halves
1 tbsp. gelatin
½ c. pineapple juice
½ c. maraschino cherries
1 c. pecans, chopped
1 c. whipping cream, whipped

Melt 8 marshmallows with pineapple over low heat. Cut up remaining marshmallows; add to apricots. Soak gelatin in pineapple juice; add to hot mixture. Stir until dissolved. Add apricot mixture, cherries and nuts. Fold in cream; chill until set. Yield: 6-8 servings.

Mrs. Martha Zimmerman, Taylorville H.S.
Taylorville, Illinois

BANANA AND CANTALOUPE SALAD

1 med. cantaloupe, peeled and diced
2 lge. bananas, sliced
1 c. miniature marshmallows
½ c. pecans
½ c. mayonnaise
½ c. strawberry ice cream
Salad greens

Combine fruits, marshmallows and nuts; mix lightly. Blend mayonnaise and ice cream; stir lightly into fruit mixture. Serve on salad greens. Yield: 6 servings.

Marian A. Henderson, Smithfield H.S.
Smithfield, Ohio

CANDLE SALAD

4 crisp lettuce leaves
1 sm. can sliced pineapple
4 bananas
4 maraschino cherries
4 tbsp. mayonnaise

Place lettuce leaves on salad plates. Lay slice of pineapple on each. Peel bananas, cutting one end evenly. Place in center of pineapple. Place cherry on banana top, making candle flame. Spread mayonnaise on sides of banana for melting wax. Chill. Serve. Yield: 4 servings.

Mrs. Christine W. Moore, Lena H.S.
Lena, Mississippi

CONGEALED FRUIT SALAD

1 lge. or 2 sm. pkg. orange Jell-O
2 c. boiling water
1 can mandarin oranges, drained
1 c. or sm. can tropical fruit, drained
1 c. crushed pineapple
½ pt. orange sherbet

(Continued on next page)

Dissolve Jell-O in boiling water; add oranges, fruit and pineapple. Add orange sherbet; stir until dissolved. Chill until congealed. Yield: 12-15 servings.

Mrs. Ruth N. Powell, Asheboro Jr. H.S.
Asheboro, North Carolina

ORANGE-BERRY SALAD

    1 pkg. strawberry gelatin
    1 pkg. frozen cranberry-orange relish,
      thawed
    1 c. finely diced apple
    2/3 c. chopped nuts
    1 tsp. lemon juice
    1/4 tsp. salt

Dissolve strawberry gelatin in 1 cup boiling water; add 1/2 cup cold water, relish, apple, nuts, juice and salt. Turn half the mixture into 1 1/2-quart mold which has been rinsed in cold water; chill until firm. Hold remaining half to use on top. Sprinkle unflavored gelatin on 3/4 cup water in saucepan; place over low heat, stirring constantly until gelatin is dissolved. Remove from heat; add orange juice concentrate, lemon juice, salt and sugar. Cool to jelly-like consistency; add cottage cheese and dry milk. Beat until smooth; pour into mold over congealed cranberry layer. Chill until firm; cover with remaining cranberry mixture. Chill until firm. Yield: 6-8 servings.

Mrs. Marie Betka, Marathon H.S.
Marathon, Wisconsin

CRANBERRY REFRIGERATOR DESSERT SALAD

    2 c. fresh or frozen cranberries,
      chopped
    1 lge. banana, diced
    White sugar
    2 c. crushed vanilla wafers
    1/2 c. margarine or butter
    1 c. powdered sugar
    1/4 tsp. vanilla
    2 eggs
    1/2 c. chopped nuts
    1 c. whipping cream
    1/4 tsp. vanilla

Mix cranberries, banana and 2/3 cup white sugar together; set aside. Place half the wafers in an 8-inch square baking dish. Cream margarine with powdered sugar. Add vanilla and eggs and beat well. Spread mixture over crumbs. Top with layer of fruit mixture and sprinkle with nuts. Add remaining wafers and remaining fruit mixture. Whip cream until it peaks and flavor with sugar and vanilla, if desired. Yield: 8-10 servings.

Mrs. Charlotte Clarke, Central H.S.
Aberdeen, South Dakota

CHRISTMAS CANDLES

    1 pkg. raspberry gelatin
    1 c. hot water
    1 c. marshmallows
    1 can whole cranberry sauce
    1 c. grated apple
    1 c. crushed pineapple
    1 c. finely chopped celery
    Almonds
    Green tinted coconut

Dissolve gelatin in hot water. Add marshmallows and stir until dissolved. Fold in remaining ingredients. Mold in 3-ounce drinking cups, which have been lightly oiled. Unmold on salad plate. Garnish with coconut at base and place sliver of almond in top for flame.

Mrs. Petrena Forsythe, Fredonia Sr. H.S.
Fredonia, Kansas

CRANBERRY-ICE CREAM SALAD

    1 can whole cranberry sauce
    2 lge. oranges
    1 tbsp. lemon juice
    1 3-oz. pkg. orange-flavored gelatin
    1 pt. vanilla ice cream
    2 tsp. orange rind
    Salad greens

Break apart cranberry sauce and drain well, reserving liquid. Peel orange and dice sections; drain well, reserving juice. Combine cranberry liquid, orange and lemon juices and enough water to make 1 cup. Heat liquid to boiling and pour over gelatin until dissolved. Add ice cream, mixing until blended. Chill until jelly-like in consistency. Fold in orange rind, diced oranges and cranberry sauce; turn into 8 individual salad molds. Chill until firm. Serve on salad greens and garnish with additional orange sections. Yield: 8 servings.

Myrtle Knutson, Fairview Jr. H.S.
St. Paul, Minnesota

CRANBERRY-ICE CREAM SALAD

    1 2-oz. can mandarin oranges
    1 can whole cranberries
    1 3-oz. box cranberry Jell-O
    1 pt. vanilla ice cream

Drain juice from mandarin oranges and cranberries. Heat juices to boiling. Dissolve Jell-O in juices. Stir until Jell-O is dissolved. Add ice cream and stir until ice cream dissolves. Mixture will be creamy and slightly thickened. Fold in fruit; pour mixture into mold slightly oiled with mayonnaise. Yield: 9 servings.

Mrs. Loretta Stock, Murdock Consol. H.S.
Murdock, Nebraska

CANDLE CRANBERRY SALAD

2 pkg. raspberry Jell-O
2 c. hot water
1 pkg. cranberries, ground
1 c. cut grapes
1 can crushed pineapple, undrained

Dissolve Jell-O in hot water; add remaining ingredients. Pour into 6-ounce juice cans; chill until firm. Unmold; place birthday candle in center. Yield: 8 molds.

Mrs. Victoria Winslow, Midland Sr. H.S.
Midland, Michigan

DESSERT FRUIT SALAD

2 apples, diced
2 bananas, diced
2 oranges, diced
4 slices pineapple, diced
¼ c. seedless raisins
20 miniature marshmallows
1 c. whipping cream
½ c. sugar

Combine first 6 ingredients. Whip cream; add sugar gradually. Fold into fruit mixture. Serve on lettuce. Garnish with coconut and red cherries. Yield: 6 servings.

Mrs. Lee Roy Snapp, Lamar Sch.
Jonesboro, Tennessee

DREAMY FRUIT SALAD

1 pkg. Dream Whip
1 pkg. strawberry Whip 'n Chill
1 can crushed pineapple
1 can fruit cocktail, drained
1 can mandarin oranges, drained
Pecans or coconut (opt.)

Follow instructions on packages of Dream Whip and Whip 'n Chill; Combine prepared Dream Whip and Whip 'n Chill. Fold in pineapple, fruit cocktail and oranges. Garnish with pecans or coconut. Yield: 10 servings.

Mrs. Lelias White, Jonesboro H.S.
Jonesboro, Texas

FROSTED HONEYDEW

1 honeydew melon
1 envelope unflavored gelatin
1 c. cold water
3 tbsp. lemon juice
1 c. blueberries
1 tsp. grated lemon rind
2 3-oz. pkg. cream cheese
2 tbsp. mayonnaise
⅛ tsp. salt
¼ tsp. Worcestershire sauce
Salad greens

Peel melon; cut slice from one end and reserve. Scoop out seeds. Drain melon, cut side down, on absorbent paper. Soften gelatin in 1/2 cup cold water. Mix remaining water, lemon juice, berries in saucepan. Bring to boil. Stir in softened gelatin. Add lemon rind. Chill until slightly thickened. Stand melon in bowl to hold upright. Fill cavity with berry mixture. Replace reserved slice and secure with toothpicks. Chill 6 hours or overnight. Frost with cream cheese softened with mayonnaise, seasoned with salt and Worcestershire sauce. Slice frosted melon. Serve on salad greens. Yield: 6-8 servings.

Sister M. Athanasius, IHM, St. Mary H.S.
Manhasset, New York

FRUIT CUP

1 slice pineapple
1 pear half
Berries to fill pear
1 leaf lemon balm or mint (opt.)

Place pineapple in bottom of serving dish; top with pear half and fill cavity with berries. Garnish with lemon or mint leaf. Yield: 1 serving.

LaBerta W. Bowler, Virgin Valley H.S.
Mesquite, Nevada

FRUIT DELIGHT

2 pkg. cherry gelatin
2 c. boiling water
2 c. soft vanilla ice cream
1 tbsp. orange juice
2 lge. bananas, sliced
1 ¼ c. crushed pineapple, drained

Dissolve gelatin in boiling water. Add ice cream; stir until melted. Add remaining ingredients. Pour into mold or oblong cake pan. Refrigerate until firm. Yield: 8-10 servings.

Mrs. Judith Wisley, Booneville H.S.
Booneville, Arkansas

FRUIT SALAD

1 can peach pie filling
1 can strawberry pie filling
3 bananas
2 c. miniature marshmallows
1 c. coconut
1 ½ c. white grapes

Combine all ingredients. Chill well. Yield: 12 servings.

Marilyn Kay Clark
U of Nebraska Sch. of Agriculture
Curtis, Nebraska

FRUIT SALAD

1 pkg. lemon Jell-O
1 c. boiling water
1 pkg. vanilla pudding
1 c. whipping cream
1 can fruit cocktail, drained
1 can mandarin oranges, drained
1 can pineapple chunks, drained
Maraschino cherries (opt.)
1 ½ c. miniature marshmallows

Dissolve Jell-O in boiling water. Cook vanilla pudding as directed on package. Mix Jell-O and pudding; refrigerate overnight. Whip cream. Beat pudding mixture; add whipped cream, fruit, cherries and marshmallows. Mix thoroughly. Serve.

Mrs. Carol Naig, Kerkhoven Sch.
Kerkhoven, Minnesota

FRUIT SALAD DELIGHT

3 c. boiling water
2 pkg. orange Jell-O
2 c. diced bananas
1 c. orange juice
1 pt. orange sherbet
1 No. 2 can crushed pineapple, drained
2 sm. cans mandarin oranges, drained
Lettuce
Sour cream

Pour boiling water over Jell-O; stir to dissolve. Cool slightly; add bananas, orange juice, sherbet, pineapple and oranges. Pour into 7 x 11-inch pan; chill until firm. Cut into squares; place on lettuce leaf. Garnish with fluff of sour cream. Yield: 10-12 servings.

Mrs. Marilyn Bell, Bakersfield H.S.
Bakersfield, California

FRUIT SALAD IN PINEAPPLE BOATS

2 pineapples, halved lengthwise
1 pkg. frozen melon balls
2 oranges, peeled and sectioned
2 bananas, sliced and chilled
1 pkg. raspberries
1 pkg. blueberries
Grapes and cherries, as desired
¼ c. mayonnaise
1 c. whipped cream

Remove hard core from pineapple using sharp knife; cut pineapple from shell, in small chunks, leaving a rim at least 1/2 inch thick. Combine pineapple and remaining fruits. Chill. Combine mayonnaise with cream; mix into fruit. Fill pineapple shells with mixture. Yield: 4 servings.

Cora Elizabeth Fairbanks, Rockport Jr.-Sr. H.S.
Rockport, Massachusetts

FRUIT SHERBET DELIGHT

1 10-oz. pkg. frozen strawberries
1 10-oz. pkg. frozen raspberries
1 10-oz. pkg. frozen melon balls
1 10-oz. pkg. frozen peaches
5 lge. lettuce leaves
1 pt. orange sherbet

Place all frozen fruit in colander. Drain for 1 hour and 30 minutes to 2 hours or until fruit is completely thawed. Stir gently. Serve on lettuce leaves. Top with sherbet. Yield: 5 servings.

Judith Dickson, Simond Jr. H.S.
Saint John, New Brunswick, Canada

GRAPEFRUIT SALAD

Grapefruit juice
½ tsp. cinnamon
½ c. brown sugar
2 tbsp. grated lemon peel
1 lge. can grapefruit sections or 4 fresh grapefruit, sectioned
1 c. sliced, pitted dates

Combine juice with cinnamon, sugar and lemon peel. Mix with fruits, tossing lightly. Bake uncovered at 350 degrees for 30 minutes. Scatter chopped pecans over top. Serve. Yield: 6 servings.

Mrs. George M. Ballard, Cumberland Jr. H.S.
Harriman, Tennessee

HALLOWEEN SPOOKY SALAD

1 lge. orange
6 pineapple slices
Raisins
¾ c. mayonnaise

Peel orange and cut crosswise into 6 slices. Place each slice on pineapple slice. Place on crisp lettuce. Make eyes, nose and mouth of face on each orange slice using raisins. Serve with mayonnaise thinned with pineapple juice. Yield: 6 servings.

Mrs. Betty M. Dillard, Marion Jr. H.S.
Marion, Virginia

HAWAIIAN CHIFFON SALAD

2 pkg. orange gelatin
2 ¼ c. boiling water
1 sm. can frozen orange juice
1 No. 2 can crushed pineapple, drained
1 can mandarin oranges, drained
1 pkg. lemon chiffon pie mix
1 pkg. Dream Whip, prepared
Cheddar cheese, grated

(Continued on next page)

Mix gelatin with boiling water; stir until dissolved. Add frozen orange juice to hot mixture; chill until partially set. Add pineapple and oranges; place in 9 x 13-inch pan until stiff. Follow directions on chiffon pie mix bowl; add prepared Dream Whip. Spread mixture over top of congealed gelatin mixture. Refrigerate. Grate cheddar cheese over top before serving. Yield: 12 servings.

Mrs. Marilyn Sieling, Audubon H.S.
Audubon, Minnesota

ICE CREAM SALAD

    2 sm. boxes lime Jell-O
    2 c. hot water
    1 qt. cherry-vanilla ice cream
    1 No. 2 can cold fruit cocktail, drained
      and juice reserved
    1 sm. can cold pineapple, drained and
      juice reserved

Dissolve Jell-O in hot water. Stir in ice cream; mix thoroughly. Add fruits and juices. Pour into 12 x 15-inch pan. Chill. Yield: 8-10 servings.

Sara Dinsmore, Crestview H.S.
Ashland, Ohio

JELL-O-FRUIT SALAD

    3 c. hot water
    1 3-oz. box lemon Jell-O
    1 3-oz. box orange Jell-O
    1 No. 2 can crushed pineapple
    2 c. miniature marshmallows
    2 bananas, chopped

Pour hot water over lemon and orange Jell-O; chill until partially set. Drain pineapple; reserve juice for topping. Add pineapple, marshmallows and bananas to Jell-O. Pour into 7 1/2 x 12-inch dish. Refrigerate.

TOPPING:

    ½ c. sugar
    3 tbsp. flour
    Reserved pineapple juice
    2 egg yolks
    ½ pt. whipping cream

Combine all ingredients except cream; cook until thick. Whip cream. Blend about 2 tablespoons whipped cream with custard, then pour custard on top of Jell-O. Spoon whipped cream onto top of custard. Chill until firm. Cut into squares. Yield: 12-15 servings.

Mrs. Wana Miller, Trenton H.S.
Trenton, Texas

LUNCHEON SALAD SUPREME

    2 cantaloupes, halved
    2 c. fresh or canned pineapple chunks
    1 c. seedless green grapes
    Grated rind and juice of 1 orange
    ¼ c. honey
    2 tsp. lemon juice
    1 c. flaked coconut
    ¼ c. dark rum (opt.)
    1 c. fresh berries
    Mint sprigs
    Sour cream or sherbet

Remove row of melon balls from around edge of each melon half. Loosen remaining flesh from rind; leave in shell. Combine melon balls, pineapple and grapes. Combine grated rind, orange juice, honey, lemon juice, coconut and rum. Mix with combined fruits and chill. Add berries, heaping onto melon halves. Place on chilled, mint-garnished salad plates. Top with sour cream. Yield: 4 servings.

Mrs. Annie Laurie Clark, Westminster Jr. H.S.
Westminster, Maryland

MOM'S SALAD

    1 3-oz. pkg. tapioca pudding mix
    1 3-oz. pkg. coconut cream pudding
      mix
    1 No. 2 can chunk pineapple, drained
    2 bananas
    1 11-oz. can mandarin oranges,
      drained
    3 c. liquid, water and juice from
      pineapple and oranges
    1 c. whipping cream
    Marshmallows and nuts (opt.)

Add pudding mixes to liquid; cook according to package directions. Chill; add remaining ingredients except whipping cream. Whip cream; fold in. Place in 9 x 12-inch pan; chill. Serve on lettuce leaf. Yield: 12-16 servings.

Ardella Johnson, Magnolia Indep. Sch.
Magnolia, Minnesota

FRUIT-FILLED ORANGES
WITH HONEY-BERRY
DRESSING

    6 lge. oranges
    3 bananas, sliced
    3 apples, sliced
    1 tsp. lemon juice

Slice tops from oranges with grapefruit knife; remove orange sections. Combine orange sections, bananas, apple slices and lemon juice. Fill oranges with fruit mixture. Serve with Honey-Berry Dressing.

(Continued on next page)

HONEY-BERRY DRESSING:

1 c. jellied cranberry sauce
½ c. honey
2 tsp. lemon juice

Beat cranberry sauce until smooth. Stir in honey and lemon juice. Pour over salad. Yield: 6 servings.

Linda Kniegge, Scranton Consolidated Sch.
Scranton, Iowa

MANDARIN DUET SALAD

2 3-oz. pkg. orange Jell-O
2 c. boiling water or fruit juice
1 pt. orange sherbet
1 11-oz. can mandarin oranges, drained
Ambrosia Fruit salad

Dissolve gelatin in boiling liquid; add sherbet, stirring until melted. Add oranges; pour into 1 1/2-quart ring mold. Chill until firm. Unmold; fill center with Ambrosia Fruit Salad.

AMBROSIA FRUIT SALAD:

1 11-oz. can mandarin oranges, drained
1 13-oz. can pineapple chunks, drained
1 c. flaked coconut
1 c. sour cream or ½ c. whipping cream
1 c. miniature marshmallows

Combine all ingredients. Chill 5 to 6 hours or overnight. Yield: 10-12 servings.

Mrs. Gerry Fanning, East Jr. H.S.
Tullahoma, Tennessee
Mrs. Linda Magnuson, Hyre Jr. H.S.
Akron, Ohio

MANDARIN ORANGE SALAD

2 3-oz. pkg. orange gelatin
2 c. hot water
1 pt. orange sherbet
1 lge. can crushed pineapple, drained
1 sm. can mandarin oranges, drained
2 bananas, diced
Chopped nuts

Dissolve gelatin in hot water; melt sherbet in gelatin mixture. Add fruit and nuts; pour mixture into 13 x 9 x 2-inch pan. Chill until firm. Yield: 6 servings.

Mrs. Mildred Tate, Henderson H.S.
Henderson, Kentucky

MANDARIN ORANGE SOUFFLE

2 pkg. orange Jell-O
1 c. hot water
1 c. orange juice
1 c. sour cream

1 pt. orange sherbet
1 c. pineapple tidbits, drained
2 c. orange sections, drained
Bibb lettuce leaves
1 c. flaked coconut
Bibb lettuce leaves

Dissolve Jell-O in hot water; add orange juice. Chill to egg white consistency; stir in sour cream and orange sherbet. Beat until thick and foamy; add pineapple and orange sections. Pour into 2-quart mold; chill 5 to 6 hours or until firm. Turn out onto platter trimmed with Bibb lettuce. Sprinkle with coconut. Yield: 10-12 servings.

Mrs. Eleanor Staszewski
Edwin Parr Composite Sch.
Athabasca, Alberta, Canada

ORANGE CREAM SALAD

4 3-oz. pkg. orange gelatin
4 ½ c. boiling water
½ c. mandarin orange juice
2 11-oz. cans mandarin oranges
½ c. pecans
2 pt. vanilla ice cream
4 med. bananas, sliced

Dissolve 2 packages gelatin in 2 1/2 cups boiling water; add orange juice. Chill until thick; add oranges and pecans. Place in 9 x 13-inch pan; chill until set. Dissolve remaining gelatin in remaining boiling water. Mix in ice cream by spoonfuls until melted; add bananas. Chill until mixture mounds on spoon; spoon onto top of congealed layer. Chill until firm. Yield: 12 servings.

Mrs. Loretta Schrowang, Hennepin Jr. H.S.
Hennepin, Illinois

ORANGE DELIGHT SALAD

2 pkg. orange Jell-O
1 ½ c. hot water
1 11-oz. can mandarin oranges with juice
½ c. broken pecans
1 pt. vanilla ice cream
1 banana, sliced and sprinkled with 3 tbsp. lemon juice to prevent darkening

Dissolve Jell-O in hot water; reserve 1/2 of the mixture for topping. Add juice from mandarin oranges to remaining Jell-O. Chill until partially set; fold in oranges and pecans. Turn into 6-cup or 10 to 12 individual molds; chill until almost firm. Add vanilla ice cream by spoonfuls to reserved hot Jell-O; stir until melted. Chill until mixture mounds on spoon; fold in banana mixture. Spoon topping over salad; chill. Yield: 10-12 servings.

Fern S. Zimmerman, Clayton H.S.
Clayton, New Mexico

ORANGE FLUFF SALAD

1 c. crushed pineapple
1 ⅓ c. sugar
2 pkg. orange Jell-O
2 c. boiling water
2 cans mandarin oranges, drained
1 pt. whipping cream, whipped
1 c. chopped nutmeats (opt.)

Combine pineapple and sugar in saucepan; cook 5 to 10 minutes. Dissolve Jell-O in boiling water; add pineapple mixture and oranges. Chill until partially set; fold in whipped cream and nutmeats. Place in 13 x 9-inch pan; chill 5 to 6 hours. Cut into squares. Yield: 12 servings.

Irene Winterfeld, John Adams Jr. H.S.
Mason City, Iowa

ORANGE SHERBET SALAD

2 pkg. orange Jell-O
2 c. boiling water
1 pt. orange sherbet
2 cans mandarin oranges
1 No. 2 can crushed pineapple, drained

Dissolve Jell-O in boiling water; add orange sherbet, stirring until melted. Chill until partially set; add mandarin oranges and pineapple. Yield: 6-8 servings.

Sandra Cuchna, Webb H.S.
Reedsburg, Wisconsin

PARTY FRUIT SALAD

1 c. peach slices
1 c. pineapple tidbits
¼ c. sliced maraschino cherries
1 c. sour cream
1 c. miniature marshmallows
1 9-in. baked pastry shell

Combine fruit, sour cream and marshmallows; pour into pastry shell. Freeze. Garnish with additional peach slices and marshmallows, if desired. Yield: 6 servings.

Ruth J. Severson, Huntley H.S.
Huntley, Illinois

PEACH MELBA MOLD

2 c. sliced peaches
4 tbsp. lemon juice
1 3-oz. pkg. lemon gelatin
2 tsp. milk
2 tbsp. salad dressing
1 3-oz. pkg. cream cheese, softened
2 tbsp. chopped pecans
1 10-oz. pkg. frozen red raspberries, thawed
1 3-oz. pkg. raspberry gelatin

Drain peaches, reserving syrup. Combine syrup and 2 tablespoons lemon juice; add cold water to make 1 cup. Dissolve lemon gelatin in 1 cup hot water; add syrup mixture. Chill until partially set; add peaches. Pour into 6 1/2-cup ring mold; chill until almost set. Mix milk, salad dressing and cream cheese; stir in pecans. Spread over peach gelatin. Drain raspberries, reserving syrup. Combine syrup and remaining lemon juice; add cold water to make 1 cup. Dissolve raspberry gelatin in 1 cup hot water; add syrup mixture. Chill until partially set; stir in raspberries. Pour over cheese. Chill until firm. Unmold. Yield: 8 servings.

Mrs. Audrey Buhl, Milaca Public Sch.
Milaca, Minnesota

SPRING DAFFODIL SALAD

1 3-oz. pkg. lime Jell-O
1 3-oz. pkg. lemon Jell-O
2 c. boiling water
2 No. 303 cans sliced peaches, diced
1 1-lb. can pineapple tidbits
¾ c. miniature marshmallows

Dissolve Jell-O in boiling water in bowl. Drain fruits well; reserve syrups. Combine 1 cup syrup and Jell-O. Chill, stirring twice, until slightly thickened. Fold in peaches and pineapple. Fold in marshmallows; turn into rinsed 9 x 13-inch salad pan. Chill until firm; spread with Cheese Topping.

CHEESE TOPPING:

¼ c. granulated sugar
2 tbsp. plus 2 tsp. flour
1 med. egg, beaten
2 tbsp. margarine
1 envelope dessert topping mix
½ c. milk
1 c. shredded cheddar cheese

Combine sugar and flour in saucepan; stir in egg. Gradually stir in 1 cup reserved syrup. Cook on low heat, stirring, until boiling and thickened. Remove; stir in margarine. Cover with waxed paper; cool. Whip dessert topping with cold milk; fold into cooled mixture. Frost salad; sprinkle with cheese. Chill. Yield: 15 servings.

Mrs. Ina P. Vance
Jefferson-Morgan Jr.-Sr. H.S.
Jefferson, Pennsylvania

TOTSIE'S PEACH SALAD

1 lge. pkg. orange Jell-O
2 c. boiling liquid, water and juice
    from drained fruit
1 lge. can crushed pineapple, drained
1 lge. can freestone peaches, drained
½ pkg. miniature marshmallows
1 c. sugar
½ c. (scant) flour
1 egg, beaten
1 pkg. Dream Whip

(Continued on next page)

Prepare Jell-O according to package directions, using boiling liquid. Chill until partially set; add fruit and marshmallows. Mix well; chill until firm. Add enough water to remaining fruit juice to make 1 cup. Combine sugar and flour; beat in egg. Add juice; mix well. Cook over low heat until thick. Chill. Prepare Dream Whip according to directions; fold into egg mixture, adding small amount of mashed peaches. Spread on top of congealed Jell-O. Refrigerate. Yield: 6-8 servings.

Mrs. Martha Brock, Rutherford H.S.
Panama City, Florida

ORANGE SHERBET SALAD

    2 pkg. orange Jell-O
    2 c. orange sherbet
    2 c. boiling water
    2 cans mandarin oranges, drained
    1 can chunk pineapple, drained
    1 can coconut
    1 c. miniature marshmallows
    1 c. pecans
    ½ pt. whipping cream, whipped

Dissolve Jell-O and orange sherbet in boiling water; pour into ring mold. Chill until set. Mix remaining ingredients into whipped cream. Unmold Jell-O; place fruit mixture in center of ring. Yield: 8-10 servings.

Eupha Watson, Liberty Eylan Jr. H.S.
Texarkana, Texas

ORANGE SHERBET SALAD

    1 6-oz. pkg. orange gelatin
    1 c. boiling water
    1 c. orange juice
    1 pt. orange sherbet
    1 11-oz. can mandarin oranges,
      drained
    1 No. 2 can pineapple rings, drained
      (8 rings)

Dissolve gelatin in boiling water; add orange juice and sherbet, stirring until sherbet is melted. Chill until partially set; add mandarin oranges to thickened gelatin mixture. Fill eight 4-ounce wide-bottom molds about 3/4 full of gelatin mixture. Place pineapple ring on top of gelatin mixture in each mold; finish filling with gelatin. Chill until completely set; unmold on salad greens. Miniature marshmallows may be added to gelatin mixture. Yield: 8 servings.

Mrs. Betty Thompson, Ferris H.S.
Ferris, Texas

ORANGE SHERBET SALAD

    1 3-oz. pkg. orange gelatin
    1 c. boiling water
    ½ c. whipping cream

    ½ c. crushed pineapple, drained
    ½ c. finely chopped celery
    ½ c. mandarin orange sections
    ½ pt. orange sherbet

Dissolve gelatin in boiling water; refrigerate until consistency of beaten egg whites. Whip Jell-O with beater until fluffy. Whip cream; add whipped cream, pineapple, celery, mandarin oranges and softened sherbet to whipped gelatin. Place in 1-quart mold; refrigerate until firm. Yield: 6 servings.

Mrs. Patricia Scott, Washington Jr. H.S.
Olympia, Washington

ORANGE TAPIOCA SALAD

    1 can pineapple tidbits
    1 can mandarin oranges
    1 pkg. orange tapioca pudding
    1 pkg. vanilla tapioca pudding

Measure juice from fruits and water to make 3 1/2 cups liquid; cook pudding according to package directions using fruit juice liquid. Cool; add oranges and pineapple. Other fruit may be added if desired. Yield: 10 servings.

Mrs. George Sanders, Hoffman Public Sch.
Hoffman, Minnesota

PARTY GRAPE SALAD

    1 6-oz. pkg. cream cheese
    Mayonnaise
    1 No. 2 ½ can pear halves, well drained
    1 lb. seedless grapes, halved
    Lettuce

Soften cheese to spreading consistency with mayonnaise; spread on round side of pear halves. Place grapes close together on pear, placing uncut side upward. Place in lettuce cup. Serve with crisp crackers. Salad needs no additional dressing. Yield: 5 servings.

Mrs. Louise B. Miller, Travelers Rest H.S.
Travelers Rest, South Carolina

PARTY SALAD

    1 egg
    ⅓ c. vinegar
    1 c. sugar
    1 c. whipped cream
    2 Delicious apples, cubed
    ¾ c. Velveeta cheese
    ¼ c. chopped pecans
    2 c. crushed pineapple, drained
    10 marshmallows, cut up

(Continued on next page)

Combine first three ingredients. Cook over low heat, stirring constantly, until thick. Cool. Season 1 cup whipped cream with dressing as desired. Combine remaining ingredients. Stir in seasoned whipped cream. Refrigerate overnight or for several hours. Serve. Yield: 8-10 servings.

Clarabel Tepe, Ft. Towson Sch.
Ft. Towson, Oklahoma

POTLUCK DESSERT SALAD

    4 c. mixed canned fruit pieces, drained
    1 pkg. lemon pudding mix
    2 envelopes Dream Whip
    ⅓ c. maraschino cherries, halved
    1 c. flaked coconut
    2 c. pineapple chunks

Cut mixed fruit into bite size pieces; set aside. Prepare pudding according to package directions. Chill. Prepare Dream Whip according to package directions. Fold cooled pudding into Dream Whip. Combine thoroughly and gently. Add mixed fruits, cherries and coconut to pudding mixture; mix lightly. Chill. Spoon into chilled sherbet dishes or baked individual tart shells. Serve. Do not prepare more than few hours before serving. Yield: 16-20 servings.

Mrs. Frederick L. Blanford, Lincoln Comm. H.S.
Lincoln, Illinois

SUNBURST SALAD

    Pineapple
    Chicory, curly
    Cream cheese rosettes
    Cherry or strawberry
    Orange, thinly sliced
    Red and green peppers
    Grapefruit
    Gold and red chopped fruit aspic

Place pineapple slice on bed of chicory. Arrange leaves of chicory to curl around edge of pineapple. Place rosette of cream cheese in center of pineapple; top with cherry. Rotate orange section from center to edge of pineapple. Repeat with red pepper slice, grapefruit section and green pepper strip. Continue arrangement all around pineapple. Pipe thin lines of mayonnaise along sides of fruits and peppers to fill in unevenness of lines and represent sun rays. Make border of aspic around edge of pineapple. Alternating strips of gold and red aspic may be used for sun rays in place of mayonnaise. Yield: 1 serving.

Ouida M. Shows, Theodore H.S.
Theodore, Alabama

RASPBERRY-BLUEBERRY-JELL-O SALAD

    2 pkg. raspberry Jell-O
    1 pt. vanilla ice cream
    1 can blueberries, drained
    1 pkg. frozen raspberries, thawed, undrained
    2 c. boiling water

Dissolve Jell-O in 2 cups boiling water. Add ice cream; stir until all ice cream is melted. Chill until partially set. Fold in blueberries and raspberries. Pour into individual molds. Chill until firm. Yield: 10 servings.

Betty M. Shuler, Narronne H.S.
Harbor City, California

RASPBERRY-LEMON MOLD

    1 pkg. instant lemon pudding
    2 c. milk
    1 c. mayonnaise
    1 envelope unflavored gelatin
    ½ c. lemon juice
    2 pkg. raspberry gelatin dessert
    1 ½ c. applesauce

Mix pudding with milk as directed on package; fold in mayonnaise. Soften gelatin in lemon juice; dissolve over low heat. Cool slightly; add to pudding mixture. Pour into 2-quart mold; allow to set. Mix raspberry gelatin dessert with 1 cup boiling water; add 1 1/2 cups cold water. Add applesauce. Allow to thicken slightly; pour over pudding mixture in mold. Chill until firm. Unmold. Other fruits may be substituted for applesauce. Yield: 10-12 servings.

Mrs. Jean Hanson, Red Lake Falls H.S.
Red Lake Falls, Minnesota

SPEEDY TWENTY-FOUR HOUR SALAD

    1 pkg. instant vanilla pudding
    1 c. whipping cream or 1 pkg. whipped topping mix, whipped
    1 1-lb. 14-oz. can fruit cocktail, drained
    1 11-oz. can mandarin oranges, drained
    1 4-oz. jar maraschino cherries, drained
    6 oz. miniature marshmallows
    2 bananas, sliced

Prepare instant pudding mix according to package directions; fold in whipped cream. Fold fruit cocktail, oranges and cherries into pudding mixture; add marshmallows and bananas. Chill thoroughly. Yield: 8-10 servings.

Mrs. Jean Hanson, Red Lake Falls H.S.
Red Lake Falls, Minnesota

(Continued on next page)

SPEEDY TWENTY-FOUR HOUR SALAD

1 pkg. instant vanilla or lemon pudding mix
1 c. whipping cream or topping mix, whipped
1 lge. can fruit cocktail, drained
1 sm. can crushed pineapple, drained
1 4-oz. jar maraschino cherries, quartered and drained
1 6-oz. pkg. miniature marshmallows
2 med. bananas, sliced

Prepare pudding mix according to directions. Fold in cream. Fold fruit, marshmallows and bananas into pudding mixture. Chill. Serve. Yield: 8-10 servings.

Mrs. Charlotte Russell, Litchfield Comm. Sch.
Litchfield, Michigan

STRAWBERRY SWEETHEART SALAD

2 3-oz. pkg. cream cheese
1 c. mayonnaise
15 marshmallows, cut fine
1 1-lb. pkg. frozen strawberries, thawed and drained and several reserved for garnish
½ c. chopped pecans
1 c. crushed pineapple
⅛ tsp. red food coloring
1 c. heavy cream, whipped

Stir cream cheese to soften; add mayonnaise, blending well. Add remaining ingredients, except whipped cream. Blend well. Fold in whipped cream. Pour into heart-shaped aluminum foil pan. Refrigerate overnight. Yield: 10-12 servings.

Mildred Snell, Austintown Fitch H.S.
Youngstown, Ohio

TAPIOCA SALAD

1 No. 2 ½ can pineapple tidbits, drained and juice reserved
1 pkg. vanilla or orange tapioca pudding
2 bananas
1 c. marshmallows

Combine juice and enough water to make 3 cups. Mix with pudding. Cook 10 minutes. Cool. Combine remaining ingredients with pudding mixture.

Mrs. Shirley Kjellberg, Woodbine Comm. Sch.
Woodbine, Iowa

MOLDED PEAR SALAD

6 lge. or 8 sm. canned pear halves
1 c. vanilla ice cream
2 3-oz. pkg. cream cheese, softened
1 pkg. lemon Jell-O
Few drops of green coloring (opt.)

Drain pears; reserve 1 1/4 cups syrup. Beat pear halves with rotary beater to remove strings of pear pulp. Heat syrup; pour over Jell-O to dissolve. Cool; beat in ice cream. Add pear pulp and cream cheese. Add food coloring. Pour into mold; chill until firm. Yield: 8 servings.

Dora E. Bean, Deerfield H.S.
Deerfield, Illinois

MRS. PROOF'S PARTY SALAD

½ c. butter, softened
2 c. powdered sugar, sifted
4 eggs
½ c. almonds
1 c. finely crushed vanilla wafers
1 c. cream, whipped
¼ c. red and green cherries

Combine butter and sugar; cream well at low speed of electric mixer. Add eggs, 1 at a time; beat vigorously. Stir in almonds. Line 9-inch square pan with 3/4 cup wafer crumbs. Spoon almond mixture into crust. Beat cream until set; fold in cherries. Spread over almond layer. Sprinkle with remaining wafers; garnish with cherries. Refrigerate for 12 hours or longer. Yield: 12 servings.

Mrs. Deborah Longbothum
Mifflinburg Area H.S.
Mifflinburg, Pennsylvania

JEAN'S ORANGE DESSERT

1 can mandarin oranges
1 pkg. orange Jell-O
1 c. orange sherbet
Ice cream or whipped cream

Drain oranges; add water to juice to make 1 cup liquid. Dissolve Jell-O in hot liquid; stir in sherbet. Add oranges. Pour into mold. Top with ice cream. Yield: 4-5 servings.

Wilma Quapp, Picture Butte H.S.
Picture Butte, Alberta, Canada

MACADAMIA NUT SALAD

1 pkg. orange-banana Jell-O
1 pkg. orange or pineapple Jell-O
2 c. boiling water
Juice of 2 oranges (opt.)
1 qt. macadamia nut ice cream
1 c. mandarin oranges
2 c. miniature marshmallows

Dissolve Jell-O in water and orange juice. Add ice cream and stir until melted and mixture begins to thicken. Add oranges and marshmallows; pour into mold and chill. Yield: 8 servings.

Lois Ellen Lakso, Ketchikan H.S.
Ketchikan, Alaska

MANDARIN DUET SALAD

2 3-oz. pkg. orange flavored Jell-O
2 c. boiling water or fruit juice
1 pt. orange sherbet
1 11-oz. can mandarin oranges, drained

Dissolve gelatin in water. Add sherbet and stir until melted. Add oranges. Pour into 1 1/2-quart ring mold and chill until firm. Unmold and fill with ambrosia fruit or salad, if desired. Yield: 10-12 servings.

Mrs. Pat Duncan, Haltom Jr. H.S.
Fort Worth, Texas
Mrs. Karen Berglund, Stowe Jr. H.S.
Duluth, Minnesota
Frances Rudd, Dir. Home Ec. Ed.
State Dept. of Ed.
Little Rock, Arkansas

ORANGE JELL-O SALAD

1 pkg. orange Jell-O
2/3 pt. orange sherbet
1 11-oz. can mandarin oranges, drained
1/4 c. chopped pecans

Dissolve Jell-O in reserved orange juice and enough water to make 2/3 cup. Add sherbet and beat until dissolved. Add oranges and pecans. Place in baking dish; refrigerate until firm. Yield: 8 servings.

Patsy Lee, Del City H.S.
Del City, Oklahoma

ORANGE JIFFY SALAD

2 11-oz. cans mandarin oranges
2 3-oz. pkg. Jell-O
1 pt. orange sherbet
1 pkg. Dream Whip, whipped

Drain oranges, saving 1 cup of juice. Heat juice to boil; add Jell-O, stirring well. Add oranges and sherbet; mix well. Let set about 10 minutes. Add Dream Whip. Place in molds and refrigerate until firm. Yield: 12-16 servings.

Mrs. Barbara Armstrong, Monona Grave H.S.
Monona, Wisconsin

ORANGE RING MOLD

2 3-oz. pkg. orange-flavored gelatin
2 c. hot water
1 pt. orange sherbet
1 can mandarin oranges, drained

Combine gelatin and water in large bowl. Liquid from mandarin oranges may be used for part of water. Cool slightly. Add sherbet and oranges. Pour into oiled 2-quart ring mold. Chill until firm. To serve, turn out on bed of lettuce leaves on large plate. Serve with mayonnaise, if desired. Yield: 6-8 servings.

Mrs. Mary Lou Siewert, McIntosh H.S.
McIntosh, South Dakota

ORANGE SHERBET GELATIN SALAD

2 3-oz. pkg. orange gelatin
1 c. boiling water
1 pt. orange sherbet
1 can mandarin oranges
1 c. heavy cream, whipped or 1 box Dream Whip

Dissolve gelatin in water. Add sherbet and mix well. When partially set, add oranges and fold in whipped cream. Pour into oiled 1 1/2-quart mold. Chill. Yield: 8 servings.

Janet Sutter, Bellflower Township H.S.
Bellflower, Illinois

ORANGE SHERBET SALAD

1 11-oz. can mandarin oranges and juice
1 pkg. orange-pineapple Jell-O or orange Jell-O
1 pt. orange sherbet
1 c. miniature marshmallows

Drain juice from mandarin oranges. Add water to syrup to measure 1 cup. Heat liquid to boiling and pour over gelatin. Stir to dissolve. Spoon in sherbet; stir until melted. Fold in oranges and marshmallows. Pour into 1-quart mold. Chill until set. Yield: 6-8 servings.

Mrs. Shirley Kiehn, Washington State U
Pullman, Washington

ORANGE SHERBET SALAD

2 boxes orange Jell-O
1 c. boiling water
1 c. miniature marshmallows
1 11-oz. can mandarin oranges,
  well-drained
½ pt. cream, whipped or sm. box Dream
  Whip
½ c. chopped pecans
1 pt. orange sherbet

Mix Jell-O and water. Add marshmallows; mix
well. Refrigerate until Jell-O begins to thicken.
Add oranges, cream, pecans and sherbet. Mix
well. Pour into 7 x 12 x 2-inch dish. Chill until
firm.

Mrs. Elizabeth B. Martin, Stewart Co. H.S.
Dover, Tennessee

ORANGE SHERBET SALAD

2 3-oz. pkg. orange gelatin
1 c. boiling water
1 pt. orange sherbet, cut into chunks
1 c. heavy cream, whipped
1 11-oz. can mandarin oranges, drained

Dissolve gelatin in water. Add sherbet and stir
until melted. When slightly thickened, fold in
whipped cream and oranges. Pour into 1 1/2-
quart ring mold or individual molds. Yield: 8
servings.

Mrs. Bobbie K. Troutman, Fairdale H.S.
Louisville, Kentucky

ORANGE SHERBET SALAD

1 family-size pkg. orange Jell-O
2 ¾ c. boiling water
1 6-oz. can frozen orange juice
1 pt. orange sherbet
3 cans mandarin oranges, drained

Dissolve Jell-O in water. Add undiluted orange
juice, sherbet and oranges. Let stand until firm.
Yield: 10-12 servings.

Mrs. Ann Eusley, Trent H.S.
Trent, Texas

ORANGE-CARROT DELIGHT

1 lge. pkg. orange Jell-O
1 ½ c. hot water
1 pt. orange sherbet
1 pkg. cream cheese (opt.)
½ c. shredded carrots
1 sm. can crushed pineapple

Dissolve Jell-O in 1 cup water; add sherbet and
the remaining water. Add softened cream cheese,
carrots and pineapple. Pour into mold; top with
mandarin oranges. Yield: 6 servings.

Mrs. Richard Daberkow, Pierce H.S.
Pierce, Nebraska

FROSTY STRAWBERRY DESSERT SALAD

1 No. 2 can pineapple tidbits, drained
1 3-oz. pkg. strawberry Jell-O
2 c. pineapple syrup and water
2 ¾ c. miniature marshmallows
1 2-oz. pkg. Dream Whip
½ c. milk
½ tsp. vanilla
9 drained maraschino cherries

Drain tidbits, reserving syrup. Add water to
syrup to make 2 cups; bring to a boil. Pour over
Jell-O; stir until completely dissolved. Add
pineapple; pour into 9 x 9 x 2-inch cold-water
rinsed pan. Cover immediately with layer of
marshmallows. Whip Dream Whip with cold milk
and vanilla in deep bowl until stiff; spoon over
marshmallows, spreading gently to cover. Chill
until firm. Cut into squares; lift onto chilled
dessert plates. Garnish with drained red cherry.
Yield: 9 servings.

Mrs. Ina P. Vance
Jefferson-Morgan Jr.-Sr. H.S.
Jefferson, Pennsylvania

GOLDEN WEDDING RING SALAD

1 pkg. orange Jell-O
½ c. hot water
1 c. crushed pineapple
¼ c. salad dressing
½ c. sour cream
1 glass pimento cheese spread

Dissolve Jell-O in hot water; blend in remaining
ingredients. Pour into individual ring molds;
freeze. Unmold on bed of shredded lettuce; serve.
Yield: 8 servings.

Mrs. A. F. Burnett, Eminence Consol. Sch.
Eminence, Indiana

HEAVENLY HASH

2 c. whipping cream
5 tbsp. powdered sugar
½ tsp. vanilla
Dash of salt
1 c. miniature marshmallows
1 c. pineapple tidbits, drained
¾ c. chopped pecans

(Continued on next page)

Whip cream; add powdered sugar, vanilla and salt. Fold in marshmallows and pineapple; add chopped pecans. Place in serving dishes; garnish with slice of orange and chopped pecans. Yield: 6 servings.

Mary E. Lash, Paramount Sr. H.S.
Paramount, California

IDAHO MOLDED ICE CREAM SALAD

    1 lge. can crushed, drained pineapple
    3 c. pineapple juice and water
    2 3-oz. pkg. flavored gelatin
    1 ⅓ c. vanilla ice cream
    1 c. shredded cheddar cheese
    1 c. chopped pecans

Heat 2 cups liquid; add Jell-O and remaining cup of liquid. Chill until syrupy; beat with rotary beater. Beat in ice cream until smooth; add pineapple, cheese and pecans. Fill molds; chill until set. Serve on Bibb lettuce; garnish with canned kumquats. Yield: 10 servings.

Lou Ann Elliott, Lima Perry H.S.
Lima, Ohio

JELL-O-ANGEL CAKE DESSERT SALAD

    2 3-oz. pkg. orange Jell-O
    1 sm. can frozen orange juice
    1 c. miniature marshmallows
    ½ sm. angel food cake
    1 pt. whipping cream, whipped
    1 No. 2 can crushed pineapple
    Maraschino cherries

Dissolve Jell-O, using small can frozen orange juice for part of liquid. Be sure Jell-O is completely dissolved before adding frozen juice. Chill until partially set; fold in whipped cream. Place broken pieces of angel food cake in 8 x 12-inch pan. Cover with pineapple, marshmallows and Jell-O mixture. Refrigerate until set. Serve with additional whipped cream with cherry on top. Yield: 12 servings.

Mrs. Esther E. Green, Hoover Jr. H.S.
Oklahoma City, Oklahoma

JELL-O DESSERT SALAD

    2 c. sugar
    4 egg yolks
    ½ lb. butter or oleo
    1 sm. pkg. strawberry Jell-O
    1 sm. pkg. raspberry Jell-O
    2 c. hot water
    2 c. crushed pineapple
    1 c. chopped pecans
    1 c. crushed vanilla wafers

Cream sugar, egg yolks and butter. Mix strawberry and raspberry Jell-O with hot water; add to creamed mixture. Add pineapple and pecans; mix well. Pour into 10 x 12-inch pan. Sprinkle vanilla wafer crumbs on top. Chill until firm. Yield: 12 servings.

Louise Paxton, Greenfield Sch.
Greenfield, Oklahoma

LIME-BUTTER PECAN SALAD

    1 lge. pkg. lime Jell-O
    2 c. hot water
    1 No. 2 can crushed pineapple
    1 pt. butter-pecan ice cream

Dissolve Jell-O in hot water; add crushed pineapple, mixing well. Add ice cream; stir until dissolved. Place in individual or large mold. Yield: 8 servings.

Mrs. Lois Sherrod, Maryville H.S.
Maryville, Tennessee

LIME-PINEAPPLE FLUFF

    2 3-oz. pkg. lime gelatin
    1 c. boiling water
    1 pt. pineapple sherbet
    ½ pt. whipped cream
    1 sm. can pineapple
    ½ c. chopped nuts

Dissolve gelatin in boiling water. Add sherbet; mix well. Chill until partially set; fold in whipped cream, pineapple and nuts. Chill until firm. Yield: 6-8 servings.

Mrs. Joan Thro, West Hardin H.S.
Stephensburg, Kentucky

MOLDED PINK SALAD

    1 3-oz. pkg. strawberry Jell-O
    1 c. hot water
    1 c. finely cut celery
    ½ c. nuts
    1 c. drained pineapple
    1 pt. vanilla ice cream

Dissolve Jell-O in hot water; cool slightly. Add celery, nuts and pineapple; fold in vanilla ice cream slowly. Pour into mold; refrigerate. Yield: 6-8 servings.

Sister M. Vincent Werner, Andale H.S.
Andale, Kansas

PARTY SALAD

    1 pkg. lime gelatin
    1 pkg. lemon gelatin
    2 c. hot water
    1 No. 2 can crushed pineapple, drained
    1 pt. cottage cheese
    1 c. nuts, chopped (opt.)
    ½ c. mayonnaise
    1 tbsp. horseradish (opt.)
    1 can sweetened condensed milk

Dissolve gelatins in hot water; cool until consistency of egg whites. Add pineapple, cottage cheese and nuts. Mix mayonnaise, horseradish and milk in small bowl until well blended. Add mayonnaise mixture to gelatins; combine well. Place in attractive container; chill until firm. Garnish with red cherry. Yield: 16 servings.

Mrs. Betty Keeney, Middleton Union H.S.
Middleton, Wisconsin

PINEAPPLE PARTY SALAD

    1 No. 2 ½ can crushed pineapple
    1 pkg. lemon gelatin
    1 pkg. lime gelatin
    ¼ tsp. salt
    1 c. dry cottage cheese
    1 c. mayonnaise
    ½ c. blanched, chopped almonds

Drain syrup from pineapple; add enough water to syrup to make 2 cups. Heat to boiling point; add gelatins, stirring until dissolved. Add salt. Cool until slightly thickened; fold in cottage cheese, mayonnaise, pineapple and almonds. Pour into 9-inch square pan. Chill until completely set. Yield: 10-12 servings.

Delores Vondrak, Elk Point Sch.
Elk Point, South Dakota

PINEAPPLE-ORANGE DELIGHT

    Pineapple rings, drained
    Orange sherbet
    Coconut

Place 1 pineapple ring on small plate. Place large round scoop of orange sherbet on top of pineapple ring. Sprinkle coconut on top. Serve immediately.

Mrs. Darlene Prashar, Astoria H.S.
Astoria, South Dakota

PINEAPPLE SUPREME SALAD

    1 box lime Jell-O
    1 box lemon Jell-O
    1 pt. hot water

    1 No.2 can crushed pineapple
    1 lb. cottage cheese
    1 c. sweetened condensed milk
    1 c. salad dressing
    2 tsp. horseradish
    Pinch of salt
    1 c. nuts (opt.)

Dissolve Jell-O as directed on package; add pineapple, cottage cheese, milk, salad dressing, horseradish, salt and nuts. Refrigerate.

Mrs. Milton McNea, Huntley Project H.S.
Worden, Montana

QUICK PINEAPPLE-LIME RINGS

    1 No. 2 can sliced pineapple
    1 3-oz. pkg. lime gelatin
    Lettuce leaves
    5 maraschino cherries, halved

Drain liquid from pineapple, leaving slices in can. Dissolve gelatin with 1 cup hot water. Carefully center slices in can; pour gelatin mixture over slices. Chill until set. Run warm water on can sides and bottom to loosen. Cut bottom from can and push mold out. Cut between pineapple slices; serve on lettuce leaf with cherry half as garnish. Yield: 5-8 servings.

Mrs. Mary Ann Schroeder, Windthorst H.S.
Windthorst, Texas

RASPBERRY DELIGHT

    1 box raspberry Jell-O
    1 c. boiling water
    1 c. vanilla ice cream
    2 tbsp. orange juice
    1 c. crushed pineapple
    ¾ c. chopped pecans

Dissolve Jell-O in boiling water. Add ice cream; stir until melted. Add orange juice; stir. Chill until partially set; blend in pineapple and pecans. Chill until set. Yield: 9 servings.

Mrs. Robert Lohse, Seaman H.S.
Seaman, Ohio

STARDUST SALAD

    1 box lemon Jell-O
    1 box orange Jell-O
    1 ½ c. hot water
    1 ½ c. cold water
    2 ½ c. crushed pineapple
    1 pkg. sm. marshmallows
    1 c. sugar
    2 tbsp. flour
    1 egg, beaten until frothy

(Continued on next page)

1 pkg. Dream Whip
1 sm. pkg. cream cheese
1 sm. pkg. cheddar cheese, finely
grated

Dissolve Jell-O's in hot water; add cold water. Drain pineapple, reserving juice; add to Jell-O. Stir in marshmallows; refrigerate until firm. Combine sugar, flour, pineapple juice and egg; cook on low heat until thick. Cool slightly; pour over congealed layer. Whip Dream Whip; blend in cream cheese. Spread Dream Whip mixture over egg mixture. Top salad with cheese. Chill. Serve as salad or dessert. Yield: 12 servings.

Lona W. Capshaw, Hermitage Springs Sch.
Red Boiling Springs, Tennessee

VENETIAN MALLOW TORTE DESSERT SALAD

1 3-oz. pkg. lime gelatin
1 3-oz. pkg. raspberry gelatin
3 c. boiling water
3 c. miniature marshmallows
1 c. drained crushed pineapple
1 c. heavy cream, whipped
12 ladyfingers, split and cut in half

Dissolve lime gelatin and raspberry gelatin separately using 1 1/2 cups boiling water for each package. Pour into separate 8-inch square pans; chill. Cut into cubes; combine with marshmallows and pineapple, mixing lightly. Fold in whipped cream; pour into 9-inch springform pan lined with ladyfingers. Chill 5 to 6 hours or overnight. Yield: 8-10 servings.

Bertha Keller Benthien
Clermont Northeastern H.S.
Batavia, Ohio

YUM YUM SALAD

1 pkg. lime Jell-O
1 pkg. lemon Jell-O
1 pt. hot water
1 carton cottage cheese
1 No. 2 can crushed pineapple
1 can sweetened condensed milk
1 c. chopped nuts
1 c. mayonnaise

Dissolve Jell-O in hot water. Add remaining ingredients; mix well. Pour into mold; chill until firm. Yield: 12 servings.

Mrs. Nadine Kaiser, Hydro H.S.
Hydro, Oklahoma

RASPBERRY RING

2 reg. pkg. raspberry Jell-O
1 c. boiling water
1 can pink lemonade concentrate, thawed

1 pt. vanilla ice cream
1 pkg. frozen raspberries, thawed
1 lb. cottage cheese

Dissolve Jell-O in boiling water; add lemonade. Add ice cream; stir until melted. Add raspberries; mix thoroughly. Pour into ring mold; chill until firm. Unmold; fill center with cottage cheese. Yield: 8-10 servings.

Clara May Charlesworth, Northeast H.S.
Pasadena, Maryland

RAGGEDY ANN LUNCHEON DISH

Hard-cooked eggs, ½ for each serving
Cloves
Pimento strips
Sliced tomatoes, 1 slice for each serving
Sliced olives
Favorite chicken salad
Lettuce leaves
Sm. sweet pickles
Celery hearts, 2 for each serving
Sliced ham
Shredded carrots

Cut eggs lengthwise; place rounded-side up with small end at bottom. Place cloves for eyes; insert pimento for nose. Place thick slice of tomato for body; place olives for buttons. Mound chicken salad below tomato for skirt; cover with lettuce leaf. Place pickle beneath skirt for each leg; use celery hearts for arms, leafy end for hands. Wrap each arm with ham. Arrange carrot around egg for hair. Serve with crackers or thinly-sliced bread.

Nancy M. Riley, Waterford H.S.
Waterford, Ohio

SPANISH CREAM

1 envelope unflavored gelatin
6 tbsp. sugar
⅛ tsp. salt
2 eggs, separated
2 c. milk
1 tsp. vanilla

Mix gelatin, 2 tablespoons sugar and salt in top of double boiler. Beat egg yolks and milk together; add to gelatin. Cook over boiling water, stirring constantly, until gelatin is dissolved, about 5 minutes. Remove from heat; stir in vanilla. Chill to unbeaten egg white consistency. Beat egg whites until stiff; beat in remaining sugar. Fold in gelatin mixture. Turn into 4-cup mold; chill until firm. Unmold on serving plate; serve plain or with whipped cream or fruit. Yield: 6 servings.

Joan Balish, Colonen Jr. H.S.
Edison, New Jersey

DESSERT FRUIT SALAD

1 c. cream cheese
1 c. whipped cream
2 c. strawberries

Mix cream cheese, whipped cream and strawberries carefully. Place in loaf pan; chill thoroughly. Cut into thin slices to serve. Yield: 6 servings.

Mrs. Ruth Aurin Jennings, Eufaula H.S.
Eufaula, Alabama

INSTANT STRAWBERRY JELL-O

2 pkg. strawberry Jell-O
1 ¾ c. boiling water
1 pkg. frozen strawberries
2 c. firmly packed vanilla ice cream

Dissolve Jell-O in boiling water. Add strawberries and ice cream. Stir until mixture is smooth; pour into mold. Refrigerate. Mixture sets very quickly. Yield: 8 servings.

Mrs. George Sanders, Hoffman Public Sch.
Hoffman, Minnesota

STRAWBERRY DELIGHT

1 pkg. strawberry Jell-O
1 c. hot water
1 pkg. frozen strawberries
1 pt. vanilla ice cream

Dissolve Jell-O in hot water. Add strawberries and ice cream; stir. Chill and serve. Any flavor may be substituted for strawberry Jell-O and frozen fruit. Yield: 6-8 servings.

Jane Parnell, Fort Sumner H.S.
Fort Sumner, New Mexico

STRAWBERRY MOUSSE

1 c. strawberries, hulled, washed and crushed
1 tsp. gelatin
½ c. sugar
1 c. whipping cream
¼ tsp. salt
2 egg whites

Drain juice from berries; sprinkle gelatin on juice. Combine sugar with strawberries. Place gelatin mixture over hot water until gelatin is melted; cool. Beat well when cool; add straw-

berry mixture. Whip cream. Add salt to egg whites; beat until stiff. Fold fruit into whipped cream; fold in egg whites. Pour into tray or jar; freeze.

Roberta S. Priestley
Brigham Young U Lab. Sch.
Provo, Utah

STRAWBERRY PARFAIT

1 pkg. strawberry gelatin
1 c. boiling water
1 10-oz. pkg. frozen strawberries
1 pt. vanilla ice cream

Dissolve gelatin in boiling water; stir in strawberries. Add vanilla ice cream cut into cubes; stir until melted. Spoon into parfait glasses; refrigerate until firm, about 30 minutes. Top with whipped cream and maraschino cherry. Yield: 6 servings.

Mary Jo Clapp, Jamaica H.S.
Sidell, Illinois

SHYNE'S BAKELESS WONDER

1 3-oz. pkg. lemon gelatin
1 c. boiling water
1 lb. cottage cheese
18 split ladyfingers
1 pt. heavy cream
½ c. strawberry preserves

Dissolve gelatin in boiling water; cool. Mix cooled gelatin with cottage cheese; chill until slightly thickened. Line angel food pan with 12 ladyfingers. Whip cream; fold into cheese mixture. Pour half the mixture into lined pan; cover with remaining ladyfingers. Spread 1/2 cup strawberry preserves on ladyfingers. Pour in remaining mixture; chill at least 3 hours. Use skimmed cottage cheese, whipped skimmed milk and low calorie preserves for low calorie dessert. Yield: 10 servings.

Sue Daye, William Floyd Sch.
Mastic Beach, New York

CUCUMBER, CELERY AND RADISH SALAD (ARMENIA)

3 med. cucumbers
16 radishes, sliced
1 c. diced celery
¼ c. chopped pistachio nuts
½ c. olive oil
2 tbsp. lemon juice
2 tsp. salt
1 c. vinegar
¼ c. sliced stuffed olives
¼ c. sliced ripe olives

371

(Continued on next page)

Foreign Salads

Peel and dice cucumbers; add radishes, celery and nuts. Beat oil, lemon juice, salt and vinegar with electric mixer or blender; combine with vegetables. Toss. Garnish with olives. Walnuts may be substituted for pistachio nuts. Yield: 6 servings.

Irene F. Payne, Shoreham H.S.
Shoreham, Vermont

FOO YUNG TOSS (CHINA)

    1 head romaine, torn in bite-sized pieces
    1 1-lb. can bean sprouts, drained
    1 5-oz. can water chestnuts, sliced
    5 slices bacon, fried and crumbled
    2 hard-cooked eggs, sliced
    Salt and pepper to taste
    1 c. salad oil
    ½ c. sugar
    ⅓ c. catsup
    ¼ c. vinegar
    2 tbsp. grated onion
    2 tsp. Worcestershire sauce

Combine romaine, bean sprouts, chestnuts, bacon and eggs in salad bowl; sprinkle with salt and pepper. Combine remaining ingredients for dressing and mix well. Add to salad; toss. Yield: 6-8 servings.

Mrs. Patsy Robertson, Ridgeroad Jr. H.S.
North Little Rock, Arkansas

COMBINATION VEGETABLE SALAD (FRANCE) SALADE NICOISE

    ½ c. olive or salad oil
    3 tbsp. red wine vinegar
    ½ tsp. salt
    1 tsp. Dijon mustard
    1 clove of garlic, pressed
    Freshly ground black pepper
    2 c. green beans, fresh, frozen or canned
    1 ½ c. cooked new potatoes, diced
    1 red or green sweet pepper
    8 anchovy fillets
    1 sm. sweet red onion
    12 sm. tomatoes, halved
    1 doz. ripe olives
    3 hard-cooked eggs, quartered

Make dressing by shaking first 6 ingredients together in jar. Cook fresh or frozen green beans in boiling salted water only until crisp-tender; drain and cool. Drizzle warm potatoes with a few drops dressing. Cut pepper into thin strips. Drain anchovies; cut into pieces. Slice and separate onion into rings. At serving time toss beans, potatoes, pepper, anchovies and onion with about half the dressing. Add salt and pepper if needed. Heap in mound on platter or arrange in shallow bowl. Garnish with tomatoes, olives and eggs. Pour remaining dressing over all. Yield: 6 servings.

Wanda J. Hamilton, Park Jr. H.S.
Kennewick, Washington

MUSHROOM SALAD (FRANCE) SALADE CHAMPIGNON

    1 ½ lb. fresh mushrooms
    1 tsp. vinegar
    Juice of 1 lemon
    2 tbsp. mayonnaise
    1 clove of garlic, minced
    ¼ tsp. salt
    ¼ tsp. freshly ground pepper
    Bibb lettuce
    Tomato slices
    Parsley sprigs

Clean mushrooms; wash in cold water to which vinegar has been added. Dry in a cloth; slice. To keep mushrooms from turning black, sprinkle with lemon juice. Toss lightly but thoroughly with mixture of mayonnaise, garlic, salt and pepper. Place in refrigerator for 1 or 2 hours; mixture will become moist from juice of mushrooms. Stir lightly several times during chilling. Serve on a bed of Bibb lettuce with tomato and parsley. Yield: 10-12 servings.

Sister Angeline Tetreault, Academie Assomption
Edmonton, Alberta, Canada

SALAD NICOISE (FRANCE)

    ¼ head lettuce
    ½ c. salad oil
    ½ c. wine vinegar
    Salt and pepper to taste
    1 sm. jar green olives
    1 can sliced potatoes
    3 hard-cooked eggs
    ½ cucumber, sliced
    2 stalks celery, sliced
    2 tomatoes, quartered
    1 sm. jar sliced beets

Arrange lettuce leaves in bottom of large salad bowl. Combine oil, vinegar and seasonings. Arrange remaining ingredients in separate layers on top of lettuce. Pour dressing over salad immediately before serving. Yield: 6-8 servings.

Mrs. Dianne Rader, Rich Central H.S.
Olympia Fields, Illinois

GURGLING CUCUMBER SALAD (GERMANY)

    2 c. sweet cream
    3 med. cucumbers
    ¼ c. sugar
    ¼ tsp. salt
    3 tsp. vinegar
    Pepper (opt.)

Chill cream. Wash and grate cucumbers; sprinkle with salt and sugar. Add vinegar; allow to stand for 10 minutes. Add sweet cream; mix. Add pepper if desired. Chill for 15 minutes. Yield: 5 servings.

Mrs. Barbara Johnson Krueger
Alderson Jr. H.S.
Lubbock, Texas

HOT POTATO SALAD (GERMANY)
WARMER KARTOFFELSALAT

6 slices bacon, diced
½ c. onion, chopped
1 tbsp. flour
1 tbsp. sugar
1 tsp. salt
½ tsp. celery seed
¼ tsp. pepper
⅓ c. vinegar
½ c. water
4 c. cooked potatoes, diced
2 tbsp. parsley, chopped
⅓ c. radishes, sliced

Fry bacon until crisp; add onion and cook until tender. Mix together flour, sugar, salt, celery seed, pepper, vinegar and water until smooth. Add to bacon and onion. Simmer, stirring, until thickened. Add potatoes. Mix gently; heat through. Toss with parsley and radishes. Yield: 4 servings.

Mrs. Virginia Darling, Olivet Sch.
Olivet, Michigan

AEGEAN SALAD BOWL WITH GREEN GODDESS DRESSING (GREECE)

Tender spinach leaves
Romaine or other salad greens
2 med. tomatoes, cut into 6 wedges each
1 med. cucumber, peeled and thinly sliced
½ c. Seven Seas Green Goddess dressing
½ lb. feta or provolone cheese, cubed (opt.)

Tear spinach leaves and salad greens into bite-sized pieces and arrange in salad bowl. Add tomato wedges and cucumber slices. Just before serving toss lightly with Green Goddess dressing. Garnish with cheese. Yield: 4 servings.

Photograph for this recipe on page 351.

MIXED SALAD (GREECE)

½ head lettuce, shredded
1 med. cucumber, sliced
2 med. tomatoes, sliced
½ green pepper, sliced
3 celery stalks and leaves, chopped fine
1 sm. onion, sliced thin
4 anchovies
8 Greek olives
4 slices feta cheese
⅓ c. pure olive oil
Juice of 1 lemon
Oregano, salt and pepper to taste

Wash and clean all vegetables. Wash anchovies thoroughly. Arrange lettuce, celery, cucumber, tomatoes, onion and green peppers on large platter. Decorate with anchovies, olives and cheese. Sprinkle olive oil, lemon juice, oregano, salt and pepper over salad.

Hazel C. Tassis, Imperial Unified H.S.
Imperial, California

VEGETABLE SALAD (GREECE)
SALATA

½ head cabbage, shredded
½ lb. string beans, cooked until tender
1 tbsp. capers
1 doz. black olives
4 lge. beets, cooked and sliced
Salt and pepper to taste
4 tbsp. vinegar
6 tbsp. olive oil
1 tsp. mustard

Mix cabbage, beans, capers, olives and beets in large bowl. Add salt and pepper. Combine vinegar, olive oil and mustard; pour over salad. Yield: 6 servings.

Hazel C. Tassis, Imperial Unified H.S.
Imperial, California

GREEN PEPPER-OLIVE SALAD (ITALY)

3 green peppers, cut into thin strips
½ c. chopped celery
1 lge. onion, sliced thin
2 lge. tomatoes, cut in wedges
1 c. stuffed green olives, cut into halves
¼ c. salad oil
¼ c. vinegar
1 tbsp. oregano
1 tsp. salt
¼ tsp. pepper

Place peppers, celery, onion, tomatoes and olives in salad bowl. Combine remaining ingredients; pour over salad. Toss gently. Yield: 6 servings.

Frances S. Zawacki, Lathrop H.S.
Fairbanks, Alaska

SQUID SALAD (ITALY)
INSALATA DI CALAMI

2 lb. squids
Salt and pepper to taste
1 clove of garlic
1 tbsp. fresh mint, chopped
4 tbsp. oil
Juice of 1 lemon

Clean squids. Cut into small pieces 2 inches long. Boil in 2 quarts water 30 minutes or until tender. Drain well; add salt. Blend remaining ingredients well; pour over squids. Marinate in cool place for several hours. Serve on lettuce leaves. Yield: 4-6 servings.

Mrs. Mary Delorme
Oppenheim-Ephratah Central Sch.
St. Johnsville, New York

RON'S ORANGE SALAD (ITALY)

4 oranges
¼ c. olive oil
½ tsp. salt
¼ tsp. pepper
½ tsp. oregano, chopped
3 cloves of garlic, chopped very fine

Section oranges into bowl. Mix olive oil, salt, pepper, oregano and garlic. Pour over oranges; toss until sections are completely coated. Let set in the refrigerator for a short time before serving. Yield: 6 servings.

Mrs. Marjorie De Leva, Pacific H.S.
San Bernardino, California

SALAD (KOREA)

2 hard-cooked eggs
1 16-oz. bag fresh young spinach, washed, drained and chilled
1 c. drained canned bean sprouts
5 strips side bacon, fried crisp and crunched
1 to 4-oz. water chestnuts, thinly sliced
French dressing

Chop eggs. Thinly slice spinach; add next 3 ingredients. Toss lightly with French dressing. One cup fresh bean sprouts, blanched in water and cooled, may be substituted for canned bean sprouts. Yield: 6 servings.

Margaret Burrow, Edmonds Jr. Sec. Sch.
Burnaby 3, British Columbia

BEAN AND FRITO SALAD (MEXICO)

1 No. 2 can Ranch Style beans
½ c. chopped onion
½ c. highly seasoned French dressing
1 head lettuce
1 c. grated strong cheddar cheese
1 3-oz. pkg. corn chips

Drain beans; combine with onion. Marinate in French dressing for a few hours or overnight. Add lettuce broken into bite-size pieces, grated cheese and corn chips broken into small pieces. Toss and serve.

Kathryn P. McElroy, La Grange H.S.
La Grange, Texas

BLUEBERRY SALAD (POLAND)

2 3-oz. pkg. lemon Jell-O
4 c. water, including liquid from fruits
1 15-oz. can blueberries
1 8-oz. can spiced grapes
Sour cream

Dissolve Jell-O in 2 cups hot water. Add 2 cups cold water. Cool. Add blueberries and grapes. Pour into ring mold. Serve with sour cream in center of ring. Yield: 8 servings.

Mrs. Jewll Vermilyea, Bondurant-Farrar H.S.
Bondurant, Iowa

ENSALADA ESPANOLA (SPAIN)

¼ c. sliced cheese
1 c. sliced salami
4 slices bacon, fried crisp
2 heads romaine, broken
6 green onions, sliced
½ c. sliced celery
¼ c. sliced green pepper
¾ c. sliced cucumber
3 med. firm tomatoes, quartered
Clove of garlic
¼ c. hot vinegar
½ c. hot bean drippings
¼ tsp. pepper
1 tsp. garlic salt
½ c. ripe black olives
3 sliced hard-boiled eggs
Garlic butter
Sour dough bread or rye bread

Cut cheese and salami into 1-inch strips. Crush bacon. Mix cheese, salami and bacon with next 6 ingredients; toss lightly in wooden bowl, rubbed with garlic. Mix next 4 ingredients and pour over salad. Decorate with olives and eggs. Serve with garlic butter on sour dough bread or rye bread. Yield: 8-10 servings.

Sister Rose Marie, Sacred Heart H.S.
East Grand Forks, Minnesota

EGGPLANT SALAD (TURKEY)

1 eggplant
¼ c. corn oil
1 lemon, squeezed
8 oz. plain yogurt
2 cloves of garlic, mashed
Salt
1 tomato
Few black olives
Parsley

With toothpick, prick eggplant in several places. Place on rack in 400-degree oven. Cook for 1 1/2 hours, turning once. Pour corn oil into small porcelain bowl or platter. When eggplant is cooked, peel while hot; mash finely in small sections on wooden board. Immerse eggplant in oil; add lemon juice to mashed eggplant to prevent darkening. Add yogurt, garlic and salt; mix well. Smooth top and garnish with sliced tomato, olives and parsley. Yield: 5 servings.

Alma Will, Mount Royal Jr. H.S.
Calgary, Alberta, Canada

INDEX

379

RECIPE FOR STUFFED EGGS CURRY ON PAGE 23

THESE ORDER BLANKS ARE NOT FOR USE BY CLUBS

FAVORITE RECIPES OF HOME ECONOMICS TEACHERS
The Most Popular Cookbook Series in America — Over 2,000 Favorite Recipes in Each Book.

ORDER BLANK
Favorite Recipes of Home Economics Teachers Cookbooks

These order blanks are not for use by clubs

Fill in number desired below:
BASIC FIVE FAVORITES

_____	Our Favorite Desserts
_____	Our Favorite Meats
_____	Our Favorite Salads
_____	Our Favorite Vegetables
_____	Our Favorite Casseroles

SPECIALTY SERIES

_____	Foreign Foods - 1967
_____	Quick and Easy Dishes - 1968
_____	Holiday Favorites (available 1969)
_____	Outdoor Cookery (available 1970)
_____	Cooking For Two or a Crowd (1971)

☐ $3.45 per book, includes mailing charge - enclosed (check or money order)

☐ Bill me at $3.95 per book (extra added for billing)

☐ $2.95 per book if 3 or more ordered, payment enclosed

Mail to:

_____
Name

_____
Address

City   State   Zip

FAVORITE RECIPES PRESS
Box 3396, Montgomery, Alabama 36109

ORDER BLANK
Favorite Recipes of Home Economics Teachers Cookbooks

These order blanks are not for use by clubs

Fill in number desired below:
BASIC FIVE FAVORITES

_____	Our Favorite Desserts
_____	Our Favorite Meats
_____	Our Favorite Salads
_____	Our Favorite Vegetables
_____	Our Favorite Casseroles

SPECIALTY SERIES

_____	Foreign Foods - 1967
_____	Quick and Easy Dishes - 1968
_____	Holiday Favorites (available 1969)
_____	Outdoor Cookery (available 1970)
_____	Cooking For Two or a Crowd (1971)

☐ $3.45 per book, includes mailing charge - enclosed (check or money order)

☐ Bill me at $3.95 per book (extra added for billing)

☐ $2.95 per book if 3 or more ordered, payment enclosed

Mail to:

_____
Name

_____
Address

City   State   Zip

FAVORITE RECIPES PRESS
Box 3396, Montgomery, Alabama 36109

Gift Order
FAVORITE RECIPES OF HOME ECONOMICS TEACHERS Cookbooks
These order blanks are not for use by clubs.

Please fill in number desired: Send (   ) Desserts (   ) Meats (   ) Salads
(   ) Vegetables (   ) Casseroles (   ) Quick and Easy (   ) Foreign Foods

☐ $3.45 Each Enclosed   ☐ Bill Me at $3.95 Each   ☐ $2.95 Each Enclosed (for 3 or more)

To: _____   _____
Name of Person to Receive Book   My Name

_____   _____
Address   Address

City   State   Zip   City   State   Zip

FAVORITE RECIPES PRESS   **P.O. BOX 3396**   **MONTGOMERY, ALABAMA 36109**